T0391451

RESISTANCE AND CHANGE IN THE INTERNATIONAL LAW ON FOREIGN INVESTMENT

Since the 1990s, conflicts within international law on foreign investment have arisen as a result of several competing interests. The neoliberal philosophy ensured inflexible investment protection given by a network of investment treaties interpreted in an expansive manner. This has led to states creating regulatory space over foreign investment. NGOs committed to single causes, such as human rights and the environment, protested against inflexible investment protection. The rise to prominence of arguments against the fragmentation of international law also affected the development of investment law as an autonomous regime. These factors have resulted in some states renouncing the system of arbitration and other states creating new treaties that undermine inflexible investment protection. The treaty-based system of investment protection has therefore become tenuous, and change has become inevitable. Emphasizing the changes resulting from resistance to a system based on neoliberal foundations, this study looks at recent developments in the area.

M. SORNARAJAH is CJ Koh Professor at the Faculty of Law of the National University of Singapore.

RESISTANCE AND CHANGE IN THE INTERNATIONAL LAW ON FOREIGN INVESTMENT

M. SORNARAJAH

CJ Koh Professor of Law, National University of Singapore

CAMBRIDGE
UNIVERSITY PRESS

University Printing House, Cambridge CB2 8BS, United Kingdom

Cambridge University Press is part of the University of Cambridge.

It furthers the University's mission by disseminating knowledge in the pursuit of education, learning and research at the highest international levels of excellence.

www.cambridge.org
Information on this title: www.cambridge.org/9781107096622

© M. Sornarajah 2015

This publication is in copyright. Subject to statutory exception and to the provisions of relevant collective licensing agreements, no reproduction of any part may take place without the written permission of Cambridge University Press.

First published 2015

A catalogue record for this publication is available from the British Library

Library of Congress Cataloging in Publication data
Sornarajah, M., author.
Resistance and change in the international law on foreign investment / M. Sornarajah.
pages cm
1. Investments, Foreign (International law)   I. Title.
K3830.4.S675   2015
346.07–dc23
2014048692

ISBN 978-1-107-09662-2 Hardback

Cambridge University Press has no responsibility for the persistence or accuracy of URLs for external or third-party internet websites referred to in this publication, and does not guarantee that any content on such websites is, or will remain, accurate or appropriate.

To Thanga

Yet again

CONTENTS

Preface   *page* xiii
Table of cases   xiv

1   Introduction   1

1.1 Neoliberalism as a driving factor   10

1.2 Explaining change   16

1.3 The phases of change   19

1.4 Earlier phases of the international law on foreign
    investment   31

    1.4.1   The first and formative phase   32

    1.4.2   The second phase of universalization of the
    conflicts   35

    1.4.3   The third phase of neoliberal change   43

        1.4.3.1   Regime formation and dissolution   44

        1.4.3.2   Expansionist norms   45

    1.4.4   The fourth and current phase   45

    1.4.5   The competing forces in the fourth phase   47

    1.4.6   Conserving the neoliberal regime   48

        1.4.6.1   New theoretical rationalizations   49

        1.4.6.2   Constancy in jurisprudence   50

        1.4.6.3   Analogical reasoning   50

        1.4.6.4   Deflecting push-backs by states   52

        1.4.6.5   Arrogation of quasi-legislative powers   53

    1.4.7   Resisting neoliberalism   54

        1.4.7.1   Push-back by states   56

        1.4.7.2   Narrowing jurisdiction   57

        1.4.7.3   Ending fragmentation   58

        1.4.7.4   Expansionism versus strict construction   61

vii

viii   CONTENTS

        1.4.7.5   Rise of corporate responsibility   63
        1.4.7.6   Other factors   64
    1.4.8   The retreat of neoliberalism?   66

1.5 The course of the fourth phase   68

1.6 The outline of the book   71

1.7 The arrangement of the book   72

2 The precursor of neoliberalism: internationalization
of foreign investment contracts   78

2.1 Future relevance   80

2.2 A brief history   81

2.3 The relationship with diplomatic protection
and state responsibility   86
    2.3.1   Diplomatic protection and state responsibility   89

2.4 The internationalization theory   94
    2.4.1   The six petroleum arbitrations   102
    2.4.2   The policy arguments for internationalization   107
    2.4.3   The Libyan arbitrations   111
    2.4.4   *Aminoil* signals change   116

2.5 Contract disputes and ICSID tribunals   122

2.6 Survival of internationalization in ICSID cases   128

2.7 The interaction between contract- and treaty-based
arbitration   130
    2.7.1   The umbrella clause   131
    2.7.2   Role of stabilization clauses under investment treaty
arbitration   132
    2.7.3   Linking the law on legitimate expectations   133

2.8 Conclusion   133

3 Creating jurisdiction beyond consent   136

3.1 The original sin: 'arbitration without privity'   139
    3.1.1   The justification of treaty-based jurisdiction:
was it faulty?   144
    3.1.2   Extreme adventurism   146

CONTENTS

3.2 Restricting arbitral adventurism 147

    3.2.1 The definition of investment and the criterion of economic development 151

    3.2.2 The requirement of an investment made in accordance with the law of the host state 164

3.3 The acme of aberrations: *Abaclat* and financial instruments 168

3.4 Corporate nationality as a vehicle for expansion 173

    3.4.1 'Round-tripping' of investments 177

    3.4.2 Migration of companies 179

3.5 The MFN clause saga 183

    3.5.1 Conclusion on expansive trends 185

    3.5.2 Trends favouring the state 186

3.6 Conclusion 188

4 The emasculation of expropriation 191

4.1 The course of expropriation law 193

4.2 The basis of expansion of expropriation 207

4.3 The revival of regulatory expropriation 212

4.4 Stemming the regulatory takings tide 220

4.5 The changing concept of property in the international law of expropriation 223

4.6 Conserving regulatory expropriation and the distinguishing criteria 237

4.7 The bridge to fair and equitable treatment 242

4.8 Conclusion 244

5 Fair and equitable treatment: conserving relevance 246

5.1 Diversity in the standard 250

5.2 Giving content to the fair and equitable standard 252

5.3 The discovery of legitimate expectations 257

5.4 The turn to administrative law 268

x CONTENTS

5.5 The contraction of legitimate expectations 272

5.6 Restrictions on legitimate expectations 273

5.6.1 There is a duty on the foreign investor to make due diligence efforts to determine whether his expectations are legitimate, reasonable and well-founded 278

5.6.2 There is a duty to have regard to the circumstances of the host state 280

5.6.3 Contractual commitments are not protected 282

5.6.4 Expectations and the stabilization commitment 284

5.6.5 Balancing of the regulatory power of the state with the legitimate expectations of the foreign investor 288

5.7 Legitimate expectations and the legitimacy crisis 291

5.7.1 Theoretical justifications for recognizing legitimate expectations 293

5.7.2 The rule of law argument 295

5.7.3 The global administrative law argument 298

5.8 Conclusion 298

6 Backlash through defences 300

6.1 The defences in the treaties and customary law 307

6.1.1 National security 308

6.1.2 Necessity 308

6.2 The expansion of defences 314

6.2.1 Human rights obligations and investor rights 318

6.2.1.1 The doctrine of permanent sovereignty over natural resources 324

6.2.2 The right to development 327

6.3 International environmental law considerations 331

6.4 Other obligations in conflict with investment protection 339

6.4.1 Cultural rights 340

6.4.2 Indigenous rights 341

6.5 Defences: evolution or erosion of investment protection? 342

6.6 Conclusion 343

CONTENTS

7 The search for balance   347

7.1 Intermediate solutions   347

7.2 Balanced treaties as the solution   348
    7.2.1 The ASEAN Investment Agreement   352
    7.2.2 The SADC Model Investment Treaty   356
    7.2.3 The Commonwealth Report and Model Treaty   362
        7.2.3.1 Change and balanced treaties   363

7.3 The proportionality rule in investment arbitration   365
    7.3.1 The public law basis of investment arbitration   369
    7.3.2 The proportionality rule   371
    7.3.3 What is the proportionality test?   373
    7.3.4 References to the proportionality test in arbitral awards   376
    7.3.5 The future of proportionality   380

7.4 Possible changes   382

8 Resistance and change in international investment law   389

8.1 Interpreting change   393

8.2 The three periods of change   394
    8.2.1 The period of explosion   395
    8.2.2 The period of conflict   399
    8.2.3 The period of uncertainties   404

8.3 The possible reforms   407
    8.3.1 The recognition that the system of investment treaties is a failure so that it should be terminated   407
    8.3.2 Establishing a screening mechanism prior to arbitration   408
    8.3.3 The responsibility of arbitral institutions   408
    8.3.4 A return to contractual methods of protection   409
    8.3.5 Controlling legal representation in investment arbitration   409

8.4 Theory of resistance and change   410
    8.4.1 There is relative certainty in the law when it is driven by an uncontested hegemonic power on the basis of an unchallenged ideology it seeks to promote   410

xii CONTENTS

8.4.2 In the economic sphere, private power acts in tandem with public to maintain international norms favourable to it 414

8.4.3 Resistance to the hegemonic order sets in when its inadequacies and injustices become apparent 415

8.4.4 The role of justice in resisting power ensures change 417

8.4.5 When resistance mounts, accommodation will be sought that may or may not ease the pressure for change. But the search for accommodation itself is change 418

8.5 Does the notion of resistance and change apply to other areas of international law? 420

Bibliography 421
Index 438

PREFACE

This book brings together some of the views that I have stated over the years in different papers published in journals. An alternative interpretation of international investment law developed in those papers finds a more complete statement in this book.

The book identifies the rapidity with which changes have occurred in the field due to the resistance that resulted from the expansion favoured by neoliberal trends within the field. Consequently, it has also been possible to study the field in the context of how an important area of the law is made in an expansive manner when a political ideology is dominant, how resistance to such expansionism emerges and how such resistance leads to change. It is possible to construct a theory of resistance and change from the events that have transpired. The last chapter presents such a theory of change in international law.

I thank my home institution, the Law School of the National University of Singapore for sabbatical leave last year, during which work on this book was done. My PhD students, Trinh Hai Yen, Prabhakar Singh and Aniruddha Rajput helped through discussions of many areas of the subject. Dr Yen's thesis is soon to be published by Martinus Nijhoff. There were many fellow travellers on my way, each of them an academic leader of this field: Peter Muchlinski, Karl Sauvant, Kenneth Vandervelde, Wenhua Shan, Gus Van Harten and David Schneiderman. I recall with joy our many conversations on this and other matters.

The support of Finola O'Sullivan and her team at Cambridge University Press for my work has always been a strength.

I wrote this book for Thanga, who has shared so much of life with me. Many readers ask of my children as they feature in the prefaces of my other books. Ahila, much to her father's delight, is an international lawyer in her own right. Ramanan, who did maths, works for the Australian Bureau of Statistics. Vaishi is on her way to becoming a medical doctor.

I am a fortunate man, given every support by family, friends, students and colleagues.

TABLE OF CASES

Abaclat v. Argentina, ICSID, Case No. ARB/07/5 (4 August 2011), 144n28, 146, 168n86, 187n128, 201n21

Abu Dhabi Arbitration (1951) 18 ILR 144, 96n41, 99, 102

Achmea v. Slovak Republic, UNCITRAL, Case No. 20133/12 (20 May 2014), 201n23

ADC v. Hungary ICSID, Case No. ARB/03/16 (2 October 2006), 295

ADF Group Inc. v. United States, ICSID, Case No. ARB(AF)/00/1, Award (9 January 2003), 52n135

AES Corp. v. Argentina, ICSID, Case No. ARB/02/17 (26 April 2005), 264n46

AGIP v. Congo (1982) 21 ILM 726, 125, 126

Aguas del Tunari SA v. Republic of Bolivia, ICSID, Case No. ARB/02/3, Decision on Respondent's Objections to Jurisdiction (21 October 2005), 7n24, 175n107, 180n116

Aguas del Tunari v. Bolivia, ICSID, Case No. ARB/03/17 (31 July 2010), 59n152, 180, 239n110, 303n7, 322, 337, 338n77

Alps Finance and Trade v. Slovak Republic, UNCITRAL Arbitration (5 March 2011), 160n69, 182

Ambiente Ufficio v. Argentina. ICSID, Case No. ARB/08/9 (8 February 2013), 146, 168n87, 187n128

Amco v. Indonesia (1988) 1 ICSID Rep. 1281, 200n18, 238n107

Aminoil v. Kuwait (1982) 21 ILM 976, 116, 117, 256n23

Amphitrite v. The King [1921] 3 KB 500, 114n87, 369n40

AMT v. Zaire (1997) 36 ILM 1534, 140, 271n56

Apotex Inc. v. United States, UNCITRAL/NAFTA, Jurisdiction (14 June 2013), 7n28, 201n22, 353n9, 384n61

Aramco v. Saudi Arabia (1963) 27 ILR 117, 96n41, 99

Argentina v. BG Group plc, US Ct. App. DC Cir. (18 January 2012), 6n20

Argentine Bribery Case, ICC, Award 1110, 321n39

Arif v. Moldova, ICSID, Case No. ARB/11/23 (8 April 2013), 167n85, 379

Armed Activities Case (Congo v. Uganda) [2005] ICJ Rep. 168, 324

Asian Agricultural Products Ltd (AAPL) v. Sri Lanka (1990) 4 ICSID Rep. 245, 2

Associated Provincial Picture Houses Ltd v. Wednesbury Corporation [1948] 1 KB 223, 374n43

Austrian Airlines v. Slovak Republic, UNCITRAL Arbitration (9 October 2009), 184n124

Azinian v. Mexico, ICSID, Case No. ARB(AF)/97/2 (1 November 1999), 14 ICSID Rep. 2, 215

xiv

TABLE OF CASES

Azurix v. Argentina, ICSID, Case No. ARB/01/12, Award (14 July 2006), 228n90, 288n88, 322n40, 378n52

Bayinder v. Pakistan, ICSID, Case No. ARB/03/29 (27 August 2009), 155n56, 282n79

Bayview Irrigation District v. Mexico, ICSID, Case No. ARB(AF)/05/1 (19 June 2007), 338n77

Belgium v. Senegal (Questions relating to the Obligation to Prosecute or Extradite), ICJ Judgment, General List No. 144 (2012), 187n132

Berschader v. Russian Federation, SCC Case No. 080/2004 (21 April 2006), 184n124

Biwater Gauff v. Tanzania, ICSID, Case No. ARB/05/22 (29 September 2006), Award (24 July 2008), 7n24, 155n59

BP Exploration Co. Ltd v. Libya, Award (1973) 53 ILR 297, 115

Brown v. United States (1921) 256 US 335, 311n21

Burimi Srl v. Albania, ICSID, Case No. ARB/11/18 (29 May 2013), 179n114

Burlington Resources v. Ecuador, ICSID, Case No. ARB/08/5 (2012), 338n78

Canadian Cattlemen for Fair Trade v. United States, NAFTA, Award on Jurisdiction (28 January 2008), 171n98

Cargill Inc. v. Mexico, ICSID, Case No. ARB(AF)/04/2 (6 September 2011), 254n19

Case Concerning the Gabikovo-Nagymaros Project [1997] ICJ Rep. 7, 308n14, 313n24, 315n26

Chandler v. Cape plc [2012] EWCA Civ. 525, 241n113

Chemtura Corp. v. Canada, UNCITRAL, Award (2 August 2010), 48n120, 338n80

Chevron v. Ecuador (31 August 2011), 7n27

Churchill Mining v. Indonesia, ICSID, Case No. ARB/12/14 (24 February 2014), 143n26, 200n18

Claimant v. Slovak Republic, UNCITRAL Ad Hoc Arbitration (5 March 2011), 153n52, 159n67, 160n69, 174n103

CME v. Czech Republic (2001) 9 ICSID Rep. 121, UNCITRAL, Award (14 March 2003), (2003) 9 ICSID Rep. 26, 38n95, 48, 209n37

CMS Gas Transmission Co. v. Argentina, (2003) 42 ILM 788, ICSID, Case No. ARB/1/8 (20 April 2004), Annulment Committee (25 September 2007), 51n130, 207n33, 265n47, 309n16

Compañiá de Aguas del Aconquija SA and Vivendi Universal SA (Vivendi Universal) v. Argentina, ICSID, Case No. ARB/97/3, Award (21 November 2000), Award (20 August 2007), 184n124

Continental Casualty v. Argentina, ICSID, Case No. ARB/03/9 (5 September 2008), 238n108, 262n42, 268n53, 274n62, 309n16, 310n19

Council of Canadians v. Attorney General of Canada [2005] OJ No. 3422, 141n16

CSOB v. Slovakia, ICSID Arbitration, Jurisdiction (21 May 1999), 152n49

Cugden Rutile (No. 2) Pty Ltd & Anor v. Gordon William Wesley Chalk [1975] AC 520, 369n40

Cyprus Popular Bank Public Co. Ltd v. Hellenic Republic, ICSID, Case No. ARB/14/16 (Pending), 310n18

DaimlerChrysler AG v. Bauman (2014) 571 US 748, 64n162

Daimler Financial Services v. Argentina, ICSID, Case No. ARB/05/1 (22 August 2012), 148n40, 187n131

Desert Line Projects LLC v. Republic of Yemen, ICSID Case No. ARB/05/17, Award (29 January 2008, 6 February 2008), 166n82, 167n84

xvi TABLE OF CASES

Deutsche Bank v. Sri Lanka, ICSID, Case No. ARB/09/02 (31 October 2012), 168n88

Doe v. Unocal (2002) 395 F.3d 230, 239n110, 317n28

Duke Energy Electroquil Partners v. Ecuador, ICSID, Case No. ARB/04/19, Award (18 August 2008), 129

EDF v. Argentina, ICSID, Case No. ARB/03/23 (2012), 79n4

EDF (Services) Ltd v. Romania, ICSID, Case No. ARB/05/13, Dissent regarding Costs (8 October 2009), 281, 285, 288n88, 294n96

El Paso v. Argentina, ICSID, Case No. ARB/03/15 (31 October 2011), 200n17, 282n78, 287n87, 297n106, 310n19

Electrabel v. Hungary, ICSID, Case No. ARB/07/19 (30 November 2012), 256n26, 276n64, 278n71

Eli Lilley v. Canada, UNCITRAL/NAFTA (2012 ongoing), 201n22

ELSI Case [1989] ICJ Rep. 15, 91, 364

Enron Corp. v. Argentina, ICSID, Case No. ARB/01/3 (2 August 2004), Award (22 May 2007), 265n47, 309n16

Ethyl v. Canada (1999) 38 ILM 708, 196n11, 204n29, 338n79

Eureko v. Poland, UNCITRAL, Ad hoc Arbitration, Partial Award (19 August 2005), 280n74

Fedax v. Venezuela, ICSID, Case No. ARB/96/3 (11 July 1997), 170n94, 397

Feldman v. Mexico, ICSID, Case No. ARB(AF)/99/1, Award (16 December 2002), 165n77, 215, 220

Fireman's Fund v. Mexico ICSID, Case No. ARB(AF)/02/1 (17 July 2006), 376

Foremost Tehran Inc. v Iran 10 Iran–US CTR 228, 209n39

Former King of Greece v. Greece, ECHR, Application No. 25701/94 (23 November 2000), 228n87,

Fraport AG v. Philippines, ICSID, Case No. ARB/03/25, Award (16 August 2007), Annulment (23 December 2010) , 78n1, 166n83, 167n84

Fredin v. Sweden, ECHR. Application No. 12033/86 (18 February 1991), 368n39

GAMI Investments Ltd v. Mexico (2004) 44 ILM 545, NAFTA Case, Award (15 November 2004), 252n16, 254n19

Garanti Koza LLP v. Turkmenistan, ICSID, Case No. ARB/11/20 (3 July 2013), 139n8, 148n41

Gas Natural v. Argentina, ICSID, Case No. ARB/03/10 (17 June 2005), 184n124

Genin v. Estonia (2002) 17 ICSID Rev. 395, 280n73

Glamis Gold Ltd v. United States (2009) 48 ILM 1035, UNCITRAL Arbitration (NAFTA), Award (8 June 2009), 53n139, 90, 247n5, 252n15, 254n19, 322, 326, 338n78, 340n88

Grand River Enterprises Six Nations Ltd v. United States, UNCITRAL, Award (12 January 2011), 338n78

Gruslin v. Malaysia, ICSID, Case No. ARB/99/3 (27 November 2000), 154n55, 167n84, 352n6

H&H Enterprises Investments Inc. v. Arab Republic of Egypt, ICSID, Case No. ARB/09/15,Decision on Respondent's Objections to Jurisdiction (5 June 2012), 166n82

Handyside v. UK, ECHR, Application No. 5493/72 Series B, No. 221975 (1975), 228n87

Harmester v. Ghana, ICSID, Case No, ARB/07/24 (18 June 2010), 283n123

TABLE OF CASES xvii

Himpurna v. Pertamina (1999) 25 YBCA 13, 116n92
ICS Inspection and Control Services Ltd v. Argentina, UNCITRAL Ad hoc Arbitration (10 February 2012), 6n20, 187n130
Impreglio v. Argentina, ICSID, Case No. ARB/07/17 (21 June 2011), 183n123
Inceysa Vallisoletana SL v. El Salvador, ICSID, Case No. ARB/03/26 (2 August 2006), 166n80, 171n95
International Bank of Washington v. OPIC (1972) 11 ILM 1216, 332n65
International Thunderbird Gaming Corp. v. Mexico, UNCITRAL Ad hoc Arbitration (NAFTA) (31 December 2005), 257
Jalapa Railroad & Power Co., American–Mexican Claims Commission (1948), 52n136
James v. United Kingdom, ECtHR (21 February 1986), 288n88, 378
Joy Mining v. Egypt, ICSID, Case No. ARB/03/11 (6 August 2004), 152n49
Karaha Bodas Co. LLC v. Pertamina & Others, 16 Int. Arb. Rep. C-2, Final Award (18 December 2000), 85n19
Kelo v. City of New London (2005) 545 US 469, 224n82
Kiobel v. Royal Dutch Shell Petroleum Co. (2013) 569 US, (2013) 133 Sup. Ct 1659, 64n162, 241n113, 317n28, 320n36, 360
Kopecki v. Slovakia (GC) ECHR 2004-IX (28 September 2004), 265n47
KT Asia v. Kazakhstan, ICSID, Case No. ARB/09/8 (17 October 2013), 175n107
Lauder v. Czech Republic, UNCITRAL Arbitration (3 September 2001), 215n58
Lena Goldfields Arbitration, The Times, 15 September 1930, 95n38, 96
LETCO v. Liberia (1986) 26 ILM 64, 127
L. F. H. Neer v. United Mexican States (1926) 4 RIAA 60 (US–Mexican General Claims Commission), 87n21
LG&E International Inc. v. Argentina, ICSID, Case No. ARB/02/1 (3 October 2006), 309n16
Libinanco v. Turkey, ICSID, Case No. ARB/06/8 (2 September 2011), 80n6
Liman Caspian Oil BV v. Kazakhstan, ICSID, Case No. ARB/07/14 (22 June 2010), 167n85, 183
Lucas v. South Carolina Coastal Council (1962) 505 US 1003, 110n78
Maffezini v. Kingdom of Spain, ICSID, Case No. ARB/97/7, Decision on Jurisdiction (25 January 2000), Award (13 November 2000), 184n124, 265n47
Malaysian Historical Salvors SDN, BHD v. Malaysia, ICSID, Case No. ARB/05/10, Jurisdiction Award (17 May 2007), Annulment Committee Decision (16 April 2009), 151n46, 154n54, 155n58
Marion Unglaube v. Costa Rica, ICSID, Case No. ARB/08/1 (16 May 2012), 333n69
McCarthy v. Minister of Education [2012] IEHC 200, 265n47
Merrill & Ring Forestry Ltd v. Canada, UNCITRAL, Award (31 March 2010), 52n136, 53, 252n15, 254n19, 262n44
Metalclad Corp. v. Mexico, ICSID Case No. ARB(AF)/97/1 (30 August 2000), (2001) 40 ILM 36, 210n42, 253n17, 260n39, 338n76
Methanex v. United States, UNCITRAL (NAFTA) Ad hoc Arbitration, Final Award (3 August 2005), 18n48, 57, 59n152, 80, 196n11, 204n29, 211n46, 216, 280n72, 303n7, 305n9, 338n79
Mihaly v. Sri Lanka, ICSID, Award (15 March 2002), (2002) 41 ILM 867, 166n81
Mobil Oil v. Venezuela, ICSID, Case No. ARB/07/27 (10 June 2010), 180

xviii TABLE OF CASES

Mondev International v. United States, ICSID, Case No. ARB(AF)/99/2 (11 October 2002), 48n120, 52n135, 90n30

MTD Equity v. Chile, ICSID, Case No. ARB/01/7 (25 May 2004), Decision on Annulment (21 March 2007), 259n35, 259n38, 279

Murphy Exploration and Production International v. Ecuador, ICSID, Case No. ARB/08/04, Award on Jurisdiction (2 June 2010), 187n129

National Grid v. Argentina, UNCITRAL, Award (20 June 2006), 184n124

Next Era Energy Global Holdings BV and Next Era Energy Spain Holdings BV v. Spain, ICSID, Case No. ARB/14/11 (Pending), 310n18

Noble Ventures Inc. v. Romania, ICSID, Case No. ARB/01/11 (17 November 2005), 281n76

Occidental Exploration and Production Co. v. Ecuador, LCIA. Case No. UN 3467, Final Award (1 July 2004), 209, 265n47

Occidental Petroleum Corp. v. Ecuador, ICSID, Case No. ARB/06/11 (5 October 2012), 377, 381

Oscar Chinn Case (1934) PCIJ Series A/B No. 63, 109n77

Parkerings-Compagniet AS v. Lithuania, ICSID, Case No. ARB/05/08, Award (11 September 2007), 7n26

Patrick Mitchell v. Congo, ICSID, Case No. ARB/99/7, Annulment Award (1 November 2006), 153n53

Penn Central Transportation Co. v. New York City (1978) 438 US 104, 237n105

Philip Morris Brands Sarl v. Uruguay, ICSID, Case No. ARB/10/7, Decision on Jurisdiction (2 July 2013), 7n25

Philip Morris v. Australia, UNCITRAL PCA. Case No. 2012-12 (2012), 7n25, 59n152, 176n109, 197n14, 198n15

Phoenix Action Ltd v. Czech Republic, ICSID, Case No. ARB/06/5 (15 April 2009), 324n51

Pierro Forresti v. South Africa, ICSID, Case No. ARB(AF)/07/01 (24 August 2010), 357n15

Pine Valley Developments Ltd v. Ireland, ECHR, Application No. 12742/87, Judgment (29 December 1991), 368n39

Ping An Life Insurance Co. of China v. Belgium, ICSID, Case No. ARB/12/2 (Pending), 169n92

Plama Consortium Ltd v. Bulgaria, ICSID, Case No. ARB/03/24, 183n122

Pope and Talbot v. Canada, UNCITRAL (NAFTA), Ad hoc Arbitration, Interim Award (2 April 2001), 208, 215n56, 305n9

Postova Bank and Istrokapital v. Greece, ICSID Arbitration (Case pending) (2014), 169n91, 196n12

PSEG Global Ltd v. Turkey, ICSID, Case No. ARB/02/5 (17 January 2007), 242, 265n47

Qatar Arbitration (1953) 20 ILR 534, 96n41, 99n49, 102

R. (on the application of SRM Global Master Fund LP) v. Treasury Commissioner [2009] EWCA Civ. 788, 375n46

Rafat Ali Rizvi v. Indonesia, ICSID, Case No. ARB/11/13 (16 July 2013), 166n81, 167n84, 174n102, 176n108, 185n127, 201n20, 352n6

Railroad Development Corp. v. Guatemala, ICSID, Case No ARB/07/23 (19 May 2010), 236n103, 255n21

TABLE OF CASES

xix

Re North and East Devon Health Authority, ex parte Coughlan [2001] QB 213, 266n51

Rederiaktiebolaget Amphitrite v. The King [1921] KB 500, 369n40

Renta 4 SVSA v. Russian Federation, SCC Case No 24/2007 (20 March 2009), 184n124

Revere Copper and Brass Inc. v. OPIC (1980) 56 ILR 258, 111n79, 217n67

Romak v. Uzbekistan, UNCITRAL PCA, Case No. AA 280, Award (26 November 2009), 160, 160n69

Rompetrol v. Romania, ICSID, Case No. ARB/06/3 (18 April 2008), 175n107, 379

RosInvest Co. UK Ltd v. Russian Federation, SCC, Case No. Arb. V079/2005, Award on Jurisdiction (October 2007), 184n124, 184n125

S. D. Myers Inc. v. Government of Canada, UNCITRAL (NAFTA), Partial Award (13 November 2000), 205n31, 215n58, 240, 260, 260n39, 302n4, 303n7, 333n67, 334n70

Saipem v. Bangladesh, ICSID, Case No. ARB/05/07 (30 June 2009), 52n137, 164n73, 322n42

Salini Construttori ApA v. Morocco, ICSID, Case No. ARB/00/4 (23 July 2001), 151n45

Saluka Investments Ltd v. Czech Republic, UNCITRAL PCA, Award (17 March 2006), ICSID, Case No. ARB/03/16 (2 October 2006), 138n8, 148n39, 180n117, 218, 256n25, 276, 276n67, 337n74

Sancheti v. United Kingdom, UNCITRAL (Pending), 55n141, 197n14

Santa Elena SA v. Costa Rica, ICSID Case No. ARB/96/1 (17 February 2000), (2002) 5 ICSID Rep. 153, 199n16, 205n31, 214, 236n104, 239n110, 240, 302n4, 303n7, 333n69, 334, 338n76, 338n81

Sapphire International Petroleums Ltd v. National Iranian Oil Co. (1963) 35 ILR 136, 113n85

Sempra Energy International v. Argentina, ICSID, Case No. ARB/02/16 (28 September 2007), 309n16

Serbian Loans Case [1929] PCIJ, Series A No. 20, 95, 103, 121

Settebello Ltd v. Baco Totta & Acores [1985] 1 WLR 1050, 369n40

Siemens AG v. Argentina, ICSID, Case No. ARB/02/8, Decision on Jurisdiction (3 August 2004), Award (6 February 2007), 52

Société Générale de Surveillance SA (SGS) v. Pakistan, ICSID, Case No. ARB/01/13 (26 August 2003), 244n115

Société Générale de Surveillance SA (SGS) v. Philippines, ICSID Case No. ARB/02/6, Decision on Jurisdiction and Admissibility (24 January 2004), 244n115

Sosa v. Alvarez Machain (2004) 542 US 692, 241n113

Southern Pacific Properties Ltd (SPP) v. Egypt (1982) 3 ICSID Rep. 131, ICSID, Case No. ARB/84/3 (30 May 1992), 3n7

Sowhoyamaxa Indigenous Community v. Paraguay, IACHR Judgment (29 March 2006), 326, 341

Sporrong and Lonnroth v. Sweden, ECHR, Series A, No. 52 (23 September 1982), 228n89

ST-AD GmbH v. Bulgaria, UNCITRAL, PCA Case No. 2011-06 (2013), 183n123

Starret Housing Corp. v Iran (1983) 4 Iran–US CTR 122, 209n38, 209n39

Suez v. Argentina, ICSID, Case No. ARB/03/19 (30 July 2010), 7n24, 263, 322n41, 338, 338n77

TABLE OF CASES

Swisslion DOO Skopje v. Macedonia, ICSID. Case No. ARB/09/16 (6 July 2012), 287n87

Tecnicas Medioambentales SA (Tecmed) v. Mexico, ICSID, Case No. ARB(AF)/00/2, Award (29 May 2003), 109n77

Telenor SA v. Hungary, ICSID, Case No. ARB/04/15 (13 September 2006), 236n103

Texas Overseas Petroleum Co. (Texaco)/California Asiatic Oil Co. (Calasiatic) v. Government of the Libyan Arab Republic (1978) 17 ILM 1, (1979) 53 ILR 389, 37n93, 113

Tippets v. Iran (1984) 6 Iran–US CTR 219, 209n39

Tokios Tokeles v. Ukraine, ICSID, Case No. ARB/02/18, Decision on Jurisdiction (29 April 2004), 175n107, 178n111, 179n115, 399

Total SA v. Argentina, ICSID, Case No. ARB/04/01 (27 December 2010), 261n40

Toto Construzioni Generali SpA v. Lebanon, ICSID, Case No. ARB/07/12 (12 May 2012), 283n80

Tza Yap Shum v. Republic of Peru, ICSID, Case No. ARB/07/6, Decision on Jurisdiction and Competence (19 June 2009), 184n124

United Kingdom Association of Fish Producers Organization v. Secretary of State for the Environment, Food and Rural Affairs [2013] EWHC 1959 (Admin), 265n47

United Mexican States v. Metalclad Corp. (2001) 14 BLR (3d) 285, [2001] BCSCR 664, 87n21, 210n43, 253n17

Vattenfall v. Germany, ICSID, Case No. ARB/09/6 (11 March 2011), 55n141, 59n152, 197n14, 198n15, 338n77, 338n81

Vava v. Anglo-American South Africa Ltd [2012] EWHC 1969 (QB), 241n113

Walter Bau v. Thailand, UNCITRAL, Award (1 July 2009), 5n17

Waste Management v. Mexico, ICSID, Case No. ARB(AF)/00/3 (30 April 2004), 217n67

Waste Management Inc. v. United States (2004) 43 ILM 967, 254n19, 254n20

White Industries v. India, UNCITRAL, Arbitration (30 November 2011), 5n17, 52n137, 160n69, 164n73, 164n74, 164n75, 322n42

Williams & Humbert v. W & H Trade Marks (Jersey) (1985) 75 ILR 268, 369n40

Wintershall v. Argentina, ICSID, Case No. ARB/04/14 (8 December 2008), 184n124

World Duty Free Ltd v. Kenya, ICSID, Case No. ARB/ 00/7 (4 October 2006), 165n78, 321n39

Yaung Chi Oo Ltd v. Myanmar (2003) 42 ILM 896, 167n84, 176n108, 177n110, 352n6

Yukos Universal Ltd v. Russia (2009) 22(2) World Trade and Arbitration Materials 279, 175n107

Zhinvali Development Ltd v. Republic of Georgia (2003) 10 ICSID Rep. 10, Award (24 January 2003), 166n81

1

Introduction

Arbitration based on investment treaties is undergoing a crisis, with many states pulling out of such arbitration.[1] Some are leaving out investor–state dispute settlement from their treaties.[2] Others are seeking to change the terms of the investment treaties, the bases of investment arbitration, so that investment protection is no longer the sole object of such treaties. The new treaties seek to preserve some regulatory space over foreign investment so as to enable them to control investments in the public interest. Other states have suspended making such treaties. Investment arbitration has seen a dramatic increase in recent years. The extent of the disenchantment caused by awards in the area, which many states feel go beyond the consent they had given the tribunals, must be explained. The resistance that has resulted is not confined to states, but extends to non-governmental organizations (NGOs), such as environmental and human rights groups. These groups believe that exclusive investment protection works to the detriment of other interests, such as the protection of human rights, the environment, cultural interests and indigenous tribal interests. This book seeks to offer an explanation of the changes that have resulted from such resistance, the reasons for such resistance and their outcomes. It examines what the future course of the law in the area should be.

A feature of investment arbitration in the last two and a half decades has been the dramatic increase in the number of arbitral awards under

---

[1] Many Latin American states have pulled out of such arbitration. Venezuela, Ecuador and Bolivia have terminated their links with the International Centre for the Settlement of Investment Disputes. Many have announced that they will not conclude any more investment treaties, including South Africa, India and Indonesia.

[2] Australia announced such a policy, but has since recanted after the change of government. Leon Trakman, 'Investor–State Arbitration: Evaluating Australia's Evolving Position', (2014) 15(1) *Journal of World Trade Law* 152. The Philippines–Japan investment treaty does not contain an investor–state dispute settlement provision. In Japan, there has been much discussion as to whether such dispute resolution should be permitted, particularly in relation to the projected Trans Pacific Pact that is being negotiated.

INTRODUCTION

investment treaties.[3] The specific year in which this explosion in treaty-based investment arbitration began can be identified as 1990. It was the year in which *Asian Agricultural Products Ltd (AAPL)* v. *Sri Lanka*[4] was decided. In that award, jurisdiction was invoked for the first time on the basis of the investor–state dispute settlement provision in an investment treaty. Since then, the majority of awards have been based on this manner of invocation of jurisdiction to settle claims of violation of the standards of protection of investment in the treaties. The impact of this development has been such that texts written on investment arbitration virtually ignore the existence of contract-based arbitration of foreign investment disputes, the older and still extant variety of investment arbitration.[5] The specialist arbitral institution for investment disputes, the International Centre for the Settlement of Investment Disputes (ICSID), set up in 1965, was designed with contract-based arbitration in mind.[6] But its workload is now largely confined to disputes arising from the violation of

---

[3] An investment treaty was usually made between a capital-exporting developed state and a capital-importing developing state, assuring protection on the basis of defined standards to foreign direct investment made by nationals and payment of compensation in the event of nationalizations. The recent treaties contain a commitment to provide unilateral recourse to arbitration to the investor in the event of a dispute. Increasingly, treaties, usually regional treaties, contain developed state partners grouped with developing states. The law is moving away from its North–South axis. Developed states often become respondents in such arbitrations, a relatively new phenomenon.

[4] (1990) 4 ICSID Rep. 245.

[5] Campbell McLachlan, Laurence Shore and Mathew Weininger, *International Investment Arbitration: Substantive Principles* (Oxford University Press, 2008). Texts on international investment law concentrate almost exclusively on investor–state arbitration as a distinct phenomenon (Christoph Schreuer and Rudolf Dolzer, *International Investment Law*, 2nd edn (Oxford University Press, 2012)). There is a spate of literature on aspects of investment treaty arbitration. For a survey of this literature, see Stephan Schill, 'Whither Fragmentation? On the Literature and Sociology of International Investment Law', (2011) 22 *European Journal of International Law* 888. A text by the present author, however, sees the law as a part of general international law and as involving other considerations besides investment protection. Muthucumaraswamy Sornarajah, *International Law on Foreign Investment* (Cambridge University Press, 1992) (its later editions are 2nd edn 2004, 3rd edn 2010).

[6] The ICSID was created in 1965 by the Convention for the Settlement of Disputes between States and Nationals of Other States (1965). The meagre caseload of the Centre from its inception to 1990 until treaty-based arbitration commenced, was based on contracts. This caseload was low. For a history of the Convention, see Antonio Parra, *The History of ICSID* (Oxford University Press, 2012). As Parra pointed out, the possibility of treaty-based consent to future arbitration was discussed during the drafting conferences on the Convention. By the end of 2013, the investment cases had reached over 568. UNCTAD, *World Investment Report* (Geneva, 2014), p. 124.

INTRODUCTION 3

investment treaties. The award in *AAPL* v. *Sri Lanka*,[7] made in 1990, identified the possibility of appropriately worded dispute settlement clauses in investment treaties as constituting indefinite offers by the host state to foreign investors of the treaty partner.[8] Such wording in investment treaties has now become commonplace. These offers could be converted into binding commitments to arbitrate. A request for arbitration would be regarded as an acceptance of the offer to arbitrate by the foreign investor. Such acceptance would create jurisdiction in the arbitration tribunal.[9] The technique triggered off a spate of investment treaty arbitrations in the succeeding years. Initially, the treaties made reference only to the ICSID, but later treaties made reference of disputes to ad hoc tribunals using UNCITRAL Rules, and to other arbitral tribunals.[10] ICSID, however, being a specialist centre dealing with disputes between foreign investors and states, has continued to attract the larger number of cases.[11]

---

[7] (1990) 4 ICSID Rep. 245. The final award was made on 27 June 1990. The view that offers of arbitration could be made to potential investors through domestic investment laws and that jurisdiction in arbitral tribunals could be created through the acceptance of these offers was stated in *Southern Pacific Properties Ltd (SPP)* v. *Egypt*, ICSID, Case No. ARB/84/3(30 May 1992). Yet none of the commentators on the British treaties made around the time identified that investment treaties had made such a momentous change, enabling an individual or a corporation to bring a state to arbitration. Two commentators participated in the negotiation of the British treaties. Eileen Denza and Shelagh Brooks, 'Investment Protection Treaties: The United Kingdom Experience', (1987) 36 *International & Comparative Law Quarterly* 908. Francis Mann, a distinguished international lawyer, wrote another. Francis Mann, 'British Treaties for the Promotion and Protection of Foreign Investments', (1981) 52 *British Yearbook of International Law* 241. Neither commentary refers to the momentous change, if a change was in fact intended. The *travaux preparatoires* of the UK–Indonesia treaty, which was made public recently under the thirty-year rule of releasing public documents previously kept secret, does not indicate that such a result was intended.

[8] The silence was not confined to British authors. Though treaties containing similar articles on dispute resolution had existed in US treaties for some time, no writer or arbitral award had suggested that such a course of securing jurisdiction purely on the basis of the treaty statement was a possibility. Some identify the first treaty containing investor–state arbitration as the investment treaty between Indonesia and the Netherlands made in 1968. By the 1980s they had become commonplace. Yet the interpretation that they would support a unilateral recourse to arbitration by the foreign investor had to await *AAPL* v. *Sri Lanka* (1990) 4 ICSID Rep. 245, which did not contain a reasoned analysis of the position. It is difficult to explain this time lapse as to why unilateral recourse to arbitration, which if it did exist as suggested, was not resorted to until 1990.

[9] For a fuller consideration of this technique, see Chapter 3.

[10] An UNCTAD study indicated that fifty-eight arbitrations were brought in 2012, the highest per year so far. In 2013, fifty-six cases were initiated. *World Investment Report* (Geneva, 2014), p. 124

[11] See at: https://icsid.worldbank.org.

4 INTRODUCTION

There are several significant factors that took place in the relatively short period of a decade in the 1990s, which was a period of intense activity in this field. First, the number of investment treaties rose from around 500 in 1990 to 2,700 by 2000. The number of bilateral investment treaties is currently over 3,236.[12] Secondly, the number of investment arbitrations, particularly arbitrations under investment treaties, rose dramatically during the decade and the trend continues. Thirdly, three distinct efforts at multilateral agreements on investments were made during this period.[13] All of them failed, but the fact is that there was a general belief in the possible success of the outcome such that efforts were attempted in quick succession within a span of ten years. The prevalent view was that a climate favourable to the making of multilateral rules on investment protection existed. Fourthly, the large number of arbitral awards under the treaties was regarded as having generated sufficient 'law' on principles of investment protection through treaties, so much so that books could be written on the basis of such 'law' as if a regime of investment protection had come into existence.[14] The different awards sought to expand significantly the scope of the treaties well beyond the intention of the states parties to the treaties. Some regard these awards as creating law through precedent. They speak in terms of constancy in arbitral jurisprudence.[15] Others question the legitimacy of the generation of law through means of precedent in investment arbitration.[16] Such questioning, however, occurred much later. During the 1990s, there was

[12] These figures are given in UNCTAD, *World Investment Report* (Geneva, 2014), p. 124. Forty-four treaties were terminated in 2014.

[13] First, the World Bank discussed such a code, but settled on guiding principles. Secondly, the OECD produced a draft of the Multilateral Agreement on Investment. Effort on the draft was abandoned due to states withdrawing from discussions in 1998. Thirdly, an instrument on investment under WTO was attempted, but these efforts were abandoned by 2000.

[14] Jeswald Salacuse, *The Law of Investment Treaties* (Oxford University Press, 2010); Jeswald Salacuse, 'The Emerging Global Regime for Investment', (2010) 51 *Harvard International Law Journal* 463; Jose Alvarez, *The Public International Law Regime Governing International Investment* (The Hague: Hague Academy of International Law, 2011); Karl Sauvant and Frederico Ortino, *Improving the International Law Policy Regime* (Helsinki: Ministry of Foreign Affairs, 2014).

[15] Christoph Schreuer and Mathew Weininger, 'A Doctrine of Precedent?' in Peter Muchlinski *et al.* (eds.), *Oxford Handbook of International Investment Law* (Oxford University Press, 2008), p. 1188.

[16] It is unlikely that there could be a constancy in jurisprudence simply because the treaty formulations are different. In *AES Corp.* v. *Argentina*, ICSID, Case No. ARB/02/17 (26 April 2005), the tribunal, following the Law of the Sea Tribunal, held that even the same provisions in different treaties need not produce the same interpretation, as the

INTRODUCTION

almost a free rein for the expansion of treaty-based investment arbitration. There were efforts to expand both the bases of jurisdiction under the treaties as well as the substantive law under the treaties through interpretation of their terms. The expansion of jurisdiction, as well as the expansion of the scope of the substantive principles in the treaties, necessarily caused discomfort to states. They had not anticipated such a course. Fifthly, over the course of time, but well after the end 1990s, disenchantment resulted with the system that had been created, resulting in a diversity of reactions from states, with some pulling out of investment arbitration altogether.[17] Often, there has been resistance to the rules that had been made in arbitral awards both by states, by arbitrators disinclined towards expansionary interpretations and by other interest groups, which stressed the importance of factors extraneous to the treaty, such as human rights, environmental protection and sustainable development. The nature of the investment treaties began to change. The newer treaties purport to be balanced treaties, seeking to reflect a resolution of the conflict between the interest of investment protection and the interest of the host state in regulating in the public interest. Some states

treaty balances differ. This is a strong argument against the treaties generating customary international law. Irene Ten Cate, 'The Costs of Consistency: Precedent in Investment Treaty Arbitration', (2013) 51 *Columbia Journal of Transnational Law* 418.

[17] In April 2007, at the 5th Summit Meeting of the Bolivarian Alliance for the Americas (ALBA), Nicaragua, Bolivia and Venezuela announced that they would withdraw from ICSID 'in order to guarantee the sovereign right of states to regulate foreign investment on their territories'. Ecuador joined ALBA and denounced ICSID. South Africa has announced that it will not renew investment treaties that have lapsed and has suspended its treaty programme. India is drafting a new model treaty that will reduce the nature of protection to foreign investment considerably. This follows the award in *White Industries* v. *India*, UNCITRAL (30 November 2011) (Brower, Rowley, Lau) where the delays in Indian courts formed the focal points of the award. Since then, there have been new disputes submitted to arbitration on the basis of the decisions of the Indian Supreme Court. Courts in South Korea and Brazil have discussed the constitutionality of the treaties. The Philippines has not signed treaties with investor–state arbitrations in the recent past. Its FTA with Japan left out the section on investor–state dispute settlement. Thailand seems to have formed negative views of investment treaties after the award in *Walter Bau* v. *Thailand*, UNCITRAL, Award (1 July 2009) (Barker, Lalonde, Bunnag). Norway has not been able to get its model treaty accepted as its balanced approach did not please all stakeholders. Norway has discontinued negotiating new treaties. In South Korea, an arbitration involving the insurance company, Lone Star, in which the general public have small investments, has caused considerable public disquiet. Yet new treaties are still being negotiated. China has made a treaty with Canada and is negotiating one with the United States. The Trans Pacific Pact, a treaty between several Pacific states, including the United States, Canada and Australia, is also being negotiated with an investment chapter.

6 INTRODUCTION

also showed a disinclination to accept arbitral awards. They have contested them through available annulment procedures.[18] Argentina has resisted enforcement of awards on various legal grounds. Attempts to seize Argentinian property for enforcement purposes have failed largely on the ground of sovereign immunity.[19] One of the Argentine awards was not enforced by the US Court of Appeal for not fulfilling the waiting period of eighteen months prior to arbitration as required by the treaty.[20] But the Supreme Court overruled the decision by a narrow majority. Argentina continues to resist enforcement despite pressure.

UNCTAD stated its displeasure with the system of investment arbitration as follows:[21]

> the public discourse about the usefulness, legitimacy and deficiencies of the investor–state dispute settlement mechanism is gaining momentum, especially given that the ISDS (Investor–State Dispute Settlement) mechanism is on the agenda in numerous bilateral and regional IIA (International Investment Agreement) negotiations. While reform options abound, their systematic assessment, including with respect to their feasibility, expected effectiveness and implementation method (e.g., at the level of international investment agreements, arbitral rules, institutions) remains wanting.

Commenting on the Bolivian withdrawal from ICSID arbitration in 2008, a leading scholar remarked that 'the future of investment arbitration is by no means certain'.[22] Since then, events have made this future even more shaky.

---

[18] Argentina has sought annulment of all awards made against it.

[19] The Law of the Sea Tribunal ordered that an Argentinian naval training ship seized in Ghana for the purposes of enforcing an arbitral award be released on the ground of sovereign immunity. *The Hindu*, 16 December 2012. The United States excluded Argentina in 2012 from the list of countries given trade preferences as a measure against non-enforcement.

[20] Argentina also resisted the enforcement of the award in the *BG Group* Award before the US courts. See *Argentina* v. *BG Group plc*, US Ct. App. DC Cir. (18 January 2012) (setting aside a US$185 million UNCITRAL award, which allowed the investor to commence arbitration without recourse to domestic courts in Argentina for eighteen months). The court said that arbitrators did not have power to decide whether investors could ignore the requirement. The Supreme Court overruled the decision by a narrow majority. Interestingly, in *ICS Inspection and Control Services Ltd* v. *Argentina*, UNCITRAL Ad hoc Arbitration (10 February 2012), the Tribunal rejected jurisdiction on the ground of non-satisfaction of the negotiation period.

[21] UNCTAD, IIA Issue Note, No. 1 (May 2013), p. 26.

[22] Christoph Schreuer in his introduction to August Reinish and Christina Knahr (eds.), *International Investment Law in Context* (Oxford University Press, 2008).

INTRODUCTION

Non-governmental organizations, interested in the impact of foreign investment on human rights, the environment and other areas, have shown concern over the impediments imposed by investment treaties on states to regulate harmful activity of foreign investors. Public anxiety has been caused as a result of huge damages awarded against states by investment tribunals.[23] Substantial disquiet exists as to the utility of investment treaty arbitration. There is an evident clash of distinct forces arraigned on different sides. One force, consisting of large multinational corporations, the law firms that advise them, their home states, large financial institutions providing investment funds, third-party funders of investment arbitration whose new business depends on investment arbitration and arbitrators inclined towards a policy of investment protection pulled the law towards inflexible investment protection on the ground that it catered to the interests of all concerned, including the developing host states, as foreign investment generally promoted economic development. The other force, supported by states affected by expansionary interpretation in arbitral awards, NGOs, arbitrators not inclined towards interpretations based solely on the policy of investment protection, and international lawyers opposing fragmentation of their discipline pulled it towards the recognition of competing regulatory interests of protection of the environment, human rights and other public interests such as health and welfare. Disputes arose which evidenced these clashes. Absolute investment protection clashed with the right to water,[24] the protection of health being affected by smoking,[25] the protection of cultural sites,[26] the protection of the rights of indigenous people,[27] the right to medicine[28] and global rights recognized by public international

---

[23] The award in *Occidental* v. *Ecuador* was for US$1.9 billion. Vulture funds which bought the awards against Argentina have refused to settle, raising the possibility of another bankruptcy in Argentina. *The Guardian*, 24 June 2014.

[24] *Aguas del Tunari SA* v. *Republic of Bolivia*, ICSID Case No. ARB/02/3 (21 October 2005); *Suez* v. *Argentina*, ICSID Case No. ARB/03/19 (30 July 2010); *Vivendi Universal* v. *Argentina*, ICSID, Case No. ARB/97/3 (20 August 2007); *Biwater Gauff* v. *Tanzania*, ICSID, Case No. ARB/05/22 (29 September 2006).

[25] *Philip Morris Brands Sarl* v. *Uruguay*, ICSID, Case No. ARB/10/7, Decision on Jurisdiction (2 July, 2013) (Bernadini, Born, Crawford); *Philip Morris* v. *Australia*, UNCITRAL PCA, Case No. 2012-12 (2012).

[26] *Parkerings-Compagniet AS* v. *Lithuania*, ICSID, Case No. ARB/05/8, Award (11 September 2007) (Levy, Lew, Lalonde).

[27] *Chevron* v. *Ecuador*, UNCITRAL PCA, Award (31 August 2011) (Bockstiegel, Brower, Van den Berg).

[28] *Apotex Inc.* v. *United States*, UNCITRAL (NAFTA), Jurisdiction (2013) (Landau, Smith, Davidson).

law. Each of these rights were espoused by different NGOs and people's pressure groups while the arbitrations were ongoing. The emergence of NGOs as actors in the field of investment law brought a countervailing power to that of multinational corporations into the field. There was also a strong pressure from within public international law to end the fragmentation of the subject by accommodating within it other principles of international law beside inflexible investment protection. These principles were increasingly concerned with issues relating to the environment, human rights and related interests. They militated against developing investment law through insulation from general principles of international law in such a manner as to accentuate a preferred objective of investment protection without heeding other international interests. In the face of such resistance, changes had to occur. These developments and the changes they provoked, which took place in a relatively short period, need an explanation.

One purpose of this book is to examine the course of developments that took place in a relatively short span of around twenty-five years, and to give explanations for the changes that took place in a rapidly evolving area of international law. It seeks an explanation in terms of the context in which the law operated, the economic and philosophical underpinnings of the important movements within the law, and the principal interests that clashed within the law. In the process, it also attempts to identify the manner in which changes take place in international law. The international law on foreign investment has hitherto been developed in a fragmented fashion, probably because of the fact that it served the specific purpose of investment protection. The strategy was to isolate it from its moorings in international law so that the focus could be on investment protection, and not on the other areas of international law that also affected the foreign investment process. To achieve the purpose of inflexible investment protection, it was necessary to keep the area insulated from other areas of international law so that the purpose of investment protection could not be diluted by other considerations. This study seeks to end the fragmented approach and to argue that the subject of investment protection under investment treaties is subject to international law principles. The solutions reached under it must always be accommodated within the general discipline of international law.

It also seeks to provide an explanation as to why the law veered out of course during the period of the last decade of the twentieth century. Explanations for this phenomenon may be sought within the law as most prefer, but the argument pursued in this work is that the explanations

INTRODUCTION 9

have to be sought outside the law as well. It suggests that the law was driven by the power of ideological changes that came about, particularly as to the structuring of the international and domestic markets. In that sense, the argument is that a set of rules came to be promoted by leading states with the instrumental purpose of ensuring the building of a law that advanced the prescriptions of an ideological preference towards the liberalization of markets, trade and investment. The view has often been taken that the decade in question was dominated politically by a single hegemonic power upholding the ideal of democratic governance as the political model, and advancing the preference for a neoliberal economic structure in which market mechanisms determined outcomes and self-corrected defects.[29] The absence of regulatory controls over market forces was a distinct feature of domestic legal systems of the period, particularly in the major developed states. This preference was transferred to the international sphere through a package of norms that reflected an ideological preference that came to be referred to as neoliberalism. In international law, this instrumental use was reflected in the expansive rule-making through arbitration to serve the ideological preference for inflexible protection of foreign investment. Neoliberalism, it is argued, becomes the central thrust behind the law that was put in place during this period.

As a prelude to the work, the next few sections of this chapter identify the primary factors that affected the law involved in investment arbitration. Section 1.1 explains how the tenets of neoliberalism were transferred into the law in the form of normative prescriptions. These were the basis on which some arbitrators made expansionist interpretations of treaty provisions. Section 1.2 demonstrates that changes that took place in the law depended on external political and economic factors, so that the changes that are taking place can be seen as a continuum of the past. Section 1.3 looks at the factors that have led to change in this area of the law and the phases of the change. Within this section, there is an examination of the clash between the aim of conserving the changes made during the neoliberal phase and the aim of change through resistance to the objectives of neoliberalism. Section 1.5 identifies the objectives to be achieved in the work. They set the background for the rest of the work, which expands on the points made, explains the resulting disenchantment with the system and suggests alternative solutions to

---

[29] Francis Fukuyama, *After the Neocons: America at the Crossroads* (New York: Profile Books, 2006).

10   INTRODUCTION

the problems created by the process. Sections 1.6 and 1.7 detail the contents of the chapters that are to follow.

1.1   Neoliberalism as a driving factor

The beginning of the 1990s witnessed the triumph of capitalism over communism after the dissolution of the Soviet Union. The Soviet Union had kept much of Eastern Europe bound to Russia and Russian communism since the end of the Second World War. During the Cold War between the Soviet Union and the United States, the two powers competed for influence in the rest of the world. They sought to spread their ideologies to other states. They created spheres of influence. The Cold War ended with the fall of the Berlin Wall in November 1989.[30] Communism, as a competing ideological force to democracy and the free market, also fell. This was trumpeted as signalling the need to organize the world on the basis of the twin philosophies of political democracy and the market-based organization of economic activity.[31] They were the twin ideologies left standing after the fall of communism. The new thinking manifested itself on international law in many ways. In the political sphere, new doctrines justifying the imposition of democracy, even by military intervention, came to be articulated. Scholarly effort was invested in the study of the influence of the single hegemonic power on the shaping of international law.[32] In the economic sphere, the preference was for the neoliberal philosophy for the ordering of both the domestic and the international economy on the basis that the market will be able to distribute resources and order economic activity more

[30] The Berlin Wall was built in August 1961 to prevent East Germans fleeing from communist rule into West Germany. Its sudden destruction symbolized the fall of communism.

[31] Francis Fukuyama, *The End of History and The Last Man* (London: Penguin, 1992); Michael Mandelbaum, *The Ideas that Conquered the World: Peace, Democracy and the Free Markets in the Twenty-First Century* (New York: Public Affairs, 2002). Fukuyama's book must have had a short shelf life as events transpired. Within six years, with the global economic crisis in 2008, the free-market ideology came to be questioned. Fukuyama was to regret his earlier, triumphant book in 2006 when he wrote *After the Neocons*. Two years later, there was the global economic crisis.

[32] Michael Byers and George Nolte (eds.), *United States Hegemony and the Foundations of International Law* (Cambridge University Press, 2003); Amy Bartholomew (ed.), *Empire's Law: The American Imperial Project and the War to Remake the World* (London: Pluto Press, 2006); Richard Burchill (ed.), *Democracy and International Law* (London: Ashgate, 2006); Shirley Scott, *International Law, US Power: The United States' Quest for Legal Security* (Cambridge University Press, 2013).

efficiently.[33] It was the basis on which international law sought to bring about new rules in international trade and investment. Neoliberalism stressed privatization of public enterprises, liberalization of flows of investment, and global governance of trade and investment. It advocated definite principles that stress trade without barriers, the flow of investments without hindrance, the protection of investment assets through secure recognition of private property, and dispute resolution mechanisms to ensure compliance with standards of governance. The ideas were not new, but they did, however, come to be tied to a programme of action referred to as the 'Washington Consensus'.[34] What was new was that after 1989 a package of norms came to be promoted as a panacea for the economic ills of the developing world by powerful states and institutions. Neoliberalism was based on minimizing the role of the state and self-regulation of the market by forces within it. The context of globalization provided a setting in which neoliberalism was seen as the glue that held the process of globalization together by bringing about a world without barriers to international trade, and a world in which there was a free movement of investments. As a result, multinational corporations were able to integrate the global economy through trade and investment. The hegemonic power, the home of the largest multinational corporations, drove globalization on the model of neoliberalism. The model was seen as the essential basis of American economic success. American national interests required such a stance. Its own economy prospered as a result of its multinational corporations being able to produce and market goods abroad and source raw materials for use at home. The United States, as the sole hegemon, drove this scheme through the instrumentality of international law.

---

[33] There were earlier phases of neoliberalism, but its peak was during the 1990s. Jamie Peck, *Constructions of Neoliberal Reason* (Oxford University Press, 2010).

[34] In the developed world, these ideas were as old as 'motherhood and apple pie'. What was new was that they were tied with the 'Washington Consensus' and promoted as a new package for economic development. The coining of the term 'Washington Consensus' is attributed to John Williamson, who described the package that constituted the Washington Consensus in his paper, 'A Short History of the Washington Consensus', republished in Narciss Serra and Joseph Stiglitz (eds.), *The Washington Consensus Reconsidered: Towards a New Global Governance* (New York: Oxford University Press, 2008), p. 14; David Harvey, *A Short History of Neo-Liberalism* (Oxford University Press, 2005). For the argument that global governance on the basis of market dominance was locked in by rules, see Stephen Gill, *Power and Resistance in the World Order*, 2nd edn (Basingstoke: Palgrave Macmillan, 2008); Alvaro Santos, 'The World Bank's Uses of the "Rule of Law" Promise in Economic Development', in David Trubek and Alvaro Santos (eds.), *The New Law and Economic Development* (Cambridge University Press, 2006), p. 253.

This drive was very evident in the resurgence of international trade law. International trade law became a force after it found sustenance in this new philosophy. The law was driven through the founding of a new institution, the World Trade Organization (WTO), replete with the most effective compliance mechanism in international law ever devised, ensuring that disputes are settled and decisions are enforced. The remit of the WTO was expanded on the ground that the disciplines of intellectual property, trade-related investments and services were intimately connected with trade. Liberalization of trade, the protection of intellectual property and the free establishment of service industries, all of which were neoliberal tenets, became central features of the new package. There was clear evidence that the new instruments, particularly those on intellectual property and trade in services, universalized the domestic law prescriptions of the United States. The manner in which the United States was able to drive its own preferred rules on intellectual property protection and services has been studied in several works.[35] These developments took place in disregard of the rights and interests of other people, particularly their right to health and access to drugs.[36] The conflicts that exist between rules of trade law and the rules of international law are repeated in the area of the law on foreign investment.[37]

There was clearly a zeal for the new wisdom in the area of foreign investment as well. The principles of the package that were relevant to foreign investment were the liberalization of the flows of inward foreign direct investment;[38] privatization of existing public corporations that supplied essential services;[39] deregulation of barriers of entry and exit;

---

[35] Susan Sell, *Private Power, Public Law: The Globalization of Intellectual Property* (Cambridge University Press, 2003).

[36] On the conflict between the right to health in international law and the TRIPS instrument, see John Tobias, *The Right to Health in International Law* (Oxford University Press, 2011) pp. 326–56. On issues of global justice and international trade law, see Frank Garcia, *Global Justice and International Economic Law: Opportunities and Prospects* (Cambridge University Press, 2012).

[37] Jan Pauwelyn, *Conflicts of Norms in Public International Law: How WTO Law Relates to Other Rules of International Law* (Cambridge University Press, 2003).

[38] The United States had formulated norms on each one of these principles. Liberalization of inward foreign investment was achieved through insistence on pre-entry national treatment in investment treaties. In GATS, it is secured through right of establishment in the services sector.

[39] Privatization was a condition for loans given by the World Bank and the International Monetary Fund (IMF). Many of the Argentine investment disputes, resulting from its economic crisis, concerned privatizations. The conditions imposed on states in crisis in

unhindered repatriation of profits; stability of the legal structure within which foreign investment functions; secure rights of property and contract; and neutral means of settlement of disputes between the host states and foreign investors.[40] Liberalization of investment flows was seen as the path to development, while competing models were regarded as unsuccessful.[41] The acceptance of this model is reflected in the policies many states took on foreign investment during the early 1990s. Thus, Argentina, the home of the 'Calvo Doctrine', which asserted the exclusive competence of local laws and local courts over the foreign investment process, gave up the doctrine in its new ardour for neoliberalism. It signed investment treaties that protected investments on the basis of external standards enforced by arbitration. Argentina was later to be inundated by over fifty claims arising from its economic crisis, itself a consequence of the adoption of neoliberal policies. The policies permitted free transfers of funds from the state, and a sudden run on the banks resulting in capital flights led to the economic crisis. Many of the neoliberal reforms in Argentina, like liberalized capital transfers and the dollar–peso parity, were undone in order to deal with the crisis. The measures violated investment treaty provisions and led to the spate of arbitrations.

The acceptance of neoliberal principles by states is an important reason for the increase in investment treaties in the 1990s, and the consequent increase in the number of investment arbitrations enabling the expansionary interpretation of the treaty principles. The states, particularly the developing states, seldom understood the nuances of the

> providing relief packages by the financial institutions have been widely criticized. John Levinson, 'Living Dangerously: Indonesia and the Reality of the Global Economic System', (1998) 7 *Journal of International Law and Practice* 437; Ross Buckley, 'The Direct Contribution of International Financial System to Global Poverty', in Krista Nadukavukaren Schefer (ed.), *Poverty and the International Economic System: Duties to the World's Poor* (Cambridge University Press, 2013), p. 278.

[40] The aim of the investment treaties and the principles formulated in awards emphasized the protection of property and contracts. The contemporary writings of Hernando de Soto stressed the importance of recording of ownership of property. Hernando de Soto, 'The Missing Ingredient: What Poor Countries will Need to Make their Markets Work', in Terry Anderson and Peter Hill (eds.), *The Privatization Process: A Worldwide Perspective* (Lanham, MD: Rowan & Littlefield, 1996), p. 19. For criticism of the law that was generated by neoliberalism during this period, see David Trubeck and Alvaro Santos (eds.), *The New Law and Economic Development: A Critical Appraisal* (Cambridge University Press, 2006).

[41] During that period, the most successful developing states, the Asian tigers, Hong Kong, Singapore, South Korea and Taiwan, did not adopt a neoliberal model, but operated a model that was based on strict regulation of the economy by the developmental state. These competing models did not come into consideration.

14 INTRODUCTION

treaties that they adopted. The assumption that underlay the making of these treaties was that they would result in the greater flow of foreign investment as the substantive provisions in the treaties give investments secure protection. It was an impression that the international financial associations carefully cultivated and propagated. They made assistance through loans conditional on the signing of investment treaties. The preambles in these treaties articulated the emphasis on investment protection. They affirmed the relevance of the treaties to greater flows of foreign investment with consequential benefits for economic development. This premise in the preambles, itself based on a neoliberal view, played a significant role in the taking of expansionary views by arbitrators in the interpretation of investment treaties. The select group of arbitrators responsible for the majority of the awards had imbibed the values of neoliberalism. They were repeatedly appointed to arbitration tribunals, where they were prepared to give effect to these principles. Their reasoning was that the effect of the treaties had to be enhanced so that the objective of economic development that underlay the treaties could be realized. It was a much contested theory of economic development, but it lay at the heart of neoliberalism. The compliance mechanism devised through compulsory arbitration ensured that there were effective sanctions against the breach of the provisions.

The assumption that investment treaties lead to greater flows of foreign investment is increasingly challenged.[42] Studies doubt that there is

---

[42] Studies discuss whether or not investment treaties promote flows of foreign investment. Though not yet inconclusive, the weight of opinion favours the view that there is little correlation between the making of the treaties and flows of foreign investment. Factors such as stability are more relevant to attracting investments. This creates considerable doubt as to whether the encroachment on sovereignty of the state involved in investment treaties can be justified by the mirage that foreign investment flows will occur as a result of the treaties and lead to economic development. There are several studies on the correlation between foreign investment flows and investment treaties. The evidence they present is not conclusive, but they throw considerable doubt on the inflexible view that foreign investment is uniformly beneficial, which is the underlying basis of investment treaties. See Karl Sauvant and Lisa Sachs (eds.), *The Effect of Treaties on Foreign Direct Investment* (New York: Oxford University Press, 2009); Susan Ackerman and Jennifer L. Tobin, 'Do BITs Benefit Developing Countries?' in Catherine A. Rogers and Roger P. Alford (eds.), *The Future of Investment Arbitrations* (New York: Oxford University Press, 2009), pp. 131–56. Some, cautiously, find a positive correlation, see Mary Hallward-Driemeier, 'Do Bilateral Investment Treaties Attract Foreign Investment? Only a Bit and They Could Bite', World Bank Policy Research Working Paper No. 3121 (Geneva: World Bank, 2003). There are an increasing number of such studies, but, due to their conflicting nature, no definite conclusions can be drawn from them. Nevertheless, the studies subject the orthodox position that BITs promote investment flows to doubt.

1.1 NEOLIBERALISM AS A DRIVING FACTOR 15

any significant link in the making of investment treaties and investment flows. It stands to reason that the symbolism of an investment treaty cannot amount to much unless the state seeking foreign investment itself has a stable system, an attractive market and a functioning judicial system. These doubts undermine the need for investment treaties as well as the law that investment arbitrators assiduously built through the interpretation of these treaties.

The 'roaring nineties', as that decade came to be referred,[43] ushered in new attitudes to the use of international law towards investment protection. The instrumental use of international law enabled it to be shaped to support the political ideologies of the hegemonic power. There were evident expansive changes taking place in the law on the use of force, international trade, the protection of intellectual property, the extraterritorial extension of laws, and in other areas. The present study focuses only on foreign investment, but this subject must also be viewed in a broader context in which the new rules that were being shaped occurred in the context of a climate of change engineered by the sole hegemonic power of a world order based on a set of norms that it preferred. There was a continuation of the dominance that the United States had exerted in this area of international law of foreign investment from the very outset.[44] United States' practice has been the dominant influence on the shaping of this aspect of international law, with Europe taking over the rules that had been designed by such practice. The United States had the opportunity to exert influence for yet another time. As stated earlier, the international financial institutions it controlled, the World Bank and the IMF supported the programme. But hegemonic order waned through overextension of military power. It was further weakened by the global economic crisis in 2008, brought about by a lack of regulatory control over lending practices of financial institutions.[45] In that context, the competing norms put forward by other interests began to have an effect on foreign investment law. The United States itself had

---

[43] Joseph Stiglitz, *The Roaring Nineties: Why We are Paying for the Greediest Decade in History* (London: Penguin, 2003).

[44] The history of the shaping of the law is stated in Charles Lipson, *Standing Guard: Protecting Foreign Capital in the Nineteenth and Twentieth Centuries* (Berkeley, CA: University of California Press, 1965). For a more recent work, see Noel Maurer, *The Empire Trap: The Rise and Fall of the US Intervention to Protect American Property Overseas, 1893–2013* (Princeton University Press, 2013). European states were later adherents to the system the United States had devised.

[45] Joseph Stiglitz, *Free Fall, America, Free Markets and the Sinking of the Economy* (London: Allen Lane, 2010).

to prepare for a change as it had become a massive importer of foreign investment. It was also facing foreign investment arbitrations in the context of NAFTA. Developing states, faced with several awards against them and further disputes pending, were busy finding ways out of the morass that faced them. New types of treaties with broad defences against state liability began to be made. The context in which these changes were taking place is relevant. They cannot be explained without having regard to the ideological underpinnings of the law that had been built up. The ebbs and flows in ideology have shaped the international law on foreign investment. This is true of other branches of international law as well. There has been an entrenched aversion to the examination of the law in its ideological and political context. This may itself have been motivated by the desire to ensure that contextual explanation of the real purpose behind the law was cloaked by a cultivated aversion. It may be possible to argue that there is clearer evidence of the decline of ideological under-pinnings of the law, leading to changes in the area of the international law on foreign investment, especially in recent times. As indicated, one aim of this book is to explain changes in this area of the law.

1.2 Explaining change

The policy reasons for the protection of foreign investment through international law were not well articulated earlier. The power context in which investments took place did not require justifications or the development of extensive rationales.[46] As these power equations began changing, it was necessary to give explanations as to why investments needed to be protected. The classical view was that flows of foreign investment led to capital formation, infusion of new technology, upgrad-ing of infrastructure, fresh employment with transfer of new skills and export earnings. The capital-exporting states espoused this classical eco-nomic explanation. The explanation sustained the making of strong norms of international law on foreign investment protection. Neoliberalism was to capitalize on this set of norms by articulating a fresh set of propositions that were favourable to foreign investment. At the least the articulation of a philosophy that gathered together existing norms in a new guise in a world that was accepting of the move to free

---

[46] European investments were made in the context of imperial systems. In Latin America, where such a system was absent, the United States had to create justifications for the protection of investments.

market economics gave vigour to the creation and expansion of new notions in the field. Such change, as already indicated, arose from momentous movements that took place at the beginning of the decade. The fall of the Soviet Union ended the competing ideology of communism, and this led to the proclamation of the triumph of the market model. The ascendancy of corporations holding capital was facilitated by the denial of aid to developing countries as a matter of policy and the drying up of excess capital in banks as a result of the sovereign debt crisis. As a result, foreign investment became important as the only source of capital inflows for developing countries. Multinational corporations holding such capital had to be courted. Developing countries were prepared to break up the cohesion they had formed in earlier decades by adopting a common policy towards foreign investment which was inherent in their efforts to bring about domestic control over foreign investment. Their efforts to create a new international economic order (NIEO),[47] with domestic control over foreign investment as one pillar of the order, was eclipsed, though during the intervening years much had been done to secure its principal tenets in constitutional provisions and foreign investment codes.[48] This effort in the immediate period after decolonization

[47] The NIEO was a package of norms stated largely through UN General Assembly resolutions, intended to bring about structural changes in the world trading system and the rules relating to foreign investment. The principal resolutions on the subject were: the Resolution on Permanent Sovereignty over Natural Resources', GA Res. 1803(XVII), 14 December 1962; the Charter on the Economic Rights and Duties of States, GA Res. 3281 (XXIX), 12 December 1974; the Declaration on the Establishment of a New International Economic Order (1974).

[48] It would be too strong a statement to say that the NIEO was given up. Some, like Jose Alvarez, have suggested that the NIEO simply faded away. Jose Alvarez, 'A BIT on Custom' (2009) 42 *International Law & Politics* 17. One could as well say that its objects had been achieved as legislation implementing the principles of the NIEO had been enacted in most states. Its principles, such as permanent sovereignty over natural resources, which was one of the chief thrusts of the NIEO, had been largely accepted both in domestic and international law. Sir Ian Brownlie, among others, regarded the permanent sovereignty doctrine as constituting *ius cogens*. Ian Brownlie, 'The Legal Status of Natural Resources in International Law', (1979) 162 *Hague Recueil des Cours* 245. The principle relating to permanent sovereignty over natural resources is stated in many constitutions. The production-sharing agreements that replaced concession agreements, in themselves a reflection of the NIEO principles, contained local law as the law applicable to the agreement. The demise of the NIEO is greatly exaggerated. The contracts of foreign investment, like the production-sharing agreement in the oil industry, reflected the idea that oil always belonged to the state, with the foreign investor being handed over a share of production once oil is put on board a nominated ship for transfer. National control over resource sectors, an objective of the NIEO, had been achieved. Given the continued existence of such legal vestiges of the NIEO, it is the better view that the NIEO continues

had the effect of creating norms that countered the existing practice of developed states on investment protection. But the competing norms associated with the NIEO went into abeyance with the advent of neoliberalism. The developing countries began to compete with each other for the limited foreign investment held by multinational corporations. The dissolution of the Soviet Union also led to the creation of new states in Eastern Europe, which adopted market economies. They increased the competition for the available foreign investment by adopting liberal policies towards entry of foreign investment. Given the prevailing belief that treaties containing protection for foreign investment were necessary to attract such investment, the newly created states of Eastern Europe added significantly to the number of investment treaties. Many arbitrations were instituted on the basis of these treaties. The Czech Republic, a part of the former Soviet Union, became one of the states against which the most number of arbitrations were brought.[49] The former Soviet Union states contributed not only to the increasing number of treaties, but also to an unprecedented growth in investment arbitration.

Simultaneously with these developments in the international economic sphere, developments took place in the political sphere. It is worth re-emphasizing these changes as they greatly assisted the acceptance of neoliberal models. In the political sphere, the hegemony of the

to have healthy existence in the domestic laws of the developing world. It could well be that its principles are revived, more probably by developed states, which are now becoming investment receiving states. Reading the US arguments in *Methanex v. United States*, seeking to assert regulatory control, is reminiscent of the arguments of the developing world. See further, Margot Salomon, 'From NIEO to Now and the Unfinishable Story of Economic Justice' (2013) 62 *International & Comparative Law Quarterly* 32. She concluded that: 'it may well be the case that it will soon be developed States that revive the NIEO's prescriptions as they may increasingly have to rely on its precepts as they become recipients of inward investments that limit their exercise of sovereignty under the very rules they fashioned' (at p. 54). Further, see Muthucumaraswamy Sornarajah, 'The Return of the NIEO and the Retreat of Neo-Liberal International Law', in Sharif Bhuiyan and Philippe Sands (eds.), *International Law and Developing Countries: Essays in Honour of Kamal Hossain* (Berlin: Brill, 2014), pp. 32–59.

[49] The Czech Republic made many treaties and was respondent later in many treaty-based arbitrations. It has not revealed the number of disputes it has against it due to fear of public protests. Tomas Fecak, 'Czech Experience with Bilateral Investment Treaties: Somewhat Bitter Taste of Investment Protection' (2011) *Czech Yearbook of International Law* 17. The Czech Republic is illustrative of the practice of the former communist states. It began its investment treaty practice in 1989, and notched up seventy-seven treaties within a short time without, according to Fecak, 'a clear idea behind their purpose'. It figures now among the states with the largest number of arbitrations (twenty to Argentina's fifty-two in 2012).

United States was paramount due to the fall of the Soviet Union. The United States increasingly sought to build its foreign policy on the basis of this hegemony by ensuring that the world order was recreated to suit its interests. Consequently, it promoted a foreign policy that was based on a preference for democratic values in the belief that the prevalence within the world of such values would enhance peace and ensure its dominance. The ideas that guided foreign policy during this period were the direct result of the triumph of the United States over communism, and they came to be termed neoconservatism.[50] The political idea of neoconservatism and the economic idea of neoliberalism worked in tandem on the ground that liberalization of markets worked best in a world organized on the basis of democracy. The considerable corporate power that existed also lobbied for outcomes that favoured corporate interests. The period was imbued with ideas that supported the evolution of a new type of world order. Clearly, international law was used to secure this world order. An attempt was made to reorient international law in many areas.[51] The present work is concerned with the area of foreign investment alone. But its reasoning is buttressed by the fact that there was a concerted drive to change international law in order to achieve certain objectives of the hegemonic power both in the political as well as in the economic sphere. In the formulation of any theory of change in international law, it will be necessary to take account of the context in which international law operated.

1.3   The phases of change

The setting in which these developments took place is necessary for the study of these changes. As a prelude, it is necessary to identify the phases of change that had taken place in the earlier course of the development of the international law on foreign investment. This examination indicates

---

[50] Justin Vaise, *Neoconservatism: The Biography of A Movement* (Cambridge, MA: Harvard University Press, 2010).

[51] There was immense activity during this period. The extent to which democracy was promoted through international law is studied in Gregory Fox and Brad Roth (eds.), *Democratic Governance and International Law* (Cambridge University Press, 2000); Byers and Nolte (eds.), *United States Hegemony and the Foundations of International Law*. Parallel developments in the area of the international law on the use of force assert US power. They were the notion that the promotion of democracy was part of international law justifying military intervention; the articulation of the Bush Doctrine on pre-emptive force; and the failure to accept accountability for war crimes by joining the International Criminal Court.

20   INTRODUCTION

the extent to which the international law on foreign investment has always been amenable to the political and economic climates in which it has operated. It also involves an implicit rejection of the positivist view that international law is a neutral discipline. Being neutral, the view was that the context in which it operated, or the interests and ideas dominant at any given time, did not affect the creation of its rules. Such a view cloaked the operation of power in shaping law. It was a convenient device to portray law as a neutral discipline so that those affected could accept its dictates without dissent. Equally, those profiting from the neutral discipline could disavow accountability for the harm they caused. Thus, the law on foreign investment protection addressed continuously the protection of the investment of multinational corporations. It seldom addressed the issue of the multinational corporation and the harm it caused to the host state through its conduct. The positivist view, which sanitized the law from its context so as to keep issues such as morality or context out, lacks substance. The changes in the international law on foreign investment can be explained only by the fact that the context in which the law operated had undergone changes as a result of the shift in power equations within that context.

The positivist view of moral and political neutrality has often been the means of hiding the interests of power and the fact that power shapes the law. It enabled the cloaking of power relationships that affect the formation of rules by ensuring that there was no need for inquiry into factors that are extraneous to the law and legal rules in studying the formation and functioning of law. This ensured that no inquiry was made as to how the rule was shaped and whose interests it served. The moral issues that may be involved in the shaping of the rules were also avoided. Since legal personality was one of the main factors in the operation of the positivist international law, a convenient way of avoiding issues was simply to regard certain actors wielding power as not having personality in terms of international law. Thus, an early multinational corporation, the British East India Company, which conquered many lands and imposed administration over them, had no personality in terms of international law.[52] It quelled rebellions, punished people, conquered lands, killed whole tribes and extorted taxes. It did all of these without personality and, hence, without accountability. Its shareholders, the most important personages

---

[52] The East India Company was not alone. There were also the Dutch East India Company, the Hudson Bay Company and several companies of entrepreneurs in colonial Africa. The holocaust in the Congo by Emperor Leopold of Belgium took place without accountability.

in Britain at the time, were similarly not accountable, though they reaped the profits of the carnage unleashed by the company. On the moral front, the justification was provided by the white man's burden of bringing civilization to India.

The modern multinational corporation similarly lacks personality according to many international texts, so that its accountability for wrongs it may commit during its operations can be avoided. It has rights but no responsibilities. It wields considerable power to effect change in both domestic and international law.[53] The changes the modern multinational corporation is instrumental in bringing about are not attributed to the exercise of its considerable power over governments, and its use of the low-order sources of international law in constructing rules favourable to it are seldom studied. Much of the international law on foreign investment was built up through the use of private power and the manipulation of the low-order sources of international law, such as the writings of 'highly qualified' publicists or the decisions of arbitral tribunals. Such positivist stances are unhelpful in the analysis of the law generally. They are particularly unhelpful in seeking explanations for changes that take place within international investment law.

In times of the wide and dominant prevalence of favourable ideology, private actors conform to and further the tenets of the dominant philosophy, either consciously or unconsciously. The contention is that given the wide prevalence of the articulation of neoliberal norms by the hegemonic power and the institutions it controlled, there was a climate conducive to the congealing of norms favourable to the interests supported by the hegemonic power. At the lower orders of application of the norms, arbitrators were intent on ensuring not only the statement of these norms in authoritative terms, but their expansion as virtue lay in bending according to the prevailing winds. This may account for the expansive interpretations that arbitrators gave to treaty provisions on standards of protection. The formation of international law in the context of prevailing conditions has been explained in other studies.[54]

---

[53] The cooperation and conflict between the public power of states and the private power of multinational corporations forms the subject of an interesting book. David Rothkopf, *Power Inc.: The Epic Rivalry Between Big Business and Government and the Reckoning that Lies Ahead* (New York: Farrar, Straus & Giroux, 2012).

[54] The New Haven School has argued consistently for taking the context and the policy of international law into account in shaping and understanding it. Michael Reisman, *The Quest for World Order and Human Dignity in the Twenty-First Century: Constitutive Process and Individual Commitment*, Hague Academy of International Law, *Collected Courses*, vol. 351 (The Hague: Martinus Nijhoff, 2012).

22   INTRODUCTION

As much as change takes place to accommodate norms favouring interests of hegemonic powers, particularly when they are consistent with the tenets of a prevailing ideology, the norms that receive such acceptance could also change when the climate supporting them changes. This happens when hegemonic power recedes and resistance to the changes build up on the basis of justice-centred ideas refuting the norms of power. The norms of the hegemonic order then are subjected to change as a result of a countervailing power exerted by the justice-centred norms usually asserted by a combination of other actors with countervailing power in the area. Change in international law takes place when changes in the moral or ideological climate either makes an existing norm undesirable (as in the making of slavery, hitherto lawful, into a universal crime), or where a new norm is brought about because of changing political and philosophical perceptions (as in the case of the recognition of self-determination in ending colonialism, the rise of international human rights law when ideas of absolute sovereignty of states recede, or international criminal law when the immunity of heads of states for genocide becomes unacceptable). When overwhelming moral support coalesces behind a norm, its maturation is sometimes explained in terms of 'norm cascades'.[55] Such phenomena usually take place in the area of human rights. But similar changes take place in other areas as well. They usually take place when resistance builds up to an existing norm, which is then perceived as unjust on the ground that it serves the interests of the few. Such changes meet with progressive acceptance within the international community as they are perceived as beneficial to the interests of the community as a whole.

Investment protection norms are advanced as cosmopolitan norms that serve global interests by promoting investment flows, which are claimed to be beneficial in promoting development. Such promotion of an idea that has scant evidence in support is accepted because it comes shrouded in an ideology that has gained prominence at a given time. But when that ideology recedes, the idea it promoted loses force and the law

---

[55] Kathryn Sikkink, *The Justice Cascade: How Human Rights Prosecutions are Changing World Politics* (New York: W. W. Norton, 2011). The work explains how norms of immunity of heads of states for domestic violations of human rights changed to impose criminal liability. The notion of norm cascades in change is derived from the writings of Cass Sunstein. For example, Cass Sunstein, *Free Markets and Social Justice* (New York: Oxford University Press, 1998). For an explanation using notions of 'tipping points', see Martha Finnemore and Kathryn Sikkink, 'Norm Dynamics and Political Change', (1998) 52 *International Organizations* 524.

built on the idea also recedes. The rise in resistance to norms of inflexible investment protection is largely based on the decline of neoliberalism, which supported the legal base on which the regime of expansionary investment protection was built. With its decline, norms that restricted the sovereignty of a state to deal with issues of public interest for the fear that it would affect foreign investment lost support.[56] The argument is also made that there is an emergence of certain norms relating to the environment and human rights as global public policy so that competing norms on investment protection had to give way. The disillusionment of states with the loss of regulatory power through an unintended and ever expanding system of investment protection led to their consideration of changes. The rise of NGOs, powerful new actors on the international scene, contributed significantly to rethinking. A new group of international lawyers seeking to end fragmentation opposed the development of autonomous areas of international law, such as that on foreign investment, without heed to its moorings in general principles of international law. A coincidence of circumstances led to change.

Changes, then, are effected in two ways. The first group of changes is associated with power. One may even argue that since custom is the most important source of public international law, the first rules of the system were established on the basis of alleged custom. The practice of hegemonic states is more likely to be followed by others and is more likely to congeal into customary law. Later changes to the rules come about as the interests of power shift. Then the states with power change the norms so that they favour their interests.[57] Such norms are maintained largely through the public power of the states or the private power of non-state entities. Public and private power can act in tandem. In many instances, the personnel who exercise them are not separate.[58] Private power can bring about norms of public international law by itself, a phenomenon positivists would be loath to admit. Private power can use low-order

---

[56] For explanations of resistance, see Rahul Rao, *Third World Resistance* (Oxford University Press, 2011).

[57] Michael Byers, *Custom, Power and the Power of Rules: International Relations and Customary International Law* (Cambridge University Press, 1999).

[58] Though more pronounced in the past, it is a visible fact that business leaders move in and out of the US administration frequently. Allegations are frequently made that the foreign policy of the United States is shaped to favour leading corporations as the administration consists of those with close links to corporations. This was particularly so during the Bush administrations, which coincide with the period studied here. Its links with the oil industry were strong. The role of pharmaceutical corporations in shaping domestic and international patent laws has been widely studied.

24   INTRODUCTION

sources to articulate norms of international law. They can invoke arbitral tribunals or use writings of 'highly qualified publicists' who could articulate norms that are partial to their interests.[59] The norms so articulated either pass into rules of international law as they come to be accepted or are resisted, in which case their acceptance will depend on the strength with which they are asserted. The legitimacy of the norm associated with power will enable its acceptance, but where it is not legitimate, in a progressively democratic world, resistance to it will build up making the norm gradually loose force. A norm made by private power favours the few and presumptively lacks democratic legitimacy. For that reason, it is an insecure norm that has to be continuously shored up and would be continuously under attack. A system of norms protecting the few foreign investors and the lucrative business of arbitrators and law firms cannot hold sway for long unless its legitimacy can be assured. The instability of norms in investment law stem from the fact that their making is associated with private power in association with low-order sources of international law. They also distribute wealth in the most unjust manner, promoting a system in which the owners of resources do not have the larger share of the benefit of their exploitation or the labour used to manufacture goods does not share proportionately in the profits.[60] Consequently, the norms generated by the system based on neoliberalism are not based on secure foundations.

Changes are made by human agency. The agents of change act consciously or unconsciously. They act consciously when they implement policy changes based on the new, preferred ideology. They act unconsciously when an ethos develops around the suggested norms based on an ideology. So, for example, judges in an age that is imbued with

[59] International lawyers turn a blind eye to the role of private power in making international law. This may be purposeful so that the authority of the norms so made is not doubted. International relations experts, however, have studied the role of multinational corporations in articulating legal norms. Claire Cutler, *Private Power and Global Authority: Transnational Merchant Law in the Global Political Economy* (Cambridge University Press, 2003). Some have claimed an independent role in law-making for international tribunals. Armin von Bogdandy and Indo Venzke, 'In Whose Name? An Investigation of International Court's Public Authority and its Democratic Justification', (2012) 23 *European Journal of International Law* 7. In the area of investment law, foreign investors can invoke tribunals that are set up with their participation and the participation of institutions that are partial to investment protection.

[60] There is extensive literature on global justice in recent times. International law has shown concern for this literature and sought to test its rules in accordance with the theories of justice. See further, Lukas Meyer (ed.), *Legitimacy, Justice and Public International Law* (Cambridge University Press, 2010).

1.3 THE PHASES OF CHANGE 25

conservative ideologies may act to curb labour rights or rights of association. At times of liberal views, the converse would happen. Judges have reflected particular economic beliefs in making decisions.[61] The same is said to happen in arbitration law when courts swing towards pro-arbitration views permitting greater freedom of decision to arbitrators, and then swing back again when such views change towards a view that seeks to control arbitration on the perception that permissiveness had made the system arrogate powers to private decision-making to the detriment of public interest.

States also act through human agency. Executive arms of states take decisions to adopt particular economic policies at the time when such policies are ascendant.[62] They do so for a variety of reasons. A conviction may be formed that they are the best policies as they are seen as successful. There could be imitation of other states, which are moving towards the policies.[63] Competition in attracting investors with other liberalizing states may provide another reason for change. There could also be indirect pressure from financial institutions, which may tie loans to the adoption of specific liberal economic policies. These various factors assisted in the adoption of neoliberal policies by states. They account for the making of a large number of bilateral investment treaties in the specific period.

At a lower level, arbitrators who interpret and apply the standards in the treaties may also be similarly affected by the prevailing economic philosophies. They may actively seek to enhance the scope of these standards through expansive interpretation, so as to give full rein to the tenets of that philosophy through formulation of legal principles.[64] Other arbitrators, showing fidelity to consent of the parties as the basis of jurisdiction, may resist such changes, leading to schisms in the law that

---

[61] Antitrust law in the United States underwent a change when important works, like Robert Bork, *The Antitrust Paradox* (New York: Basic Books, 1976), and Richard Posner, *Antitrust Law* (University of Chicago Press, 2001), advocated that courts should interpret the Sherman Act through the prism of price theory. This was another legal triumph for market-based economics.

[62] An example would be the adoption of the open-door policy by China in 1979.

[63] The Chinese open-door policy was imitated by Vietnam. A so-called 'wild geese in flight' pattern takes place when states follow a successful leader and adopt similar policies. Tax incentives are another example. There is no evidence that tax incentives attract investments, but once a state grants them, others follow in the belief that if they did not, the investor would establish in the state that grants them the incentive.

[64] Examples of this would be introduction of the rules on legitimate expectations into fair and equitable standards. See Chapter 5.

is developed through arbitral precedents. Such schisms also undermine the legitimacy of the law, making resistance to earlier established norms succeed more easily.

The manner in which hegemonic powers seek to process the norm they wish to promote as law is relevant. The laundering of the norms through judicial or processes resembling judicial processes is important in ensuring the acceptance of the law by the community affected by the norms. Because such processes are regarded as neutral, there is an easier acceptance of the norms created through judicial processes than through legislation passed by politicians, increasingly seen as flawed. The laundering of a norm through a judicial or a like process hides the power element in its making and gives it a cloak of legitimacy.[65] The visibility of such law creation is also low. There is an increasing tendency among international lawyers to argue that, once established, an international tribunal has a life of its own. It has the power, it is argued, to develop the law in the area. On this view, investment arbitrators would have the ability to develop the law even against the wishes of the states that created jurisdiction in them.

The strategy of using arbitration in investment disputes is to employ a similar technique. The assumption is that it may be easier to sell the law that is processed through a system of arbitration. There was much talk of the 'depoliticization' of the law at the time investment arbitration arose to prominence.[66] The argument was that a judicial-like process would remove the power equation from the settlement of investment disputes. It could also assuage public disquiet about outcome. The argument, however, ignores the fact that the arbitration system could also involve itself in ideological predisposition towards favourable stances to particular interest groups.[67] This could be particularly so where an arbitral institution functions within an institutional system given to the propagation of certain economic models. ICSID is the classic example for it works

---

[65] Compare the argument that elites insulate policy-making from discussions as to distributive justice by transferring decision-making to the courts. Ran Hirschl, *Towards Juristocracy: The Origins and Consequences of New Constitutionalism* (Cambridge, MA: Harvard University Press, 2007).

[66] This was a view assiduously promoted by the World Bank. The argument is that by moving disputes to a neutral forum like arbitration, the power element that might otherwise be used in settling it is reduced. World Bank, *Towards a Greater Depoliticization of Investment Disputes: ICSID and MIGA* (Washington, DC: World Bank, 1992)

[67] Further, see David Schneiderman, *Constitutionalizing Economic Globalization: Investment Rules and Democracy's Promise* (Cambridge University Press, 2008).

1.3   THE PHASES OF CHANGE

within the World Bank system that advances certain preferred economic solutions. The institutional bias affects arbitration under the system.

Arbitrators themselves are predisposed towards solutions that favour commercial stability as they come from a background of commercial arbitration. This may be acceptable when they operate in a purely commercial environment, but, even then, neutrality is not assured as each arbitrator carries with him prejudices towards solutions.[68] But investment arbitration involves deeply political issues that concern both the domestic and the international public where human rights or environmental concerns are involved.[69] Depoliticization conceives the law itself as neutral when in fact it is laden with values that favour particular solutions. The counterpart in international trade was the argument that the rules of trade replace the rules of power.[70] At the time this view was formulated, it was also stated that the process of arbitration was based on the rule of law.

In the case of international law on foreign investment, the period of neoliberalism witnessed such changes in that there was an accentuation of the principles on investment protection on the basis of the view that flows of foreign investment were uniformly beneficial to economic development. An ideological climate was created in which a small arbitral community acted in the conviction that it was interpreting and applying a law in order to advance the tenets of an ideology that advocated that promotion of the flows of foreign investment through creative interpretations of the investment treaties was a mission that was mandated by a treaty system and advanced the interests of the global community. The fact that they operated in the context of an institutional system committed to this mission further entrenched this attitude.[71] This articulated premise became the justification for the maintenance of a system of expansionary law of investment protection. The small group of arbitrators who administered the system imbibed the culture of the system and reinforced the belief of each other. Following the package of rules also

---

[68] Yves Dezaley and Bruce Garth, *Dealing in Virtue: International Commercial Arbitration and the Construction of a Transnational Legal Order* (University of Chicago Press, 1996).

[69] Gus Van Harten, *Investment Treaty Arbitration and Public Law* (Oxford University Press, 2007); Andreas Kulick, *Global Public Interests in International Investment Law* (Cambridge University Press, 2012).

[70] John Jackson, *The World Trading System: Law and Policy of International Economic Relations* (Cambridge, MA: MIT Press, 1996), p. 109.

[71] ICSID itself was founded on the basis that the existence of a secure system of investment arbitration ensured flows of foreign investment necessary for economic development. The preamble of the ICSID Convention implicitly states the link.

happened to be personally profitable to them.[72] It is perfectly possible that other arbitrators were acculturated into the beliefs held by this small group of arbitrators or complacently followed the exclusive band. In any event, in the recent phase of the law a small group of arbitrators were able to expand the meaning of treaties to accommodate ideas of investment protection in a manner that could not have been intended by the states making the treaty, precipitating a crisis in the subject. This was resisted by another group of arbitrators, who believed that going beyond the rules to which parties had agreed to would undermine the fundamental tenet of arbitration that consent provided the basis of arbitration. These internal clashes within the system precipitated a situation of norm clashes that will have to result in accommodation or change. One could argue that these clashes also represent clashes between norms of power and norms of justice in that the major group represents the interests of expansionism enhancing the norms dictated by power, while the other group resists such expansionism on the ground of restricting interpretation to the strict intention of the parties to the treaties. A few within the latter group may want to accommodate global public interests manifested in environmental issues, human rights and other concerns. The schisms that have opened up may lead to the dismantling of the rules established by neoliberal expansionism. This may be an optimistic prediction as the vitality of neoliberalism remains despite reversals. The private power of multinational corporations still remains tenacious enough to ensure that change is not effected easily.[73] But they cannot resist states that either pull out of the system individually or act collectively or regionally to bring about change. An intermediate solution they have adopted is to bring about balanced treaties conserving regulatory space.

---

[72] An OECD study suggested that twelve arbitrators were involved in 60 per cent of 263 ICSID tribunals. OECD, 'Investor–State Dispute Settlement', Public Consultation Paper, 16 May 2012–9 July 2012 (Paris: OECD, 2012), at para. 120. Studies found that eighteen arbitrators are 'at the core of the social structure of investor–state arbitrators'. It is significant that the core clusters emerged during the 'roaring nineties'. Corporate Europe Observatory, *How Law Firms, Arbitrators and Financiers are Fuelling an Investment Arbitration Boom* (London: Corporate Europe Observatory, 2012). Practitioners have pointed out similar tendencies. George Kahale, the managing partner of the legal firm, Curtis, New York, referred to a club of arbitrators in a keynote speech at the 8th Annual Investment Treaty Arbitration Forum, 28 March 2014, developing the law in this area by citing each other's awards.

[73] Colin Crouch, *The Strange Non-Death of Neoliberalism* (Cambridge: Polity Press, 2011), where the argument is made that neoliberalism may be kept alive through the power of multinational corporations.

1.3 THE PHASES OF CHANGE 29

International lawyers were generally willing supporters of the expansionist tendencies. As Falk pointed out, there is a tendency on the part of international law and lawyers to 'often follow prevailing lines of power and wealth'.[74] There was a willing acquiescence to the neoliberal trends of the times, despite the fact that the law was deviating from its moorings in notions of justice that should have geared the law to securing interests of poverty reduction, environmental protection and the promotion of human rights. In this instance, international lawyers largely went along with the dictates of power rather than standing as 'an invisible college' that provides a bulwark against instrumental use of international law. Their mercenary interests displaced the sanctity of their discipline. In this area, this is an indictment that international lawyers must face.

There were academic rationalizations for what was being done. The role of the academic lawyer in providing justifications for the emerging system must also be noted. Often, academics also sat as arbitrators so that there was mutual reinforcement of ideas in awards and in academic writings. At the height of hegemonic power, there was a willing consensus formed in order to support the norms of power.

One academic claim was that the law on investment protection was a self-contained regime dedicated to the protection of foreign investment.[75] Regimes are autonomous. They could be hived off and developed separately by those with esoteric knowledge. As a machination of power for the development of esoteric knowledge, this in itself requires time for study and research. Only the developed states and their international lawyers could participate in the venture of developing and maintaining the autonomous regime. Universities in the developed world churned out doctoral theses on minute aspects of the law, contributing to the creation of a neoliberal regime on the protection of foreign investment. Equally, there were also responses to this phenomenon from a sufficient number of academic writers, who maintained a viewpoint that sought to regard investment protection as an aspect of international law that had to be fitted into the general structure of international law's growing interest in the fast developing areas of environmental protection, human rights and indigenous rights. The utopian sentiments that have always characterized thinking in international law were never dimmed and remained bright in

---

[74] Richard Falk, 'A New Paradigm for International Legal Studies: Prospects and Proposals', (1975) 84 *Yale Law Journal* 969, at 970.

[75] Jeswald Salacuse, *The Three Laws of International Investment: National, Contractual, and International Frameworks for Foreign Capital* (New York: Oxford University Press, 2013).

30   INTRODUCTION

the universities of the world. Its productive capacity though did not equal the writings in support of the neoliberal regime.

In a contentious area, the existence of prolific academic writings that showed partiality to the dominant ideological view had the effect of reinforcing the existing leanings towards these viewpoints. There was support for the view that the law should be developed as such without recourse to any other related disciplines. The difficulties that arose could be explained as teething problems common to all systems of law, especially in their initial phases. The explanation takes the law as a new body of principles that is still in a state of formation. In course of time, the explanation suggests, it would internalize and accommodate competing interests within it. But such explanations do not accord with the changes that are taking place in the area or the extent of the disagreements that exist within it. The reaction to the situation comes not so much from within the regime as from those outside who seek transformations that require replacement of the tenets on which the regime is founded. Non-governmental actors and others resisting the expansionist visions of investment protection are not internal to the regime. Their resistance is external and cannot be accommodated within the existing system unless the exclusive character of the regime gives way to an inclusive system that takes in normative values other than investment protection. Unless these organizations are able to exercise countervailing power to neutralize the private power of multinational corporations, the neoliberal regime will not change. The signs of such change are now evident as such countervailing power has been built up.

What is important is that the law in this area has always been subject to the political and economic winds of the times. It is necessary to reiterate this point so as to understand the present morass in which the law finds itself. If the ideological and other pulls that affect the law are understood, it would be easier to explain the law and find solutions to the difficulties it presents. The understanding of the conflicts of interest can lead to finding solutions through the accommodation of the different interests at a balancing point, if one can be found. If a sufficient reconciliation of these interests is not possible within the system, alternatives to it must be sought. It is therefore important to look more systematically at the different periods of change through which the law has moved. It is possible to identify significant phases in the development of the international law on foreign investment in the context of the developments discussed above. Each of these phases involved intense conflicts of interest between different groups and the changes that resulted to accommodate those conflicts. Each of these phases involved resistance to the rules

1.4 EARLIER PHASES OF INTERNATIONAL LAW   31

developed by power. In each of the phases, the law had to undergo a change as a result of the resistance. Resistance has a transformational capacity.[76]

Unlike past phases, in the present phase the resistance is global as the interests espoused by NGOs transcend state boundaries and are global.[77] Several actors – developing states affected by the law being constructed, NGOs and people's groups – coalesced in the resistance. Such resistance is global and is also internal to the powerful states that support the law. When such resistance takes place, the powerful states will be caught up in an ambivalent position in which they may veer towards the public interest due to political necessity. Besides losing power, the strong states of the Western world are now fast becoming the recipients of foreign investment and the targets of foreign investment arbitration.[78] These states have had to take defensive positions. They may veer towards the public interest rather than support private power as they have in the past, thereby precipitating changes. The balanced treaties of the United States and Canada are symbolic of such changes. The different phases of change in the past will illustrate the significance of external factors in the changes that come about.

1.4 Earlier phases of the international law on foreign investment

Intensity of normative conflicts has been a characteristic of the international law on foreign investment from its inception. The understanding of this conflict requires an identification of the different interests that came into conflict. In early phases, the conflict was between the interests of capital-exporting states in developing external norms to protect foreign investment through international law, and the interests of capital-importing states in the assertion of total domestic control of incoming foreign investment. In the past, the law had been constructed on the premise that any dispute involved only the host state and the home state, the injured foreign investor supplying the medium through which a claim arises. But in later phases, the direct interest of the foreign investor in bringing claims came to be recognized. The attempt at externalization of the foreign investment process through its removal from control by the

---

[76] Neta Crawford, *Argument and Change in World Politics: Ethics, Decolonization and Humanitarian Intervention* (Cambridge University Press, 2002).

[77] On resistance to power in international relations, see Gill, *Power and Resistance in the New World Order*.

[78] The significant opposition to NAFTA and other investment treaties was evident during the discussion of the drafting of the new US Model Treaty, 2012.

INTRODUCTION

host state's laws has been the principal feature of all the phases of the development of the law. In that context, the struggle throughout the phases has been between the interest in externalization and the interest in ensuring local control over the investment process.

1.4.1   The first and formative phase

In the first and formative phase of the law, the contest was confined to North and South America.[79] Investments in the rest of the world largely took place within the colonial context. In that situation, the imperial law settled disputes in a manner advantageous to the interests of the metropolitan capital from which the investment came. The situation was different in the Americas. The United States was intent on externalizing the protection of the massive foreign investment its nationals had made in the Latin American states by creating an international minimum standard according to which such investments should be protected. This body of law was to be built into the rules on diplomatic protection of nationals abroad. The strategy was to ensure that the United States had the competence to intervene to protect the physical person of its nationals as well as their property from wrongful treatment by the host state. If diplomatic intervention on behalf of the national failed, the idea was to ensure that the dispute was internationalized and subjected to decision according to international legal principles by an external tribunal. The rationale was that the domestic, internal law would be partial to the host state or could be changed so as to protect local interests. The local courts would side with the state, especially in states where a system of separation of powers did not exist. In the Latin America of that period dictatorships were common, so making this assumption was sound. The international minimum standard mandated that disputes between foreign investors and host states in Latin America should be settled in accordance with such an external standard by neutral tribunals sitting overseas.[80] The Latin American states, the recipients of American

---

[79] The history of US contribution to the law is dealt with in Lipson, *Standing Guard*; Maurer, *The Empire Trap*; Kate Miles, *The Origins of International Investment Law: Empire, Environment and the Safeguarding of Capital* (Cambridge University Press, 2013).

[80] The early development of this set of norms can be traced through the writings of scholars: Edwin Borchard, *The Diplomatic Protection of Citizens Abroad* (1915, reissued, New York: Kraus & Co., 1970); Alwyn Freeman, *The International Responsibility of States for Denial of Justice* (New York: Longman, Green, 1938); Andreas Roth, *The Minimum Standard of Treatment as Applied to Aliens* (Leiden: Sijhoff, 1949).

1.4 EARLIER PHASES OF INTERNATIONAL LAW

investment, rejected this view. They argued that a national treatment standard applied and that this standard of treatment permitted national courts to dispose of disputes between foreign investors and their host states according to national law. International law had no role to play. If it did, it merely referred the disputes back to national law to be settled by national courts as the final arbiters. The standard was no different from that applied to local investors. Equal treatment of the foreign investor with the national investor justified such a course. The foreign investor came voluntarily into the host state and could not, therefore, argue that he should be subject to an external system. The Latin American view was stated in the form of the Calvo Doctrine.[81] A clause excluding the jurisdiction of foreign tribunals, known as a Calvo Clause, was often introduced into Latin American concession contracts.

The contest between these two sets of norms were played out in the context of the rising power of the United States and the economic dependence of the Latin American states on foreign investment from their neighbour. Gradually, rules were developed that provided a compromise. The notion of denial of justice confined recourse to international law only in circumstances where the foreign investor had not been provided a remedy by the local courts or the remedy provided was egregiously insufficient. The rule was that local remedies must first be exhausted and that there must be such a denial of justice by the local courts so as to require the intervention of an international court or tribunal.[82] The *Neer* Claim (1926)[83] asserted a high standard for the violation of the international minimum standard by requiring that the denial of justice must be such as would shock a reasonable bystander. The Commission stated that 'the treatment of the alien, in order to constitute an international delinquency, should amount to an outrage, to bad faith, to wilful neglect of duty, or to an insufficiency of governmental action so far short of international standards that every reasonable and impartial person would readily recognize its insufficiency'. It is not a standard that can be easily satisfied. It is evident that the law did evolve in a manner that responded to the conflict through compromises, though not in a manner that fully satisfied either group of contestants.

---

[81] The doctrine is attributed to Carlos Calvo, an Argentinian jurist. Donald Shea, *The Calvo Clause: A Problem of Inter-American and International Law and Diplomacy* (Minneapolis, MN: University of Minnesota Press, 1955).

[82] Chitharanjan Amerasinghe, *Local Remedies Rule*, 2nd edn (Cambridge University Press, 2008).

[83] (1926) 4 RIAA 60 (US–Mexican General Claims Commission).

34 INTRODUCTION

The United States was the dominant regional power during this phase. It often used force to settle foreign investment disputes. It was able to exert sufficient pressure to ensure the settlement of the disputes that arose in relation to American foreign investment in the different Latin American states through claims commissions, which ensured certain legality to outcomes. The claims commissions were set up when crises within states gave rise to a large number of claims resulting in damage to American lives or property. These commissions articulated legal principles that largely used the norms preferred by the United States, ensuring that precedents were built up that enabled the statement of principles of investment protection. Yet, despite this evolution, few principles could be identified as constituting the content of the international minimum standard. Beyond the need for recourse to local courts first, the notion of denial of justice, the payment of compensation for expropriation and liability for foreign property destroyed due to the failure of the host state authorities to provide adequate protection and security, the framework of a certain content of the standard did not exist.

Outside personal injuries, the focus of attention of the law was largely on the expropriation of American property. The American practice on this became progressively clearer. By the time of the Mexican expropriations of 1938, the indicia of lawful expropriation had been set out as far as US practice was concerned. Such practice indicated the content of the international minimum standard, with the payment of full compensation upon expropriation as its most important requirement. The first articulation in literature on the international minimum standard commences around the beginning of the nineteenth century, continues through the twentieth century and into the twenty-first century. Outside expropriation and the strict rules on denial of justice, the content of the standard has remained elusive despite over a century of evolution. The standard was continuously opposed by the Latin American states, so that it would be facile to state that it had become a principle of customary international law, despite contrary assertions in American and European textbooks.[84] There was persistent objection to the principle by all Latin American states, so that it could not become a principle of universal international

---

[84] Thus, Schreuer's and Dolzer's statement in their 2012 text that there was a 'widespread sense that the alien is protected against unacceptable measures of the host state by rules of international law' depends on what the unacceptable measures are. Dolzer and Schreuer, *International Investment Law*, at p. 3. This widespread sense was confined to the United States and Europe, and can hardly be said to constitute customary international law. Expropriation, not any 'unacceptable measure', was the focus of the practice.

1.4 EARLIER PHASES OF INTERNATIONAL LAW

law. Many Latin American expropriations were confiscatory in nature and were clearly unlawful. The Mexican expropriations, the focus of much attention, were in pursuance of economic reform and were quite distinct. One wonders how the expropriations would have fared before a modern tribunal. They became significant for the articulation of the Hull standard of full compensation.

1.4.2 The second phase of universalization of the conflicts

The conflict in the first phase of international investment law became internationalized with the decolonization of African and Asian states. The universalization of the conflict marks the second phase of the international law on foreign investment. The African and Asian states espoused the Latin American view that there must be exclusive national control over foreign investment, whereas the former colonial powers of Europe adopted the American position that an international minimum standard should protect foreign investments. During both phases, the focus of attention was on the expropriation of the property of the foreign investor and the extent of the compensation that must be paid in the event of the expropriation. The United States and its allies insisted on the hallowed Hull formula of 'prompt, adequate and effective' compensation, while the developing states argued that issues of compensation should be settled by national courts applying national laws. The first phase ended when the law became truly universal upon decolonization of Africa and Asia. New actors joined the scene when movement of foreign investment ceased to be within the imperial system. The new states wished to recover control over their economies from their erstwhile masters.

It is during the second phase that the newly independent states of Africa and Asia, along with those of Latin American, espoused the NIEO, which, among other things, sought to universalize the Calvo Doctrine. The NIEO was contained in a UN General Assembly resolution. The affirmation of the Calvo Doctrine was even stronger in the associated resolutions containing the Charter of Economic Rights and Duties of States.[85] The developing states had over the years also passed resolutions

---

[85] Particularly in Article 2(2)(3) of the Charter, which declared that issues relating to compensation for nationalization of foreign property were entirely for national courts to settle according to national law. Charter of Economic Rights and Duties of States, UN General Assembly, Resolution 3281(xxix), 12 December 1974, UN GAOR, 29th Sess., Supp. No. 31 (1974) 50, UN Doc. A/963, reproduced in 14 ILM 251 (1975) (120 votes in favour, six against, ten abstentions).

asserting the doctrine of permanent sovereignty over natural resources.[86] These developments were hotly resisted by the developed states. Thus, the compromise resolution accepting permanent sovereignty over natural resources contained the promise that contracts should be honoured and that disputes arising from the violation of contracts should be settled in accordance with international law.[87] The existence of a compromise resolution is an indication of the reconciliation of clashing interests. But this compromise did not last long. The permanent sovereignty doctrine continued to be asserted in the UN General Assembly resolutions without the compromise formula. The exact status of the doctrine of permanent sovereignty over natural resources has remained a matter of controversy. Some regard it as a principle of *ius cogens*;[88] others doubt this assessment.[89]

But the doctrine has had definite impacts. There have been repeated resolutions affirming the significance of the doctrine.[90] States have adopted the principle of permanent sovereignty over natural resources in their national constitutions and in their domestic legislation, such as foreign investment codes and mining acts.[91] In the petroleum sector,

---

[86] Nico Schrijver, *Permanent Sovereignty over Natural Resources: Balancing Rights and Duties* (Cambridge University Press, 1997). The rule that a state has complete control over resources within its territory merely states a truism. Jurisdictional principles of international law always recognized that all persons and property within a state are subject to the control of that state. It was necessary to state the notion of permanent sovereignty because of the capture of the resources by multinational corporations and the need to end such capture. For the statement of the rule by developed states, see Article 18 of the European Charter Treaty.

[87] Resolution 1803 (1964).

[88] One view regards the doctrine as constituting *ius cogens*. Brownlie, 'Legal Status of Natural Resources in International Law', at p.255.

[89] Generally, see Schrijver, *Permanent Sovereignty over Natural Resources*.

[90] The principal resolutions are the Charter of Economic Rights and Duties of States, UN General Assembly Resolution 3281(xxix), 12 December 1974, UN GAOR, 29th Sess., Supp. No. 31 (1974) 50, UN Doc. A/9631, reproduced in 14 ILM 251 (1975) (120 votes in favour, six against, ten abstentions); UN General Assembly Resolution 3201 (S-VI), 1 May 1974 on the New International Economic Order, UN Doc. A/res/S-6/3201, text at (1974) 13 ILM 715. The major countries that did not subscribe must be regarded as persistent objectors subscribing to the alternate system of investment protection. This supports the view regarding normlessness.

[91] See, e.g., Article 13 of the Constitution of Uganda; Article 33(3) of the Constitution of Indonesia. Both affirm sovereignty over natural resources. There are similar statements in most constitutions of the newly independent states of Asia and Africa. They constitute general principles of law and amount to state practice based on norms these states supported at the General Assembly. In any event, such sovereignty over resources in the territory of a state is a statement of a self-evident principle.

1.4 EARLIER PHASES OF INTERNATIONAL LAW 37

where the changes were marked, they established state corporations vesting ownership rights in petroleum resources in these corporations. The sector so dominated by state corporations was operated through contracts, such as the production-sharing agreement, which ensured that control over operations and the ownership of oil remained with the state corporations. The changes occurred at three levels. First, the newly independent states sought to change international law through the resolutions on the NIEO. Secondly, they changed their constitutions and instituted foreign investment codes, which incorporated the principle of permanent sovereignty over natural resources. Thirdly, contracts in the sector underwent changes transferring control over operations from the foreign corporation to the state corporation, which had monopoly powers over the sector. The production-sharing agreement, universally adopted as the contract that is used in the oil industry, reflects this change in that it vests control from initial stages of oil exploration to the final stages of exploitation in the state oil company. The interaction between these three levels entrenched the law at each level. State practice was consistent in that the assertion of the principle of permanent sovereignty was followed by enactment of domestic law and, subsequently, by the creation of contractual mechanisms to give effect to that practice. If practice of states makes international law, then, the uniform practice of the oil-producing states, which are the only states capable of engaging in practice relating to the oil sector, must make international law.

The developed states sought to blunt these changes. There were discussions as to whether international norms could be created by resolutions of the UN General Assembly.[92] The writings of the period and statements in arbitral awards[93] challenged the changes that the developing countries proposed and characterized them as aspirations (*lex ferenda*) rather than real law.[94] During this second phase, the law was kept in a fine balance, for much of the law that had been built up by the

---

[92] Blaine Sloan, *United Nations General Assembly Resolutions in Our Changing World* (New York: Transnational, 1991).

[93] In *Texas Overseas Petroleum Co. (Texaco)/California Asiatic Oil Co. (Calasiatic) v. Government of the Libyan Arab Republic* (1978) 17 ILM 1, at 88, the resolutions were regarded as *lex ferenda*. Arbitrator Dupuy purposefully set out to demolish the efforts of the developing states in his award. This has led to trenchant criticisms of the award by developing country international lawyers.

[94] In the light of later criticisms and developments, Professor Dupuy was concerned with the impact his award, debunking the efforts of the developing world to create an NIEO, would have on his legacy. He explained away the impact that *Texaco* should have on the law. Antonio Cassese, *Five Masters of International Law* (Oxford: Hart, 2011).

developed states also relied on weak sources of international law. They were contained in arbitral awards and in the writings of publicists, which in terms of opposability would be weaker law creating sources than solemn resolutions of states made at the General Assembly indicating what their preferred norms of law are, backed up by their practice.

The new edition of *Brownlie's* text on public international law suggests that the controversy has become passé as a result of the large number of bilateral investment treaties that assert both the international minimum standard as well as the Hull formula on compensation for expropriation.[95] It refers to a 'BITs revolution'. There is no uniformity within international law as to whether the norms resulting from BITs have general acceptance. Each BIT involves a carefully negotiated balance. Some protect only approved investments. The covered or protected investments under treaties vary. There is no uniformity even in the practice of single states. There are changes being effected to the newer investment treaties,[96] with the new treaties providing for extensive defences based on the protection of the public interest.

They undermine the so-called 'BIT revolution' that the new edition of *Brownlie* speaks of. BITs have evolved through so many phases that there is no consistency in them to be able to speak in terms of any revolution. The thesis as to the 'BIT revolution' is based on the wrong assumption that all BITs subscribe to the same principles. The newer treaties contain many sovereignty-based defences. They make imposition of responsibility difficult. In that context, the 'BIT revolution' is a myth. It is as exaggerated as the demise of the NIEO. The making of these efforts at depreciating the norms of the NIEO show the extent of the controversy and the absence of clarity in the law brought about by consistent conflicts in norms.

The BITs could be grouped into three types. In the first period (1959–90), the BITs that were made did not have strong statements. They were more intent on creating stances favourable to the reception of investments or the making of associations. Germany, which began BITs practice in 1959 with its treaty with Pakistan, was keener to develop

---

[95] James Crawford, *Brownlie's Principles of Public International Law*, 8th edn (Oxford University Press, 2012), at p. 626. Brownlie himself took a different position, as stated in the new edition, and in his dissent in *CME* v. *Czech Republic* (2003) 9 ICSID Rep. 264.

[96] The carve-out of regulatory expropriation is a major blow to any settled practice as to expropriation. Some states, like India, are likely to return to other formulae relating to compensation. In any event, 3,000 treaties with widely differing formulations as to what types of investment are protected cannot create any uniform practice that could lead to custom.

1.4 EARLIER PHASES OF INTERNATIONAL LAW 39

associations with investment-receiving states than it was to assert rules of protection of investments. Less than 500 treaties were made during this period. Many of these treaties were damp squibs, incapable of making any revolution. Many did not contain compulsory arbitration or any other compliance mechanism. It was in the neoliberal phase (1990–2004) that harder treaties with strong and inflexible rules on investment protection came to be made. The treaty practice also reached the 3,000 mark during this time. The 2,000 diverse treaties during this period could hardly have created customary international law. The third phase began with the 'balanced' treaties, the 2004 US Model Treaty being the example. Around that period, treaties had begun to shed the inflexibility as to investment protection and had come to recognize limits based on domestic and global public interests. As these balanced treaties sought to recover regulatory control over foreign investments, it may well be argued that they are more consistent with the norms of the NIEO, with its emphasis on state sovereignty and control. A decline in the number of BITs also has been noted. In 2013, there were forty-four withdrawals from treaties.[97] In this context of the multifaceted nature of approaches to investment treaty practice, the notion of a 'BITs revolution' is farfetched. Such a revolution never took place.

Contestation among states has been the feature of the formation of international law. The dominance of positivism, which has concentrated on the formation of rules through the examination of sources of international law, has hidden the extent of the role of power in the shaping of law. The contest between hegemonic power and the collective power harnessed through cooperation and recourse to justice-oriented arguments of opposing interests, brings about either an accommodation or the momentary triumph of a preferred set of rules. The different phases of the development of the international law on foreign investment illustrate this phenomenon. No other rule does this better than the rule on compensation where the struggle between just compensation, preferred by the developing states because it enables the context of the expropriation to be taken into account, and the conflicting standard of full compensation, which emphasizes that the market value of the property must be the standard of compensation as an immediate value is created in the taker of the property, was never resolved. Despite the acceptance of the market value as the standard in a large number of investment treaties, the debate can, by no means, be seen as settled in terms of general

---

[97] UNCTAD, *World Investment Report* (Geneva, 2014), p. 124.

40   INTRODUCTION

international law.[98] Investment treaties do not settle the debate simply because they apply only to protected investments as defined in the treaties. That, again, is a reason why arguments cannot be made as to customary international law on the basis of investment treaties as they do not apply to all foreign investments made within host states. They often heavily qualify the foreign investment entitled to their protection. They require approval procedures or conformity with domestic laws prior to protection.

The refusal to accept the personality of entities other than states and international organizations, which states created, enabled the continued maintenance of a curtain so that abuses by multinational corporations could remain beyond scrutiny.[99] In the second phase, though the contest was largely between states, it occurred in the context of decolonization, which resulted from large movements for liberation initiated by people against colonial states. The international law formulated in the context of decolonization centred on the rights of people rather than those of states, an idea that brought discomfort to the traditional Western international lawyers, who found it difficult to accommodate the notion that people's movements could lead to the creation of doctrines in international law, and that, too, one so fundamental as the principle of self-determination extended to colonial peoples. The dawn of a people-centred approach to international law must be seen in the early freedom struggles to recover both political rights to freedom and economic rights to resources that people had lost. Its rise was coterminous with the human rights movement. But the notion of collective rights of large groups sat uneasily with the Western liberal tradition that rights were entirely individual to the owner. Thus, international lawyers from developed states contested the central right in investment law developed during this phase, the right of permanent sovereignty over natural resources, as a right of the peoples. But the articulation of the new law had considerably dented any existing

---

[98] The treaties are not uniform in stating the Hull formula. Many of them do not apply to all investments, qualifying the investments to which they apply. The view is still articulated that the context of each situation is the determinant of the amount of compensation due on expropriation. Crawford, *Brownlie's Principles of Public International Law*, p. 626.

[99] Movements in the literature indicate increasing recognition of the need to discuss the liability of multinational corporations. Jennifer Zerk, *Multinational Corporations and Corporate Social Responsibility: Limitations and Opportunities in International Law* (Cambridge University Press, 2006); Adefolake Adekunle, *Corporate Social Responsibility of Multinational Corporations in Developing Countries* (Cambridge University Press, 2012).

1.4 EARLIER PHASES OF INTERNATIONAL LAW 41

norms on investment protection, which, resting on weak sources, hardly had superior claims to legitimacy.

The newly independent states also argued that they had suffered deprivations during the era of colonialism. They argued that the deprivations that led to their underdevelopment and the consequent prosperity of Europe should be rectified through the recognition of a right to development.[100] The articulation of a right to development again created oppositional norms that contested the premises that foreign investment protection could be the sole object of international law. The dominant views in international law were averse to the recognition of the existence of such a right in international law.[101] The dominant thinking in the law was not prepared for the next two phases of challenge. The dominant thinking was structured entirely on the twin objects of ensuring protection of investments and of the contracts that initiated them.

The insulation of the law on foreign investment from the developments that were taking place in international law was seen as desirable in the dominant view. This objective began early as a result of competing considerations developing within international law.[102] The object of foreign investment protection was attacked during the second phase with norms articulated through valid law-making sources of international law. It was difficult to ignore these counter-norms. These norms came to be supported by the emergence of strong, new non-state actors in the form of NGOs in the fields of human rights and the environment. But these new actors were yet to gather the strength they came to exert in international relations in later times.

One has to concede that the international law during this phase was unclear as a result of the contest between two sets of norms. This provides the perfect setting for the emergence of bilateral investment treaties. Given that the norms at the international level were uncertain, states began making investment treaties on a bilateral basis, ironing out their

---

[100] For a recent survey of the international law on development, see Isabelle Bunn, *The Right to Development and International Economic Law: Legal and Moral Dimensions* (Oxford: Hart, 2012). Poverty alleviation must be considered a central tenet of the increasing concern with the articulation of developmental goals. Krista Nadakavukaren Schefer (ed.), *Poverty and the International Economic Legal System: Duties to the World's Poor* (Cambridge University Press, 2013).

[101] Bunn, *The Right to Development and International Economic Law*, marshals the authorities supporting the existence of the right.

[102] The movement against fragmentation was to come later. The silent fragmentation of the law had begun in this field when the developing states began to construct counter-norms.

42 INTRODUCTION

agreement as to what the law between them was.[103] At the multilateral level, developing states maintained a cohesive view supporting the counter-norms, but they were able to deviate from these norms at the bilateral level in bargains they struck with developed states in the belief that such bargains giving investment protection through treaties were necessary to promote of foreign investment. It was a belief that was fostered by leading economic institutions at the time. These institutions advocated multilateral agreements between states on foreign investment.[104] Such multilateral treaties were unsuccessful.[105] The alternative was the making of as many bilateral treaties as possible. This provides an explanation for the growth of bilateral investment treaties. The practice began in 1959.[106] In the first twenty years of this treaty practice not more than 500 treaties had been concluded, but the amount was to increase exponentially in the third phase of the law. The early treaties were not uniform. Many did not contain unilateral offers of arbitration to foreign investors.[107]

---

[103] There are other explanations for the profusion of investment treaties and why developing countries make them. One is that developing countries compete among themselves and make treaties so as not to lose out to other states in attracting foreign investment. Andrew Guzman, Zachary Elkins and Beth Simmons, 'Competing for Capital: The Diffusion of Bilateral Investment Treaties', (2006) 60 *International Organization* 811. The more likely explanation is the belief that investment flows will occur if treaties are signed. This accounts for the spurt in the number of treaties during the neoliberal era. There is also the fact that institutions pressured states into signing them. The IMF made it a condition for loans that treaties are signed. It is said that UNCTAD held 'mass weddings' at which developing countries were herded in to sign such treaties after conferences on investment treaties, so accounting for the fact that many treaties were signed on the same day.

[104] The OECD promoted a multilateral agreement in 1961 based on the Abs–Shawcross Convention drafted in 1959, reputedly the basis of the first ever investment treaty between Germany and Pakistan (1959). It never materialized, but it provided the basis for many bilateral investment treaties, including the British investment treaties. Denza and Brooks, 'Investment Treaties: The United Kingdom Experience'.

[105] Successive efforts at multilateral agreements on investment failed. The World Bank's attempt resulted in non-binding principles in 1991. The OECD effort in 1995 failed. It was confined to developed states. The effort to make an instrument on investment within the WTO also failed.

[106] The first treaty was the treaty between Germany and Pakistan in 1959.

[107] Germany was to sign 139 investment treaties. Among them, the first to include investor–state dispute settlement was the German treaty with Romania in 1979, which was confined to disputes involving compensation only. A comprehensive dispute settlement clause was included in 1986 in the treaty with Nepal. Tillman Braun, 'Globalization: The Driving Force in International Investment Law', in Michael Waibel *et al.* (eds.), *The Backlash Against Investment Arbitration* (The Hague: Kluwer, 2010).

1.4   EARLIER PHASES OF INTERNATIONAL LAW   43

1.4.3   The third phase of neoliberal change

The third phase related to the changes that the preference towards market-based solutions brought about. The triumph of neoliberalism can be dated from the dissolution of the Soviet Union as it signalled the end of communism. The fall of communism left democracy and its economic concomitant, the free market theory, as the prevailing philosophies that were left standing at the end of the Cold War. Ideas shape events. The events on the economic front in the last decade of the twentieth century were very much shaped by the ideas generated by neoliberalism. The Western liberal state was advanced as the model for governance.[108] There was a package of economic attributes associated with neoliberalism. The triumph of this idea brought about another phase in the international law on foreign investment.

The ascendancy of neoliberalism ensured that a halt was put on the movement in the developing world towards sovereign control over foreign investment. Dominant ideas give impetus to the shaping of norms and policies. Neoliberalism gave impetus to the policy that free movement of investment was facilitated through secure norms of investment protection, and that such movements of investment promoted economic development. It was argued that the creation of secure regimes of investment protection was necessary for such flows to take place and that, without such regimes in place, the necessary foreign investment flows, promoting economic development, would not take place. This argument, as already indicated, came to be espoused by the World Bank and the IMF, making it a part of the 'Washington Consensus'. UNCTAD, a body created to aid the poorer states, fell in line and assiduously promoted the making of investment treaties. The reality of institutional capture was very evident in these instances. It was also argued that the unstoppable force of globalization made liberalization of flows of capital, assets, technology, trade and investments inevitable.

The notion that neoliberal globalization was an unstoppable force finds reflection in thinking in international investment law. The acceptance of the solution that market-led forces are necessary for economic development became the rationale for arguments that were floated as to developments within the law. It was suggested that the growing number

---

[108] A liberal state is defined as a state 'with some form of representative democracy, a market economy based on private property rights and constitutional protection of civil and political rights'. Anne-Marie Slaughter, 'International Law in a World of Liberal States' (1995) 6 *European Journal of International Law* 1.

44 INTRODUCTION

of investment treaties, nearly 3,000 of them, indicated the trend towards standardization of international law through custom,[109] even though almost seven times that number of uniform treaties was necessary to achieve global coverage.[110] The treaties, as already pointed out, were by no means uniform. They could not create custom.

In the preambles of most of these treaties, the link between investment flows, economic development and the regime of investment protection contained in the treaty are linked. Such linkage promoted the view that the provisions in the treaties on investment protection should be interpreted expansively so that their objective of economic development through investment flows generated by investment protection could be realized. This sparked off an attempt to create a firm body of rules on investment protection through arbitral activity. The preambles were seen as a licence to promote a teleological interpretation of the treaty provisions, favouring investment protection. The link between economic development and investment treaties is heavily contested in the literature on the subject.[111]

The spate of new investment treaties, and the arbitral awards based on them, were regarded as creating new forms of law. These new laws moved away from the previous era of developing country resistance marked by the NIEO principles. As one writer put it, the change was needed as developing countries 'came to realize that an attractive investment climate would be needed if they were to advance up the economic ladder through inflow of foreign capital'.[112] These views were the basis of the 'BITs revolution'. This was the climate that prevailed during this period and it gave rise to certain phenomena.

1.4.3.1 Regime formation and dissolution

Such beliefs promoted attempts at regime formation in the area in the reified belief that a single model of inflexible investment protection, mandated by neoliberalism, was needed to ensure economic progress. Some thought this had come into existence as a result of the increasing

---

[109] Stephen M. Schwebel, 'The Influence of Bilateral Investment Treaties on Customary International Law', (2004) 98 *ASIL Proceedings* 27.

[110] Tarcisco Gazzini, 'The Role of Customary International Law in the Field of Foreign Investment', (2007) 8 *Journal of World Trade Law* 691.

[111] See fn. 41.

[112] Andreas F. Lowenfeld, 'Investment Agreements and International Law', (2003) 42 *Columbia Journal of Transnational Law* 123; see also Schwebel, 'The Influence of Bilateral Investment Treaties on Customary International Law', p. 27. Alvarez, ' A BIT on Custom', wrote in agreement.

network of investment treaties. Neoliberalism decried plurality of visions, instead it mandated a single universal prescription for all economic malaise. Consistent with this vision, factors were mobilized to construct a regime. A select group of arbitrators emerged who would take the rules of investment protection to the limits. Optimistic visions of a law being built on precedent came to be stated.[113] Even as the third phase belonged to regime-building, the next phase resulted in the collapse of the regime. But, before then, the expansionary norms of the regime had come to be articulated.

1.4.3.2 Expansionist norms

This period resulted in the creation of expansionist norms based on the belief that the treaties gave arbitral tribunals a mandate to create such law as their bases lay in the creation of norms of protection of the investment so that flows of investment were promoted. Giving this objective as a rationale, arbitrators reinterpreted phrases in the treaties well beyond the intention of the states to create rules of secure investment protection. Thus, the provision on full protection and security was regarded as requiring a stable climate for investment to thrive. The fair and equitable standard was interpreted as requiring that legitimate expectations, created at the time of the investment, are not thwarted. Mere depreciation of the value of investments caused by government measures came to be regarded as tantamount to expropriation. The structure that was being created disconcerted the states, and they reacted adversely to the system that was emerging. These developments agitated NGOs, which saw the norms as bringing about a regulatory chill, so objectives that they sought to promote could not be furthered. Along with states which saw their regulatory space diminishing, they mounted a counterattack on the rules engendered through expansionism.

1.4.4 The fourth and current phase

Regimes can unravel as fast as they are created. The classic regime that lasts must be founded on coincidence of the national interests of the member states and other stakeholders.[114] Such coincidence of interests is

---

[113] Christoph Schreuer and Mathew Weininger, 'Conversations across Cases: Is there a Doctrine of Precedent in Investment Arbitration?' in Peter Muchlinski *et al.* (eds.), *The Oxford Handbook of International Investment Law* (Oxford University Press, 2008), p. 1211.

[114] Volker Rittburger, *Regime Theory and International Relations* (Oxford University Press, 1993). Regimes in the area of maritime navigation, postal services and health are based

46 INTRODUCTION

lacking in the area of foreign investment. It is difficult to build up a strong regime in the area. The universality of norms, created at a time of dominance of a philosophical or economic idea, will crumble when the faults of that idea are demonstrated by events. As a succession of economic crises swept across the world, the faults of neoliberalism were revealed. The norms based on it then start to crumble. As the process does not take place immediately, there is a slow descent into chaos or normlessness.[115]

The fourth phase began around 2004 when the balanced treaties, moving away from the treaties based on inflexible norms of investment protection, came to be made.[116] Neoliberal expansionism went on after the dawn of the twenty-first century. The best evidence of it was the revival of fair and equitable standards in the early Argentine awards dealing with the financial crisis. It was revived and given meaning within the first five years of this century. Schisms, which began to develop between arbitrators, came to be entrenched around this time, though they had begun a few years earlier towards the end of the third phase. As the 'core' of arbitrators stuck together sustaining the expansions they had made, those on the periphery rebelled against the expansionism that characterized the work of the core. Such expansionism was inconsistent with the basic rationale in arbitration that the award should not go beyond the consent of states. Consequently, a periphery within investment arbitration rebelled by requiring interpretations of the treaty provisions that reflect the intention of the states making the treaties, thereby provoking a schism among arbitrators and a profusion of inconsistent awards that weakened regime-building considerably.[117] States,

on mutual interests. They have a lasting quality as mutual interests sustain them. Others are based on willing dependence on hegemonic powers. The regime on foreign investment protection is built on interests that do not coincide.

[115] Optimists define the collapse in terms of a process of adaptation. Joost Pauwelyn, 'The Edge of Chaos: Emergence and Change in International Investment Law' (2013) SSRN-id 2271869. But when large groups of states desert the system, it can no longer be described as a system of international law.

[116] Purists decried this move away from inflexible investment protection. Stephen Schwebel, 'The United States 2004 Model Treaty and Denial of Justice in International Law', in Christina Binder *et al.* (eds.), *International Investment Law for the Twenty-First Century: Essays in Honour of Christoph Schreuer* (Cambridge University Press, 2010), p. 519.

[117] The terms activism and conservatism used in the context of judicial attitudes cannot be used to describe arbitral law-making, as activist judges are generally considered progressives extending the law to favour a social cause. In the case of investment arbitration, the 'core' arbitrators were intent on favouring the interests of the minority of multinational corporations against the public interest by extending the rules of investment protection. In that sense, they were conserving and extending the original purpose of inflexible investment protection.

1.4   EARLIER PHASES OF INTERNATIONAL LAW   47

disillusioned by expansionist awards began to withdraw from treaties and arbitration based on them. Regime collapse was imminent. It was furthered by several factors. Two competing forces characterized the beginning of the fourth phase. One shored up the formation of a regime, while the other sought to dismantle it. The competing forces at work need to be identified.

1.4.5   The competing forces in the fourth phase

The tenets of neoliberalism came to be challenged towards the end of the third phase, after they had become somewhat established. They became stronger as the fourth phase began. The precise time of the transition between the two phases is difficult to identify. Disenchantment with neoliberalism had already begun before the end of the millennium. This is demonstrated by several factors. The effort at a multilateral investment agreement failed in 1998. Successive economic crises occurred in states adopting neoliberalism in Asia in around the same year. The cases resulting from the economic crisis in Argentina had begun around 2000. But, confining the third phase to the height of neoliberalism and remembering that the third and the fourth phases shade into each other, 2004 may be taken roughly as the year when the fourth phase began. It was the year when the United States changed its Model Treaty to accommodate other interests and to create defences to liability for violations of treaty standards. The Model Treaty did not please the promoters of the third phase. The broadly similar Canadian Model Treaty was also made in 2004. Around that the time, economic studies began appearing contesting whether or not investment treaties had a role to play in contributing to the flow of foreign investment.

Doubts began to appear as to the viability of a system built upon the uniform prescription that the protection of foreign investment will ineluctably lead to economic development.[118] Economists have invested much effort in disproving the myth that there is a definite correlation between investment flows and the making of investment treaties.[119] The substantial

---

[118] Hallward-Driemeier, 'Do Bilateral Investment Treaties Attract Foreign Investment? Only a Bit and They Could Bite'.

[119] There is an increasing amount of literature being generated on this topic. See above at fn. 36. UNCTAD, *The Role of International Investment Agreements in Attracting Foreign Direct Investment to Developing Countries* (UNCTAD: Geneva, 2009); Emma Aisbett doubted any correlation. Emma Aisbett, 'Bilateral Investment Treaties and Foreign Direct Investment: Correlation Versus Causation', in Karl Sauvant and Lisa Sachs

48 INTRODUCTION

surrender of regulatory sovereignty that the treaties involve were justified on the basis that the protection they offer to foreign investment was necessary to ensure flows of foreign investment. There is now increasing literature which disputes whether the assumptions relating to the link between treaties and foreign investment flows were correct.

In the context of these developments, there emerged two competing trends. The first sought to conserve the neoliberal regime that had been so assiduously built up in the third phase. The second sought to displace it completely or effect changes that moved it away from its sole purpose in investment protection. These two competing trends characterize the current phase of the international law on foreign investment.

1.4.6   Conserving the neoliberal regime

Towards the end of the third phase, trends that were intended to shore up the gains made by the expansionist views of investment treaties against erosion are visible. These trends show desperation in the construction of theories to indicate the viability of the regime. These trends went on into the fourth phase as well, when the conflict between the different interests became acute. In many arbitral awards, the treaties are represented as being 'truly universal in their reach and essential provisions'.[120] The view on the 'BITs revolution' criticized above is a manifestation of this trend. Similar views are also taken in different forms in some writings. They suggest that the BITs and the awards based on them are a contribution to a possible multilateralization of the norms of international investment law.[121] These views were challenged, but, nevertheless, they continue to be asserted. Well into the fourth and present phase, there are

---

(eds.), *The Effect of Treaties on Foreign Direct Investments* (Oxford University Press, 2009), p. 395. Jason Yackee, 'Do Bilateral Investment Treaties Promote Foreign Direct Investments?' (2010) 51 *Virginia Journal of International Law* 397. Ackerman and Tobin, 'Do BITs Benefit Developing Countries?' (indicating their marginal utility depending on a variety of circumstances). Todd Allee and Clint Peinhardt, 'Contingent Credibility: The Impact of Investment Treaty Violations on Foreign Direct Investment', (2011) 65 *International Organization* 401. Due to their conflicting nature, no definite conclusions can be drawn from these studies. Nevertheless, the studies subject the orthodox position that BITs promote investment flows to doubt.

[120] *CME v. Czech Republic*, UNCITRAL, Award (14 March 2003), at para. 497; also *Mondev International v. United States*, ICSID, Case No. ARB(AF)/99/2 (11 October 2002), at para. 117, and *Chemtura Corp. v Canada*, UNCITRAL, Award (2 August 2010), para. 121.

[121] Stephan Schill, *The Multilateralization of International Investment Law* (Cambridge University Press, 2009).

1.4 EARLIER PHASES OF INTERNATIONAL LAW 49

rationalizations advanced to keep the neoliberal advances made in the third phase intact. They include the following:

1.4.6.1 New theoretical rationalizations

As fissures in the regime began to appear, there were several new efforts to shore up the expansionist regime by providing it with new theoretical justifications. Every effort was made to shore up a system that had begun to fray. There was a return of the religious zeal in advocating the prescriptions of investment protection as the only means of salvation for poor states. The defenders of the regime argued that such a system was necessary for economic development. The increase in treaty-based investment arbitration that occurred provided evidence of the viability of the system. Quick theoretical rationalizations for building up a regime followed. It was argued that the system indicated the formation of a global administrative law that supervised decisions made by domestic authorities through investment arbitration to ensure that standards such as fair and equitable treatment of foreign investment were provided, contributing to effective global governance of beneficial foreign investment flows.[122] Such standards of global governance made it politically easier for developing countries to make the relevant changes in their domestic laws through reliance on the external standards articulated at the international level. It was claimed that these standards could be discovered through a comparative study of public law systems, the only systems studied being confined to Europe.[123] The hallowed doctrine of the rule of law, designed to protect the weak from the mighty, was reinterpreted as recognizing the right to property (on a standard higher than even that of US law, according to some American scholars[124]) and the right to contract.[125] The system bypassed national courts as the settlers of disputes on foreign investment by entrusting the task to foreign arbitration, thereby

---

[122] Benedict Kingsbury, Nico Krisch and Richard Stewart, 'The Emergence of Global Administrative Law', (2005) 68 *Law and Contemporary Problems* 15; for a critical view, see Gus Van Harten and Martin Loughlin, 'Investment Treaty Arbitration as a Species of Global Administrative Law', (2006) 17 *European Journal of International Law* 121.

[123] Stephan Schill (ed.), *International Investment Law and Comparative Public Law* (Oxford University Press, 2010).

[124] Vicki Bean and Joel Beauvais, 'The Global Fifth Amendment?' (2003) 78 *New York University Law Review* 30.

[125] Stephen Humphries, *The Theatre of the Rule of Law: Transnational Legal Intervention in Theory and Practice* (Cambridge University Press, 2010). Traditional statements on the rule of law hardly refer to the right to property or the right to contract at all. Lord Bingham, *The Rule of Law* (London: Penguin, 2010).

50 INTRODUCTION

preventing robust judicial institutions overseeing foreign investment being built up within developing countries.[126] The assumption was that these states were incapable of creating adequate systems that would provide justice to the foreign investors. Rather than serving the rule of law in these states, the system had the opposite effect of impeding the formation of effective court systems to deal with issues of foreign investment.

1.4.6.2 Constancy in jurisprudence

There were claims that what was happening had congealed into law through the building up of precedent.[127] Efforts were made to construct precedents to support the view that precedents created a coherent body of rules and that tribunals had a role to play in the creation of international law. Attempts were made to reach into the past to demonstrate that the rules of the system were really reinterpretations that existed in the traditional rules, such as those on state responsibility. Repetition, a technique of imperial law,[128] was used to reinforce these justifications. They were often repetitions by the same individual arbitrator, sitting with different combinations of fellow arbitrators featuring a limited number of like-minded lawyers.[129]

1.4.6.3 Analogical reasoning

When analogical reasoning was sought in support of norms that were being used, they were found in single systems of Western law. But the law is often found selectively to support a conclusion that has already been drawn. Thus, in searching for legitimate expectations as a basis for the fair and equitable treatment in support of the view that expectations created at the time of entry by the host state should not be violated by its subsequent measures, authority was found for its supposed existence in English law. In English law, there is little authority for the use of

---

[126] Michael Trebilcock and Ronald Daniels, *Rule of Law Reform and Development: Charting the Fragile Path of Progress* (Cheltenham: Edward Elgar, 2008).

[127] Yas Banifatemi, *Precedent in International Investment Law* (New York: Juris Publishing, 2008): 'Legally bankrupt decisions are cited in subsequent cases involving the same issue in the hope that a new legal principle will emerge, and suddenly a theory that couldn't be taken seriously in any classroom is hailed in conferences like this and imbued with a certain legitimacy.'

[128] Lauren Benton, *Law and Colonial Cultures: Legal Regimes in World History 1400–1900* (Cambridge University Press, 2001).

[129] George Kahale was scathing in his keynote speech to the 8th Investment Arbitration Forum, 28 March 2014, observing: 'Legally bankrupt decisions are cited in subsequent cases involving the same issue in the hope that a new legal principle will emerge, and suddenly a theory that couldn't be taken seriously in any classroom is hailed in conferences like this and imbued with a certain legitimacy.'

1.4 EARLIER PHASES OF INTERNATIONAL LAW 51

legitimate expectations to establish substantive liability or to review the legislation of the state on the basis of legitimate expectations. It is largely used to give procedural protection against decisions of subordinate decision-makers. This little difficulty was not allowed to stand in the way of the formulation of the doctrine as a part of the nebulous standard of fair and equitable treatment. As an afterthought, there was a search in other legal systems besides English law for such a doctrine.[130] Similarly, the use of the doctrine of proportionality, as limiting the exercise of legislative power by the state, was justified on the basis of its use in German law and its later acceptance in European Community law. It is not a general principle of law. Within just one system, the common law, there is considerable doubt as to whether it should be accommodated.[131] The rationalizations were reminiscent of the search for general principles of law in the civilized nations of the world in an earlier age when such 'civilization' was confined to Europe. It would be difficult to demonstrate that all the civilized or Western systems subscribed to the law that was discovered and applied.[132] Comparative law reasoning in the area has been selective to such an extent that it leaves out even the systems of the state that gave birth to the law on foreign investment. The proportionality rule has little resonance in US law.[133] It is also reminiscent of developing country efforts in the past to argue that foreign investment contracts were located in public law.[134] This was strenuously denied as the idea did not favour investment protection. Now, since it is necessary to have recourse

---

[130] Professor Orrego-Vicuna had found authority for the proposition in English law in a speech to the American Society of International Law. It was later stated in *CMS Gas Transmission Co.* v. *Argentina* (2003), an award by a tribunal he chaired. It was much later in *Total* v. *Argentina*, ICSID, Case No. ARB/04/01 (27 December 2010) that a feeble effort was made to find a rational basis for the use of the doctrine in European comparative law. See further in Chapter 5.

[131] Sir Philip Sales, 'Rationality, Proportionality and the Development of the Law', (2013) 129 *Law Quarterly Review* 223, for views on whether the rule of rationality used in the English law should be replaced by proportionality.

[132] The theme of analogical reasoning on the basis of domestic legal systems is developed in Chapter 5 when dealing with the fair and equitable treatment, and in Chapter 7 when dealing with the proportionality rule. On the use of analogy in investment law, see Anthea Roberts, 'Clash of Paradigms: Actors and Analogies Shaping the Investment Treaty System', (2013) 107 *American Journal of International Law* 45.

[133] In US law, there is difficulty in applying the proportionality rule due to the existence of the doctrine of separation of powers. The proportionality rule is a problem in other common law jurisdictions such as Australia for similar reasons.

[134] The argument that the foreign investment contract was an administrative contract was rejected on the ground that it was a peculiarity of French law when in fact it was not. For its existence in English law, see Colin Turpin, *State Contracts* (London: Penguin, 1972).

52 INTRODUCTION

to public law to keep investment protection relevant, there is a return to selective principles of public law.

1.4.6.4   Deflecting push-backs by states

As states began to react to arbitral expansionism by the rediscovery of regulatory expropriation or the redefinition of the fair and equitable clause by tying it to customary international law, expansionist arbitrators responded by stating laxer causes of action that could be accommodated within the treaty. Thus, for example, the notion of denial of justice was the basis for the violation of the international minimum standard. The application of the rule required exhaustion of local remedies and an egregious denial of justice by domestic courts for a claim to arise. The standard required for denial of justice was interpreted as based on a lower standard in modern times due to developments in the area of human rights. The *Neer* Claim (1926)[135] was mugged. It had required a high standard of violation, that is, such egregious denial of justice as would shock a bystander. The old standard would make it difficult for the foreign investor to succeed in claims. So the a standard was dismissed as an anachronism in an age where the world had moved towards better standards of governance. The rule had to be more lax in the modern world; it was made lax. Other contemporary cases were found that stated the proposition using looser formulae.[136] Denial of justice came to be reinterpreted so as to embrace arbitrary acts of states and other infractions that did not amount to the high standards that had enabled review of the decisions of domestic courts by international tribunals in the past.[137] The arbitration tribunals converted themselves into appellate

---

[135] (1926) 4 UNRIIA 60. The standard was violated if there was 'wilful neglect of duty, or to an insufficiency of governmental action so far short of international standards that every reasonable and impartial man would readily accept'. In *Mondev International* v. *United States*, ICSID, Case No ARB(AF)/99/2 (11 October 2002), the tribunal referred to the 'evolutionary potential' of the rule, suggesting that tribunals had the power to identify its later contents. Similar views were stated in *ADF Group Inc.* v. *United States*, ICSID Case No. ARB(AF)/00/1 (9 January 2003).

[136] In *Jalapa Railroad & Power Co.*, American–Mexican Claims Commission (1948), 'arbitrary acts' were referred to. It is used in the *Vivendi* v. *Argentina*, ICSID, Case No. ARB/97/3 (20 August 2007), para. 7.5.9, and in *Siemens AG* v. *Argentina*, ICSID, Case No. ARB/02/8, Award (6 February 2007), para. 251, to suggest a lower standard. David Schneiderman, *Resisting Economic Globalization* (Basingstoke: Palgrave Macmillan, 2013), p. 61. Other cases are used in *Merrill & Ring Forestry Ltd* v. *Canada*, UNCITRAL (31 March 2010), para. 2008.

[137] Such review became a feature of the developments. In *Saipem* v. *Bangladesh* and *White Industries* v. *India*, tribunals reviewed the conduct of domestic courts.

1.4 EARLIER PHASES OF INTERNATIONAL LAW 53

courts with the power to review decisions of domestic courts.[138] They were clearly exceeding the mandate given to them.

1.4.6.5 Arrogation of quasi-legislative powers

Consistent with the view that the standards of treatment evolve, some arbitration tribunals arrogated to themselves a quasi-legislative role. On the theory that standards are evolutionary or that they had been entrusted to administer a vague standard such as the fair and equitable standard, arbitrators assumed the power to interpret the provisions in accordance with what they saw as the object of the treaties, which was investment protection. It was thought that standards such as the international minimum standard, which could evolve, and vague standards such the fair and equitable standard were entrusted to arbitrators to create a course of precedents through interpretation of the terms of the treaties. It has been suggested that the continuous pronouncements of arbitral tribunals create custom. In this way, the law on the subject could be created, vesting arbitration tribunals with legislative authority to create international law, a power that was not given even to the International Court of Justice (ICJ). Some tribunals have reacted by stating that only the states through their practice could indicate what changes have taken place as to the meaning of the standards of treatment recognized in customary international law.[139] The treatment of *Neer* within the NAFTA context indicates the extent of the divisions that have come about between arbitration tribunals. The division is explicable on the basis that there was a rampant desire in some of the tribunals to extend the law towards greater investment protection, whereas other tribunals, understanding the political context of the situation and fearing the reaction of the states, were reluctant to embark on such adventures. Unlike in the case of judicial activism in domestic legal systems that seek progressive changes, arbitral expansionism in investment arbitration sought to conserve the interests of private power.

---

[138] Michael Goldhaber, 'The Rise of Arbitral Power over Domestic Legislation', (2012) 1 *Stanford Journal of Complex Litigation* 374.

[139] *Glamis Gold Ltd* v. *United States*, UNCITRAL Arbitration, Award (8 June 2009). But the tribunal in *Merrill & Ring Forestry Ltd* v. *Canada* (Orrego-Vicuna, Dam, Rowley) contested this view, asserting its competence to declare what the nature of the standard was in the light of earlier jurisprudence, confining *Neer*, which had wide acceptance in NAFTA awards, to situations of denial of justice. The statements were gratuitous and purposeful statements of broad viewpoints as there were no findings of violations of any standards by Canada.

54   INTRODUCTION

Even as the fourth phase witnessed efforts at conservation of the advances of the third phase of neoliberalism, there were competing tendencies at work denying the legitimacy of the law on which expansionary rules of investment protection had been created. It was clear that the tendencies described above had used international law as an instrument through which a dominant philosophy could be advanced and its gains conserved. But these tendencies are clearly undergoing resistance. It could well be that the principles established during this period could retreat. It may be possible to demonstrate that other hegemonic principles advanced during the period were being dismantled.[140] But the tenacity of neoliberal principles will remain as long as the systemic community of arbitrators, academics, lawyers, economists and others continue to support it. They have valid intellectual as well as mercenary reasons to support the principles. Even as these arguments were being put up in support of the retention of the neoliberal regime, attacks on it emerged with vigour as the fourth phase gathered momentum and increased in strength, particularly after the global economic crisis in 2008. That crisis forced developed states to move away from market economics and to adopt regulatory measures in order to deal with it, including the nationalization of failing financial institutions. Neoliberalism was shaken at its foundations by the global crisis, though it remained tenacious despite it. It will remain tenacious, despite the demystifying of neoliberalism, because the locus of private power, which resides in multinational corporations, has not shifted. Such power will vigorously resist change. Section 1.4.7 describes the competing tendencies that emerged during the fourth phase.

1.4.7   Resisting neoliberalism

The rationalizations of the neoliberal principles were inconsistent with the rapid changes that were taking place within the normative structure. These changes rapidly eroded the efforts at regime creation. The resistance came from some unlikely quarters. The United States and Europe were intent on moving away from inflexible investment protection for a variety of reasons, not least of which was that they found themselves as respondents in cases in a law that was intended to be used as a sword

---

[140] An example is that the Bush Doctrine on pre-emptive force has been sufficiently attacked that it may have lost significance. Christine Gray, *International Law and the Use of Force*, 2nd edn (Oxford University Press, 2012), pp. 209–16.

1.4   EARLIER PHASES OF INTERNATIONAL LAW   55

against other states, especially developing states.[141] The global picture of investment flows was changing, with the industrializing states of the South, especially China and India, and smaller states like Singapore, South Korea and Taiwan, becoming massive exporters of investment capital. The developed world was in need of shields. International law itself was changing from a unipolar order to a multipolar order.[142] Interestingly, China, in expanding its foreign investment in search of energy and markets, was also in need of swords.[143] The resistance came from several quarters. States were changing course to conserve regulatory space. New actors on the scene; NGOs committed to specific sectors, such as the environment, human rights and labour standards, began arguing against inflexible investment protection. Scholars against fragmentation of international law wanted to ensure that other areas that impacted on foreign investment were included in the consideration of the protection of foreign investment, so that the exclusivity of foreign investment protection was ended. Interest in global corporate social responsibility

---

[141] Quite apart from the NAFTA cases against the United States, Germany became respondent in the high-profile *Vattenfall* v. *Germany* Case (ICSID, Case No. ARB/09/6 (11 March 2011)), involving the legislative decision to phase out the use of nuclear power by 2022. The claim was based on breaches of provisions of the Energy Charter Treaty. In the earlier case (2009), Vattenfall had challenged licensing policies under environmental legislation. The United Kingdom was respondent in an arbitration brought by an Indian lawyer: *Sancheti* v. *United Kingdom*, UNCITRAL (Pending). The United States and Canada had faced a series of NAFTA arbitrations, while Australia was faced with the *Philip Morris Tobacco* litigation.

[142] Muthucumaraswamy Sornarajah, 'The Role of the BRICS in International Law in a Multipolar World', in Vai Io Lo and Mary Hiscock (eds.), *The Rise of the BRICS in the Global Political Economy: Changing Paradigms?* (Cheltenham: Edward Elgar, 2014), p. 288.

[143] China's treaty practice changed. It had hitherto submitted only the issue of the quantum of expropriation in its investment treaties to external arbitration. In its treaty with Germany (2005), it began the practice of submitting disputes violating all treaty standards to foreign arbitration. Norah Gallagher and Wenhua Shan, *Chinese Investment Treaties: Policies and Practice* (Oxford University Press, 2008). Though Alvarez used this new Chinese practice to argue that BITs were not 'tools of a hegemonic empire', the contrary may be the case. As Chinese investment expansion takes hold and it emerges as a powerhouse in trade and investment, if not in military might, it will act like other hegemonic states. Jose Alvarez, 'The Once and Future Foreign Investment Regime', in Mahnoush Arsanjani *et al.* (eds.), *Looking to the Future: Essays in International Law in Honour of Michael Reisman* (Leiden: Martinus Nijhoff, 2010), p. 607. China's own sketchy internal regime of property protection is not reflected in its international stances. As it rises in wealth, it may well join the rest of the gang of promoters of the neoliberal system. China is currently negotiating a free trade agreement with the United States, which will contain an investment chapter, no doubt with strong investment protection, based on the US Model Treaty 2004. But its absence from the list of states negotiating the Trans Pacific Pact may indicate a strategy of keeping China out.

56 INTRODUCTION

increased, with the United Nations chipping in to appoint a rapporteur to study the subject of business and human rights.[144]

1.4.7.1 Push-back by states

The dominance of the United States as the single hegemonic power in a rapidly globalizing world ensured that it was able to push through norms based on its own political and economic system during every phase of international law.[145] During these periods, the role that the hegemonic power had in shaping international law through infusion of its preferred norms is evident in many areas.[146] This included the international law on foreign investment. The US Model Treaty of 1987, which immediately preceded the third phase and was a dominant instrument during that phase, contains inflexible provisions on investment protection. The phases of the evolution of the US model treaties are reflective of different phases. The Model Treaty was revised in 2004 and then again in 2012. The 1987 Model Treaty reflects the ascendancy of the United States and its insistence on strong standards of investment protection, while the later models show a departure from such standards. In the cases arising from the Argentine economic crisis, as well as in the NAFTA investment cases, the provisions contained in the 1987 model played an important role. Certainly, the thinking of the United States played a dominant role in the shaping of the law in this period. The United States was reluctant to move away from the norm of inflexible protection during the 1990s, the highpoint of neoliberalism. It refused to accede to Argentina's request to indicate that the Argentine–US treaty, which was silent on the point, contained a subjective understanding of the national security provision.

But with several cases being brought under NAFTA against the United States and mounting internal criticism of the treaties, the United States began to backtrack. This retreat is evident in the model treaties that were made in 2004 and 2012. The arguments that the United States made in the cases in which it was respondent smack of heavy emphasis on

---

[144] The Rapporteur on Business and Human Rights, John Ruggie, issued a report. He has described his work in John Ruggie, *Just Business: Multinational Corporations and Human Rights* (New York: W. W. Norton, 2013).

[145] Fox and Roth (eds.), *Democratic Governance and International Law*; Scott, *International Law, US Power*.

[146] The role that the hegemonic power plays in bringing about regimes has been widely studied. In the period, the most significant change was the establishment of the WTO with instruments on intellectual property, services and government procurement. The role of the neoliberal tenets in shaping international trade law thereafter has been widely studied.

1.4 EARLIER PHASES OF INTERNATIONAL LAW 57

sovereign rights of regulatory control over foreign investments. *Methanex* v. *United States* (2005) was a successful assertion of the regulatory right of a state to control foreign investment in order to safeguard public health. As pointed out earlier, the emphasis on sovereignty and regulatory control over investment are reminiscent of the claims of developing states under the NIEO. Wits would have it that the United States is moving towards the Calvo Doctrine. This may be an overstatement. The regulatory expropriation rule remained eclipsed during the neoliberal phase, but it was always part of US views on expropriation.[147] In 2004, it moved to a more central position.

Similar processes were at work in other states and regions. The new approaches that were being adopted showed the need to preserve state control over foreign investment rather than surrender such power to an international regime. Withdrawals from existing arrangements were initiated. States avoided signing treaties with investor–state arbitration provisions. New regional treaties contained wide defences to liability that considerably eroded the aim of investment protection. The broad defences in the 'balanced' treaties undermined the notion of inflexible investment protection. Though existing treaties could not be withdrawn in respect of ongoing investments, the new tendencies showed that states wished to withdraw from any notion of a regime of investment protection. These developments are dealt with in Chapters 6 and 7.

1.4.7.2 Narrowing jurisdiction

There was also an effort to curtail the expansionist attitudes to jurisdiction, but with limited success. Thus, the use of incorporation as a method of obtaining jurisdiction through insertion of sandwich companies or the round-tripping of investments from a domestic state through a corporation established in a treaty state, was dealt with through denial of benefit provisions that enabled the state to avoid jurisdiction in such evidently fraudulent attempts at obtaining jurisdiction. But the success of this depended on how arbitrators interpreted the provisions. Likewise, states have successfully contested jurisdiction on the basis of the dispute arising from a transaction that does not fall within the definition of an investment. Again, the extent of the context that has developed in the area shows that the fourth phase is a period of contest between norms rather

---

[147] The American Restatement on Foreign Relations Law stated the rule, as did Sohn's and Baxter's draft code on state responsibility.

58   INTRODUCTION

than one in which there is certainty. The issues that have arisen in
jurisdiction are more fully dealt with in Chapter 3.

1.4.7.3   Ending fragmentation

Trends within international law also favoured the change that was taking
place.[148] The over-fragmentation that has taken place in the field has
resulted in a plethora of works that have looked at the subject in isolation
from the general principles of international law, and without regard to
the changes that were taking place in the climate in which international
law had to operate.[149] This fragmentation enabled the law to be developed as a self-contained regime intended to advance foreign investment
protection to the exclusion of other considerations. Not only did it ignore
general international law, but it also avoided consideration of other
regimes in other areas, such as human rights, which may conflict with
the rules of inflexible investment protection.[150] As argued earlier, such
compartmentalization of international law was a strategy that favoured
the hegemonic power, for it was only a large power that could provide the
capacity and expertise to maintain the high degree of sophistication
necessary to ensure the development of the law in the narrow areas that
such compartmentalization creates. This process would also be facilitated
by the fact that arbitrators, academics and law firms capable of acquiring
the necessary expertise are largely located in the hegemonic state and its
allies.[151] A regime desired by global private power could be constructed
within international law if the area in which it operates is hived off from
international law and is developed separately through the use of low-
order sources of international law, such as the decisions of tribunals and
the writings of 'highly qualified publicists' who may be no more than

---

[148] International Law Commission, 'Fragmentation of International Law: Difficulties
Arising from the Diversification and Expansion of International Law', A/CN.4/L.682
(New York: ILC, 2006).

[149] These works were largely concerned with arbitration of investment disputes under
treaties, and concentrated on explaining the treaty principles and their interpretation
by arbitral awards. See Schreuer and Dolzer, *International Investment Law*; McLachlan
et al., International Investment Arbitration. The general tenor of these works was that
international investment law could, through internal processes of adjustment, accommodate within it external factors such as human rights and environmental
considerations.

[150] On conflict between regimes, see Margaret Young (ed.), *Regime Interaction in
International Law: Facing Fragmentation* (Cambridge University Press, 2012).

[151] Within this 'industry' there are persons who wear all three hats, sitting as arbitrators, are
professors and are members of law firms. Their role has often led to challenges on the
basis of bias, giving rise to many decisions by national courts as well as arbitral tribunals.

hired guns often converting an opinion given in a dispute into an academic article. The groups supporting regime creation work in tandem in promoting the preferred norms of the hegemonic power, as well as of the private power of multinational corporations. Multinational corporations have a distinct interest in ensuring the creation of a regime of inflexible investment protection. They also exert pressure to ensure that the hegemonic state supports the norms they prefer. The coalition between the state, business, international financial institutions, law firms and the arbitration sector played a powerful role in the shaping of the law. It would be difficult for developing countries to create such capacity or expertise to match or provide counterarguments as to why the law should not take a particular course. The more esoteric a narrowly created area becomes, the easier it is to keep others, particularly the weak whose knowledge base is deficient, out of the process of participation. The role of power in shaping the law becomes enhanced. Democratic legitimacy suffers, but the low visibility of this phenomenon does not attract attention until spectacular events draw attention to developments that are detrimental to the public interest.[152] Later events, such as the Argentinian cases arising from the economic crisis, the *Cochahamba* water dispute, investments in nuclear plants and the prohibition of smoking resulting in investment claims, attracted universal public attention. The rise of NGOs pursuing single issues, in which they also came to garner expertise, changed the course of the law in the current phase.[153] If a project of regime formation existed, it became stunted as a result.

As a result of fragmentation, the law on investment protection came to be dominated by arbitrators and commentators who did not have much grounding in public international law, but were more inclined to see it as an extension of international commercial law.[154] Procedure and form in

---

[152] There were disputes that caught world attention. Examples are the Bolivian water dispute (*Aguas del Tunari* v. *Bolivia*), the cigarette labelling disputes in Australia and Ecuador (*Philip Morris* v. *Australia*), the nuclear reactor in Germany (*Vattenfall* v. *Germany*) and carcinogens in petrol in California (*Methanex* v. *United States*). Many of these cases concerned developed states.

[153] For the role of Amnesty International in opposing stabilization clauses in mining contracts, see Sheldon Leader, 'Human Rights, Risks and New Strategies for Global Investment', (2006) 9 *Journal of International Economic Law* 657. The impact of NGOs working in the environment field has been well explored. Jorge Vinuales, *Foreign Investment and the Environment in International Law* (Cambridge University Press, 2012).

[154] Van Harten, *Investment Treaty Arbitration and Public Law*.

investment arbitration was similar to commercial arbitration. This helped to entrench the tendency to regard them as similar. Consequently, contract-based solutions dominated over concerns with the public interest of states.

International lawyers who sat as arbitrators were prone to positivist analyses, so that the resulting awards were based on the analytical dissection of the texts of treaties on which the awards were based. It was possible to rely on the premise that foreign investment promoted economic development as the formulations on the treaties or other relevant documents, such as the ICSID Convention, contained references to the link between foreign investment flows, settlement of disputes and economic development. Again, technically competent arbitrators are more prone to interpret the words of the relevant contracts and treaties without regard to the outcomes in the law that seek to accommodate interests that are reflected in other areas of international law. Though reliance is often placed on the Vienna Convention on the Law of Treaties for the interpretive techniques that are used, there is little evidence that the convention's prescriptions were followed in the awards. Rather, the convention has often been used to buttress preconceived decisions. Often, in commercial arbitration, the only preferable outcome arbitrators have in mind is to ensure that the contract is given effect on the ground that international commerce cannot function unless parties respect the obligations they assumed. So, too, when interpreting a treaty the superficial objective of which would appear to be the protection of foreign investment, arbitrators were inclined to move towards this objective than to seek to examine the public interests of the state in taking measures that violated the treaty. Arbitrators with such inclinations were unlikely to look into other disciplines. Such disciplines may impact on the obligations under the investment treaties. For this reason, they would be inclined to promote fragmentation. Such fragmentation could be opposed not only by other arbitrators, but by an increasingly vocal group of NGOs, political groups and academic writers. Consequently, the pressure to end fragmentation posed a threat to the view that the dominant theme of investment arbitration should be the inflexible protection of foreign investment. There was a burst of academic writings seeking to end fragmentation in the area. Their demand that competing considerations of environmental law, human rights, cultural heritage and sustainable development was to have a considerable effect on the shaping

1.4 EARLIER PHASES OF INTERNATIONAL LAW 61

of the law.[155] As public opinion changed, states, including developed states, had to pay heed to these competing considerations. The old view regarding the inflexibility of investment protection as the basis of law had to undergo a change.

1.4.7.4 Expansionism versus strict construction

There were other considerations that dictated outcomes that favoured the foreign investor.[156] These relate to the preconceptions that arbitrators bring to their decision-making. In practising a profession that depended on influence and patronage, many arbitrators were influenced by the prevailing political tendencies geared to the views favourable to international business and ignored the higher values of the profession such as neutrality and fidelity to the trust placed in them by the parties,[157] or the higher values of human rights and environmental protection to which the international community aspired.[158] As already indicated, there was a limited group of professional arbitrators involved in investment arbitration, so the process of socialization into a value system was not difficult. Such socialization is an observed facet in many professional groups.[159] Success within the group depends on conformity to the values of the group. So even if arbitrators may not understand the technical aspects of an ideological predisposition such as neoliberalism, its basic values could have been transferred within the select group through association or

---

[155] Pierre-Marie Dupuy and Jorge Vinuales (eds.), *Harnessing Foreign Investment to Promote Environmental Protection* (Cambridge University Press, 2013); Valentina Vadi, *Cultural Heritage in International Investment Law and Arbitration* (Cambridge University Press, 2014); Kulick, *Global Public Interest in International Investment Law.*

[156] There is debate as to whether it is statistically demonstrable that investment treaty arbitration has favoured the foreign investor.

[157] Dezaley and Garth, *Dealing in Virtue.*

[158] Moshe Hirsch, 'The Interaction between International Investment Law and Human Rights Treaties: A Sociological Perspective', in Tomer Broude and Yuval Shany (eds.), *Multi-Sourced Equivalent Norms in International Law* (Oxford: Hart Publishing, 2011), p. 211. Hirsch argued that arbitrators belonged to a systemic community different from human rights lawyers, and subscribed to a different set of values promoting stability in contracts and certainty of business norms. They believed in capital flows, legal predictability and market economy ideology, while others, such as human rights lawyers, had universal values based on the primacy of human rights. This is a kinder explanation than one based on sheer prejudice.

[159] Even deviant behaviour is learned through association. Sutherland's theory of differential association was based on explaining teenage criminal gangs on the basis of learned behaviour through association. Edwin Sutherland, *Principles of Criminology* (Philadelphia, PA: Lippincot, 1966). He extended this view to white-collar crimes.

62   INTRODUCTION

through the institutional culture within which such arbitration operates. This may happen despite the fact that the learned values may not be consistent with the rules of the system. A subculture may behave according to its own norms.

The professed values of the system of arbitration require neutrality. The rejection of a political or economic ideology such as neoliberalism was an important tenet of arbitration. If it can be shown that arbitrators had imbibed such a philosophy even subconsciously and were acting in accordance with it, then, they were not acting in accordance with the spirit of arbitration. Yet the evidence seems to suggest that in the narrow field of investment treaty arbitration a significant number of arbitrators were affected by the prevailing mood of the times, and were making expansionary decisions that accorded with the dominant neoliberal views. They were prone to making expansionary interpretations of treaty provisions so as to increase the jurisdictional scope of the treaty provisions on dispute settlement as well as the substantive law provisions.

It cannot be said that all in the profession were similarly tainted. As in domestic law, where observers speak of activist judges and strict constructionists, it is clear that a similar distinction has emerged in investment arbitration between expansionist arbitrators and those with fidelity to the system based on the consent of the parties. Whereas activist judges are admired as they extend the law in order to meet social needs, expansionist arbitrators seek to advance the interests of the powerful few over the interests of the multitude.

The schisms that have arisen in the field of investment arbitration are best explained in the context of the attitudinal differences that have characterized developments in this area of the law. There was a struggle between two camps. There were those committed to neoliberal views, which required the expansion of a system of foreign investment protection based on the values of promoting the free market ideals of sanctity of property, the importance of preserving commercial obligations and free flows of investment. These arbitrators permitted jurisdictional expansions such as through the use of the most favoured nation (MFN) clause or through manipulations of corporate nationality.[160] They expanded substantive principles of liability, principally through the use of the fair and equitable treatment provision in the investment treaties, finding in it an obligation to respect the legitimate expectations of the foreign investor. The use of the umbrella clause and the exploration of the phrase

---

[160] See Chapter 5.

1.4 EARLIER PHASES OF INTERNATIONAL LAW 63

'tantamount to an expropriation' are other instances of such an expansionary tendency.[161] A fervour for neoliberalism neatly accounts for the expansionary trends that were initiated in the field. In finding policy justification for the extensions they were making, the argument most often used was that the statement in the preamble that the treaty's objective was economic development justified the expansive interpretation that was being made. The uniform neoliberal vision was that all foreign investment was beneficial and had to be protected.

The second group of arbitrators saw their duty as insisting on fidelity to the exact terms of the consent of the parties and an absence of bias which the system of arbitration mandated. This group of arbitrators was wary of transgressing into areas of policy. They also used teleological interpretations based on the assumed intention of the states. But they were not limited by the singular vision of neoliberal arbitrators. In considering the issues arising from the definition of investment, they took into account whether or not the investment had the potential to promote economic development. Caution was expressed that expansion would affect the state's willingness to permit entry to foreign investment. The need to take heed of human rights and *ius cogens* principles was stated. They adopted a pragmatic approach. They were able to see that states would react to the expansive interpretations that were being made and that such intervention would damage the system of arbitration.

1.4.7.5 Rise of corporate responsibility

A careful effort has been made to ensure that the stream of the law relating to corporate responsibility for international wrongs committed by multinational corporations does not mix with the law on investment arbitration. It ensures that the purity of the multinational corporation as a virginal force for economic development is unsullied so that the rationale for investment protection could be maintained. All the while, there has been a separate development of a heavily contested law that seeks to ensure that there is responsibility in the multinational corporations for the international wrongs in their conduct abroad.

The imposition of such responsibility on multinational corporations has been heavily contested. This in itself shows the extent of the power that multinational corporations possess. The long history of litigation in

---

[161] See Chapter 4.

64 INTRODUCTION

the United States under the Alien Tort Claims Act attests to the hesitant development of the recognition of such responsibility by the domestic courts of the multinational corporations.[162] There is every possibility that the law on multinational responsibility and the law on state responsibility for foreign investors will meet when the law on counterclaims under investment arbitration comes to be developed. Counterclaims will become the norm in future. The existence of circumstances justifying counterclaims is a way of distinguishing between regulatory expropriations and compensable expropriation. The existence of defences to responsibility in the newer treaties also points in that direction. When the two streams of investment protection and corporate responsibility meet and mix, it will be difficult to maintain a system of inflexible investment protection. When this happens, it could well be that the fervour for investment arbitration will also abate. Few multinational corporations would want to see their misdeeds publicly paraded. The rule of law arguments requires equal treatment of all actors. It is not possible to treat the multinational corporation as incapable of fault and maintain an investment treaty system under which only the multinational corporation can sue the state. Developed countries have opposed a binding code of conduct for multinational corporations. The effort to draft an investment discipline under the WTO failed because of the insistence by developing countries that the discipline should include provisions on misconduct of multinational corporations. The recognition of the existence of defences goes some way in pleading the misconduct of multinational corporations before arbitral tribunals, though it does not go towards bringing claims against them for such misconduct. But the rule of law argument that is so often raised in defence of investment protection must logically lead to the situation that recognizes that such claims are made possible. The law will move towards that direction.

1.4.7.6 Other factors

There were those outside the immediate field of arbitration who had an impact on the outcomes. They also split into two groups. The large law firms, a result of globalization of the 1990s,[163] aggressively courted

---

[162] The recent judgment of the Supreme Court in *Kiobel* v. *Royal Dutch Shell Petroleum Co.* (2013) 569 US. The decision required contact with the US territory for the violation to be subject to jurisdiction. There is another case currently before the Supreme Court: *DaimlerChrysler AG* v. *Bauman* (2014) 571 US 748.

[163] Yves Dezaley, *The Internationalization of the Practice of Law* (The Hague: Kluwer, 2001). These firms also helped in the transportation of legal values and fashions. Yves Dezaley

1.4 EARLIER PHASES OF INTERNATIONAL LAW   65

investment arbitration. These firms saw expansions in the field as a way of enlarging the market for their services. There was also the growth of a new business of third-party funding for investment arbitration, the effect of which was to ensure that both the grounds of jurisdiction as well as the substantive law in the area were broadened. Academics, who also saw a lucrative supplementation of their otherwise meagre incomes, joined the bandwagon as experts and advisers. Law schools, sad to say, hastened to associate themselves with law firms, which had set up sections on investment arbitration, held out professorships to practitioners to teach courses offered by them in the law school curriculum. There are accusations of a vulture culture within the legal profession in the manner in which they pursued states in economic distress and made creative use of provisions of the treaties to base claims.[164] Vulture funds have bought up awards both in efforts to enforce them as well as to settle them at a profit. They also fund new arbitrations. These are undesirable results that will have the effect of states acting to prevent further arbitration of investment disputes. Even if the treaties did not lead to the economic development of the poor, they certainly did lead to the economic development of arbitrators and lawyers.

On the opposing side, there were the non-governmental groups, academics and others disturbed by the fact that the law that was being created concentrated solely on the protection of foreign investment to the detriment of other values, such as the protection of the environment,[165] human rights,[166] corporate social responsibility,[167] sustainable development[168] and the primacy that must be attached to *ius cogens* principles of international law.[169] The idea that investment protection

---

and Bruce Garth, *Global Prescriptions: The Production, Exportation and Importation of a New Legal Orthodoxy* (Ann Arbor, MI: University of Michigan Press, 2005).

[164] Kevin Gallagher, 'The New Vulture Culture: Sovereign Debt Restructuring and Investment Treaty Arbitration', Tufts University Ideas Working Paper 02/2011 (2011).

[165] Kyla Tienhaara, *The Expropriation of Environmental Governance: Protecting Foreign Investors at the Expense of Public Policy* (Cambridge University Press, 2009); Vinuales, *Foreign Investment and the Environment in International Law*.

[166] David Kinley, *Civilising Globalization: Human Rights and the Global Economy* (Cambridge University Press, 2009); Pierre-Marie Dupuy *et al.* (eds.), *Human Rights in International Investment Law and Arbitration* (Oxford University Press, 2009).

[167] Zerk, *Multinational Corporations and Corporate Social Responsibility*; Adekunle, *Corporate Social Responsibility of Multinational Corporations in Developing Countries*.

[168] Marie Cordonier Segger *et al.* (eds.), *Sustainable Development in World Investment Law* (The Hague: Wolters Kluwer, 2010).

[169] Muthucumaraswamy Sornarajah, *The Settlement of Foreign Investment Disputes* (The Hague: Kluwer, 2001), argued that *ius cogens* principles created a doctrine of arbitrability

66 INTRODUCTION

had to operate within a system of international law, which had hierarchies of interests and conflicting obligations, did not come easily to commercial arbitrators to whom contractual sanctity was the major determinant. It was natural that other camps should emerge, both within arbitration and outside it, which gave priority to competing values found within the international system over the values of neoliberalism. Equally, there were networks created by foreign investment interests that worked to stabilize the norms of investment protection.[170] The fact that arbitrators brought different visions to their tasks resulted in wide divergences in the law stated in their awards.

1.4.8 The retreat of neoliberalism?

As neoliberalism retreated, with increasing evidence of failure manifested in a succession of economic crises in Asia and Latin America and finally in the global economic crisis in 2008, the schism within investment treaty arbitration became more pronounced, with some arbitrators showing a willingness to beat back the gains that neoliberalism had made within the field.[171] States also became intent on curbing the excesses that had taken place. They saw the need to recover their regulatory powers in order to deal with economic crises. They began to make new treaties that sought to curtail the possibility of expansion through interpretation. States that were totally dissatisfied simply announced their withdrawal. The possibility of the Latin American states going back to the Calvo Doctrine has become real.[172]

One may argue that the internal schisms among arbitrators are a credit to the system and that it is capable of self-correction. Apologists for the system suggest that all areas of the law go through periods of

for foreign investment arbitration. The view was that certain disputes involving violations of *ius cogens* principles like allegations of torture and genocide were not arbitrable by tribunals set up under investment treaties.

[170] On competition between NGOs on the different sides, see Clifford Bob, *The Global Right Wing and the Clash of World Politics* (Cambridge University Press, 2012). There is a clash of networks in global politics. In foreign investment, networks supporting business clash with NGOs working on poverty, human rights and the environment.

[171] This statement is made on reliance of restrictions that arbitrators began to place on legitimate expectations requiring examination of conditions in the state at time of entry, the existence of business risks and the extension of notions of regulatory measures in the public interest as being justifications for the measures. These are discussed in Chapter 5.

[172] Argentina has yet to pay on any of the awards against it in cases arising from its economic crisis. One can expect further litigation arising from awards against Ecuador and other Latin American states.

experimentation and that choice of rules that are workable. But such self-correction has not happened and is unlikely to happen. The system is not geared to self-correction as actors within it, both arbitrators and counsel (and, now, third-party funders), benefit through maintaining an expansionist position. States had to intervene to accomplish a significant movement away from the base of inflexible investment protection to an entirely different system that accommodates greater space for regulatory measures of the state in certain contingencies.

The reaction of states was the most important as they make international law more effectively and swiftly. The expansionist law that was made by arbitrators and the scholars supporting them, with all the brave face put on a *jurisprudence constante* and the eminence of writers, are based on low-order sources. It is a charade to argue that tribunals are capable of creating custom. Tribunals cannot create international law that is not supported by states. States began to assert themselves by pursuing vigorous and ingenious defences to liability found both within treaties as well as within international law, as a result of which arbitrators had to decide issues in a context outside the ambit of an inflexible and absolute law on investment protection.[173] The Argentine cases resulted in the exploration of the scope of necessity in general international law outside its formulation in the treaty.[174] Around the same time, there was increasing questioning of the benefits of entering into investment treaties generated by economists. Quite apart from this literature, which discussed whether investment treaties in fact lead to greater inflows of foreign investment justifying the surrender of sovereignty to secure such investment flows, there was visible demonstration that arbitrations were costly,[175] and that a state could stand in peril of losing large sums by way of damages.[176]

Despite these developments, the retreat of neoliberalism has not completely taken place. It is clear that neoliberalism will survive because of its

---

[173] The Argentinian awards show the best evidence of this. The various aspects of the defence of necessity become prominent in these awards. The rediscovery of regulatory takings as non-compensable also is essentially a revival of an old customary law principle that sovereign functions done in pursuance of police powers of a state are not reviewable. But jurisdictional defences, such as whether the investment was made in accordance with the foreign investment laws of the host state, also became prominent. These issues are discussed in subsequent chapters.

[174] The Argentinian cases on necessity are discussed in Chapter 7.

[175] Reports in the Philippines suggest that *Fraport* v. *Philippines* cost the government over US$56 million. The litigation still continues in various fora.

[176] This again proved to be contentious, with some arguing that the damages were not heavy and others arguing that they were.

68   INTRODUCTION

adaptive capacity and its ability to morph into different forms when faced with criticism. Thus, regulatory expropriation may provide release of space for the states, but there is a strike-back through the limitation introduced that a proportionality test has to be satisfied. The ability of neoliberalism to forestall changes against its preferred structure and initiated changes that preserve its essential framework is great. Yet the fact is that there is considerable disarray that has resulted in the structure of absolute foreign investment clearly being displaced. In that sense, there is a retreat of neoliberalism, but no definite system has replaced the system that was built up in the context of neoliberalism. Some states have cut the Gordian knot, but others seek to keep the system going.

1.5 The course of the fourth phase

The vestiges of the law created through neoliberal thinking will remain tenacious until fully dismantled, if that is possible. A norm created on the basis of a prevalent disposition that protects bases of power cannot be easily displaced unless there is countervailing power, or dominant ideas emerge in support of an opposing norm. Until such overwhelming power emerges, the tenacity of the older norms will remain. They will remain also because the ideas that led to their creation will continue to have sway, and may return to favour at some future time. The cyclical nature of the decline and return to favour of ideas is an observable phenomenon in the history of politics as well as of law.[177] Besides, once established, a norm will become difficult to dislodge. The prevalence still of ideas that were created during the first phase of the law of foreign investment indicate how old norms retain vitality and cannot easily be displaced until more vigorous norms take over. Arguments that are made in favour of change will be met, turning the arguments on their head, to support old norms. Thus, one can witness the phenomenon of human rights arguments for changes in inflexible investment protection being met with arguments within the human rights field based on the right to property.[178] There are considerable neoliberal features that have been inserted into these related disciplines, so that accommodating them into the neoliberal structure of investment protection may not be difficult. The debate will go on and resistance to change will be strong. In such situations, change may be

---

[177] The cyclical nature of the phenomenon of nationalizations in economic history was identified by Edith Penrose, 'Nationalization of Foreign Owned Property for Public Purpose', (1992) 55 *Modern Law Review* 1.

[178] The legitimacy of this view is considered in Chapter 5.

1.5 THE COURSE OF THE FOURTH PHASE 69

difficult. Until change takes place, the contest between norms will continue with the law being in a state of 'normlessness'.

One may argue that notions of sovereignty inherent in the NIEO, whose demise was gleefully announced earlier, have resurfaced in modern times in new guises. The drive towards greater regulatory control over foreign investment that one finds now in modern treaties is reflective of asserting control over natural resources and foreign investment that was a feature of the NIEO. The argument that there is a moral duty not to make laws that work against the poor finds acceptance in the philosophical writings of many modern thinkers.[179] The NIEO sought the recognition of a legal rather than a moral duty. It could well be that such ideas may return, with developed states also evincing a desire to assert control over foreign investment. The idea that globalization led to the erosion of the sovereignty of states may well prove to be an overstatement.[180] The return of the state and with it the return of ideas of the NIEO could yet take place.

As time passes, the advances that were made during the ascendancy of the period of neoliberal thinking will be subjected to greater scrutiny. Though the principles may not disappear altogether, their force will come to be dented considerably. One may even argue that it would be so dented that foreign investors may not have the same confidence in treaty-based arbitration that they initially had, and will look to contractual and other means of protecting their investments. With the increasing number of defences to liability, the chances of success for foreign investors in arbitration under treaties are diminishing. The grant of costs against the losing party will also deter such arbitrations. The law would then have undergone a full cycle. There will be a return to contract-based arbitration.

The recent episodes will remain important in studying how a vibrant field of international law was affected by an idea that was espoused by the hegemonic power acting in the interest of its multinational corporations, and how competing ideas brought about change. The role that arbitrators, academics, law firms, negotiators of treaties and NGOs played in the successive changes are areas that are worthy of study. The change was also brought about by the fact that the initial success of the application of neoliberal theories did not eventually succeed. The successive economic

---

[179] Thomas Pogge, *World Poverty and Human Rights: Cosmopolitan Responsibility and Reforms*, 2nd edn (Cambridge: Polity, 2008).

[180] Jose Alvarez, 'Sovereignty is not Withering Away', in Antonio Cassese (ed.), *Realizing Utopia* (Oxford University Press, 2012), p. 26.

crises, precipitated by the adoption of neoliberal policies, resulted in rethinking on unregulated market solutions, bringing back the idea that without state regulation markets cannot function smoothly. The return to regulation made investment protection based on market based theories unsound. The regulatory power of the state became central to economic functioning, and the treaty principles, which hindered the exercise of such regulatory power, had to be changed.

The processes of such change in the phases create opportunity for the study of the law in manifold areas of activity. The episodes concern arbitration as a mechanism of protection, the response of the legal profession to the creation of a new area of expertise, the role of the arbitrators acting both in an expansionist and in a conservative manner and the role of the academic commentators in shaping the law. The interactions that took place in the different phases indicate that the international law on foreign investment will always remain a controversial area of international law where ideological and other conflicts continuously shape the course of law. The law cannot be understood except in the context of its ideological and political context.

This book is a study in changes in the law fluctuating in accordance with the dominance of competing ideologies at different periods and the manner of the resolution of conflicts of interests. It indicates that in this, as in other areas of international law, the tendency of international law to be put to instrumental use is great. When such instrumental use becomes pronounced, reactions to it produce resistance as those who do not believe in the objectives of such instrumental use seek to check the progress of the objectives. Those who do so are themselves putting the law to instrumental use in that they seek to correct or counter certain biases. The resulting schism itself will bring about changes by seeking new accommodations within the law or leading to the weakening of the system through withdrawals and dissent. This introductory chapter has defined the broad views that stood in opposition to each other during the period of the ascendancy of neoliberalism. The chapters that follow look at specific instances of the conflicts and change.

This work concentrates on the changes that took place in the third and fourth phases that have been described. This period began in 1990 and continues to the present. They are rapid changes that took place in a short period of time. The work seeks to explain those changes and to find a theoretical basis for understanding such changes in terms of power and resistance to power.

1.6 The outline of the book

This book is a study of changes in the international law on foreign investment as contained in investment treaties, and the creation of law on the basis of such treaties through interpretations of their provisions by arbitration tribunals. Resistance to the expansionist interpretation of arbitrators curtailing the regulatory sovereignty of states led to resistance and brought about changes. The events enable contemplation of a theory of how changes occur in an area of international law. It indicates that there is evidence that when any ideological position is taken by a significant hegemonic power, the propositions that advance that ideology find expression through international law, and that there are willing institutions, agencies and persons to transfer the prescriptions into norms of international law. The willingness ensues either because the institutions have been captured by the hegemonic power or were originally set up in order to carry out its preferences. Agents support such ventures largely because they serve their own interests.

The study also enables consideration of the extent to which the developments, which have taken place on the basis of neoliberal prescriptions, are consistent with the principles of justice in international law. Justice in itself is a subjective consideration, and arguments based on it are avoided simply because of the lack of objectivity in the selection of the norms of justice on which arguments or justifications are based.[181] But this criticism is unjustified in the area under consideration. It would be difficult to show that the neoliberal advances were rooted in justice. They privileged large multinational corporations on the pretext that the investments they brought would create wealth for the people of the poorer world. That premise has been shown to be false. Successive economic crises have shown that unregulated market capitalism created harm for all people, those at home as well as abroad. The nationalizations of banks that took place in the richer states indicated that the techniques used for recovery of control were reminiscent of conduct that developing states had used when faced with similar problems. It was difficult to maintain the pretence that international law should be different for different people. The situation then gives rise also to a debate about the justice of the results that the neoliberal order sought to achieve. A law that is unjust lacks

---

[181] This is the classic reason for justifying positivist preferences. Kelsen's pure theory is often explained on the ground that prescriptions based on justice are based on subjective preferences and have no objective basis.

legitimacy. Resistance to it will result in change. These and other debates that need airing are given space in this book.

The book concentrates on the period between 1990 and the present. It explores some themes in the law that developed and progressively weakened. It explores the extent to which neoliberal views were given expression through awards based on investment treaties. It indicates the rise of competing interests that sought to check the advance of these neoliberal tendencies both within arbitration as well as in the reaction of states to the excessive extensions of treaty principles through interpretation. It tests the justice of the neoliberal order that was constructed through arbitral awards. To the extent that it can be found to be unjust, the case for repeating the construction of such an order through the means of arbitration or through multilateral means must be considered weak. It explores and explains a theory of change in one area of international law and examines whether that theory of change can be applied to the whole of international law.

1.7 The arrangement of the book

This introductory chapter has looked at the changes that occurred in the 'roaring nineties'. It sought to provide the setting in which the developments of the last few years took place. International law in the first part of this period was characterized by the euphoria that resulted from the dissolution of the Soviet Union. The triumph of market capitalism over state-controlled socialism signalled a new age in which the neoliberal ideology took hold. While that ideology provided the fundamental base for the argument that the free market should be the determinant of economic decisions, the political counterpart of the neoliberal vision was that government must be organized on democratic ideals. The twin considerations of promoting market capitalism and political democracy were the objectives to be achieved. International law was seen as the means through which these objectives were to be achieved. The dissolution of the Soviet Union also witnessed the emergence of a single hegemonic power, the United States. The United States, along with its allies and the institutions it controlled, drove the agenda of neoliberalism and its political counterpart, neoconservatism. This chapter noted these developments and concluded that international law was put to an instrumental use in this period to secure the objectives of the single hegemonic power and its allies. There was a definite project to build up strong norms of investment protection through treaties and through the interpretation

1.7 THE ARRANGEMENT OF THE BOOK 73

of those treaties through interpretation. The role of private power in using low-order sources to advance the instrumental objectives of inflexible investment protection through international law was emphasized. The project achieved a large measure of success as a result of the rapid proliferation of treaties and the expansive interpretation made of its jurisdictional and substantive principles by arbitral tribunals. But disenchantment soon set in. The emergence of new actors like NGOs and citizens groups within states began to query the developments that left the states without sufficient regulatory power to deal with domestic public interest issues. The hegemonic vision of the world order in investment relationships was met with resistance both within the arbitral system as well as outside it. A crisis resulted that had to result in change. The chapter establishes the setting for the discussion of the problems that arose.

Chapter 2 identifies existing patterns that had already emerged within the area of international law on foreign investment that were hospitable to the advancement of the neoliberal tenets. It deals with the earlier and still existing type of arbitration of investment disputes arising from contracts. It identifies policy rationales that were made by arbitrators as well as commentators in such arbitrations that facilitated the later neoliberal thrust that was to be made in the area of treaty-based arbitration. These occurred largely in shaping protection through international law for the foreign investment contract. It is important to assess the nature of the contractual protection that had been devised through the internationalization of the foreign investment contract, which rested on premises that were similar to those used by arbitrators dealing with investment treaties. This process itself required considerable mental feats as one of the parties was not subject to international law as it existed at the time, and possibly still is not. There were no procedural rules for the making of foreign investment contracts and no substantive law that applied to them in terms of international law. Despite these theoretical difficulties, a law was created in order to protect the foreign investment contract. This was an early instance of the use of private power to establish a system in terms of international law for the protection of foreign investment. It dragged in principles of state responsibility, reshaped them and created new rules, so that an autonomous regime for the protection of foreign investment contract was created in terms of international law. This experience gave the lead for later adventures in the field. The theoretical justifications that were formulated in elevating the foreign investment contract into the international sphere lay the foundations for similar endeavours in

74 INTRODUCTION

investment treaty arbitrations. There was also the need to conserve the advances that had been made in the field of contractual protection through the new rules on protection through investment treaty principles. The interaction between the two systems itself is an example not only of private power at work, but the ideological underpinnings fashioning a law to ensure that its aims were advanced.

The thesis advanced in Chapter 2 is that a climate has been created for the ready acceptance of extensions of the law relating to the protection of foreign investment as the rationale for such inflexible protection of foreign investment had already become well-articulated in awards that were made in contract-based disputes. They pre-dated the major thrust that took place in the 1990s to stabilize a regime of investment protection. The theory of internationalization of foreign investment contracts that was developed through a series of arbitrations provided the setting in which it was possible to extend the legal principles under investment treaties towards the realization of neoliberal ends. The resistance that built up to the internationalization of foreign investment contracts is also significant in understanding later resistance to expansionism in investment treaty arbitration.

Chapter 3 deals with the expansive interpretations made to the dispute settlement provision in the treaty as a means of establishing jurisdiction of the tribunal. Expansionary jurisdiction was necessary in order to establish a bridgehead for advancing the expansion of the substantive provisions of the treaty. The schisms that resulted and the reaction of the states and other actors to such arbitral adventurism are analysed in this chapter.

Chapter 4 deals with expropriation. Expropriation was the most important cause of action in investment arbitration. The chapter details the nature of efforts to expand the scope of expropriation and the resultant reactions both on the part of arbitrators opposed to such expansionism as well as of states. States argued for limitations and introduced restrictions in the newer treaties. They restricted the scope of expropriation. The chapter demonstrates that the significance of expropriation, the mainstay of investment protection law, has been greatly reduced in modern times as a result of the recognition that regulatory takings are usually non-compensable. As a result, once the door of expropriation began closing, it was necessary from the point of view of the viability of the investment arbitration system to open another door through the awakening of the, hitherto dormant, fair and equitable standard and the quick attribution of meaning to it. There may be fresh

1.7 THE ARRANGEMENT OF THE BOOK

attempts to revive the basis of expropriation law through new techniques. These are also explored in the chapter.

Chapter 5 deals with the process of shifting importance onto the fair and equitable standard. The standard of fair and equitable treatment has become of central importance, and has undergone surprising innovations unknown at the time treaty practice was initiated. Several book-length treatments of this specific clause have appeared seeking to explain the nature of the interpretation of this provision.[182] The emergence in importance of this clause by itself attests to the important changes that have been occurring within investment arbitration. The schisms that have emerged on the interpretation of this provision also attest to the fact that there are many ideological attitudes to the emergence of the law and theoretical difficulties as to the power of arbitrators to give meanings to phrases in a manner that parties could not possibly have intended.

Chapter 6 analyses the response of states to expansionism through the creation of new defences to liability. It concludes that the creation of defences to liability, both during pleadings and through newer treaties, creates such uncertainty in the law that there is a return to the same normlessness that characterized the law on investment protection as existed in the law prior to the making of investment treaties. It then speculates as to the continued utility of the treaties as a means of investment protection. Changes in investment patterns that have made newly industrializing states such as China, India and Brazil the exporters of capital to the traditional capital exporting states – the United States and the states of western Europe – will add further strains to the existing law, making it depart from the neoliberal project of emphasizing investment protection. The increasing demands for the balancing of investment protection with other aims of international law, such as the eradication of poverty, the protection of the environment and the promotion of human rights, will further erode the considerations of investment protection.[183]

Chapter 7 considers the new types of treaty that are now being made. They are referred to as balanced treaties as they seek to retain within them the same standards of foreign investment protection while

---

[182] Ioana Tudor, *The Fair and Equitable Treatment Standard in the International Law of Foreign Investment* (Oxford University Press, 2008); Martin Paparinskis, *The International Minimum Standard and Fair and Equitable Treatment* (Oxford University Press 2012); Roland Klager, *Fair and Equitable Treatment in International Investment Law* (Cambridge University Press, 2011).

[183] Vinuales, *Foreign Investment and the Environment in International Law.*

simultaneously ensuring regulatory space for the state to protect the public interest in broadly identified circumstances. The marriage of these two inconsistent notions would seem unworkable. Anticipating such changes, the response has been to make use of the proportionality doctrine that is used in European systems in order to balance rights with the interests of the state in acting to conserve the public interest. The chapter seeks to make an analysis of the workability of the test in situations of investment disputes. It sees in the introduction of the doctrine an effort on the part of arbitrators to be relevant in the face of change.

The Chapter 8 contemplates the significance of these rapid changes for international law. For one thing, the changes had much to do with both hegemonic power as well as with private power. They indicate how the ideological preferences of the dominant hegemonic power are translated into propositions of international law. They also indicate how, at the micro-level, these propositions are stabilized through the use of low-order sources of international law, such as the decisions of arbitral tribunals and the writings of 'highly qualified publicists', which largely favour the positions that advance private power. This fact calls into question the extent to which weight should be given to these sources in the formation of public international law. The chapter also considers the extent to which the developments that took place are consistent with theories of justice in international law, and queries whether the acceptability of rules formulated by tribunals should be tested on external criteria such as their concordance with accepted norms of justice. It seeks to formulate a theory of change in international law by pointing out that international law is a process that balances different interests, and that hence norms that receive dominant support undergo decline when resistance to the norms emerges. Such resistance results in a process of rebalancing the interests at conflict in the course of which the different norms in conflict are reordered and a new structure given to the law.

The Western philosophical approach to poverty is based on blaming the poor for their plight, an idea that is applied to their own poor who are seen as idle and as not exerting themselves to rise out of their situation. In times when neoliberalism, which promotes individual effort towards wealth creation and ownership, is in the ascendancy such ideas become well entrenched in the domestic sphere. But even at other times, the duty to the remote poor is not recognized, either on the grounds that such poverty is the fault of states in mismanaging their resources or that it is some 'cosmic injustice' that cannot be attributed to the rich. The moral duty to assist the remote poor did not arise. It is suggested that global justice lies in changing this entrenched attitude and recognizing that a moral duty to assist such poor is recognized. The chapter argues that the legitimacy of the existing law fails when considered in the light of notions of fairness and global justice, and, hence, needs to be replaced with a law that takes human needs into account rather than caters to the human greed of a few. Prescriptions necessary to change the law towards this objective are stated.

2

The precursor of neoliberalism: internationalization of foreign investment contracts

Contractual protection of foreign investment was a precursor to treaty-based protection. Many of the techniques that were used in structuring the protection of foreign investment contracts, which were essentially made in the context of a domestic legal system, were later transported into investment treaty arbitration. It is unfortunate that modern treatments of the law on foreign investment protection concentrate on treaty principles and arbitration based on them without considering the links between such principles and the principles of the earlier means of contractual protection. The two are linked. The theoretical structure and policy reasons for foreign investment protection were first worked out in the context of arbitration based on contracts. Contractual arbitration still continues to exist as the entry of foreign investment is largely based on initial contracts the foreign investor makes with the state or state entities.[1] The contract will contain its own mechanisms for the protection of the foreign investment. Arbitration remains the main contractual technique through which such protection is accomplished. The manner of building up the rules on investment protection through contract-based arbitration is instructive in that several theoretical hurdles had to be surmounted before such a project could be accomplished. The existence of these hurdles did not deter the building up of the system. It provides an illustration of how such a system, which flies in the face of fundamental theoretical premises of international law, could be constructed and maintained through frequent repetition in awards and writings based on such awards. The schisms that exist within such arbitration is reflective of the schisms that later characterized investment treaty

---

[1] Sometimes, the two forms of arbitration are brought in tandem in respect of the same dispute. For example, in the long-standing *Fraport* v. *Philippines* dispute, there was both an ICC arbitration as well as an ICSID arbitration going on simultaneously. The ICC award was challenged before the Singapore High Court. The award was annulled in full. *Fraport AG* v. *Philippines*, ICSID, Case No ARB/03/25, Annulment (23 December 2010). The cost of the litigation exceeded US$58 million for the Philippines.

arbitration. In every sense, contract-based arbitration is very much the forerunner of investment treaty arbitration. It is a phenomenon that undermines international law as an internally coherent system. It demonstrates that private power can wield significant authority in constructing systems of rules within international law, even if they run counter to its essential theoretical base.[2] The phenomenon should be studied as it is constantly repeated in other areas where capture of institutions or authority makes it possible for rules to be made that have to be followed by those without power to resist their formation. It demonstrates that systems of rules could be created and maintained despite their being inconsistent with international law as long as a base of power supports the venture. When actors with power use international law to achieve objectives, changes may be effected, though such changes may have an ephemeral effect due to constant challenge and resistance.

The structure of contract-based investment protection was constructed prior to the ascendancy of neoliberalism. But, as scholars point out, the tenets of neoliberalism were present from much earlier times. Their virulent rise was during the 1990s when a confluence of circumstance made it possible for the tenets of neoliberalism to be advanced through the law to create a treaty-based system of investment protection. But the idea of creating such a system had been simmering for some time. The significance of contract-based arbitration is that it paved the way for the later success of treaty-based arbitration. Due to low visibility,[3] the number of contract-based arbitrations are uncertain, but there are a significant number of awards that are publicly available. The rules of contractual protection through 'international law' provide an alternative and older method of investment protection. Increasingly, an effort is made to ensure that contracts come to be protected through treaty provisions as well.[4]

---

[2] Thus, at the time such contractual protection was conceived, international law did not recognize the personality of multinational corporations and did not conceive of their ability to sue states. Neither had it conceived of principles that could be applied to foreign investment contracts.

[3] There is now a tendency to publish treaty-based awards as the public interest in such disputes are acknowledged. Many states disclose all information, including papers filed in the course of arbitrations. They are available freely on several websites. The picture is different in the case of contract-based arbitration where awards are seldom released.

[4] The umbrella clause which involves the protection of commitments made to the foreign investor has been held to protect contracts. *SGS* v. *Philippines*, ICSID, Case No. ARB/02/6, Decision on Jurisdiction and Admissibility (24 January 2004); *EDF* v. *Argentina*, ICSID, Case ARB/03/23 (2012), at para. 884. The stabilization clause in the contract has been held

80   THE PRECURSOR OF NEOLIBERALISM

2.1   Future relevance

It is likely that the number of contract-based arbitrations will increase in the future for a variety of reasons. The first among them is the fact that as treaties increasingly refer to a wide variety of preclusionary measures, such as national security and defences such as measures taken to protect interests in health, morals and public welfare, there will be greater uncertainty as to the scope of treaty protection. The second is that an increasing range of interests, such as labour standards, human rights, the environment and public interest concerns, are included in treaties. Such inclusion ensures that investment protection ceases to be the sole concern of investment treaties. The introduction of these interests ensures that measures of states violating treaty standards will be regarded as regulatory non-compensable violations of the standards. The third is the possibility of counterclaims in investment treaty arbitration to meet arguments based on fairness by showing that the foreign investor engaged in unfair practices justifies the state measures. Inflexible statement of the rules on investment protection has made treaties attractive to foreign investors so far. The law was based on the assumption that the state was erring in imposing measures interfering with the investment. That attitude is on the wane. With the emphasis in the newer treaties shifting to the accommodation of regulatory interests of states,[5] treaty-based arbitration may lose its glamour. A fourth development is that frivolous resort to treaty-based arbitration is often met with the award of costs against the claimant.[6] For these reasons, it is important to consider the continuing relevance of contract-based arbitration. The significance to this work is not that contract-based arbitration will retain its importance, but that it is the older variety of investment arbitration and that the theoretical justifications advanced for it continue to animate justifications for expansionist techniques used in treaty-based arbitration. This variety of foreign investment arbitration influenced later attitudes greatly through the formulation of ideas that were the forerunners of neoliberal tenets that drove treaty-based investment arbitration. It also

---

to be protected by the fair and equitable standard of treatment on the ground that it creates a legitimate expectation. It has also been suggested that the violation of a stabilization clause is an exception to the rule relating to indirect regulatory expropriations not being compensable. *Methanex* v. *United States* (3 August 2005).

[5] See Chapter 9.

[6] For example, *Libinanco* v. *Turkey*, ICSID, Case No. ARB/06/8 (2 September 2011), which resulted in an award of US$25 million against the claimant on the ground that the claim was frivolous.

2.2 A BRIEF HISTORY

demonstrates that historically very similar ideas have been used in order to construct foreign investment protection. As it is said, the past is simply the future waiting to happen. For a variety of reasons that type of arbitration is a necessary prelude to any discussion of treaty-based investment arbitration, not the fact that contract-based arbitration will recover its prominence. Recent literature manifests the increasing spotlight that is being thrown on arbitrations arising from state contracts.[7]

2.2 A brief history

Though the focus of this work is on the recent period of developments relating to investment treaty arbitration, it must be recognized that the foundations for the thrust that was made of the ideological view that privileged foreign investment by multinational corporations over the interests of the people of the host states, dates back to a considerably longer period of time. In that sense, the neoliberal philosophy that animates modern foreign investment protection law had its roots in an earlier classical view that foreign investment is uniformly beneficial to economic development due to the benefits its flows create so to be worthy of protection.[8] Early justifications, such as the sanctity of contracts, the sanctity of property, the need for stability of investment and the protection of the property against expropriation through damages for future profits, were thought up in the context of contractual arbitration. They are similar to the neoliberal justifications for the expansionary interpretations in investment treaty arbitration. From very early times, international law has been associated with debates involving trade and investment. Justifications had to be provided for colonial expansion and the subjugation of non-European people to European control. Since resources and wealth had to be transported from the colonies to fuel industrial expansion as well as ensure economic power, it became necessary to ensure colonial expansion. During this period, sheer force ensured the protection of investment. The argument is made that the

---

[7] Ivar Alvik, *Contracting with Sovereignty: State Contracts and International Arbitration* (Oxford: Hart, 2011); Jan Ole Voss, *The Impact of Investment Treaties on Contracts between Host States and Foreign Investors* (Leiden: Martinus Nijhoff, 2011).

[8] The classical view on foreign investment was that such investment was uniformly beneficial to developing countries as it led to asset flows, transfer of technology, opportunity for export income and other advantages. For a description of the classical view, see Muthucumaraswamy Sornarajah, *The International Law on Foreign Investment*, 3rd edn (Cambridge University Press, 2010), pp. 82–8.

THE PRECURSOR OF NEOLIBERALISM

existence of rules and principles on foreign investment protection enforced through arbitration brought an end to the gun-boat diplomacy that was the characteristic method of dispute resolution in the earlier period of investment disputes.[9] So it was argued that secure rules protecting the contracts would end the use of force by requiring settlement through legal rules applied by a neutral tribunals, an argument that was to find resonance in the notion of the 'depoliticization' of investment disputes in later times.[10] Law becomes a substitute for the use of force. Gun-boat diplomacy comes to be replaced by arbitration. Yet the rules of the new system may bring about the results desired by power through power-based laws that are sustained by the mechanism of arbitration. The rules can be presented as value neutral norms. The mechanism used to apply them, arbitration, can be presented as a neutral forum. For this reason, the neutrality of the system has to be carefully cultivated. The fact that both the formation of the rules as well their application by arbitration tribunals, or even the constitution of the tribunal, can be manipulated to serve the interests of power must be carefully hidden. The suggestion that the system that replaced gun-boat diplomacy was no less power-based in that the same results are now achieved under the cloak of legality has credibility. Dezaley and Garth have explored the manner in which the neutrality of the system of arbitration is a carefully cultivated myth.[11] Powerful states, in combination with powerful private interests within states, could create international systems that are favourable to their interests.[12] The distinction between the state and the private interests is often tenuous.[13] In these circumstances, the law

[9] Jan Paulsson, 'Third World Participation in Investment Arbitration', (1987) 2 *ICSID Review* 1. The view is that there is a rule-based system that has supplanted a power-based system. The question is always, who makes the rules? If the rules are made through power, then, the aims are realized through means that appear to be lawful, but are nevertheless power-based. The same argument is made regarding international trade.

[10] In promoting ICSID arbitration, it was argued that it would 'depoliticize' issues by removing the powerful home state from the dispute. The home state's pressures through diplomatic interference are eliminated with the foreign investor being given direct access to arbitration. Under the ICSID Convention, diplomatic protection remains suspended while the arbitration is pending.

[11] Dezaley and Garth, *Dealing in Virtue*.

[12] For the role of power in creating normative orders, see Claire Cutler, *The Emergence of Private Authority in Global Governance* (Cambridge University Press, 2003).

[13] Historically, the classic example is provided by the British East India Company, which was formed by the ruling cabal of Britain. The company achieved the conquest of India before India was brought under imperial control in 1858 after the First War of Indian Independence. Likewise, the role of the Hudson Bay Company in Canada and Rhodes in southern Africa were crucial in acquiring new territory. The power of modern

2.2 A BRIEF HISTORY 83

becomes a cloak for the exercise of power. The chances of such subversion of the law are great.[14] The course of history of the development of the international law on foreign investment indicates that this is what took place. When gun-boat diplomacy ended, force ceased to be used. But the laws that replaced such gun-boat diplomacy may equally well be founded in rules based on power. They act as a substitute for force, particularly when they are enforced through means that employ coercion, such as denial of aid, loans or access to markets. They also are enforced through seizure of assets in pursuance of the enforcement of awards, with the legal correctness of the award no longer subject to any challenge. Most arbitration rules ensure that arbitral awards can be challenged only on grounds of procedural irregularity.[15]

Ideas relating to the free movement of trade and investments were laid by the rise of Spain during the fifteenth and sixteenth centuries. Spanish expansion into the newly discovered regions of North America resulted in debates about the justice in conquering people in these regions, destroying their culture, their way of life and, more importantly, the slaughtering of large numbers of people. It is easy to forget the human costs that attended this expansion of trade and investment. The Spanish invaders destroyed the identities and cultures of a people who lived in communities that had as much claim to organizational standards of living as the European invaders. Yet Spanish jurists justified the conquest

multinational corporations is no less. They act in tandem with state power. Sometimes, they act independently to enhance their own power. For example, Steve Coll, *Private Empire: Exxon Mobil and American Power* (London: Penguin, 2013).

[14] The links between business and the state are as strong now as they were in the past. The role of the East India Company is described in an article in *The Economist* thus: 'The Company created a powerful East India lobby in Parliament, a caucus of MPs who had either directly or indirectly profited from its business and who constituted, in Edmund Burke's opinion, one of the most united and formidable forces in British politics. It also made regular gifts to the Court: "All who could help or hurt at Court", wrote Lord Macaulay, "ministers, mistresses, priests, were kept in good humour by presents of shawls and silks, birds' nests and attar of roses, diamonds and bags of guineas". The Company even sought to give an English virgin as a bribe to the Sultan of Achin', *The Economist*, 'Company that Ruled the Waves', 17 December 2011. In the United States, as in other parts of the world, business leaders often spend time in administration. US Vice President Cheney was only a recent example of a prominent leader transferring from business into politics. Both Presidents Bush had connections with oil companies.

[15] Under the New York Convention on the Enforcement of Foreign Arbitral Awards (1957), an enforcement of a foreign arbitral award can be challenged only on the basis of procedural irregularity not on grounds of error in the application of the substantive law. The position is similar in the case of the widely adopted UNCITRAL Model Law on International Commercial Arbitration.

84   THE PRECURSOR OF NEOLIBERALISM

on the basis of freedom of trade, the inferiority of indigenous culture and the brotherhood of man, sanctimonious notions that cloaked conquest through unspeakable brutalities.[16] It is clear that in every age of exploitation, altruistic reasons have been given for the plunder and pillage of other peoples. In the age of the Dutch and British colonial expansions, similar justifications were used both to promote such expansion, as well as to justify the control of lands that had been conquered. It is worth considering whether the modern justification of economic development that proceeds from trade and investment also cloaks similar inequities on the peoples of the host states. Over the years of resource exploitation, economic development cannot be proved to have occurred. Rather, it ensured the depletion of the resources and the continued poverty of the people of resource-rich lands.

The hiding of imperial dominance through altruistic arguments relating to the brotherhood of man, the freedom of trade and the raising of other peoples to European standards of civilization was the feature of international law of the colonial period.[17] The legitimacy of law is employed in such a manner as to create an aura of legality over events that were inherently unjust. The employment of the law and the giving of altruistic motives enable the explanation of the unjust events in a manner that seemed acceptable. The argument that it was the 'white man's burden' to bring other races to civilization hid the imbalances in trade and investment between the colonies and the imperial states. It could well be argued that the same situation continues to be a feature of modern international law. It is arguable that the modern international law on foreign investment continues disparities between the developed and developing states, has little ethical merit and cloaks many injustices through rules that promote foreign investments to the detriment of other interests, such as human rights or the environment.[18] In its historical context, it is not too much to claim that rules on investment law and foreign investment arbitration were devised to promote the interests of the United States and the European states, which were the traditional exporters of capital. The ideological base for the rules was provided by

---

[16] Miles, *The Origins of International Investment Law*; Gerrit Gong, *The Standard of Civilization in International Society* (Oxford University Press, 1984).

[17] The point is conceded by developed country lawyers, who would argue that the situation has now changed. The only change is that now there is the rule of law and the standard of governance replacing the old platitudes.

[18] See, e.g., Cordonier Segger *et al.* (eds.), *Sustainable Development in World Investment Law*; Vinuales, *Foreign Investment and the Environment in International Law*.

theories of economic development based on showing that benefits flowed from the formulation of rules on the protection of foreign investment. The principal benefit alleged was the greater flows of foreign investment. It was seen as beneficial in the carefully cultivated economic argument that its flow brought prosperity to the developing countries. Attendant benefits claimed were the immediate creation of new capital assets, the flow of new technology, the creation of new jobs, the upgrading of infrastructure and greater export earnings. The price that was to be paid in the depletion of natural resources, the repatriation of profits, environmental degradation and the violation of indigenous rights were concealed.

Early investment was exploitative. It was intent on finding resources to fuel industries in the metropolitan states and markets for their finished products in the colonies. The investment took place under the imperial legal system. That system ensured complete protection for such investment. The picture should have changed after decolonization. However, once the element of control that was at the heart of the imperial system had ended, it was necessary to find a substitute for it so that the imperial economic system could be continued. The contention in this chapter is that international law became an instrument through which such a system could be established by the use of private power. That is what sets contract-based arbitration apart from investment treaty arbitration. It was built up entirely through the exercise of private power, whereas state participation through the making of investment rules in treaties is basic to treaty arbitration. Investment treaties are made by states. State consent is the basis of arbitration under them. The consent is given in advance to a third party, the national of the home state of the investor, so that he could have unilateral recourse to an arbitral tribunal before which he could allege violations of the treaty standards of protection granted him by treaty. Contract-based arbitration is different in that the foreign party negotiates the protection for itself. It is entirely a function of private power. The rules created thereafter to afford protection to the foreign investment through arbitration also depend on private processes, though their effectiveness may rely for enforceability on systems that states have created.[19]

---

[19] The most important means of enforcement would be through the mechanism of the New York Convention for the Enforcement of Foreign Arbitral Awards, 1957, which imposes a reciprocal duty on the part of member states to enforce arbitral awards made in each other's states. The *Karaha Bodas Co. LLC* v. *Pertamina & Others*, 16 Int. Arb. Rep. C-2, Final Award (18 December 2000), a contract award against Indonesia, was enforced by three courts in the United States, Hong Kong and Singapore.

This chapter looks at the manner in which such a system was accomplished by arguing that international law protected foreign investment contracts by insulating them from local laws and by subjecting dispute resolution from such contracts to foreign arbitration tribunals. This central theme, which existed from the period after decolonization, found firmer theoretical expression under investment treaty arbitration. The idea became more refined and better articulated during the period of the ascendance of neoliberalism in the 1990s. There is continuity from the decolonization period through contract-based protection and then to treaty-based investment arbitration. The rationalization for the protection of foreign investment has remained the same, though it has become more refined with the passage of time. Such rationalization became most intense in the period of neoliberalism when supported by international institutions and hegemonic power.

The growth of contract-based arbitration as a prelude to investment treaty arbitration is important because the contract remains the basis of investment entry, and the extension of protection of the treaty to the contractual obligations has been an aim of expansionist interpretations of the treaty so that the treaty principles could be given wider coverage. It is difficult to understand the contextual basis of treaty-based investment arbitration without first discussing contract-based arbitration. Quite apart from the umbrella clause in the treaty that is claimed to protect the investment contract, arguments have been made as to the extent to which the stabilization clause creates legitimate expectations under fair and equitable treatment and provides an exception to regulatory takings. As a result of later developments, the two types of arbitrations have many features in common. There is a definite effort to ensure that the treaty-based arbitration protects several features of the foreign investment contract.

2.3 The relationship with diplomatic protection and state responsibility

The technique of protection of the foreign investment contract relied heavily on arbitration. The central feature of the law that was created was the manipulation of diplomatic protection and the rules of the international minimum standard that was to be applied by external arbitration tribunals. In historical terms such arbitration of investment disputes began as the period of colonialism ended, though in the context of another unequal relationship – that between the United States and

2.3 THE RELATIONSHIP WITH DIPLOMATIC PROTECTION 87

Latin America – the law had been developed along lines of American practice. Arbitrations by mixed claims commissions set up by treaties between the United States and different Latin American states provided the genesis of some of the early law that was applied.[20] The system originally operated within the rules on diplomatic protection of aliens and their property by their home states. It was a system that was based on states and was consistent with the idea that only states had personality in international law. The construction of the international minimum standard became a central feature of the system. The survival of this standard, as stated in the *Neer* Claim (1926)[21] decided by the Mexican Claims Commission, into modern times is an indication of the influence of the law that was made in this period.[22] This system provides the context within which the international law on foreign investment has been built. It still functions as the basis of the rules for investment protection. Some of its rules have been taken into modern investment treaty arbitration through their statement in the investment treaties. In fact, the major purpose of the investment treaties was to state the rules of customary law, as developed by the Western states, on which there was considerable doubt due to the challenges made by the developing states. The description of the theory that has come to be known as the theory of internationalization of foreign investment contracts is a necessary prelude to any discussion of foreign investment protection. The manner of the making of the rules of such arbitration indicates a problem of legitimacy that existed at the outset. It flawed the subject from the time of its formation. There had been no willingness on the part of international lawyers to discuss the schisms that have developed as a result of the development of such arbitration. Instead, modern international lawyers proved to be no different from the early imperial writers on international law. They favoured the creation of rules that protected foreign investors despite the fact that it supported only the interests of those with power. They supported the rules despite the theoretical flaws in them rather than

---

[20] Jackson Ralston, *The Law and Procedure of International Tribunals* (Stanford University Press, 1926).

[21] *L. F. H. Neer* v. *United Mexican States* (1926) 4 RIAA 60 (US–Mexico General Claims Commission).

[22] The *Neer* standard did not permit intervention by an international tribunal unless there was a denial of justice as would shock the conscience of a bystander. In modern times, the standard has been considered to be too high and that it should evolve into a lower standard (*Mondev*, para. 116). But this view is not uniformly accepted. In the Draft Code of the South African Development Commission, the *Neer* standard is codified almost in the exact terms as it was stated.

adopting an objective, justice-based attitude towards the creation of such rules. They emphasized investment protection to the detriment of other areas of international law, such as human rights and environmental protection. They downplayed the role of the state in protecting the public interests that were involved in these areas, concentrating entirely on the sanctity of the foreign investment contract and its terms. The 'international law' that was developed on investment contracts privileged considerations of investment protection over all other interests, including those relating to control of resources by the state, payment of fair price for the resources, and environmental and human rights standards. The developing states sought to counterbalance the efforts of the former colonies to recover control over their economies through an alternative structure of law associated with the NIEO, but there was resistance to the acceptance of the NIEO and its norms. Such resistance also has significance for the resistance of the powerful and will ensure that competing norms do not surface, even if stated. The creation of a law on internationalization was intended to stem the creation of an NIEO.

This chapter deals with the emergence of norms advanced by developing states. State entities took over the running of the natural resource industries from foreign multinational corporations, particularly in the oil industry. The emergence of a tussle in this area of law is evident from the arguments that resulted as to the legitimacy of the new rival theory that denied competence to external systems and tribunals in settling investment disputes. The response to this change is assessed in section 2.4, and the efforts to keep alive the theory of internationalization despite the changes effected both in the domestic laws of host states as well as in international law is then examined. Emphasis is placed on the vitality of the policy reasons given by the older writers and the tenacity of their survival. It is a conflict that goes on in the law, possibly without a solution. The conflict was infused into treaty-based investment arbitration when it became more common in the mid-1990s. In understanding the conflicts that arose under treaty-based arbitration, it is important to keep in mind the conflicting views that had already emerged in the law earlier. The ideological underpinnings of the conflicting viewpoints must be understood. In that sense, contract-based arbitration is not only an alternative, but is a prelude to investment treaty arbitration. It will interact with treaty-based arbitration, and treaty-based arbitration will be extended, if possible, to conserve the foreign investment contract. Most of the justifications for expansionary rules in investment treaty arbitration had been thought up during the period of emergence of contract-based arbitration.

2.3.1 Diplomatic protection and state responsibility

The primary method of investment protection that has been developed within international law involved diplomatic intervention by the home state to protect the alien who suffers injury at the hands of the host state. The intervention was justified on the basis of the link of nationality between the alien and his home state.[23] The theory on which the law operated was that an injury to the alien was an injury to his home state. This concept of mediate injury was necessitated by the fact that the alien did not have personality in international law.[24] The injury arose when the host state violated an international minimum standard of protection that it owed to the alien. The content of this standard has never been precisely worked out, despite being in existence for over a century.[25] It stands in contrast to the fair and equitable standard, which was given definite content after its resuscitation in a few years. Since the international minimum standard was external, the violation of the standard had to be pronounced upon by an external tribunal, usually an arbitration tribunal. The norms had been worked out in American practice largely in connection with the protection of its nationals in Latin American states. The Latin American states had always contested the law as stated by the United States and by American writers on the basis of US practice.[26] The Latin American states insisted that an alien was always subject to their local laws, had to be given only national treatment, and that disputes relating to their treatment were subject only to their national courts. In the context of this controversy, it is unlikely that any customary international law could have arisen. When it is stated that the international minimum standard constitutes customary international law, it is a mere statement of the preferences of the Western international lawyers based on American practice. The controversy continued as the Asian and African states espoused the stance of the Latin American states after decolonization. In that context, it is futile to talk in terms of the existence of any universal customary international law concerning the rule.

---

[23] The link of nationality remained important under treaties though the devise of corporate nationality came to be abused in seeking jurisdiction for arbitration tribunals.

[24] Chitharanjan Amerasinghe, *State Responsibility for Injuries to Aliens* (Oxford University Press, 1964).

[25] Some would stay that it has still not been worked out. Matthew Porterfield, 'An International Common Law of Investor Rights?' (2006) 27 *University of Pennsylvania Journal of International Economic Law* 79.

[26] Further see Santiago Montt, *State Liability in Investment Treaty Arbitration* (Oxford: Hart, 2009).

90 THE PRECURSOR OF NEOLIBERALISM

Responsibility could arise in international law only as between states, an important rule that was overcome when investor–state arbitration became possible under treaties. The seriousness involved in the acceptance of such arbitration must be kept in mind, for it pushes aside accepted theories of international law. It is not that treaties cannot do this, but the extent of the change must be scrutinized with care when it occurs as it involves a derogation of sovereignty over a purely internal matter. This is particularly so when states objected to the creation of even basic rules on state responsibility for injuries to aliens. The customary law on the subject does not rest on firm foundations. The International Law Commission (ILC) was unable to codify the primary rules on state responsibility. The secondary rules it assembled in a draft code are also contested.

Conflicts result in accommodation. To the extent there was an accommodation, the law came to recognize that the remedies provided by the host state must be exhausted before recourse could be had to remedies in international law recognizing state responsibility, except where the remedies provided by the local tribunals are illusory due to the courts being controlled by a dictator or by the executive of the state.[27] The *Neer* Claim[28] stated that the denial of justice must be egregious in order to give rise to state responsibility. The formula it used in the test was as follows:

> the treatment of an alien, in order to constitute an international delinquency, should amount to an outrage, to bad faith, to wilful neglect of duty, or to an insufficiency of governmental action so far short of international standards that every reasonable and impartial man would readily recognize its insufficiency.

The ICJ used similar words in stating the extent of the denial of justice that gives rise to state responsibility. The Court stated, in defining arbitrariness, that:[29]

> It is a wilful disregard of due process of law, an act which shocks, or at lease surprises, a sense of judicial propriety.

Later, a view was stated that there is a difference between the formulations and that the ICJ's formulation is more lax, permitting a lesser test of the standard of justice on the ground that decades of evolution has resulted in changes to the standard that is required.[30] This view has not

---

[27] Chitharanjan Amerasinghe, *The Local Remedies in International Law*, 2nd edn (Cambridge University Press, 2004).
[28] (1926) 4 RIAA 60.   [29] [1989] ICJ Rep. 15.
[30] *Mondev International* v. *United States*, ICSID, Case No. ARB(AF)/99/2 (11 October 2002). *Glamis Gold Ltd* v. *United States*, UNCITRAL Arbitration, Award (NAFTA) (8

2.3 THE RELATIONSHIP WITH DIPLOMATIC PROTECTION 91

received uniform acceptance. But it is clear that the lessening of the bar to find a denial of justice is also a sign of the pro-investor climate of a given period.

In the *ELSI* Case,[31] the ICJ held that the rule relating to the exhaustion of local remedies must be read into a treaty that is silent on the point. This rule, of course, meant that domestic tribunals of the host court should have the opportunity to speak on the issue before an international tribunal does, for it is only upon the denial of justice by the local courts that an allegation of responsibility can be invoked before an international tribunal. It is only in circumstances where the remedy provided by the local courts is so inadequate as to shock the conscience of any third-party onlooker that responsibility of the state could arise.

The rule is one relating to the practice of states. A rule that is based on a primary source, such as custom, cannot be easily changed by a subsidiary source, such as an arbitral decision. It is obvious that arbitrators, whose competence in matters of international law is of varied quality, certainly cannot make such changes to customary principles. It was understood in international law that state responsibility should not be lightly imposed.[32] The argument in some recent awards that consistent practice among arbitral tribunals can create customary law is one that is made without an adequate understanding of international law. It arrogates a power to a group of individuals which the ICJ itself has not claimed. It is an elementary proposition that awards of tribunals are but 'subsidiary sources' of international law.

The procedural limitation was that local remedies should be satisfied, and that the outcome of the local court's decision should indicate a denial of justice resulting from an egregious misapplication of the law. The substantive rule was that state responsibility required the violation of an international minimum standard best shown by a denial of justice. This implied the need for a decision by a local court. It is the court's denial of justice that gives a claim to the foreign investor. The law was largely formulated in the context of expropriations, which provided the

---

June 2009) accepted the US argument that there must be 'concordant practice' of states to effect change. The tribunal noted, regarding views that standards have changed since 1926, that 'arbitral awards do not constitute State practice and thus cannot create or prove customary international law'.

[31] [1989] ICJ Rep. 15.

[32] It is another reason why the new awards in investment treaty arbitration seek to place emphasis on the more laxly stated fair and equitable standard of treatment. The United States and other states sought to curb this trend by tying the fair and equitable standard to the international minimum standard, but this has not met with uniform success.

most usual context for the development of the law. The US practice had devised firm, but still contested, rules. The law on expropriation had come to be defined with some certainty, though there was no agreement as to the standard of compensation. In this practice, due process was a requirement for expropriation. Absence of due process made the expropriation unlawful. Due process would result in a judicial resolution of the dispute. It is only if the judicial remedy provided was not in accordance with the international minimum standard that liability arose in the state. This again was a confirmation of the rule that required satisfaction of local remedies. From the American point of view, there should be full compensation made. This was the standard that existed in American constitutional law, which demanded high standards of property protection. The Latin Americans consistently rejected this view until their acceptance of bilateral investment treaties in the 1990s. Even then, at the multilateral level, there was no consensus as to any legal rule. Likewise, African and Asian states espoused the view of the Latin American states as representing the general international law. The making of bilateral investment treaties was a way of resolving this impasse. Despite the making of the bilateral treaties, there is no evidence that these states were prepared to change their views at the multilateral level. It may be because they sought to adhere to their original views as to the international minimum standard that they preferred to deal with the situation through bilateral treaties so that the obligation created is as between the two states making such treaties.

It would be an error to state that there ever was certain and clear customary international law relating to state responsibility. The law on the protection of investments made by aliens constituted the bulk of the precedents on state responsibility. When the ILC came to draft a code on the law, the schisms that emerged frustrated the efforts of the early rapporteurs. Eventually, the secondary rules on state responsibility came to be codified. This may have been a ruse attempted in order to facilitate the later emergence of a statement of the primary rules through arbitral awards and commentaries. The assumption was that once the secondary rules were stated, their use by tribunals would lead to statements of the primary rules, which could be identified through the use of the secondary rules. The strategy worked to some extent, as an increasing number of arbitral awards used the draft articles on state responsibility and went on to make statements on the substantive law. However, they also exposed the limitations of the statement of the law in

2.3 THE RELATIONSHIP WITH DIPLOMATIC PROTECTION 93

the draft articles.[33] Despite the draft articles of the ILC, the area of state responsibility, particularly that area in connection with state responsibility arising from injuries to aliens, still remains controversial.[34]

The discussions as to the law disclosed an important area of dissent. This related to the view taken by some writers who urged that the breach of a foreign investment contract would, *per se*, create state responsibility. The recognition of such a situation would have resulted in a major victory for foreign investment protection. But there was reluctance to move in the direction of recognizing such a rule, as this would elevate the foreign investment contract from an instrument located within municipal law to an instrument governed by international law immediately upon its breach. This issue remains unresolved. The controversy was deepened under the law on treaty protection when several inconsistent awards in investment treaty arbitration resulted on the precise status of a breach of a foreign investment contract. The umbrella clause contained in some investment treaties protected all commitments that the host state had made to the foreign investor. It was a neatly tucked-away clause in investment treaties that was suddenly discovered. In a sense, the umbrella clause was a confirmation of the view that a breach of an investment contract was a violation of the law *per se*. That provision had been used to argue that contractual commitments were covered by the umbrella clauses. Initially, some tribunals accepted this view, but more recent tribunals have moved away from it as they seek a rigorous distinction between treaty violations, which alone are subject to investment treaty arbitration, and the disputes arising from the violation of the investment contract, which must be subjected to arbitration devised by the provisions in the contract. The general tendency has been to steer clear of the broad view taken in *SGS* v. *Philippines* that the umbrella clause elevated foreign investment contracts into the realm of treaty protection. Recent awards accepting the relevance of umbrella clauses to the protection of contracts have kept the controversy alive. But the use of the umbrella clause in order to protect contracts must be seen as a part of the expansionist tendencies that characterized the sway of neoliberalism in the period of its ascendance in international investment law.

As can be seen from this brief account, the area of responsibility for interference with the property of an alien has always been a subject of

---

[33] As the Argentinian awards demonstrated, the statement of the defence of necessity was too rigid to be accepted. See below, Chapter 7.

[34] For a recent exposition of the law, see James Crawford, *State Responsibility* (Cambridge University Press, 2013).

94 THE PRECURSOR OF NEOLIBERALISM

dissension. It is a consistent error that is made in the major textbooks to present the law as if the European–American position constitutes uncontested international law. It was never so. It was due to the inability to devise clear norms on foreign investment protection that efforts had to be made by those who supported foreign investors to advance other techniques to deal with the problem. There were two such techniques. The first was the effort at the internationalization of the foreign investment contract. This is dealt with in the present chapter. The second is the protection of investment through bilateral and regional investment treaties, which forms the major subject of the book. As indicated, the consideration of the law on contract-based protection is to serve as a prelude to the broader consideration of the expansionist techniques in treaty-based arbitration, the resistance to it and the changes that have been generated as a result of such resistance.

2.4   The internationalization theory

Contracts of foreign investment are the medium through which investment entry takes place. It is logical to assume that the foreign investor who enters a state is subject to its laws, and that the contract he makes, especially with the state or its entity, is made in accordance with the law of that state. The law of procedure that applies to the making of the contract has to be the law of the host state, for there can be no other law that is relevant in prescribing the manner in which such a contract is to be made. It is equally logical that the substantive law that applies to the contract is also the law of that state. The contract is made and is to be performed on the territory of the state. Every theory of conflict of laws points to the application of the host state's laws to the performance of the contract. International law has no role to play in the process of the making of the contract and its subsequent performance, both of which are subject to domestic law. There is no relevant international law on either area. The only relevant rule of international law at the stage of entry is that every state has the right to keep any alien out of its territory and to control his entry as well as his subsequent state within its territory.[35] If a state decides to permit a foreign investor entry, it may subject the investor to any condition it desires, subject to contrary

---

[35] Except in the situation where there is a right of establishment provided for by treaty. The practice of the United States, which is followed by Canada, Japan and South Korea, is to require such a right of establishment or the right of pre-entry national treatment.

2.4 THE INTERNATIONALIZATION THEORY 95

treaty obligations. International law has a law on treaties, but no law on contracts made between a private entity and a state. Besides, the orthodoxy was that multinational corporations, which conclude the contracts, did not have personality to be subject to international law. In pure theory, the application of international law to the foreign investment contract was remote.

This was the position taken in early authoritative pronouncements. In the *Serbian Loans* Case (1921), the Permanent Court of International Justice stated that 'a contract between a state and a private person is subject to municipal law' of a state. The Mexican Claims Commission applied the law of Mexico to the claims before it.[36] A study of the League of Nations on loan contracts with states concluded that the law that applied had to be the law of the state party to the contract, despite the fact that, as a receiver of the loan, it hardly had any bargaining power.[37] There was overwhelming evidence that international law had no bearing on foreign investment contracts.

The genesis of a possible contrary view can be seen in the *Lena Goldfields* Arbitration.[38] The case arose from the nationalization of a gold mine after the Russian Revolution. The arbitration tribunal sat in London and held that compensation was due. The Russian arbitrator withdrew from the case. It was left to the remaining arbitrators, 'a famed German professor of metallurgy' and an English lawyer 'of such distinction that he sits upon His Majesty's Privy Council', to announce 'this awful decision'.[39] The idea that there was a breach of contract that should be compensated was set out in the award. The award was not later relied on in any significant way in the leading cases that constructed the theory of internationalization. The *Lena Goldfields* Award against Russia, which Russia simply ignored, did not have much effect on the later development of the law, though it has been hunted up and used in more recent times to support the theory of internationalization. The Award did not speak about international law. It is a fact that an arbitration tribunal provided relief for a breach of contract by the Russian state. Russia did not pay. Yet

---

[36] A. H. Feller, *The Mexican Claims Commission: 1923–1934* (New York: Macmillan, 1935), p. 178.

[37] League of Nations, *Report of the Committee of the League of Nationals Studying Loan Contracts*, Doc. C.145.M 93 1939 II.A, League of Nations Publications, Economic & Financial (Geneva: League of Nations, 1939), p. 21.

[38] There are no official records of the award. An excellent restating of the facts and the award are to be found in V. Veeder, 'The Lena Goldfields Arbitration: The Historical Roots of Three Ideas' (1998) 47 *International & Comparative Law Quarterly* 747.

[39] *The Times*, 15 September 1930, as cited in Maurer, *The Empire Trap*, at p. 522.

96   THE PRECURSOR OF NEOLIBERALISM

it would be inexact to elevate the *Lena Goldfields* Arbitration as being the forerunner of the internationalization theory. It was an aberration that was seized upon later to make exorbitant claims.[40]

The turning point came with awards in three Middle Eastern arbitrations, made in the 1950s and involving concession agreements in the petroleum sector.[41] The three awards recognized that the law that would apply to petroleum-related contracts would normally be the law of the host state, but argued that since the Islamic law of the states was not mature enough to be applied to sophisticated petroleum contracts, they would have to use general principles of law to deal with disputes that arose in such states. It is unlikely that the contract laws of the European states were any more sophisticated. One learned English contract law well after the 1960s from cases that dealt with the hiring of deck chairs at seaside resorts or the selling of carbolic smoke balls, not from petroleum contracts. Islamic scholars have spent much effort demonstrating that the absence of Islamic law principles was just a fallacy to cloak the application of a non-host state law by the arbitrators and that Islamic law, like the law of Western states, had no specific rules on petroleum contracts. But, as in the case of Western laws, its principles were capable of being applied to petroleum contracts through analogical reasoning.[42] What the arbitrators were intent on doing in their assertion of the superiority of European laws was to provide a cover for the creation of a new scheme to keep the petroleum resources of the Middle Eastern states tied up through contracts with European and American multinational companies that operated in the oil sector. The petroleum awards and academic commentaries on them facilitated the idea of the existence of an external system that could be created to apply to foreign investment contracts, particularly petroleum contracts. It was a subtle way of ensuring that national control over petroleum resources was countermanded by contractual principles that could be enforced through foreign arbitration.

The rationalization was made that the arbitrators had found contractual sanctity as the basic norm that applied to foreign investment

---

[40] Maurer, *The Empire Trap*, p. 390.

[41] *Abu Dhabi* Arbitration (1951) 18 ILR 144; *Qatar* Arbitration (1953) 20 ILR 534; *Aramco v. Saudi Arabia* (1963) 27 ILR 117.

[42] A. el Chiati, 'Protection of Foreign Investment in the Context of Petroleum Agreements', (1987) 204 *Hague Recueil des Cours* 1. In *Abu Dhabi*, Lord Asquith regarded Abu Dhabi as 'a primitive region'. It does not appear to be so any more. In any event, the reasoning based on the absence of rules in the domestic systems has no relevance in modern times when all states have sophisticated foreign investment laws. But, despite this, the internationalization theory has not become defunct.

2.4 THE INTERNATIONALIZATION THEORY 97

contracts. This basic norm was identified as a general principle of law. Such a general principle, being a source of international law within the terms of Article 38(1) of the Statute of the ICJ, was elevated to the only rule of international law that applied to foreign investment contracts.[43] The linking of *pacta sunt servanda*, thought of as the basic norm of international law, with contractual sanctity was another technique that was resorted to.[44]

Such reasoning was unsound for a variety of reasons. The awards themselves do not show that a meaningful exercise had been performed to isolate contractual sanctity as a general principle of law applicable uniformly to all foreign investment contracts. Contractual sanctity was more in line with the *laissez faire* system that existed in earlier times. The interventionist welfare state was more concerned with constructing a just system that accorded with the interests of the weaker sections of the community with less bargaining power. Modern contract law systems have moved away from the notion of sanctity of contracts. In fact, some would argue that progress in the law of contracts is achieved only when it moves away from notions of the sanctity of contracts and begins to inquire into circumstances of inequality between parties and the effect of unfair terms being introduced into the contract through overweening bargaining power.[45] That process had started in the law well before the 1950s. Besides, even if sanctity of contracts was an inflexible rule, there is nothing to suggest that it applied to a contract made by a state within its own territory. Constitutional theory would not permit a state to divest itself of the power to perform the public functions of the state by the making of a contract with a foreign private party.[46] There is no inquiry

---

[43] The link was provided by the concession agreement between Iran and the Anglo-Persian Oil Company, which required disputes to be decided 'on juridical principles contained in Article 38 of the Statute of the Permanent Court of International Justice'. Francis Mann, 'The Proper Law of Contracts Concluded by International Persons', (1959) 35 *British Yearbook of International Law* 34, at p. 51. The *Sapphire* Arbitration (1963) 35 ILR 136, made no reference to domestic law. It accepted that the law applicable was the general principles of law.

[44] Alfred Verdross, 'Quasi-international Agreements and International Economic Transactions', (1964) 18 *Yearbook of World Affairs* 230. A later attempt was made to work out the same result through arguments relating to the *lex mercatoria*. Voss, *The Impact of Investment Treaties on Contracts between Host States and Foreign Investors*, p. 31.

[45] Patrick Atiyah, *The Rise and Fall of the Freedom of Contract* (Oxford University Press, 1986).

[46] In the age of privatization of state functions, it is argued that a state may transfer public functions it had performed in the past. The dismantling of the welfare state through privatization is based on such power. But the extent to which the state can transfer certain

98 THE PRECURSOR OF NEOLIBERALISM

made as to whether national systems permit the sovereign state to relinquish regulatory control over such contracts. The idea that the sovereign regulatory powers of a state can be restricted by contract, a private law instrument, would sit uneasily with the public law theory of many state systems. It would be contrary to the general principles of law. It is a well-accepted principle that mandatory principles of domestic public law cannot be defeated by the exercise of private party autonomy involved in the making of a contract.[47] It is likely to be a general principle that states could interfere in contracts that turn out to be against their public interest. It has never been explained how this constitutional power of a state can be displaced by contractual techniques. The foreign investment contract can be founded only on the basis of a domestic legal system and exists only to the extent permitted by that legal system. The reasoning in the petroleum awards of the 1950s is defective for a variety of reasons, but they are regarded as the basis of new law in the area. This is simply because it suited the interests of the dominant players on the political scene.

The theoretical objections were not permitted to stand in the way of achieving the objective of investment protection. Later one finds in treaty-based arbitration that there are similar problems with the gradua-tion of the notion of legitimate expectations or of the proportionality rule. But these are minor irritants that can be swept away through the overwhelming weight of the opinions of 'highly qualified publicists'. A select group of arbitrators agreeing on a rule is seen as elevating that rule into law. It is easy to see this happening in the later course of the internationalization theory.

There were six awards that played an important role in the creation of the theory of internationalization of foreign investment contracts.[48] The first three awards were made in the 1950s. They involved the three Middle Eastern oil-producing states discussed above. The second set consisted of three Libyan awards that were made in the early 1970s. The two sets of cases form the basis of the theory of internationalization

---

public law functions, such as the right to punish or the power to interfere to protect the public, is still contentious. The better view is that there is a certain reserve of powers which cannot be privatized.

[47] Peter Nygh, *Autonomy in International Contracts* (Oxford University Press, 1999).

[48] There were other awards that supported the theory of internationalization made during the period. *Sapphire International Petroleum Ltd* v. *National Iranian Oil Co.* (1963) 35 ILR 136.

2.4 THE INTERNATIONALIZATION THEORY

Both sets of awards concerned arbitrations in the petroleum industry arising from concession agreements.[49] Concession agreements involved the virtual surrender of sovereignty over vast tracts of land in the state for a long period of time so that the foreign oil company could explore for oil and exploit it, if found, for a payment of royalty to the ruler. There were no democratic governments in the region.[50] In many of these Middle Eastern kingdoms, the British had imposed a system of extraterritoriality.[51] The effect of this was that the principle insulated the British traders from the jurisdiction of the local courts and subjected them to the jurisdiction of British courts, sitting within the kingdoms and applying British law. Such an insulation of trading and traders from the local courts is an interesting notion. It was based on the existence of power and the use of naked force. The system of extraterritoriality could be maintained in China after the Opium War and in the Middle East only because of the extent of British and American power. But such power was declining. A similar system had to be created that had a semblance of legal credibility. One function of international law was to devise systems that gave a semblance of legitimacy for arrangements that are made by the powerful. After extraterritoriality, the theory of internationalization provided a rationale for the continued maintenance of control over resources through contractual means, supported by arbitration to provide a compliance mechanism. They provided insulation for the foreign investment contract in much the same way as extraterritoriality did in that it enabled disputes to be settled by external tribunals applying external laws.

Extraterritoriality was achieved through treaties.[52] But internationalization of foreign investment contracts was achieved through private power seeking to create norms through the use of low-order sources of law, such as general principles of law or the writings of 'highly qualified

---

[49] The first three awards were the *Abu Dhabi* Arbitration (1951) 18 ILR 144; *Qatar* Arbitration (1953) 20 ILR 534; *Aramco* v. *Saudi Arabia* (1963) 27 ILR 117 (which concerned a concession to transport oil from Saudi Arabia).

[50] The kingdoms, often small, were ruled by sheikhs. The influence of Britain in the area was great, some of the kingdoms being British protectorates.

[51] Extraterritoriality was a system that insulated European traders from the laws of certain host countries that were not colonized. It was maintained by power and was an institution that was a symbol of control. It continues to be reviled in the areas which were subjected to it. The main areas were China, Thailand and some Middle Eastern states.

[52] The Chinese notion of unequal treaties, rejecting treaties obtained through asymmetries in power, was formulated largely in the context of treaties that imposed extraterritoriality after the Opium Wars, such as the Treaty of Nanjing (1848).

100 THE PRECURSOR OF NEOLIBERALISM

publicists'.[53] It was possible for private power to manipulate these low-order sources to create international law. It demonstrates that international law was not always created by states or by international institutions to which they had delegated power. It was possible, to reiterate again, for multinational corporations, long-time wielders of power,[54] to create international law through the use of low-order sources, as the creation of the theory of internationalization demonstrates.

It is a subtlety to say that international law was made by states when the fact is that the early purveyors of colonialism were not states, but large corporations such as the British and Dutch East India companies. Colonialism, as maintained by large corporations, existed for over a century until imperial administrations were established. It would be difficult to deny that these corporations were not actors in international law. But such a denial became commonplace, and is maintained to this day despite the extent of the power that multinational corporations wield in international affairs. The denial of the personality in terms of multinational corporations cloaks the exercise of private power by these institutions. They are able to argue the case for theories like internationalization when it suits them, but deny any accountability for any effects of their conduct on the basis that they do not have personality in terms of the law. They seek rights to assert obligations in international law towards them, but they deny there are obligations binding on them. Having power without responsibility is indeed a privileged position to be in. Systems of investment protection that have been devised enable the foreign investor to sue without providing for counterclaims against the foreign investor or the possibility of direct actions, a position still retained in investment treaty arbitration.

---

[53] It is difficult to know whether these 'highly qualified publicists' were carrying on a long tradition, initiated by Grotius, of working to further the interests of multinational corporations in the expectation of monetary rewards. Grotius wrote his tract on Prize to justify the claims of his employer, the Dutch East India Company, to the cargo in the *Santa Katarina* which sank in action in the Straits of Malacca. Grotius, much praised as the founder of international law, could as well have been a mercenary charlatan. Peter Borschberg, *Hugo Grotius, the Portuguese and Free Trade in the East Indies* (Singapore: NUS Press, 2011). The role that 'highly qualified publicists' have played from early times is suspect.

[54] Rothkopf, *Power Inc.*, is an interesting study of the role of private power in historical and modern times. It has a striking quote from 'Lord' Clive: 'When I think, of the marvellous riches of that country (India) and the comparatively small part of which I took away, I am astonished at my own moderation' (p. 117).

2.4 THE INTERNATIONALIZATION THEORY 101

The idea that international law was made only by states was a subterfuge that camouflaged the fact that power was exercised by private individuals and corporations in global affairs and that such power created norms of international law. The course of the structuring of the internationalization theory is a demonstration of the extent to which private power could be used to construct mechanisms of protection of private assets through norms of international law.

International lawyers have shied away from understanding the role of private power in the making of international law. Recognition of the role of private power is destructive of the carefully built assumptions relating to the creation of international law by states through custom, treaties and the lesser sources of law, such as general principles,[55] writings of publicists and awards of tribunals. The extent to which the lesser sources can be manipulated by private power, wielded by multinational corporations or even single individuals exercising inordinate power,[56] to secure ends, with the willing participation of home states in which public power resides, is seldom accepted. In many situations, private power influences states to act so as to bring about principles of international law, which promote the interests of such power.[57] In other situations, as in the case of the internationalization of foreign investment contracts, private power directly creates favourable regimes of legal principles that are to its advantage. The instrumentality of the law becomes a powerful device for justification of a system, which hinders the exercise of host state power in the public interest. That such a system could be constructed through contracts involving the exercise of private power is in itself a revelation of how such private power can directly construct international law favourable to its interests. International law texts, unfortunately, continue to state the

---

[55] Soviet jurists did not regard general principles of law as sources because they lacked the consent of states. They can also be manipulated easily. The general principles, to this day, are sought from selected legal systems, as the creation of rules relating to legitimate expectations or the proportionality rule demonstrate.

[56] The ultimate control of multinational corporations is often with single individuals. Rhodes was an early example, but in the modern world examples are too numerous to be listed. The extent of control of the media, the stock markets and politics by these single individuals is enormous.

[57] A widely studied instance would be the use of private power to bring about rules on intellectual property that apply globally as a result of the efforts of the United States to bring about secure rules through the Trade Related Intellectual Property Measures attached to the WTO. The lobbying of the American government by the pharmaceutical and entertainment industries to secure this instrument was extensive.

102 THE PRECURSOR OF NEOLIBERALISM

fallacy that international law is made, principally, by states through custom and treaties, with a subsidiary role for other sources, which are generally held to be impartial sources.

The attempt to change the rule that foreign investment contracts are usually subject to the laws of the host state and subject them to international law through arbitral awards provides clear evidence of the formation of rules through the exercise of private power.[58] Of the first two sets of arbitration that attempted the change, the first group acknowledged the existence of the rule that the law of the host state governed foreign investment contracts. Yet they also bypassed the need to apply the local laws on the untested assumption that no principles could be found in them to settle disputes arising from sophisticated contracts. The six awards, which are crucial to the theory of internationalization, merit further analysis.

2.4.1   The six petroleum arbitrations

A deeper examination of the awards indicates the technique of construction of the doctrine of internationalization. The first three arbitrations relating to the oil industry took place in the 1950s.[59] The *Abu Dhabi* Arbitration (1951),[60] the *Qatar* Arbitration (1953),[61] and the *Aramco* Arbitration (1958)[62] laid the foundations for the theory of internationalization. In all three arbitrations, it was accepted that the law applicable to the disputes arising from a foreign investment contract between the state – in this case, the sheikh or absolute ruler of the state – and the foreign oil company was the law of the host state.[63] They are primarily affirmations of the existing rule that international law had no relevance to foreign investment contracts.

In all these arbitrations, which were decided by sole arbitrators, the arbitrators accepted the rule that the law of the host state should be applied when resolving a dispute arising from the foreign investment contract. In the *Abu Dhabi* Arbitration, Lord Asquith said:

---

[58] Some theorists, having regard to the fact that international law applied only to states, regarded the system that applied to foreign investment contracts as transnational law. Phillip Jessup, *Transnational Law* (New York: Columbia University Press, 1948).

[59] The *Aramco* Arbitration concerned a concession for the transport of oil.

[60] (1951) 18 ILR 534 (Lord Asquith of Bishopstone).

[61] (1953) 20 ILR 534 (Sir Alfred Bucknill).

[62] (1958) 27 ILR 117 (Professor Sauser-Hall).

[63] In the first two arbitrations, a concession agreement, which transferred absolute control over tracts of land in exchange for payment of royalty per barrel of oil if oil was found was involved. The third concerned a concession to transfer oil through tankers.

2.4 THE INTERNATIONALIZATION THEORY 103

This is a contract made in Abu Dhabi and wholly to be performed in that country. If any municipal system were applicable, it would, prima facie, be that of Abu Dhabi.

Professor Sauser-Hall, the arbitrator in the *Aramco* Arbitration stated:

> The law in force in Saudi Arabia should be applied to the content of the concession because this state is a party to the agreement, as grantor, and because it is generally admitted, in private international law, that a sovereign state is presumed, unless the contrary is proved, to have subjected its undertakings to its own legal system. This principle was mentioned by the Permanent Court of Justice in its judgment in the *Serbian Loans Case*.

Despite the unanimity in the awards that the law applicable should be the law of the host state, the three arbitrators concluded that the law of the three Middle Eastern states – Islamic law – was not sophisticated enough to deal with complex issues of petroleum contracts. Hence, they applied what they termed general principles of law, culled from the Western systems, which they said emphasized contractual sanctity. There is no indication as to how the exercise was performed. The conclusions may have been coloured by a tinge of racial superiority or by inclinations towards definite results. The assumption was that Islamic law could not possibly provide for sophisticated contracts like petroleum contracts.

The three arbitrations were premised on the absence of any host state law to deal with the issues raised. It is clear that if there was such law, it had to be applied to the exclusion of any other law. In any case, all three awards expressly acknowledged that the law of the host state should normally be applied, and one of them cited the *Serbian Loans* Case as authority. International law clearly required that domestic law be applied to state contracts. Three single arbitrators could not have changed the existing international law. Lord McNair, commenting on these arbitrations, pointed out in a seminal article written in 1958 that the awards were formulating a rule to be applied in the event of *lacunae* in the host state's law.[64] McNair supported the use of general principles in the three awards, but was careful to note that the technique of using general principles is confined to the 'situation where the legal system of the country in which for the most part the contract is to be performed is not sufficiently modernized for the purpose of regulating this type of contract'.[65] Modernity comes into the picture. The reasoning

---

[64] Lord McNair, 'General Principles of Law Recognized by Civilised Nations', (1958) 33 *British Yearbook of International Law* 1.

[65] McNair, 'General Principles of Law Recognized by Civilised Nations', at p. 19.

104   THE PRECURSOR OF NEOLIBERALISM

characterizes those opposite as primitive, whose laws need to be supplanted with modern notions. It is reminiscent of the exclusion of the large majority of human beings on the basis of a false standard of civilization in an earlier period of international law. But Lord McNair was emphatic that the 'legal system appropriate to the contract under consideration is not public international law'.[66] Yet the arbitrations were to become the launch-pad for the theory of internationalization. They were later taken to mean that general principles of law, a source of international law, was to be applied to foreign investment contracts and that, as a result, the foreign investment contract was transferred from the control of the host state's law and subjected to the regime of international law. There is no textual base for such a reading in the awards themselves or in the manner in which contemporary commentators, like McNair, understood the awards.

It has to be observed that this transference from the domestic sphere into the international sphere is the essence of the process of internationalization. It lies at the root of all the strategies of investment protection that have been attempted. The theory of internationalization involved the subjection of a foreign investment contract, which could not have had an objective existence except under the host state's law, to a supranational system administered through arbitration. Later, with investment treaty arbitration, a formalized set of external standards, created by treaties and administered by arbitrators, displaced the host state's laws and its courts.

In arriving at the internationalization theory, the limitations contained in the three awards that the host state law would normally apply suffered an ellipsis with the application of general principles coming to be emphasized. Writers latched onto the use of general principles to argue that foreign investment contracts made in developing countries were subject to general principles of law, and that as general principles of law were sources of public international law these contracts were subject to international law. The foreign investment contracts were re-designated as economic development agreements so as to capture the idea that they were made in developing countries in need of investments and lacking in secure laws protecting such investments.[67] Their usefulness to the

---

[66] McNair, 'General Principles of Law Recognized by Civilised Nations', at p. 6.
[67] C. Curtis, 'The Legal Security of Economic Development Agreements', (1988) 29 *Harvard International Law Journal* 317; Rudolf Geiger, 'The Unilateral Change of Economic Development Agreements', (1974) 23 *International & Comparative Law Quarterly* 73 (Geiger suggested that sanctity of contracts 'seems to be nothing less than a subtle form of colonialism'); Pierre Lalive, 'Contracts between a State or a State Agency and a Foreign Company', (1964) 13 *International & Comparative Law Quarterly* 987.

2.4 THE INTERNATIONALIZATION THEORY 105

developing countries in promoting economic development was stressed, again an argument that was resorted to in of support of investment treaty arbitration.

Internationalization was not supportable by any dicta in the three awards, but the conversion was quickly made as it suited the interests of large foreign investors, particularly the petroleum corporations. The process presaged the arguments that were to be made in investment treaty arbitration in later times. The eminence of the arbitrators was emphasized.[68] The policy of the law was indicated as the protection of investment, and a result conducive to foreign investment protection was achieved. It is interesting to view the history of the transformation as it shows the manner in which bases of private power were mobilized. The coinciding interests of academic leaders of international law, ruling elites and those wielding commercial power used the three awards to argue for a system of foreign investment protection. The construction of fresh authority in law, the ability of those wielding private power to employ those with esoteric knowledge of international law, the willingness of academics to be so employed, and the support of the developed states to facilitate the process enabled the building of the theory of internationalization. These were techniques later employed in treaty-based arbitration. There was a willing chain of agents working towards the elevation of certain notions that served the interests of particular groups into international law. Equally, the formation of the law was facilitated by the lack of legal knowledge in developing countries and the inability to resist the commercially strong companies. By 1965, the relevance of public international law as law applicable to foreign investment contracts came to be established when the ICSID Convention stated it as the default law in Article 42(1).[69]

The theory of internationalization is defective when looked at in the context of private international law. The primary rule recognized by this system is that parties are free to choose the legal system that should apply to the contract. But they cannot displace mandatorily applicable law through the choice of law device. These are the rules that are applied to transnational contracts between private parties. But a foreign investment contract is different in that it always involves a state or a state entity as a party. In these circumstances, it would be logical that the law of the host

---

[68] Of the three arbitrators, Professor Sauser-Hall alone had claims to competence in international law.

[69] See further on the case law on Article 42(1), Christoph Schreuer, *The ICSID Convention: A Commentary*, 2nd edn (Cambridge University Press, 2009).

THE PRECURSOR OF NEOLIBERALISM

state should apply for a variety of reasons. First, the state would not normally accept the law of another state as applicable to its contracts. Secondly, even if does accept international law, there is no body of concrete principles of international law that could apply to contracts, foreign investment contracts or any other variety. As Feller, studying the work of the Mexican Claims Commission (1923–1934), pointed out on the basis of practice:[70]

> International law contains no rules for the controversies involving breach of such contracts. All that can be found in international law is a reference back to municipal law.

Stephen Toope stated the same, writing fifty-five years later that:[71]

> A purely practical objection to the application of international law is that the corpus of public international law simply does not contain rules that are applicable to the regulation of complex private contractual relationships.

It is very much a moot point whether international law has in the intervening period thrown up rules on foreign investment contracts. In fact, even during the present stage of its development through treaty law and the clear elevation of protection of investment into the international sphere through investment treaties, domestic law has to be looked at to provide for basic issues relating to the law on foreign investment contracts.[72] Despite years of arbitration of foreign investment disputes, outside treaty rules on investment protection, which were not designed to apply to contracts, there is little agreement as to any specific rules that have been recognized as constituting an international law on foreign investment contracts. Though, technically, an uncertain body of rules such as general principles of law can be chosen, the question of whether these rules constitute international law when identified by arbitrators as general principles remains uncertain. Arbitrators do not have the power to create international law, particularly if states mandate the application of their own domestic law rules to foreign investment contracts. At the least, the technique of identifying the general principles of law must be stated so that it is open to objective analysis.

---

[70] Feller, *The Mexican Claims Commission: 1923–1934*, p. 178.

[71] Stephen Toope, *Mixed International Arbitration* (Cambridge: Grotius Publications, 1990), at p. 78.

[72] Monique Sasson, *The Substantive Law of Investment Arbitration: The Unsettled Relationship between Municipal Law and International Law* (The Hague: Kluwer, 2010).

2.4 THE INTERNATIONALIZATION THEORY

By the time the Libyan arbitrations appear on the scene, sufficient spadework had been done to stabilize the possible argument that there was an international law that applied to foreign investment contract. There was considerable academic writing that had been generated.[73] As indicated, Article 42(1) contains reference to the relevance of international law to the settlement of investment disputes. The Libyan arbitrations confirmed trends that had already been initiated. Before considering them, the policy justifications that were coming to be articulated in justification of internationalization may be briefly considered.

2.4.2 The policy arguments for internationalization

Independently of the structuring of the theory of internationalization of foreign investment contracts through the inclusion of appropriate clauses that increase the external contacts of the contracts, policy grounds have been developed to justify the theory of internationalization. The policy grounds are founded in clearly classical economic views that foreign investment brings unmitigated blessings to a developing country, and that flows of such investment should be promoted through legal protection given through international law. In modern times, these policy preferences have acquired greater vigour due to their assimilation with neoliberal trends. They presage the later neoliberal justifications of expansionist interpretations of principles of investment treaties.

---

[73] There were occasional queries. Bowett expressed puzzlement that the law created was applied only to developing countries. Derek Bowett, 'Claims between States and Private Entities: The Twilight Zone of International Law', (1986) 35 *Catholic University Law Review* 929. But this is not too problematic as the answer would be that deficient laws that had to be supplemented with general principles are found only in developing countries. For this reason, the agreements were renamed 'economic development agreements'. The term also encapsulated the economic rationale behind the exceptional treatment. Richard Lillich, 'The Law Governing Disputes under Economic Development Agreements', in Richard Lillich and Charles Brower (eds.), *International Arbitration for the Twentieth Century* (Irvington, NY: Transnational, 1993). As Elisabeth Kjos stated, the theory is 'controversial'. Elisabeth Kjos, *Applicable Law in Investor–State Arbitration* (Oxford University Press, 2013), pp. 215–16. Nagla Nassar, *Sanctity of Contracts Revisited: A Study in the Theory and Practice of Long-Term International Contracts* (The Hague: Martinus Nijhoff, 1995). As Delaume asked, 'Why should a different solution prevail when the contracting state is a developing nation whose law is capable of supplying the basic legal framework of the transaction?' Delaume, 'State Contracts and Transnational Arbitration', *American Journal of International Law* 140. One has to have a peculiar notion of the rule of law to accept that developing countries should not be treated equally.

The justifications concentrate on the benefits of foreign investment. The benefits brought by foreign investment include technical assistance, transfer of new technology, the building of infrastructure and new employment for local personnel. Such flows would not take place if there was instability in the legal regime that covered the foreign investment. The considerable financial risks involved in making investments in sectors like petroleum require that there should be security for such investments. Security and stability are essential because of the long duration of the contract. Since the laws of the host state were inherently unstable, it was necessary to rectify this situation by constructing stable rules that promoted contractual stability. These are long-standing justifications for the protection of foreign investment through internationalization.

They are the main basis for taking inflexible stances on the validity of the stabilization clauses in contracts. Great importance was attached to the stabilization clause, which sought to freeze the law of the host state as at the time of entry. The aim of the clause was to ensure that the law so frozen continued to apply to the contract despite later changes to the host state's law. This insulation of the contract through the stabilization clause flew in the face of fundamental notions of constitutional law. It was not possible to freeze the law by private consent as the legislative sovereignty of the state to change the law could not be contained by private agreement, even if a state entity participates in the contract. These legal considerations have been displaced through policy considerations.

An example of where these policy reasons are stated is the following passage in the *Texaco* Award:[74]

> Several elements characterize these arrangements: in the first place, their subject matter is particularly broad: they are not concerned only with an isolated purchase or performance, but tend to bring to developing countries investment and technical assistance, particularly in the field of research and exploitation of mineral resources or in the construction of factories on a turnkey basis. Thus, they assume a real importance in the development of the country where they are performed ... In the second place, the long duration of these contracts implies close cooperation between the state and the contracting party.

The formulation of the policy justification for the internationalization anticipates some of the justifications that were to be advanced by those who favoured the creation of neoliberal principles under investment treaties. What is observable is that the policy justification for preserving

---

[74] Paragraph 45 of *Texaco* Award.

2.4 THE INTERNATIONALIZATION THEORY   109

the force of the stabilization clause continues to influence the shaping of foreign investment protection to this day. The justification may be put with greater sophistication perhaps, but the argument for foreign investment protection through the stabilization clause and its later elevation to protected status by an investment treaty are still firmly based on the view that foreign investment brings economic development to the host state and that, therefore, the protection of the stabilization clause through its internationalization either under the old view or under the investment treaty is a desirable result. Many economists doubt this policy reasoning. Many lawyers also doubt the policy justification because the restriction of the state's regulatory power to act in the public interest rests on unsupportable economic hypotheses and is not supportable in terms of constitutional theory.[75] Not all foreign investment benefits host states. It is difficult in logic to support an inflexible rule on investment protection brought about by private contracts.

The theory of internationalization rests heavily on the stabilization clause. The stabilization clauses prevented changes being effected to the contract through subsequent legislation by freezing the legislation and other law existing at the time of entry in the host state as applying throughout the life of the contract.[76]

Furthermore, the extent to which a contractual mechanism can eliminate a state's police powers to protect public interests when circumstances change and require the exercise of such powers must be considered.[77] A contract system cannot exist within domestic law unless the state permits it to exist. A state cannot relinquish its own regulatory powers merely by concluding a private contract with a foreign party.[78] An inclusion of a

---

[75] For recent doubts on the efficacy of the theory, see Kjos, *Applicable Law in Investor–State Arbitration*, p. 222.

[76] See further, Nassar, *Sanctity of Contracts Revisited*; Munir Maniruzzaman, 'Stabilization in Investment Contracts and Change of Rules by Host Countries', Association of International Petroleum Negotiators, Houston, Texas, 2007. Professor Maniruzzaman has written extensively in this area.

[77] The existence of such police powers in the state has been regarded as 'indisputable'. *Tecnicas Medioambentales SA (Tecmed) v. Mexico*, ICSID, Case No. ARB(AF)/00/2 (29 May 2003), para. 115. It has been generally accepted in recent awards. It is restated as a rule in recent investment treaties, which concede that indirect expropriation, which is regulatory in character, cannot generally give rise to compensation. The terminology of police powers is derived from American law. Its content has been known to international law. The state's regulatory powers are an aspect of its sovereignty. *Oscar Chinn* Case (1934) PCIJ Series A/B No. 63.

[78] Alvik, *Contracting with Sovereignty*, pp. 261–72. The limitation is often considered to be inherent in the concept of property itself. The concept of property is created by public law

stabilization clause cannot be said to be valid for the duration of the contract, for the state could not possibly have contemplated all the possible changes to the surrounding circumstances of the contract affecting the public interest and excluded the application of its police powers in response to such situations. Yet the impact of police powers on stabilization clauses has seldom been considered in arbitration simply because arbitral tribunals cannot accommodate notions of police powers within the theory of internationalization.

Foreign investors in certain sectors such as petroleum had long-term contracts. They sought stability for their contracts and the stabilization clauses were regarded as necessary to achieve this aim. It was necessary to create theory in order to support the notion that the stabilization clause would have the effect of freezing the contract and giving it immunity from future changes through legislation. The theory of internationalization provides the basis on which the stabilization clause could operate so as to provide stability for the contract as well as protection in the event of its breach. The presence of an arbitration clause ensured that the breach resulted in a remedy being provided through arbitration held outside the host state. The choice of law clause, the stabilization clause and the arbitration clause worked in tandem. They provided the foundation of internationalization on the basis that the three clauses maximize the external contacts in the contract.

The presence of the clauses created the view that parties had agreed to internationalize the contract, for the stabilization clause could have no effect unless subjected to a system higher than the domestic law of the state agreeing to its inclusion. The presence of a choice of law clause indicating the applicability to the contract of such a supranational system reinforces the internationalization of the contract. The ideal conditions for the employment of the theory of internationalization, if one concedes its existence, would be the existence of three clauses in the contract: a stabilization clause effectively freezing the law as at the time of entry; a choice of law clause indicating general principles of law or some identifiable supranational system of laws; and an arbitration clause mandating overseas arbitration in the event of a dispute. Some would argue that the

---

to be defeasible in the ultimate public interest. For a recent discussion, see Jeremy Waldron, *The Rule of Law and the Measure of Property* (Cambridge University Press, 2012). See also *Lucas* v. *South Carolina Coastal Council* (1962) 505 US 1003. The US Supreme Court said: 'property rights are arbitrary assemblages of rights that the state creates for its own instrumental purposes, and which it can undo almost at will for the same instrumental ends'.

2.4 THE INTERNATIONALIZATION THEORY 111

existence of an arbitration clause by itself would suffice as it indicates a desire to externalize the contract.[79] The internationalization process then becomes a matter of inference by the arbitration tribunal. Nevertheless, the optimum condition for the operation of internationalization depends on the existence of the three clauses and the argument that their presence indicates an agreement by the parties to subject the contract to an external mechanism of protection.

2.4.3 The Libyan arbitrations

The second set of the six arbitrations arose from disputes with Libya following the Arab–Israeli conflict, and provide a stronger basis for the theory of internationalization. In all these arbitrations, there were stabilization clauses as well as clear choice of law clauses. These factors set the Libyan cases apart from the earlier group of cases in that they contained stronger factors that the arbitrators could employ in resorting to a theory of internationalization.

The three Libyan arbitrations provided a more substantial basis for the theory of internationalization, but, as will be seen, the foundation they provided for the theory was rather shaky. In any event, the type of concession contracts on the basis of which the theory was constructed hardly exists in modern times.[80] Yet there were important features that set the Libyan arbitrations apart from the earlier arbitrations and facilitated the application of the theory of internationalization to them. The outcomes and reasoning in all three arbitrations were different, thus presaging the conflicting awards that were to come about in investment treaty arbitrations.[81]

---

[79] As was accepted in *Revere Copper and Brass Inc.* v. *OPIC* (1980) 56 ILR 258. But this was not an arbitral award, it was part of an internal procedure of OPIC, a body that provides insurance for outward foreign investments. It makes an assessment as to whether a claim is payable on the ground that an expropriation has occurred. The decision is doled out as if it was an award in later writings. Elisabeth Kjos refuted this view: 'The sole insertion of an arbitration clause would appear insufficient', Kjos, *Applicable Law in Investor–State Arbitration*, at p. 222.

[80] In the petroleum sector, the concession agreement has been displaced by the production-sharing agreement, which is based on the total control of operations by the state oil company, the foreign corporation merely sharing in the profits and being eventually phased out after reasonable profits have been made during a fixed period of operation.

[81] Robin White, 'Expropriation of the Libyan Oil Concessions: Two Conflicting International Arbitrations', (1981) 30 *International & Comparative Law Quarterly* 1. All three were in conflict. Texaco supported internationalization fully. *BP* proceeded on the basis that the nationalization was illegal as it was by way of reprisal. *Liamco* found that it was lawful, but had to be compensated.

First, there were strong, express stabilization clauses in all three of the Libyan cases. Secondly, there were express choice of law clauses that made reference to general principles of law. In *Texaco*,[82] the choice of law clause specifically stated that Libyan law, which conforms with international law, was to be applied. The award that is considered the highpoint of the internationalization theory was intended to apply only to those contracts that contained a specific type of choice of law clause. Thirdly, they all required settlement of any disputes by ad hoc arbitration outside Libya. It was only the third element that was present in the earlier set of cases. These were strong circumstances for the drawing of inferences that the parties had created sufficient external links that indicated that the contract was to be internationalized. Equally, there were strong circumstances against the notion of internationalization. The resolutions on the NIEO were reaching a high point as the Libyan cases were being decided. The developing countries were asserting permanent sovereignty over natural resources, particularly over oil. Subsequent events ensured that national legislation and the form of contracts in the petroleum sector were changed to reflect national control over petroleum resources. A tussle was on. The Libyan cases were decided in the context of that tussle. Professor Dupuy, who made the award in *Texaco*, weighed in heavily against the trends that developing countries had initiated by formulating arguments against them in his award.[83]

Despite the presence of strong elements supporting internationalization, the three sole arbitrators disagreed as to the process through which relief should be provided. Libya did not contest the arbitrations. The sole arbitrators appointed by the oil companies, using the default procedure in the arbitration clauses, made each of the awards. The awards then suffer from an inherent weakness in that they rest on the assumption that the party-appointed arbitrators would take neutral stances. It is evident that in the *Texaco* Award, the arbitrator took an advocacy position supporting the internationalization.[84] He considered the arguments

---

[82] *Texaco* v. *Libya* (1978) 17 ILM 1.

[83] Professor Dupuy dismissed the role of the UN General Assembly in creating law in the area, regarded the prescriptions in the Assembly resolutions on the NIEO as creating only *lex ferenda* and dismissed the argument that the oil concessions were administrative contracts on the ground that the distinction relating to administrative contracts was a peculiarity of French law. None of these positions would be accepted in modern times. The award is much criticized.

[84] For a recent evaluation of the case, see Julien Cantegreil, 'The Audacity of the *Texaco/Calasiatic Award*: Rene-Jean Dupuy and the Internationalization of Foreign Investment Law' (2011) *European Journal of International Law* 441.

2.4 THE INTERNATIONALIZATION THEORY 113

contrary to internationalization and dismissed them, deliberately taking a position favourable to the internationalization theory. The award of the peculiar remedy of specific performance was granted so that the strategy of pursuing the oil from the Libyan fields could be facilitated. The weakness of the cases flows from the fact that the Libya refused to participate in the arbitrations. It thereby permitted the arbitrator in *Texaco* to state what was effectively the case for the oil company as his award. The conclusions of the arbitrators differed on similar facts, a situation that was later to plague arbitrations under investment treaties. It is interesting to note this in view of the fact that the claim is made that these differences flow from prior partiality for certain standpoints as to investment protection. Certainly, *Texaco* v. *Libya* demonstrates a prior partiality in that it contains a virtual acceptance of the case for the claimant and a purposeful debunking of possible arguments in favour of Libya.

The strongest support for internationalization comes from *Texaco* v. *Libya*.[85] The claimants had sought the unusual remedy of specific performance, which would have required a holding of illegality of the expropriation and the continued validity of the concession agreements. The unusual remedy was requested so that the claimant company could, armed with the award, pursue title to Libyan oil through the domestic courts of states to which it was sent.[86] The arbitrator held that the Libyan nationalization measures were illegal because they violated the stabilization clause. To arrive at this conclusion, it was necessary for the arbitrator to hold that the contract existed in a supranational system, for if the law applicable to the contract was Libyan law, the nationalization decree would have extinguished the contract. Professor Dupuy, the sole arbitrator appointed through default procedure by the president of the ICJ, discarded all the sovereignty-based arguments that could have been put. He rehearsed every argument that existed against internationalization of foreign investment agreements at that time and rejected them. Much praised by some, the award can equally well be charged with bias towards the claimant as well as an eagerness to bolster the theory of

---

[85] Sometimes referred to as *Topco* v. *Libya*, the name of the claimant company being Texas Overseas Petroleum Corporation, abbreviated as Topco or Texaco. Calasiatic (California Asiatic Oil Company) was the other claimant. The award is reported at (1979) 53 ILR 389. The earlier award by Judge Cavin in *Sapphire International Petroleums Ltd* v. *National Iranian Oil Co.* (1963) 35 ILR 136, was a precursor.

[86] For the working out of this strategy, see Muthucumaraswamy Sornarajah, *The Pursuit of Nationalized Property* (The Hague: Martinus Nijhoff, 1986).

114   THE PRECURSOR OF NEOLIBERALISM

internationalization. Every facet of the award has been subject to later criticism. Professor Dupuy, an eminent French international lawyer, held that the notion of administrative contracts, which permitted a state to intervene in state contracts in the public interest, was a peculiarity of French law not found in other legal systems. That view seems unacceptable as the defeasibility of state contracts in the public interest is accepted in many legal systems.[87] He found that the repeated resolutions on permanent sovereignty over natural resources at the UN General Assembly constituted *lex ferenda* and not *lex lata*. Many respectable international lawyers have regarded the doctrine not only as *lex lata*, but as constituting a principle of *ius cogens*.[88] In any event, the territorial sovereignty of subsoil resources is a principle that has been stated from Roman times. It was necessary for developing states to restate it only because colonialism had subverted the notion to advance its own interests. The rule was an affirmation of a central proposition of international law. The substantive content of permanent sovereignty over natural resources was always accepted in domestic systems of law. The mere fact that it was being conveyed through the UN General Assembly did not make it any less a law. Contemporary literature did recognize a qualified competence in the General Assembly to make international law.[89] Such capacity is now well accepted, leaving Professor Dupuy's comments on such capacity no longer tenable.

In the process, Professor Dupuy upheld the notion of internationalization of the foreign investment contract, which enabled him to find an illegality, a condition precedent for the granting of the remedy of specific performance sought by the claimant. His award rested on the fact that the contract itself contained relevant clauses indicating an intention of the parties to externalize the contract, as well as on policy grounds such as that economic development, which is the objective of foreign investment contracts in the petroleum sector, could not be achieved without

---

[87] French writers contest the proposition that the defeasibility rule is uniquely French as Dupuy suggested. Bernard Audit, *Transnational Arbitration and State Contracts* (The Hague: Martinus Nijhoff, 1988), p. 108 The common law recognizes the defeasibility of state contracts. *Amphitrite v. The King* [1921] 3 KB 500. In *BP*, Judge Lagergren accepted the view that state contracts are subject to the principle of governmental effectiveness. *BP* Award (1973) 53 ILR 297, at 349.

[88] Crawford, *Brownlie's Principles of Public International Law*, p. 489.

[89] At the time of the discussion of the internationalization theory, there were doubts as to the law-making capacity of the General Assembly resolutions. Blaine Sloan, *The Binding Force of the Recommendations of the General Assembly of the United Nations* (Oxford University Press, 1948). The legal significance of these resolutions is now well accepted.

2.4 THE INTERNATIONALIZATION THEORY 115

internationalization of the contract. The need to ensure an equilibrium between the power of the state to change the contract and the stability that is required for the investor's capital outlay to succeed required the protection of the investment through an external mechanism. It is a nakedly prejudiced award. It sought to argue the case for internationalization. It virtually established that the breach of a foreign investment contract amounted *per se* to an illegality, a position that foreign investors wanted to establish. In later times, knowing that his great legacy in international law will be marred by the award, Professor Dupuy sought to explain away its effects.[90]

Professor Dupuy's views in *Texaco* were not followed in the other two Libyan arbitrations. The premises in *Texaco* are considerably weakened by the fact that the neither the claims advanced by *BP* and *Liamco* nor the course taken by the arbitrators in the two awards on basically similar facts corresponded in any significant manner to the views in *Texaco*. They portend the later schisms that developed in investment arbitration. In *BP* v. *Libya*, Judge Lagegren did find illegality, but that the nationalization was an act of reprisal against US support for Israel.[91] Nationalizations by way of reprisals are considered illegal in international law. He awarded damages on the basis of this illegality. It was unnecessary for him to invoke the stabilization clause or the theory of internationalization to arrive at this conclusion. Equally, departing from the analysis in *Texaco*, Professor Mahmassani ruled in *Liamco* v. *Libya* that there was no

---

[90] Professor Dupuy was concerned with the manner in which the *Texaco* Award would affect his legacy as the leading French international lawyer of his times. He was almost apologetic about the award. He sought to explain the award's impact by pointing out that it dealt with the old style concession contract, which has no significance in modern times. This is not an appropriate explanation. The central feature of the award was reasoning on internationalization, which could apply to any foreign investment contract. He saw a need to explain away the award as it was not consistent with liberal stances in terms of international law. As time passed, many propositions in the award, such as the *lex ferenda* effect of General Assembly resolutions, the view that administrative contracts were peculiar to French law or the effect of the stabilization clause, had become outdated. Professor Dupuy, like many academics later on, served the interests of private power to the detriment of fairness in international law by upholding doctrines that flew in the face of efforts by developing states to advance interests that had been thwarted during colonialism. *Texaco* was a blot on a great career. In Cassese, *Five Masters of International Law*, pp. 33–5, Professor Dupuy stated his apologetic view of *Texaco*. It would be interesting to see how history regards the contributions of several other academics who have ventured into this field.

[91] Judge Lagegren said that the nationalization was made for the 'purely extraneous political reasons and was arbitrary and discriminatory in character'. The focus was on the illegality of the expropriation.

116 THE PRECURSOR OF NEOLIBERALISM

illegality as a state was perfectly entitled to nationalize foreign property, but had to pay compensation to the foreigner whose property is taken. On that basis, he awarded damages to the claimant.[92]

It is evident that the Libyan cases do not provide uniform support to the theory of internationalization. They also indicate arbitrator preferences for definite solutions. Yet, on close examination, the choice of law clauses indicated the application of international law. There appear to be no cases, even after the Libyan awards, where international law was applied in the face of a clear choice of domestic law in ad hoc arbitration. There was no *jurisprudence constante* in support of internationalization, but this did not seem to matter at all, the six Libyan cases being taken as uniformly supporting the theory of internationalization. Arbitrator preferences for distinct theories and results played a role in the outcome. Professor Dupuy took an extreme position that favoured internationalization, and went out his way to promote the theory as well as further the interests of Texaco, which had devised a strategy of pursuing Libyan oil through domestic courts.[93] The award was made in such a manner as would facilitate the strategy of the claimant, permitting the unusual remedy of specific performance to signal that property in the oil had not passed to the state as a result of the nationalization. It is interesting that in the later literature *Texaco* has received greater attention. Despite the criticisms it received from writers, its reasoning was preserved so that the internationalization theory it advocated could be reinforced.[94]

2.4.4 Aminoil *signals change*

A significant change occurred from this line of cases, which laid a shaky foundation for a theory of internationalization, in *Aminoil* v. *Kuwait*.[95] The cases rose from a classic concession agreement. Concession agreements were based on the foreign petroleum company being given a *carte blanche* over oil exploration and exploitation covering vast tracts

---

[92] Later awards in the area are seldom in the public domain. Even those with limited experience in practice know that there are awards following the internationalization theory. Some awards are available. *Himpurna* v. *Pertamina* (1999) 25 YBCA 13. The *Karaha Bodas* v. *Pertamina* Award, which arose from similar facts to those that arose during the Indonesian economic crisis, resulting in state measures terminating contracts, also employed the internationalization theory. This case is known as enforcement proceedings took place in the United States, Hong Kong and Singapore.

[93] On pursuit litigation, see Sornarajah, *The Pursuit of Nationalized Property*.

[94] Curtis, 'The Legal Security of Economic Development Agreements'.

[95] (1982) 21 ILM 976.

2.4 THE INTERNATIONALIZATION THEORY 117

of land for a long period of time in return for royalties per barrel of oil exported. The pattern began to change dramatically when the oil-exporting states wished to change the dominance of the oil companies and recover control of the sector. *Aminoil* occurred at a time of such change. Whereas *Texaco* may be interpreted as an effort to staunch the change through rejection of arguments relating to the power of the UN General Assembly to create law relating to control over natural resources and through confining, incorrectly, the notion of administrative contracts to French law, events in the petroleum sector had moved more inexorably towards state control by the time *Aminoil* came to be decided.

Aminoil v. *Kuwait* is a precursor to the change.[96] It arose out of the usual concession agreement, but at a time when changes were being effected to transfer control over the petroleum industry to the state. Adverting to the changes that the concession contract had undergone, the tribunal said: 'These changes have not been the consequence of accidental or special factors, but of a profound or general transformation in terms of oil concessions that occurred in the Middle East, and later throughout the world.'[97] The formation of the Organization of Oil Exporting Countries (OPEC) was a reality and the rise in oil prices, which gave rise to the dispute in *Aminoil*, was a consequence of the oil-producing countries acting collectively through OPEC to increase the price of oil. As a result, the producer was able to sell oil at high prices. Kuwait wanted some of the profits and sought renegotiation of the contract. Aminoil refused. Kuwait nationalized the property of Aminoil. Aminoil predictably relied on the stabilization clause and argued that the contract was an internationalized contract. Kuwait appeared before the tribunal and vigorously asserted its right to terminate the concession agreement under the circumstances.[98] The majority in the *Aminoil* tribunal cast considerable doubt on the earlier awards. They did not regard the stabilization clause as having value except to protect the investment during its early stages of implementation and as having an effect on calculation of damages. The clause did not prevent the state from rescinding the contract. They recognized the regulatory power of the state to act in the public interest and saw that power as diminishing

---

[96] Schreuer and Dolzer, stated that *Aminoil* marked a clear change from the earlier cases. Schreuer and Dolzer, *International Investment Law*, pp. 75–7.

[97] Paragraph 97 of the *Aminoil* Award.

[98] The vigorous argument in the case had an impact. See the article written by one of the counsel, explaining the case. Alan Redfern, 'The Arbitration between the Government of Kuwait and Aminoil', (1985) *British Yearbook of International Law* 6.

the force of the stabilization clause. The tribunal also said that a state should have the opportunity to respond to changed circumstances, the increase in oil prices being such a circumstance. *Aminoil* took a more conciliatory stance. It could not deny the obvious fact that control had passed from the foreign oil companies to the states in the natural resources sectors. That transfer of power had taken effect more conclusively in the petroleum sector.

Aminoil stated progressive views, which were in advance of its time. It signalled the need for regulatory space in the state to ensure that public interests were protected when the circumstances of a contract changed and proved disadvantageous. The *Aminoil* tribunal considered termination, despite the existence of a stabilization clause, as legitimate if made in the light of 'exigencies connected with essential state functioning'. It recognized that there was a public law prerogative in the state to terminate a contract. Though subject to the need to pay appropriate compensation, there was in the host state regulatory powers that flowed from its territorial sovereignty over the foreign investment process. It presaged the prominence of the regulatory expropriation rule in investment treaty arbitration.[99]

Despite *Aminoil*, the theory of internationalization has continued to retain a tenacious vitality. The tenacity it has within investment arbitration is a continuing indication of the philosophical differences among arbitrators as to the policy reasons behind investment protection. From this point of view, the early awards have relevance for the divisions that are now taking place in treaty-based investment arbitration. There is an inherent clash of attitudes that produces discordant results.

Texaco was the product of an arbitrator convinced that foreign investment promotes economic development. He subscribed to the view that 'economic development agreements' required protection through internationalization because that is the only way to achieve the economic objective of development. *Aminoil*, on the other hand, showed that arbitrators are capable of assessing issues in the context of the circumstances of changes that were taking place. Within this range of different views, the early awards, though much fewer in number, exhibit differing tendencies that reflect predispositions to results. These predispositions continue to be the reason for the schisms that occur in investment arbitration. They are ultimately traceable to the political and ideological stances that arbitrators take as to the utility of foreign

---

[99] Ahmed el-Kosheri and Tarek Riad, 'The Law Governing a New Generation of Petroleum Agreements: Changes in the Arbitration Process', (1986) 1 *ICSID Review* 257.

2.4 THE INTERNATIONALIZATION THEORY 119

investment. It is too facile to rationalize the differences as being teething problems when they have had a continuous existence for over six decades.[100] The differences became accentuated in more recent times as the ideological viewpoints became stronger in the 1990s. Attitudes in investment treaty arbitration are a continuation of those formed in the prior period of contract-based foreign investment arbitration. These attitudes continue to cross-fertilize each other.

The first six cases arose in the petroleum industry at a time when the contract used was the concession agreement. Under the concession agreement, the form which was used widely within the industry, it was usual to include stabilization clauses, choice of law clauses indicating general principles of law and a foreign arbitration clause. These clauses maximized the contacts the contract had with external factors so that an inference to promote the contract out of the territorial control of the host state could be assumed to fall within the principle of party autonomy. Theory was made to support the process of internationalization. Party autonomy came to be extolled in this as well as in other business transactions. It was suggested that the lack of personality in the foreign investor could not stand in the way of internationalization, as the state could confer the extent of the personality required by the foreign investor and thereby subject the agreement to international law. The view was stated, on the basis of *Wimbledon*, that a state, being sovereign, had the sovereign right to surrender its sovereignty in any manner it pleased.[101] These are novel notions seeking to justify the theoretical deficiencies that were present.[102] In *Texaco* itself, Professor Dupuy suggested that the claimant companies 'had certain capacities which enable them to act internationally in order to invoke the rights which result from an internationalized contract', recourse to arbitration being one of them. He,

---

[100] The Indonesian arbitrations attest to the vitality of the internationalization theory. In *Himpurna* and *Karaha Bodas*, the contractual provisions were upheld despite the fact that there was an ongoing economic crisis, and the IMF advice to Indonesia was to cease the large projects that had been started by the previous government of Suharto. Cameron refers to some other awards, the reports of which are not in the public domain, asserting the existence of the theory of internationalization. Peter Cameron, *International Energy Investment Law: The Pursuit of Stability* (Oxford University Press, 2010).

[101] *Wimbledon* does not supply authority for surrendering sovereignty otherwise than by treaty to a non-sovereign. *Wimbledon* is not sound authority, though Dupuy and others have used it in this context.

[102] There was considerable contemporary discussion of these theoretical difficulties. See Cantegreil, 'The Audacity of *Texaco/Calasiatic* Award: Rene-Jean Dupuy and the Internationalization of Foreign Investment Law', at p. 454.

thus, anticipated the unilateral invocation of such a right by the investor under investment treaties. But the theoretical objections to internationalization are many. Even if sound, the theory, which is reliant on international law as the applicable law, would have to accommodate the whole of international law, including human rights, environmental rights and a package of other principles that assert the regulatory power of the state to act in the public interest. The public welfare of the people, whose resources are affected, needs to be taken into account.[103] The theory of internationalization was conceptualized in a different age when concern with the construction of an international law that conserved the dominance of multinational corporations was the only value that guided the law. In modern times, international law has developed to include concern for a diversity of other factors that are inconsistent with the emphasis on the sole value of investment protection. Internationalization may not provide a secure system of investment protection as the makers of the theory envisaged.

In relation to the stabilization clause, which is the linchpin of the internationalization theory, authorities overwhelmingly doubt its efficacy in curtailing a state's power to act in the public interest. Thus, Bernadini observed:[104]

> The effectiveness of such provisions may be doubted whenever they purport to limit the States' inalienable prerogatives, as it would be the case of a stabilization clause providing for the prohibition of nationalization or expropriation. It is a principle of public international law that States may not renounce sovereign prerogatives, the exercise of which is instrumental to the pursuance of the country's essential public objectives. A stabilization clause contradicting mandatory rules of international law (*jus cogens*) may not therefore produce its typical effects. The principle of permanent sovereignty of each State over its natural resources assumes in this context a significant relevance. The qualification of the State's sovereignty as *permanent* has led States to consider that the right to exploit the natural resources is inalienable so that it cannot be hindered or restricted by commitments conventionally undertaken *vis-à-vis* other States or private parties.

Redfern and Hunter stated in their text on *International Commercial Arbitration*:

---

[103] Lorenzo Cotula, 'The New Enclosures? Polanyi, International Investment Law and the Global Land Rush', (2013) 34 *Third World Quarterly* 1605.

[104] Piero Bernadini, 'Stabilization and Adaptation in Oil and Gas Contracts', (2008) 1 *Journal of World Energy Law & Business* 98–112.

2.4 THE INTERNATIONALIZATION THEORY 121

> However, stabilization clauses have come under increasing scrutiny and pressure from civil society groups who argue that private investors should not be in a position to limit a host State's ability to modernize its laws. Indeed, some have criticized the stabilization clauses as being responsible for the so-called regulatory chill. In this sense, Aminoil marked a turning point in the treatment of long term contracts for the exploitation of natural resources although the debate has now widened and encompasses other contracts and industries.

It is strange that the stabilization clause now has greater significance in investment arbitration despite the fact that its significance has been dented in contract-based arbitration. In investment arbitration, it is touted as a limit to regulatory expropriation.[105] It forms the basis of raising legitimate expectations protected by fair and equitable treatment. In the eyes of some arbitrators it is protected by the umbrella clause. The significance of the stabilization clause in treaty arbitration when its significance is diminished in contract-based arbitration is again an idea to keep alive notions of investment protection through untenable means.

Events have dented the relevance of the internationalization theory considerably, though the theory continues to be invoked. Its success depends largely on the inclinations of the particular arbitration tribunal before which it is invoked. States now have legislation ensuring the monopoly of oil and other natural resource sectors in their state corporations. The forms of contract the state corporations enter into are not concession agreements, but agreements, such as the production-sharing agreements, which ensure that the state entity closely supervises production, has ownership of the resource up to the point of delivery and terminates the agreement at a stated time. There are effective domestic investment codes that control the whole process of foreign investment. The role for internationalization in such agreements has diminished.

But the tenacity in the idea of internationalization remains. *Texaco* itself had indicated means of keeping the relevance of international law alive. In seeking to reconcile the old rule in the *Serbian Loans* Case[106] as to the relevance of the domestic law of the contracting state, Professor Dupuy suggested that the domestic system of a state contained public international law within its principles. The genesis of later interpretations of Article 42(1) of the ICSID Convention, which refers both to national and international law, lies in the proposition that domestic law itself

---

[105] The crucial passage in *Methanex* stated the stabilization clause as an exception to regulatory expropriation without citing any authority.

[106] [1929] PCIJ, Series A, No. 20.

contains the international law proposition relating to contractual sanctity. This permitted the monistic view that international law, understood as containing the sole norm of contractual sanctity, played a supervisory role and counteracted any contrary domestic law that applied.[107] This, of course, depends on the notion that contractual sanctity is a dominant principle in the different legal systems of the world and forms part of international law. It also excludes the vast body of relevant law on the environment and human rights which may support state intervention in the public interest. It calls for a selective view of international law in a manner that would secure investment protection. International law that is considered cannot be selective. If it is relevant, it cannot be constructed on the doubtful notion relating to sanctity of contracts. It must take into account all the developments, such as those relating to permanent sovereignty over natural resources and the principle of economic self-determination. More importantly, it must take into account the whole range of international law relating to the environment and human rights, as well as basic rules that a state should not be prevented from acting in the public interest.[108] At the least, they constitute more forceful principles than those fobbed off as general principles of law. The avenues of introducing internationalization through the back door is not a promising venture. But the ICSID cases based on contracts indicate that the internationalization theory has life left in it yet, as they are based on a selective understanding of international law.

2.5 Contract disputes and ICSID tribunals

ICSID tribunals were originally created with contract disputes in mind, though much of the ICSID's work is now devoted to treaty-based arbitration. Investment treaty arbitration was an interloper, which reduced the significance of the original role of the ICSID. It could well happen that the role of the ICSID in contract arbitration could come back into favour, if treaty-based arbitration declines as a result of disenchantment with the system. Also, with extensive defences to liability of the state being provided in the newer treaties, it may become more prudent for

---

[107] Munir Maniruzzaman, 'State Contracts in Contemporary International Law: Monist versus Dualist Controversies', (2001) 12 *European Journal of International Law* 309.

[108] The UN Secretary General's Special Rapporteur on Business and Human Rights was scathing on the role of stabilization clauses. He regarded the clauses as infringing on the 'required policy space to pursue bona fide human rights obligations'. SRSG Report, 9 April 2010, p. 6

2.5 CONTRACT DISPUTES AND ICSID TRIBUNALS 123

investors to rely on contract-based arbitration rather than the uncertainties involved in treaty-based arbitration.

It is clear that the formulation in the ICSID Convention relating to the choice of law in contracts is based on the theory of internationalization. The significance of this fact seems to have been little understood by the parties, particularly developing states that signed the ICSID Convention. ICSID tribunals have been aided in applying the internationalization theory by the fact that the ICSID Convention specifically refers to international law in Article 42. The Article deals with applicable law. Article 42(1) reads:

> The Tribunal shall decide a dispute in accordance with such rules of law as may be agreed by the parties. In the absence of such agreement, the Tribunal shall apply the law of the Contracting State party to the dispute (including its rules on the conflict of laws) and such rules of international law as may be applicable.

One major problem in this formulation is that, though the provision makes international law relevant, it does not indicate any means of identifying the relevant international law. The relevance of international law arises only if there is no express choice of law clause. A prudent host state should technically be able to escape the application of international law by mandating the application of its own law to every foreign investment contract. But, as will be seen, arbitrators have ensured, through interpretation, that international law would still be the controlling factor. Interpretation, thus, plays a crucial role in both contract and treaty arbitration. Such interpretation in contract arbitration is a forerunner to the more rampant interpretations that arbitrators placed on treaty provisions in investment treaty arbitrations so that the scope of protection of investment is increased. The arbitral understanding of international law is that international law's only role is to promote contractual sanctity, and that it has a controlling role to play in respect of the foreign investment process.

It is clear that the first part of Article 42 accepts the primacy of party autonomy and ensures that the law chosen by the parties is the law applicable to the contract. On any reading of the second part of Article 42, it would be apparent that the second part can have operation only if there is no express choice of law. But that is not how ICSID tribunals have read Article 42. They have read it in a manner that makes Article 42 and its reference to international law relevant even if there is an express choice of law clause so as to keep the theory of internationalization alive. It is not the natural reading of the provision, which clearly contemplates the use of the second clause only in circumstances where there is no express choice of law. It is also not how the World Bank sold the ICSID Convention to developing countries. Arbitral adventurism is not a novelty that arose in treaty arbitration.

The first clause regards a choice of law by the parties as conclusive. The second clause makes the host state's law as applicable and, apologetically, refers to the relevance of international law. But rules of interpretation have not deterred arbitrators from giving expression to their preconceptions. Here again, arbitral results supply fodder to the criticism that arbitrators have a preference for solutions that offer protection to foreign investors and will not be hindered by the rules of interpretation in achieving their purpose.

Where there is an express choice of law clause in modern agreements, it is unlikely that the law chosen to apply to contracts made with states is likely to be anything other than the law of the host state. The internal laws of most states, both developed and developing, would mandate that the law applicable to such contracts be the law of the host state. There may still be contracts that choose a neutral systems of law, but, given internal laws that mandate the application of host state law, this would be unlikely. The choice of such neutral or external systems would violate internal laws and the foreign investor is committed to not violating such laws.[109] Many of these laws, particularly relating to natural resources, are contained in constitutions. In any event, the arbitrator would be under a duty not to avoid the application of a mandatory law as to do so would be in violation of the public policy of the state. Given this situation, one would expect that the role that the second limb of Article 42 would play would be extremely limited, given that states will not deviate from their foreign investment laws mandating the use of their own legal systems as the applicable law.

---

[109] The argument was that such a choice would be *ultra vires*. Those who support the internationalization theory meet this argument by holding that the state should have known what its law was and that it could not rely on its internal laws to rescind an obligation it had undertaken. This is a principle of the international law of treaties and hardly has relevance to a contract, even though it is one of the parties. The argument could equally be made that the foreign investor has a duty to know and abide by the laws of the host state and should not have agreed to a term that is in breach of the law. Every legal system expects that an alien who enters its jurisdiction knows and abides by the law, ignorance of it being no excuse. This is also a very basic general principle of law. Again, general principles of law are selectively chosen according to the preferences of arbitrators.

2.5 CONTRACT DISPUTES AND ICSID TRIBUNALS 125

Several ICSID tribunals have stated the view that international law was relevant, even where there is a clear choice of the host state's law by the parties. Such a position was taken in open defiance of the written words in Article 42. The Article makes the choice of the parties as to applicable law conclusive. The only explanation that can possibly be given is that the arbitrators expressing this view wanted to gear the interpretation of Article 42 to a position that was favourable to investment protection by adopting the position that the foreign investment contract was internationalized through reference to ICSID arbitration, and that international law was therefore relevant to the contract as providing a supervisory function.

It is interesting to note that once the view is expressed in an arbitration, it takes hold in academic writings as well as in other arbitral awards. It is like a one-sided rugby scrum with a unidirectional push overcoming a usually non-existent opposition with overwhelming weight. Repetitive assertions add further weight. The opposition is absent or is small and less weighty either because, as usually happens, it is unaware of what is happening or because it has no avenues through which it could express dissent. Deficiency in knowledge, absence of avenues for dissent and lack of personnel aware of the arcane trends in investment arbitration in developing countries are major reasons why the views of those seeking to conserve the interests of the foreign investors have triumphed over the years. There are no glossy arbitration journals servicing the like-minded which would publish contrary views. On occasion, Western writers have been inclined to spot what is happening and point out the error, but such writings are few.[110] They can and are ignored. The episode of this change may be set out to demonstrate how erroneous opinions favourable to foreign investment protection became entrenched.

The problem begins with *AGIP* v. *Congo*.[111] Professor Dupuy, who decided *Texaco*, sat as a party-appointed arbitrator. The law that was chosen to apply to the contract was 'Congolese law, *supplemented if necessary by any principle of international law*'. Here, the parties specifically referred to international law. It was not a case for the application of the second part of Article 42(1) as international law was a part of the law chosen by the parties. It would be wrong to regard the case as having stated that international law would be relevant even where

---

[110] Some leading scholars had reservations about what was taking place. Oscar Schachter, *Sharing the World's Resources* (New York: University of Columbia Press, 1977).

[111] (1982) 21 ILM 726 (emphasis added).

the law of the host state is chosen as the applicable law. The tribunal itself indicated that it was applying the first part of Article 42(1) as the parties had themselves chosen the law.[112] Despite the express reference to international law in the contract itself, in listing the laws the tribunal indicated only the laws of Congo as relevant.[113] Yet, later in the award, the tribunal considered the relevance of international law as a general proposition. It stated that the reference to the Congolese law being 'supplemented by international law' in the choice of law provision 'means that there can be recourse to the principles of international law either to fill a gap in Congolese law or to supplement it if necessary'. Here, the tribunal was merely interpreting a provision in the contract. But the tribunal went on to say that 'the unilaterally-decided dissolution which took place ... represented a repudiation of these stability clauses, whose applicability results not from the automatic play of the sovereignty of the contracting State but from the common will of the parties expressed at the level of the international juridical order'.[114] This is not an interpretation of Article 42, but a straight adoption of the internationalization theory that when there is a stabilization clause, the contract is elevated to the international juridical order. The clear implication is that whatever the choice of law may be, the presence of a stabilization clause in the contract means that that clause is protected through the elevation of the contract into the international juridical order.[115] On this basis, *AGIP* v. *Congo* can be interpreted as a straightforward application of the internationalization theory without recourse to Article 42. It is possible to read *AGIP* v. *Congo* as having held that, even absent a specific reference to international law in the choice of law provision, where there is a stabilization clause in the contract international law will always be relevant in upholding that clause on the ground that the presence of the clause indicates that the contract operated in an international sphere. The protection of the clause is not possible unless such a view is taken. According to the award, the mere presence of the stabilization clause links the contract to the international legal order. The interpretation keeps alive the prospect that the internationalization theory is alive and well under the ICSID Convention.

---

[112] At para. 43.
[113] At paras. 45–46. It referred to the French law that existed at the time of independence and to relevant provision of the Constitution of Congo.
[114] Paragraph 85.
[115] 'It is in regard to such clauses that the principles of international law supplement the rules of Congolese law' (para. 88).

2.5 CONTRACT DISPUTES AND ICSID TRIBUNALS   127

Later ICSID tribunals sought to confirm the relevance of international law, even where there was an express choice of the host state's law. The next case is *LETCO* v. *Liberia*. This, again, was an arbitration based on contract under the ICSID Convention. The law chosen by the parties was Liberian law. The tribunal discussed the question of whether Liberian law was exclusive. It said:[116]

> The only question is whether Liberian law is applied on its own (as the law chosen by the parties) or in conjunction with applicable principles of public international law.

The tribunal then referred to Article 42, and stated that the provision required that in the absence of a choice the tribunal should apply domestic law and international law. It adverted to the dispute as to whether international law was in such circumstances a regulator of the national system and stated that 'no such problem arises in the present case; the Tribunal is satisfied that the rules and principles of Liberian law are in conformity with generally accepted principles of public international law'. The latter observation is of little value. Under Article 42(1) if there is a clear choice of law, that law has to be applied. There is no requirement that one should proceed to the second limb and inquire into international law. In any event, it was Liberian law, the law of the host state and the internal provisions of the contract that were applied to the dispute. But the award does create the impression that even where there is an express choice of law, there is a further need to examine whether the law of the host state was consistent with the principles of public international law.

It may be that the significance of the stabilization clause will diminish with the increasing acceptance of the view that the host state's regulatory power cannot be displaced by a mere contractual device. It could be argued that this is the position in international law, which concedes the regulatory power of the state in matters of its public interest. As a result, the old style stabilization clause is seldom used in modern contracts. Re-negotiation clauses are becoming more the standard clause that deals with changes effected by legislation. It is becoming increasingly difficult to reconcile the mandatory application of host states' laws with stabilization clauses. The reference to international law, when it is referred to as applicable, is increasingly taken to include not only stability of business, but also other standards relating to human rights and the

---

[116] (1986) 26 ILM 64, at p. 18.

128 THE PRECURSOR OF NEOLIBERALISM

environment.[117] In this evolving context, the stabilization clause cannot be construed to support the theory of internationalization. Though still used, the interpretation that would be placed on a stabilization clause in modern times may well differ, given the fact that new notions such as regulatory expropriation permits a state to intervene in contracts in the public interest.

2.6 Survival of internationalization in ICSID cases

Once the ICSID tribunals had held that even despite the clear choice of host state law, international law is relevant as providing a supervisory rule so as to control the host state law, the avenue was opened to revive the theory of internationalization. The difficulty, of course, was that international law, strictly speaking, was unclear as there was clear evidence that international law itself made a reference to the host state law. But this inconvenient view had to be discarded in the reconstruction of the internationalization theory. They latched on to the erroneous interpretation that had been made in some of the ICSID tribunals as to Article 42, which asserted the relevance of international law despite the choice of the host state's law.

Discarding the fact that Article 42 could only be used by ICSID tribunals operating on the basis of an international convention, they argued that the same avenue was open to all tribunals, ad hoc or institutional, even though such tribunals operated on the basis of rules that were made by private entities such as the International Chamber of Commerce, or used rules such as the UNCITRAL Rules, which could be chosen by tribunals or by the parties as the procedural rules to be used.

There is recognition in the literature that the use of Article 42 of the ICSID Convention to support the internationalization theory is erroneous. Thus, Delaume has observed:[118]

> This is an issue that has been clarified by subsequent awards rendered in the context of ICSID arbitration. In this respect, it should be recalled that under Article 42(1) of the ICSID Convention, and failing express stipulation of applicable law, an arbitral tribunal is under a mandate to apply in the first place the law of the Contracting State party to the dispute, however, testing the results of its findings against international law.

---

[117] See, e.g., Lorenzo Cotula, 'Reconciling Regulatory Stability and Evolution of Environmental Standard in Investment Contracts: Towards a Rethink of Stabilization Clauses', (2008) 1(2) *Journal of World Energy Law and Business* 121.

[118] Georges Delaume, 'The Proper Law of State Contracts Revisited', (1997) 12 *ICSID Review* 1.

2.6 SURVIVAL OF INTERNATIONALIZATION IN ICSID 129

Given these guidelines, it is interesting to note that, although, there was a stipulation of applicable law in the majority of cases registered by ICSID and a number of stipulations combined references to the host state law and to international law, arbitral tribunals have not shown a particular eagerness to rely on international law. In most cases, the tribunals elected to resolve the dispute on the basis of domestic law either because it was felt that there was no need to apply international norms or because it was found that the local law was in harmony with international law.

Also noteworthy is the fact that no attempt has been made to duplicate the ruling made in the *Topco Award*,[119] that submission to international arbitration might constitute implicit choice of international law as the law applicable to the substance of the dispute. The *Topco* assumption was an extreme example of internationalization philosophy that inspired certain arbitrators in the years past.

One has to view the decisions on internationalization under the ICSID Convention as being in conflict. Dicta in awards such as *Duke Energy Electroquil Partners* v. *Ecuador*[120] does make international law relevant, even in situations where there is a clear choice of law provision requiring the application of the domestic law of the host state. But these are dicta and are not the outcome of the award, which itself was based on the domestic law. The process of internationalization depends very much on the stabilization clause. Given the fact the host state's mandatory laws exclude the possibility of such a clause, the modern developments are towards new types of balancing clauses that seek to restore the contractual equilibrium through negotiation. Though the theory of internationalization has been dented, it still hovers about waiting to be rekindled in appropriate circumstances. All one can say is that the present moment is not propitious for that to happen, even in ICSID jurisprudence.

In the separate world of contract-based investment arbitration, the theory of internationalization and the stabilization clause on which it depends will have a continuing role to play. But as its significance recedes due to states making their laws applicable to natural resources contracts,[121] its inclusion may yet be significant as avenues of giving it

---

[119] The *Topco* Award referred to here is the same as the *Texaco* Award.

[120] ICSID, Case No. ARB/04/19 (18 August 2008).

[121] The use of the stabilization clause of the old variety is also less in modern contracts. Changes in operating circumstances are dealt with in modern contracts through re-negotiation clauses or equilibrium clauses, which trigger off contractual adaptation when changes occur. But stabilization clauses continue to be included in contracts. Two instances of its inclusion, the Mittal–Liberia contract and the Baku–Tbilisi–Ceyhan Pipeline contract, have received comment. The human rights and environmental

protection under the distinct category of investment treaty-based arbitration will remain.

The stabilization clause's ability to prevent the exercise of the regulatory power of the state has also been increasingly queried.[122] As in the case of expropriation under investment treaties, strong opinion has now emerged challenging the freezing effect that the stabilization clause can bring about. The reasoning is that a state cannot be contained in exercising regulatory powers necessary to protect public interests. The further argument, which takes a different tack, is that contractual sanctity is not the only concern of modern international law. It recognizes prior and more dominant concerns, such as those concerning human rights, environmental obligations, labour rights, rights in cultural heritage and the rights of indigenous people. These concerns can displace contractual obligations contained in stabilization clauses. Increasingly, financial institutions take such considerations into account even at the preliminary stages of contract formation. It is clear that if international law is applicable, its content will include not only notions of relevant contract principles, but the increasing body of environmental and human rights law that impacts on foreign investment. In the face of such onslaught, the significance of the stabilization clause as a contractual means of protection may diminish. But the means of protection of the clause have now been shifted to a different arena, that of investment treaty arbitration.

2.7   The interaction between contract- and treaty-based arbitration

Treaty-based arbitration contains more secure standards on investment protection. As a result, investment protection would be enhanced if the foreign investment contract itself can be protected by treaty arbitration. Arbitrators have made efforts to ensure this. But as the *Vivendi* Annulment Tribunal clearly indicated, the treaty was intended to apply only to instances where there had been abuse by the state of the rights of the investor in violation of the treaty standards and was not concerned with mere breaches of contract. At the same time, the tribunal pointed out that there could be violations of the contract that could take place

---

implications of such contracts are studied in the different papers collected in Sheldon Leader and David Ong (eds.), *Global Project Finance, Human Rights and Project Finance* (Cambridge University Press, 2011).

[122] Leader and Ong (eds.), *Global Project Finance, Human Rights and Project Finance*.

2.7 CONTRACT- AND TREATY-BASED ARBITRATION 131

directly as a consequence of governmental measures that violate the treaty provisions as well. The scope for expansion had been left open. Investment protection would be enhanced if the instances in which a breach of the contract could amount to a violation of the treaty can be explored and identified. One aspect of the expansionary phase of investment treaty arbitration has been to identify instances in which a link could be created between the protection of the foreign investment contract and the treaty standards. The instances in which the violation of the contract could amount to the violation of the treaty were identified in the awards, thereby enhancing the neoliberal project of investment protection.

2.7.1 The umbrella clause

The most obvious instance would be where the treaty contains an umbrella clause. Such a clause states that all commitments made by the state should be honoured. The clause does not appear in all investment treaties. Its use is avoided in the more recent treaties. But it does appear in many treaties. In these instances, it has been argued that a breach of a foreign investment contract would violate the umbrella clause as the contract qualifies as a commitment. The tribunals have been divided on whether this argument should be accepted. In *SGS* v. *Pakistan*, the tribunal refused to accept the argument on the ground that the umbrella clause should not be given any effect. The tribunal suggested that the parties did not intend to elevate the contract into a situation giving it treaty protection. But the opposite conclusion was reached in *SGS* v. *Philippines*. Tribunals, which have considered the clause in later cases, have been almost evenly divided, opening up another area in which there has been disagreement among them. The disagreement may be explained consistently with the view that the use of the umbrella clause, a clause that has hitherto remained dormant, to secure protection for the contract is further evidence of an expansionary trend that is induced by an ideological preference for investment protection. On the other hand, the contrary view is that the tribunals have no alternative but to interpret the treaty as they find it. The difference of views on the umbrella clause is an ongoing one.[123]

---

[123] But see Voss, *The Impact of Investment Treaties on Contracts between Host States and Foreign Investors*, pp. 271–2.

132   THE PRECURSOR OF NEOLIBERALISM

2.7.2   Role of stabilization clauses under investment treaty arbitration

The stabilization clause plays a significant role in the theory of internationalization. It is said that the clause is not used in modern contracts. The newer contracts are more realistic in that they use techniques that contemplate a contractual equilibrium and the adjustment of the equilibrium through negotiation in the event that any change affects the equilibrium. Damages result only if the state fails to negotiate or does not agree on an appropriate new equilibrium. Whatever the significance of the newer types of clauses is, the clauses still seek to protect the bargain that was struck at the time of the original contract.

There have been views expressed that a state's regulatory power to deal with matters relating to the public interest could not be restricted by the inclusion the stabilization clause. The emergence of the view that regulatory powers of states must be preserved has significantly affected the scope of the stabilization clause. There is an increasing view that stabilization clauses should not be used to fetter the right of the state to take measures to meet public interest objectives in situations that involve the environment and human rights.[124] Despite this view emerging in contract arbitration, the effort in treaty-based arbitration has been to treat the existence of the stabilization clause as an exception to the situation of a regulatory expropriation. There is no authority is support of this view stated in a crucial passage in the *Methanex* Award.[125]

Those who advocate inflexible investment protection will not give up the utility of the stabilization clause easily. As its significance in contract-based arbitration recedes, they have studied ways of keeping the stabilization clause relevant by exploring means by which it could be protected by the investment treaties.

The argument is made that the basis of fair and equitable treatment that the presence of a stabilization clause provides, gives rise to a

---

[124] Amnesty International, 'Human Rights, Trade and Investment Matters' (London: Amnesty International, 2006). Andrea Shemberg, 'Stabilization Clauses and Human Rights', Research Paper for the United Nations Representative on Business and Human Rights (New York: United Nations, 2008).

[125] The passage reads: 'as a matter of general international law, a non-discriminatory regulation for a public purpose, which is enacted in accordance with due process and, which affects, *inter alios*, a foreign investor or investment is not deemed expropriatory and compensable unless specific commitments had been given by the regulating government to the then putative foreign investor contemplating investment that the government would refrain from such regulation' (*Methanex* Award, Pt IV, ch. D, p. 3).

legitimate expectation that the legal circumstances at the time of the contract remain unaffected. The issue becomes one of whether the legitimate expectation must be maintained even where a situation has changed so as to call for measures that interfere with the expectations of the investor. The fact that there is a stabilization clause would not affect the conclusion that a regulatory interference is justified. If a regulatory interference is not protected under contract arbitration, there is no reason why it should be protected by treaty principles.

2.7.3 Linking the law on legitimate expectations

Clearly, the most rapid expansion in investment treaty arbitration was in the creation of a law based on the legitimate expectations. Though it cannot be demonstrated that the rule on legitimate expectations is a general principle of international law, it was quickly received into investment treaty arbitration as a part of fair and equitable treatment. Knowing that investment treaty arbitration will fade away due to its future uncertainties, the transference of its gains into contract-based arbitration will be assiduously pursued. One technique would be to argue that the foreign investor is entitled to protection under the international minimum standard and that this now includes the case law principles under the fair and equitable standard, including the development of the rule on legitimate expectations.[126] This is a futile argument. There is nothing in the internationalization theory to show that the international minimum standard, which could be invoked only by states under the rules on diplomatic protection or by an investor under an investment treaty, could be used in contract arbitration. The manner of the breach may involve a breach of a treaty standard, but this is not a matter for contract arbitration.

2.8 Conclusion

The experience of contract-based arbitration is interesting as it is a precursor to many of the aspects and techniques of investment-based arbitration. There was a group of arbitrators, academics and institutions that sought to construct a structure or a 'regime' that protects foreign investment through the theory of internationalization. The notion of a

---

[126] The argument is foreshadowed in *Duke Energy* v. *Ecuador*, ICSID, Case No. ARB/03/28 (18 August 2008), para. 268; the argument of the claimant to this effect was made in reliance on an expert opinion which the tribunal did not have to consider as it found breach on other grounds.

regime of investment treaty arbitration is an idea that is frequently raised. It is not a new effort. Internationalization was worked out through arbitral awards with the support of academic writings. The experience is repeated in investment treaty arbitration. There was academic support for what was theoretically unsupportable. The phenomenon is common to both types of investment arbitration. Academics often serve as arbitrators or are involved as experts. The making of the law is based on low-order sources –arbitral awards and writings of publicists – both of which are amenable to the influence of private power.

The genesis of many ideas of foreign investment protection that were later used can be found in the manner in which the internationalization theory was developed and used. The techniques of development and the extension of inflexible investment protection used later in investment treaty arbitration were developed in the context of contract-based arbitration. Policy justifications are advanced as if the assumptions of economic development on which they are based are beyond reproach or are an incontestable truth. It is a view that is nurtured by the leading international financial institutions. The ICSID Convention rests on this premise. The solitary norm of contractual sanctity is isolated and maintained as a general principle and as a part of international law. The fact that there could be competing international law principles is ignored. These are difficult exercises to perform within a system that professes neutrality. Consequently, schisms are bound to develop. The gap between investment protection and the promotion of other interests, such as human rights and the environment, ensures that there will always be schisms in the area

The differences in views within investment arbitration developed quite early, as attested by the Libyan cases, decided on virtually the same facts. It indicated that preferences of individual arbitrators and their economic and political visions as to the role of foreign investment is the better explanation for the schism than is any division as to what the law is. Professor Dupuy, a leading academic international lawyer, wrote an award that contained what would now be considered indefensible propositions. There are preferences for certain outcomes conducive to investment protection. Such a tendency was formed in this area of arbitration quite early. Arbitrators preferring an absolutist theory of foreign investment protection have not been deterred by rules of interpretation of treaties from arriving at solutions that are favourable to foreign investors. They have grasped at every technique that enables the objective of inflexible investment protection to be kept alive.

The relevance of international law has also become moot with the passing of time as it is difficult to determine the nature of the international law that is to be applied. Initially, it was possible to isolate sanctity of contracts as the primary and only relevant principle that could constitute international law. With the advent of the NIEO principles, this view was challenged. If a rule formed by a few arbitral awards by single arbitrators and the writings of publicists can constitute international law, then the solemnly passed resolutions of the UN General Assembly on the NIEO also can constitute international law. There are in effect two or more sets of international law, both, perhaps, based on weak sources of law. The problem is further complicated by the rapid rise in modern times of international law on a range of relevant areas, including the environment, human rights, cultural property, indigenous people and natural resources. In that context, the international law that may apply to foreign investment contracts cannot be confined to the rule on sanctity of property. The thrust of the theory of internationalization is very much dented as a result of these developments. The revival of the view in *Aminoil* that regulatory intervention despite the existence of a stabilization clause is justified in terms of international law undermines internationalization considerably. But this will not deter the arbitrators who are inclined to support the theory to focus only on contractual sanctity. Because of the low visibility of contract-based investment arbitration, there is still the possibility that awards based on the classic formula of internationalized contracts will continue to be made. They are also more likely to be enforced through the network of legislation based on the New York Convention on the Reciprocal Enforcement of Arbitral Awards. It may be what proves contract-based arbitration to be more attractive to the foreign investor than treaty-based arbitration. But the low visibility of such arbitration also will become less as a result of the awareness of the significance of such arbitration to the economic and political processes within states. The NGOs that operate in the field are also unlikely not to spot instances where the interests they pursue are affected by the existence of such arbitrations. Contract-based arbitration will also encounter the problems that afflict investment treaty arbitration.

3

Creating jurisdiction beyond consent

The massive increase in treaty-based investment arbitration has had much to do with the expansion of the bases of jurisdiction well beyond what was originally intended by the parties to investment treaties. The basic principle of arbitration is that jurisdiction is conferred on the arbitral tribunal by the consent of the parties. It is also the basis of jurisdiction of every international tribunal, including the ICJ.[1] Through processes of creative interpretation of the treaties, some arbitral tribunals have extended the bases of their jurisdiction so that they could provide relief for the violation of the substantive provisions of the treaties. The substantive provisions also came to be expanded significantly. The securing of jurisdiction enabled the expansion of substantive principles and the attempt at the building up a law of investment protection that some have described as a regime[2] and others as a multilateral framework that is global in application.[3] There is a carefully orchestrated pattern towards the building of a regime. The aim of those who argue for such a global regime is to secure high standards of investment protection, uniformly applicable around the world. The project has nearly broken down due to resistance and withdrawals from the regime. But the manner of its building is worthy of study as a failed experiment in creating norms that had considerable support at first, but is nearing collapse due to the failure of the ideological basis on which the attempt rested.

The techniques of enhancement of jurisdiction and the manner of their reasoning require explanation. As an episode in international law, the expansion and the later contraction of jurisdiction in investment arbitration is worthy of study. The finding of jurisdiction becomes the first step towards the expansionist adventure in substantive law. The

---

[1] In *Armed Activities on the Territory of the Congo* [2006] ICJ Rep. para. 88, the ICJ said that 'its jurisdiction is based on the consent of the parties and is confined to the extent accepted by them', and that ;any conditions to which such consent is subject must be regarded as constituting the limits thereon'.

[2] Salacuse, *The Law of Investment Treaties*, pp. 6–16.

[3] Schill, *The Multilateralization of International Investment Law*.

CREATING JURISDICTION BEYOND CONSENT 137

project required the expansion of jurisdiction beyond what was intended by the parties to the treaties under which such jurisdiction was claimed. It is necessary to understand the techniques used in obtaining jurisdiction and the resulting resistance to the use of such techniques before proceeding to deal with the nature of the expansions in substantive law. The expansive bases of jurisdiction that were created through interpretation were later contested, either through state intervention making the original intention clear, as, for instance, in the denial of benefits provisions of investment treaties, which prevented the use of corporate nationality as a basis for expansion,[4] or through subsequent awards casting doubts on the earlier extensions. Though it may be argued that the system was correcting itself, the fact is that tensions, created by the assumption of jurisdiction on the basis of expansive interpretations, led some states to withdraw from the system altogether. Some tribunals found ways of bypassing the rectifications that the states have sought by interpreting the new provisions narrowly, as happened with the denial of benefits provisions. The legitimacy of the system came to be doubted with both tribunals and states reacting in different ways. The expansion of the jurisdictional bases is dealt with in this chapter. The subsequent chapters deal with the expansion of the substantive rules in the treaties.

Explanations have to be advanced for the rapid construction of the law on foreign investment protection through investment treaties within a relatively short period of time. It is possible to identify 1990, the year of *AAPL v. Sri Lanka*,[5] when dispute settlement provisions in investment treaties were first recognized as giving jurisdiction to arbitration tribunals, as the year in which the trends commenced. As suggested in Chapter 1, an explanation that could be advanced for both types of expansion is that there was an ideological climate favourable to investment protection, which enabled such extensions to take place without much protest for a sufficient period of time. During this time, the expansionary rules of investment protection took hold. There was a climate of exuberance for solutions based on liberalization of flows of foreign investment that investment protection was thought to promote, which supported these moves. In that climate, the extensions were justified on the ground that they promoted the flow of foreign investment by guaranteeing a definite basis on which investments could be protected. There was an euphoric climate that was conducive to the making of this

---

[4] As will be seen, the reaction of the arbitrators was to interpret such provisions narrowly.
[5] (1990) 4 ICSID Rep. 245.

138 CREATING JURISDICTION BEYOND CONSENT

expansionist law. In this climate, the ascendancy of the view that investment protection must have priority over other objectives took hold.

The system of investment arbitration was in many ways geared to the acceptance of such an ideological stance. Its constitutive documents, such as the conventions creating the arbitral institution and treaties creating jurisdiction in them, embodied such a preference. The preamble of the ICSID Convention links arbitration and investment protection with flows of foreign investment that is said to facilitate economic development.[6] The natural inclination of arbitrators was to adopt pro-investment stances.[7] The institutional context in which the arbitrations took place required such attitudes. Arbitrators and lawyers may construct systems in a manner consistent with the major interests they serve, particularly when the direction the law is to take is suggested in the constituent instruments of the institutions within which they operate. With the turn towards a global acceptance of market theories, a pro-investment climate came to exist, particularly in the last decade of the twentieth century. States initially accepted the expansions simply because the climate was such that there was a general belief that the existence of the system achieved mutual benefits by encouraging investment flows. It took time for them to realize that the expansionary rules created by arbitrators eroded their sovereignty more significantly than they had consented to in the treaties. Whatever benefits the system brought were countermanded by the immense costs it involved.

The expansion of the rules of jurisdiction became the first crucial step in the establishment of a neoliberal system of investment protection. It met with resistance both from arbitrators, who resisted the expansions as being inconsistent with the fundamental tenet of arbitration that jurisdiction should be based on the consent of the parties, and states, who resisted the expansion on the ground that they eroded their sovereignty in areas beyond their consent.[8] The resulting tussle brought out the

---

[6] The very first sentence of the ICSID Convention links economic development and foreign investment. It reads: 'Considering the need for international cooperation for economic development, and the role of private international investment therein.' It was premised on the classical economic view that investment promoted economic development. The Convention functions within the World Bank system, which was part of the 'Washington Consensus'. Other arbitral tribunals, such as those operating within the ICC system, were committed to ensuring that business functioned efficiently through contracts made being kept.

[7] Dezaley and Garth, *Dealing in Virtue*.

[8] Often, the arbitrators who resisted expansionary interpretation disclose the reasons for such resistance. There are many examples. In *Saluka Investments Ltd* v. *Czech Republic*, UNCITRAL PCA, Award (17 March 2006) (Watts, Fortier, Behrens), at para. 300, the

3.1 THE ORIGINAL SIN 139

tensions within the area. This chapter details the expansionary trends as to jurisdiction and the manner in which resistance to such trends built up. It begins with the consideration of an idea that opened the flood-gates of jurisdictional expansion.

3.1 The original sin[9]: 'arbitration without privity'

The major themes that are looked at in this chapter begin with a consideration of the treaty provisions, which have been held to create a unilateral right of recourse to arbitration in the foreign investor. All arbitration depends on the consent of the parties. Consent provides legitimacy to arbitration. Unlike in the case of a judge, the only condition of legitimacy of an arbitrator is the consent of the parties. It defines the extent of the powers of the arbitrators. An award that goes beyond consent loses legitimacy. The rules of all arbitral institutions uniformly recognize this most basic principle of arbitration.[10] Arbitrators are conscious that, whatever the type of arbitration, their awards become subject to challenge as having been made in excess of jurisdiction if they go beyond the power of decision the parties had entrusted to them. The resulting awards would become null and void. Early investment treaties advert to the use of arbitration as the means of settlement of disputes resulting from alleged the violations of their provisions. Some required separate agreements to arbitrate after the alleged violation had taken place.[11] In later treaties, this requirement was dispensed with and the language used indicated that such arbitrations could take place without

tribunal thought that expansion of jurisdiction would deter states from accepting investment under the treaties. The tribunal stated that 'an interpretation that exaggerates the protection to be accorded foreign investments may serve to dissuade host States from admitting investments'. In the dissent in a recent award against the use of an MFN clause to expand jurisdiction, the arbitrator stated that the 'concern that the rights and legal interests of both parties are unaltered' by interpretation. Dissent of Professor Laurence de Chazournes in *Garanti Koza LLP* v. *Turkmenistan*, ICSID, Case No. ARB/11/20 (3 July 2013).

[9] The original sin in investment arbitration was committed in *AAPL* v. *Sri Lanka*.

[10] For example, the Preamble of the ICSID Convention states: 'no Contracting State shall by the mere fact of its ratification, acceptance or approval of this Convention and without its consent be deemed to be under any obligation to submit any particular dispute to conciliation or arbitration'. The requirement of consent is dealt with again in Article 25 of the Convention.

[11] The different types of formulations on dispute settlement in early investment treaties are dealt with by Aron Broches, 'Bilateral Investment Treaties and Arbitration of Investment Disputes', in Jan C. Schultz *et al.* (eds.), *The Art of Arbitration* (Deventer: Kluwer, 1982), p. 132. They seldom contained an offer of arbitration.

140 CREATING JURISDICTION BEYOND CONSENT

an intervening agreement on arbitration. The assumption was that an unilateral offer is made as to such arbitration in investment treaties; this offer is subsequently converted to an agreement when the foreign investor accepts that unilateral offer of arbitration through a request for arbitration. This is the explanation that has been given in the different arbitral awards that have assumed jurisdiction on the basis of treaties since *AAPL* v. *Sri Lanka* (1990),[12] the first award in which the technique was used. The respondent state did not challenge jurisdiction in *AAPL* v. *Sri Lanka*. Jurisdiction was simply assumed, the tribunal observing that the cooling off period in the treaty had passed and that as a result the claimant 'became entitled to institute the ICSID proceedings'. As later explained in *AMT* v. *Zaire* (1997),[13] such jurisdiction is based on the view that the consent that is given need not be in the same instrument. Usually, consent to arbitration is contained in a single instrument, but this is not a requirement. It could be pieced together in a series of documents. In investment treaty arbitration, a series of instruments – the unilateral offer in the treaty and the recourse to arbitration made by initiation of proceedings – are connected together in creating jurisdiction in a tribunal. Such an explanation is now commonplace.[14] Whenever recourse was had to creating jurisdiction on the basis of treaty provisions, every effort was made to create privity through the process of creating consent through a chain of documents. Alternatively, there is an exchange of consents involved in two separate documents: one a treaty expressing the state's consent, and the other the consent of the foreign investor contained in the request for arbitrations. Later arbitrations assumed that this process was understood whenever recourse was had to the appropriately worded dispute settlement provision of an investment treaty.

But, early on, the phenomenon of acquiring jurisdiction through investment treaties was not explained as being consistent with the existence of an agreement and, hence, not a deviation of the general rule. It was regarded as an innovation in international arbitration akin to the domestic law situation where a consumer sues a manufacturer without

---

[12] The case was commenced in 1987 and the award was made 1990; (1990) 4 ICSID Rep. 245.

[13] ICSID Award, 21 February 1997, paras. 5.17–5.23.

[14] But later awards, at the instance of respondent states, examine the language of the dispute settlement provision in the treaty more closely. *Churchill* v. *Indonesia*, unreported ICSID Award (2014), indicates when there is appropriate language recourse that could be had to this technique. It was the view of the tribunal in the award that many Australian treaties lacked the necessary language to create automatic jurisdiction.

3.1 THE ORIGINAL SIN 141

having any privity with him. It was referred to as an instance of 'arbitration without privity'.[15] The term sacrifices accuracy for flamboyance. It set the context of exorbitant claims to arbitration that was to characterize the later course of events.

The terminology of 'arbitration without privity' suggested laxity in the manner in which jurisdiction was created. The policy justifications that were given to it accentuated this laxity. In fact, an absence of privity was contemplated when the article with the title 'arbitration without privity' stated 'that another citadel of privity is proving pregnable, this time in the realm of international arbitration'.[16] It suggested the use of an unorthodox technique when in fact a rather conventional technique of piecing together different documents to create consent was the explanation. The terminology of 'arbitration without privity' implied a startlingly permissive notion as to creation of jurisdiction on the basis of treaties. The policy justifications given enhanced such permissiveness. The policy justification was that in 'this new world of arbitration',[17] the expansion of arbitral jurisdiction over foreign investment disputes was to be welcomed. The brave new world depended on the processes of globalization, which around that time had come to be spoken of as presaging significant changes. Such a justification set the stage for a lack of future restraint in establishing jurisdiction through processes of creative interpretation of the relevant provisions of the treaty. The trend that was set has to be looked at in the light of prevailing moods. There was a preoccupation with globalization and the command of that process by markets. Foreign investment protection was linked to these trends. A euphoric belief that the coming of globalization would bring about a system of secure investment protection through arbitral tribunals having the means to obtain jurisdiction by relying on a network of investment treaties underlies the justification. As Paulsson put it, the developments 'could presage an

---

[15] As originally conceived, the term included two instances: (1) where a treaty offers arbitration to settle disputes to all foreign investors; and (2) where the domestic investment code offers such arbitration. Jan Paulsson, 'Arbitration without Privity' (1995) 10 *ICSID Review* 232.

[16] Paulsson, 'Arbitration without Privity', at p. 255. The other citadel referred to was the rule that a consumer need not show privity with a manufacturer of defective goods to institute proceedings for harm caused by use of such goods. A Canadian court suggested that in the case of NAFTA, 'there is no necessary privity between an investor and the respondent'. *Council of Canadians* v. *Attorney General of Canada* [2005] OJ No. 3422 (SCJ), at p. 31.

[17] Paulsson, 'Arbitration without Privity', at p. 232. The imagery of discovery of land is invoked. 'They have already landed on a few islands, and they have prepared maps showing a vast continent beyond.'

epochal extension of compulsory arbitral jurisdiction over states, at the behest of private litigants who wish to rely on governmental undertakings even though they have not contracted for a forum'. In 1990, the article recounted, there were 358 treaties on record.[18] It was on the basis of this number, existing at the time of *AAPL* v. *Sri Lanka*, that the permissive thesis was made. The numbers boomeranged to nearly 3,000 by the end of the decade, providing greater justification for permissiveness.

Euphoria attending globalization soon faded when its limits came to be realized. The policy justification that was advanced was hollow. Globalization, as its past history shows, is an ephemeral phenomenon. It provides an unsound basis on which to hang a whole theory that seeks to change the basis of jurisdiction in the settlement of investment disputes. Discontent with globalization was present right from the origin of its modern phase, but it set in firmly after the global economic crisis in 2008. Passion for globalization, liberalization and the free market do not exist to any considerable degree any more.[19] Interventionist policies in the United States and Europe, taken in the context of the economic crisis, indicated that the regulatory state is very much back in fashion. State capitalism practised in China indicates that there are other methods of organizing business that may lead to economic success and development.[20] This may mean that the deflation of the policy justification given for the so-called 'arbitration without privity' will result in the technique itself being scrutinized with greater care. If ideologues in favour of unlimited globalization and liberalization of flows of foreign investment had thought that foreign investors stood 'on a broad highway',[21] the fact is that the highway is now beginning to shrink in the course of the search for limits on jurisdiction.[22]

---

[18] The article stated: 'A recent survey noted that of 891 BITs on record, 533 were signed or entered into force after January 1990'.

[19] Stiglitz, *Free Fall*.

[20] China has consistently argued for other political and economic models. Stefan Halper, *Beijing Consensus: How China's Economic Model will Dominate the Twenty First Century* (New York: Basic Books, 2010).

[21] Paulsson, 'Arbitration without Privity'.

[22] Paulsson stated in 1995 that 'with most BITs, the investor is standing on a broad highway'. But the breadth of the highway has progressively diminished. In some treaties, they have become non-existent with no reference to investor–state arbitration. For example, the Japan–Philippines FTA. Australia announced that it would not make treaties with investor–state arbitration, though with a change of government it now states that it will consider inclusion of such provisions on a case-by-case basis. As indicated earlier, states have pulled out of investment arbitration. Many, like India, South Africa and Indonesia, have announced the freezing of their investment treaty programmes.

3.1 THE ORIGINAL SIN 143

Paulsson prophetically concluded his seminal article on 'arbitration without privity' with the following remarks:[23]

> Future prospects for this development in international arbitration may depend on whether national governments – many of whom may not have appreciated the full implications of the new treaty obligations discussed in this article[24] – take fright and reverse their tracks. That may in turn depend on the degree of sophistication shown by arbitrators when called upon to pass judgment on governmental actions. Arbitration without privity is a delicate mechanism. A single incident of an adventurist arbitrator may be sufficient to generate a backlash. But if the mechanism is applied judiciously, it will help fill a void that now exists in the absence of compulsory jurisdiction, and thus contribute to enhancing the legal security of international economic life.

There was not just a single incident of arbitral adventurism, but an avalanche of such incidents. Adventurist arbitrators proliferated. This has triggered a significant backlash against investment arbitration.[25]

The extent of the limits of the unilateral offer of arbitration has not been stated in many treaties.[26] A re-examination of the various methods that have been adopted on the basis of 'arbitration without privity' and other ways in which jurisdiction was expanded becomes necessary to ascertain the impact these awards have made on the development of the law. If assumption of jurisdiction was indeed faulty, serious doubts would remain as to the validity of these awards in setting the course of the law.

---

[23] Paulsson, 'Arbitration without Privity'.

[24] This is a fair statement. Even developed states like the United Kingdom may not have appreciated the extent of their treaty formulations. No writer who considered the British treaties containing language similar to the UK–Sri Lanka treaty adverted to what would have been a momentous change in terms of international law: the right of an individual to bring an action against a state unilaterally. The commentaries on the contemporary British treaties included Denza and Brooks, 'Investment Protection Treaties: The United Kingdom'. Dr Mann, a percipient observer, did not think that the language used in UK treaties was sufficient for the invocation of jurisdiction without a further agreement made by the investor. He observed that: 'The Investment Protection Agreement is a treaty between the High Contracting Parties, from which the private investor is unlikely to be able to derive any benefit unless he ensures the inclusion of a corresponding clause in the document to which he is a party.' He was analysing the UK–Philippines Treaty. Francis Mann, *Further Studies in International Law* (Oxford University Press, 1990), p. 244.

[25] Waibel *et al.* (eds.), *Backlash against Investment*.

[26] *Churchill Mining* v. *Indonesia*, ICSID, Case No. ARB/12/14 (24 February 2014), has doubted whether the formula used in some Australian treaties is correct.

3.1.1 The justification of treaty-based jurisdiction: was it faulty?

The so-called notion of 'arbitration without privity' is resorted to in two circumstances. The first is under the dispute settlement provision of a treaty. The second is under the foreign investment laws of a state when these laws hold out an offer of arbitration to all foreign investors entering the state in the belief that the protection so offered would act as an incentive to foreign investment. The second method, which is infrequent, can be dealt with briefly. In a limited number of cases, arbitral tribunals have found jurisdiction where the foreign investment laws of a host state hold out the promise to all future investors that the state will ensure the settlement of any dispute that may arise with them through arbitration. In the event of a dispute arising, it has been held that such a promise could be the foundation for jurisdiction.[27] The state, if it finds the basis of such jurisdiction unacceptable, can withdraw the unilateral offer simply by changing its own legislation.

The idea of a unilateral offer held out to third parties, which, in technical terms, did not have any standing in the context of international law,[28] would have been a strange idea not only in terms of international law, but also in terms of most, if not all, municipal legal systems of the world. The old rule in both the common law and civil law systems was that a benefit could not be conferred on a third party through contract. That being so, an offer, to all in a country, would be a legal fantasy. It would be more like an invitation to treat than an offer.[29] The common law systems, at least in 1990, did not permit stipulations in favour of third parties due to the doctrine of consideration. Legislative change was brought about to this situation in English law in 1996, well after *AAPL*

---

[27] *SPP* v. *Egypt* (1982) 3 ICSID Rep. 131.

[28] It would be difficult to analyse the status of the offer in terms of international law. The idea of such an offer being held out to an indefinite number of individuals who had uncertain status in terms of international law is a difficult one. Clearly, the offer existed only in terms of domestic law. There may be a treaty obligation to hold out such offers through domestic law to individuals who are nationals of the other contracting state. But whether such offers could be made in terms of domestic systems to yet unidentified, and unidentifiable third parties remains conjectural. Such issues have never been raised in employing this technique. Yet *Abaclat* v. *Argentina* (2012) brings out the fact that large numbers of potentially unidentifiable persons could be held to be protected through such a technique, which would be considered absurd in terms of domestic legal systems.

[29] A display of goods in the shop window is not an offer, but an invitation to treat, indicating that the goods on display are for sale.

3.1 THE ORIGINAL SIN

v. *Sri Lanka*.[30] It is difficult to understand how a British treaty could adopt the technique of an offer of arbitration to all when such a contract resulting from an acceptance by a third party is not possible in terms of the English law. Both the United Kingdom and Sri Lanka are common law countries, though Sri Lanka also has a Roman Dutch basis.[31] In the Roman Dutch Law, as applied in Sri Lanka, the Roman law view that a *stipulatio alteri* could not be made, except in certain limited circumstances, has continued to hold.[32] Such stipulations are permitted under stringently controlled circumstances. Yet, in 1990, we have the situation, in a weak legal system – international law – of investment treaties creating stipulations in favour of foreign investment corporations, which have limited, or, some would say, no, personality in terms of international law and are a potentially unknowable entity to the host state until after the investment is made, being given the unique advantage of an hitherto unknown idea of having a unilateral recourse to arbitration against a state.[33] Several hurdles would have to be jumped to reach such a unique situation. No international lawyer paused to consider the monumental steps that had been taken to achieve this situation relating to 'arbitration without privity'.[34] It is legitimate to question why there was such silence in the face of such a seemingly major advancement in the law.

Recourse to international tribunals to remedy abuse was not unknown to international law. In the area of human rights law, in exceptional instances, it is possible for an individual, in certain more advanced regional systems, to petition human rights courts specially set up by regional treaties. Here more important values, such as the fundamental rights of an individual, are threatened.[35] Yet the machinery devised in the

---

[30] Reform of the English law followed upon the presentation of a report by the Law Revision Committee on the subject. Law Revision Committee, *The Third Party Rule of Contract for Benefit of the Third Party*, Law Comm. No. 242, Law Commission, London, 1996.

[31] In the Roman Dutch law, as introduced in Sri Lanka, there was a strong prohibition against the *stipulatio alteri*. Robert Warden Lee, *Introduction to Roman Dutch Law* (Oxford University Press, 1962), Appendix 1.

[32] In the Roman law, a principal exception to the rule, *nemo potest stipulatio alteri* is the *donatio mortis causa* and possibly the *fideicommissum*. Both are testamentary devices.

[33] Comparison with regional human rights law is not apposite. The citizen of the state is known to the state. The state's local remedies have to be exhausted. There are filters before the matter could be raised before the regional human rights court.

[34] Article 36 of the Vienna Convention on the Law of Treaties deals with treaties made in favour of third states, but the position of an individual having rights under a treaty is not contemplated.

[35] There were some justificatory writings in which the right to property under investment treaties was compared with the rights under the human rights conventions. The defects in

regional treaties on human rights carefully circumscribes the right of petition. There is no right of petition unless it can be shown that local remedies have been exhausted. Jurisdiction is not automatic. A commission would ensure that there is a case to argue. Where the state takes measures necessary to protect its national security or to regulate its public interests, the courts have ruled that a wide margin of appreciation should be given to the state to determine the need for such measures. The law that has been developed in the regions of the Western world in safeguarding more valuable interests than foreign investment seems to require higher jurisdictional standards than those devised for multinational corporations operating in developing countries. The comparison also calls for the questioning of the disparity in the standards applied in the two areas. There has been an unquestioning attitude on the part of European and American international lawyers, where such human rights systems operate, to the system of virtually unlimited jurisdiction under investment treaties.

Progressively, there were limitations on arbitral adventurism that sought to extend the scope of 'arbitration without privity'. They can be attributed perhaps to a realization that without limits the notion of expansive jurisdiction will do damage to the system and will amount to assumption of jurisdiction without the consent of the parties. States were naturally interested in bringing about change, at least in their newer treaties in which they spelled out changes restricting the broad interpretations made by arbitral tribunals. Some arbitrators saw the damage the broad interpretation, unsupported by principle, was doing to the system and sought to rein in the excesses.

3.1.2 Extreme adventurism

Despite strains within the system, such arbitral adventurism relating to jurisdiction has not ended. *Abaclat* v. *Argentina* (2012)[36] represents the most recent and damaging of the arbitral adventures. Its confirmation in *Ambiente Ufficio* v. *Argentina* (2013)[37] compounds the problem. Both

---

such comparisons were obvious. Recourse was had to a permanent system of courts, like the European Court. There was a duty to exhaust local remedies. There was a screening process through the office of the Advocate General.

[36] (2011) ICSID, Case No. ARB/07/5 (4 August 2011) (Tercier, Van den Berg; Abi-Saab, dissenting).

[37] ICSID Case No. ARB/08/9 (8 February 2013) (Simma, Bockstiegel; Torres Bernadez, dissenting).

had strong dissenting opinions. Both held that Italian holders of financial instruments issued by Argentina could bring class actions under the Argentina–Italian investment treaty. The awards not only recognize that financial instruments constitute investments, but also that their holders could collectively bring an arbitration against the issuing state. The awards in *Abaclat* and *Ambiente Ufficio* were made in full awareness of the difficulties that investment arbitration was facing. They added two heavy straws to the camel's creaking back. *Abaclat* and *Ambiente* provoked strong dissent. The two recent awards need separate treatment. But it is important to flag the cases for the reason that they signal that the tendencies towards neoliberal adventurism are by no means ended. The extent of this adventurism and the efforts to end it require attention.

3.2 Restricting arbitral adventurism

There were several major restrictions on jurisdiction under treaties that had developed which need examination, as the making of these exceptions indicated a tussle between contending ideas representing different visions of investment arbitration. Expansive jurisdiction would have diminished the significance of these limitations, whereas fidelity to the norms of arbitration that required jurisdiction to be founded on the basis of strict consent would have supported the making of these restrictions. The restrictions that came to be recognized need consideration in order to show that they also involved a competition between distinct approaches.

The schisms that have developed in treaty-based investment arbitration are deep. In explaining them, it is too facile an argument to say that every dispute involves a choice between two equally tenable, competing rights.[38] This notion is a subterfuge to preserve the neutrality of the law and the idea that the decision-maker applies the law in a neutral fashion, making a difficult choice between two tenable views. They also call for an assumption of the equal validity of either solution. In the situation of jurisdiction in arbitration, particularly against a sovereign state, the consent of the state to arbitration has to be clearly demonstrated. The idea that there is a conflict between two contending interests or rights is inapposite. The existence of two equally permissible solutions is the dominant, positivist explanation used to portray the law as a neutral

[38] Andres Rigo-Sureda, *Investment Treaty Arbitration: Judging under Uncertainty* (Cambridge University Press, 2012).

148 CREATING JURISDICTION BEYOND CONSENT

purveyor of values, and the decision-maker as a disinterested applier of the law to the dispute before him. It is a fiction that hides the power considerations that shape the legal principle and the prejudices that influence the decision-maker in applying such law. In the instances of expansion of jurisdictional notions in investment arbitrations, many arbitrators expanded the law in a way that served their philosophical and ideological inclinations. The explanation that is advanced in this work is that this group of arbitrators subscribed to the instrumental use of the law so as to devise a strong system of investment protection in keeping with the neoliberal sentiments of the times. There were, equally, arbitrators who were conscious of the damage such expansionist views would cause to the system and resisted such expansions. In *Saluka*, for example, the tribunal stated that 'an interpretation that exaggerates the protection to be accorded foreign investments may serve to dissuade host States from admitting investments'.[39] The result, it appears, could be worse. They could exit the system altogether.

Some arbitrators have recognized a conflict between two positions. They suggested a Taoist balance to reconcile the conflict between investment protection and the extent of the state consent: 'These two aspects must always be held in tension. They are the *yin* and *yang* of bilateral investment treaties and cannot be separated without doing violence to the will of the states that conclude such treaties.'[40] It is obviously inappropriate on this view to upset the balance by tilting it in favour of investment protection.

Arbitrators with expertise in jurisdiction of international tribunals have been concerned with the manner in which their counterparts have been extending jurisdiction beyond the consent of states. One arbitrator, Professor Laurence Boisson de Chazournes, was constrained to state the first principles of jurisdiction in disputes involving states as follows:[41]

> The trust and confidence in third-party adjudication is dependent on the respect by international courts and tribunals of the limits to the jurisdiction conferred upon them. Tribunals should not create a *de facto* system of compulsory jurisdiction, which in the present stage of positive international law remains the exception. The international legal order still rests largely on a system of facultative jurisdiction, and because of that essential

[39] *Saluka Investments* v. *Czech Republic*, UNCITRAL PCA, Award (17 March 2006), para. 300.
[40] *Daimler Financial Services* v. *Argentina*, ICSID, Case No. ARB/05/1 (22 August 2012), para. 161 (Dupuy, Janeiro; Brower dissenting).
[41] Dissent in *Garanti Koza LLP* v. *Turkmenistan*, ICSID, Case No. ARB/11/20 (3 July 2013).

3.2 RESTRICTING ARBITRAL ADVENTURISM 149

characteristic, a tribunal should never attempt to impose its jurisdiction and adjudicate the merits of a dispute when the parties have not consented to its jurisdiction. The ICSID arbitration system is not an exception to that approach. BITs were never concluded by sovereign states with the idea that a third-party adjudicator would then empower himself or herself with the authority to embark on 'consent shopping'.

There was an obvious need to restate such an elementary proposition only because the practice in investment arbitration was moving away from the conventional wisdom in arbitration. The law became a tussle between two groups of arbitrators, one tending towards expansion on the ground that the objective of investment protection justifies such a course, and the other maintaining that fidelity to the system requires strict construction of the extent of the consent. This is demonstrated in the contest between arbitrators that is triggered when expansionary interpretations of the treaty bases of jurisdiction are made.

The tussle took place in the principal areas dealt with below. In these areas, expansionist tendencies confronted strict fidelity to discovering consent. In both circumstances, it is interesting to note that parties had recourse to determining the real intention of the states using the rules of interpretation of treaties. Both groups of arbitrators resorted to the principles in the Vienna Convention on the Law of Treaties in arriving at starkly contrasting results.[42]

The techniques of interpretation used by the two groups vary. Both use teleological interpretations when it suits them. Equally, both groups are strict constructionists when their aims are furthered by strict construction. This selective use of the different techniques of interpretation needs explanation. The explanation that is offered here is on the basis of the tussle between two ideological positions rather than on the basis of legal techniques of interpretation. Expediency dictates the selection of the rule of interpretation rather than principle. In the tussle between the two opposing camps, there is a selective use of the techniques of interpretation, indicating an alarming deviation from the norms of interpretation prescribed in international law. This deviation can only be explained on non-legal grounds where there is such subjectivity in decisions in investment arbitration that much depends on the ideological predisposition of

---

[42] For studies on the use of the Vienna Convention on the Law of Treaties, see Romesh Weeramantry, *Treaty Interpretation in Investment Arbitration* (Oxford University Press, 2012); Trin Hai Yen, 'Interpretations of Investment Treaties', PhD dissertation, Faculty of Law, National University of Singapore, 2013 (forthcoming as a book published by Martinus Nijhoff).

the arbitrators who constitute the tribunals. This chapter is concerned with how these techniques are used in jurisdiction.

The first of the areas in which a challenge arose was that the claimant must prove that the transaction he or she made was in fact an investment both in terms of the treaty and the ICSID Convention. In this area, there is a definite clash between the two views. Arbitrators who favour the narrower definition of investment that foreign investment must contain economic development as a characteristic use a teleological interpretation founded in the preamble of the treaty that identifies economic development as its object. Arbitrators who rely on the definition in the treaty provisions take the view that one must construe the provisions on the definition of investments in order to find the characteristics of the protected investment. The second area relates to the requirement that the investment should be made in accordance with the laws of the host state. The third, to the manipulation of the concept of corporate nationality so as to enhance forum shopping. The fourth, to the extension of protection to a wider category of persons deemed to be foreign investors, including those who held minority shares in privatized industries. The fifth, to the use of the MFN clause in investment treaties so that the foreign investor could either enhance jurisdictional choices or the nature of the substantive rules of protection by latching onto other treaties of the host state containing more preferable standards of treatment. The sixth, relates to recent trends to expand protection to financial instruments.

The trends discussed in each of these areas indicates a tussle between two binary tendencies within investment arbitration. Each of the areas deserves more elaborate treatment than is given here. But the purpose in considering them is to illustrate the extent of the changes effected on the treaty principles and the nature of the resistance that resulted from the changes. Since the expansive interpretation was the more prominent of the tendencies, state intervention was often necessary to redress the changes. As will be shown, mere intervention by states to amend treaty provisions to restrict expansionism did not always have the desired effect of curbing arbitral expansionism. Often, the arbitrators ensured that the efforts states made to curb the expansions through alterations in the treaty terms were thwarted through reinterpretation, reducing the significance of the changes.[43]

---

[43] An example is the introduction of the denial of benefits provision into the treaty.

3.2 RESTRICTING ARBITRAL ADVENTURISM 151

3.2.1 The definition of investment and the criterion of economic development

Investment treaties contain definitions of protected investments. Treaties create jurisdiction only if the disputes arise from investments as defined in the treaties. Where the jurisdiction of an ICSID tribunal is invoked, there is the additional requirement under Article 25(1) of the ICSID Convention that the dispute submitted to resolution by an ICSID tribunal must arise from an investment. The ICSID Convention leaves investment undefined. The investment treaty, on the other hand, usually contains a very comprehensive definition of a protected investment, referring to tangible and intangible rights of the foreign investor and including any business concession obtained from the host state. The concept of an investment therefore becomes crucial for jurisdiction.[44] The subject matter of the dispute must qualify as arising from an investment. The issue has therefore become doubly significant before ICSID tribunals. This does not mean that it is not significant for other tribunals.

The objective criteria identified in the *Salini* Award[45] for determining whether the transaction amounted to an investment for determining jurisdiction of an ICSID tribunal has been the subject of much controversy. The problem arises as a result of a 'double-barrel' approach in ICSID disputes.[46] Though the investment may satisfy the broad definition of an investment in the investment treaty so as to fall within the scope of the state's consent to jurisdiction, for ICSID jurisdiction it must also satisfy the requirement mandated by the ICSID Convention in Article 25(1). Article 25(1) confines the jurisdiction of an ICSID tribunal to 'any legal dispute arising directly out of an investment'. The term 'investment' is left undefined in the Convention.[47] Though investment treaties define investments broadly as including any type of assets and usually list the assets included in the definition of assets, the problem created is that transactions that would not normally be considered investments are included in the definition. Thus, claims to money are included in the treaty list but, clearly such claims to money could arise

---

[44] Schreuer, *The ICSID Convention: A Commentary*.

[45] *Salini Construttori ApA* v. *Morocco*, ICSID, Case No. ARB/00/4 (23 July 2001).

[46] *Malaysian Historical Salvors SDN, BHD* v, *Malaysia*, ICSID, Case No. ARB/05/10, Jurisdiction Award (17 May 2007), para. 55.

[47] There was disagreement as to the definition. It was a deliberate decision to leave the term undefined. Schreuer, *The ICSID Convention: A Commentary*, p. 115.

152   CREATING JURISDICTION BEYOND CONSENT

from transactions that could not be considered investments.[48] Tribunals agree that there is an objective meaning of an investment. Such a meaning cannot be changed by the agreement of the parties.[49] As a result, as far as ICSID arbitration is concerned, some tribunals, such the one in *Salini*, have attempted to define the characteristics of an investment by identifying indicia that are contained in an investment. They are: 'contributions, a certain duration of performance of the contract and a participation in the risks of the transaction'.[50] These criteria themselves are controversial, there being a strong view that the criteria merely provide guidance and are not to be treated as inflexible factors in determining whether a transaction is an investment.[51] But the *Salini* tribunal added a fourth criterion, which has proved even more controversial. The tribunal stated that 'in reading the Convention's preamble, one may add the contribution to the economic development of the host state of the investment as an additional condition'. This is a relevant criterion as both the ICSID Convention and investment treaties are premised on the belief that foreign investments lead to the economic development of the host state. In fact, the World Bank would have no mandate to run an arbitration facility like ICSID unless it is connected to economic development. It has no mandate to run general arbitration facilities. The carrot that was continuously held out to developing states when negotiating the ICSID Convention was that the existence of secure facilities for dispute settlement would promote their economic development through flows of foreign investment. The argument would be that if the investment is shown to be incapable of securing such economic development, then, it ceases to be a protected investment under the treaty, as the aim of economic development as an object appears in the preamble of the treaties. It also ceases to be an investment in respect of which consent

---

[48] An example is where the underlying transaction from which the claim to money arises does not fall within the definition of investment.

[49] *CSOB v. Slovakia*, ICSID Arbitration, Jurisdiction (21 May 1999), para. 55; *Joy Mining v. Egypt*, ICSID, Case No. ARB/03/11 (6 August 2004), para. 50.

[50] Contribution and duration of at least five years are stated as indicia in the first draft of the ICSID Convention. Schreuer, *The ICSID Convention: A Commentary*, p. 115. Schreuer relied on *CSOB* in suggesting that there must be significant contributions to the host state's economy.

[51] There is much literature on definition of an investment. See, e.g., David Williams and Simon Foote, 'Recent Developments in the Approach to Identifying "Investment" Pursuant to Article 25(1) of the ICSID Convention', in Chester Brown and Kate Miles (eds.), *Evolution in Investment Treaty Law and Arbitration* (Cambridge University Press, 2011), p. 42.

was given under Article 25 of the ICSID Convention, as an investment relevant under the Convention must promote economic development as such development is an object of the Convention. The view that this criterion could apply only to ICSID arbitration and not to other arbitration under ad hoc tribunals using the UNCITRAL Rules is misplaced, as investment treaties are also premised on the notion that investment flows that the treaties promote would result in economic development.[52] Besides, as UNCITRAL tribunals have pointed out, investment has an objective meaning, which includes economic development as a criterion.

The issue of whether economic development is a necessary consideration in determining jurisdiction has become a hotly debated one, resulting in inconsistent arbitral awards. Another schism has been opened up in the area on an initial issue relating to the assumption of jurisdiction not foreseen at the time of the euphoric pronouncement as to arbitration without privity. The issue ultimately boils down to whether consent for arbitration of that type of transaction was in fact contemplated by the parties. The argument is that the agreement, both under the ICSID Convention as well as under the investment treaties, was to protect only such investments as would promote the economic development of the host state. Expansionist views, however, do not accept the making of this requirement, taking the view that once the investment treaty defines investment in wide terms, the definition is reflective of the necessary consent of the states and that it is impermissible to look to the preamble to discover additional factors. This does not, however, get over the hurdle presented by Article 25 of the ICSID Convention. The expansionists tend to soft-pedal the fact that Article 25 and the ICSID Convention may be premised on economic development. Instead, they emphasize the paramountcy of the treaty definition. The schism can be expected to continue.

Among the awards that require economic development as an indicator of an investment is the annulment decision in *Mitchell v. Congo*.[53]

---

[52] Emmanuelle Cabrol, '*Pren Nreka* v. *Czech Republic* and the Notion of Investment under Bilateral Investment Treaties', (2010) 2 *Yearbook of International Investment Law* 217. *Claimant* v. *Slovak Republic*, UNCITRAL Ad Hoc Arbitration (Crivallaro, Stuber, Klein) (5 March 2011), indicated that unless there is economic development ensuing from the contract, the investment would fall outside the purpose of the treaty and would not be a protected investment.

[53] *Patrick Mitchell* v. *Congo*, ICSID, Case No. ARB/99/7, Annulment Award (1 November 2006) (Dimolistsa, Dossou, Giardina). The Committee cited (at para. 31) Schreuer's view that the 'only possible objective meaning that can be gleaned from the Convention is contained in the Preamble's first sentence which speaks of the "need for international cooperation for economic development and the role of private international investment

154 CREATING JURISDICTION BEYOND CONSENT

Essentially, it held that provision of legal services does not contribute to the economic development of the state and hence could not amount to an investment justifying assumption of jurisdiction.

The *Malaysian Salvors* case could be taken as a setting for the discussion of the issue. The question was whether a contract for services for the salvage of artefacts of archaeological significance from an historical wreck made with a government agency could be regarded as an investment qualifying for protection under the investment treaty. The award in *Malaysian Salvors* v. *Malaysia* characterized a salvage contract as a services contract and not an investment.[54] In doing so, it surveyed the existing awards on the definition of an investment and found that there was disagreement on the requirement of economic development.

The sole arbitrator could more easily have dealt with the issue as to whether there was an approved investment involved in terms of the treaty, as there was already an award involving Malaysia, *Gruslin* v. *Malaysia*,[55] which denied jurisdiction under the same UK–Malaysia treaty on the ground that there was no approved investment for purposes of protection under the treaty. Malaysia had pleaded absence of approval as a jurisdictional defence. Instead, the arbitrator chose to deal with the issue of investment, which was the first issue presented to him.

The sole arbitrator analysed the existing cases and discovered two approaches, one tending to place great emphasis on the hallmarks necessary for an investment, the other inclining to regard them as providing guidance only. He conceded that the both approaches required a practical outcome. He then interpreted existing cases in the light of his own two-type construct. To that extent, the discussion and analysis of the trends is otiose and of little utility to the more crucial issue of whether economic development was a necessary component of an investment for purposes of the jurisdiction of an ICSID tribunal. The sole arbitrator recognized this when he said: 'In practice, it is unlikely that any difference in juristic analysis would make any significant difference to the ultimate finding of the tribunal.'

---

therein ... ". Therefore, it may be argued that the Convention's object and purpose indicate that there should be some positive impact on development.'

[54] *Malaysian Historical Salvors SDN, BHD* v. *Malaysia*, ICSID, Case No. ARB/05/10 (17 May 2007) (Hwang, sole arbitrator).

[55] *Gruslin* v. *Malaysia*, ICSID, Case No. ARB/99/3 (27 November 2000) (Griffith, sole arbitrator).

3.2 RESTRICTING ARBITRAL ADVENTURISM   155

The crucial issue was the discussion as to whether the need for economic development was a constituent element of an investment. On this, the sole arbitrator found that the existing awards were in agreement that this component was necessary. The only disagreement was whether it was a separate component or whether it was already included in the elements of substantial contribution, duration and risk.[56] The annulment award in *Patrick Mitchell* was clear in requiring that economic development was a necessary and independent component of an investment. The sole arbitrator concluded that an economic contribution was an essential component of the investment necessary for jurisdiction.[57] As he had concluded that the first three requirements had been marginally satisfied, he was left to consider whether a significant contribution to economic development was a necessary component and whether it had been satisfied on the facts of the case. He concluded that what was involved was a service contract and that it was unlikely to constitute a significant contribution to the economy of the host state. This constituted the basis of the award. The finding was the focus of the annulment award. It would have been simpler if the decision was that a service contract did not constitute an investment.

But the Annulment Committee[58] decided that economic development was not a necessary criterion for an investment, the criteria listed in the different awards being indicative only and not final determinations.[59] Judge Schwebel, a former President of the ICJ, chaired the Annulment Committee in *Malaysian Salvors*. Judge Tomka, the current President of the ICJ, joined with him in making the award. Judge Shahabudeen, a former Judge of the ICJ, dissented.[60] Judge Schwebel has emphasized the importance of investment treaties in investment protection. His views on investment law have generally favoured regarding the investment treaties

---

[56] *Bayinder* v. *Pakistan*, ICSID, Case No. ARB/03/29 (Kaufman-Kohler, Berman, Bockstiegel), stated that economic development could be subsumed under the other criteria, but thought that there may be instances where the issue may arise independently and economic development may become an issue.

[57] 'The Tribunal considers that the weight of the authorities cited above swings in favour of requiring a significant contribution to be made to the host State's economy', *Malaysian Salvors* v. *Malaysia* (17 May 2007) (Hwang, sole arbitrator), para. 123.

[58] *Malaysian Historical Salvors SDN, BHD* v. *Malaysia*, ICSID Case No. ARB/05/10, Annulment Committee Decision (16 April 2009) (Schwebel, Tomka; Shahabudeen dissenting).

[59] Also see *Biwater Gauff* v. *Tanzania*, ICSID, Case No. ARB/05/22, Award (24 July 2008).

[60] An issue of concern is whether judges, present and past, of the ICJ should sit on such arbitrations, which call for expression of ideological biases.

156   CREATING JURISDICTION BEYOND CONSENT

as customary law and as providing a strong framework for the protection of investments.[61] The Annulment Report stated:[62]

> While it may not have been foreseen at the time of the adoption of the ICSID Convention, when the number of bilateral investment treaties in force were few, since that date some 2,800 bilateral, and three important multilateral, treaties have been concluded, which characteristically define investment in broad, inclusive terms such as those illustrated by the above-quoted Article 1 of the Agreement between Malaysia and the United Kingdom. Some 1,700 of those treaties are in force, and the multilateral treaties, particularly the Energy Charter Treaty, which are in force, by themselves endow ICSID with an important jurisdictional reach. It is those bilateral and multilateral treaties, which today are the engine of ICSID's effective jurisdiction. To ignore or depreciate the importance of the jurisdiction they bestow upon ICSID, and rather to embroider upon questionable interpretations of the term 'investment' as found in Article 25(1) of the Convention, risks crippling the institution.

On this teleological reasoning that the jurisdiction of the ICSID should be conserved and expanded, priority has to be given to the definition in the investment treaty. There is nothing in the ICSID Convention or the investment treaties that justify the interpretation. It is the assumption that in view of the increasing number of investment treaties, the jurisdiction of the ICSID should be expanded and not contracted, even if there is no textual authority for this view. It is at best a subjective policy preference. The reasoning is faulty, as the Malaysia–UK treaty does not protect all investments defined as investments under the treaty, but only 'approved investments', thereby requiring an additional criterion of approval prior to protection being granted. Neither do all treaties protect all investments uniformly so that customary international law could evolve. The premises on which Judge Schwebel's reasoning rest do not support that a uniform rule as to the protected investments could be drawn. It is based on the fallacy that all treaties are alike when they are not, and that all treaties provide for arbitration without privity to the same extent.

Treaties do not protect investments that prove to be harmful to the state. Certainly, the new balanced treaties are premised on many defences that would exclude the possibility of harmful investments being the basis

---

[61] He has indicated displeasure with the new 2004 US Model Treaty, which departs from the earlier emphasis on investment protection, lowers standards of treatment and contains preclusionary factors that enable the avoidance of responsibility. Schwebel, 'The Influence of Bilateral Investment Treaties on Customary International Law', 27.

[62] *Malaysian Salvors* v. *Malaysia*, Annulment Committee Decision, Report, para. 75.

3.2 RESTRICTING ARBITRAL ADVENTURISM 157

of responsibility. The requirement of economic development seeks, *in limine*, to pursue the question at a later stage of the arbitration. The nature of the investment may be visible at the outset by having regard to the investment and the circumstances that gave rise to the dispute. By requiring the proof of the element of economic development as a characteristic of foreign investment, the dispute as to the worthiness of the investment for protection is merely being advanced to the jurisdictional phase so that it could be disposed of early. This may not be to the personal advantage of arbitrators, but it is certainly a rule that promotes the interests of investment arbitration, which is confined to settlement of disputes that arise from investments protected on the basis of their capacity to generate economic development and not from deleterious investments.

Judge Shahabudeen, in his dissenting opinion, stated the position that economic development is an essential criterion for an investment. He drew this conclusion for a variety of reasons. The first was that an investment that maximized the wealth of the foreign investor without profiting the host state would receive protection contrary to the purpose of the investment treaty as well as the ICSID Convention, if economic development was not a criterion of the protected investment.[63] The second was that 'the preamble reflects an inference that the very purpose of an ICSID investment is to contribute to the economic development of the host State'.[64] As indicated earlier, the crucial factor is that ICSID itself was created for the purpose of fostering economic development, and that the World Bank has no mandate to run arbitral services if not for the connection, tenuous or not, between arbitration of investment disputes and economic development. Besides, ICSID was touted to the developing states as necessary for their economic development on the ground that the provision of secure settlement of foreign investment disputes would enable flows of foreign investment into states otherwise thought of as lacking in neutral facilities for dispute settlement.

The four arbitrators involved in *Malaysian Salvors* split equally on the need for economic development as a criterion of a protected investment. Mr Hwang, the sole arbitrator making the initial jurisdictional award, and Judge Shahabudeen of the Annulment Committee who required that there be proof that the investment promoted economic development. Judges Schwebel and Tomka, who constituted the majority on the Annulment Committee, took the opposite view. The case is interesting

---

[63] Paragraph 22 of the dissenting report.   [64] Paragraph 28 of the dissenting report.

as it brings into profile the nature of the dissension that takes place among arbitrators, ultimately traceable to their preferred ideological approaches to foreign investment protection and to international law.

Whether the annulment award could focus on this issue under the terms of its powers as specified in Article 52 of the ICSID Convention is contentious. The Annulment Committee may interfere only on the basis of the violation of some specified procedural requirements in the making of the award. The Committee sought to pronounce on a purely legal view taken by the sole arbitrator. His view was taken on the basis of existing authority. The award was based on a logical basis of reasoning and was a very possible view. Annulment is permissible under the ICSID Convention only on the basis of the procedural faults stated in Article 51 of the Convention and not on the basis of the merits of the award. Yet much of the Annulment Committee's decision focuses on the legal issue of whether the additional requirement of a contribution to the economy of the host state was a necessary component of an investment under Article 25(1) of the ICSID Convention. An error as to law cannot amount to a manifest excess of jurisdiction in the normal course. Given the number of awards which supported the sole arbitrator, it would be difficult to regard his award as an error of law. In any event, such an error is not a manifest excess of jurisdiction justifying annulment.[65] The Annulment Committee was in error in suggesting annulment.

The majority of the annulment tribunal gave priority to the definition of investment contained in the investment treaty itself, and marked the failure of the sole arbitrator to deal with the treaty definition as a manifest error. By giving priority to the investment agreement over the jurisdictional provision of the ICSID Convention, the majority report was able to shift the focus onto the broader definition of the investment in the investment treaty. This may not be a permissible technique, for Article 25 states that the consent of the parties, here evinced in the investment treaty, cannot broaden the jurisdiction of the ICSID tribunal. The majority report points out that that the investment agreement between Malaysia and the United Kingdom defines an investment very broadly to include claims to money and a performance under contract having financial value. The contract of salvage may qualify as an investment on this ground. The reasoning is faulty as it looks only at the provision

---

[65] In *CMS* v. *Argentina*, ICSID, Case No. ARB/01/8 (25 September 2007) (Guillaume, Elaraby and Crawford), the Annulment Committee found several errors in the application of the law, but denied it had the power to interfere with the award.

3.2 RESTRICTING ARBITRAL ADVENTURISM 159

defining an investment and fails to read the investment treaty as a whole. The preamble to the investment treaty states that the parties made the treaty in the belief that the investment flow would secure economic prosperity to the parties. It states the belief that the protection of the investment will secure 'the economic prosperity of both states'. Clearly, a contract that does not contribute to the economic prosperity of the state is excluded. The investment is protected only if it is approved. The implication is that such investments will not be approved unless there is significant economic benefits that are brought to the host state. The majority report does not look at the definition of investment in the context of the express provisions of the treaty or its purpose of obtaining flows of beneficial investments through the protection provided by the treaty. It is not any investment that is protected, but investments that advance economic prosperity, as the preamble states. There must be a quid pro quo for the treaty, which involves a surrender of sovereign rights of the state. The protection of all investments does not, by itself, secure the extent of the benefit that justifies the surrender of sovereign rights of control over that investment through the treaty. Though much is made of principles of interpretation of treaties in the majority report in *Malaysian Salvors*, the report ignores the need to read the treaty in the context of its other provisions as well as its purpose.[66] The Award is an instance where the Vienna Convention on the Law of Treaties is called in aid to support pre-arrived conclusions that do not fit in with its prescription that the provisions of the treaty are paramount in determining their meaning, and that the treaty must be interpreted having its purpose in view. An investment treaty was never intended to protect an investment from which 'its economy received no benefit whatsoever'.[67]

There is selectivity shown in the argument of the majority in stating that the only avenue for redress under the investment treaty is through ICSID arbitration provided in Article 7, and that not providing such arbitration would make the treaty redundant. This gives an impression that tribunals belonging to other institutions do not require the satisfaction of objective criteria of investment. Practice shows otherwise.[68]

---

[66] The majority report states that 'the Committee is unable to see what support the Sole Arbitrator could have mustered to sustain the conclusion that the Contract and its implementation did not constitute an investment within the meaning of that Agreement'. This is untrue. As suggested, the preamble of the investment treaty could have been relied on. The respondent had raised the need for approval.

[67] *Claimant* v. *Slovak Republic*, at para. 235.

[68] Cabrol, '*Prem Nreka* v. *Czech Republic* and the Notion of Investment'.

CREATING JURISDICTION BEYOND CONSENT

UNCITRAL tribunals, which have now garnered a substantial number of investment treaty arbitrations, require an objective basis for an investment so that jurisdiction can be satisfied.[69] An UNCITRAL tribunal in *Romak* v. *Uzbekistan* specifically rejected the reasoning of the majority of the Annulment Committee. The *Romak* tribunal, considering the view that there was broader jurisdiction under the terms of other institutional tribunals than in the case of the ICSID because of issues relating to the definition of jurisdiction in Article 25 of the ICSID Convention, said that such views 'would imply that the substantive protection offered by the BIT would be narrowed or widened, as the case may be, merely by virtue of a choice between the various dispute resolution mechanisms sponsored by the Treaty. This would be both absurd and unreasonable.'[70] The objective requirement of an investment for purposes of investment treaty arbitration requires economic development as a criterion simply because investment treaties are made on the assumption that the investment flows that take place contribute to the economic prosperity of the host state.

The majority report in *Malaysian Salvors* also stresses the *travaux preparatoires* of the ICSID Convention and the reason for the absence of a definition of investment in Article 25. There was clear disagreement among the delegates as to the definition of an investment. The decision to leave the concept undefined in the belief that the necessary qualifying investment can be recognized requires conclusions to be drawn as to the type of investment from the nature of both the Convention as well as the investment treaty. It was always assumed that objective, inherent criteria exist for an investment and practice also shows it.[71]

---

[69] *Romak* v. *Uzbekistan*, UNCITRAL PCA, Case AA 280, Award (26 November 2009) (Mantilla-Serano, Rubins, Molfessis), refused to assume jurisdiction over a wheat supply contract under the Switzerland–Uzbekistan treaty. Further, see Judith Levine, 'Navigating the Parallel Universe of Investor–State Arbitrations under UNCITRAL Rules', in Chester Brown and Kate Miles (eds.), *Evolution in Investment Treaty Law and Arbitration* (Cambridge University Press, 2011), p. 368, at pp. 398–9. See also for a later UNCITRAL case, *Alps Finance and Trade* v. *Slovak Republic*, UNCITRAL Arbitration (Stuber, Klein, Crivellaro (5 March 2011). Also see to a similar effect, *Claimant* v. *Slovak Republic*, UNCITRAL Ad Hoc Arbitration (5 March 2011). *Alps Finance* concluded that this is also the outcome under customary international law as well as under the treaties. But *White Industries* v. *India*, UNCITRAL, Arbitration (30 November 2011) (Rowley, Brower, Lau), took a different position relying entirely on the definition in the treaty.

[70] The tribunal was here speaking of a treaty that gave an option between ICSID and UNCITRAL arbitration. But the reasoning would apply where only ICSID arbitration was chosen. A BIT is also conditioned on economic development.

[71] Awards rely on the fact that the secretary general had on one occasion refused to register a dispute arising from a sale of goods agreement. See *Salini* v. *Morocco*, para. 52.

3.2 RESTRICTING ARBITRAL ADVENTURISM 161

The reference in the majority report to the existence of a large number of investment treaties having broad definitions of investment is not convincing, and is again made on a superficial assumption that investment treaties are uniform. The definition of investments that are protected by the treaty are qualified in various ways. As in the case of the UK–Malaysia treaty involved in *Malaysian Salvors*, many treaties protect only approved investments. Other treaties provide protection only to treaties made 'in accordance with the laws and regulations' of each state party. Given such uncertainty, the point made that there is a large network of treaties creating jurisdiction in the ICSID does not add much except to indicate that Judge Schwebel's unacceptable view that the bilateral investment treaties, because of their sameness, contribute to customary international law finds resonance in the award. With the increasing trend towards so-called 'balanced treaties', with the balance struck differently in each treaty, the view taken by Judge Schwebel will become even more tenuous.

The strong dissent of Judge Shahabudeen from the majority report of the Annulment Committee considerably weakens the force of the majority report. He believes that to begin the consideration with the investment treaty is 'to stand the analysis on its head'. He also thought that there was no manifest excess of powers justifying annulment. Having observed that the 'context does speak', he found that the context of the ICSID Convention, the parties to the Convention, 'fell to be considered as having impliedly accepted that an ICSID Convention must contribute to the economic development of the host state'.

One aspect of that context was that ICSID arbitration was administered by the International Bank of Reconstruction and Development. Article 2 of the ICSID Convention stated that the seat of the centre shall be at the International Bank of Reconstruction and Development. This indicated that the subject matter of the arbitrations conducted by the ICSID had to do with the functions of the bank, which were reconstruction and development. Member states had an obligation to defray deficits of the ICSID. Such a burden would not have been undertaken to benefit private contractors seeking their own profits. As stated, there was no intention on the part of the states that created the bank to provide general arbitration facilities, but to provide for the creation of the ICSID on the ground that it would promote economic development by facilitating the settlement of investment disputes.

There was a need to join battle on this crucial issue, and the battle lines were divided on ideological grounds. Clearly, those seeking to advance investment protection saw the need for wide definitions of investment and sought arguments that would favour such wide definitions so as to broaden the scope of the jurisdiction of investment tribunals over larger categories of transactions. Those seeking to protect the interests of states wanted to restrict jurisdiction by insisting on the qualification relating to economic development. The latter group showed greater fidelity to the rules of interpretation of the investment treaty, which required that they be given 'their ordinary meaning' in 'their context and in the light of their object and purpose'.

The division of opinion strikes at the very root of foreign investment arbitration. If such arbitration is confined to those investments that are beneficial to the host state, two inroads, one by a jurisdictional defence on the ground that the element of economic development is missing, and the other a defence on merits that the investment proved harmful to the economic interests of the host state and therefore justified regulatory intervention, could be made.[72] Both types of defence could be seen as diminishing the system of absolute investment protection. The possible operation of the jurisdictional defence has already been explored in the award of *Malaysian Salvors*. The defence on the basis of merits is the more interesting one. In order to forestall the possibility of a jurisdictional defence based on economic development some tribunals argued that economic development must only be a consequence of the investment. But such transference of the criterion to the merits may not provide a feasible answer unless there is a way of invoking a defence based on the absence of economic development flowing from the investment. Such defences are provided in the new balanced treaties, but not in the old treaties, which provide inflexible investment protection. Tribunals must be willing to infer the existence of the defence in the older treaties, which would depend on the persuasion of these who sit on them. The inclusion of the criteria of economic development as a component of a protected investment would forestall the need for defences at the merits phase and enable the disposal of the dispute at the jurisdictional phase.

In *Phoenix*, it was pointed out that economic development, in terms of economics, is a highly complicated subject and cannot be easily dealt with in this area of the law. The nature of the economics necessary to

---

[72] This would be so in cases where the proceedings are grounded on expropriation or the violation of the fair and equitable treatment.

find out whether the investment was harmful is not exacting. It depends on fairly visible circumstances, such as environmental pollution, violation of human rights, raising of domestic capital to fund the investment or rapid depletion of resources. In the context, of the classical theory employed by the World Bank, there is at least some material benefit that foreign investment brings to the host state by way of improvement that did not exist before its flow. The investment treaties are based on the premise of such benefits. This is easy to quantify. The type of economic harm that Judge Shahabudeen contemplated, such as pollution or the causing of economic disadvantages such as resource depletion without at least some benefits resulting to the host state, are visibly identifiable. It is a test that is easy to apply at the initial phase of the arbitration.

The episode regarding differences of opinion on the definition of investment shows that expansionism has an adverse effect on investment arbitration. If tribunals go beyond the meaning that states ascribed to investments and take an all-embracing view on the topic, states will always hit back by simply refusing to abide by the award and by questioning the need for investment treaties. The stance that expansionist arbitrators take is counterproductive.

It is not far-fetched to argue that there is an ideological schism that dominates the debate on the definition of investment. Those who seek to confine the jurisdiction of tribunals would seek to define consent of states as being confined to investments that clearly promote economic development, whereas the expansionists would not like to see jurisdiction limited in this manner. The explanation of the rift between these two views does not turn only on the interpretation of words, but on the imputation of policy objectives. Arbitrators have predetermined positions on policy objectives before they sit on the panels. Some have indicated their preference through their writings. It would be easy to predict how a particular arbitrator would decide having regard to his past writings or record. In this sense, it may be possible to argue that decisions are based on biases towards the predetermined positions of arbitrators, taking neutrality in the system into the realm of fiction.

Expansionism in this area has taken curious turns. One is that a commercial arbitration award based on contracts for services has been held to be an investment, so that delay by the courts in enforcing the award could be construed as a violation of the treaty. Such a course is dependent on characterizing the arbitration award and the underlying contract on which it was based as investments.[73] It is difficult to see how an arbitration award could be construed to be an investment, even in the case of the underlying contract qualifying as an investment. In this manner, it has been possible for expansionist arbitrators to enable another innovation of using investment treaties and arbitration under them as a way of enforcing arbitral awards.[74] The result of the technique has been to ensure that the affected state withholds from making new treaties and putting its treaty programme on hold.[75] The strategy has not brought benefits to the system of investment arbitration, though it was momentarily thought of as a clever innovation. It will prove to be a Pyrrhic victory for the expansionists. Such an innovation was not clearly within the contemplation of the states that signed the treaty. They will react in a manner adverse to the interests of investment arbitration.

The next qualification that the investment must accord with the host state's laws is closely tied with the issue of the definition of investment. The host state's laws often institute administrative screening devices to ensure that only beneficial investments are given entry and also protection under the treaties. Again, the existence of this limitation establishes the need for economic development as a criterion for the definition of investments as the host country's laws are tuned to the admission of only such investments as are economically beneficial.

3.2.2 The requirement of an investment made in accordance with the law of the host state

An investment is not a concept of international law. International law is not strong on notions of property, except when it comes to the recognition of a heavily qualified right to property in terms of human rights, the property of refugees, or the protection of civilian property in times of war or civil strife. Property exists largely within territories of states, and it is left for the municipal law of every state to identify such property and create rights as to such property. The presence of foreign investments

---

[73] *Saipem* v. *Bangladesh*, ICSID, Case No ARB/05/07 (30 June 2009). (Kauffman-Kohler, Schreuer, Otton); *White Industries* v. *India*, UNCITRAL, Arbitration (30 November 2011) (Rowley, Brower, Lau).

[74] *White Industries* v. *India*, UNCITRAL, Arbitration (30 November 2011) (Rowley, Brower, Lau).

[75] India has put its treaty programme on hold. It is unclear whether it honoured the award in *White Industries* v. *India*, UNCITRAL, Arbitration (30 November 2011) (Rowley, Brower, Lau); Shruti Iyer, 'Redefining Investment Regime in India: Post White Industries', (2013) 14 *Journal of World Investment & Trade* 595.

3.2 RESTRICTING ARBITRAL ADVENTURISM 165

within the territory of a state must depend to a large extent on the domestic law of the host state. For purposes of what investment is protected in any system, the domestic laws of the host state must remain the first reference point. It is such law that creates the right in property. That right may be protected through international means, but the creation and extent of that right is always a matter for domestic law. As Monique Sasson stated, regarding ICSID arbitration:[76]

> Article 25 of the ICSID Convention does not create an autonomous and self-contained concept of 'investment' that somehow floats apart from the underlying rights that may exist under municipal law in relation to 'investment'. Article 25 defined the nature of the disputes referable to the Centre as any 'legal dispute' arising from an 'investment'. These two terms require, in the absence of any express definition in the investment treaty, a *renvoi* to the substantive regulation contained in municipal law.

Investment treaties merely itemize types of property or rights created by domestic law for protection through international mechanisms. When, for example, an investment treaty protects the intellectual property of the foreign investor, it is apparent that such property is created in terms of domestic law. All investment that enters a state exists and functions only because the state permits it to enter and function. The rights created in that investment are created by domestic law and exist in accordance with domestic law. The notion is inherent in all foreign investment.

Investment entry is usually made through an investment contract. It is obvious that the validity of that contract depends entirely on domestic law. Thus, where it is affected by bribery, fraud or any other defect in formation under domestic law, the contract could become a nullity and it would be obvious that a treaty cannot protect an investment made through such invalid means.[77] It is superfluous to say that bribery provides a situation of illegality in transnational law as the contract's only location of existence is domestic law.[78] Transnational law cannot be the basis on which contracts are created. If such a law exists, it has no

---

[76] Sasson, *The Substantive Law in Investment Treaty Arbitration*, p. 34.

[77] *Feldman* v. *Mexico*, ICSID, Case No. ARB(AF)/99/1 (16 December 2002).

[78] The effort to develop bribery as a principle of transnational illegality is superfluous. As an offence, it can function only in terms of domestic law. There could be international standards and rules advocated in conventions such as the United Nations Bribery Convention, but they merely provide models for domestic law. For an instance of bribery as a notion of transnational illegality, see *World Duty Free Ltd* v. *Kenya*, ICSID, Case No. ARB/00/7 (4 October 2006).

166   CREATING JURISDICTION BEYOND CONSENT

known rules on the formation of contracts. Domestic laws guide the making of a contract on foreign investment that is the starting point of foreign investment.

In many states, the entry of foreign investment is subjected to administrative controls. The law sets up machinery that screens foreign investment to ensure that such investments contribute to economic development.[79] Some treaties specify that the protected investments are confined to those made 'in accordance with the laws and regulations of the host state'. The view has been taken in *Inceysa*[80] that the absence of such a provision relating to the conformity of the investment to the local laws and regulations is not necessary as the parties could not have intended to protect an investment that is not made in accordance with the laws and regulations of the host state.[81] In *Desert Line* v. *Yemen*,[82] the tribunal pointed out the more specific references to the entry laws that must be satisfied pose greater barriers to jurisdiction than the mere reference to the satisfaction of the laws of the host state. Efforts to bypass the satisfaction of requirements of the entry laws involve illegality, particularly when there is a criminal proscription attached to such evasion. It is clear that jurisdiction will not be assumed in these instances.[83]

Yet it is when treaties spell out an additional requirement not for entry but for the purpose of protection of the treaty, that issues have arisen as to the effect of non-satisfaction of the requirement. In many treaties, it is stated that only investments 'approved' by a designated authority are protected. In these situations, it is obvious that jurisdiction will not arise where there is no approval has been given for purposes of treaty protection. Efforts had been made to soft-pedal such requirements by stating that deviations, as where consent by the high authorities of the state rather than the body designated by the treaty, can be shown. But these are evidence of instances where arbitrators have strained to find jurisdiction

---

[79] Thomas Pollan, *The Entry of Foreign Investments* (Utrecht: Eleven Publishers, 2006).

[80] *Inceysa Vallisoletana SL* v. *El Salvador*, ICSID, Case No. ARB/03/26 (2 August 2006).

[81] *Mihaly* v. *Sri Lanka*, ICSID, Award (15 March 2002), (2002) 41 ILM 867; also see *Zhinvali Development Ltd* v. *Republic of Georgia* (2003) 10 ICSID Rep. 10, Award (24 January 2003); *Rafat Ali Rizvi* v. *Indonesia*, ICSID, Case No. ARB/11/13 (16 July 2013).

[82] *Desert Line Projects LLC* v. *Republic of Yemen*, Award, ICSID. Case No. ARB/05/17 (29 January 2008). *H&H Enterprises Investments Inc.* v. *Arab Republic of Egypt*, ICSID, Case No. ARB/09/15, Decision on Respondent's Objections to Jurisdiction (5 June 2012). Both these awards involved liberal interpretations construing contacts at high levels of administration in the process of entry as amounting to admission in the context of the looser criteria for admission contained in the provision on admission.

[83] *Fraport AG* v. *Philippines*, ICSID, Case No. ARB/03/25, Award (16 August 2007).

3.2 RESTRICTING ARBITRAL ADVENTURISM 167

beyond the consent of the state and add to the evidence of expansionary trends. The limitation provides another example of the fact that treaties are not uniform and do not contribute to customary international law, as their application is only to the type of investment that had obtained the specific approval. Obviously, investments that do not have such approval will exist within the state, but will not be protected by the treaty but through other means, including diplomatic protection under customary international law.[84]

The investment contracts on the basis of which entry was made would be void *ab initio* if the manner of their making did not accord with local law. Yet some tribunals have suggested that this point should be overlooked, particularly in circumstances where the foreign investment had been allowed to commence operations. A distinction is drawn between situations of bribery where the illegality flows from transnational public policy, and illegality arising from domestic law.[85] The view that there is no jurisdiction applies only in the case of the former, but not in the case of the latter. This, again, is difficult reasoning, unless, of course, one believes, first, in a transnational legal order in which the offence of bribery is founded, and, secondly, in the idea that investments exist otherwise than in the realm of domestic law.

Despite these frictions, it is clear that tribunals seldom bypass local laws. Jurisdiction that is assumed without taking the restrictions on the protected investment in the treaty should be regarded as invalid. Apart from the annulment procedure, there does not seem to be any way of redress to the state where this is done. Since the matter of the legality of the investment is a matter of domestic law, what the local courts have to say about the issue should be given great weight.

A third related situation in which there is expansion of jurisdiction concerns financial instruments. These have been considered to fall within the definition of protected investments in a series of recent awards, considered in section 3.3, below.

---

[84] *Gruslin v. Malaysia*, ICSID, Case No. ARB/99/3 (27 November 2000); *Yaung Chi Oo Ltd v. Myanmar* (2003) 42 ILM 896; *Desert Line Projects LLC v. Yemen*, ICSID, Case No. ARB/05/17 (6 February 2008); *Fraport AG v. Philippines*, ICSID, Case No. ARB/03/25 (16 August 2007); *Rafat Ali Rizvi v. Indonesia*, ICSID, Case No. ARB/11/13 (16 July 2013).

[85] *Liman Caspian Oil BV v. Kazakhstan*, ICSID, Case No. ARB/07/14 (22 June 2010); *Arif v. Moldova*, ICSID, Case No. ARB/11/23 (8 April 2013), para. 347, where a surprising proposition was advanced that unlawful and *ultra vires* acts could still give rise to legitimate expectations. This would stump any public lawyer under any system (except investment arbitration).

3.3 The acme of aberrations: *Abaclat* and financial instruments

The jurisdictional award of the tribunal in *Abaclat* v. *Argentina*[86] brings together all the doubts that have existed about the new-found theories of jurisdiction, which made the spurt in investment arbitration possible. The doubts were compounded when the same views were taken in *Ambiente Ufficio* v. *Argentina*[87] by the majority virtually following the view of the majority in *Abaclat*, with a strong dissent along the same lines as in *Abaclat*. It was followed by an award in *Deutsche Bank* v. *Sri Lanka*,[88] involving financial instruments, again with a strong dissent. The three awards with three dissents show the extent of the discord that attends a fresh effort of trying to include a new category of disputes arising from financial instruments within investment treaty arbitration. They are done on the basis that the financial instruments involved qualify as protected investments under the treaty. *Abaclat* and *Ambiente* also raise issues as to whether class actions were within the contemplation of states when they made treaties.[89]

The tribunal in *Abaclat* was divided on many issues.[90] The strong dissent on all issues by the third arbitrator, Professor Abi-Saab, shreds the hypotheses on which the majority award rested and undermines the award severely. The award is replete with abnormalities. The first abnormality is that the arbitration was brought as a class action in which some 1,800 persons and corporations were represented. The idea that class actions could be brought was not even thought of by states at the time investment treaties were signed. Class actions are known to American law and but are new to other legal systems. The conversion of that idea, which could not have been even remotely thought of by the parties to the ICSID Convention or the investment treaties into investment arbitration, is a feat that required the fecund imagination of the two arbitrators who made the award. Again, it is an expansion of the law well beyond what the parties to the investment treaty contemplated. The legitimacy of the authority of the tribunal to make such an extension

---

[86] *Abaclat* v. *Argentina* (2011) ICSID Case ARB/07/5 (4 August 2011).

[87] *Ambiente Ufficio* v. *Argentina*, ICSID Case No. ARB/08/9 (8 February 2013).

[88] *Deutsche Bank* v. *Sri Lanka*, ICISD, Case No. ARB/09/02 (31 October 2012).

[89] As the dissenting arbitrators pointed out, the respondent state could not possibly have thought of and consented to such actions. Berk Demirkol, 'Does an Investment Treaty Tribunal need Special Consent for Mass Claims?' (2013) 2 Cambridge *Journal of International & Comparative Law* 612.

[90] The majority consisted of Professor Pierre Tercier and Professor Albert Van den Berg. Professor Georges Abi-Saab dissented.

3.3 THE ACME OF ABERRATIONS

that well beyond the consent of the states making the treaties must be open to question.

The purpose of the decision could only have been to facilitate claims against states in economic crises facing difficulties in servicing the bonds they had issued. The award was made at a time when several European states were also facing financial crises.[91] Such a result can hardly facilitate solutions to the difficulties that are faced by countries going through economic crises. Now that economic crises brought about through neo-liberalism have affected Europe and moved closer to the developed states, one may think that a different result would eventuate. But *Abaclat* and *Ambiente* demonstrate that there is an 'excessive zeal' for the business of investment arbitration to be continuously broadened.[92] Clearly, the law needs to be changed, if, indeed, the law is what the majority in *Abaclat* stated it to be. The increasing facility with which new directions of litigation are thought up and supported by arbitrators will add to the need for states to rethink the system of investment arbitration.[93]

The second abnormality is that a state's responsibility can arise only in respect of persons to whom it owes some duty of protection or some duty to provide a standard of treatment. It cannot possibly owe such a duty to bondholders, who keep changing continuously and who never entered its

[91] Referred to as PIGS (Portugal, Ireland, Greece and Spain), these states faced severe economic crises, much to the delight of law firms preparing themselves for another spate of arbitrations similar to those in Argentina. The arbitrations did not eventuate. The enthusiasm was dimmed by the fact that most European states had taken measures similar to that of Argentina in dealing with the crises that affected all of them in different degrees. *Postova Bank and Istrokapital* v. *Greece* (2014), is pending before the ICSID. Other arbitrations are threatened.

[92] There were gleeful prognostications as to the number of arbitrations that would be generated by the failure of the PIGS (Portugal, Ireland, Greece and Spain) states similar to those generated by the Argentinian crisis. Big firms were gearing up for such business. Tomaso Fernando, '*Abaclat* Legacy: Investment Arbitration as an Obstacle to Greek Recovery', 27 February 2012, posted at www.criticallegalthinking.com. In his dissent in *Ambiente*, Arbitrator Torres spoke of the 'excessive zeal' of the majority of the tribunal to follow *Abaclat*. There have been many pending arbitrations brought against European states traceable to the 2008 global economic crisis. *Ping An Life Insurance Co. of China* v. *Belgium*, ICSID Case No. ARB/12/2 (Pending). Withdrawal of incentives have resulted in seven cases against Spain and another seven against the Czech Republic. Anne de Luca, 'Withdrawing Incentives to Attract Foreign Investments', Columbia FDI Perspectives, No. 125, 7 July 2014.

[93] The China–Canada investment treaty (2014) specifically states that a loan or a debt security issued by a financial institution is an investment only when the loan or debt security is treated as regulatory capital by the contracting party in whose territory the financial institution is located. The requirement is that the original maturity of the loan should be over three years.

territory. A state has no ready means of identifying such bondholders, who would be a shifting group. Though in *Fedax* v. *Venezuela*,[94] such an abnormality had already been initiated, the notion that foreign bondholders are subject to the protection of an investment treaty is irksome simply because of the fact that the state did not even know to whom it owed a duty of treaty protection. Quite apart from this, there is the problem of whether the state could have consented to arbitration to persons or entities of whom the state had no knowledge and who had never entered the state. The rules of state responsibility work on the basis that the state owes a duty of protection to an alien who is on the territory of the state. Investment treaties never sought to go beyond the ambit of such law. The state knows of that person's existence and has a commitment owed to his home state to give protection. The violation of the treatment standard must occur on the territory of the state. The investment treaty supplants that duty of protection and works on the same principle that the investor has entered the territory of the host state. This was the assumption on which the treaty was made. It is a subversion of principle to hold that the treaty protects bondholders who have no presence in the state and do not contribute to the economic development of the state through their presence and work.

The third abnormality is that the award decided that bonds that were sold in Italy subject to Italian law amounted to protected investments under the Argentina–Italy investment treaty. Clearly, there was an action available in terms of Italian law against the banks that sold the bonds. The organization of the group of bondholders to sue Argentina by the banks could well be, as alleged by Argentina, to avoid suits against the banks under Italian law. The bondholders had assigned their rights to an entity organized by the banks so that the class action could be brought.

In addition to these abnormalities, there are contested issues relating to the law. The first among them was whether the bonds that were the subject matter of the dispute could amount to investments protected by the treaty. Here, the tribunal applied a mechanical test stating that bonds and securities create economic rights of value or obligations, and that these rights and obligations are listed in the treaty as investments. This ignores the fact that the rights and obligations are protected because they

---

[94] *Fedax* v. *Venezuela*, ICSID, Case No. ARB/96/3 (11 July 1997). Clearly, an expansionist award which went unnoticed at the time, it was based on acquiring jurisdiction over bonds initially issued to Venezuelan nationals, then to Dutch nationals whose home state had a treaty with Venezuela. It was a clear instance of creation of jurisdiction through transfer. The issue was hardly raised.

3.3 THE ACME OF ABERRATIONS

arise as incidental to the original investment made in the form of a corporate entity or other vehicle for the investment upon entry. It is not possible to enter the state as an investor through obligations or economic rights such as securities sold on foreign stock markets. A person, possessing shares, obligations and economic rights associated with an entity functioning within the state, would have rights protected as those of an investment or investor. Besides, investment is defined as being subject to the laws of the state, which are usually the entry laws of the investment. If there is no such definition in the treaty itself, it has to be inferred that the investment enters subject to the laws of the host state.[95] The requirement presupposes that entry had been made in accordance with these laws and the rights had been created in accordance with the laws applicable to foreign investments.[96] It presupposes contact with the legal system of the host state and the creation of rights by the legal system of that state. There must be a possibility of relief being provided to the investors by the local courts so that international responsibility could be avoided by the home state. Bonds sold by foreign banks on their internal markets do not create economic rights within Argentina. Such rights are contractual rights between the vendor banks and the buyers to whom securities have been transferred, in this case, under Italian law.[97] They do not have any territorial nexus with Argentina. Argentinian courts will not be able to provide relief in respect of a transaction located entirely in Italy. As an ICSID tribunal put it, 'in accordance with normal principles of treaty interpretation, investments made outside the territory of the Respondent State, however beneficial to it, would not be covered by the BIT'.[98] Economic rights independent of such rights have not qualified as investments in the earlier cases with the exception of *Fedax*,[99] also a unique award initiating extreme adventurism.

---

[95] *Inceysa Vallisoletana SL* v. *El Salvador*, ICSID, Case No. ARB/03/26 (2 August 2006).

[96] In fairness, it must be pointed out that each of the categories, as defined in the specific Argentina–Italy investment treaty seem to be stand-alone categories, making the interpretation of the tribunal a possibility.

[97] Michael Waibel, 'Opening the Pandora's Box: Sovereign Bonds in International Arbitration', (2007) 101 *American Journal of International Law* 711.

[98] *SGS* v. *Philippines*, ICSID, Case No. ARB/02/6, Decision on Jurisdiction and Admissibility (24 January 2004), para. 99; see also *Canadian Cattlemen for Fair Trade* v. *United States*, NAFTA, Award on Jurisdiction (28 January 2008), para. 127. As cited by Professor Abi-Saab in dissent in *Abaclat*

[99] Professor Abi-Saab points out that '*Fedax* is an isolated case. It is an outlier.' The plain fact is that *Fedax* was wrongly decided. Abi-Saab also pointed out that the three cases cited by the majority, *Fedax* and the two *SGS* cases, are distinguishable as the tribunals had held that the underlying transactions were territorially based.

Having held that the bonds were investments under the treaty, the tribunal found that the double-barrel test was satisfied as any contribution that creates value would qualify as an investment under Article 25 of the ICSID Convention. Again, this is a new meaning of investment under Article 25 that has no support in the evolution of that concept under the ICSID Convention. It is a result that depends entirely on the assumption by the tribunal that the highly subjective assessment of the tribunal that fairness requires such a result. Bonds, which involve funds in free circulation, cannot be regarded as foreign investment protected by the treaties. There is no evidence that such funds that move about freely bring any economic benefits to any host state. Rather, the rapid pull-out of such funds precipitate economic crises. They do not bring durable economic benefits to the economy to be regarded as protected investments. The new Canada–China treaty (2014) overcomes this problem by requiring that the maturity of the loan should be at least three years.[100]

As Professor Abi Saab pointed out in his dissenting award, the majority award is guided largely by policy considerations supported by the two arbitrators. It is a conclusion that ties in nicely with a thesis of this work that neoliberalism provided an impetus for the expansionist awards that were made during the period of the ascendancy of this philosophy, which included within it an ideal model of investment protection. *Abaclat* constitutes an extreme example of this phenomenon at the end stages of neoliberalism, perhaps demonstrating that the ideas still continue to glow in investment arbitration, though its fire may have died out elsewhere or, possibly, that they kick harder when they are about to expire.

The majority award in *Abaclat* is naked in making subjective assumptions of fairness in overcoming the hurdles that stood in the way of finding jurisdiction. It overcame the difficulty of the absence of territoriality, the lack of satisfaction of the definition of investment and the absence of consent of the parties to the institution of class action by appealing to the spirit of the ICSID Convention and the investment treaties. This invocation of the spirits to justify jurisdiction must have involved an esoteric knowledge of a mystic world known only to the select few. The spirit that animated the award is that there should be inflexible investment protection. This spirit is stated as animating the ICSID Convention and the investment treaty system. There is no such spirit discernible to the objective observer. The Convention's *travaux preparatoires* demonstrate a careful consideration of objective

---

[100] Canada–China treaty (2014), Article 1(1)(d).

3.4 CORPORATE NATIONALITY AS A VEHICLE 173

circumstances of factors that should be taken into account, such as, of course, the customary law basis on which the Convention was built, the economic development of the host state, the reason for the existence of the World Bank, which sponsored the ICSID Convention, and the most paramount factor, that consent must exist for interference with the sovereignty of the state that foreign arbitration involves. *Abaclat* and *Ambiente* are aberrations that show neoliberalism at its apogee. The tenacity of neoliberalism in investment arbitration may be due to other factors, such as professional interest in maintaining an inflexible system of investment arbitration and the continuation of the interests of private power, including that of the small community of arbitrators and lawyers who service the industry of investment arbitration, in secure systems of investment protection.[101] *Abaclat* removes investment arbitration from the orbit of legitimacy created by free consent and thereby moves investment arbitration away from acceptance by affected states. It provokes resistance and undermines the voluntary basis on which arbitration rests. It may profit those immediately concerned in the arbitration, but the overall damage it causes to the system of investment arbitration is yet to be seen.

3.4 Corporate nationality as a vehicle for expansion

The capricious use of the notion of corporate nationality in establishing jurisdiction is another area that has brought investment arbitration into disrepute. States, again, have reacted in various ways to counter the use of corporate nationality to engage in forum shopping by claimants. Lawyers also encouraged the view that favourable means of protection could be obtained through the insertion of a subsidiary company in a jurisdiction that maintained incorporation as the method of acquiring corporate nationality and had investment treaties with effective standards of protection. Such services were euphemistically referred to a corporate planning when their true purpose was obtaining jurisdiction through means not intended by the states making the treaty. The strategy known as the 'Dutch Sandwich' evolved.[102] But, as with all unscrupulous

---

[101] The legal costs in *Abaclat* are instructive. They are stated at para. 682 of the Award. The claimant submitted claims for US$18,707,679 and €7,169,125. Argentina's cost were US$12,420,340. The tribunal's cost were US$1,331,960.

[102] So termed because Holland, which maintained favourable investment treaties, was a place used to adopt this strategy. Other small states, like Mauritius (for India), Singapore (for China and the Asian hinterland) and Hong Kong (for China) are gateway or

schemes,[103] the creative use of corporate nationality had to flounder when states sought to plug the loopholes in the strictest manner possible, or simply used it as another excuse for withdrawing from the system. First, it is necessary to describe the schisms that arose in the course of the efforts at the use of corporate nationality to invoke jurisdiction in a manner not intended by the parties to the treaty. Though the literal interpretation of the treaties may have permitted the various scams that were attempted, the purpose of the treaties militated against the use to which they were put.

It is well known that a corporation being a creature of the law of a state obtains the nationality of the state. Except in the treaties of civil law countries,[104] this rule as to corporate nationality is used in the investment treaties. The treaties permit standing to a corporation of a state, which is a party to the investment treaty, to enjoy the rights under the treaty arising from its investments in the other state party. It is possible for any multi-national corporation of any third state to obtain corporate nationality of a treaty state simply by incorporating in that state.

Standing to commence arbitration was given to natural persons who were citizens of either state or to corporate nationals of either state. There were few problems with natural persons. They related to issues of dual nationality and the relevant time at which nationality was acquired. It is corporate nationality that has proved to be the more difficult problem. It was capable of creative use in a manner that could not possibly have been contemplated by the states at the time they made the treaties. This point is made in *Claimant v. Slovak Republic*, in which the tribunal stated:

> platform states. They encourage foreign investors to incorporate in their territories before proceeding to other countries. For the foreign investor, an advantage, besides the stability of banking etc., is the protection given by the investment treaty systems these small states maintain. Recently disclosed negotiating papers of the UK–Indonesia treaty (1975) indicate Indonesian fears that Indonesian Chinese would redirect or 'round-trip' investments through Hong Kong with protection of the UK–Indonesia treaty. For this reason, Indonesia argued that indirect investments through Hong Kong should not be protected. The recently disclosed negotiating history of the treaty was used in *Rafat Ali Rizvi v. Indonesia*, ICSID, Case No. ARB/11/13 (16 July 2013).

[103] The scheme subverts the objective of economic cooperation that investment treaties profess to promote. *Claimant v. Slovak Republic*, UNCITRAL Ad Hoc Arbitration (Crivallaro, Stuber, Klein) (5 March 2011).

[104] The civil law countries use the alternative *siège social* theory, requiring that the seat of management be also in the state of incorporation for there to be corporate nationality. Consequently, treaties of civil law states have not attracted any abuse. Holland, though a civilian country, uses incorporation as the test.

3.4 CORPORATE NATIONALITY AS A VEHICLE 175

> It is illogical to assume that the goals (of fostering mutual benefit and economic prosperity) could be achieved by giving treaty protection or by attracting into the host country 'shell companies' which are unable to establish the kind and level of activities that they conduct in their own state.

Unfortunately, the life of the law is not logic. Expediency and considerations of mercenary profit seem to guide the life of international investment law. Several awards exploited the notion of incorporation as the test of nationality in expanding the scope of their jurisdiction. They permitted shell companies to claim jurisdiction.

A commentary on investment treaties by Dolzer and Stevens published in 1995 did not even contemplate the possibility of any deviant use of corporate nationality.[105] In 1995, corporate nationality in investment treaties was a quiescent doctrine. It took another nine years before it was woken up and put to creative uses in establishing jurisdiction. The first creative use of corporate nationality was in *Tokios Tokeles* v. *Ukraine*, decided in 2004. There was little anticipation of the creative uses to which the incorporation theory could be put. The states that used incorporation to identify corporate nationality hardly contemplated the possibility of its later use in expanding the scope of jurisdiction. It is again an instance where an unexpected expansion took place with the objective of expanding investment protection well beyond the consent of the states that made the treaties.[106]

The innocence on corporate nationality was to be shattered, and within a few years.[107] Corporate nationality assumed a significance it

---

[105] The treatment of corporate nationality in the work recounts the type of clauses that are used to define corporate nationality in the various treaties. Rudolf Dolzer and Margrete Stevens, *Bilateral Investment Treaties* (The Hague: Martinus Nijhoff, 1995).

[106] UNCTAD studies on investment treaties also did not anticipate this creative use of corporate nationality. Such use can only be attributed to the creativity of law firms interested in expanding the scope of investment arbitration and arbitrators who willingly embraced such creativity.

[107] The period begins with cases like *Tokios Tokeles* v. *Ukraine*, ICSID, Case No. ARB/02/18 (29 April 2004) and *Aguas del Tunari SA* v. *Republic of Bolivia*, ICSID, Case No. ARB/ 02/3, Decision on Respondent's Objections to Jurisdiction (21 October 2005). *Tokios Tokeles* has been followed in *Rompetrol* v. *Romania*, ICSID, Case No. ARB/06/3 (18 April 2008) and the *Yukos Universal Ltd* v. *Russia* (2009) 22(2) World Trade and Arbitration Materials 279, awards. *Tokios Tokeles* was followed in *KT Asia* v. *Kazakhstan*, ICSID, Case No. ARB/09/8 (17 October 2013), on the ground that the words in the treaty adopting the incorporation test are clear and that there was no room to look at the purpose of the treaty. This was despite the fact that the claimant was a shell company incorporated in the Netherlands by a national of the respondent state. The award held that corporate veil would be pierced only in circumstances where the corporate

176   CREATING JURISDICTION BEYOND CONSENT

was never thought to have had in the previous years of its existence, again, signifying that there were major changes that occurred in the law which require explanation. The explanation that an ideological and attitudinal change took place in this period is an explanation that best fits the frenetic change that occurred in this area. There were arbitrators who were willing to depart from the existing moorings of the law and take it on a course of expansion hitherto unthought of. The climate was receptive to the making of such extensions.

There were two major experiments attempted. The first situation is where the nationals of a state incorporate a company in a state with which their home state has an investment treaty and channel investments through that company into their home states. In this way, they hope to secure the protection of the treaty of the state of incorporation through which they channel the funds they have taken there, despite the fact that their home state was the origin of the funds. Obviously, there is no benefit for the home state in giving such treaty protection to funds that originated from within it. This practice of 'round-tripping' is common.[108]

The second was for multinational companies that had commenced an investment in a host state to incorporate in a state with a favourable treaty when a dispute was anticipated. This was done either because the home state of the corporation did not have a treaty or because a third state in which the fresh incorporation took place had a treaty with better standards of protection. Multinational corporations could also create holding companies in states with strong treaties so that they could take advantage of the treaty protection when occasion arises.[109] Likewise, multinational corporations may seek advantages through incorporation of small subsidiaries, or even post-box companies, so that they can exploit the advantages of the investment treaties of these states. The system undermines the old rules on diplomatic protection, which required a definite link of nationality on the basis of which protection was offered. It also defeats the purported purpose of creating economic cooperation and

---

formalities were misused. One would think that there was misuse when the purpose of incorporation was merely to treaty-shop.

[108] It is said that a significant number of the investments in China consist of round-tripping of Chinese assets through Hong Kong. Indonesia feared that its Chinese minority would round-trip their assets through Hong Kong, then a British protectorate, and wanted to take precautions against it. *Rafat Ali Rizvi* v. *Indonesia*. The suggestion of round-tripping was also made in *Yaung Chi Oo Ltd* v. *Myanmar* (2003) 42 ILM 896.

[109] As in *Philip Morris* v. *Australia*, UNCITRAL PCA, Case No. 2012-12 (2012) (ongoing), where the arbitration is based on the Hong Kong–Australia treaty, the claimant having a subsidiary in Hong Kong.

3.4 CORPORATE NATIONALITY AS A VEHICLE 177

promoting economic development, which post-box companies cannot achieve. Post-box companies also cannot contribute to the economic development of the host state. These are minor irritants to overcome when they stand in the way of an arbitrator who goes into bat with the intention of advancing investment protection. The notions of 'migration of companies' and 'corporate restructuring' innocently encapsulated the different creative techniques through which incorporation could be exploited. The state of incorporation may not have sufficient links to offer diplomatic protection to the foreign corporation, but the mere fact of incorporation enables the foreign corporation to exploit the advantages provided by the state's investment treaties, particularly where the state's treaties have an adequate global coverage or target certain countries with large markets or natural resources. In the light of experience, there were later formulations to avoid these possibilities.[110] But even these later formulations have been narrowly construed. One wonders about the good faith of the states that allow their treaties, indeed design their treaties, to permit such abuse.

These two situations represent creative uses of corporate nationality in order to obtain jurisdiction in a manner that goes beyond the intention of the parties in agreeing to the investment treaty. They are considered in the following pages.

3.4.1 'Round-tripping' of investments

As explained, round-tripping of investments occurs where nationals of a state take assets into a state with which their home state has an investment treaty, vest the assets in a corporation they create in that host state, and route the investment through that corporate entity back into their home state. The strategy would then be that the investment treaty between the home and the host states would protect the assets, which had originated in the home state, on the ground that the new corporation so created is a national of the other state. This amounts to a fraud on the law of the home state in that the investment treaty was designed to promote flows of foreign funds from the home state through offer of protection to funds originating from that state. The clear intention was to give protection to foreign funds that flow from external sources, not

---

[110] Thus, for example, incorporation was combined with a test of management in Asian treaties, but the test of management that was used by investment treaties was not very stringent. In *Yaung Chi Oo Ltd* v. *Myanmar* (2003) 42 ILM 896, it was held that satisfaction of reporting requirements satisfied the required management criteria.

178   CREATING JURISDICTION BEYOND CONSENT

funds that origin within the state. The policy objective of promoting flows of foreign investment is also frustrated as assets that flow back are the assets of the home state. But on the ordinary interpretation of the treaty, it would appear permissible that such protection should be provided to the assets simply because of the fact that the only test of corporate nationality is incorporation. Such an interpretation clearly defeats the purpose of the treaty. Good faith considerations are negated when such an attempt is permitted to succeed. Yet that is what is accomplished in some awards.

In *Tokios Tokeles* v. *Ukraine*,[111] Ukrainian nationals incorporated a company in Lithuania, a state with which Ukraine had an investment treaty, and invested funds they had taken from Ukraine in that Lithuanian company. The company they incorporated in Lithuania was held to be entitled to claim the protection of the treaty on the ground that the company was a national of Lithuania, though they were nationals of the respondent state.[112] Investment treaties are intended by the parties to promote foreign investment. The ICSID Convention promotes investment flows from other countries and settles disputes, as the title to the Convention itself suggests, between states and nationals of other states.[113] All investment treaties are also premised on a similar objective. In this case, there was no foreign investment as nationals were taking assets from their own home country, vesting them in a company incorporated in a treaty state and bringing them back as protected foreign investment. The protection of such 'round-tripping' could never have been the intention of any state in making investment treaties, and cannot be supported on the basis of any policy. Clearly, there could have been no intention on the part of Ukraine to protect such investment, which brought it no benefit. But the tribunal held that such 'round-tripping' of assets would be protected if funds had been vested in a company incorporated in a treaty partner state. This reading may satisfy the words of the treaty, but not its intended meaning. In this situation, the majority used a strict construction of the treaty in order to expand the meaning beyond what the parties to the treaty had intended.

---

[111] *Tokios Tokeles* v. *Ukraine*, ICSID, Case No. ARB/02/18, Decision on Jurisdiction (29 April 2004) (Bernadini, Price, majority award; Weil, the president, minority award – he resigned from the tribunal).

[112] Ukrainian nationals owned 99 per cent of the shares in the Lithuanian company.

[113] The first sentence of the preamble to the ICSID Convention refers to the 'need for international cooperation for economic development, and the role of private international investment therein'.

3.4 CORPORATE NATIONALITY AS A VEHICLE 179

The strong dissent of the president of the tribunal, Professor Prosper Weil, indicated the extent of the departure from principle that the jurisdictional award in *Tokios Tokeles* was making. His dissenting award pointed out that the purpose of both the ICSID Convention and the investment treaty was to promote flows of foreign investment into the state. Interestingly, both the majority award and the minority award used purposive arguments. For the majority, the ICSID Convention and the investment treaty were premised on investment protection, justifying a definition of the corporation that qualifies for protection on the basis of its incorporation in the foreign state without any need to lift the corporate veil to examine who its shareholders were. For the minority award, the purpose of the two instruments was the flow of assets owned by non-nationals. Round-tripping would defeat that aim.[114]

It is yet another instance of pro-investment arbitrators twisting the treaty to benefit investors. As Professor Weil suggested, the award may well 'jeopardize the future' of ICSID.[115] It shows the willingness of arbitrators to interpret treaties so as to enhance the aims of investment protection despite the fact that the clear purpose of the treaty was not to give protection to assets, which had originated in the host state. The origin of an investment is clearly important having regard to both the ICSID Convention and the investment treaty, both of which are posited on the encouragement of flows of overseas funds into a country. The 'round-tripping' of funds originating in the country can hardly be said to effect this purpose.

3.4.2 Migration of companies

The error in *Tokios Tokeles* was compounded when it was held that a company could, in anticipation of a dispute, 'migrate' to another country offering higher standards of protection in its treaty with the host state.

---

[114] Also see *Burimi Srl* v. *Albania*, ICSID, Case No. ARB/11/18 (29 May 2013) (Price, Cremades, Fadlallah), where the tribunal frowned on any effort for dual nationals to steer around obstacles through use of incorporation.

[115] Professor Weil dissented and resigned from the tribunal. He observed that 'the approach taken by the Tribunal on the issue of principle raised in this case for the first time in ICSID's history is in my view at odds with the object and purpose of the ICSID Convention and might jeopardize the future of the institution'. *Tokios Tokeles* v. *Ukraine*, ICSID, Case No. ARB/02/18, Decision on Jurisdiction, Dissenting Opinion (29 April 2004), at p. 1.

180   CREATING JURISDICTION BEYOND CONSENT

Aguas del Tunari v. *Bolivia*[116] was a case that was watched with great interest around the world because it involved water privatization in Bolivia. The litigation generated massive protests against it. The litigation strategy contained an even more startling proposition involving corporate nationality. It was suggested that, as in the case of ordinary persons, corporations could also migrate to more salubrious places so as to enjoy the benefits of treaty protection of the new state in which they locate. At the time of the investment in that dispute, ICSID arbitration could not have been invoked either under treaty or under contract. But the suggestion was that the foreign investor could insert a new corporation into its corporate holding structure at an intermediate level by incorporating a new company in a state (the Netherlands) with which the host state (Bolivia) had a favourable investment treaty.[117] This could be done in order to benefit from better investment protection or from investment protection only available in the treaty of a state in anticipation of a dispute, or, as in *Aguas del Tunari*,[118] in the course of the dispute. This view makes a mockery of investment treaty arbitration. The aim of any investment treaty is to ensure the flows of investment from the state to the other through securing treaty protection for companies located within it and having a link of nationality with it, not to provide unrelated companies with secure jurisdiction simply through incorporation and the insertion of a new subsidiary in the chain in order to acquire jurisdiction.

In *Mobil Oil* v. *Venezuela*,[119] the situation was rationalized on the basis that corporate reorganization was always possible, even in spite of the fact

---

[116] *Aguas del Tunari SA* v. *Republic of Bolivia*, ICSID Case No. ARB/02/3, Decision on Respondent's Objections to Jurisdiction (21 October 2005).

[117] In *Saluka Investments* v. *Czech Republic*, the tribunal assumed jurisdiction over another situation in which the funds did not proceed from the state, which was party to the treaty. A Japanese company had made the original investment, but its shares were transferred to the Dutch subsidiary for purposes of satisfying jurisdiction under the Dutch–Czech Republic treaty. Japan did not have a treaty with the Czech Republic. What made *Aguas del Tunari* different was that the creation of the intermediate company was in anticipation of the dispute.

[118] In *Aguas del Tunari*, Bolivian law prevented changes in the corporate structure without the consent of the administrative authorities. The laws of Luxembourg, however, permitted migration of companies. There was no arbitration clause in the agreement, as Bolivia had maintained that there could not be foreign arbitration of a dispute in an essential sector under Bolivian law. The right of shareholders to bring arbitration was recognized. This is an anomalous situation as it raises the question as to whether the shareholders can act independently of the company.

[119] ICSID, Case No. ARB/07/27 (10 June 2010).

that such reorganization was done in order to obtain jurisdiction, which would otherwise have not existed, through the incorporation of a new company in the Netherlands. The object of the treaty could only have been to promote investment flows from the Netherlands into Venezuela, not to make the Netherlands the place where companies incorporate only to secure jurisdiction before an arbitration tribunal. The strategy of the Netherlands may be to profit from such treaties as it attracts foreign companies to incorporate in there and use it as a platform for launching investments. But bringing such profit to the Netherlands is not the object of the treaty. Whether the Netherlands should lend itself to such unsavoury schemes designed to circumvent the objectives of its treaty partners is a matter for that state to decide. The incorporation of shell companies within the corporate structure cannot satisfy the objects of investment treaties in that such companies cannot promote economic development or economic cooperation between the states. As Professor Weil stated in the dissenting award in *Tokios Tokeles*, such schemes put the success of ICSID arbitration 'at risk by extending its scope and application beyond the limits so carefully assigned to it by the Convention'. One must note that such predictions have increased in recent times.

The extensions frustrate the objectives of both the investment treaty and the ICSID Convention, which protect only investment flows and not the fictional re-routing of existing foreign investment through other states simply to achieve protection. The objects of the treaty from the point of view of the host country would not in any way have been furthered by the notion of corporate migration or corporate restructuring. The fact that a company 'migrates' so as to benefit from a treaty by the simple act of incorporation can bring no economic development to the host country, which is the main purpose of any investment treaty as well as of ICSID arbitration. It only creates economic hardship to a host state as an unanticipated method of arbitration is created. This idea will lead to widespread treaty shopping and creates doubts about the treaty regime as a whole, as the uncertainties that are involved will lead states to rethink the wisdom of entering into treaties that are capable of infinite extensions and that create liability to an unlimited number of corporations. As Bolivia argued, this interpretation would mean that the Netherlands–Bolivia treaty would become 'a treaty between Bolivia and the world' as every foreign investor could 'migrate' a post-box, subsidiary company into the Netherlands and secure the protection of the treaty, hardly a result

182   CREATING JURISDICTION BEYOND CONSENT

that Bolivia could have intended when signing a bilateral investment treaty. If this does lead to a multilateralization of treaties, the result is achieved through fraudulent means that would not have been contemplated by the states making the treaties.

If what was intended as a bilateral treaty was converted into a multilateral treaty, it is a result that would greatly enhance neoliberal strategies. That indeed was the justification given by the tribunal, for it said:[120]

> This Decision reflects the growing web of treaty-based referrals to arbitration of certain investment disputes. Although titled 'bilateral' investment treaties, this case makes clear that which has been clear to negotiating states for some time, namely, that through the definition of 'national' or 'investor', such treaties serve in many cases more broadly as portals through which investments are structured, organized, and, most importantly, encouraged through the availability of a neutral forum. The language of the definition of national in many BITs evidences that such national routing of investment is entirely in keeping with the purpose of the instruments and the motivations of the state parties.

The only object of such rationalizations is to ensure that there is broad latitude provided for treaty shopping by multinational corporations. They have nothing at all to do with the original purpose of the investment treaty or of the ICSID Convention. In these circumstances, one must query whether there is an institutional duty on the part of ICSID to take a stance as to the appropriateness of the interpretation as it is obviously condoning a situation that had not been anticipated by the parties or by the institution.

In *Alps Finance and Trade v. Slovak Republic*,[121] the tribunal was conscious of the harm that the emphasis on incorporation and the expansion of jurisdiction could bring about. The tribunal held that more than mere incorporation was required to establish corporate nationality. The provision must be interpreted in good faith. Shell companies could not satisfy the objects of the treaty, which was to bring about greater economic cooperation between the states and economic benefits that the preamble of the treaty mentions. The tribunal took a contrary view to those adopt the expansionist view. One could, then, in this area as well, clearly distinguish between expansionist tribunals and tribunals that show fidelity to the limits of jurisdiction expressed in the consent of the parties.

---

[120] At para. 332.
[121] UNCITRAL Ad hoc Arbitration (2011) (Crivellaro, Stutter and Klein).

3.5 THE MFN CLAUSE SAGA

States reacted to this situation by incorporating denial of benefits clauses into their new investment treaties. But arbitration tribunals have reacted by construing these provisions narrowly so as not to affect investment protection. In *Liman Caspian Oil BV* v. *Kazakhstan*, the tribunal held that the denial of benefits clause could not be used where Dutch companies brought the claim though the real controllers were Canadian. The tribunal suggested that the facts should have been known to the respondent state at the time of the request for arbitration, and the issue as to denial of benefits should have been brought at that time and not one year later, during the jurisdictional phase. This is difficult reasoning and one deliberately calculated to ensure that the investor benefits despite the fact that the provision itself does not specify that it is time limited. It is another instance of tribunals adopting strict constructions when it favours the investor and purposive interpretations when it does not.[122]

3.5 The MFN clause saga

> The ongoing technique of obtaining jurisdiction through construction is further illustrated in the use of the most favoured nation clause. The clause is used to expand the jurisdiction given by the treaty by using better standards in the treaties of the host state granting jurisdiction to third parties on more favourable procedural terms. It is also used to argue that better standards of protection in other treaties could be utilized by an investor protected by a treaty with an most favoured nation clause. The technique is a departure from existing international law. The approach to most favoured notion clauses (MFN clauses) had hitherto been to refuse to rely on the MFN clause to expand the jurisdiction of an international tribunal. As Professor Brigitte Stern pointed out,[123] 'across hundreds of years of activity of international courts and tribunals leading up to *Maffezini*, there had only been judicial pronouncement against such a device'.

In *Maffezini*, the tribunal held that it was possible through the use of the MFN clause in one treaty to obtain the better protection in other treaties

---

[122] Further see *Plama Consortium Ltd* v. *Bulgaria*, ICSID, Case No. ARB/03/24, where a similar reasoning was used and the denial of benefits provision was held not to operate retrospectively.

[123] Separate and Dissenting Opinion of Brigitte Stern in *Impreglio* v. *Argentina*, ICSID, Case No. ARB/07/17 (21 June 2011). See also *ST-AD GmbH* v. *Bulgaria*, UNCITRAL, PCA Case No. 2011-06 (2013), the later award in which she was the presiding arbitrator where the issue is discussed. She has also pointed out that that the awards which use the MFN clause to extend jurisdiction were made by the same arbitrators sitting in different tribunals.

184 CREATING JURISDICTION BEYOND CONSENT

made by the same state. In this case, the technique was used to overcome the requirement of an eighteen-month negotiating period prior to the initiation of arbitration that was found in the treaty between Spain and Argentina, on the basis that such a limitation was not contained in Spain's treaty with Chile. *Maffezini* was rejected in *Plama* in no uncertain terms. Later awards have divided behind the two distinct views in the awards.[124] As Professor Stern pointed out in her dissent, the number of awards do not count, as the personnel of the tribunal making the awards following *Maffezini* were often the same, illustrating the problem in investment arbitration that the expansionist decisions have largely been made by a handful of persons and, equally, those who reject them are also made by the same few. It is again a schism that needs explanation. It is best explained on the view suggested in this work that there was a clear division based on expansionist arbitrators who were bent on creating a particular regime of investment protection and those who showed fidelity to the scope of consent. The further suggestion is that the split is on ideological predispositions. The MFN saga also supports this analysis.

It is evident that the expansionists have strained the law in order to advance their thesis as to the use of the MFN clause to bolster the extent of protection of investment. The use of the provisions of another unconnected treaty goes well beyond the construction of consent that is involved when jurisdiction is claimed on the basis of an investment treaty. It seeks to link the consent in an entirely unrelated treaty to the foreign investor when there is no logical chain that connects the two treaties. Studies show that the wording of the treaties do not have such effect.[125] What has mattered is the composition of the tribunal. The

[124] *Maffezini* was followed in *Siemens* v. *Argentina*, ICSID, Case No. ARB/02/8 (3 August 2004); *Gas Natural* v. *Argentina*, ICSID, Case No. ARB/03/10 (17 June 2005); *National Grid* v. *Argentina*, UNCITRAL, Award (20 June 2006); *Compañiá de Aguas del Aconquija SA (Vivendi)* v. *Argentina*, ICSID ARB/97/3 (21 November 2000); and *RosInvest. Plama* was followed in *Telenor; Berschader* v. *Russian Federation*, SCC Case No. 080/2004 (21 April 2006); *Wintershall* v. *Argentina*, ICSID, Case No. ARB/04/14 (8 December 2008); *Renta 4 SVSA* v. *Russian Federation*, SCC Case No 24/2007 (20 March 2009); *Tza Yap Shum*; and *Austrian Airlines* v. *Slovak Republic*, UNCITRAL Arbitration (9 October 2009). *Maffezini* v. *Kingdom of Spain*, ICSID, Case No. ARB/97/7, Decision on Jurisdiction (25 January 2000). Compare *Tza Yap Shum* v. *Republic of Peru*, ICSID, Case No. ARB/07/6, Decision on Jurisdiction and Competence (19 June 2009), with *RosInvest Co. UK Ltd* v. *Russian Federation*, SCC, Case No. V079/2005, Award on Jurisdiction (October 2007).

[125] Julie Maupin, 'MFN-based Jurisdiction in Investor–State Arbitration: Is there any Hope for a Consistent Approach?' (2011) 14 *Journal of International Economic Law* 157. The award in *RosInvest Co. UK Ltd* v. *Russian Federation, op. cit.*, contains a statement of the

3.5 THE MFN CLAUSE SAGA

outcomes are linked to the personal preferences of the individual arbitrator. The use of the MFN clause in order to employ better substantive provisions of other treaties is connected to the argument relating to the multilateralization of international investment law.[126] These are departures from what the parties had intended. They are used in order to expand jurisdiction and substantive law so as to achieve the objectives of neoliberal governance of the global investment process. In the area of the use of the MFN clause, the battle is between neoliberal expansionism and the conventional view that unless the words of the treaty are clear, the MFN clause should not be used to expand jurisdiction. The episode illustrates that the tussle between neoliberal expansionism and the conservative position that consent must not be imported from other treaties continues.

Logic requires that the MFN clause can be employed only by an investor who is qualified for protection under the treaty. The clause cannot be used to acquire jurisdiction when the claimant cannot independently establish standing to be present before the tribunal.[127] Logic notwithstanding, the disagreement will continue as it stems from predisposed views as to whether an expansionary view is to be preferred or not.

3.5.1 Conclusion on expansive trends

The efforts on the part of those who supported expansionist interpretations to the dispute settlement provisions in investment treaties resulted in resistance from others involved in investment arbitration. The extent of the situations listed above indicate a purposeful agenda to bring about a situation that would secure methods of obtaining jurisdiction over a wider field than was intended by the parties to investment treaties or by

---

two lines of argument of the awards. Several articles have been written on this issue, most of them seeking to conserve the integrity of the regime by explaining the difference on the basis of the difference in words employed in the different treaties. Dana H. Freyer and David Herlihy, 'Most-favoured-nation Treatment and Dispute Settlement in Investment Arbitration: Just How "Favoured" is "Most Favoured"?' (2005) 20 *ICSID Review* 58. But this explanation is not sound as there seems to be no significant variation in language used to justify this appeasement of an untenable position. Zachary Douglas demonstrated the incompatibility of the arguments used in cases using the MFN clause to expand jurisdiction with principles of treaty interpretation in international law. Zachary Douglas, 'The MFN Clause in Investment Treaty Arbitration: Treaty Interpretation off the Rails', (2011) 2 *Journal of International Dispute Settlement* 97.

[126] Schill, *The Multilateralization of International Investment Law.*

[127] *Rafat Ali Rizvi* v. *Indonesia*, ICSID, Case No. ARB/11/13 (16 July 2013).

the institution providing the arbitration facilities. The agenda was driven by motives of securing investment and personal profit rather than by the aim of economic development that underlay the objectives behind investment treaties and the ICSID Convention. It was a sham to say that wider expansion of the system of investment arbitration brought about greater flows of foreign investment. The arbitrators were not given a mandate to construct a system that promoted private power on the basis of an unprovable assumption. What has happened has undermined a system that was supposedly built to secure advantages for the world's poor. What eventuated was that the system was undermined. The rules of interpretation were used haphazardly. The expansionists used strict construction when permitting jurisdiction on the basis of round-tripping, but found justification in using a purposive interpretation when considering the definition of an investment or in extending jurisdiction to those holding financial instruments. Likewise, those who sought to narrow the base of jurisdiction also employed purposive interpretations when they sought to include economic development in the definition of investment or sought to deny jurisdiction in situations of round-tripping. The schism is not explicable on the basis of the use of different interpretive techniques, but on the fact that arbitrators sought to achieve different objectives and these objectives were predetermined by their ideological stances to foreign investment protection. The schism is more pronounced in the manner in which substantive propositions are considered, but it is as evident in the approach to issues of jurisdiction. Arbitrators who sought to confine jurisdiction also have contributed to the schism by striking out on their own and restricting the scope of jurisdiction through articulation of new notions or the rediscovery of old ones. This tendency exacerbates the division that has come about.

3.5.2   Trends favouring the state

As much as there are expansionary trends, either made directly or made in the context of efforts to curtail jurisdiction, there are more direct efforts to curtail the scope of jurisdiction by formulating views that impede the exercise of jurisdiction in the face of certain circumstances inherent either in the dispute or in the procedures that need to be satisfied before the right to an arbitration arises. Expansionist arbitrators would find them irksome. Again, battle is joined as to such requirements.

Most modern treaties require that there be prior consultations and negotiations for a specified period of time. These requirements were

3.5   THE MFN CLAUSE SAGA   187

largely found in Chinese treaties, but have now become a norm in investment treaty practice. Sometimes, there is a requirement that domestic courts should have been invoked for a period of time. The obvious intention behind these measures is that a good faith effort at solving the dispute through domestic means should first have been attempted before recourse to international means of settlement. But claimants have often ignored these prescriptions, and the practice of tribunals has been to condone the failure to have recourse to negotiations for the specified period, usually on the ground that such negotiations are not mandatory. Some awards involving the Argentine crisis have gone further and ignored the requirement in the treaties that required remedies before local courts to be tried for a period of eighteen months.[128] The taking of such views ignores the peremptory language in the treaties.[129] This may be another instance where tribunals hold out for a strict interpretation of treaty terms relating to jurisdiction when it favours the foreign investors, but do not do so when it does not favour their interests.

An UNCITRAL award involving Argentina, *ICS Inspection* v. *Argentina*,[130] refused jurisdiction on the ground that no prior negotiations had been attempted. *Daimler Financial Services* v. *Argentina*,[131] decided immediately after by an ICSID tribunal agreed with this view. In the dissenting award in *Abaclat*, Professor Abi-Saab criticized the majority award for ignoring the requirement of negotiations and the eighteen-month period for trying out local remedies on the ground that it was not mandatory. He viewed the requirement as a condition of the consent. The overwhelming authority in international law, including decisions of the ICJ,[132] support Professor Abi-Saab's view.[133]

---

[128] *Abaclat* v. *Argentina*, ICSID, Case No. ARB/07/5 (4 August 2011) (Tercier, Van den Berg; Abi-Saab, dissenting); *Ambiente Ufficio* v. *Argentina*, ICSID Case No. ARB/08/9 (8 February 2013). These cases largely rely on the lack of utility in using negotiations or litigation.

[129] *Murphy Exploration and Production International* v. *Ecuador*, ICSID, Case No. ARB/08/04, Award on Jurisdiction (2 June 2010); Richard Deutsch, 'An ICSID Tribunal Denies Jurisdiction for Failure to Satisfy BIT's Cooling Off Period: Further Evidence of a Sea Change in Investor–State Arbitration or a Meaningless Ripple?' (2011) *Houston Journal of International Law* 589.

[130] *ICS Inspection and Control Services Ltd* v. *Argentina*, UNCITRAL Ad hoc Arbitration (10 February 2012).

[131] *Daimler Financial Services* v. *Argentina*, ICSID, Case No. ARB/05/1 (22 August 2012).

[132] *Belgium* v. *Senegal* (Questions relating to the Obligation to Prosecute or Extradite), ICJ Judgment, General List No. 144 (2012).

[133] Further see Samuel Worthstone, 'Jurisdiction, Admissibility and Pre-conditions to Arbitration', (2012) 27 *ICSID Review* 255.

In the later *Ambiente* award, virtually following *Abaclat*, the view that there should be a waiting period during which local courts should have been approached was ignored on the ground that it may be an unrealistic restriction in situations where it is patently obvious, having regard to past experience, that the courts of a state would provide relief within the eighteen-month period. This is reminiscent of the local remedies rule which need not be followed where the remedies suggested in local law are illusory. They provided for situations, common in Latin America at the time the local remedies rule was formulated, where the judiciary was patently tied to the executive to such an extent that it would not provide a remedy that transgressed the wishes of the executive. Such a situation has no relevance in states with functioning democracies. Besides, the treaties containing such provisions are couched in mandatory terms and contain a pre-emptive direction as to negotiation and prior efforts at litigation before commencing arbitration. There is no room in these circumstances for the tribunal to find a way out of the precedent requirements.

3.6   Conclusion

The early euphoria regarding 'arbitration without privity' was misplaced. Leaving aside the fact that states are withdrawing from the system of investment arbitration, other states have sought to argue for exceptions to jurisdictions based on the formulations in the treaty or to introduce changes in the new treaties they make. More states will withdraw if tribunals interpret jurisdictional provisions in an expansive manner. Some arbitral tribunals have warned of this consequence. They have pointed out that if treaties are not interpreted in good faith, there will be adverse consequences on the system.[134] It may have proved harmful to the system of investment arbitration that this euphoria led to the view that there would be an almost unrestricted right to sue states under treaties that could be exploited in creative ways. With that in mind, several ingenious ways of invoking jurisdiction under the treaties were attempted, bringing about a reaction from states that had to respond by restricting the right either through challenging jurisdiction before tribunals on a variety of grounds, by modification of treaties or by withdrawal from arbitration. Within the system of arbitration itself, a schism resulted between those arbitrators who favoured expansionist views and those who showed fidelity to the idea that strict consent must exist prior to the

---

[134] *Alps Finance.*

3.6 CONCLUSION   189

finding of jurisdiction. Both groups found support in the rules on interpretation of treaties, which they used as it suited their objectives rather than in any principled way. Consequently, divisions developed which led to concern with the system. This disenchantment, both in states as well as within the arbitration community, became accentuated where various other factors relating to jurisdiction were also exploited in ways that were not originally intended by the framers of the treaties. These areas were identified above.

The expansionism was sudden and in a period of time that was characterized by a move for liberalization of flows of assets around the world during the dominance of a market-oriented economy. One may say that the reactions against these moves also took hold when a reaction set in against such expansionism. The reaction did not come from resistance by external actors, as this area, being technical, was of low visibility. The challenges to expansionism were internal to the system. It came from arbitrators, who saw in expansionism a threat to the system in that interpretations designed to benefit foreign investment protection in a manner that did not reflect the intention of the parties not only deviated from the central tenet of arbitration, which required consent as the basis of jurisdiction, but also offended rules of treaty interpretation. Resistance also came from states. The system of investment arbitration depends on states. If expansionism is sufficiently resented, states will respond either through withdrawal or through changes to the treaty system.

Changes that states have sought to make have not entirely worked. Thus, a response of the states to expansionism through corporate nationality has been to introduce the denial of benefits provision. But expansionist tribunals have sought to interpret such provisions as narrowly as possible, thereby accentuating the problem of biased interpretations. Besides, the language in which the change is couched may not achieve the desired result.[135] There is a disparity in effectiveness of negotiators and the ability to respond to developments in the field. In any event, given the prevalence of the pro-investment trend, it is likely that methods of surmounting efforts at restriction would be overcome. If this happens, the withdrawal from the system may be the only way open to the states. It

---

[135] Thus, the ASEAN investment treaty's denial of benefits provision (Article 19) makes the operation of the provision conditional on notification of the home state of misrepresentation of ownership of investment in areas reserved for nationals. This could hardly have been the reason for a denial of benefits provision, which has been watered down during negotiations. Obviously, all states do not have equal knowledge of the implications of the provisions in a regional treaty.

provides a reason for ensuring that good faith is strictly adhered to in making interpretations. Fidelity to the arbitral function also requires such a course. It is difficult to argue that the use of the incorporation theory to permit round-trippers to benefit from the treaties or the use of the MFN clause to widen the scope of arbitration are based on good faith principles. They offend good sense.

One deterrent that is being provided is that when claimants have recourse to arbitration without adequate cause and attempt exorbitant methods of arguing for jurisdiction tribunals, which reject arbitration, are allowing costs against such arbitration.[136] One way forward is to provide security for costs in situations where there are reasons to believe that the jurisdictional grounds are weak. There are well-worn arguments against this, but the need to provide a deterrent for weak jurisdictional arguments justifies such a course.

There is a need also to revive the exhaustion of remedies rule and state a category of non-arbitrable disputes[137] with greater precision. The return to the local remedies rule holds out possibilities. The preamble to the ICSID Convention itself indicates that the Convention did not seek to displace domestic courts. Greater use of domestic courts should be mandatory. The law was made at time when the justice provided by some domestic courts was illusory. But that situation has changed. Recognizing the initial competence of domestic courts and confining remedies to situations of denial of justice will be good starting points to get out of the present malaise created by expansive awards on jurisdiction. It must be tied to the development of an arbitrability doctrine having regard to the increasing significance of other areas of international law that impact on foreign investment so that the greater competence of other tribunals to deal with disputes implicating foreign investments comes to be recognized.

[136] A recent instance is the award in *Achmea* v. *Slovak*, UNCITRAL Case No. 20133/12 (20 May 2014), where the tribunal held that there was no jurisdiction on the ground that the claimant did not have a *prima facie* case and ordered costs against the claimant.

[137] A way was opened for possibility of non-arbitrability in *Desert Line* v. *Yemen* when the issue of *ius cogens* principles clashing with investment protection was considered.

4

The emasculation of expropriation

There is general acceptance that the purpose of the provisions on expropriation in the older investment treaties is to conserve the understanding of capital-exporting states as to what the constituents of a lawful expropriation in customary international law are. Yet these provisions do not create customary international law as not only are the provisions not similar, but the protection that they give to types of investments are qualified in various ways.[1] The primary thrust of customary law, as developed in the practice of developed states, related to the requirement to pay full compensation upon a lawful expropriation. The situations in which expropriation became unlawful were also stated as part of this customary law. These requirements included a public purpose for the expropriation, an absence of discrimination between foreign investors from different home states, the duty to provide due process prior to the expropriation and the payment of compensation.

The drive of the developed states to create a customary body of law on expropriation had been contested by the Latin American states through the Calvo Doctrine, which had asserted exclusive national competence over investment disputes. It was then contested by the developing states after decolonization. The newly independent states espoused the Calvo Doctrine and rejected the competence of international law to deal with issues relating to foreign investment, which was considered an entirely territorial process over which state sovereignty required the exclusiveness of domestic law.[2] Customary law, as conceived by the developed states,

---

[1] As seen in Chapter 3, treaties qualify investments that are protected. They, e.g., protect 'approved' investments only or investments 'admitted in accordance with' specified laws. The internal balance in each treaty varies. The fact that their form is similar does not mean that their substance is the same.

[2] The highpoint was the Charter of Economic Rights and Duties of States (CERDS), Article 2(2)(c) of which asserted domestic competence over all issues of foreign investment. CERDS was embodied in a UN General Assembly resolution. It forms a group of General Assembly resolutions associated with the NIEO, which sought to rebalance the

192 THE EMASCULATION OF EXPROPRIATION

was assailed at a more global level during the articulation of the NIEO[3] and the doctrine of permanent sovereignty over natural resources.[4] The emphasis in the conflict was largely on the standard of compensation, with the developing states advancing 'appropriate compensation' as the new standard, and the developed states adhering to the Hull formula of 'prompt, adequate and effective' compensation.[5] The significance of this debate has abated considerably. The existence of the divergence of views may have been the reason for the making of investment treaties. Expropriation was the central feature of the disputes that took place within the foreign investment process at the time the early treaties were made. Existing standards of treatment, principally the international minimum standard, also showed preoccupation with expropriation, with the standard of compensation as its component

Through investment treaties, states sought to iron out bilaterally what the law relating to expropriation is. Expropriation was the primary concern of the law at the time of the older treaties, and remained so until the period when concern with lesser measures taken by states, which did not amount to expropriation and did not involve dispossession, became prevalent. This did not take place until the mid-1990s. Even when they did take place, some found comfort in the belief that the phrase 'tantamount to an expropriation', used in the treaties to describe a third category of expropriatory acts, would be sufficient to include such measures within the law of expropriation and also to expand the scope of expropriation law. But this belief was soon rejected. Such measures did not affect possession of the investment by the foreign investor. They left possession intact. They did not fall within the paradigm involving dispossession that formed the basis of the law on expropriation. Hence, it became necessary to find other avenues of seeking redress in situations where there were interferences with foreign investment, leaving

---

structure of the international economic order on the assumption that the existing order, built in the time of colonialism, was weighted in favour of the former colonial powers.

[3] The NIEO articulated norms that were intended to redress structural imbalances they argued existed in the international economy. The norms were articulated in the form of a series of General Assembly resolutions, which included, in effect, the Calvo Doctrine and the permanent sovereignty over natural resources.

[4] See Schrijver, *Permanent Sovereignty over Natural Resources*.

[5] The best-known conflict from which the Hull standard originated concerned the Mexican expropriations of 1938 when Cordel Hull, the then US Secretary of State, used the formula 'prompt, adequate and effective compensation' to describe the compensation due to American foreign investors.

4.1 THE COURSE OF EXPROPRIATION LAW

possession of the foreign investment intact. They could not be found in expropriation law. These developments need to be examined.

4.1 The course of expropriation law

The large majority of the investment treaties accept the Hull formula, requiring payment of full compensation immediately in fully transportable currency.[6] Though it is far-fetched to say that such acceptance makes it a part of customary international law, the Hull standard of compensation applies to investments protected under the many treaties that contain a statement of the formula.[7] The rules relating to compensation on expropriation have also been stated in a large number of awards, which have attracted a considerable amount of literature. It is too premature to pronounce the Hull standard as having passed into customary international law on the basis of consistent acceptance in the investment treaties and in arbitral awards. But it is fair to say that the issue is no longer the one that is controversial in the law relating to the expropriation of foreign investment in situations where the treaties state the applicable standard of compensation.

It is, however, worth noting in passing that capital-exporting states always considered that an expropriation effected in the exercise of police powers against specific persons and their property was not only legitimate, but did not carry a duty to pay compensation.[8] The rule was frequently stated, but did not arouse controversy as the law at the time of its formulation was concerned with expropriation of foreign property

---

[6] Some argue that this makes the Hull standard customary law. But this is not correct. Investment treaties only protect investments identified for protection. Restrictions qualify the type of investments that are protected. For example, the treaties may require the investments to be approved or made in accordance with the laws of the host state. Non-approved foreign investments have to be protected by means other than by the treaty law. It would be futile to make the numerical argument that because there are many treaties on investment, they make customary international law. It is necessary to look at the nuances of each treaty. Each treaty contains a carefully negotiated balance.

[7] Quite apart from the fact that the 3,000 odd treaties are not sufficient to create custom, even if they uniformly adopt the standard, there are the problems stated above that most treaties qualify, and qualify differently, the types of investments that are protected under them. This simple fact makes the possibility of custom in this area remote. Custom simply cannot arise in such situations.

[8] Thus, in the draft of the rules on state responsibility made by Sohn and Baxter, the authors recognized takings effected in the exercise of police powers. The American Law Institute's 'Third Restatement on the Foreign Relations Law of the United States' also recognized such takings and gave instances of it as including takings in the exercise of antitrust or customs powers and the imposition of fines for violation of laws.

that took place in pursuance of nationalization programmes that affected the whole economy or sectors of the economy. In the context of such nationalizations, there was an insistence on the payment of compensation by the capital-exporting states despite the fact that there could not have been a better example of a regulatory expropriation than when a former colonial state seeks to change the basis of control of its economy from foreign hands. It is a function of power, perhaps, resulting from imbalance in knowledge that the situation was not considered along those lines. Looked at with hindsight, the whole debate on compensation for foreign property affected in order to change the economic structure of a state freed from exploitative control of investors from the imperial powers appears to be quintessentially regulatory. The reduction of foreign control of the economy resulted in dispossession of the foreign monopolistic owners in some sectors. The aim of the project was the recovery of economic control by the state. If so, the issue of whether such wholesale nationalizations required compensation raises issues different from those that were discussed then. It is also a symbol of change that the episode is now a matter of relative insignificance as the compensation debate is of little significance in the modern law.

New issues have been thrown up as a result of changing circumstances and concerns. Perhaps because outright expropriations seldom take place in modern times to the same extent, compensation for such expropriation is no longer considered as controversial as it was only a few decades ago. In any event, investment treaties were specifically designed with such expropriations in mind. The treaties have settled the standard of compensation that would be paid in the event of the violation of their provisions. Investment law has moved out of the paradigm situation in the context of which the treaty formulation was stated. Treaties designed with outright expropriations in mind have to cater to entirely new situations. The straitjacket of the old formulations in the law remained. There was no intention on the part of the states to deviate from the pattern of customary international law positions as understood by the capital-exporting states. The investment treaties, primarily, did not seek to create new law, but to conserve the Western understanding of what international law on investment protection was.

The need to attract foreign investment was strongly felt during the period of market liberalization, which had accelerated in the 1990s. There was intense competition for such investment, increased by the arrival of the former Soviet bloc states, which had also adopted liberal policies on foreign investment and made investment treaties, giving a further spurt

4.1   THE COURSE OF EXPROPRIATION LAW   195

to the number of such treaties. For them, the investment treaties served the added function that they had left behind communist ideological positions and had embraced capitalism. In that context of competition for foreign investment, outright expropriations became rare. States cannot carry the ignominy of uncompensated expropriation of foreign property and at the same time court foreign investment. In addition to maintaining a front against expropriation through legislative promises not to expropriate foreign property without compensation, states were keen to display hospitability to foreign investment through a slew of measures that showed liberalization of the law on foreign investment. They were part of the neoliberal measures that were advocated by the international financial institutions.[9]

In the past, expropriation had a pejorative connotation. It was discussed by lawyers of the traditional capital-exporting states in the context of the belief that expropriation was confined to socialist states motivated by ideology or to developing states motivated considerations of narrow nationalism. This view was formed at a time when direct expropriations were common. But interferences with the property and contractual rights of foreign investors became more frequent as a result of the need to exercise regulatory powers of states for economic as well as national security reasons within Western states. Developed countries, too, saw the need to exercise such measures of control.[10] As a consequence, they too took measures that amounted to expropriations. The North American Free Trade Agreement (NAFTA), which contained an investment chapter very similar to the US Model Investment Treaty, became the focus of many claims for expropriation against the United States and Canada. The mechanism that was devised against the developing states now began to be used against the developed states, and in the context of these claims the outer extent of the expropriation law formulated in the

---

[9] The role of the World Bank and the IMF in the adoption of market-oriented economies by developing countries and the role of these policies in precipitating economic crises is dealt with in various texts. See Chapter 1.

[10] Both the United Kingdom and Canada rescinded and remade petroleum contracts that they perceived as disadvantageous. Peter Cameron, *Property Rights and Sovereign Rights: The Case of North Sea Oil* (London: Academic Press, 1983). In the context of the global economic crisis, the measures taken by some states have been regarded as expropriatory. See Jason Calamita, 'British Bank Nationalizations: An International Perspective', (2009) 58 *International & Comparative Law Quarterly* 119. The fear expressed in this article was unfounded. No foreign bank sued the British government, for it seemed to have been accepted that the bank nationalizations were necessary regulatory acts. There is currently an arbitration against Greece and others are contemplated.

196   THE EMASCULATION OF EXPROPRIATION

investment treaties came to be explored. The strategies of litigation that were adopted began to be based on extreme theories that could not possibly have been contemplated by the state when making the treaties.

Aggressive theories of litigation were adopted in the North American context. Thus, it was claimed that any act of the state, even a statement of a minister announcing a future intention relating to a measure controlling the production of a potentially carcinogenic substance manufactured by a foreign investor, could be regarded as an expropriation if the value of the enterprise or of the shares in the enterprise fell as a result.[11] This was so despite the fact that the measure was intended to protect the health of the people from the use of the carcinogenic substance. The globalization of the law firms meant that these aggressive litigation techniques began to permeate into other legal cultures.

The focus of expropriation law changed dramatically after the global economic crisis of 2008. European states and the United States took expropriatory measures, particularly in the banking sector. Despite the fact that foreign investment was involved in many of the banks that were taken over by states, no claims for expropriation ensued because of the obvious fact that they constituted regulatory measures to forestall greater economic calamities. Yet Argentina had faced an economic crisis and over fifty cases were brought against it. The two situations stand in marked contrast. There needs to be a credible explanation as to why Argentina had to face this prolonged course of litigation when other states in similar situations did not have to.[12] The Argentine cases and the inconsistent awards arising out of them are burning wide holes in the system of investment arbitration as well as in the theory of expropriation. In the context of these developments, earlier inflexible attitudes to expropriation as a negative practice of developing states had to be given up. Expropriation had to be viewed not as the practice of states that wavered from the straight path of governance standards dictated by the West, but as the practice of prudent developed and developing states ending the excesses of the neoliberal age, which resulted in the absence of regulatory control over financial and economic institutions and precipitated economic crises. Taking these

[11] This was the theory on which *Ethyl* v. *Canada* (1999) 38 ILM 708 and *Methanex* v. *United States,* UNCITRAL (NAFTA), Award (3 August 2005) were brought. In the first case, Canada settled by paying compensation. The claimant lost the second case.

[12] Now Greece, consequent on the global crisis, faces claims based on expropriation under investment treaties. *Postova Bank and Istrokapital* v. *Greece* is a case pending before ICSID arising from sovereign bonds issued by Greece.

4.1 THE COURSE OF EXPROPRIATION LAW 197

banks and other financial corporations into public control and ensuring that they are restored to health became necessary functions of the affected states. Expropriations were obviously a feature of economic regulation, a necessary means of correcting market failures and imperfections in any economic society. In the context of this attitudinal change, it was difficult to maintain the inflexible rules on expropriation built up largely to deter developing states from interfering with foreign investment in the post-colonial phase.

The playing field and the players were also becoming different. Supercilious preaching regarding the reckless nationalists of the developing world had to give way as there was heavy penetration of the economies of the developed states by foreign investors from the newly industrializing BRICS states.[13] Defensive conduct against such economic penetration became necessary, sometimes for precisely the same narrow nationalistic concerns that the developing countries were accused of. The United States, the progenitor of many of the rules of investment protection for over two centuries, stood on the threshold of change in its attitudes to foreign investment as the largest importer of foreign investment capital. Europe is undergoing a similar experience. The possibility that they may have to keep out foreign investment or nationalize existing foreign investment that they find deleterious to their economies is a real fact in these developed states. Expropriation law has lost its place as the natural battleground between the developed and the developing world, with the developed states well on the back-foot on many issues in the area. The pejorative notion that expropriation as the refuge of recalcitrant states bent on harm to the foreign investor while in the throes of nationalist or socialist fervour is not a baggage the law carries any more as the states that claim higher propriety in standards of property protection are now more prone to engage in direct expropriations than developing states. The issues in modern expropriation law are as much issues that affect developed countries, which are increasingly becoming respondents in claims,[14] as they do developing countries. What is more, multinational corporations from developed states are bringing claims

---

[13] BRICS is an acronym for Brazil, Russia, India, China and South Africa. These newly industrializing countries were exporting foreign investment to the erstwhile capital-exporting states, which, sometimes, have had to protect themselves from such penetration on grounds of national security.

[14] Initially, such claims arose in the context of NAFTA. But claims against developed states under other treaties have begun and will increase. See *Vattenfall* v. *Germany; Sancheti* v. *United Kingdom* and *Philip Morris* v. *Australia.*

198 THE EMASCULATION OF EXPROPRIATION

against developed states.[15] In that context, what would be explored most in expropriation law would not be the old rules relating to standards of compensation, but new issues as to what would amount to a taking and how a regulatory taking, which does not involve compensation, is to be identified and differentiated from compensable expropriation.

A related issue is whether there could be circumstances in which a regulatory expropriation carries a duty to pay compensation on the basis of a proportionality test. A compensation debate of a different type arises in this situation. Strangely, if compensation becomes permissible on the basis of a proportionality test, it would mean that the compensation that is granted would be similar to appropriate compensation rather than full compensation, the balance required taking into effect the past factors attending the course of the investment. The law is veering to the view that was taken by the developing states.

Arbitrators who had formed their views in a different period of history were unable to shake off their prejudices when novel solutions were needed to address issues relating to regulatory interference. They had been schooled in international commercial arbitration where property and contract were sacrosanct. Many were brought up in the context of the Iran–US Claims Tribunal, which seldom veered from providing relief to American claimants who had been dispossessed of their property during the Iranian Revolution from Iranian funds that had been seized by the US government. The formula that had to be applied by the Iran–US Claims Tribunal was more extensive than expropriation in that the tribunal was directed to consider the law stated in the text of the Algiers Accord, which gave it jurisdiction to deal with contract disputes as well as those arising from 'expropriation or other measures affecting property rights' according to commercial or international law. As a result, the awards of the Iran–US Claims Tribunal are not directly transferable into other contexts of expropriation as the tribunal had a wider ambit than investment tribunals. Many arbitrators who served on the Iran–US Claims Tribunal transferred into investment arbitration, transporting the law developed by the tribunal into the law applied by investment tribunals, despite the fact that the mandates given to the tribunals were not the same. The mind-set of the arbitrators was tuned to consider the wrongfulness of expropriation. In that context, in the early phases the central emphasis continued to be on property protection, even if there were public and societal interests that required

[15] *Vattenfall* v. *Germany*, ICSID, Case No. ARB/09/6 (11 March 2011); *Philip Morris* v. *Australia*, UNCITRAL, PCA, Case 2012-12 (2012) (ongoing).

4.1 THE COURSE OF EXPROPRIATION LAW 199

protection.[16] Until a schism developed between arbitrators wedded to the cause of investment protection and those who were accommodative of the international law contained in other areas such as human rights, the trend to frown upon expropriations continued.

The nature of the assets that were held in the hands of foreign investors had also undergone changes due to domestic laws on foreign investment. These laws ensured that foreign investors no longer had absolute control over the operations of business, as was the case in the past when the usual situation involved the taking of physical property wholly owned by the foreign investor. The law had to move away to a new paradigm in which the property involved was often intangible property involving rights of control through shareholdings rather than ownership. The foreign investment laws of host states often required foreign investment to operate in association with local business in joint ventures and other forms of associations. The wave of privatizations resulting from the adoption of neoliberal policies resulted in the holding of shares in public corporations by foreign investors, often as minority shareholders. As a result, a significant amount of foreign investment was through the holding of shares in locally incorporated companies, which may not give direct control over the corporations, especially if only minority participation was permitted to foreign investors. A large number of the cases that arose during this period dealt with measures affecting the profitability or value of these shares. When government interventions with business took place in such circumstances, there was no crude taking of assets of the foreign investor, but interference in the manner of the operation of the business or in the exercise of the rights of the shareholders. The situation called for changes to a law that was constructed on the basis of the outright taking of ownership of property. The law on expropriation had to reflect the new reality that in a large number of circumstances total ownership was not affected. The foreign investor's right to his shares was seldom affected. The business was permitted to carry on. The shares may have lost their value, but they still remained with the foreign investors. Also, the position of the foreign investor was no worse and no better than that of the local investor as a result of the intervention. The issue of the foreign investor's protection, especially through the law on expropriation, would be difficult in such circumstances as his position was no worse than that of the local investor in

---

[16] See, e.g., *Santa Elena* v. *Costa Rica*, which was decided by a tribunal that had arbitrators who had sat on the Iran–US Claims Tribunal. A much quoted passage in it emphasizes the cause of investment protection over other considerations.

200 THE EMASCULATION OF EXPROPRIATION

the same corporation. The law on expropriation was not designed to deal with such situations where no dispossession from property was involved. Arbitrators found other ways of dealing with the situation, but carefully avoided using expropriation simply because it would have defied logic if they were to do so. Arbitrators, quite logically, held that mere loss of value cannot amount to expropriation, thus stunting a development of the view that any depreciation in value caused as a result of a measure of the state could amount to expropriation. The recognition of regulatory expropriation further dented the value of expropriation law.[17]

The law had to grapple increasingly with notions of domestic administrative law and concepts of public law. Here again, a change had to occur. Whereas in the past, there had been a preoccupation with contract-based notions, such as the sanctity of contracts, the old moorings in contract were cast aside as it was increasingly clear that what was becoming important was the employment of administrative control mechanisms of the domestic public law. Licensing regimes that were instituted ensured that a new class of property, referred to as 'new property' by administrative lawyers, became significant in investment law. These consisted of administrative permits, clearances for hiring labour, planning permissions for factories, licences for exports and environmental clearances. It was not possible to engage in the process of foreign investment without such administrative permissions. Such devices were enmeshed in local public law and did not exist in any external system. Though the treaty does seek to list concessions given by local law as a part of the protected investment, it is unclear what exactly this meant. The notion of new property did not refer to the physical property or the corporate mechanisms through which property was held, but rather to the administrative preconditions that were necessary to put the property to use, as well as their continued supervision to ensure that the process of investment conformed to the law and the conditions attached to the entry. The conditions could apply not only at the point of entry, but to the later performance of the investment process.[18]

---

[17] For example, *El Paso* v. *Argentina*, ICSID, Case No. ARB/03/5 (31 August 2011), para. 240: 'In principle, general non-discriminatory regulatory measures, adopted in accordance with the rules of good faith and due process, do not entail a duty of compensation.'

[18] In *Amco* v. *Indonesia* (1988) 1 ICSID Rep. 1281, capitalization requirements were involved. The tribunal held that the manner of interference for their breach was unlawful. Obviously, there could have been a lawful interference with the investment for non-performance of the requirement. The later tribunal, *Churchill Mining* v. *Indonesia*, ICSID, Case No. ARB/12/14 (24 February 2014), found that the Indonesian entry laws dealt with admission only. This is incorrect. As *Amco* showed, conditions could be imposed by an

4.1 THE COURSE OF EXPROPRIATION LAW

201

The traditional notions of property remained important, but their use was conditioned on the existence of rules requiring administrative permissions before such could be put to profitable use. Thus, numerous control devices, such as the requirement of planning permissions, environmental permissions such as permission for emissions from industrial sites, capitalization requirements, the permission for the use of infrastructure facilities and permissions to export finished products, were instances of control that the administrative state increasingly employed. They were instituted through licensing systems. Such controls were imposed on national as well as foreign investors, but in developing countries, where the scale of operation of a foreign investor was likely to be larger, the manner in which such controls affected the foreign investor was more visible. Since foreign investment could not be carried out without these administrative permissions, and their withdrawal would affect the carrying out of the foreign investment, issues relating to the proper exercise of regulatory controls assumed significance. The answer that withdrawal of such licences amounted to expropriation was too simplistic as it did not examine the regulatory purpose behind the licensing scheme. Likewise, there were regulatory interferences by states in a large manner of circumstances, such as environmental controls, the distribution of water resources, controls over the price of commodities and export controls. Control over such areas as telecommunications,[19] banking,[20] financial markets,[21] pharmaceuticals,[22] blood banks[23] and conservation of cultural property[24] are also among the areas in which foreign investment disputes have arisen due to regulatory controls. The law of expropriation failed to anticipate these developments, and it was not possible to accommodate the new developments within the old customary law on expropriation stated in the treaties.

---

admissions agency as to how the foreign investor should thereafter operate prior to admission.

[19] *Telekom Malaysia* v. *Ghana*, UNCITRAL (2004). Facts were stated in the challenge to the arbitrator in Dutch proceedings, District Court of the Hague, 18 October 2004. The arbitrator nominated had acted as counsel in another arbitration having similar issues. The few arbitrators who dominate the area also play a multiplicity of roles, adding to criticisms of the system.

[20] *Rafat Ali Rizvi* v. *Indonesia*, ICSID, Case No. ARB/11/13 (16 July 2013).

[21] *Abaclat* v. *Argentina*, ICSID, Case No. ARB/07/5 (4 August 2011).

[22] *Eli Lilley* v. *Canada*, UNCITRAL (NAFTA) (2012 ongoing); *Apotex Inc.* v. *United States*, UNCITRAL (NAFTA), Jurisdiction (14 June 2013). Jurisdiction was not found in the latter case as local remedies had not been exhausted.

[23] *Achmea* v. *Slovak Republic*, UNCITRAL, Case No. 20133/12 (20 May 2014).

[24] *Malaysian Salvors* v. *Malaysia*, ICSID, Case No. ARB/05/10 (17 May 2007); *Parkerings* v. *Lithuania*, ICSID, Case No. ARB/05/8 (11 September 2007).

For a variety of reasons, after the immediate decolonization phase in which direct takings of property ended the economic dominance of the companies of the former colonial powers, emphasis shifted to the question of what types of act could be considered takings for the purpose of compensation, and whether certain types of expropriation did not require the payment of compensation due to their overwhelming public benefit or because public interest in the avoidance of harmful effects required state intervention. The central feature of the developments had to deal with situations in which the governmental measure did not lead to dispossession of property, though there was a diminution of the rights in the property, a fall in its value or the ability to secure the same level of profits as before ceased to exist.

There were two distinct phases of the law in the course of its development beyond the post-colonial nationalizations. The first phase involved incidents in Iran triggered by the downfall of the shah and the setting up of a revolutionary government hostile to the United States. American business fled Iran and was taken over when its owners did not return. There was widespread restructuring of businesses. Some involved the appointment of new Iranian managers. The Iran–US Claims Tribunal was set up to assess compensation for these separate incidents. The tribunal made an expansive interpretation as to what amounted to a taking of property to trigger the expropriation provision in the investment treaties. Such expansive interpretation was justified by the terms of the Algiers Accord. The Iran–US Claims Tribunal's mandate was specified in its founding documents. It was to deal with 'expropriations and other measures affecting property rights', giving rise to the idea that any interference with property rights could be assimilated to an expropriation due to the reference to the 'other measures' in the provision.[25] The tribunal had a specific mandate to take the view that 'other measures affecting property rights' were to be treated like expropriations. The tribunal was to dissect the notion of property into its constituent components and hold that any adverse effect on any aspect of such unbundled property rights would amount to an expropriation justifying compensation.[26] The reasoning was justified in the context of the specific

[25] Article 2 of the Declaration on the Settlement of Claims attached to the Algiers Accord, 19 January 1981.
[26] It was common to regard property as a bundle of rights rather than as a single right as the concept could be split. Servitudes could be granted. Leases could be made. The explanation in terms of a bundle of rights was considered appropriate as property could be split with ownership in one person and lesser rights created by the owner in others. Later, the

formulation in the Algiers Accord. It was not an idea that was transportable into investment treaties, which were not similarly worded. Yet, since personnel in the Iran–US Claims Tribunal were to later decide cases arising from investment treaties, the transportation came to be too readily made, befuddling the law under the investment treaties. Awards made under the Iran–US Claims Agreement came to be used as precedents to be followed in investment arbitration.

The second phase concerned the transference of the Iran–US Claims Awards into customary international law despite the fact that such a transference is not theoretically possible. Awards made on the basis of an accord between two states can hardly constitute state practice. The awards could not create law that applies to third states. Some texts on general international law began to use the cases decided by the Iran–US Claims Tribunal indiscriminately as reflecting customary international law on expropriation without regard to the specific powers that had been given to that tribunal by its constituent treaty.[27] The transference was wrongly thought to be justified by the threefold classification of taking in investment treaties as direct and indirect takings with the addition of a third potentially wide category providing for acts 'tantamount to' or 'equivalent to' takings. The formulation was entirely different from that in the Algiers Accord, which included 'measures affecting property' within expropriation. In this phase of expansion not only were ideas propounded by awards of the Iran–US Claims Tribunal carried into investment treaty arbitration, but increasingly creative interpretations were made in devising fascinating litigation strategies that states could never have contemplated as capable of being accommodated within the framework they had stated in the formulae used to define the acts that could amount to takings. The second phase was expansionary. It focused on the expansion of the third limb regarding acts that were 'tantamount' to arbitration. This formulation made creativity possible, and a tendency began to appear under which any measure that led to the depreciation in the value of the investment could amount to expropriation. If this view

---

state came to acquire power over property for planning, environmental and other reasons. This was explained as affecting some of the rights in the bundle.

[27] Thus, e.g., the popular casebook on international law, David Harris, *Cases and Materials on International Law*, 7th edn (London: Sweet & Maxwell, 2010), includes several pages of materials from the Iran–US Claims Tribunal on expropriation in illustrating the rules on state responsibility without paying any heed to the fact that the cases were based on the peculiar wording of an accord, and could hardly give rise to customary international law on state responsibility or illustrate principles of expropriation within international law. No explanation is given as to how this was accomplished.

was possible, it would be broad enough to capture the developments relating to measures states were taking in order to deal with social and welfare problems, as well as regulation of shares and interests in locally incorporated companies. It was confidently predicted in 2004 that the future course of expropriation law would be based on the scope of the third limb, 'tantamount to an expropriation' in the definition of takings.[28] The tendencies can be said to promote neoliberal visions of foreign investment protection in that the coverage of protection came to be greatly extended beyond what had been originally intended by the parties to the treaty on the basis that policy objectives required the making of such extensions.

The prediction went awry in the very year the US Model Treaty (2004) indicated that regulatory takings were not to be considered indirect takings except in very exceptional circumstances. The states immediately affected by this trend were the developed states, as the expansion was initially tried out in the NAFTA context.[29] Its initial success in *Ethyl* was scotched in the later *Methanex* case.

The first part of this chapter deals with these expansionary trends. The second part deals with the return to the old wisdom that only physical dispossession was relevant for the application of the expropriation provisions of the treaty. The need to return to the old model of expropriation must be explained, for it constituted a sudden reversal of the way the law was heading. This reversal was an evident reaction to the expansionary trend initiated by adventurous arbitrators and lawyers bent on expanding expropriation as a cause of action to meet new situations involving administrative interferences in property, which were on the increase. To some extent, the reversal was brought about by new provisions on regulatory expropriations in investment treaties. But some arbitrators began to baulk at the expansive interpretations. As explained previously, expropriation law was not constructed with such situations in mind. The backlash that took place concentrated on the paradigm situation of the need for physical dispossession for there to be expropriation. It

---

[28] Michael Reisman and Robert Sloane, 'Indirect Expropriation and its Valuation in the BIT Generation', (2004) 75 *British Yearbook of International Law* 115.

[29] The initial success was in the case against Canada. *Ethyl* v. *Canada* (1999) 38 ILM 708, where a statement made as to a future possible ban on the manufacture of a chemical additive to petrol was considered tantamount to an expropriation was the basis of the claim. Canada, reportedly settled by paying several million dollars by way of damages. *Methanex* v. *United States* (2005) had similar facts, but the United States succeeded with the argument that the measures were regulatory in nature.

4.1 THE COURSE OF EXPROPRIATION LAW

sought to curb the excessive interpretation by concentrating on the original model on the basis of which the law was created. The natural meaning of 'tantamount to an expropriation' also required that there should be similarity with the situation of an actual dispossession. Expropriation could not apply to a situation where the foreign investor was still holding the property that was the subject of the alleged expropriation. The reaction of states was to effectively emasculate the law on expropriation. The third category of 'tantamount to' takings was often removed from the newer treaties. More tellingly, a new provision was introduced into the taking provision that indirect regulatory takings were not compensable except in exceptional circumstances. The law underwent a definite transformation, resulting from the reactions of states as well as to the arguments that excessive protection of foreign investment led to sacrificing social, environmental and human rights interests.

The entry of both NGOs and international lawyers with interests in related fields of human rights,[30] the environment[31] and cultural property[32] had the effect of conserving the category of regulatory expropriations. The clash of interests in this field with that of property protection had to be accommodated. Cases increasingly reflected this clash. The revival of regulatory expropriation enabled the accommodation of these interests as their existence, as the purpose of state measures, enabled them to be characterized as regulatory expropriations. They moved out of the law on compensable expropriation.

The episodes powerfully demonstrate how emphasis on the objective of exclusive property protection leads to the resistance of interest groups concerned with conflicting issues, and how the law reacts by seeking an accommodation of these interests within it by relinquishing absolute emphasis on one interest in order to accommodate other equally valid interests. It also shows that fragmentation of international law will come to be resisted when the law is compartmentalized so as to prefer investment protection to the exclusion of other legal areas, such as those relating to environmental and human rights. It demonstrates the cyclical movements in the law, where the emphasis on foreign investment

---

[30] Dupuy *et al.*, (eds.), *Human Rights in International Investment Law and Arbitration.*

[31] *Santa Elena* v. *Costa Rica* was a case where the environmental concern was pleaded unsuccessfully. *S. D. Myers* v. *Canada*, UNCITRAL (NAFTA) (13 November 2000); the several awards involving environmental considerations are conveniently discussed in Vinuales, *Foreign Investment and Environment in International Law.*

[32] Valentina Vadi's work contains a discussion of the awards and the law involving cultural property. Vadi, *Cultural Heritage in International Investment Law and Arbitration.*

protection in times of the ascendancy of neoliberal views emphasizing property and contract rights leads to absolute protection, only to be replaced by more accommodative norms recognizing competing interests when resistance to neoliberalism develops as a result of its visible failures. The neoliberal ideas do not die out altogether. They are kept alive. No idea is completely vanquished. The end of history never occurs. Neoliberal views are too powerful and tenacious to be eliminated altogether. Vestiges of their past success will remain, and they could be resurrected if changes in circumstances were to present opportunities in the future. Evidence of this is provided in this area by the resurgence of arbitral competence over regulatory expropriation through the application of the proportionality test. The pendulum keeps swinging. It does not stop.

Arbitrators, too, are sensitive to these changes. The increasing understanding of the role of public law in the area of investment arbitration has led to the acceptance of the view that regulatory space has to be created for the state to ensure the performance of its basic task of protecting public interests. It could well be that arbitrators steeped in the tradition of commercial arbitration may be resistant to such trends, but other arbitrators within investment arbitration are more conscious of the need to recognize that investment arbitration does have to accommodate the public interests. When such understanding comes about, accepting the changing attitudes to expropriation are easy. Yet some arbitrators will not want to travel this path. They would prefer to cling onto the old orthodoxy of absolute investment protection against expropriation. Schisms develop among arbitration awards as a result. But with the acceptance that the role for the old law on expropriation in situations of regulatory takings has diminished, there has been a reduction in recent times of such schisms. State intervention to change treaties to ensure that regulatory interventions are excluded from the scope of expropriation has assisted this process. But arbitrators intent on investment protection have opened up an escape route through the development of the fair and equitable standard to accommodate concerns caused by administrative measures. They have also had recourse to the notion of proportionality to reserve a competence to decide whether or not the measure adopted was necessary in the circumstances and, where necessary, was it proportionate to the benefit secured or the harm avoided through the infringement of the property right. The view on which this review is based is that unreasonable and disproportionate regulatory measures of interference should carry a duty to compensate.

4.2 THE BASIS OF EXPANSION OF EXPROPRIATION 207

It is necessary to understand the developments in the area of expropriation to understand why the formerly dormant standard of fair and equitable treatment has become the central focus of the current law on investment treaty arbitration. The shift is explicable largely on the basis of the events leading to the emasculation of expropriation. As expropriation law becomes restricted through an emphasis on actual dispossession and the need to create regulatory space for the state to protect public interests, newer theories and views had to be formulated to keep the objective of investment protection alive. Another door had to be opened for this to be achieved. That door was the hitherto dormant standard of fair and equitable treatment. The discovery and expansion of that standard within a short span of a few years,[33] dealt with in Chapter 5, was seen as the way out of the problem for investment protection created by the emasculation of expropriation. Though initially the fair and equitable standard was stated in an all-embracing fashion to encompass regulatory measures, its scope has also progressively been whittled down. This process itself reflected a need to seek an accommodation between the objective of investment protection and the state's right to exercise its regulatory function. This process is considered in Chapter 5. For the reason that it is the emasculation of expropriation that led to the opening up of the new cause of action under the fair and equitable treatment, the analysis of expropriation in this chapter forms a prelude to the next, which deals with the rise to prominence of the standard of fair and equitable treatment and the tussles that have resulted in determining its scope. In the light of trends in expropriation law, it is of significance to inquire whether the sudden expansion of the fair and equitable standard will also prove to be of ephemeral significance.

4.2 The basis of expansion of expropriation

The threefold formulation of a taking as 'direct, indirect or an act tantamount (or equivalent) to a taking' provided the basis for an expansionist interpretation. The second category of indirect takings had itself moved the law away from its original moorings in deprivation of physical possession that is involved in a direct taking. Newcombe, after surveying

---

[33] A five-year period is calculated on the basis of its acceptance in *CMS Gas Transmission Co. v. Argentina* (2003), and the assessment by Schreuer that the fair and equitable standard had become an autonomous standard in an article in 2005. Christoph Schreuer, 'Fair and Equitable Treatment in Arbitral Practice', (2005) 6 *Journal of World Investment and Trade* 357.

208 THE EMASCULATION OF EXPROPRIATION

the then existing authorities, concluded that there is 'overwhelming authority for the proposition that an indirect expropriation occurs where the state acquires the control, use or enjoyment of property through the exercise of state powers'.[34] That is a conclusion dependent on treating property as having constituent rights. It also worked on the notion that the right of management and control was central to ownership of interests in a company. The change was necessary as the host law often mandated that locally incorporated companies operate foreign investments. What was affected was the power of the foreign investor to control the corporation. It was a response to a phenomenon at a particular stage of the law. One important factor in this line of cases is that the state did stand to gain as a result of the measures it had adopted, as the control over the company that was in possession of the assets went into the hands of the state or its nominees. In such circumstances, there was a moral and a legal duty to compensate. These cases may have been instances of regulatory takings in the sense that if the state did not take over and run the businesses, they would have been left unattended or would have failed. In the context of the Iranian Revolution, many of the American owners of companies had fled the country, leaving the companies without management. The state usually took over the running of the companies, and in that sense profited from the taking. Such a profit element in the state was lacking when ownership of the shares were left intact in the hands of the foreign investor and the company was running as before, though the measures taken by the state, often in response to economic crises, had led to reduction of profits. This was a situation that could not have been covered by the older cases.

In the older awards, expropriation was found even in clear situations which had a regulatory purpose. Thus, in *Metalclad v. Mexico*,[35] the tribunal held that the deprivation of the 'use or reasonably to be expected economic benefits of the property' is sufficient to find expropriation. But in the same year, *Pope and Talbot v. Canada*[36] used a restrictive test emphasizing the intensity of the deprivation as a requirement, a mere lessening of benefits flowing from the governmental measure not being sufficient. A division in attitudes had emerged.

---

[34] Andrew Newcombe, 'Boundaries of Regulatory Expropriation in International Law', (2005)20 *ICSID Review* 1, at p. 21. See, generally, Ursula Kriebaum, 'Regulatory Takings: Balancing the Interests of the Investor and the State', (2007)8 *Journal of World Investment and Trade* 717.

[35] ICSID, Case No. ARB/97/1 (30 August 2000), (2001) 40 ILM 36.

[36] UNCITRAL (NAFTA), Ad hoc Arbitration (2 April 2001).

4.2 THE BASIS OF EXPANSION OF EXPROPRIATION 209

The loosening of the requirements for establishing indirect expropriation was also accomplished by emphasizing the effect a measure had on the investment, rather than by examining the intent of the state in adopting the measure. This facilitated a measure to be considered as expropriation on the ground that it affected the exercise of a right or caused a depreciation in value despite the fact that it was not the intention of the state to produce such a result, but was a by-product of the measures it had taken to achieve an objective in the public interest. The strategy was to argue that the impact of the measure on the investment was what mattered. The awards responded with wide definitions of indirect expropriation that emphasized 'the neutralizing of the benefit of the property rights of the foreign owner'.[37] The best authority for expropriation as consisting of measures that reduce the enjoyment of benefits comes from the awards of the Iran–US Claims Tribunal, which, as indicated, rested on a different formulation in the Algiers Accord. In *Starret Housing* v. *Iran*,[38] the tribunal spoke of measures 'rendering rights useless that they must be deemed to have been expropriated, even though the State does not purport to have expropriated them'.[39] In *Occidental Exploration and Production Co.* v. *Ecuador*,[40] the broad statement is made on reliance of the Iran–US Claims Tribunal awards that 'a deprivation of taking may occur under international law through interference by a state in the use of that property or with the enjoyment of its benefits, even where legal title to the property is not affected'. The tribunal in *Occidental* stated it as a proposition of general international law, not as law under the treaty, and showed a willingness to state general international law so widely without sufficient authority from sources other than the Iran–US Claims Tribunal, which was given the specific power of treating measures affecting property as equivalent with expropriation.

The laxity introduced into the law brought about tensions. Restrictions widening of the scope of the expropriation law attempted in the earlier awards in the 1990s had begun to appear. Clearly, some arbitrators

---

[37] *CME* v. *Czech Republic* (2001) 9 ICSID Rep. 121, at 236.

[38] *Starret Housing Corp.* v *Iran* (1983) 4 Iran–US CTR 122.

[39] *Starret Housing Corp.* v *Iran; Tippets* v. *Iran* (1984) 6 Iran–US CTR 219; *Foremost Tehran Inc.* v. *Iran* (1987) 10 Iran–US CTR 228, where the tribunal said that 'it is well settled, in this Tribunal's practice as elsewhere, that property may be taken under international law through interference by a State in the use of that property or with the enjoyment of its benefits'. The statement may be correct as to the Tribunal's practice grounded in the formulation under the treaty creating it, but whether it is true 'elsewhere' is contentious. The tribunal was creating a mirage that it was applying a universally accepted principle.

[40] LCIA No. UN3 467 (1 July 2004) (Orrego-Vicuna, Brower, Sweeney).

recanted in the belief that the law had been extended beyond the intention of the parties and that this would produce a backlash against investment arbitration unless stopped. The awards based on the discovery of regulatory expropriation may be taken as indications of a withdrawal by some arbitrators from the over-zealous approach that took the law away from its original base.

The third category of measures 'tantamount to an expropriation' provided scope for expansion in the context of developments relating to regulation of sectors that were becoming increasingly common due to greater concern with environmental problems, human rights and labour rights. The distinction between indirect expropriation and the third category of acts 'tantamount to an expropriation' had not been clearly worked out. It provided an enormous scope for expansion and was probably intended to do so by the draftsmen who introduced the phrase into the treaties.[41] It obviously was not taken from any domestic system, but was purposely introduced to ensure as complete a protection as possible. It provided a reserve category which enabled the foreign investors to go to arbitration if governmental measures affected their interests even minimally by producing effects they considered to be undesirable.

Awards such as *Metalclad* and the litigation strategy in *Ethyl* indicated that efforts were being focused on this provision to found a broad theory that any regulatory measure that depreciates the value of the foreign investment would amount to an expropriation. *Metalclad*'s broad definition of indirect expropriation that the deprivation of the 'use or reasonably to be expected economic benefits of the property' amounted to expropriation,[42] though widely criticized,[43] reflected the mood of the times. Writing in 2004, Reisman and Sloane found that the third limb – 'tantamount to a taking' – would be the focus of the future development

---

[41] The exact time of such introduction is difficult to identify. Dolzer and Stephens, *Bilateral Investment Treaties*, do not make reference to the term 'tantamount to an expropriation' in their survey of investment treaties. Focus on the phrase came later and lasted for a very short period, demonstrating passing facets in the law.

[42] *Metalclad Corp.* v. *Mexico*, ICSID, Case No. ARB(AF)/97/1 (30 August 2000): 'expropriation under NAFTA includes not only open, deliberate and acknowledged takings of property, such as outright seizure or formal or obligatory transfer of title in favour of the host State, but also covert or incidental interference with the use of property which has the effect of depriving the owner, in whole or in significant part, of the use or reasonably-to-be-expected economic benefit of property even if not necessarily to the obvious benefit of the host State'. Such broad definitions link expropriation with the fair and equitable treatment.

[43] The British Columbia court which had supervisory jurisdiction over the award vacated this part of the award. *United Mexican States* v. *Metalclad Corp.* (2001) 14 BLR (3d) 285.

4.2 THE BASIS OF EXPANSION OF EXPROPRIATION 211

of expropriation law. They suggested that 'the major innovation of the "tantamount clause", found in almost all BITs, therefore consists in extending the concept of indirect expropriation to an egregious failure to create or maintain the normative favourable conditions in the host state'.[44] It took the law beyond the already expansionist meaning of indirect expropriation into an area yet to be charted. It coincided with efforts at the time to deem that any measure that interfered with the stability of the investment would be a violation of the treaty.[45] At the least, the existence of such a vast residual category condoned the expansion of the category of indirect expropriations that had already been made. In that very year, the prediction was shattered with the US Model Treaty, which contained a provision that regulatory expropriations protecting or promoting public welfare should be regarded as non-compensable.[46] It also did not include the wording regarding acts tantamount to an expropriation in the main article on expropriation, thus evincing a clear desire to restrict the adventurism that had been initiated through the imaginative strategies that sought to extend 'tantamount to a taking' to all measures of the state that caused any depreciation to the property, even where such depreciation was an unintended consequence of the measure taken. This stymied the hopes of the expansionists in using the third limb of the definition of takings.

The rule that indirect regulatory expropriation is part of investment law has been confirmed through awards as well as through its inclusion in treaties. Yet the possibility of relief through expropriation was provided through the argument that the formulation does not prevent a tribunal from giving compensation on the basis of assessments as to the proportionality of the regulatory measure in the context of the harm it sought to cure and the effect of the measure on the foreign investor. The importation of the proportionality doctrine into investment law is intended to keep alive the idea that compensation is possible even in the case of regulatory expropriations. The proportionality doctrine itself has no basis in the language of the formulation of expropriation in the

---

[44] Reisman and Sloane, 'Indirect Expropriation and its Valuation in the BIT Generation', at p. 116.

[45] Three separate strands of the idea were present at the time. Apart from acts interfering with stability being regarded as expropriation, such measures were regarded as affecting the protection of security of the investment and the fair and equitable standard.

[46] The influence of *Methanex* v. *United States* was obvious. The brunt of the US argument was that there was sovereign power in the United States to regulate in the public interest and forbid the manufacture and use of substances which are injurious to public health notwithstanding the NAFTA prohibition on expropriation without compensation.

212   THE EMASCULATION OF EXPROPRIATION

treaty. The impact of the introduction of the proportionality rule is considered in greater detail in Chapter 8. It is an innovation that is intended to keep the relevance of expropriation in the fact of the exception of regulatory expropriation, which is the more usual form of state interference with foreign investment in modern times.

4.3   The revival of regulatory expropriation

The idea that expropriation in the exercise of police powers of a state was not compensable always existed in the constitutional laws of Western states and passed into the statement of the international law on expropriation. Its clearest expression is in American constitutional law. It is the American rule on regulatory expropriation that has been imported into the modern treaties. The best statement of the rule is in the American Restatement on the Foreign Relations Law of the United States.[47] The examples that were given in the Restatement of regulatory expropriation were criminal fines, which involved confiscation of property after conviction, taxation measures, charges accompanying customs measures, taxation and antitrust interventions. The list was not intended to be exhaustive. Antitrust measures, for example, were largely American as many legal systems at the time of the Restatement, did not have such laws.[48] The examples were made at a time when other regulatory devices, such as those relating to the environment and human rights, were uncommon.

In later times, states became interventionary. The welfare state as a provider of facilities and services to the community intervened regularly in the market place.[49] There concerns were introduced through the interaction of international and domestic norms. Legal areas, non-existent in the past, developed as a result of the concern of societies

---

[47] American Law Institute, Second Restatement on the Foreign Relations Law of the United States.

[48] The Sherman Act was the basis of American antitrust law aimed at monopolization and price fixing. European systems recognized a law on restrictive practices in contracts, but a fully-fledged antitrust law appeared only with Articles 85 and 86 of the Treaty of Rome.

[49] Some early works were Lord Hewart, *The New Despotism* (London: Ernest Benn, 1929); Wolfgang Friedmann, *The Rule of Law in a Mixed Economy* (London: Stevens, 1971), identifying the emergence of a more active state with the advent of socialism in Europe. But the extent of state control considerably accelerated after the Second World War until the advent of Thatcherism in Britain and its European counterparts. After a dormant period in which free market capitalism stunted regulation, regulatory interventions have become more frequent.

4.3 THE REVIVAL OF REGULATORY EXPROPRIATION 213

with new issues that confronted them globally as well as domestically. These related to the promotion of human rights, the protection of the environment, the recognition of labour rights, the promotion of corporate responsibility, prevention of corruption, taxation of excessive profits, protection of cultural property, the conservation of indigenous rights to land, and the protection of the health and welfare of society. The intensity of these concerns hardly existed at the time that investment treaties came to be made. Concern with these interests grew more intense than concern for investment protection, which constituted the interests of a smaller group within the international community. The interests were global interests, whereas the interests of foreign investors were those of a limited group. In the hierarchy of interests, it could well be argued that the global interests create obligations of greater intensity. They have the capacity to displace the obligations owed by states to foreign investors.[50]

Each of these areas involving global interests were addressed through international law, but also addressed through domestic law. The domestic law on them was often constructed on the basis of international documents. But sometimes they were of domestic origin. The law on expropriation that had been formed in the context of the capricious confiscations of dictators and later the nationalistic takings of newly independent states, had to cope with the entirely new phenomena of state interventions motivated by genuine public interest reasons arising from new developments. Public concern with these new areas was stoked by the rise of NGOs with single agendas to promote the interest they espoused. They advocated that states should regulate areas in which their concerns are affected. They often wielded as much power within states as multinational corporations. They were able to meet the interests advanced within the domestic political sphere by multinational corporations with equal vigour. The NGOs argued that the regulatory chill that foreign investment protection, mandated by investment treaties, brought about thwarted the global interests in several areas.[51] As much as investment protection was furthered by multinational cooperation, the competing interests of the protection of the environment, of human rights, of corporate responsibility and other matters were furthered by different groups of NGOs. The power that multinational corporations could wield to promote investment protection came to be neutralized by the pressure that NGOs could exert to bring about regulatory measures affecting

---

[50] Kulick, *Global Public Interest in International Investment Law.*
[51] Tienhaara, *The Expropriation of Environmental Governance.*

214 THE EMASCULATION OF EXPROPRIATION

foreign investment. This contest was repeated at the global level as well. NGOs were able to summon sufficient numbers of protestors and lobbying power to prevent efforts that states took to advance the interests of multinational corporations. In the trade sphere, the Doha Development Round and the endless protests at different meetings of the WTO are symbols of such pressure to bring about changes to laws that had entirely favoured the interests of multinational corporations. The pressure brought about to change aspects of the WTO law on intellectual property involving pharmaceutical drugs is an instance of the success of such resistance. Similar trends were at work in international investment law.

Neoliberalism in the 1990s eclipsed these interests as the state was to refrain from regulation of markets. This hands off approach led to failure. As the failure became evident, the breach that was made against neoliberalism burst out, resulting in the resurgence of the competing interests of different groups pressing for regulation of foreign investment. The onslaught of these interests was such that change had to occur.

Both developed and developing states were subjected to such pressures. The state's right to regulate in the public interest came into collision with the inflexible aim of investment protection. Investment protection dictated the inflexible preservation of the old law on expropriation. Reality dictated changes to the old law, for the developed states themselves were engaging in takings that reflected the new concerns. In that context, it was not possible to retain the law inspired by the neoliberal viewpoint, which rested on the neoliberal policy assumption that the aim of the investment treaties was to create 'a control mechanism over government' and contribute to the acceptance of common international standards of governance.[52]

Some arbitral tribunals sought to preserve the old law in the initial stages. They went along with the notion that the regulatory purpose behind the taking would not be relevant. It was stated that regulatory expropriation, particularly environmental measures taken in the public interest or in pursuance of obligations created by environmental treaties, will not provide an excuse. In *Santa Elena* v. *Costa Rica*,[53] the award expressly stated that the environmental reasons for the taking should not be considered as relevant. It said:[54]

---

[52] Reisman and Sloane, 'Indirect Expropriation and Its Valuation in the BIT Generation', at p. 117.

[53] ICSID, Case No. ARB/96/1 (17 February 2000), at para. 72.

[54] The context was the emphasis on effect rather than the purpose of the measure. In this, the tribunal was following the finding in *Tippets*, an Iran–US Claims Tribunal, that 'the intent

4.3 THE REVIVAL OF REGULATORY EXPROPRIATION 215

Expropriatory environmental measures – no matter how laudable and beneficial to society as a whole – are, in this respect, similar to any other expropriatory measures that a state may take in order to implement its policies: where property is expropriated, even for environmental purposes, whether domestic or international, the states obligation to pay compensation remains.

Likewise, in the *Tecmed* Award, made in 2003, the tribunal stated:[55]

> We find no principle stating that regulatory administrative actions are *per se* excluded from the scope of the Agreement, even if beneficial to society as a whole – such as environmental protection – particularly if the negative economic impact of such action on the financial position of the investor is sufficient to neutralize in full the value, or economic or commercial use of its investment without receiving any compensation whatsoever.

In *Pope and Talbot* v. *Canada*, the tribunal stated that 'a blanket exception for regulatory measures would create a gaping loophole in international protection against expropriation'.[56]

A 'gaping loophole' was in fact foreshadowed even as awards like *Tecmed* were delivered. In *Feldman* v. *Mexico*,[57] decided in 2002, the tribunal signalled the notion that regulatory interventions need not amount to expropriation under the investment chapter of NAFTA.[58] In doing so, the tribunal indicated that it was paraphrasing what had been said in *Azinian* v. *Mexico* (1999).[59] The tribunal in *Feldman* said:[60]

---

[55] of the government is less important than the effects of the measures on the owner, and the form of the measures of control or interference is less important than the reality of their impact' (para. 77).

[55] *Tecmed* v. *Mexico*, ICSID, Case No. ARB(AF)/00/2 (29 May 2003), para. 121.

[56] *Pope and Talbot* v. *Canada*, UNCITRAL (NAFTA), Ad hoc Arbitration, Interim Award (2 April 2001), para. 99.

[57] ICSID, Case No. ARB(AF)/99/1, Award (16 December 2002), para. 112 (Kerameus, Bravo, Gantz).

[58] Earlier, in *Lauder* v. *Czech Republic*, UNCITRAL Arbitration (3 September 2001) (Briner, Cutler, Klein), the tribunal, in an arbitration under the Netherlands–Czech BIT, stated that 'bona fide regulation within the accepted police powers of the state' was not expropriation. In *S. D. Myers* v. *Canada*, the tribunal stated that 'parties are not liable for economic injury that is the consequence of bona fide regulation within the accepted police powers of the State'.

[59] ICSID, Case No. ARB(AF)/97/2 (1 November 1999), (1999) 14 ICSID Rep. 2, at para. 83 (Paulsson, Civiletti, von Wobeser). The sentence paraphrased was innocuous. It read: 'It is a fact of life everywhere that individuals may be disappointed in their dealings with public authorities.'

[60] The tribunal relied on the American Restatement on the Foreign Relations Law of the United States in identifying the measure as 'undeniably a measure of general taxation of the kind envisaged by Restatement Comment (g)'.

216   THE EMASCULATION OF EXPROPRIATION

> To paraphrase *Azinian*, not all government regulatory activity that makes
> it difficult or impossible for an investor to carry out a particular business,
> change in the law or change in the application of existing laws that makes
> it uneconomical to continue a particular business, is an expropriation
> under Article 1110. Governments, in their exercise of regulatory power,
> frequently change their laws and regulations in response to changing
> economic circumstances or changing political, economic or social con-
> siderations. Those changes may well make certain activities less profitable
> or even uneconomic to continue.

In arriving at this conclusion, the tribunal had indicated that it was
stating customary international law. It said:[61]

> governments must agree to act in the broader public interest through
> protection of the environment, new or modified tax regimes, the granting
> or withdrawal of government subsidies, reductions or increases in tariff
> levels, imposition of zoning restrictions and the like. Reasonable govern-
> mental regulation of this type cannot be achieved if any business that is
> adversely affected may seek compensation, and it is safe to say that
> customary international law recognized this.

The view stated in *Tecmed* was not consistent with some existing awards,
which had begun to recognize that regulatory takings were not compensable. These awards must be taken as another instance of conflicting
awards in the area of investment arbitration. But *Methanex* v. *United
States*, decided in 2005, put an end to any contrary views.

In *Methanex* v. *United States*,[62] the claimant's argument was that there
was a taking as the ban on its production of methanol had diverted the
market to competitors manufacturing an equivalent chemical product,
ethanol. The manufacture of methanol had been banned due to a finding
that it was carcinogenic. A University of California study supported this
finding. The claimant relied on the argument that the ban was 'tantamount to expropriation'. The argument, in effect, was that the diminution of the market value of the investment was an expropriation. The
tribunal recognized that a regulatory expropriation protecting public
health was not compensable in the context of NAFTA. The tribunal in
Methanex stated the rule on regulatory takings thus:[63]

> as a matter of general international law, a non-discriminatory regulation for
> a public purpose, which is enacted in accordance with due process and which

---

[61] At para. 105. American Restatement, section 712, comment (g), that bona fide general
taxation is within the police powers of a state is reproduced in the paragraph.
[62] UNCITRAL (NAFTA) Ad hoc Arbitration, 3 August 2005 (Veeder, Rowley, Reisman).
[63] Pt IV, ch. D, p. 3.

4.3 THE REVIVAL OF REGULATORY EXPROPRIATION 217

affects, *inter alios*, a foreign investor or investment is not deemed expropriatory and compensable unless specific commitments had been given by the regulating government to the then putative foreign investor contemplating investment that the government would refrain from such regulation.

The proviso relating to specific commitments was supported by the statement in *Revere Copper and Brass Inc.* v. *OPIC*,[64] which is cited as authority for it, but the case does not form a part of general international law. The status of the case, an OPIC award,[65] in terms of international law is doubtful, and there is no authority in general international law for any exception to the rule that a non-discriminatory expropriation for a public purpose is not expropriatory. The American Restatement, which is considered the best statement of police powers, contains no exceptions to the rule. The fact that commitments may have been given will make no difference to the rule. It simply would not matter if commitments had been made to the claimant. It is now accepted that a stabilization clause in a contract, which is the strongest form of commitment a state could make, cannot stand in the way of a state acting in the public interest.[66] The two awards[67] cited cannot affect the validity of the general rule on regulatory expropriation, which has always been stated without qualification. In any event, the tribunal found that:[68]

> No such commitments were given to *Methanex*. *Methanex* entered a political economy in which it was widely known, if not notorious, that governmental and environmental and health protection institutions at the federal level, operating under the vigilant eyes of the media, interested corporations and non-governmental organizations and politically active electorate, continuously monitored the use and impact of chemical compounds for environmental and health reasons.

The rule, so formulated, 'as a matter of general international law' is accurate, but the exception in the formulation that commitments made

---

[64] (1980) 56 ILR 258.

[65] OPIC (Overseas Private Investment Corporation), an arm of the US Department of State, provides facilities for insuring foreign investment. Before payment, an internal OPIC tribunal determines whether there was an expropriation. The significance of such tribunals in contributing to international law in the area would be tenuous.

[66] See discussion in Chapter 2.

[67] *Revere Copper and Brass Inc.* v. *OPIC* (1980) 56 ILR 258 and *Waste Management* v. *Mexico*, ICSID, Case No. ARB(AF)/00/3 (30 April 2004). *Waste Management* relied on *Revere Copper* for the exception. *Revere Copper* was an internal decision of a government insurance corporation, given an undue status in arbitration literature as it favours certain views.

[68] Pt IV, ch. D, p. 5.

to the putative investor are protected from regulatory intervention has no basis in general international law whatsoever. The formulation of an exception to regulatory expectations on the basis of commitments to putative investors is an invention to conserve the protection of the stabilization clause, and foreshadows commitments made to the foreign investor giving rise to legitimate expectations. It is an infusion of a neoliberal thought, seeking to preserve what could be preserved for the cause of investment protection. For the reinvention of regulatory expropriation was truly an emasculation of expropriation law. Yet the exception made is faulty. If there are public purpose justifications for state interference, there is no reason why such commitments should attract the application of any exception. The tribunals' solicitude to commitments made to the foreign investor is without merit. The tribunal in *Methanex* had no option but to uphold the law on regulatory expropriation, rediscovered and pleaded by the United States. There was no basis in the law for making this exception, apart from a particular policy preference of the particular tribunal.

The exception is not stated in the later awards affirming that regulatory takings are not compensable. The year after *Methanex, Saluka Investments* v. *Czech Republic* (2006)[69] affirmed this position by stating that all treaties, even those that did not contain an exception relating to regulatory expropriations, were subject to the rule that a taking in the exercise of the police powers of the state was non-compensable. The tribunal said that 'it is now established in international law that states are not liable to pay compensation to a foreign investor when, in the normal exercise of their regulatory powers, they adopt in a non-discriminatory manner *bona fide* regulations that are aimed at the general welfare'.[70] The tribunal adverted to the existence of a difficulty in drawing a 'bright line' separating regulatory non-compensable taking from compensable taking, but affirmed the existence of the rule. The regulatory takings rule was

---

[69] UNCITRAL PCA, Award (17 March 2006) (Watts, Fortier, Behrens).

[70] Paragraph 255. The tribunal used the statement in the Harvard Draft Convention on the International Responsibility of States for Injuries to Aliens as authority. The Draft stated: 'an uncompensated taking of an alien property or a deprivation of the use or enjoyment of the property of the alien which results from the execution of tax laws; from a general change in the value of currency; from the action of the competent authorities of the state in the maintenance of public order, heath or morality; or from the valid exercise of belligerent rights or otherwise incidental to the normal operation of the laws of the State shall not be considered wrongful'. Louis Sohn and Richard Baxter, 'Responsibility of States for Injuries to the Economic Interests of Aliens', (1961) 55 *American Journal of International Law* 515.

4.3 THE REVIVAL OF REGULATORY EXPROPRIATION   219

confirmed in the US and Canadian Model Investment treaties (2004), which contained similar formulations of regulatory expropriation. The provision in Annexe B of the US Model Treaty reads:[71]

> Except in rare circumstances, non-discriminatory regulatory actions by a Party that are designed and applied to protect legitimate public welfare objectives, such as public health, safety, and the environment, do not constitute indirect expropriations.

The formula is widely used in many recent treaties. But whether expressly stated or not, it must now be taken that the statement on expropriation in investment treaties would be read subject to the rule relating to regulatory expropriations as being non-compensable. The rediscovery of regulatory expropriation emasculates the law on expropriation, or creates such a large 'gaping loophole' that it makes many of the inflexible rules of the old model of expropriation law redundant. The earlier views that regulatory expropriations do not constitute an exception were obviously formed at a time when market-oriented policies frowned upon government interventions and sought to eliminate such interventions on the basis that market mechanisms did not require them. But with the increasing failure of market-based policies following successive economic crises, regulatory interventions have become necessary. Historically, economic crises have attracted government intervention as they signal the failure of market-oriented policies that advocated the reduction of government intervention. State intervention is justified in the context of market failures or impending economic crises. Besides, the increasing protests of environmental and other groups, which viewed the inflexible character of investment protection as antithetical to the interests of the protection of public welfare, required changes in attitudes to regulatory expropriation. These groups were joined by other groups, which also had their own concerns for human rights, labour standards, the promotion of corporate responsibility, the prevention of corruption and the protection of cultural property.[72] Taxation was another issue, as states used taxation to remedy situations of acquisition of profits in the resources that flowed due to purely exogenous factors unrelated to any merit on the part of the investor.

---

[71] Article 1 of Annex B declares that the principles it contains are customary international law, thus locating regulatory expropriations in customary international law. See Annex B, Article 6 of the Model Treaty, which covers expropriation.

[72] Freya Baetens (ed.), *Investment Law within International Law: Integrationist Perspectives* (Cambridge University Press, 2013), contains chapters on the impact of other disciplines within international law on issues of foreign investment.

220   THE EMASCULATION OF EXPROPRIATION

Tribunals have continued to affirm the regulatory takings rule. In *Chemtura* v. *Canada*,[73] cancellation of licences for harmful pesticides was held to be within the regulatory powers of the state. The statements in the later awards confirming the rule that a 'State does not commit an expropriation and is thus not liable to pay compensation to a dispossessed alien investor when it adopts general regulations that are accepted as within the police powers of state forms part of customary international law today'[74] do not contain any exceptions as to commitments given to putative investors. Though the 'bright line' dividing regulatory expropriation and compensable expropriation may be difficult to draw, it is clear that the modern state will seldom engage in measures affecting property rights unless there is a public welfare reason. To that extent, the relevance of expropriation law has considerably diminished.

4.4 Stemming the regulatory takings tide

The broadness of the regulatory takings rule emaciates the law on expropriation. The 'gaping loophole' had to plugged. Efforts have been made to limit it either on the basis of a notion of reasonableness or through the introduction of the idea prevalent in European human rights law that requires a balance between the harm caused by the taking to the investor and the social benefit that accrues to society. Earlier, in a holding action seeking to stem the possibility of the recognition of an exception of regulatory expropriation, the tribunal in *Feldman* v. *Mexico*[75] sought to distinguish between types of regulation on the basis of reasonableness. But the formulation itself disclosed the inconsistencies involved in the identification of which regulation constitutes expropriation and which does not. The *Feldman* tribunal had said:[76]

> In the past, confiscatory taxation, denial of access to infrastructure or necessary raw materials, imposition of unreasonable regulatory regimes,

---

[73] UNCITRAL, Award (2 August 2010) (Kaufmann-Kohler, Brower, Crawford), at para. 266.

[74] *Saluka* Award, at para. 262. In *Chemtura* (para. 266n), the tribunal found that the ban on the chemical substance lindane was 'motivated by the increasing awareness of the dangers [presented by lindane for human health and the environment]. A measure adopted under such circumstances is a valid exercise of the State's police powers and, as a result, does not constitute an expropriation.'

[75] ICSID, Case No. ARB(AF)/99/1 (16 December 2002) (Kerameus, Bravo, Gantz).

[76] ICSID, Case No. ARB(AF)/99/1 (16 December 2002).

4.4 STEMMING THE REGULATORY TAKINGS TIDE 221

among others, have been considered to be expropriatory acts. At the same time, governments must be free to act in the broader public interest through protection of the environment, new or modified tax regimes, the granting or withdrawal of government subsidies, reduction or increases in tariff levels, imposition of zoning restrictions and the like. Reasonable governmental regulation of this type cannot be achieved if any business that is adversely affected may seek compensation, and it is safe to say that customary international law recognizes this.

This is an obviously confused statement, which provides little guidance on the reasonableness of the regulation. It seeks to categorize instances of lawful regulation, which has been done many times over, but to identify unreasonable regulation is a more difficult task. This is borne out by the inclusion of taxation in both categories. The extent to which taxation is reasonable and when it becomes unreasonable is a matter of subjective assessment. Some recent treaties provide for a separate handling of the issue of taxation by subjecting the question of when taxation is unreasonable to a joint committee set up by the two states.[77] Reasonableness does not provide a meaningful way of distinguishing between different types of expropriations or of limiting the scope of regulatory expropriation. But the search for a way of limiting the scope of regulatory expropriation has continued. Since denial of its existence was no longer feasible, there was concentration on finding means of limiting its scope.

The criteria of reasonableness will be satisfied where there is a public interest reason that avoids harm of a severe nature or provides significant benefit to the public. It is inherent in the concept of property that the individual enjoyment of it is subject to the public interest. Much of the regulatory activity took place either in the context of economic crises or when a state took measures to deal with environmental or human rights concerns. The measures taken applied uniformly to both local and foreign investors. The non-discriminatory nature of the measures in the context of the crisis or public need made the measures reasonable. There was a perception of inequity in a situation where the foreign investor was protected, but the local investor was not.[78] The notion of reasonableness is possibly derived from English administrative law,

---

[77] See, e.g., the US Model Treaty 2004.

[78] The Trade Policy Statement of the Australian Government (12 April 2011) stated that such protection 'would confer greater legal rights on foreign business than those available to domestic businesses'. Constraint on the making of laws to promote public interest is the other reason given in the Australian Statement for dispensing with investor–state arbitration in future investment treaties.

which does not easily permit the decision of an administrator to be interfered with.

The second type of effort to restrict the regulatory takings rule is the use of the proportionality test. This test determines whether there is a balance between the regulatory objective and the taking that is put into effect. The test is taken from public law systems of Europe, principally Germany, and the case law of the European Court of Human Rights. There is no authority for either test in customary international law. The test is not stated in the text of the treaty. They are innovations of arbitrators who see a predicament in the restriction on expropriation that terminates the expansive notions that were attempted earlier. The legitimacy of importing such rules into investment arbitration is questionable. There are also many theoretical difficulties that attend the application of these limiting rules in expropriation law. These are explored in Chapter 7.

Where state measures are a reaction to a situation brought about by the foreign investor (as where the foreign investor causes massive pollution), the idea that there should be compensation paid by the state for intervening to remedy the harm involved in the situation would be to reward the harm-doer. It would be as ludicrous as saying that an offender who has been fined for a violation of a criminal prohibition should be compensated to the extent of the fine or some percentage of it as there is a taking of his property. In these circumstances, the taking would be clearly regulatory.

In other circumstances, the classification of the taking as regulatory will depend upon the circumstances. The situation is reminiscent of the old debate between full compensation and appropriate compensation, except that it is the camp that is solicitous of the foreign investor that now argues for something akin to appropriate compensation in the event of a regulatory expropriation on the basis of reasonableness or a proportionality test. The argument has come in many guises. It has taken the guise of arguing that the concept of property, as well as the constitutional rules guaranteeing it, require that regulatory expropriation is assessed on the basis of the extent to which it is necessary and whether the onus could be borne by the state for some compensation in that the public benefit involved may have to be borne disproportionately by the single owner. The proportionality test is also an argument for the payment of appropriate compensation in the sense that the tribunal is required to balance the interests of the state against those of the foreign investor, having regard to the purpose of the taking. These arguments are premised on notions of the function of property and the extent of a right to property.

4.5 The changing concept of property in the international law of expropriation

The view that some compensation is due even in the event of a regulatory taking is based on the belief that it is inherent in the concept of property that the rights in property are not violated unless some compensation is paid, even where there is a regulatory taking as the owner has to suffer a disproportionate harm so that the rest of society benefits. This in itself is a neoliberal notion. The competing social democratic view does not contain a reference to any compensation. The social democratic view is the basis of the statement of the right to property in the First Protocol to the European Convention on Human Rights, which does not refer to the requirement for compensation.[79]

If it is inherent in the concept of property that the individual owner's rights must give way to superior claims of the public, then the argument for supporting compensation is negligible. If the concept talks in terms of a hierarchical gradation of the nature of public interests that can displace the claims of the owner, then it can be said that there is a moving mark within the concept of property that requires an objective calculation of the relevant merits of the interests so that appropriate compensation can be fixed for the interference with the interests of the individual. In any event, the test is not external but internal to the concept of property. Such a notion of property contrasts with an absolutist vision in which the individual right to property is sacrosanct. In this vision of property, there must be payment of full compensation if the state interferes with property rights.

The concept of property that has been used in formulating the early international law on expropriation in the practice of capital-exporting states is based on an absolutist vision of property, which requires that there be no intervention in the individual right to property except upon payment of compensation in the event there is a need for the state to take such property. It is the vision of property that is contained in the international minimum standard of protection espoused by the United States in its practice and later by the European states. It is a particularly Lockean vision in which the acquisition of property through labour was seen as the object of individual effort, and that property so acquired must be kept for the exclusive use of the person acquiring it.[80] The function of

---

[79] Tom Allen, 'Liberalism, Social Democracy and the Value of Property under the European Convention on Human Rights', (2010) 59 *International & Comparative Law Quarterly* 1053.

[80] John Locke, *The Fragment on Property in Two Treatises on Government* (1690).

the state is to protect the property so acquired. The Fifth Amendment of the US Bill of Rights best reflects the position. The reference in it to property reads: 'Nor shall [anyone] be deprived of life, liberty, or property without due process of law; Nor shall private property be taken for public use without just compensation.' The extent to which it has influenced the statement of the expropriation law is clear. The language of due process and full compensation used in investment treaties is clearly derived from American law. But, despite this ideal of absolute protection, it was never the situation in American law that taking of property must always be compensated. There was a gap between the ideal and what was done in practice.

Property theories exist in different types of political systems. It was in its origin conceptualized in the context of capitalist systems. The world has never been confined to such systems. It has always had a plurality of systems. Property is about the just distribution of wealth within society. The social function it performs has been widely recognized. That function cannot be the same in every political community. Different political systems take different views as to the extent of the protection of property rights. The concept does not remain static even within a single legal system. Its scope changes with circumstances.[81] The construction of an idea of property within international law cannot be based on just one political base. As such, the notion that there could be a global rule or a standard of governance in respect of the way a state interferes with property rights is unacceptable. This is the principal difficulty in the international law of foreign investment. It is put to an instrumental use when mandating a uniform principle of property protection, often in excess of even the best constitutional system of protection that exist.[82] Given the plurality of attitudes that exist in the world, it would be difficult to cull a single rule that has universal acceptance. The project to create a global rule of governance in this area suffers from the non-acceptability of single visions of property. Some American constitutional law writers believe that the investment treaty standards on property protection are in

---

[81] The clearest example comes from American law where absolutist notions were given up after the New Deal. They returned somewhat during the period of neoliberalism. Some regard property protection in international investment law to be in excess of standards of American law.

[82] There is argument as to whether there was a uniform view of property in American legal history. For views as to the social function of property with the rights of the state to interfere as opposed to an absolute right, see *Kelo* v. *City of New London* (2005) 545 US 469. Nestor Davidson, 'Sketches for a Hamiltonian Vernacular as a Social Function of Property', (2011) 80 *Fordham Law Review* 1053.

4.5 THE CHANGING CONCEPT OF PROPERTY 225

excess of those in American constitutional law, which is thought of as being closest to the absolutist vision.[83]

The absolutist vision was emphasized during the neoliberal period of the 1990s when strict protection of property was emphasized as necessary to promote the flows of foreign investment. The theory was that it was the absence of effective protection of property that hindered developing states from economic progress.[84] It was possible to formulate this as the policy rationale for such protection through the provisions on expropriation treaties.

In this absolutist vision of property, there is little role for regulatory expropriation. Theorists who support this view would include regulatory expropriation within the general concept of expropriation by disaggregating property into a bundle of constituent rights so that any measure, regulatory or otherwise, interfering with any of the disaggregated rights would appear more drastic and could be dressed up as akin to expropriation. The measure would destroy that specific constituent right that has been isolated and converted into a property right. This strategy was widely employed by the US–Iran Claims Commission where the tribunals recognized interference with the right to management and the right to attend shareholder meetings as amounting to expropriation. The strategy has little basis in the domestic legal systems of different states. What was suggested as international law was in excess of the law that prevailed in the domestic systems of the capital-exporting states, all of which recognized exceptions to the law on expropriation enabling states wide discretion to interfere with property rights in the public interest.

Western scholars writing on the international law on expropriation have relied largely on the liberal view of property in arguing for full compensation upon expropriation. They have seldom addressed alternative views relating to property despite the fact that such views had been articulated both within the United States and Europe. Socialist notions were strong within Europe, so much so that the initial draft of the European Convention on Human Rights did not contain a statement of the right to property. The vision of property as having a social function that may trump individual rights when inconsistent with the objectives that society may wish to pursue through the use of such property, or the

---

[83] Bean and Beauvais, 'Global Fifth Amendment?'.

[84] The literature produced by the institutions associated with the Washington Consensus emphasized the absence of such property protection as a defect that stood in the way of economic progress. It also indicated an absence of the rule of law in the society, property protection forming a central element of this reinterpreted rule of law.

duty of the owner of property to ensure that it is put to active use so as to benefit social aims have seldom informed discussions of the international law on expropriation. Rather, a narrow, untested economic vision that is based on the supposed capacity of absolute property protection to facilitate the flows of foreign investment has been the policy justification advanced to support the view that an inflexible rule on full compensation for expropriation must be maintained at the international level. Investment treaties are premised on this view. It has been bolstered by the unproven hypothesis that such property protection is a general principle of law and hence must have relevance in the formulation of international law.

In this sense, the quest for a uniform vision of property may be fruitless as each society would have its own aim as to how property should be used conditioned by its own history, culture and political ideology. The unilateral vision of an absolute right sits uneasily with the pluralist vision of property that each society has a multitude of visions as to how property should be employed in the advancement of its members. By founding the law on expropriation on the absolute right to property, the interests of the foreign investor are no doubt secured, but it does not secure the interests of the host societies in which the investment has been made. This disregard of the interests of the host communities is a defect in the law. It is addressed through the recognition of the state to exercise regulatory powers over foreign investment without being deterred by the need to pay compensation.

While the law of expropriation was firmly fixed on absolutist notions of property, this does not appear to have been the case in the consideration of the right to property by human rights courts or by writers on international human rights. It is important to look at human rights law. Those who argue that disproportionate regulatory expropriation carries with it a duty to compensate rely to a large extent on human rights law, especially the jurisprudence of the European Court of Human Rights. The notion of proportionality is specifically addressed in the case law of the European Court. Parallels are drawn despite the fact that human rights law and investment law have systemic and historical differences.

It was once thought that human rights arguments could be used to buttress absolute protection of foreign investment. Given the impact of the argument that human rights effects on investment protection must be taken into account, the absolutist vision of the right to property as a counter to this argument has resurfaced. The increasing number of cases, interpreting the right to property in the various human rights

4.5 THE CHANGING CONCEPT OF PROPERTY 227

documents, belies that possibility. Article 1 of the First Protocol to the European Convention itself is a neutral statement of the right with a change being that it refers to international law.[85] It specifically refers to the right of the state to control property 'in accordance with the general interest, the right of taxation and the exaction of other contributions and penalties'. Regulatory expropriation in the public interest is recognised from the outset. Its subjection of the right to conditions provided by 'general principles of international law' is a curiosity as it would be difficult to ascertain what are these general principles of international law. Does one include the communist systems in ascertaining these general principles? It is also instructive that the statement contained no reference to the payment of compensation. Allen has pointed out that this is due to the prevailing social democratic vision of property at the time the Protocol was drafted.[86]

The European Court of Human Rights has nevertheless addressed the issue as to whether the owner of the property should be given compensation even in situations of regulatory expropriation. The requirement of compensation is inserted into the law through judicial interpretation. The European Court gives a wide margin of appreciation as to the social purposes given by the state for the taking of the property. It is after giving a wide margin of appreciation that the Court considers whether the taking

[85] Article 1 of the First Protocol reads: 'Every natural or legal person is entitled to the peaceful enjoyment of his possession. No one shall be deprived of his possessions except in the public interest and subject to the conditions provided for by law and by general principles of international law. The preceding provisions shall not, however, in any way impair the right of a State to enforce such laws as it deems necessary to control the use of property in accordance with the general interest or to secure the payment of taxes or other contributions or penalties.'

[86] Allen, 'Liberalism, Social Democracy and the Value of Property under the European Convention on Human Rights'. Allen observed the interpretive movement of the provisions founded on socialist principles towards a law based on neoliberal principles. The cross-fertilization of investment law and European human rights law may be favoured for neoliberal reasons. European human rights law has comparative law value, but does not constitute law from which international law principles can be queried. Overmuch discussion of this area as if it has great relevance to investment law may be reminiscent of the days when European law constituted the general principles of 'civilized legal systems'. The search for parallels between European law and investment law accords with the neoliberal project. The link is made in recent literature. Paparinskis, *The International Minimum Standard and the Fair and Equitable Treatment*, pp. 232–40. Likewise, American international lawyers draw parallels between constitutional protection of property in US law and investment protection. Property has different connotations in the different legal systems of the world. The constitutional treatment of property and the balances that are struck between individual rights and social necessities varies in different legal systems of the world.

228   THE EMASCULATION OF EXPROPRIATION

produced disproportionate effects on the owner of the property.[87] The state is subject to conditions of legality and proportionality so that the individual's interest in the property must be balanced against the public interest. The fair balance requires that the owner is not made to bear an excessive burden. In this process, full compensation of the property is not guaranteed. Yet non-payment is justifiable only in exceptional circumstances.[88] The notion of balancing is strong in the European system. It is inferred from the structure of Article 1 of the First Protocol, which, after stating the right to property, subjects the right to the general public interest.[89] European writers would seek to universalize the European position, but it may not accord with the position that is accepted in other jurisdictions so as to make it general principle. It is judge-made law based on the neoliberal inclinations that became widespread after the first formulation of the First Protocol. Investment tribunals have sought to adopt this notion of proportionality and balancing without indicating the basis on which it could be included in the treaty statement of expropriation.[90] The investment treaties mandate payment of full compensation upon expropriation. With the rediscovery of the rule on regulatory expropriation, the position is that no compensation needs to be paid in the event of a regulatory expropriation, except in exceptional circumstances which the treaty formulation does not identify. If the rule on proportionality is to be adopted, it would mean that there is an intermediate category which requires payment of less than full compensation for a regulatory but disproportionate taking. The nature of the compensation would vary in accordance with the degree of disproportionality. Such a rule is not stated in the treaty, which only talks of the payment of full compensation (or no compensation in the event of a regulatory expropriation). Such a rule relating to an intermediate type of compensation has to be created, in a manner similar to the insertion of the requirement of compensation into the right to property stated in the European Convention on Human Rights. While the European Court has a mandate to do what it did, it does not fall within the powers of arbitration tribunals to create such a rule. The power

---

[87] *Handyside* v. *UK*, ECHR, Application No. 5493/72 Series B, No. 221975 (1975); *Former King of Greece* v. *Greece*, ECHR, Application No. 25701/94 (23 November 2000).

[88] Luis Wildhaber and Isabelle Wildhaber, 'Recent Case Law on the Protection of Property in the European Convention on Human Rights', in Christina Binder (ed.), *International Investment for the 21st Century* (Oxford University Press, 2009), p. 657.

[89] *Former King of Greece* v. *Greece*, ECHR, Application No. 25701/94 (23 November 2000); *Sporrong and Lonnroth* v. *Sweden*, ECHR, Series A, No. 52 (23 September 1982).

[90] For example, *Tecmed* v. *Mexico*, ICSID ARB(AF)/00/2, Award (29 May 2009); and *Azurix* v. *Argentina*, ICSID, Case No. ARB/01/12, Award (14 July 2006).

4.5 THE CHANGING CONCEPT OF PROPERTY 229

of the arbitration tribunal is derived from consent. Tribunals have no powers to insert any concept into the law they were given the power to apply. It is not a part of customary international law. Neither can it be said that the proportionality rule is a general principle of law. Within the common law itself, there are judges and writers who oppose the acceptance of the proportionality rule.

When constitutional systems are brought to the aid of a vision that favours property rights in international investment law, there is an inclination to study only those constitutional systems that incline towards compensation or some compromise towards balancing and proportionality.[91] There is no explanation as to why a solution that is adopted by a regional court should be elevated to an international law principle.

The views on proportionality and balancing are strong in German law, which is the genesis of the views of the European Court of Human Rights. Article 14 of the German Basic Law begins with a statement of an absolute right to property. But this is immediately qualified by the obligation that property must serve a social function, thus indicating a tension between the absolute right and the social function of property. Article 14(3) of the Basic Law states that proportionality and balancing are requirements of expropriation.[92] These are formulations of German law made in 1949 in the context of Germany's historical experiences. Germany is inclined towards a monistic system, which received international law principles into its domestic law. There is little reason why such compromises should form the basis of other domestic legal systems or be converted into rules of international law.[93]

Constitutional systems around the world do not accept an absolute right to property. The text of the Canadian Bill of Rights does not contain a statement of the right. The Singapore Constitution does not mention the right to property at all. Different constitutions have different statements of the right. They do not have uniform views as to how any tension

---

[91] For example, Schill (ed.), *International Investment Law and Comparative Public Law*. The work, which purports to be a comparative study, hardly extends beyond European systems.

[92] 'Expropriation shall only be permissible in the public interest. It may only be ordered by or pursuant to a law, which determines the nature and extent of compensation. Compensation shall reflect a fair balance between the public interest and the interests of those affected. In the case of disputes regarding compensation recourse may be had to the ordinary courts.'

[93] See the statement of German law in Andre Van der Walt, *Constitutional Property Clauses: A Comparative Analysis* (The Hague: Kluwer, 1999), p. 121.

230   THE EMASCULATION OF EXPROPRIATION

between the right to property and the social function of property is to be resolved. It would be difficult to posit a rule of international law only on the basis of the practice of a single country or a regional grouping.

Most constitutional systems recognize a wide right in the state to take measures affecting in the public interest without payment of compensation. Professor Van der Walt, in his survey of the right to property in different constitutional systems of the world,[94] pointed out that most systems recognize the distinction between takings effected in terms of the power of eminent domain and those in the exercise of the police powers of the state. The latter are not compensable. He points out, however, that the distinction between the two types of expropriations is a grey area. Constitutional systems have the same difficulty in drawing the 'bright line' between regulatory takings and compensable takings. No definitive test has been provided to solve this issue. The distinction, widely based on American law, has been arrived at independently in many jurisdictions.

In the constitutions of new states, there is great scope for regulatory takings simply because of the fact that newly independent states would have a greater need to effect measures that would interfere with property rights. The creation of infrastructure, the need for frequent changes in economic policies and a greater frequency of economic crises make rapid regulatory changes necessary. This was very much so in the founding history of the United States, when property rights were not allowed to hinder the creation of infrastructure and other development projects. Attitudes to property have varied between countries and between historical periods within countries. The practice ranges from not stating a right to property to the recognition of regulatory takings in respect of which no compensation needs to be paid.

In most legal provisions, an effort is made to state definite instances of regulatory takings. Thus, takings of property causing injury to public health or the health of animals or plants are regarded as non-compensable. In any event, if there is no express provision, there is an implied right in the state to terminate rights in such property or to prevent the use of property in a manner that is injurious to the public. The Nigerian Bill of Rights, an example of the laws of a newly decolonized state, attempts a lengthy list of police powers, including taxation, penalties, bankruptcies, execution of judgments, dealing with property injurious to human beings, plants or animals, taking of enemy property, governance of trust property and

---

[94] Van der Walt, *Constitutional Property Clauses*, p. 19.

4.5 THE CHANGING CONCEPT OF PROPERTY 231

property of public bodies, interference for investigation or inquiry, and soil conservation. This legislation provided a model for the bills of rights for over twenty Commonwealth countries. Obviously, measures affecting property that fall under the listed categories will not carry an obligation to pay compensation. It is interesting to note that the lists in these documents are considerably longer than those in the American Law Institute's Restatement on the Foreign Relations Law of the United States. Clearly, if the measures affecting property fall within the categories, analysis would end there and the measure would be deemed regulatory and not compensable. The drawing of a 'bright line' between compensable and regulatory takings does become a possibility if the constitutional documents of different countries are looked at for guidance.

The South African Constitution, made after the ending of apartheid, is particularly instructive of how historical tensions relating to the concept of property, ownership of which was confined on racial grounds, need to be resolved. Property figures very much in the configuration of social relations between racial groups within society. In apartheid South Africa, the whites were dominant precisely because they had exclusive rights to property. For that reason, basic notions of equality have much to do with ownership of property, as black history in the United States demonstrates. There cannot be uniform theories of property simply because of the different historical, social, political and other circumstances of societies. The argument that there could be universal constitutionalism created on the basis of the European experience is a non-starter, and is unlikely to gain acceptance in other parts of the world. The historical problems had impacts on South Africa's attitudes to investment treaties.[95]

The South African Constitution recognized the distinction between deprivations of property in the exercise of police powers and expropriation in terms of the power of eminent domain. Though a balancing test is suggested in Article 25(3), the factors listed clearly tilt the balance more in favour of the state than the owner. The balancing has to be effected 'having regard to all relevant circumstances'. The circumstances are listed to include the current use of the property, the history of the acquisition and use of the property, the market value of the property, the extent of direct state investment and subsidy in the acquisition and beneficial capital improvement of the property, and the

---

[95] Particularly in relation to the Black Empowerment Act, which sought to give privileges to the black community. South Africa was averse to the making of investment treaties as they did not provide adequate means of ensuring such reforms.

purpose of the expropriation. Public interest is defined as including 'the nation's commitment to land reform, and to reforms to bring about equitable access to all of South Africa's natural resources'. The provision on property encourages the redress of past racial discrimination and the restitution of land seized after 1913 to persons or communities dispossessed of such property. But there is a general derogation clause in Article 36, which requires that all measures must be tested on a standard of reasonableness. It is unlikely that courts will interfere with state regulations which the state determines are required to effect changes to the property structure in the country. The provision recognizes the past inequities in the distribution of property and desires rectification of the situation.

In what satisfactory way can it be argued that standards of global governance require that South Africa should conform to the uniform ideas that are contained in European law? In whose favour would such standards of global governance work? Can racial peace be maintained in South Africa if the uniform standards of constitutionalism are adopted? It is for each state and each region to decide how it is to treat the concept of property and to devise rules as to its protection in the context of its history, social circumstances and ideological preferences.

This would be so for every constitutional system. While ostensibly, the US Constitution requires the payment of just compensation for the taking of property, the case law that has developed deviates significantly from an absolutist vision. It may even be incorrect to view the Constitution as being animated by a desire to project an absolutist vision of property. The US Supreme Court has generally been favourable to regulatory interferences with property rights. It would be intellectually dishonest to project any legal system as being based on a uniform concept of property that remained unchanged in the face of historical circumstances.[96] That being the case, there cannot be any basis on which a particular theory or the application of its resulting norms must be solitary guides for the formation of international norms on property.[97]

---

[96] Schneiderman, *Constitutionalizing Economic Globalization*, p. 3.

[97] Gregory Alexander, *Global Debate over Constitutional Property: Lessons from American Takings Jurisprudence* (University of Chicago Press, 2001), at p. 21, states: 'In its failure to openly recognize that individual owners owe duties to maintain the common welfare of their communities, the American constitutional property clause lags behind the rest of the world. It is time to catch up.'

4.5 THE CHANGING CONCEPT OF PROPERTY 233

Allen observed that 'Commonwealth constitutions do not require compensation for every state action that affects property. Consequently, legislation may affect a great many property owners adversely, but only a small number may be entitled to compensation.'[98] Allen concedes that the difficult distinction between regulatory and non-regulatory expropriation has eluded the Commonwealth courts. These writers have largely compared the liberal systems of the common law world. One has to remember that there are still communist states that are members of the international community. If a comparative study is relevant to the international law on this subject, it has to be made without the inclination to believe that what the European courts decide is international law. The notion that the practice within Europe can be multilateralized, despite the fact that the rest of the world does not accord with such practice, should be abandoned. The old notion that it is only the general principles recognized by civilized nations that constitute international law is hardly acceptable in the modern world in which Europe has been reduced to relative insignificance.

The view that some compensation is payable in the event of regulatory takings that one finds in human rights precedents was taken largely in cases of expropriation of land, not in the case of expropriations of in the business or industrial sectors. The large majority of cases that occur in the area of foreign investment do not involve expropriation of land, but intervention by the state in vital sectors of the economy, such as the provision of services relating to water or controls imposed on businesses to prevent market failures brought about by external circumstances or to channel them in a manner consistent with the economic development of the host state. It is unlikely that principles derived from comparative law would support payment of compensation in situations of interference in these circumstances. What is created on the basis of European comparative law is the mirage that principles exist within it that require the application of proportionality tests when this may be difficult to establish as an inflexible rule. In any event, as indicated, even if such a rule exists in European public law, the conversion of that rule into international law would be inappropriate as it cannot be demonstrated that other public law systems in the world subscribe to a similar principle.[99]

---

[98] Tom Allen, *The Right to Property in Commonwealth Constitutions* (Cambridge University Press, 2000), at p. 162.

[99] Hannoch Dagan, 'Reimagining Takings Law', in Gregory Alexander and Eduardo Penalver (eds.), *Property and Community* (New York: Oxford University Press, 2009), pp. 203–24, supports partial or differential compensation.

234 THE EMASCULATION OF EXPROPRIATION

The proportionality analysis is applied in many areas of human rights, particularly in cases where personal liberty is denied in situations where people are detained following allegations of terrorism. It is difficult to argue that rules created for the protection of the rights of the disadvantaged faced with the oppressive power of the state should be extended into the realm of property protection where the considerations are different. The right to life and the right to liberty stand higher in the hierarchy of rights. The International Covenant on Civil and Political Rights does not even feature the right to property. It constructs a hierarchy of rights in that some of the rights it states are regarded as non-derogable.[100] It is largely in respect of non-derogable rights that courts adopt the proportionality rule in order to determine whether, in the extreme instances of public necessity, such rights may be interfered with. In these instances, the courts begin with a margin of appreciation given to the decision of the state. The analogy with investment disputes and human rights cases involving personal liberties is grossly improper. The right to property is not of the same quality as non-derogable rights. The analysis in the human rights sphere is different in that the rights dealt with are inalienable rights, unlike the rights of the foreign investor which are conferred on him by the domestic law of the host state and are created largely by virtue of the foreign investment contract and the entry laws of the host state. If analogical reasoning is proper in the situation of international investment law, as no doubt it is, the two instances that are analogized must be in reasonable parity.

In the situation of foreign investment disputes, the state takes measures that affect a few in the face of situations that pose a threat to the interests of the many. Such threats involve those to the environment, human rights and national security. In such situations, even if a balancing test is applied, the result would usually favour the state as the values supporting state intervention far outweigh interests in property, particularly where the measures are applied in a non-discriminatory fashion. Where the state is willing to show that its measures prevent harmful practices by the foreign investor, the result in favour of regulation would be clear. The state must provide a justification for its action, and its

---

[100] The ICCP states in Article 4 that certain rights it recognizes are non-derogable. These are the right to life (Article 5), the right not to be tortured (Article 6), the right not to be enslaved (Article 7), the right not to be imprisoned for a contract debt (Article 11), right not to be held liable for a crime not in existence at the time of its commission (*nullum crimen sine lege*; Article 15), the right to recognition as a person (Article 16) and the right to religion (Article 18).

4.5 THE CHANGING CONCEPT OF PROPERTY 235

explanation would have to be accepted in most circumstances. If an analogy exists with human rights cases, one must recognize that the cases permit a wide margin of appreciation to the state.

This is not to say that the state is always right. The law must recognize, as it does, that there are 'exceptional cases' in which relief must be provided. The criteria of such an exceptional case would be elusive. It must involve a taking that visibly lacks any semblance of public purpose or the public purpose appears minimal. In these situations, the taking becomes more akin to a confiscation rather than an expropriation. The law already provides for the obvious situations, such as where the taking is racially motivated. If a public purpose is lacking, the expropriation becomes illegal. Ultimately, it is the quality of the public purpose that makes the distinction between a regulatory taking and a compensable taking. In determining these exceptional cases, the tribunal must assess the state's justification for its measures, the fault of the foreign investor that triggered those measures, and the extent of the harm that is sought to be averted or the benefit resulting to the public by the taking. As always, the state's understanding and response must be given due weight and should not be displaced by the tribunal unless circumstances warrant it. Exceptional cases will be rare. The tribunal must indicate why it displaces the state's appreciation of the need for the regulation with its own view that it was unnecessary or disproportionate. In that sense, the opportunity for assessing partial compensation in circumstances where the taking is disproportionate to the benefit achieved does arise. This is a matter of factual assessment. In this sense, the investment tribunal still has a role to play in situations of regulatory takings.

The primary rule in the treaty formulation is that regulatory takings are non-compensable. In certain areas, there is a conclusiveness that attaches to this rule. These areas include, as identified in customary international law and in international conventions, areas of taxation unless exorbitant, changes in values in currency, maintenance of public order, national security, preservation of health and morality, protection of the environment, and the protection of indigenous and tribal groups. There is adequate customary international law that supports the identification of measures in these areas as regulatory and, hence, non-compensable.[101] The list cannot be exhaustive. In the modern

---

[101] The evidence for customary law is contained in the American Law Institute's Third Restatement on the Foreign Relations Law of the United States, and in the Harvard Draft on State Responsibility, Article 10(5). A list could be compiled on the basis of the statements in these formulations, which have been in existence for several decades. To

investment treaties, many of these instances would be provided as instances precluding liability. The subjective formulation of the national security exception and the scope of this exception impacts the consideration of whether a measure is regulatory or not. It provides an argument for excluding the discretion of the tribunal altogether in certain circumstances.[102]

There is a list of concerns that arise from international concerns with domestic incidents. In addition to domestic concerns, one has to add to the list the areas of international concern that often run in parallel to those of domestic concern. These concerns arise out of international conventions on the protection of the environment, on human rights and on cultural property. These concerns are relatively new. This category of international concerns is relevant in identifying non-compensable regulatory takings. Together with domestic concerns, these international concerns provide criteria for distinguishing regulatory takings from compensable takings. These international concerns are identifiable on the basis of treaty principles, such as those in the fields of human rights, environmental protection, the protection of cultural property and the protection of indigenous rights. Takings made in pursuance of these international treaty principles must also be considered regulatory takings. In the hierarchy of interests, they must rank higher than the protection of investment.[103]

Some difficulty may exist in early documents on human rights and the environment in that they contain hazy statements of the obligations, but the obligations they seek to impose will become progressively more clearly identified.[104] Equally, in the new balanced treaties, the defences based on the environment and labour rights do not contain firm requirements. But one can anticipate that pressure from activist groups will result in future treaties having firmer statements of defences relating to such interests. There may also be rudimentary emergence of obligations on multinational corporations not to seek exemptions from certain types of regulatory norms. Thus, the OECD Guidelines on Multinational Corporations require that these corporations should not accept or seek

---

these, the list in the constitutional documents will have to be added as indicating general principles of law. The constitutional documents, particularly those of developing states such as Nigeria, must be taken into account as these are states in need of development. Investment treaties are about development.

[102] See further Chapter 7.

[103] *Railroad Development Corp.* v. *Guatemala*, ICSID, Case No ARB/07/23 (29 June 2012) (Sureda, Eizensat, Crawford), para. 151; *Telenor SA* v. *Hungary*, ICSID, Case No. ARB/04/15 (13 September 2006).

[104] Thus, the environmental convention in the *Santa Elena* v. *Costa Rica*.

'exemptions not contemplated in the statutory or regulatory framework related to human rights, environmental, health, safety labour, taxation, financial incentives or other issues'. It will become increasingly possible to construct a list of areas in which legislative measures affecting the property rights of investors will presumptively amount to regulatory takings.

4.6 Conserving regulatory expropriation and the distinguishing criteria

The modern-day reality is that states seldom adopt measures affecting property rights except when the interests of public welfare require it. So far, both in domestic constitutional systems as well in international law, no general principles that provide criteria for the distinction between compensable expropriation and non-compensable regulatory expropriation has been found.[105] As the *Saluka* Award put it, international law has yet 'to draw a bright and easily distinguishable line between non-compensable regulations, on the one hand, and, on the other, measures that have the effect of depriving foreign investor of their investment and are thus unlawful and compensable in international law'.[106]

Yet there are indicia that attach to regulatory expropriations. First, a regulatory expropriation seldom involves the transfer of rights to the state or to a third party. In *Methanex*, the state did not profit from the banning of the business of the foreign investor. In taxation, there is a direct profit that is made by the state, but the profit motive is secondary given that the purpose of taxation is that the moneys derived be channelled for the public good. The second has been to look at the primary purpose behind the taking. There is always a dominant motive that benefits a public interest supported by a value higher than the property interests of individuals or groups. In the context of foreign investment laws relating to entry and operation, one has to include within it the range of functions that an administrative authority performs in relation to foreign investment. These have already been identified in the law, and interference for the purposes stated in the entry legislation cannot come

---

[105] Much discussion has focused on American constitutional law and its concept of regulatory takings. The language of police powers is a distinct feature of US law. The wide belief that the US Model Treaty formulation is based on the US case on regulatory takings, *Penn Central Transportation Co. v. New York City* (1978) 438 US 104, has driven much of the discussion by American writers.

[106] *Saluka* Award, para. 263.

as a surprise to the foreign investor. Thus, requirements relating to capitalization, use of local materials or labour, export of percentages of production, and location in certain areas may be mandated by entry laws or may be conditions on which entry is permitted. Takings effected as a result of a failure to conform to these requirements must be regarded as regulatory takings brought about through fault of the foreign investor. The foreign investment functions within the state on the condition that the requirements as to the entry laws and administrative guidance given under them are complied with. In particular, where conditions are imposed on entry and these are transgressed, interference should be considered as an exercise of a regulatory function, provided due process conditions are satisfied.[107] As indicated earlier, besides the traditional categories of regulatory takings, a further list could be made on the basis of constitutional provisions permitting taking of property that are common to several countries.

Where the state is responding to a situation of necessity, clearly, the measures it takes must be regarded as regulatory. The Bhopal disaster provides the extreme example. It cannot credibly be suggested that any measure that the Indian government took to reduce the effects of the gas emission could be anything but regulatory. In lesser situations, too, the objective situation of necessity would require that state measures be regarded as regulatory. Both in terms of the national security defence, which is subjectively stated in many treaties, and the general defence of necessity in customary international law will liability be excluded from such regulatory measures. There is an interaction between the notion of regulatory takings and the situation of necessity and national security.[108]

Outside these categories, the new categories are justifiable on the basis of international multilateral conventions addressing global interests in a variety of areas. The existence of these conventions create normative conflicts between the interests they identify with the interest in investment protection. Thus, the categories relating to the environment, human rights, labour standards, indigenous rights and cultural property are based on obligations created by international conventions. They involve conflicts between obligations that arise from multilateral

---

[107] *Amco* v. *Indonesia*, which involved capitalization measures extending beyond the initial investment. The final outcome was that damages were based on failure to provide due process before cancellation of the licence.

[108] In *Continental Casualty* v. *Argentina*, ICSID, Case No. ARB/03/9 (5 September 2008), para. 175, it was stated that necessity can be invoked 'to protect a wide variety of interests, including the safeguarding the environment'.

4.6 CONSERVING REGULATORY EXPROPRIATION 239

investment treaties and bilateral and regional investment treaties. Two means have been suggested by which this conflict can be resolved, both of which depend on the creation of hierarchies as to these treaties and the creation of an order of precedence among the obligations created by the different treaties.

The first is the suggestion that some obligations created by multilateral conventions are created in such a manner as to involve obligations of a fundamental character so as to qualify as *ius cogens* obligations. If they do so qualify, the competing obligations in the investment treaties are clearly rendered otiose simply because they must yield place in the event of such a conflict. So, too, even where the multilateral obligations are not *ius cogens*, they may have precedence because of their importance in securing the global interests of the international community.[109] There must be a decision as to whether the global interests in multilateral conventions have a hierarchical precedence over the interests of the foreign investor under the investment treaty. One result of this is that the conflict between these multilateral obligations concerning global interests and the obligations in bilateral investment treaties protecting the narrower interests of foreign investors are not arbitrable before tribunals set up by investment treaties between the two states or between few states of a region, but should be settled by an international tribunal such as the ICJ, which can adequately and competently settle the conflicts involving global interest. Alternatively, the matter should be dealt with as a dispute between states and be settled by a tribunal set up by the states. This is a jurisdictional issue that has to be settled at the outset when a claim is made that the alleged measure violating the expropriation provision is regulatory on the ground that it promotes a global interest. There is increasing authority for this approach.[110]

---

[109] Vinuales, *Foreign Investment and the Environment in International Law.*

[110] Sornarajah, *The Settlement of Foreign Investment Disputes*, pp. 186–92, where the argument on the non-arbitrability of *ius cogens* obligations and multilateral obligations by an investment tribunal is made. *Desert Line* v. *Yemen* considered an investment agreement involving genocide or slavery as violating *ius cogens*. In litigation under the Alien Tort Claims Act, cases have featured forced labour (*Doe* v. *Unocal* (2002) 395 F.3d 230), torture, and violation of aboriginal rights. Such accusations have not yet arisen in investment arbitration. But the scope for it will increase as corporate responsibility norms become better articulated. Jeffrey Davis, *Justice Across Borders: The Struggle for Human Rights in US Courts* (New York: Cambridge University Press, 2007). The two strands of corporate liability and investment protection will have to be reconciled at some stage. Investment disputes have also skirted on rights such as native rights, the right to water (*Aguas del Tunari* v. *Bolivia*), the right to cultural property (*Malaysian Salvors; Parkerings*) and the right to the environment (*Santa Elena* v. *Costa Rica*). See further Chapter 6.

240   THE EMASCULATION OF EXPROPRIATION

The second approach is to argue that areas relating to the environment, human rights and cultural property are obligations owed to the international community, which, on a hierarchy of obligations, take precedence over obligations owed to foreign investors under investment treaties. So far, arbitral tribunals have not taken kindly to this argument, but the arguments have been raised in disputes to which the old style investment treaties apply, which contained absolute standards of investment protection. With the newer treaties recognizing a wide array of defences, including measures relating to the environment, labour standards, national security, health, morals and welfare, the treaty itself mandates the acceptance of such justifications. Yet the argument that the justifications operate independently of the statement of the defences in the investment treaties must be examined as such an argument strengthens the case for the acceptance of these defences, which are based on the idea that measures taken in pursuance of the objectives on which they are based must be considered non-compensable regulatory expropriations. The defences are inherent in the notion of regulatory expropriation. This requires examination of each of the areas on which the defences are based.

A state that takes property in order to ensure that it conforms to an obligation under international environmental law or treaty need not pay compensation for the taking. The rule must favour non-payment of compensation as the state is conforming to an obligation that it owes to the international community and in the process violates an obligation it owes to the foreign investor under a bilateral agreement. The awards in *Santa Elena* v. *Costa Rica* and *S. D. Myers* v. *Canada* contain views that this is not the case. But they may be explained as older cases in which priority was given to investment protection over domestic environmental legislation, or on the basis that the facts gave rise to protectionism with environmental reasons as a cover. The creation of a hierarchy of obligations is necessary, and an environmental obligation must have precedence, particularly where it is stated in a multilateral convention in concrete terms.[111]

A similar analysis could be made of international human rights law and labour standards. Here again, there are obligations that arise through the existence of multilateral documents. As against the individual rights of the investor under the investment treaties, human rights concerns should have priority, especially in situations where the foreign investor is

---

[111] Vinuales, *Foreign Investment and the Environment in International Law.*

4.6 CONSERVING REGULATORY EXPROPRIATION 241

seen to be the violator of human rights. Even otherwise, it could be argued that some of the human rights, especially if they flow from *ius cogens* principles or stand in a higher degree of normativity, override the rights of the foreign investor drawn from a bilateral treaty. For this reason, a taking in reliance of a human rights norm should have precedence over the rights of the foreign investor.[112]

In the case of takings based on purely domestic concerns, the regulatory nature of the taking has to be judged on its merits. A margin of appreciation has to be given to the state in deciding whether such a taking was necessary and in the public interest. If it appeared necessary, the analysis should end there. The issue as to the extent to which a tribunal could thereafter examine the reasonableness of the expropriation remains.

It is also necessary to have regard to the developments that are taking place in considering the liability of multinational corporations for harm they cause in their host states. The United Nations has considered this issue and has come up with the notion of a responsibility to protect the interests of the host state. Notions of corporate responsibility for ensuring the welfare of the community within which investment functions are coming to be recognized both in domestic and international law. In the United States, the Alien Tort Claims Act has resulted in many civil actions being brought by affected citizens of host states against parent companies present within the United States. The US Supreme Court permitted such actions provided part of the conduct complained of took place within US territory or a clear nexus with the US jurisdiction existed.[113] The possibility of such actions in other jurisdictions exists and is being explored. In the context of this growing trend towards liability of multinational corporations, a blanket proposition that foreign investment that is expropriated must uniformly be compensated becomes difficult to maintain. It is necessary to examine how the multinational corporation functioned within the host state. If it caused harm to the host

---

[112] Jeff Waincymer, 'Balancing Property Rights and Human Rights in Expropriation', in Pierre-Marie Dupuy *et al.* (eds.), *Human Rights in International Investment Law and Arbitration* (Oxford University Press, 2009), p. 276.

[113] The US Supreme Court's decision in *Kiobel* v. *Royal Dutch Shell Petroleum Co.* (2013) 569 US, may result in subsiding, but not removing, such litigation. The majority decision left open the possibility of such litigation where part of the conduct was done on US territory. The minority referred to an earlier Supreme Court decision, *Sosa* v. *Alvarez Machain* (2004) 542 US 692, where a torturer was assimilated to a pirate and jurisdiction was permitted. English courts would allow parent responsibility for acts of subsidiaries committed abroad. *Chandler* v. *Cape plc* [2012] EWCA Civ. 525; *Vava* v. *Anglo-American South Africa Ltd* [2012] EWHC 1969 (QB).

242   THE EMASCULATION OF EXPROPRIATION

economy, it is difficult to argue that the corporation must be given compensation when the harm is terminated by the host state. The measure that is taken by the state to counteract the harm must be regarded as regulatory expropriation.

It would appear that the alternative formula of appropriate compensation, which already exists within international law, may be preferable in such circumstances as it enables an assessment of compensation in the light of the performance of the multinational corporation. The notion of appropriate compensation itself was based on a balance in that the appropriateness would have to be determined by consideration of past performance, past and potential harm caused by the investment, profits and other circumstances of the affected foreign investment. Clearly, a meritorious foreign investment that had meshed with the development goals of a host state would deserve full compensation. Likewise, an investment that had been attracted into the host state and was taken as it was about to bear profits would merit future profits being included in the compensation. Equally, a persistently deleterious investment that is terminated would not receive any compensation as clearly the taking would be regulatory. The notion of appropriate compensation is a manipulable device that could supplant the idea of balancing as that notion is inherent in it. But given that the investment treaties mandate full compensation, it is difficult to see how a tribunal can award lesser compensation.

4.7   The bridge to fair and equitable treatment

The progressive emasculation of expropriation that has taken place as result of the rigorous arguments made by states, as well as through their entrenchment of the doctrine of regulatory expropriation along with other factors, has led to the opening of new avenues of keeping investment protection under treaties alive. The need for the creation of new avenues of protection of foreign investment had to be explored. The tribunal in *PSEG Global Ltd* v. *Turkey* stated this need in the following terms:[114]

> The standard of fair and equitable treatment has acquired prominence in investment arbitration as a consequence of the fact that other standards traditionally provided by international law might not in the circumstances

[114] ICSID, Case No. ARB/02/5 (17 January 2007) (Orrego-Vicuna, Fortier, Kaufmann-Kohler), at paras. 238–239.

4.7 THE BRIDGE TO FAIR AND EQUITABLE TREATMENT 243

of each case be entirely appropriate. This is particularly the case when the facts of the dispute do not clearly support the claim for direct expropriation, but when there are notwithstanding events that need to be assessed under a different standard to provide redress in the event that the rights of the investor have been breached.

Because the role of fair and equitable treatment changes from case to case, it is sometimes not as precise as would be desirable. Yet it clearly does allow for justice to be done in the absence of the more traditional breaches of international law standards. This role has resulted in the concept of fair and equitable treatment acquiring a standing on its own, separate and distinct from that of other standards, albeit many times closely related to them, and thus ensuring that the protection granted to the investment is fully safeguarded.

The constriction of expropriation through the rediscovery of the regulatory takings exception resulted in the exploration of new avenues for finding liability for what was perceived as arbitrary behaviour on the part of the host state. Such an avenue was provided by the presence in the investment treaties of the amorphous phrase, 'fair and equitable treatment'. The focus of interpretation of that provision came to be the formulation of the rule that the treatment does not detract from the basic expectations on which the foreign investor made its investment. The other attempt was the use of the umbrella clause in the treaty, a throw-away provision that reiterated the requirement to keep all commitments made to the foreign investor.

Two factors within expropriation law accelerated the trend towards discovering new causes of action. The first is that direct expropriation lost its significance. The same reason for investment treaties, the attracting of investments, simply meant that states did not want to engage in direct expropriations and scare away foreign investors. Domestic foreign investment laws were also structured such that controlling ownership in projects was less likely so that what was usually affected were the share interests of the foreign investor in the project. Direct expropriation could not provide for this situation. Indirect expropriation also became less useful with the recognition of regulatory takings as almost always such takings would have regulatory features. There was a need to look elsewhere to maintain a system of foreign investment protection.

The resuscitation of dormant clauses in the investment treaties – the umbrella clause and the fair and equitable clause – provided the avenues for such a project. The fair and equitable clause was dusted up and given an array of meanings. The most important among them was the inclusion into the fair and equitable standard of the legitimate expectations rule. It

244 THE EMASCULATION OF EXPROPRIATION

was also possible to read into the fair and equitable standard a whole list of transgressions by the host state. One finds that expansiveness in this area is quite extensive. It can be explained only on the basis of the earnestness of the search for new and alternative bases of liability to keep the law on foreign investment protection alive. It required a creative exercise, which was provided by a select group of arbitrators who sat in a series of arbitrations, often together, to build a new area of liability. As did happen, not all arbitrators joined in wholeheartedly. The more cautious did not undermine the project, but stated the rules, such as the rule of legitimate expectations, more cautiously.

To a lesser extent, the umbrella clause also provided an avenue for alternative basis of liability. But the umbrella clause did not appear in all treaties. Besides, the schism as to the scope of the umbrella clause appeared at the very beginning of the effort to use it, so that there was a division as to the use to which the clause could be put from the very beginning. The awards on the umbrella clauses have split on the basis of the initial differences that arose in the two *SGS* arbitrations,[115] one giving no significance to it, and the other recognising it as a basis of liability.

The equitable treatment provision is either left out or appears qualified by the statement that it is no different from the customary international law minimum standard. It is a mystery that the treaties that contain this qualification continue to state both types of treatment standards. Though expropriation still has life, the controversies concerning it have, to a large extent, run their course. The more vibrant path that has opened up is through fair and equitable treatment. This path is explored in Chapter 5.

4.8 Conclusion

This chapter set out the changes that have taken place in expropriation under investment treaties. From being the focal point of investment law expropriation has undergone changes that presage its virtual extinction. The controversy shifted from the extent of compensation to what amounts to a taking. This was due to the elimination of an ideology which denied any compensation as well as to the decline in the

---

[115] *Société Générale de Surveillance SA (SGS)* v. *Pakistan*, ICSID, Case No. ARB/01/13 (26 August 2003); *Société Générale de Surveillance SA (SGS)* v. *Philippines*, ICSID, Case No. ARB/02/6 (24 January 2004).

4.8 CONCLUSION 245

developing states' eagerness to support norms of the NIEO. The interest then shifted to what amounted to a taking. The desire was to enlarge the scope of taking through formulation of new categories such as creeping expropriation, and what amounted to the categories of acts 'tantamount to a taking'. States reacted to these moves by reviving the doctrine of regulatory takings both in their arguments in arbitrations as well as in treaties they made. Non-governmental organizations and other interest groups joined in by articulating the view that governmental measures to protect the environment, to promote human rights or similar interests should not be regarded as expropriation. Indicia of what amounted to regulatory takings were explored. The consequent emasculation of expropriation required the opening of new avenues of creating remedies for foreign investors. The efforts to breathe life into expropriation through the proportionality rule is flawed and will prove to be short-lived. The change of emphasis to the fair and equitable standard was the principal means of keeping investment arbitration alive.

5

Fair and equitable treatment: conserving relevance

Few instances illustrate the rapidity of law-making in international law as the emergence into prominence of the fair and equitable standard from out of the shadows of over half a century of disuse,[1] with content attributed to it in six short years. The international minimum standard, which the United States had sought to assert in investment protection for over a century, remains uncertain in content. But the claim is made that the fair and equitable standard has, within a few years of its rediscovery, established itself as an autonomous standard with a specific content. The developments involving the fair and equitable standard began with the new millennium, seeking to keep open avenues of protection for investors when the most potent basis of such protection – expropriation – had been shut due to stringent requirements as to the extent of the deprivation necessary for a finding of expropriation and the recognition of regulatory expropriation as non-compensable taking. The recognition of regulatory expropriation as non-compensable taking created a 'gaping hole' in the strategy of investment protection through treaties.

A new door had to be opened if investment arbitration was to remain viable. Investment arbitration supported many lawyers, arbitrators, arbitral institutions and academics. It would be cynical to say that it was their interests alone that led to the creation of a new law that enabled investment arbitration to live on. Clearly, the need to preserve a law that was conducive to investment protection was the motivating factor for the exploration of a new avenue of protection. The new door that was opened was through the fair and equitable standard.[2] It was opened largely

---

[1] The clause was used in the Havana Charter in 1948. The Charter was to have established the International Trade Organization. It is found in the OECD Draft Convention on Investment 1957. It thereafter passed into investment treaties, but remained unused until awards in the early years of the present millennium. It was attributed content in these awards and a full set of meanings had come to be ascribed to it by 2005.

[2] The fact that the statement of the fair and equitable treatment is disparate has not deterred this development. The UNCTAD *World Investment Report* (2014) indicated that

FAIR AND EQUITABLE TREATMENT

through the awards of individual arbitrators who had a dominant influence in shaping its early course.

The law on the fair and equitable standard is of recent vintage, created largely through interpretations placed on the phrase by arbitrators who favoured expansion. In a leading article on the clause written in 1999, Vasciannie found it difficult to identify the content of the fair and equitable standard of treatment.[3] Yet writing six years later, Schreuer maintained that the standard had been fleshed out with sufficient meaning within that period by arbitral awards.[4] If correct, it is an interesting phenomenon, for the precise content of the international minimum standard, which has been around for over a century, is still a matter of conjecture. The formation of law has been swift indeed. But, whereas international minimum standard has relied primarily on state practice for its creation, the fair and equitable standard has relied on arbitral awards and the writings of 'highly qualified publicists', both subsidiary sources of international law.[5] The law on it has been made by agencies of private power. The current importance of the standard is attested to by the extensive literature that has resulted from the few awards in existence.[6]

The creation of a law based on the fair and equitable standard is a vindication of the view presented in this work that the primary thrust in investment arbitration has been to promote investment protection according to a desired model, and not to bring about a law that balances the interests of the foreign investor with other interests of the host state, its people and the international community as a whole. The revival of a

---

'formulations remain varied'. This has not deterred uniform conclusions from being drawn by arbitral tribunals from these provisions or a system of precedent being built.

[3] Stephen Vasciannie, 'The Fair and Equitable Standard in International Investment Law and Practice', (1999) 70 *British Yearbook of International Law* 99. Vasciannie also observed that it would be 'artificial' to argue that anything in investment treaties could be customary law as developing countries had little option but to accept the formulations of the developed states.

[4] Schreuer, 'Fair and Equitable Treatment in Arbitral Practice'.

[5] *Glamis Gold Ltd* v. *United States* (2009) 48 ILM 1035. The embarrassment that the law was made through weaker sources led to even more embarrassing theory that arbitration tribunals can create customary international law.

[6] There are an increasing number of book-length treatments based on doctoral theses, and there several more doctoral theses in the making. Tudor, *The Fair and Equitable Standard in International Foreign Investment Law*; Klager, *Fair and Equitable Treatment in International Investment Law*; Alexandra Diehl, *The Core Standard of International Investment Protection* (The Hague: Kluwer, 2012); Paparinskis, *International Minimum Standard and the Fair and Equitable Treatment*.

clause that had gone into desuetude had the solitary purpose of catering for the new situation where expropriation law had floundered on the rocks of regulatory expropriation principle, and there was a need for an alternative hook on which to hang responsibility of the state for measures detrimental to the interests of the foreign investor. The expansionist arbitrators were playing a quasi-legislative role for which they had no authority in law. They were motivated by the desire to promote investment protection without any care for the underlying values in international law that sought to promote other global interests. Equally, there was resistance from arbitrators who, though they joined in the expansion, yet were cautious to restrict the new doctrines being articulated by having regard to the restrictions on the doctrine that existed in their domestic law sources. In this episode, too, there is a clear demonstration of the schism between expansionary arbitrators and those averse to expansion.

The developments that have taken place in this area provide an obvious example of the differences in attitudes internal to investment arbitration. It also shows that resistance to the trend developed outside it as a backlash resulted against the capricious move towards the creation of principles that had no backing in the intention of the parties who had made the treaties and were averse to interests other than investment protection in which different groups had concerns. This area is the best example of these two tendencies at work within the investment arbitration system

International tribunals have powers of control over decisions of national legislatures and judiciaries, if treaties vest such power in them. But the issue is whether these tribunals have the power to exceed the limits of consent, which underlies their jurisdiction.[7] The struggle was between law-making through arbitral adventurism with the object of promoting a new liberal vision, and arbitral restraint that showed a need to keep within the limits of jurisdiction created by the investment treaty. The incorporation of the legitimate expectations rule in the fair and equitable standard is the most glaring example of expansionary activism. Despite apologetic statements that arbitrators do show restraint and adopt deference to the interests of states,[8] there is no objective evidence of this having happened in many arbitral awards which have adopted the legitimate expectations rule. The second group of arbitrators

---

[7] Gus Van Harten, *Sovereign Choices and Sovereign Constraints: Judicial Restraint in Investment Treaty Arbitration* (Oxford University Press, 2013).

[8] Stephan Schill, 'Deference in Investment Treaty Arbitration', (2012) 3 *Journal of International Dispute Settlement* 577.

did not question the expansion of the fair and equitable standard. They sought to limit the effect of the rules identified in an acceptable manner. They went along with arbitral adventurism part of the way, though not the whole way. The option that the expansion was untenable was not even considered. Thus, both groups of arbitrators agree that the rule on legitimate expectations constituted part of the fair and equitable standard despite the fact that it required considerable creativity to make it part of the standard. Few tribunals have considered the legitimacy of the adventurist interpretation. In that sense, there was no restraint in either group. The restraint of one group is to search for the limits to the application of the rule in specific circumstances and some cursory investigation as to what the source of the rule could be.

The conflict is a reverse of the debate as to judicial law-making within democratic states. In judicial law-making, activist judges extend the law in order to meet valid social objectives or to accommodate social changes within the law on the basis of an assumed legislative intent, whereas conservative judges seek to promote the status quo. The exact reverse takes place in investment arbitration. What the small group of expansionist arbitrators promotes is the conservative object of investment protection favoured by private power. The arbitrators with fidelity to the limits of jurisdiction stated in the treaties go some way towards acceptance of the interpretation, but hold back with caution in order not to provoke a reaction from states. But the law was made by the larger majority of arbitrators who either belonged to the 'club' that has dominated investment arbitration, or were aspirants to membership with an eagerness to participate in arbitral adventurism in the hope of admission to the club.

But arbitrators who performed a restraining function did not question the legitimacy of the trends that had been initiated. A further problem was that the transference to fair and equitable treatment required a radical change from what was earlier perceived as the private law moorings of the law to principles of review that were found in the public law. They were called upon to apply administrative law principles, which had been imported into the application of the fair and equitable standard by the activist arbitrators. Many arbitrators had private law backgrounds. Steeped in commercial law arbitration, they had difficulty in dealing with public law ideas.[9] The result of the disputes was conceived in private law terms and rationalized in terms of the public law. The reasoning in some of the awards lacked coherence as a result.

---

[9] Van Harten, *Investment Treaty Arbitration and Public Law.*

The inconsistency between the awards undermines the course of the developments towards the recognition of the standard as an autonomous category. The entry of the fair and equitable standard was seen as a new dawn, but as time went on attacks on it became vigorous. Since notions of fairness and equity cut both ways, the standard opened up defences to liability enabling the foreign investor to be cast in bad light.[10] It does not provide a sound basis on which investment protection can be built. Furthermore, states themselves began attacking these trends in their new treaties. The tying of the standard to the customary international minimum standard, adopted principally in the US treaties, undermined significantly the possible uses of the fair and equitable standard. Some new treaties simply leave the fair and equitable standard out.

These trends and issues form the basis of this chapter. It begins with the examination of the difference in statements of the fair and equitable standard in the treaties, giving rise to the possible conclusion that uniform law on the standard is precluded by the very diversity in the manner of the statement of the standard in different treaties. The great rush to argue that a *jurisprudence constante* has been developed in the area is foreclosed from the very beginning simply because of the fact that the standard has taken different guises in different treaties. The argument about the possibility of a *jurisprudence constante* is akin to the argument that bilateral investment treaties create customary international law. The project of converting the norms into customary international law, as if through the wave of a magic wand, and securing the multilateralization of investment norms is one that lies at the heart of the neoliberal plan. Neither is possible. There is no constant jurisprudence. There is no constancy in the statement of the standard such as to create a basis for customary law. The nuance of the words in the formulation of the fair and equitable standard in particular, and the investment treaties in general, make the evolution of a uniform standard difficult.

5.1 Diversity in the standard

Ioana Tudor, in her 2008 study of the fair and equitable treatment clause, compared 358 treaties among the then extant treaties, numbering around

---

[10] Muthucumaraswamy Sornarajah, 'Fair and Equitable Treatment: Whose Fairness? Whose Equity?' in Frederico Ortino (ed.), *Investment Treaty Law: Current Issues* (London: BIICL, 2007); Peter Muchlinski, 'Caveat Investor? The Relevance of the Conduct of the Investor under the Fair and Equitable Standard', (2006) 55 *International & Comparative Law Quarterly* 527.

5.1 DIVERSITY IN THE STANDARD 251

2,500, and found that the statement of the fair and equitable clause varied markedly among the treaties she studied. The 'number of variations assigns different meanings to the fair and equitable standard'.[11] In her book, she found five principal variants of the clause. An UNCTAD study found seven different types of provision.[12] In this rich disarray in the statement of the standard, it would be fanciful to construct a *jurisprudence constante* on the basis of the awards interpreting the different treaties.

There are several forms the fair and equitable standard takes. It often appears in the preamble. The preamble is intended to state the object of the treaty and not to state binding obligations. Its appearance in the preamble merely states an aspiration that the objective is to attain standards of fairness and equity. In some treaties, particularly after the interpretive note of the NAFTA Commission requiring that the fair and equitable standard of treatment should be treated as no more than the international minimum standard, it is stated as tied to the customary international law. The American and Canadian model treaties of 2004 contain examples of such tying, but such a method is by no means confined to these two states. After the expansive interpretations became common, many states have limited the possibility of such interpretations by tying the fair and equitable treatment to the international minimum standard contained in customary international law. But tribunals have split on whether the standard is affected by the tying.[13] There are treaties in which the fair and equitable standard is tied to other standards, such as non-discrimination, denial of justice, full protection and security and national treatment.

But, most importantly, there are treaties in which the fair and equitable standard is not included. Tudor found nineteen treaties in her study, but these are older treaties. In the newer ones, they are not included precisely because of the controversial interpretations that have been placed on them. Where they are included, they are tied to customary international

---

[11] Ioana Tudor, 'The Fair and Equitable Treatment Standards and Human Rights Norms', in Pierre-Marie Dupuy *et al.* (eds.), *Human Rights in International Investment Law and Arbitration* (Oxford University Press, 2009), p. 310, at p. 312. Tudor concluded at p. 316 that the 'study of the bilateral, regional and multilateral treaties leads to the conclusion that there are different levels of treatment corresponding to the FET standard'. The UNCTAD study found seven different types of fair and equitable standard provisions.

[12] UNCTAD, *Fair and Equitable Treatment: Sequel* (Geneva: UNCTAD, 2012).

[13] The phrase appears without such limitations in some treaties. In such instances, it is a moot point as to whether it provides a higher standard than the international minimum standard.

law or to the international minimum standard.[14] In some recent treaties, the standard is tied to denial of justice, ensuring that there is a pronouncement of the domestic court prior to arbitration so that liability can arise only from the egregious failure of the court to provide justice. It is an obvious reaction to arbitral adventurism in the area. Some states respond simply by making such adventurism not possible by leaving the clause out altogether. It is an unheeded signal to arbitrators to desist from their adventures. Yet it does not seem to have had any effect on some tribunals.[15] The fact of these variations does not deter commentators and arbitrators inclined towards the broad construction of the fair and equitable standard as an autonomous standard to desist from adventurism.

5.2 Giving content to the fair and equitable standard

Given this divergence in the statement of the standard in the different treaties, there could be two approaches possible. The first is that each dispute under each treaty should be considered separately, so that a decision could be arrived at on the basis of the provisions of the specific treaty. This view is supported not only by the differences in the treaty formulations, but also by the fact that the provision calls for the application of an amorphous standard. The approach does not depend on following precedent, but on deciding appropriately, given the different formulations in the treaties reflecting the bargain struck between the two parties as well as the fact situations of each dispute. Several tribunals have indicated this flexibility in approach. Given the 'abstractions'[16] in the clause, such flexibility is seen as necessary. The result, however, does not support the creation of a firm law on the standard, but depends on a case-by-case approach.

The other approach is to argue that the awards have created a constant jurisprudence on the fair and equitable standard. Neoliberalism demands such an approach so that a concrete system of investment protection is built up once more after the erosion of the safeguards provided by the law

---

[14] The Canadian and US Model treaties of 2004 are examples. Several treaties made by the two states follow these models.

[15] The conflict is evident in the NAFTA awards. Compare *Glamis Gold Ltd* v. *United States*, UNCITRAL Arbitration, Award (8 June 2009) and *Merrill & Ring Forestry Ltd* v. *Canada*, UNCITRAL, ICSID (31 March 2010).

[16] *GAMI Investments Ltd* v. *Mexico* (2004) 44 ILM 545, NAFTA Case, Award (15 November 2004), para. 92.

5.2 GIVING CONTENT TO FAIR AND EQUITABLE STANDARD 253

on expropriation. This approach focuses on the evolutionary nature of the law and seeks to conserve the gains made in the existing awards. This approach is geared to the formation of a law that furthers investment protection by almost restating the principles of investment protection through the amorphous formulation of the fair and equitable standard. The mere presence of the clause in the treaty makes it possible to invoke the earlier case law, regardless of the nuances in the language. The justification is that this enables the building up of a consistent body of case law on the application of the standard. The precedents are said to support a series of situations in which the violations of the treatment standard could be found. These include the identification of objective situations in which the tribunal had found violations of the standard.

There have been attempts to compile a set of content. Textual authority for the suggested content is non-existent as the treaties themselves are silent as to the content of the standard. As a result, much creativity has to be used in constructing the content of the clause. The legitimacy of this exercise is open to doubt. The treaties do not invest arbitration tribunals with authority to create the law they apply to the investment dispute. When innovating on the basis of the clause, the arbitral tribunals perform quasi-legislative functions lacking any basis in the consent of the states that vest jurisdiction in them. The manner in which the content of the standard has been constructed has not been clearly explained in any award. The hint that the principal rule suggested as constituting the content –the rule on legitimate expectations – constitutes a general principle of law has not been convincingly demonstrated.

The expansive view has attributed definite content to the fair and equitable standard. The content has been stated in terms of definite rules. Thus, the absence of transparency in the law applied has been held to violate the standard, creating a new head of violation to be grouped under the fair and equitable standard.[17] The technique for discovery of the content of the standard has been to use principles of interpretation of treaties in a creative manner. The choice of the rules of interpretation for this purpose has itself been queried. The technique is to argue that the rules permit a purposive interpretation. The purpose of the treaty is said to be found in the preamble. The awards identify stability

---

[17] *Metalclad Corp.* v. *Mexico*, ICSID, Case No. ARB(AF)97/1 (30 August 2000). The British Columbia Supreme Court, which had jurisdiction to review the award, did not uphold this part of the award on the ground that the transparency requirement was imported from another part of NAFTA. *United Mexican States* v. *Metalclad Corp.* [2001] BCSCR 664.

254 FAIR AND EQUITABLE TREATMENT

and economic development as the main purposes of the treaty. The conclusion is then drawn that the clause will accommodate principles that promote the stability of the investment relationship that has been formed.

Using the same technique, a compilation of circumstances, which would call for the determination of the violation of the standard, has been made. Awards have elevated situations involving the violation of due process, harassment of the investor by state agencies, discriminatory treatment and violation of legitimate expectations as instances of violations of the fair and equitable standard. The UNCTAD Study (2011) listed five categories under which these developments could be grouped.[18] They included arbitrariness, denial of justice, discrimination, abusive treatment and violation of legitimate expectations.[19] Apart from the category of legitimate expectations, the other categories are based on the existing international minimum standard, giving rise to the impression that the four categories are included only to bolster the claim of legitimate expectations to be one of the categories. Leaving the four categories aside, as they are separately provided for in treaties either under the international minimum standard or individually, it is only the legitimate expectations category that can be offered as a distinct content of the fair and equitable treatment standard.

A list is also provided in the award in *Waste Management II*:[20]

---

[18] UNCTAD, *Fair and Equitable Treatment: Sequel.*

[19] Later NAFTA cases did not deviate from the requirement of a high threshold for finding liability, indicating that mere deviations from the applications of administrative law would not create liability. They follow the high threshold in the *Neer* formulation as the test, while paying lip-service to the possibility of evolution of the standard. *GAMI Investments Ltd v. Mexico* (2004) 44 ILM 545; *Cargill Inc. v. Mexico*, ICSID, Case No. ARB(AF)/04/2 (6 September 2011); *Glamis Gold Ltd v. United States* (2009) 48 ILM 1035. According to *Glamis*, the level of scrutiny remains the same as in 1926, but what is considered egregious conduct in modern times may be different. 'The minimum standard of treatment of fair and equitable treatment is infringed by conduct attributable to the State and harmful to the claimant if the conduct is arbitrary, grossly unfair, unjust or idiosyncratic, is discriminatory and exposes the claimant to sectional or racial prejudice, or involves a lack of due process leading to an outcome which offends judicial propriety – as might be the case with a manifest failure of natural justice in judicial proceedings or a complete lack of transparency and candour in an administrative process' (*Glamis Gold*, para. 626). The passage is a mere repetition of the statement of the content in *Waste Management Inc. v. United States* (2004) 43 ILM 967. But *Merrill & Ring Forestry Ltd v. Canada*, UNCITRAL (31 March 2010), departs from these views in holding that the fair and equitable treatment has become customary international law.

[20] *Waste Management Inc. v. United States* (2004) 43 ILM 967.

5.2 GIVING CONTENT TO FAIR AND EQUITABLE STANDARD 255

> The minimum standard of treatment of fair and equitable treatment is infringed by conduct attributable to the State and harmful to the claimant if the conduct is arbitrary, grossly unfair, unjust or idiosyncratic, is discriminatory and exposes the claimant to sectional or racial prejudice, or involves a lack of due process leading to an outcome which offends judicial propriety – as might be the case with a manifest failure of natural justice in judicial proceedings or a complete lack of transparency and candour in an administrative process.[21]

Except for the inclusion of the amorphous words 'grossly unfair, unjust or idiosyncratic', which merely paraphrase and compound the already hazy formula of fair and equitable treatment, the formulation does not indicate categories that cannot be fitted into other provisions of the investment treaty. One might be forgiven for the cynicism in feeling that the list as is so large the whole area of investment law is captured within it. On this basis, the investment treaty might be shorter if one just has a reference to the fair and equitable standard and the dispute settlement provision and allows the adventurous arbitrator accomplish his task of expansive definition of the standard without restraint. If the laundry list in *Waste Management II* is the meaning of the fair and equitable clause, it encapsulates within it virtually the whole of international investment law.

Presumably, the categories could be stabilized when precedents grow. But the difficulty of the existing categories is that, with the exception of legitimate expectations, a category not supported by the language in any treaty, the other categories in the list are otiose as they clearly fall under older and more established treaty principles. Failure to provide due process in situations of expropriations clearly violates a customary norm as well as the provision on expropriation in the treaty. Similarly, harassment of the investor is a violation of the duty to provide full protection and security. Non-discrimination is also separately provided for in the national treatment standard.[22] Racial discrimination is prohibited by international law as a violation of a *ius cogens* principle. It hardly requires statement and is never specifically referred to in investment treaties. Where an expropriation is racially discriminatory, it would be clearly unlawful in terms of customary international law. The effort of drawing the content of fair and equitable standard lacks cogency in that it restates existing rules, except when it comes to the notion of legitimate

---

[21] The list was approved in *Railroad Development Corp. v. Guatemala* (2010) ICSID ARB/07/23 (19 May 2010), para. 219.

[22] UNCTAD, *Fair and Equitable Treatment: Sequel.*

256   FAIR AND EQUITABLE TREATMENT

expectations, a category hitherto unknown to the law on foreign investment protection through investment treaties.[23] The effort is merely to
show that the fair and equitable standard is somehow larger than it is
when, in fact, the only important advancement that has been suggested is
that the violation of the legitimate expectations of the foreign investor is a
violation of the fair and equitable standard. This ground stands on
uncertain foundations. It is in order to strengthen the inclusion of the
rule that the standard appears with a larger cast than justified in the hope
that unity will give it strength. It is difficult to understand how a dormant
standard could suddenly explode into life unless supported by a concerted effort to blow it up into an all-embracing standard encapsulating
virtually every aspect of international investment law so that in the dust
that is raised, the principal norm that is being created relating to legitimate expectations passes without much scrutiny. As the UNCTAD
Report rightly puts it, the category of legitimate expectations is an
innovation. It is, in effect, the only innovation accomplished through
the revival of the fair and equitable standard. It is a category that could
not have been contemplated by the parties to the treaties.[24] It is not even
established that the terminology exists in all legal systems. Its use extends
beyond the consent of the parties and is inherently suspect. The main
thrust of the discovery of the fair and equitable standard has been to
formulate the rule as to legitimate expectations. It is the 'dominant
element of that standard'.[25] Protection of legitimate expectations is the
'most important function' of the fair and equitable standard.[26] It is the
principal basis on transferring investment arbitration from a private law
base to public law as it calls for the judging of the validity of a governmental act in the context of its past promises and its past conduct.[27] It is

[23] It has been mentioned in some awards on contract-based arbitration such as *Aminoil* v.
Kuwait in the context of calculation of damages.
[24] The Annulment Committee in *MTD* v. *Chile*, ICSID, Case No. ARB/01/7, Decision on
Annulment (21 March 2007) (Guillaume, Crawford, Ordonez Noriega), paras. 67–69.
The Committee warned that 'the obligations of the host state towards foreign investors
derive from the terms of the applicable investment treaty and not from any set of
expectations investors may have or claim to have. A tribunal which sought to generate
from such expectations a set of rights different from those contained in or enforceable
under the BIT might well exceed its powers, and if the difference were material might do
so manifestly.' But the Committee accepted that legitimate expectations grounded in the
conduct of the authorities of the host state are relevant.
[25] *Saluka Investments* v. *Czech Republic*, para. 301.
[26] *Electrabel* v. *Hungary*, ICSID, Case No. ARB/07/19 (30 November 2012), para. 7.75.
[27] That idea is inherent in the formulation of the *Neer* standard, which spoke of an
'insufficiency of governmental action'. The formulation proceeded: 'Whether the

5.3 The discovery of legitimate expectations

an important conduit for imposing standards of governance. It is the ford for the reformation of the law so that its neoliberal basis could be continued. The focus of attention must therefore be on that notion.

5.3 The discovery of legitimate expectations

The notion of legitimate expectations was unknown to international investment law in the form in which it has come to be used in recent times.[28] Its precise use in the context of investment law is defined by the tribunal in *International Thunderbird Gaming Corp.* v. *Mexico*[29] as follows: 'the concept of legitimate expectations' relates to 'a situation where a Contracting Party's conduct creates reasonable and justifiable expectations on the part of an investor to act in reliance on the said conduct, such that a failure by the Party to honour those expectations could cause the investor to suffer damages'. It has not been used in this sense hitherto in international law. There are a few references to the idea of legitimate expectations in the literature of international law. It does not appear that these past references indicate the formulation of any particular legal principle.[30]

There are two possible bases for the origin of the notion of legitimate expectations in international investment law. One is in the idea of good faith. The awards in *Tecmed*[31] and *Thunderbird* v. *Mexico*[32] find the origin of legitimate expectations in good faith. This does not seem plausible. The finding of bad faith in the circumstances of investment law would be difficult even if the host state had applied its own law incorrectly. In terms of international law, it is a particularly serious matter to attribute bad faith to a state. The founding of the rule in good faith may serve to dispel the criticism that the tribunal was creating new

---

insufficiency proceeds from deficient execution of an intelligent law or from the fact that the laws of the country do not empower the authorities to measure up to international standards is immaterial' (*Neer*, para. 4). One does not need the fair and equitable standard to convert the treaty standards into a public law inquiry as to whether external governmental standards were not complied with by a respondent state. The idea was always there.

[28] There are references to the phrase in some earlier awards involving contract disputes. The *Aminoil* Award contains references, but the terminology is not used in the modern sense.

[29] UNCITRAL Ad hoc Arbitration (31 December 2005).

[30] Chester Brown, 'Protection of Legitimate Expectations as a "General Principle of Law": Some Preliminary Thoughts', (2009) 6(1) *Transnational Dispute Management* 3.

[31] *Tecmed* v. *Mexico*, ICSID, Case No. ARB(AF)/00/2 (29 May 2003) (Naon, Fernandez Rozas, Verea).

[32] UNCITRAL Ad hoc Arbitration (31 December 2005).

258   FAIR AND EQUITABLE TREATMENT

doctrine and, hence, was deviating from the intention of the parties. For that reason, many early cases – the story beginning only in 2000 – refer to good faith as the basis of the rule.

In the *Tecmed* Award,[33] a highpoint of the definition of the legitimate expectations rule, the origin of the rule and its content are explained in what was for some time – until dismissed as containing standards unattainable by any state – a frequently quoted passage. It reads as follows:

> The Arbitral Tribunal considers that this provision of the Agreement, in light of the good faith principle established by international law, requires the Contracting Parties to provide to international investments treatment that does not affect the basic expectations that were taken into account by the foreign investor to make the investment. The foreign investor expects the host State to act in a consistent manner, free from ambiguity and totally transparently in its relations with the foreign investor, so that it may know beforehand any and all rules and regulations that will govern its investments, as well as the goals of the relevant policies and administrative practices or directives, to be able to plan its investment and comply with such regulations. Any and all State actions conforming to such criteria should relate not only to the guidelines, directives or requirements issued, or the resolutions approved thereunder, but also to the goals underlying such regulations. The foreign investor also expects the host State to act consistently, i.e., without arbitrarily revoking any pre-existing decisions or permits issued by the State that were relied upon by the investor to assume its commitments as well as to plan and launch its commercial and business activities. The investor also expects the State to use the legal instruments that govern the actions of the investor or the investment in conformity with the function usually assigned to such instruments, and not to deprive the investor of its investment without the required compensation. In fact, failure by the host State to comply with such pattern of conduct with respect to the foreign investor or its investments affects the investor's ability to measure the treatment and protection awarded by the host State and to determine whether the actions of the host State conform to the fair and equitable treatment principle. Therefore, compliance by the host State with such a pattern of conduct is closely related to the above-mentioned principle, to the actual chances of enforcing such principle, and to excluding the possibility that state action be characterized as arbitrary; i.e. as presenting insufficiencies that would be recognized ... 'by any reasonable and impartial man' or, although not in violation of specific regulations as being contrary to the law because: 'it shocks, or least surprises, a sense of juridical propriety'.[34]

---

[33] Paragraph 154.
[34] The quotations are from the *Neer* formulation of the international minimum standard.

5.3 THE DISCOVERY OF LEGITIMATE EXPECTATIONS 259

Despite its profession that the fair and equitable standard as interpreted in this paragraph is an autonomous standard, the fact is that it draws support from the *Neer* Claim for the broad statement. The passage has been cited and followed,[35] but, as will be seen, there has been a progressive departure from the stringent standards that it seeks to impose on states. It is unlikely that the idyllic standards in the passage could be met by even the most perfect of states. The tribunal does not say from where and how it conjured up these standards, which hardly any state can be expected to meet. As Douglas put it, 'the *Tecmed* "standard" is actually not a standard at all; it is rather a description of perfect public regulation in a perfect world, to which all states should aspire but very few (if any) will ever attain'.[36] The *El Paso* Tribunal said of the passage: 'Sometimes, the description of what FET implies looks like *a programme of good governance that no State in the world is capable of guaranteeing at all times.*'[37]

The Annulment Committee in *MTD* pointed out that *Tecmed*'s 'apparent reliance on the investor's expectations as the source of the host State's obligations is questionable. The obligations of the host State towards foreign investors derive from the terms of the applicable investment treaty and not from any set of expectations investors may have or claim to have.'[38]

But, even while founding the law in good faith, the tribunal was conscious of the extension to the law it was making, for the very next paragraph in the award is a rationalization of the extension as consistent with the intention of the parties. The tribunal stated that:

> 'by including this provision in the Agreement, the parties intended to strengthen and increase the security and trust of foreign investors that invest in the member States, thus maximizing the use of the economic resources of each Contracting Party by facilitating the economic contributions of their economic operators. This is the goal of such undertaking in light of the Agreement's preambular paragraphs which express the will and intention of the member States to 'intensify economic cooperation for the benefit of both countries . . .', and the resolve of the member States,

---

[35] *MTD Equity* v. *Chile*, ICSID, Case No. ARB/01/7 (25 May 2004) (Sureda, Lalonde, Blanco).

[36] Zachary Douglas, *International Law of Investment Claims* (Cambridge University Press, 2009), p. 28.

[37] *El Paso*, at para. 342 (emphasis added).

[38] *MTD Equity* v. *Chile*, ICSID, Case No. ARB/01/7, Decision on Annulment (21 March 2007), at para. 66.

within such framework, 'to create favourable conditions for investments made by each of the Contracting Parties in the territory of the other'.

Such wisdom had escaped the arbitrators in the past. The concern for rationalization is due to the consciousness that a major deviation from the language of the text is being made. It was also selectively made as not all foreign investment can increase economic cooperation or prosperity. The Malaysia–Chile investment treaty also states in its preamble that the investment flows contemplated should lead to the economic prosperity of both countries. The teleological interpretation is possible that the only investments that the treaty protects are investments leading to such economic prosperity and development. It is unclear how the particular project involved in the dispute, the building of a housing complex, could have led to the economic prosperity of Chile.

A proposition that all investment is protected by an inflexible standard can hardly be drawn from the preamble. If the parties did intend to accept ideal standards, they would have stated it in more certain terms rather than leave the meaning to be determined by a tribunal several years after the making of the treaty from a clause that had hardly ever been used. Not only is a slumbering clause being awakened, but a new content undiscoverable in terms of its language is being introduced as the dominant content of the clause. Indeed, no academic commentary on investment treaties had anticipated such an interpretation until the awards interpreting the clause came about around the turn of the millennium.

The good faith origin does not provide a credible explanation of the term 'legitimate expectations'. Early NAFTA tribunals – and by early here is meant around the year 2000 – had begun to find the rule rooted in equally amorphous notions. Thus, in *S. D. Myers* v. *Canada*, the tribunal stated that the rule is to be founded in ' the international law requirements of due process, economic rights, obligations of good faith and natural justice'.[39] While scratching around for equations with equally vague notions, there had been no concrete concept with which an association had been made. But the states, to whose intention the expansion was being attributed, would have none of it. It is now well known that within NAFTA the attempt at law creation was brought to a sudden

---

[39] *S. D. Myers Inc.* v. *Government of Canada*, UNCITRAL (NAFTA), Partial Award (13 November 2000), para. 134, p. 29, at: http://www.naftalaw.org. Also see *Metalclad Corp.* v. *Mexico*, ICSID, Case No. ARB(AF)/97/1 (30 August 2000): 'Metalclad was merely acting prudently and in the full expectation that the permit would be granted' (para. 89).

5.3 THE DISCOVERY OF LEGITIMATE EXPECTATIONS 261

halt by the Interpretive Note of the NAFTA Commission, which stated that the fair and equitable treatment provision is no different from the customary law principle of international minimum standard. Within the NAFTA context itself, it is still a possibility that, despite the interpretive note, the international minimum standard of customary law could be expanded to include notions such as legitimate expectations on the basis that the international minimum standard is an evolutionary standard. The tying of the two standards has not eliminated the possibility of this expansive interpretation. The tussle still goes on within the NAFTA context despite the interpretive note.

The tying of the fair and equitable standard to administrative law principles was a slightly later development. It was made without much examination of the link between the standard and the legitimate expectation principle in administrative law that was to form its cardinal base.

Total v. *Argentina*[40] is one of the few awards in which the tribunal attempted a comparative study of the legitimate expectations principle. It found that 'it appears that only exceptionally has the concept of legitimate expectations been the basis of redress when legislative action by a State was at stake'. This is so in domestic legal systems. As a matter of Commonwealth law based on the English common law system, this statement represents the law. Courts have reviewed through the principle of legitimate expectations the decisions taken by local councils, licensing authorities and administrative officials. When a remedy had to be given, the remedy has usually been a procedural remedy that requires a hearing to be given to the affected party. But when a legislature or government interferes through measures that affect all citizens, the review takes a constitutional dimension and moves out of the sphere of administrative law. The legitimate expectations of a citizen are not something against which legislation is tested. Such an idea would go against the legislative sovereignty of the state. Even where the review remains administrative, the court would take into account, as the *Total* Tribunal pointed out, 'the reasons and features for changes and the public interest involved ... in order to evaluate whether an individual who incurred financial obligations on the basis of the decisions and representations of public authorities that were later revoked should be entitled to a form of

---

[40] *Total SA* v. *Argentina*, ICSID, Case No. ARB/04/01 (27 December 2010). The tribunal attempted a comparative study of largely of European law. It suggested that the doctrine had its origin in German law and in European systems (para. 128). There was no effort to go beyond these systems, though the tribunal suggested that there was a need to balance the expectations of the investor with the public interest.

262   FAIR AND EQUITABLE TREATMENT

redress'.[41] Relief was never automatic. In *Continental Casualty*,[42] the tribunal challenged the basic premise on which the application of legitimate expectation rested when it said that it would be 'unconscionable for a country to promise not to change its legislation as time and need change or even more to tie its hands by such a kind of stipulation in case a crisis of any type or origin arose'.

What many arbitration tribunals, which accepted the notion, have done is to create a virtual right of substantive redress for the investor through a legitimate expectations rule. The tribunals, which recognized the notion of legitimate expectations as a part of the fair and equitable standard, were creating a remedy that seldom existed in domestic legal systems in respect of policy changes effected by the state. Though in exceptional instances, where specific commitments had been made to specific individuals, legitimate expectations have created substantive remedies for individuals in domestic legal systems, there is no such remedy when public policy was changed especially to meet situations of public necessity or to forestall damage to the public interest. In creating a substantive remedy quite readily, investment tribunals showed a definite bias towards investor protection at the cost of sacrificing legitimacy. They have not clearly demonstrated how the rule comes to be a part of the treaty law.

Whatever the outcome of these tussles, two factors are clear. First, there are expansionary notions at work for the reading of meanings that could not have been contemplated at the time of the drafting of the treaties by the parties.[43] Such expansionary meanings may signify that the neoliberal motives of advancing investment protection are at work so that a new front for investment protection could be opened up now that regulatory intervention had dried up the possibility of expansions in the law on expropriation. In the context of the extent of the creativity in the area, it is a reasonable inference to draw. Arbitrators who subscribe to such views will hold on to them even if states intervene in order to redefine the scope of fair and equitable treatment.[44] The second is that

---

[41] *Total* v. *Argentina*, ICSID, Case No. ARB/04/01 (27 December 2010), para. 129. The relevance of unilateral commitments made by states in public international law (para. 132) provides little similarity as the commitment is not made to a state, but to an investor within the territory of the state.

[42] *Continental Casualty* v. *Argentina*, ICSID, Case No. ARB/03/9 (5 September 2008).

[43] Muthucumaraswamy Sornarajah, 'A Coming Crisis: Expansionary Trends in Investment Treaty Arbitration', in Karl Sauvant (ed.), *Appeals Mechanism in International Investment Disputes* (Oxford University Press, 2008), p. 39.

[44] *Merrill & Ring Forestry Ltd* v. *Canada*, UNCITRAL (31 March 2010).

5.3 THE DISCOVERY OF LEGITIMATE EXPECTATIONS 263

there was a need to find a more concrete peg on which to hang the fair and equitable standard beside nebulous notions such as good faith. This was found in the rule relating to legitimate expectations, a phrase that had a clear meaning in English and European administrative law. Yet the manner of the construction of the doctrine in investment arbitration, though initially justified on the basis of its existence in domestic law, is very much at variance with domestic principles, which are more prone to give procedural rather than substantive remedies in the event of the violation of legitimate expectations. But these minor inconveniences have never stood in the way of the project of the creating secure protection for foreign investment.

No canon of treaty interpretation can support the view that the term 'fair and equitable treatment' can include any reference to the protection of the legitimate expectations of the foreign investor. It is not the natural meaning of the term. It has to be conjured through a mystical process of divining the intention of the parties from the preamble and infusing the intention into the fair and equitable standard. When the attempt is made to give the term a teleological interpretation to make it consistent with investment stability that is referred to in the preamble, the interpretation is contrived. Any rule on legitimate expectations would have been furthest from the intention of the states that made the treaties, and its introduction into the law had an obvious history, which is traced below. As Judge Nikken, in his dissent in *Suez* v. *Argentina* pointed out, the interpretation 'goes beyond the normal meaning of the terms of the BITs and the intention of the parties'. He observed further:[45]

> The assertion that fair and equitable treatment includes an obligation to satisfy and not to frustrate the legitimate expectations of the investor at the time of his/her investment does not correspond, in any language, to the ordinary meaning to be given to the terms 'fair and equitable'. Therefore, prima facie, such a conception of fair and equitable treatment is at odds with the rule of interpretation of international customary law expressed in Article 31(1) of the Vienna Convention on the Law of Treaties. In addition, I think that the interpretation that tends to give the standard of fair and equitable treatment the effect of a legal stability provision has no basis in the BITs or on the international customary rules applicable to the interpretation of treaties.

It is interesting that arbitrators belonging to the different camps can invoke the same techniques of interpretation to support their

---

[45] ICSID, Case No. ARB/03/19 (30 July 2010).

preconceived views on the objects the investment treaties. The line of cases that have made legitimate expectations the central feature of the fair and equitable treatment have a short and contested lineage.

The inclusion of the rule on legitimate expectations within the fair and equitable treatment not only protects commitments made both through contracts and through extracontractual assurances, but also amounts to the recognition of the immutability of a stabilization mechanism contained in the foreign investment contract. There has been little discussion regarding the place of the fair and equitable standard in customary international law.[46] The attempt to give protection to the stabilization clause in contracts through the legitimate expectations rule will become a feature of further expansion both in contract arbitration as well as in investment arbitration. In contract arbitration, the argument will be made that legitimate expectations is the part of the law that is to be applied to the internationalized contract. In treaty arbitration, the presence of a stabilization clause is the instance of a clear commitment that gives rise to expectations.

In determining that liability is founded on the violation of legitimate expectations created at the time of the entry, the tribunals were in fact creating new law not applying an existing doctrine or the intention of the parties. The origin of the notion of legitimate expectations is to be found in rather recent academic writings and arbitral awards.[47] The early

---

[46] In *ADF Group Inc.* v. *United States*, ICSID Case No. ARB(AF)/00/1, Award (9 January 2003), the tribunal stated that there had been no adequate demonstration as to the status of the fair and equitable treatment as a part of customary international law. For a history in other areas of the use of the term, see Mona Pinchis, 'The Ancestry of Equitable Treatment in Trade Lessons from the League of Nations during the Inter-War Period', (2014) 15(1) *Journal of World Investment & Trade* 13.

[47] Early justification for the use of legitimate expectations is to be found largely in the writings of Professor Orrego-Vicuna. His view was that 'Fair and equitable treatment is not really different from the legitimate expectations doctrine developed, for example by the English courts and also recently by the World Bank Administrative Tribunal.' Francisco Orrego-Vicuna, 'Foreign Investment Law: How Customary is Custom?' (2005) *ASIL Proceedings* 98. In another article, referring to the *Coughlan* Case, decided by the English Court of Appeal in 1999, a singular instance in which the English courts used legitimate expectations as a substantive principle, he said: 'The situation is not altogether different in international law. Governments and international institutions may undertake changes of policy in their continuing need to search for the best choices in the discharge of their functions. However, to the extent that policies in force earlier might have created legitimate expectations both of a procedural and of a substantive nature, for citizens, investors, traders or other persons, these may not be abandoned if the result will be so unfair as to amount to an abuse of power.' Francisco Orrego-Vicuna, 'Regulatory

5.3 THE DISCOVERY OF LEGITIMATE EXPECTATIONS 265

consolidation of the law on legitimate expectations was in awards on the disputes relating to the Argentine economic crisis.

There were the many theoretical justifications advanced in order to support the changes that were being made. The separate opinion in *Thunderbird* v. *Mexico*[48] by Professor Thomas Walde made an influential effort to rationalize the change both in terms of the shift of investment arbitration to a public law base and in terms of an emerging notion of a standard of administrative governance. The Opinion stated that the 'abuse of governmental power is not an issue in commercial arbitration, but it is at the core of the good-governance standards embodied in investment protection treaties'. It sought to find the genesis of legitimate expectations that lies at the core of this standard in a diversity of rules, including good faith, estoppel and comparative public law.[49]

Around this time, there were also particular tendencies within international law that showed an inclination towards the constitutionalization of

---

Authority and Legitimate Expectations: Balancing the Rights of the State and the Individual under International Law in a Global Society', (2003) 5 *International Law Forum* 180, at p. 194. Professor Orrego-Vicuna presided over or participated in many arbitrations in which legitimate expectations were used. *Occidental Exploration and Production Co. v. Ecuador*, LCIA, Case No. UN 3467, Final Award (1 July 2004) (Orrego-Vicuna, Brower, Sweeney) (he also presided over *CMS Gas Transmission Co. v. Argentina* (2003) 42 ILM 788; *Enron Corp. v. Argentina*, ICSID, Case No. ARB/01/3 (2 August 2004); *Sempra v. Argentina*, ICSID, Case No. ARB/02/16 (28 September 2007); and *PSEG Global Ltd v. Turkey*, ICSID, Case No. ARB/02/5 (17 January 2007) (Orrego-Vicuna, Fortier, Kaufman-Kohler) and *Maffezini v. Kingdom of Spain*, ICSID, Case No. ARB/97/7, Award (13 November 2000), para. 83 (Orrego-Vicuna, Buergenthal, Wolff)). In *Merrill & Ring* (2010), where Professor Orrego-Vicuna was chairman of the tribunal, the tribunal said that 'there is still a broad and unsettled discussion about the proper law applicable to the standard' and that 'the difficulties . . . are further compounded because of the need to determine the specific content of the standard'. The premise of finding the doctrine in English common law is an error. The common law does not permit public interests to be thwarted by any legitimate expectations that had been raised earlier. *McCarthy v. Minister of Education* [2012] IEHC 200 ('Even had the applicants such an expectation, overwhelming considerations of the public interest would outweigh it in the light of the dire financial circumstances facing this country at the time the decision was made'). *United Kingdom Association of Fish Producers Organization v. Secretary of State for the Environment, Food and Rural Affairs* [2013] EWHC 1959 (Admin). For European law, see *Kopecki v. Slovakia* (GC) ECHR 2004-IX (28 September 2004). Luis Wildhaber, 'The Protection of Legitimate Expectations in European Human Rights Law', in M. Monti *et al.* (eds.), *Economic Law and Justice in Times of Globalisation: Festschrift for Carl Baudenbacher* (Baden-Baden: Nomos, 2007), p. 121.

[48] *Thunderbird v. Mexico*, Separate Opinion (31 December 2005), at para. 14. Award dated 26 January 2006 was by Ariosa and Van den Berg.

[49] The Award initiated a trend to look to public law in finding principles of investment treaty arbitration. Schill (ed.), *International Investment Law and Comparative Public Law*.

266 FAIR AND EQUITABLE TREATMENT

international law. Professor Orrego-Vicuna was a contributor to such views. In the Hersch Lauterpacht Lectures he delivered at Cambridge in 2001,[50] he announced that in the context of globalization, there was an interlinking of the emergence of constitution-like principles, access of individuals to tribunals to enforce them and privatization. In the area of foreign investment, the new approach was that: 'States are accountable to foreign investors to the extent that wrongful State action interferes with their rights as provided for in national legislation, treaties and contracts'. Recognizing that 'outright expropriations were exceptional', the problem in modern times was identified as protection against regulatory measures taken by the states. Professor Orrego-Vicuna identified legitimate expectations as a means through which this could be solved. He relied on English case law to support his view, though in English law legitimate expectation is seldom used to provide a substantive remedy.[51] It normally results in a procedural remedy requiring a prior hearing before a right is rescinded by an administrative authority. It is only exceptionally that a substantive remedy is provided.

The facts of the Argentine disputes, resulting in over fifty requests for arbitration, were broadly similar and lent themselves to an argument based on legitimate expectations. The situation was that Argentina, in order to recover from economic setbacks in the 1980s, had, in the early 1990s, embarked on a programme based on neoliberal reforms. It courted foreign investment vigorously and at the same time privatized its essential service industries, including gas and electricity. It invited foreign investment from the United States by promising parity between the US dollar and the Argentine peso. It pegged the price of commodities to the American price indices. The then president made promotional trips to the United States advertising the same promises. A brochure, published by the government, contained references to the dollar–peso parity and the fixing of prices to the American price indices. A programme was also announced to privatize existing state corporations. The foreign investors who came into Argentina entered largely as minority shareholders in the privatized state companies of Argentina.

---

[50] Francisco Orrego-Vicuna, *International Dispute Settlement in an Evolving Global Society: Constitutionalization, Accessibility, Privatization* (Cambridge University Press, 2004).

[51] The case he relied on, *Re North and East Devon Health Authority, ex parte Coughlan* [2001] QB 213, is unique in being the first and rare case that permitted the use of legitimate expectations to found a substantive remedy for damages. The usual rule is that it provides a procedural remedy by way of a hearing only. Later English courts have assiduously distinguished the case on its facts and have not drawn any general principle from it.

5.3 THE DISCOVERY OF LEGITIMATE EXPECTATIONS 267

Around the same time, Argentina, the home of the Calvo Doctrine, had also signed investment treaties with the United States and some European states accepting standards of investment protection that it had earlier rejected on the ground of primacy of its own laws over foreign investment within Argentina. The economy improved as a result of the reforms, but capital liberalization also saw capital flight when slightly adverse trends developed. Excessive capital flight led to an economic crisis in 2000, which caused widespread riots, extensive poverty and political instability and resulted in five governments changing within one week. Argentina, which had hitherto followed the prescriptions of the IMF to meet the crisis, deviated from them when they did not work. It took a different course. It devalued the peso, dropping its value to one-third of a US dollar and controlled the transfer of money out of Argentina. These were violations of promises that Argentina had held out in order to attract foreign investors. The uniform argument in the disputes that ensued was that the devaluation of the peso and the depreciation in the value of the shares amounted to an expropriation; an argument that was quickly dismissed in the awards as there had been no ensuing dispossession following the measures. The foreign investors still remained shareholders. They had the option to sell the shares and move out.[52] The main argument that the foreign investors were left with was that they had legitimate expectations at the time of entry that they would not be subjected to adverse measures during the course of their investments as the dollar–peso parity was to be maintained and the energy prices were to be tied to the American indices.

CMS v. *Argentina* was the first award involving the Argentine crisis. It considered and accepted the view that the foreign investor's legitimate expectations had been flouted by the measures taken by Argentina. Consequently, there was a violation of the fair and equitable treatment. It signalled the adoption of an administrative law approach. In the Argentine cases, the focus of attention became not the violation of contracts or expropriation, but the failure of the government to meet the expectations its promises, at the time of entry, had raised in the foreign investor.

The general tenor of the later awards that were made in some of the Argentine cases have adopted the view that, though expropriation claims were not maintainable, the violation of the fair and equitable standard would provide remedies on the facts of the cases. With the exception of

---

[52] *CMS*, 42 ILM 788 (2003), paras. 263–265.

268   FAIR AND EQUITABLE TREATMENT

cases that allowed the plea of necessity for the duration of the crisis,[53] the existing awards helped to establish legitimate expectations as a basis of claims, though the nuances adopted vary. They are time-based in that enthusiasm for the initial upholding of claims on the basis of legitimate expectations progressively waned. As the Western states undergoing a global economic crisis began to take measures that were akin to those taken by Argentina, the fervour was dented when realization dawned that measures such as expropriation or devaluation were necessary tools for states faced with an economic crisis. Tribunals began to consider defences to responsibility such as necessity favourably. Understanding of fairness and equity changes when the boot is on the other foot.

5.4 The turn to administrative law

The early awards on legitimate expectations do not provide much analysis on how the category can be conjured out of the clause on fair and equitable treatment in an investment treaty. Once the category is used in an award, it is followed in later awards that purport to follow earlier ones. Anthea Roberts has been kind in her observation that the early awards are like a pack of cards, building up on each other on unstable foundations.[54] A less kind observer would suggest that, since the citations of earlier awards are by a small group of persons, numerical authority was being created on the basis of erroneous understandings of what amounts to legitimate expectations in the domestic legal systems that were used as the basis of the articulation of the rule. Even the maxim *communis error ius facit* will not apply as a virtually identical group of arbitrators was engaging in the *communis error* so that the error cannot be described as a common error among a large number of disaggregated decision-makers not influenced by ideological predispositions.

The legitimate expectations of the foreign investor were given a meaning akin to that it had in administrative law systems involving the review of subordinate decision-makers, enabling a distinct line of argument to be made in response to the fact that most interferences that were taking place with foreign investment were through regulatory measures. But awards seldom contain discussions of the limited extent to which the rule relating to legitimate expectations operates in domestic administrative

---

[53] *Total; Continental Casualty; El Paso.*
[54] Roberts, 'Clash of Paradigms: Actors and Analogies Shaping the Investment Treaty System'.

systems. Such discussions took place later in awards such as *El Paso* and *Total*. The discussions in them are not too convincing. The earlier awards are weak on explanations as to how the concept could become part of the fair and equitable standard. Where domestic administrative systems recognize the rule, the studies made of it do not show that damages result from the violation of legitimate expectations as a matter of course. Rather, the remedy, if a violation of legitimate expectations is established, is either procedural or, rarely, the nullity of the administrative decision that was made. In investment arbitration, there is an inflexible result of the creation of responsibility leading to damages upon proof of the violation of legitimate expectations. Besides, administrative law dealt with the judicial review of actions of subordinate decision-makers, whereas in the case of investment disputes, what was involved was legislation of the state, not a subordinate but a sovereign body. In domestic systems, courts review such sovereign legislative acts for compliance with definite constitutional standards. Judicial review of such legislation was possible on the ground of its constitutionality. Nowhere has it been suggested that such legislation can be reviewed on the ground that it violates legitimate expectations or that damages flow from such violations.

The rationale is provided in the separate opinion in *Thunderbird* that investment treaties created a standard of governance that arbitration tribunals maintained. It will be difficult to reconcile this with the intention of the states making such treaties. It would come as news to them that they gave such an exorbitant power to the arbitration tribunals over internal processes of decision-making. The shift to public law is also equally difficult to reconcile with the intention of the parties to the treaties. There are issues of legitimacy when such far-reaching assumptions are made in the light of later events. Yet the notion of legitimate expectations has now emerged as the single most important basis of claims in investment arbitration.

The moorings of international investment law were shifted considerably in taking the theme of legitimate expectations further. The viability of the concept of legitimate expectations must be scrutinized with care as it forms the vanguard of a new thrust. The great difficulty in the acceptance of the concept is that no satisfactory explanation could be found of introducing it into the standard of fair and equitable treatment.

The effort to secure its base in comparative public law seems to be a non-starter. It is difficult to find a system that permits inflexibly the award of damages for the violation of legitimate expectations. As already pointed out, English law, which was the font of the original wisdom, contains very few cases in which damages have flowed from the violation of legitimate expectations. It is unlikely that courts in any system would accept legitimate expectations as fettering a state which acts in the public interest. An investment tribunal finding domestic law analogies in administrative law on the review of lower functionaries and bodies using discretionary powers embarks on a false path, as it does not provide a parallel with a state legislating a public interest measure that affects the foreign investor.

The similarities between this project and the effort to give sanctity to the stabilization clause negotiated in a foreign investment contract, discussed in Chapter 2, is startling. The stabilization clause gave inflexibility to the original terms that had been agreed between the parties. It was the cornerstone of investment protection under the law prior to the advent of the investment treaty system until *Aminoil* subjected it to an analysis that made variance of the contract in response to changing circumstances possible, particularly if it was effected through the exercise of a regulatory power in the public interest. The rule on legitimate expectations attempted to give even more secure protection, as it seeks to ensure that unilateral assurances made by government officials at the time of entry of the investment give stability to the foreign investment transaction throughout the course of its operation. This would happen even if the assurances are not given in any formal document, unlike a stabilization clause which is always in a contract that is addressed to a specific party. The stability of the legal framework is deemed to be a legitimate expectation if assurances of such stability have been made in the treaty. For some time, the view was taken in awards that the clause on full protection and security ensured that the state had committed itself it maintaining a stable investment climate.[55] This view was too atrocious to maintain as the full protection and security clause was founded on customary international law, which confined it to the protection of the physical security of the foreign investment. This untenable interpretation, another instance of expansionism, was soon abandoned, but its short existence shows the desire to construct a new law on investment protection through the interpretation of hitherto unused provisions of

---

[55] This was an obvious instance of an exercise of an assumed quasi-legislative power. The clause is based on customary international law that a state owes an obligation of protection against violence to the alien. The rule is stated in the treaties. It has been interpreted well beyond its ambit as establishing an obligation to provide legal stability to the investment.

5.4 THE TURN TO ADMINISTRATIVE LAW 271

investment treaties.[56] But the view that legal stability was an expectation of foreign investment continued to be maintained. Legitimate expectations are elevated to property rights, so that if they are affected even by regulatory change then compensation will follow.

Even more startling, is that despite the NAFTA states contesting the validity of the expansive notion of the fair and equitable standard, the tribunal in *Merrill & Ring* v. *Canada*, suggested that 'the fair and equitable treatment has emerged to make possible the consideration of inappropriate behaviour of a sort, which while difficult to define, may still be regarded as unfair, inequitable or unreasonable'. As a definition, the statement is worthless. A rule that has no certainty cannot guide behaviour and cannot credibly be a basis of an action for its violation. It provides no guidance to states as to what sort of behaviour they must avoid. It leaves such identification to the caprice of individual arbitrators. There seems to be a need to switch to a new basis for the fair and equitable standard as its basis on legitimate expectations becomes increasingly shaky. But there do not seem to be too many takers for this new and even broader basis. To the extent that no violation of the standard was found in the dispute against Canada, the dicta in the award, which is a fresh effort to ensure the viability of the violation of the fair and equitable treatment clause as a cause of action, can be taken as an escapade in fantasy.

The tenacity of the attitude in finding new and flexible notions to establish liability for violations of standards of investment stability persists. The role of an international tribunal, once established, could assume unintended guises. There are extensive visions of the role of international tribunals. Their increase has led to crediting them with the role of developing international law well beyond the consent of the states that created jurisdiction in them. But most of the tribunals, like the Law of the Sea Tribunal or the WTO Dispute Settlement Board, were international tribunals, with a definite membership and appointed through elections. They were created by multilateral conventions. The investment tribunals are largely ad hoc tribunals. They act under the auspices of existing centres, like ICSID or the PCA, which provide only procedural rules. Other international tribunals have substantive laws stated in the conventions that create them. Whatever the role of the other international tribunals, the role of the investment tribunal is necessarily limited. Other international tribunals interpret what are

---

[56] In *AAPL* v. *Sri Lanka*, the clause had been used in its customary law sense. Also in *AMT* v. *Zaire* (1997) 36 ILM 1534.

272 FAIR AND EQUITABLE TREATMENT

effectively constituent documents of institutional regimes. Investment tribunals are different in that they do not have a single instrument that controls the substantive law they apply so that they could create law through interpretation with a possible base in legitimacy. Such tribunals are not tasked with the interpretation of treaties so as to give them unintended meanings and justify the meanings through argument. It is necessary for investment treaty tribunals to demonstrate that any innovation that they make is founded in the treaty or, at least, is a possible interpretation that is generated by an accepted source of international law. Investment tribunals that apply the concept of legitimate expectations are unable to do this.

5.5 The contraction of legitimate expectations

It may well be that legitimate expectations may, as in the case of expropriation law, go through a process of contraction. The first phase of legitimate expectations consisted of the awards in which the concept was given wide scope. It spoke of requiring consistency of state measures with an external standard of administration that the foreign investor was led to expect at the time of his entry. Its best representation is in the oft-cited passage in *Tecmed* (2003), which elevated investor expectations at the time of entry to near perfect conditions of stability and gave immutability to such standards. The Argentine awards in *CMS, Enron* and *Sempra* gave it further impetus.[57] There are other awards that similarly seek to establish the requirement of stability in the legal framework on the basis of the expectations of the foreign investor.[58] But commentators began to raise doubts as to the viability of the elevation of legitimate expectations in particular, and the fair and equitable standard in general, as autonomous principles of investment protection.[59] Slowly, the

---

[57] The separate opinion in *Thunderbird* should be included in this group of awards for its major impact on later theoretical developments. Its impact on shifting focus onto public law is acknowledged by later writers in the field. It attempts an incomplete survey of comparative administrative law as the basis of legitimate expectations. It anticipates issues such as legitimacy and gives legitimate expectations, inconsistently perhaps, its origin in good faith and its result an explanation in estoppel. It gives it a policy base in core standards of governance. It is an early exploration of themes and, without doubt, a contribution to the critical explanation of the trends at work. Later writers, inclined to follow, have built much on the basis of the ideas in this separate opinion.

[58] *PSEG* v. *Turkey; Occidental* v. *Ecuador*.

[59] Muchlinski, 'Caveat Investor? The Relevance of the Conduct of the Investor under the Fair and Equitable Standard'.

5.6 RESTRICTIONS ON LEGITIMATE EXPECTATIONS 273

legitimate expectation standard came to be whittled down in scope. The process resulted in considerable schisms among arbitral awards, which prevents the emergence of constancy in jurisprudence in the area.[60] These schisms are downplayed in some writings. But they seem too fundamental to be ignored. The imposition of conditions for the application of legitimate expectations in some arbitral awards track the manner in which the emasculation of expropriation came about. A significant feature of the later contraction is that arbitrators felt, as they did in the case of indirect expropriation, that it was necessary to provide space for regulation of foreign investment in the public interest. The reconciliation of these two incompatible interests led to the formulation of a series of restrictions on the legitimate expectations rule.

5.6 Restrictions on legitimate expectations

The legitimate expectations rule focuses on the commitments made at the time of entry of the foreign investment. There are two types of commitments that would create expectations. These relate to general promises that the state makes to all potential investors in the hope that they would bring investments into the state. Such general promises are not relevant to the creation of legitimate expectations. In the Argentinian awards, they had significance because of the fact that the general promises were translated into contractual promises. The awards indicate that the peso–dollar parity and the parity of prices for gas with the American price index were written into contracts. The promise was made to specific investors and not to a general group.[61] In domestic law, too, there is a requirement that legitimate expectation should be created in a specific individual or in a definite group by commitments addressed to them. The

---

[60] There is an absolute misunderstanding of international law in some statements made in the area. Thus, the separate opinion in *Thunderbird* (para. 16) stated, referring to awards on legitimate expectations, that: 'if an authoritative jurisprudence evolves, it will acquire the character of customary international law and must be respected'. It is basic that judicial decisions are only a subsidiary source of law and cannot constitute customary international law. The effort to elevate the ability of tribunals to make customary international law is found in the award of *Merrill & Ring* v. *Canada* as well. It is difficult to see how pronouncements on disparate treaty formulations of the standard made by arbitrators not conforming to the same viewpoints on interpretation can give rise to uniform views, let alone give rise to international custom. This is wishful thinking on the part of those whose understanding of the formation of rules through custom is weak.

[61] Reliance was not placed on the promotional literature generated by the Argentine government.

second situation is also contractual in that the commitment would be contained in a stabilization clause giving assurances that the contract would be insulated from legislative changes. The only expectations that are created in the foreign investor relate to the making of the contract and the specific promises made to him at the time of entry. The Argentinian cases are nevertheless embarrassments to the law. What they essentially involved were state measures that were responses to an economic crisis. They are quintessential instances of regulatory measures that fall within the police powers of the state. One may see an effort to isolate the Argentinian awards from the rest of the case law on the subject. The euphoria for neoliberalism found in the facts of the cases a context for the statement of the law in wide terms, but fervour for such broad expansion diminished as the cases went through later tribunals.

Yet the new developments put the foreign investor at an advantage in that he or she can seek a remedy before an arbitral tribunal under the dispute settlement provision of the investment treaty for administrative measures that are in breach of his expectations. Since the claim of expropriation stands little chance of success in circumstances of regulatory controls, an alternative avenue through the newly rediscovered fair and equitable treatment provision is sought. The early attempt was to bring about a situation that would give virtually watertight protection through the protection of legitimate expectations by emphasizing the notion that stability was what was crucial and the commitments, either through officials or through the legal framework on foreign investment, would have promised such stability. The preambles in some treaties also referred to stability as a reason for the treaty, thus enabling the reinforcement of this view. From the presence of such preambles and the inclusion of the fair and equitable provision, conclusions were drawn that treaty provisions protect legitimate expectations.[62] A fresh category deals with the legislative framework at the time of entry. The framework is read as creating legitimate expectations on the assumption that the foreign investor would have considered its entry in the light of this framework. This extends the notion of legitimate expectations even to legislation as the assumption is that expectations of stability are to be derived from the legal framework also cannot be changed by later legislation, a result that

---

[62] In *Continental Casualty* the tribunal doubted this use of the preamble. It questioned whether a state can in fact make a promise not to change its laws in the public interest. The tribunal declared that 'it would be unconscionable for a country to promise not to change its legislation as time and needs change'. *Continental Casualty* v. *Argentina*, ICSID, Case No. ARB/03/9, Award (5 September 2008), para. 258.

5.6 RESTRICTIONS ON LEGITIMATE EXPECTATIONS 275

sits uneasily with domestic rules that do not so fetter the legislative power of states. Such a situation would have been even better than having a stabilization clause in the contract and would more effectively have fettered any regulatory intervention the state made with the foreign investment. Clearly, these trends indicate that there was a preference for bringing about a law that so the entrenched the rights of the foreign investor were immutable even in situations where changing circumstances required the state's regulatory intervention. The danger to the system of investment arbitration that these developments posed was clear. The law was being built on the basis of extensions beyond the consent of the states. As has been pointed out, it is unthinkable that states could have agreed to such an outcome. States were bound to react, undermining the system of investment arbitration.

The UNCTAD Report (2012) characteristically understated the issue when it observed:

> In these cases, tribunals have gone so far as to suggest that any adverse change in the business or legal framework of the host country may give rise to a breach of the FET standard in that the investors' legitimate expectations of predictability and stability are thereby undermined. This approach is unjustified, as it would potentially prevent the host State from introducing any legitimate regulatory change, let alone from undertaking a regulatory reform that may be called for. It ignores the fact that investors should legitimately expect regulations to change over time as an aspect of the normal operation of legal and policy processes of the economy they operate in. Considerations of this kind have led some tribunals to require further qualifying elements to the notion of investors' legitimate expectations.

Predictably, some arbitrators found it difficult to go along with the scheme of the law that was being built. Schisms began to develop. The idea that these schisms would heal and that they are teething problems that bring about 'some unevenness'[63] which would disappear as the law settles is not an appropriate analysis. The schisms are the result of attitudinal stances and therefore cannot be easily healed. When the strand favourable to investment protection becomes dominant within investment arbitration, the whole balance in the investment treaty becomes upset. States will react to the situation. Many have. The reaction from states that chose to remain within the system have varied from leaving the fair and equitable standard out altogether to tying it with

---

[63] McLachlan *et al.*, *International Investment Arbitration*, p. 225.

276 FAIR AND EQUITABLE TREATMENT

customary law. Arbitrators showing fidelity to the actual consent of states will also stand away from expansionary views of the law, thus entrenching the schism. The expansionary position will have to recede in the face of such opposition.

Inflexible views that any infraction of legitimate expectations will result in liability were the basis of the older arbitral awards. But there is a movement away from this inflexible stance.[64] The progressive building up of exceptions to the expansionary view both on the basis of the need for factual bases and on the basis of principle is visible in the later awards. These awards accept the existence of legitimate expectations as the core element in the standard on fair and equitable treatment, but seek to restrict its scope. Such acceptance itself is questionable. It could well be that arbitrators did not want to question the validity of the expansion because of the overwhelming support that had been built up. The technique was to accept the expansion, but to restrict its scope.

In *Saluka Investments* v. *Czech Republic*,[65] after observing that 'legitimate expectations is the dominant element' of the standard of fair and equitable treatment, the tribunal stated that this did not mean that the dicta in past awards[66] that gave the impression that it was an inflexible standard should be given effect. Referring to these statements, the tribunal said:[67]

> This tribunal would observe, however, that while it subscribes to the general thrust of these and similar statements,[68] it may be that, if their terms were to be taken too literally, they would impose upon host States' obligations which would be inappropriate and unrealistic. Moreover, the scope of the Treaty's protection of foreign investment against unfair and inequitable treatment cannot exclusively be determined by foreign investors' subjective motivations and considerations. Their expectations, in order for them to be protected, must rise to the level of legitimacy and reasonableness *in the light of the circumstances*.
>
> No investor may reasonably expect that the circumstances prevailing at the time the investment is made remain totally unchanged. In order to

---

[64] *Electrabel* v. *Hungary*, ICSID, Case No. ARB/07/19 (30 November 2012), where the tribunal spoke of the need to show reasonableness in legitimate expectations. Regulatory pricing of electricity was a state power subject to a reasonable margin of appreciation (para. 8.35).

[65] ICSID, Case No. ARB/03/16 (2 October 2006).

[66] The dicta were from *Tecmed; CME; Waste Management*.

[67] *Saluka Investments* v. *Czech Republic,*, UNCITRAL PCA (17 March 2006), paras. 304–305 (Watts, Fortier, Behrens).

[68] The tribunal was referring to statements of the rule in *CME, Waste Management* and *Tecmed*.

5.6 RESTRICTIONS ON LEGITIMATE EXPECTATIONS   277

determine whether frustration of the foreign investor's expectations was justified and reasonable, the host State's legitimate right to subsequently to regulate domestic matters in the public interest must be taken into consideration as well. As the *S. D. Myers* tribunal has stated, 'the determination of the breach of the obligation of fair and equitable by the host state must be made in the light of the high measure of deference that international law generally extends to the right of domestic authorities to regulate matters within their own borders'.

The award in *Duke Energy* v. *Ecuador*[69] echoed these views. The tribunal had stated in its award:

> The stability of the legal and business environment is directly linked to the investor's justified expectations. The Tribunal acknowledges that such expectations are an important element of fair and equitable treatment. At the same time, it is mindful of their limitations. To be protected, the investor's expectations must be legitimate and reasonable at the time when the investor makes the investment. The assessment of the reasonableness or legitimacy must take into account all circumstances, including not only the facts surrounding the investment, but also the political, socioeconomic, cultural and historical conditions prevailing in the host State. In addition, such expectations must arise from the conditions that the State offered the investor and the latter must have relied upon them when deciding to invest.

These passages in the *Saluka* and the *Duke Energy* Awards presage important limitations within a few years of the beginning of the notion of legitimate expectations. The expectations have to be objectively founded. They must have legitimacy in the light of the circumstances. The commitments must have been addressed specifically to the foreign investors. There was an onus on the foreign investor to consider the risks of change prior to entry in the light of the past history of the state,[70] the cycle of economic changes that occurred and cultural attitudes to foreign investment. For example, Argentina, the home of the Calvo Doctrine and ever-present cycles of economic change, did not present a good context for the foreign investor to have the legitimate expectations that were claimed in the Argentine cases. Such a factor was not taken into account in the early Argentine cases when legitimate expectations were considered. There was

---

[69] ICSID, Case No. ARB/04/19, Award (18 August 2008) (Kaufman-Kohler, Pinson, Van den Berg), para. 340. Despite this dicta, there was a reluctance to depart from the earlier views in the older awards relating to stability. The award cites *Tecmed, CMS* and *Occidental* without comment.

[70] In *Methanex*, it was stated that the great concern shown for the environment in the United States should have been known to the foreign investor.

no duty to reward the foreign investor for being an innocent or for permitting him to bail out of the situation at the expense of the state through the formulation of a hazy doctrine of legitimate expectations. Most importantly, the tribunals recognized that there could be justifications for interfering with the expectations on the ground that regulation in the public interest was necessary. As it was put in *Electrabel*,[71] 'while the investor is promised protection against unfair changes, it is well-established that the host State is entitled to maintain a reasonable degree of regulatory flexibility to respond to changing circumstances in the public interest'. In determining such a justification, it was necessary to give the state 'a high measure of deference' or what in EU law would be termed a margin of appreciation. These are important qualifications. The parallel between the modern qualifications on expropriation and those that are coming to be imposed on the use of the fair and equitable doctrine cannot escape notice. It could well be that this newly discovered standard could become as circumscribed as expropriation with the passage of time.

The qualifications of the rule also indicate that an idea of a counterclaim is inherent in the idea of fair and equitable treatment in that if the new circumstances were brought about by the foreign investor's conduct, the regulatory interference would become more than justified. Not only that, the justification could give rise to counterclaims. It would be difficult to say that the interference was unfair if it was in response to the misconduct of the foreign investor. So far, tribunals have been divided on the issue of counterclaims. But the very argument as to fairness and equity presupposes the existence of a defence in that the affected state could always argue that the context of the measure must be relevant in assessing the fairness and equity involved in the measure it took. As the consideration of the rule relating to legitimate expectations increased, the restrictions on it became more stringent. The themes that were stated in cases such as *Saluka* have been refined in later awards. They must be considered.

5.6.1 *There is a duty on the foreign investor to make due diligence efforts to determine whether his expectations are legitimate, reasonable and well-founded*

The older awards draw an inflexible conclusion as to legitimate expectation from the fact that assurances were given to the foreign investor.

---

[71] *Electrabel* v. *Hungary*, ICSID, Case No. ARB/07/19 (30 November 2012), at para. 7.77.

5.6 RESTRICTIONS ON LEGITIMATE EXPECTATIONS 279

These assurances could be contained in the foreign investment laws or in the contract of investment. The impression given in these awards is that the tribunal would draw legitimate expectations of the foreign investor that stable conditions would be maintained for the investment from a wide variety of other sources. The standard argument used to support this view is that the preamble of the treaties refers to enhancing investment flows. This objective would require stability. Liability arose where these expectations were sundered and changes made to the expected framework of the operating conditions of the investment.

There was no requirement that the foreign investor should have paused to consider whether the assurances were well founded in fact or history. In the Argentine situation, the expectations that the foreign investor could have had did not support the view that the laws will not be changed or the external situation would remain constant. The economic and political history of Argentina belies the reasonableness of such expectations. Argentina was a country of constant economic fluctuations. It was questionable that expectations could have been formed as to the stability of the state merely from the changes made by one administration to the laws or promises given by a president. An investor who enters an unstable country in the hope of quick profits and the absence of competition should not be insured against his risk through the legitimate expectation rule.

The formulation of a principle that assurances could give rise to expectations that, when violated, will result in damages being granted to the foreign investor is to absolve him of all risk in relation to his investment. As some tribunals have stated, such a rule amounts to converting investment arbitration into a scheme for risk insurance. The onus is always on the investor to make his own assessment as much as the onus is on any buyer to recognize the puff of a commercial item and make up his own mind independently as to purchase.

In *MTD Equity* v. *Chile*, the tribunal recognized that the onus was on the foreign investor to inquire as to the lawfulness of the commitments that had been made to him. Its technique of reducing damages on this account, after finding a violation of the fair and equitable standard, is questionable. The issue was whether or not a legitimate expectation could arise under the circumstances. The tribunal clearly favoured treating the legitimate expectation rule as inflexible. Its decision to reduce damages indicates unease with the application of the rule.

In every system of law there is a presumption that those who function within it know the laws of that system. The foreign investor, like the

280   FAIR AND EQUITABLE TREATMENT

citizen, must be taken as knowing the laws of the state. *Ignorantia juris non excusat*. He cannot pretend ignorance of the law. In a different context, the tribunal in *Methanex* made the point as follows when stating that the claimant had entered a country 'in which it was widely known, if not notorious, that governmental environmental and health protection institutions at the federal and state level continuously monitored the use and impact of chemical compounds and commonly prohibited or restricted the use of some of those compounds for environmental and/ or health reasons'.[72] It is difficult to escape the conclusion that the foreign investor must anticipate the making of changes to the law as conditions change.

5.6.2   There is a duty to have regard to the circumstances of the host state

Some later tribunals have stated that the legitimacy of the expectations that are formed depend on the circumstances of the state that the foreign investor had entered. This view is consistent with the view that the expectations must be founded on objective factors. The view has most often been stated in relation to the economies of East European states which were adjusting to their emergence from the Soviet communism as independent states forming market economies.[73] A corresponding idea is that if the foreign investor fishes in the troubled waters of a country expecting to profit from the instability, then he cannot at the same time rely on expectations of stability.

The view that the circumstances of the state are relevant to the formation of expectations has been stated in several awards. In *Genin v. Estonia*,[74] there was a revocation of a banking licence. In considering the fairness of the revocation, the tribunal said that it was 'imperative to recall the particular context in which the dispute arose, namely, that of a nascent independent state, coming rapidly to grips with the reality of modern financial, commercial and banking practices and the emergence

---

[72] *Methanex* v. *United States*, UNCITRAL (NAFTA), Ad hoc Arbitration, Final Award (3 August 2005), Pt IV, ch. D, para. 10.

[73] *Parkerings* v. *Lithuania; Genin* v. *Estonia*.

[74] (2002) 17 ICSID Rev. 395. In *Eureko* v. *Poland*, UNCITRAL, Ad hoc Arbitration, Partial Award, (19 August 2005) (n. 70, above), paras. 232 *et seq.*, the tribunal held that there could be good reasons for violating the legitimate expectations of the foreign investor, thus recognizing defences internal to the rule.

5.6 RESTRICTIONS ON LEGITIMATE EXPECTATIONS 281

of state institutions responsible for overseeing and regulating areas of activity, perhaps previously unknown'.

The view is made clearer with respect to legitimate expectations in some later awards involving East European states. In *Parkerings* v. *Lithuania*,[75] the tribunal took into account that Lithuania was in political transition, and that the strength of the commitments it made had to be taken in that context as rapid changes to the law are more likely during such transition. *Parkerings* v. *Lithuania*, *Saluka* v. *Czech Republic* and *EDF* v. *Romania* are awards made in the context of economies in transition. The tribunals were sensitive to the fact that they were economies in which changes would be rapid. Inefficiencies are to be expected in certain types of states. It cannot be expected that all countries, particularly those changing to market economies or developing countries without adequate administrative facilities, can have the same standard of efficiency.[76] The notion of an inflexible standard of governance that underlay some early views on legitimate expectations is belied by this trend.[77] The arbitrators clearly did not believe in imposing a single, global standard of governance.

All surrounding circumstances accompanying the measure of the state are relevant. The tribunal in *Duke Energy* v. *Ecuador* stated that in using the rule, the tribunal should 'take into account all relevant circumstances, including not only the facts surrounding the investment but also the political, socioeconomic, cultural and historical conditions prevailing in the host state'. Such a view is a limitation on the use of the legitimate expectations rule. If the tribunal stops with the analysis that the measure is justified as a response to the prevailing conditions brought about by the foreign investor or by external circumstances, there could be no criticism of the formulation. But, usually, the tribunal makes the context the opportunity for applying the balancing test so as to keep alive its competence to provide a remedy.

The recognition of a diversity of standards in the context of which legitimate expectations are to be assessed is a reversal for neoliberalism, and the theories that are used to support the existence of a uniform standard are vital to the pursuit of a neoliberal framework. The existence of this diversity in standards makes the explanation of the law on a standard of governance or of a uniform notion of a rule of law not possible. The

---

[75] ICSID, Case No. ARB/05/08 (Kaufmann-Kohler, Pinson, Van den Berg).
[76] In *Noble Ventures Inc.* v. *Romania*, ICSID, Case No. ARB/01/11 (17 November 2005), the tribunal pointed out that Romania could not be expected to be like Switzerland. The recognition of diversity of standards is a relevant consideration.
[77] For example, separate opinion in *Thunderbird*.

expansionary arbitrators sought an inflexible rule on legitimate expectations. Other arbitrators, while not rejecting the rule, have confined it by looking at the circumstances in which such expectations could arise.

The emergence of this group of cases that indicate that in considering the legitimate expectations rule, the situation of the host state should be taken into account flies in the face of the neoliberal notion that there must be standards set through the uniform rule that the expectations of the investor created at the time of entry must be respected. The view that there should be a standard-setting function that is performed in requiring all states to conform with the rule on legitimate expectations that characterized the view taken particularly by earlier tribunals interpreting the fair and equitable standard, has now been challenged by awards that take into account the social and political situation at the time of entry of the investor. An investor who seeks to fish in troubled waters should not have too high expectations.

In some later awards, the context of the economic or political crisis was taken into account when considering the arguments based on the legitimate expectations rule. In *El Paso*, there was a firm declaration that 'there can be no legitimate expectation for anyone that the legal framework will remain unchanged in the face of an extremely severe economic crisis'.[78] The fact that a host state was emerging from communist rule had been a consideration in taking expectations into account.[79] In *Bayinder* v. *Pakistan*, the political circumstances in the host state were considered relevant. While these tribunals did not raise the more important issue as to whether the fair and equitable standard included a notion of legitimate expectations, they did indicate that they would not approve an inflexible view that notional legitimate expectations formed at the time of entry constitute an inflexible fetter on the ability of a host state to change the law applying to the foreign investment when changing circumstances justify such a course. To hold otherwise would be to construct an unwritten stabilization clause that would give an absolute protection to the foreign investment.

5.6.3   *Contractual commitments are not protected*

Some tribunals have stated that contractual commitments are not protected by the rule on legitimate expectations. Contractual

---

[78]   *El Paso* v. *Argentina*, ICSID, Case No. ARB/03/15 (31 October 2011) (Caflish, Bernadini, Stern).

[79]   *Parkerings* v. *Lithuania*; *Bayinder* v. *Pakistan*, ICSID, Case No. ARB/03/29 (27 August 2009).

5.6 RESTRICTIONS ON LEGITIMATE EXPECTATIONS 283

commitments are made in the context of commercial relationships, and the aim of the treaties is to protect against governmental conduct.[80] Hence, there is an aversion to protect commitments that are made in the context of the contract and do not implicate administrative or governmental functions. The assumption is that such commitments included in contracts must be protected through mechanisms that are devised in the contract, the treaty itself protecting only governmental commitments and their breaches. But such a view flies in the face of the contrary view that the best example of commitments would be stabilization clauses in contracts.

The award in *Harmester* v. *Ghana*[81] concerned a claim relating to a joint venture between the Cocoa Board of Ghana, which both controlled the market and traded in the cocoa market as a monopolist. The tribunal held that the dealings complained of involved purely commercial conduct on the part of the Cocoa Board and could not be attributed to the state. Such contractual claims could not be dressed up as treaty claims. The fact that assurances had been made in the context of commercial dealings does not mean that the claim could be dressed up as a treaty claim on the ground that the assurances gave rise to legitimate expectations. The tribunal cited with approval the following passage in *Parkerings* v. *Lithuania*:[82]

> It is evident that not every hope amounts to an expectation under international law. The expectation a party to an agreement may have of the regular fulfilment of the obligation by the other party is not necessarily an expectation protected by international law. In other words, contracts involve intrinsic expectations from each party that do not amount to expectations as understood in international law.

This is an obviously sensible rule. Neither customary law nor the law under the treaties is concerned with the conduct of entities, which, though having governmental functions, act in a purely commercial capacity in entering into contracts or commitments in relation to the

---

[80] *Toto Construzioni Generali SpA* v. *Lebanon*, ICSID, Case No. ARB/07/12 (12 May 2012), at para. 161, the tribunal said: 'As was found in *Impreglio SpA* v. *Pakistan*, in order that the alleged breach of contract may constitute a violation of the BIT, it must be the result of behaviour going beyond that which an ordinary contracting party could adopt. Only the state in the exercise of its sovereign authority ("*puissance publique*"), and not as a contracting party, may breach the obligations assumed under the BIT.'

[81] ICSID, Case No, ARB/07/24 (18 June 2010) (Stern, Cremades, Landau).

[82] *Parkerings* v. *Lithuania*, ICSID, Case No. ARB/05/8, Award (11 September 2007), para. 344.

284 FAIR AND EQUITABLE TREATMENT

contracts, even in a situation where there is an umbrella clause.[83] Where the breaches of contracts do not implicate governmental functions, there can be no liability under investment treaties. The distinction between governmental and commercial acts have been made in other areas of international law, principally in the area of sovereign immunity. One potential exception indicated in some awards relates to the situation where there is a stabilization clause in the foreign investment contract.

5.6.4 Expectations and the stabilization commitment

It has been suggested in some awards that expectations arise when a contract or extracontractual documents contain a stabilization clause immunizing the contract to future changes in the law. Those awards, which adopt stricter analysis of legitimate expectations, do so after a preservation of the situation where there is a stabilization clause in the contract. This view is based on the notion that a stabilization clause is a direct assurance given to the specific foreign investor. The technique of investment protection through contract and the importance of the role that stabilization clauses play in it has been dealt with in Chapter 2. The effort to preserve the sanctity of this provision through the treaty system has continued in several awards. When the rule relating to regulatory expropriations treating such expropriations as non-compensable was stated in *Methanex*, the possibility of the stabilization clause providing relief even in the context of regulatory expropriations was retained. This solicitude for the stabilization clause was continued in the context of the formulation of restrictions to the developing rule on legitimate expectations.

Something akin to the rule on regulatory expropriation as non-compensable expropriation has been formulated as a restriction on the legitimate expectations notion. There is recognition that where the purpose of the interference by the state is regulatory, legitimate expectations of the foreign investor cannot stand in the way of that interference. This again accords with the domestic public law principle that measures in the public interest can be taken despite interference with existing legitimate expectations of individuals. It is necessary to state the instances where such an exception is made. This recognizes the right of the state to regulate without hindrance once the need based on public interest can be shown.

---

[83] But see *Duke Energy* v. *Ecuador*, ICSID, Case No. ARB/04/19, Award (18 August 2008).

5.6 RESTRICTIONS ON LEGITIMATE EXPECTATIONS 285

As in the case of the statement of regulatory expropriations, the tribunal in *Parkerings* proclaimed the absolute right of a state to regulate in the public interest even where legitimate expectations of a foreign investor are violated, but reserved an exception for the stabilization clause. The reasoning behind the exception is not explained. The two notions are irreconcilable. One would have thought that if an exception was to be made, it has to be explained. The tribunal stated:[84]

> A State has the right to enact, modify or cancel a law at its own discretion. Save for the existence of an agreement, in the form of a stabilization clause or otherwise, there is nothing objectionable about the amendment brought to the regulatory framework existing at the time an investor made its investment.

Here, again, theoretical conflict splits the arbitrators and the awards. Even when making a departure from the view of strict protection of investment, there is reluctance to move away from making an exception for which there is no authority. There is an eagerness on the part of some arbitrators to separate stabilization clauses, even though they can only be part of a contract and were intended to protect the contract. Even so, there is no authority to suggest that the stabilization clause is binding in the face of a situation that requires change in the public interest. There is no rationalization that has been provided for this separation, but a bald declaration as to the exception of the stabilization clause is made.

In *EDF v. Romania*,[85] a similar preservation of specific commitments is made, not confining the commitment as being made in a contract. It is a looser formulation. The tribunal stated:

> Except where specific promises or representations are made by the State to the investor, the latter may not rely on a bilateral investment treaty as a kind of insurance policy against the risk of any changes in the host State's legal and economic framework. Such expectation would be neither legitimate nor reasonable.

---

[84] *Parkerings v. Lithuania*, ICSID, Case No. ARB/05/08, para. 344.

[85] ICSID, Case No. ARB/05/13 (8 October 2009) (Bernadini, Rovine, Derains), at para. 217: 'The idea that legitimate expectations and therefore FET, imply the ability of the legal and business framework, may not be correct if stated in an overly-broad and unqualified formulation. The FET might then mean the virtual freezing of the legal regulation of economic activities, in contrast with the State's normal regulatory power and the evolutionary character of economic life. Except where specific promises or representations are made by the State to the investor, the latter may not rely on a bilateral investment treaty as a kind of insurance policy against the risk of any changes in the host State's legal and economic framework. Such expectation would be neither legitimate nor reasonable.'

286 FAIR AND EQUITABLE TREATMENT

Tribunals, considering the regulatory power of the state, have stated it in absolute terms, but yet have made exceptions of stabilization clauses. Thus, to cite *Parkerings* again, the tribunal stated the right to regulate in extensive terms, but also observed that it would be 'unconscionable for a country to promise not to change its legislation as time and needs change or even move to its hands by such a kind of stipulation in case a crisis of any type or origin arose'. This is a blanket affirmation of the regulatory right of the state. Yet the same tribunal makes an exception as to the stabilization clause.[86] The question then arises as to how an exception to the right could be rationalized. The onus is on the tribunal asserting the exception to rationalize it either in terms of logic or authority. It is an exception that limits sovereignty and has to be rationalized with care if it is to be applied.

The exception is an obvious carry-over from the protection of stabilization clauses in contractual disputes. The presence of arbitrators who are zealous of foreign investment protection enables the continuation of the hoary hallmark of past foreign investment law, which enables a contractual term to stand against the regulatory needs of a state. This is so when the theory of the stabilization clause itself has undergone change. Modern views regard the clause as not imposing a fetter on the state, but read it as commercial obligation to renegotiate the contract in the light of legislative or regulatory changes. But the obligation to pay damages is attenuated if there are strong public interest reasons as to why there should be an interference with the contract. The new theory does not affect or deny the power of the state to regulate, but creates a contractual obligation on the part of the state entity to rectify the loss that ensues as a result of the change in proportion to the deprivation caused to the foreign investor and the benefit accruing to the public. The risk of change is passed to the state entity. But this risk allocation takes place within the context of the contract and has little relevance to the treaty. The power of the state is not denied and, in constitutional theory, cannot be denied. Unfortunately, investment treaty arbitration continues to treat the stabilization clause as a fetter on legislative sovereignty while at the same time declaring the power of regulation in the state. This, again, can be seen as

---

[86] *Parkerings* v. *Lithuania*, ICSID, Case No. ARB/05/08, para. 332: 'It is each State's undeniable right and privilege to exercise its sovereign legislative power. A State has the right to enact, modify or cancel a law at its own discretion. Save for the existence of an agreement, in the form of a stabilization clause or otherwise, there is nothing objectionable about the amendment brought to the regulatory framework existing at the time an investor made his investment.'

5.6 RESTRICTIONS ON LEGITIMATE EXPECTATIONS 287

the planting of the seeds of the neoliberal agenda in every progressive change that is made. It shows the continuing vitality of that agenda in that changes cannot be made except through accommodation of ideas of the contested neoliberal regime within the new changed rules.

It is also inconsistent that tribunals maintain the distinction between commercial and sovereign acts while at the same time the role of the stabilization clause is treated as an exception. The negotiation of a stabilization clause is very much part of the negotiation of the contract and is quintessentially a commercial act. The stabilization clause is often justified in terms of party autonomy in contract. As such, it would be difficult to concede how the stabilization clause, a part of the contract, can have a status within investment treaty arbitration so as to constitute an exception to the exercise of the regulatory power of the state. The origin of the exception is in the *Methanex* Award. Yet none of the authorities cited in *Methanex* to state the rule relating to non-compensability of regulatory expropriation refer to an exception relating to stabilization clauses.

Though the erosion of the scope of fair and equitable treatment began with the statement of restrictive principles limiting the scope of legitimate expectations, the tenacity of the aim of investment protection ensures that there is still preservation of old notions of investment protection. If the wholescale emasculation of the fair and equitable standard ensues, investment arbitration would be left without sufficiently tenable bases on which arbitration could be brought. The *El Paso* Award is an example where the state's case received sympathetic treatment, but new doctrine was created as to the cumulative effect of the conduct of the state as being violations of the standard.[87] Such notions are indicative of the reluctance of arbitrators to let go of the system of absolute protection, so that even arbitrators inclined to more liberal stances conserve or create rules that preserve the viability of a new front that has been created.

The most glaring instance of the tenacity of the goal of investment protection is the statement that, though the regulatory power of the state has to be recognized, there must be a balancing of that power with that of the interests and rights of the foreign investor under the investment treaty. Tribunals that have started to recognize the exercise of the regulatory power of the state as an exception to the rule on legitimate

---

[87] *El Paso* v. *Argentina*. This view was followed in *Swisslion DOO Skopje* v. *Macedonia*, ICSID, Case No. ARB/09/16 (6 July 2012). *PSEG* v. *Turkey* also spoke of the aggregate of situations that contributed to lack of stability.

expectation, still seek to subject it to a proportionality analysis. Hitherto, the rule relating to the exercise of the regulatory power of the state has been stated as a rule that admits of no restriction in expropriation law. But, suddenly, there appeared on the scene the idea that the rule is subject to a balancing test that ensures that there is a reasonable proportion between the public interest secured and the deprivation of the foreign investor. Such a qualification has no basis either in customary international law relating to the exercise of the police powers of the state or in treaty law. It is conjured up as a limitation largely on the basis of its existence in domestic public law of some European states. As in the case of regulatory expropriation, the test of proportionality is to be used as a way in which a limit can be found to the regulatory power of the state so that relief could be provided in the event of a regulatory measure found to be in breach of legitimate expectations.[88]

5.6.5 Balancing of the regulatory power of the state with the legitimate expectations of the foreign investor

Unlike the early tribunals, which recognized liability for the mere violation of the legitimate expectations on the ground that the violation of the stability that is required justified such liability, the later tribunals recognized the regulatory right of the state to change laws despite such expectations. But, at the same time, they required that this regulatory power must be balanced against the rights of the foreign investor to the standards of treatment promised by the treaty. The parallel to the manner in which the proportionality rule is used to limit regulatory takings is clear. But, whereas the proportionality test in regulatory takings is founded in the practice of the European law, there is no authority provided for the use of the test in limiting the rule on legitimate expectations. But the tribunals regard the expropriation law as supplying deficiencies in using the legitimate expectations rule in investment arbitration. There being no rule on the calculation of damages for violation of legitimate expectations, the rule that is used is the rule in

---

[88] *EDF* v. *Romania*, at para. 293: 'As held by other tribunals, in addition to a legitimate aim in the public interest there must be a "reasonable relationship of proportionality between the means employed and the aim sought to be realized: that proportionality is lacking if the person involved" bears an individual and excessive burden.' The tribunal cited *Azurix* v. *Argentina* at para. 311, citing the European Court of Human Rights case *James* v. *United Kingdom*, ECtHR (21 February 1986), at paras. 50 and 63.

5.6 RESTRICTIONS ON LEGITIMATE EXPECTATIONS 289

expropriation law. The position is similar when it comes to the situation of a clash between regulatory interferences and the proportionality rule.

The proposition was formulated in the *Saluka* Award thus: 'The determination of a breach of Article 3.1 by the Czech Republic therefore requires a weighing of the Claimant's legitimate and reasonable expectations on the one hand and the Respondent's legitimate regulatory interests on the other.' There is a balancing to be effected. Having formulated restrictions on the earlier absolute vision of stability, the tribunals now introduce another means of keeping alive the possibility of the foreign investor's interests and, of course, assert a continuing role for themselves by this balancing test.

It is an interesting evolution. An absolute regulatory power in the state would have closed avenues of remedy for the foreign investor. It would also have killed off investment arbitration. This is a new front that has been opened up to keep investment arbitration alive and with it, possibly, the interests of the foreign investor. Another 'gaping hole' would open up in this new front, rendering the innovation of legitimate expectations useless unless the proportionality rule was fashioned. It also shifts the moorings of investment law entirely to public law, where the balancing test is most often employed. European public law uses it in a variety of instances, and it is not confined to measures affecting property rights alone.

To a lesser extent, both the ideas relating to a margin of appreciation and balancing have been used by the European Court in dealing with the First Protocol of the European Convention on Human Rights. The First Protocol contains the right to property. In the hierarchy of rights, the right to property comes much lower than the personal rights which concerned the courts that have used the balancing test. The leading text on proportionality, *Proportionality: Constitutional Rights and Limitations*, by the former Israeli Chief Justice, Aron Barak, does not even mention the right to property. Not all rights are equal. The right to property is the least of the rights that have attracted the theorists on proportionality simply because it was always a right that was defeasible in the public interest. Yet it is becoming the centrepiece of investment arbitration as it searches for principles to keep it viable. The public law project in investment arbitration seeks the incorporation of the proportionality rule into investment arbitration. It enables investment arbitration to function as a court of review that oversees the legality of the internal public administration of a state. But the administrative review of domestic courts is confined to the review of subordinate tribunals and decision-makers, not the function of a sovereign state acting in the public interest. The analogy with domestic administrative review simply does not hold.

On the basis of domestic administrative review, the argument is made that an investment tribunal has the task of judicial review of every regulatory measure affecting the foreign investment, so that a balance can be struck between the right of the foreign investor to protection under the investment treaty and the exercise of the regulatory power by the state in the public interest. The argument is enhanced in circumstances where the right of the foreign investor arose through assurances given as to the stability of the investment to the foreign investor at the time of entry as they create legitimate expectations. Such legitimate expectations are protected through judicial review by domestic courts. The claim is made on the basis of the assimilation of the position before investment arbitration tribunals and the domestic courts that the arbitral tribunal has the power to act in the same manner in exercising the review function over state measures.

The reliance on European law may not be apposite. The European Court can be invoked only after domestic remedies have been exhausted. No such requirement exists in investment arbitration. The analogy fails because of this important requirement as the domestic courts would first have pronounced on the issue of legitimate expectations. Finally, the disputes that arise before the European courts have largely dealt with the deprivation of land of individual citizens or families where fairness considerations would have a greater relative merit as the source of housing, income and livelihood are being deprived. It is different in the case of a multinational corporation, which conducts large business sectors and may also have conducted itself in such a manner as to attract the measures complained of. There is no dispossession that takes place. The foreign investor usually holds shares that he could continue to hold despite the state's measures, but instead voluntarily transfers them because their income-producing levels have diminished as a result of the measures. The cause for relief in the circumstances is minimal even on any proportionality criterion.

Given that in such interference by the state, the public interest element will always be present, the balancing test, if applied, will generally tilt the decision in favour of the state. The issue is whether the balancing test should be applied when the formulation of the right to property, unlike the non-derogable right to life and liberty, is stated as subject to the public interest in every constitutional system that recognizes the right. Such a public interest is inherent in the very concept of property itself. It

5.7 Legitimate expectations and the legitimacy crisis

is not external to it so that it is balanced against some other right. It is never stated as an inflexible or a non-derogable right and has never been treated as such in any constitutional system. What is called for in any public law system is an analysis internal to the right to property, which requires that its proper exercise depends on the existence of an overwhelming public interest.

5.7 Legitimate expectations and the legitimacy crisis

Consent is the bedrock of arbitration. It is the same with investment arbitration. Leaving aside the dubious nature of the notion of arbitration without privity,[89] it is not appropriate for tribunals, which are based on the consent of the parties, to apply a law that is not founded in the consent of the parties. The tribunals cannot discover law and apply these discovered principles to the dispute. Legitimate expectations are a conjured notion of arbitrators. It plainly depends on the creative construction of the arbitrators who set out to attribute meanings to the fair and equitable treatment clause. As indicated above, the meaning may have been constructed on the basis of the mis-appreciation of the rule on legitimate expectations in English administrative law by a very small group of arbitrators.

In the context of the proliferation of international tribunals, their juridical nature as well as the role of those who sit on them is increasingly scrutinized. Of all those who sit on these tribunals, the competence of those who sit on investment tribunals is the most questionable. While other tribunals are permanent bodies, apply a law that is usually firmly stated and have a mandate provided by a multilateral treaty, the investment treaty tribunal is weak in such attributes. It is appointed for a specific case, usually applies norms of a bilateral treaty, and was devised at a time when treaties were rarer and the notion of treaty-based jurisdiction had not been articulated. Also, to the extent that the tribunals have been seen as extensions of commercial arbitration tribunals, the validity of commercial lawyers applying principles of public law or public international law has been suspect.[90] There is a legitimacy issue built into investment tribunals, which becomes accentuated when they embark on exorbitant courses beyond what states ascribed to them. A classic instance of such an exorbitant course is the discovery of the fair and

---

[89] This was dealt with in Chapter 2.
[90] Van Harten, *Investment Treaty Arbitration and Public Law*.

equitable standard, the attributions of new meanings into it and the building of a new law on investment protection beyond the prescription of the parties to the treaties.

In domestic law, judicial activism is tolerated because it often takes the law further towards reform, appeals to democratic legitimacy in that it may influence larger groups and is heavily reasoned to support the change that is being made. More importantly, a higher court within the appellate system could halt the change. If the higher court has approved and the change is inconsistent with the views of the elected representatives of the people, it could be set right through legislation. It is possible to justify judicial activism as consistent with democratic theory in the domestic sphere. The public authority of a state is embedded within a political system that supplies legitimacy to them. International tribunals, which have some permanence,[91] have some authority vested in them by their institutional regimes. These safeguards are absent when it comes to arbitration of investment disputes. There is no appellate system. The building up of an appellate system on the present foundations will only enhance the faults of the system. The annulment tribunal within the ICSID system does not have the power to interfere with decisions as to the substantive issues, even where wrongly made.[92]

Legitimacy for changes is derived from the strength of the reasoning that is provided and the existence of authority supporting it. In the situation of legitimate expectations and the fair and equitable clause, such legitimacy is lacking as there has never been a comprehensive examination of the extent to which legitimate expectations can be the dominant feature of fair and equitable treatment. The academic rationalizations of it seem hollow. The founding of the notion in English law is weak.[93] Equally weak is the notion that legitimate expectation exists in the manner in which it is used in investment arbitration. Most legal systems use the notion to deal with measures that target specific and not general measures.[94] The measures that are targeted in investment arbitration, as in the Argentinian cases, are general measures adopted to deal with an economic crisis. If legitimate expectations are to be

---

[91] The Law of the Sea Tribunal and the dispute settlement system of the WTO are located within institutional structures created by the international community. Their judges are elected.

[92] *CMS* Annulment Decision.

[93] As indicated above, English law does not support a substantive right resulting in damages even in the exceptional cases.

[94] Diehl, *The Core Standard of International Investment Protection*, p. 398.

5.7 LEGITIMATE EXPECTATIONS AND LEGITIMACY CRISIS 293

drawn from general principles of law, this must be demonstrated. The doctrine is used to review subordinate decision-makers not the general legislation of a sovereign state. That is a constitutional function performed by courts applying constitutional limitations on the legislature. It works within a system of separation of powers. The situation does not provide a parallel.

In academic literature, there are few successful efforts at showing that legitimate expectations have sufficient acceptance as a general principle. There is an examination of European systems, but hardly any reference to other 'civilized' legal systems, including that of the United States. The world does include other systems besides the European systems and no effort seems to have been made to study these different systems. But the rule, whenever recognized, is subject to a heavy qualification regarding public interest. More research is necessary to determine whether the rule can be established as a general principle. The legitimacy that can be derived from solid authority is lacking in the expansion that the arbitral tribunals have sought to make regarding legitimate expectations. Several attempts have been made to overcome the legitimacy problem.

5.7.1 Theoretical justifications for recognizing legitimate expectations

There are many theoretical justifications advanced for the acceptance of the legitimate expectations rule. They flow largely from neoliberal notions. The most often used justification is that the system of investment treaties seeks to promote a standard of governance. Clearly, the viewpoint draws on the neoliberal vision that rules on investment protection have to be maximized so as to maintain optimum conditions for the flow and maintenance of foreign investment, particularly in developing countries. But its transference to the international sphere, which consists of a plurality of systems of governance, is fraught with difficulty for it cannot be said that the free market model which it purveys is the only model that is appropriate for economic development.[95] Neither is it the function of investment tribunals to impose standards of governance on states.

From this idea of governance, there have followed similar rationalizations of the changes made on the basis of fair and equitable treatment. The notion of the rules of governance is drawn from the single vision of the world organized on the basis of democracy and market capitalism.

---

[95] Dani Rodrik, *The Globalization Paradox* (New York: Oxford University Press, 2011).

It is evident that world is not such a place. The state that is capable of being among the largest investors, China, does not care much about the standards of Western governance and cannot be forced into so caring despite the fact that it is the largest maker of investment treaties. Economists are divided on whether there could be any single economic theory that provides a panacea for the problems of the world. Neither is there evidence to show that a system that is organized on the basis of such principles is the better system. The global financial crisis, which is in effect an American and European crisis, is widely attributed to the adoption of neoliberal theories. There is no reason why the rest of the world must adopt theories that have failed in these states. The attempt to impose the standards of Western liberalism on the rest of the world is akin to the earlier efforts to impose standards of civilization through international law. They are bound to face resistance. States that entered into bilateral investment treaties did not do so on the understanding that political and economic philosophies could be imposed on them through arbitration of disputes under the treaties.

The idea relating to the standards of governance has taken new forms. They emphasize that the central purpose of the fair and equitable standard and the rule of legitimate expectations is to ensure that stability given to the foreign investment. Stability becomes the cornerstone of the rule on legitimate expectations as applied by the tribunals. The notion is largely drawn from the preamble to the treaties. The preamble states other objectives such as economic development and cooperation. Stability of the investment is not to be the sole object of the treaty to be achieved at all costs.[96] Stability, as the aim of the standard of governance, is open to the criticism that it involves the imposition of a normative order from above on states, which have not given consent to such an imposition, particularly by investment arbitration tribunals. The tribunals are not created for that purpose. They lack competence to do so. Yet the suggestions have attracted much attention in the literature. They are justified on two main grounds. The developments are justified on the basis of the rule of law or on the basis of an emerging global administrative law.

---

[96] In *EDF* v. *Romania*, the Arbitration Tribunal held that: 'the idea that legitimate expectations, and therefore, FET, imply the stability of the legal and business framework, may not be correct if stated in an overly-broad and unqualified formulation. The FET might then mean the virtual freezing of the legal regulation of economic activities, in contrast with the State's normal regulatory power and the evolutionary character of economic life.'

5.7 LEGITIMATE EXPECTATIONS AND LEGITIMACY CRISIS 295

5.7.2 *The rule of law argument*

The rule of law argument seeks to maintain legitimate expectations against the regulatory power of the state. The tribunal in *ADC* v. *Hungary*[97] suggested that the 'while a sovereign State possesses the inherent right to regulate its domestic affairs, the right is not unlimited and must have its boundaries'. The tribunal said that 'the rule of law, which includes treaty obligations, provides such boundaries', so that a state that enters into an investment treaty must honour the obligations rather than plead its right to regulate against the performance of such obligations. The rule of law proposal is based on the idea that the rule of law is common to domestic legal systems and its content can be determined through comparison of the different domestic public law systems.[98] The principles so derived are general principles of law and constitute a source of international law. But, as with all the exercises to discover general principles in the past of international law, only European systems are taken into account in constructing the core of general principles. The work of the European Court of Human Rights is held out as a quarry for the principles. The hoary neoliberal policy justification regarding the promotion of foreign investment flows through stability, and the economic development that such flows bring to development is doled out despite the fact that this policy justification has come to be increasingly contested in economic literature. That policy justification can hardly support the extension of the treaty prescriptions beyond the intention of the parties. The need to restrict public power is emphasized without providing for circumstances when extensive private power that holds the state hostage, as happens when multinational investors capture an economic sector, is not provided for. The rule of law also is an abstraction that can be manipulated to serve the neoliberal cause. If public power needs to be restricted, so does the power of the large multinational corporation. The best exponents of the rule of law would require it to capture essential human values within the concept. The protection of foreign investment at the cost of public interest cannot capture such values. The problem of controlling exorbitant private power in international relations is not factored into the rule of law arguments.

---

[97] ICSID, Case No. ARB/03/16 (2 October 2006).
[98] Stephan Schill, 'Fair and Equitable Treatment: The Rule of Law and Comparative Public Law', In Stephan Schill (ed.), *International Investment Law and Comparative Public Law* (Oxford University Press, 2010), p. 151.

296   FAIR AND EQUITABLE TREATMENT

The global economic crisis in the rich states of Europe has demonstrated that the power of the large banks and corporations has to be controlled. The need for the regulatory power of the state has been reasserted after a period of market domination.

There are expansive theories afloat as to the public authority of international tribunals. The view is that these tribunals are vested with an authority that results from the structure of the international society's plural and globalized state. Their function has been to drive towards securing global norms. This is a fanciful theory without adequate foundations. Uncontrolled power in the hands of the few will irk a system founded on state sovereignty unless the states have a say, as they do within regimes of institutional order, in correcting the course taken by the tribunals. No such system exists within what some have optimistically described as the 'regime' of investment protection law. Whatever truth it may have in the case of other tribunals, the investment tribunals are ad hoc tribunals deriving their authority from the direct consent of states manifested in the investment treaty and not from any institutional arrangement with substantive laws. They do not have the power to extend their authority into the realm of activist law-making as is done in the case of legitimate expectations.

The literature that is rolled out to support the vision consists entirely of what is used to support the neoliberal vision or is generated by the agencies such as the World Bank, known purveyors of this single vision of development. The usual writers, Adam Smith, Max Weber, Frederik Hayek and Richard Posner, are used in support. Thus, Schill stated that 'Scholars in this field particularly emphasize the significance for economic growth and development of a well-functioning legal system that embodies the rule of law.'[99] There is selectivity in the use of the scholars.[100] The existence of those who support other views are not considered. In Chapter 1, the division of views between scholars has been indicated. It is only necessary to point out that there is cogent economic literature that supports other views.

The view as to the rule of law does not accord with the practice of many states. It cannot be said that when China signed its 180 investment treaties, it agreed to abide by the rule of law as understood in the West. It cannot be said that the spectacular economic development achieved by

---

[99] Schill, 'Fair and Equitable Treatment', at p. 181.

[100] There is economic literature against the imposition of single visions. Rodrik, *The Globalization Paradox*; Stigliz, *Free Fall*.

5.7 LEGITIMATE EXPECTATIONS AND LEGITIMACY CRISIS 297

China is based on the rule of law as understood in the West.[101] Some would argue that it is based on the negation of the rule of law in that the economic achievements of China are due to a state that directs its economy strictly and ensures that its controlled programme works. Its laws do not permit the admittance of foreign investment without regulation. This could be said of many other states, which are based on economies based on state-directed companies. The ascendancy of the economies of the BRICS[102] states shows the diversity that exists in the systems of these states. Not all of them are liberal democracies pursuing the rule of law.[103] Their diversity belies the fact that it is necessary to have a single standard of governance for progress to be achieved.[104] Neither can uniformity, a Western drive from colonial times,[105] be imposed on states in the present era where a multipolar world replaces the hegemonic order of the unipolar world. In the particular context of fair and equitable statement, the rule of law provides little policy justification for the nature of the expansions that have been made and could be made so as to erode the sovereignty of states making investment treaties. It is a castle in the air. It rests on no foundations but the imaginations of arbitrators, quickly followed by writings that rationalize the views that they have sought to establish. The surprising contortions in the law that arbitral tribunals perform enhance the disbelief that the rule of law has anything to do with this exercise.[106] A system that has not devised any settled rules cannot be said to promote the rule of law. There is an absence of equality in that local entrepreneurs do not have access to foreign tribunals. One may also argue that since the rules are made through processes of private power, there is no rule of law in the system but a rule of power that cannot be controlled.

---

[101] Randall Peerenbohm, *China's Long March toward the Rule of Law* (Cambridge University Press, 2007).

[102] Brazil, Russia, India, China and South Africa. Soon to be joined perhaps by Indonesia, these countries are not based on Western liberalism to any significant extent, except possibly India and perhaps South Africa.

[103] Sornarajah, 'The Role of the BRICS in International Law of the Multipolar World'.

[104] Brazil has no investment treaties. Russia is a totalitarian state. India is a democracy that is corrupt at its base. China is communist and corrupt. South Africa has decided against investment treaties.

[105] Benton, *Law and Colonial Cultures*, at pp. 18–20, deals with how property concepts in the colonies were changed to favour market mechanisms and institutional stability.

[106] For example, see *El Paso*, where the tribunal held that every act of Argentina was legitimate, but that there cumulative effect justified a finding of a breach of the fair and equitable treatment. *El Paso* v. *Argentina*, ICSID, Case No. ARB/03/15 (31 October 2011).

298   FAIR AND EQUITABLE TREATMENT

5.7.3   The global administrative law argument

The effort to construct a global administrative law is a wider effort, but is based on the ability of international tribunals to supervise the administrative decisions made by domestic administrative machinery so that these decisions accord with external standards derived from notions of good governance. Again, the project is open to the criticism as to how these standards of good governance are to be decided on. But, despite this initial criticism, the project will remain an important attempt to conserve the developments relating to the fair and equitable standard.[107] The notion is driven more by developments in areas such as international environmental law, but there are efforts to extend it into international investment law. A principal thrust is based on the developments relating to review based on the failure to respect legitimate expectations. As indicated, the soundness of this extension still remains to be established. It is jumping the gun to speak optimistically of the evolution of a global administrative law in the area of investment law by clutching at hollow straws.

5.8   Conclusion

The turn to the fair and equitable treatment standard was necessary as the wind had been knocked out of expropriation law through the recognition of the principle on regulatory takings. In seeking to create a new peg on which to hang claims, arbitrators sought actively to create law that could provide a future impetus for investment arbitration based on treaties. They revived the fair and equitable treatment, making legitimate expectations the centre point of that standard of treatment. Unfortunately, there has been no success in grounding it in any substantial source in the law or in establishing the legitimacy of the process through which the clause in the treaties could be extended to cover the protection of legitimate expectations. It has been difficult to show that the legitimate expectations rule

---

[107] Benedict Kingsbury and Stephan Schill, 'Investor–State Arbitration as Governance: Fair and Equitable Treatment, Proportionality, and the Emerging Global Administrative Law', in Albert Jan Van Den Berg (ed.), *50 Years of the New York Convention* (Alphen aan den Rijn: Kluwer, 2009), p. 5; Benedict Kingsbury and Stephan Schill, 'Public Law Concepts to Balance Investors' Rights with State Regulatory Actions in the Public Interest: The Concept of Proportionality', in Stephan Schill (ed.), *International Investment Law and Comparative Public Law* (Oxford University Press, 2010), p. 75; Alec Stone Sweet, 'Investor–State Arbitration: Proportionality's New Frontier', (2010) 4 *Law and Ethics of Human Rights* 47; Benedict Kingsbury, 'The Concept of "Law" in Global Administrative Law', (2009) 20 *European Journal of International Law* 1.

5.8 CONCLUSION

commands such acceptance that it is a general principle of law. The policy rationale that investment stability requires the rule also sounds weak, as stability is not the only rationale that lies behind investment treaties.

The dalliance with the legitimate expectations rule illustrates the paucity of grounds on which the treaty system is workable as a basis for giving protection to the foreign investor after its base in expropriation law had been virtually eliminated. The frenetic search for a new base in the legitimate expectations rule has opened up schisms in investment arbitration that expose its many weaknesses. The continued uncertainty that arises with each new decision on legitimate expectations will serve neither states nor foreign investors.

The authority of an investment treaty tribunal is dependent on the consent of the states. It also is dependent on the making of decisions that are right and are demonstrably anchored in the law. When a tribunal exceeds the limits of the consent and extends the law on demonstrably inadequate authority, the legitimacy of the exercise it performs becomes suspect. The tribunal ceases to have legitimacy and the law it formulates itself is not founded in authority. It is this double illegitimacy that taints the use of the rule on legitimate expectations. Its continued use will undermine investment arbitration even further.

The episode relating legitimate expectations also illustrates the unsavoury instances of attempting to foist a law lacking authority as if it is a well-founded assumption. It is made on insufficient authority by a handful of arbitrators willing to follow each other. A course of precedent is established. The argument is raised that a line of authority is being followed in the later cases. There is then a search for possible ways of rationalizing the development. 'Scholars' join in the endeavour with the same degree of self-citations and following of other like-minded scholars. Law then is created on the basis of this overwhelming numerical accumulation of evidence of awards and 'scholarly' commentary. Many of the 'scholars' have given expert testimony to various tribunals. It is their expert opinions that are transferred into learned articles published in journals run by those possessed with the same esoteric wisdom. These journals do not carry articles stating a contrary argument. So is the law made. The acceptance of such law will come to be challenged increasingly. The fact that law should be made that caters only to the interests of sectional groups and profits those making the law brings the law into disrepute.

6

Backlash through defences

One evident backlash against the expansionism of the neoliberal period has been the discovery of new defences to liability under the investment treaties. The neoliberal emphasis on investor protection to the exclusion of all other interests is no longer the policy goal on which the law rests. Thus, the European Commission in announcing its policy objectives in the sphere of foreign investment stated:[1]

> Investors are not the only beneficiaries of investment agreements. Investment, being an important driver for economic and social development, equally benefits all stakeholders. Thus, protection of investors' rights is not an aim in itself, but serves a wider objective: to enhance investment and contribute to the well-being of society.

Obviously, changes are afoot. There is a discovery of new aims which compete with the interest in inflexible investment protection. Newer treaties have begun to recognize defences based on the need of the state to regulate in the public interest. They are not based on the solitary objective of investment protection. The recognition of defences is an intermediate solution. It keeps the treaty system alive. It is premised on the possibility of liability. It avoids the exclusion of investor–state arbitration from treaties or the total termination of treaty practice, which are more extreme solutions adopted by some states.[2]

---

[1] European Commission, Investment, Memorandum, Brussels, 7 July 2010, 'Q&A: Commission Launches Comprehensive European international investment policy.' On the internal tussles within the European Community, see Mark Clodfelter, 'The Future Directions of Investment Agreements within the European Community' (2013) 12 *Santa Clara Journal of International Law* 183.

[2] Some states, like South Africa, have terminated treaties after their initial periods and have announced that they will sign treaties only if some overwhelming benefit can be demonstrated. Some, like Australia, have announced that they would sign future treaties with investor–state arbitration clauses. Australia has since retracted from this position, but its earlier stance marked out such an option. Philippines did not include an investor–state dispute settlement provision in its treaty with Japan. Some Latin American states have pulled out of the investment arbitration system. These reactions have been recounted more fully elsewhere in this book.

300

There is a need to examine the changes effected to the treaty system itself in a proclaimed effort to bring about a balance in the treaties between investment protection and regulatory space in the host state to act in the public interest. The issue has to be raised as to whether such 'balanced' treaties are useful in reconciling the conflict between investment protection and the regulatory needs of the state, or whether they are of limited use as the uncertainties as to result they generate neither serve the purpose of investment protection nor facilitate the state's purpose of attracting investments. It can no longer be said that their task is the promotion of flows of foreign investment into developing countries as no inflexible protection is granted. Rather, uncertainty is created as to the extent of the protection. The issue has to be squarely faced that regulatory space for the state cannot be achieved without sacrificing inflexible investment protection. This discussion is deferred to Chapter 7.

The present chapter deals with the emergence of defences to liability in existing case law and academic discussion. Academic discussion is important as it increasingly seeks to reintegrate investment protection within existing international law relating to emerging fields of human rights, the environment, indigenous rights and cultural heritage.[3] As the insulation of investment protection ends through its reintegration with other areas of international law, new defences will have to emerge even if arbitrators may show resistance to such a course. States will assist in this process as it enables them to resist ongoing litigation by advancing new defences on the basis of this reintegration process. In advancing a case for interference on the ground of public interest, states will present their cases in the form of defences based on existing international conventions dealing with public health, social welfare and human rights.

The focus in this chapter is on the defences that have been attempted in arbitral jurisprudence that rely on existing treaty formulations, as well as those discovered through the use of principles to be found in customary international law, such as the necessity defence. As indicated, they also involve defences suggested in academic literature. These defences find expression in the newer treaties. The existence of these defences precluding responsibility tilts the balance in favour of the state, if they are applied without bias by arbitration tribunals. But one has to be conscious

---

[3] Reinisch Hofman and Christofer Tams (eds.), *International Investment Law and General International Law: From Clinical Isolation to Systemic Integration* (Baden-Baden: Nomos, 2011); Baetens (ed.), *Investment Law within International Law: Integrationist Perspectives.*

of the fact that arbitration tribunals have restricted the scope of any rule that is adverse to the interests of investment protection by interpreting such rules as narrowly as possible.[4]

The discussion and recognition of these defences in recent awards has made investor protection more uncertain. It has made the law move from a position of absolute protection to a situation of qualified protection. They arise at a time when the new investment treaties are beginning to formulate defences based on domestic and global regulatory interests. These defences create more uncertainty. They add to the existing uncertainties created by the schisms within investment arbitration. The policy rationale of the system of investment treaties was the unprovable assumption that the certainty of protection given to foreign investors through the treaties boosted flows of foreign investment due to the confidence given by the treaties that neutral arbitral fora would settle disputes. That certainty is no longer exists. The untestable premises that support the system of investment arbitration have been undermined by the fact that the increasing number of defences to liability has removed any certainty about outcomes as regards investment protection. An increasing number of defences to liability will add to the existing confusion, thereby accentuating the present instability in the law. Argentina had explored many jurisdictional and substantive defences in the arbitrations it has had to face. The developed states like the United States, faced anew with arbitrations against them under NAFTA, sought to develop others, such as the revival of the exception of regulatory expropriation.[5] The creation of these defences curb the law that resulted from expansionary interpretation of investment treaties. In that sense, they are a response to arbitral excesses of the past.

Resistance to inflexible investment protection by pressure groups concerned with abuses of human rights and the environment by

---

[4] Tribunals have seldom been faced with the 'balanced treaties'. It is likely that the defences will be interpreted restrictively. The charge is not loosely made. There are several instances of this happening within the existing system. Tribunals have not treated treaty conflicts with favour, giving priority to the investment treaty (e.g., *Santa Elena* v. *Costa Rica; S. D. Myers* v. *Canada*). The restriction of fair and equitable treatment by tying it with customary international law has been restrictively interpreted by some tribunals. Similarly, the denial of benefits provision to curtail the use of corporate nationality has been restrictively interpreted. The plea of necessity has been restricted by finding alternative avenues of escaping the situation, though these alternatives may not have been feasible. Many other instances are referred to in this work.

[5] To the extent that it is an exception to the main rule, the regulatory expropriation rule could be taken as a defence.

multinational companies also promoted the recognition of defences. Several writers and groups argue for change in the context of the development of sustainable development as a concept in international law.[6] The capacity of that concept to create new defences seems limitless as it embraces a wide variety of obligations it imposes on a foreign investor, including, but not confined to, duties recognized by international environmental law and human rights law.

International lawyers have also turned their attention to the issue of fragmentation. Investment arbitration has attracted their attention as it has hitherto been developed as an autonomous regime. There is now an insistence that international investment law and arbitration must take into account the obligations that arise under other areas of international law. These obligations go beyond the areas of human rights and the environment.[7] The view that the regime of investment law and arbitration are *sui generis* and are based on *lex specialis* that enables this regime to pick and choose the rules of general international law that are to be admitted is a defensive response that is unlikely to be accepted. These trends also open up the possibility of new defences being thrown up as a result of conflicting norms, and the possibility that the norms of these other areas may have supremacy over investment treaty obligations. The construction of theories relating to a hierarchy of norms that are

[6] Cordonier Segger *et al.* (eds.), *Sustainable Development in World Investment Law.* The Columbia-Vale Centre of Sustainable Investment works in the field of formulating principles of foreign investment and sustainable development. UNCTAD, *World Investment Report* (Geneva, 2014) noted (p. 116): 'A review of the 18 IIAs concluded in 2013 for which texts are available (11 BITs and 7 FTAs with substantive investment provisions), shows that most of the treaties include sustainable development-oriented features, such as those identified in UNCTAD's Investment Policy Framework for Sustainable Development (IPFSD) and in *WIR12* and *WIR13.56*. Of these agreements, 15 have general exceptions – for example, for the protection of human, animal or plant life or health, or the conservation of exhaustible natural resources – and 13 refer in their preambles to the protection of health and safety, labour rights, the environment or sustainable development.' Such formulations remain to be considered in arbitrations.

[7] They include, to give some examples and indicative cases, the protection of cultural property (*Parkerings* v. *Lithuania, Malaysian Salvors* v. *Malaysia, SPP* v. *Egypt*) the rights of indigenous people, the right to resources such as water (*Aguas del Tunari* v. *Bolivia*), the protection of wildlife species (*Santa Elena* v. *Costa Rica*), transport of hazardous waste (*S. D. Myers* v. *Canada*), public health (*Methanex* v. *United States*), the environment, etc. Disputes that have arisen involve such areas, but have received little attention from the point of view of the clashes they present with investment protection. As these awards involving interests competing with those of investment protection increased, academic commentaries on specific issues also increased. See Vinuales, *Foreign Investment and the Environment in International Law*; Vadi, *Cultural Heritage in International Investment Law and Arbitration.*

in conflict may see the demotion of the protection of foreign investment to a lower status so that the precedence given to higher norms will displace investment protection, thereby providing defences (if they are the appropriate technique for the accommodation of these higher norms). Chapter 7 points out that the future course of development in this area is that a new generation of treaties will contain formulations of larger categories of defences and move away from investment protection as the sole basis of investment treaties. When this trend takes hold, the issue has to be squarely faced as to whether the investment treaty system should be dismantled as its objectives have become so contradictory that they may be unworkable. This issue is also addressed in Chapter 7.

The first section of this chapter provides a setting for the emergence of exculpatory defences. It then identifies the substantive defences that have emerged and the possible uses to which the defences could be put. The factors ousting jurisdiction, which are also an important way of avoiding responsibility, have already been covered in Chapter 3. It is important to keep them in mind in considering the extent to which the neoliberal fervour for extending the law has come to be dented. They add to the erosion of an inflexible system of investment protection that had been the original aim of the system of investment treaties. The undermining of the system through the recognition of substantive defences to state liability is a greater blow to the effectiveness of investment treaties in providing protection to foreign investment. The chances are that the longer the system lasts and cases are brought, the greater would be the tendency to explore the limits of these defences and, possibly, also the discovery of new defences. There may be a creation of an expansionary law in reverse, made largely through academic discussions, lobby groups and state action. As foreign investors, their advisers and arbitrators sought to expand the bases of protection under the treaties, academics, states and their advisers have responded and will respond in full measure by exploring new avenues for avoiding liability on the basis of conflict of norms. This trend benefits neither the states nor the investors.

The changes in the climate that brought about a revision in the system must be kept in mind. This is not as a result of the reaction of the states to arbitral activism alone, but also due to structural changes that were taking place within the system of the international law relating to foreign investment. These changes were multifarious. They included the fact that developed states were coming to be affected by the protective principles on foreign investment that they had designed. As they increasingly became recipients of capital from newly emerging economies such as China, India and Brazil, the possibility of finding themselves as respondents in investment arbitration increased.[8] States which devised swords now had to devise shields. In the context of NAFTA, this has already begun to happen, and developed states had to take defensive stances.[9] Having the experience of the pain they had so far inflicted on the developing states, there was a new learning experience.[10] The context of these different interests impacting on investment protection is necessary for the understanding of the developments in the field and the future changes that may be generated as a result of the conflict of these different interests on the law.

Fragmentation of international law helped the powerful states to hive off areas of international law and to develop them as regimes with specialist expertise with which those lacking similar expertise could not compete on equal terms. Private power that operated in the field of foreign investment protection benefited greatly as a result of this fragmentation. Unlike in other fields, fragmentation aided law-making through private means as the decision-making in the area had been delegated to tribunals that did not function under the supervision of public institutions nor were they subject to regulation by institutionally legitimized agencies. The ending of fragmentation challenged the rules that had been made through the techniques of law-making through the exercise of private power. That process itself led to the search for new defences so that the old law created through expansionary techniques could be ended.

The first part of the chapter deals with the defences that are based in the treaties themselves. The obvious defence is national security. It is provided for in some treaties. The second section consists of defences

---

[8] Economic power is passing to the hands of the BRIC states. It is estimated that Brazil, Russia, India and China have a combined gross domestic product of 24.5 per cent, whereas the share of the four big European economies (Germany, France, Britain and Italy) is 13.4 per cent. Robert Wade, 'IMF Needs a Reset', *International New York Times*, 5 February 2014.

[9] NAFTA arbitrations resulted in the articulation of the rule on regulatory expropriation (*Methanex* v. *United States*) and led to the restriction of fair and equitable treatment by tying it to customary international law. The latter resulted from an interpretive note of the NAFTA Commission, while the argument in *Pope and Talbot* based on the notion of a higher standard was being put before the tribunal in that arbitration.

[10] Arbitrations under NAFTA are listed on the website of the US Trade Representative. In Europe, arbitrations have been brought against Britain (*Sancheti*) and Germany (*Vattenfall*). There are arbitrations that will arise against Spain and Greece resulting from the measures they had taken to deal with their respective economic crises.

that are drawn from customary international law. The principal defence in this category is necessity. It exists as a defence, apart from the defence of national security, which is stated in the treaty. It is a true defence in that it is relevant only after state responsibility is established. The defence is broader and its exact limits are as yet uncertain. The revival of old customary law rules, such as the rule on the non-compensability of regulatory expropriation, could be regarded as defences in that the rule is taken up as a defence after expropriation is shown. The rule has been already been dealt with under expropriation.

The third part of the chapter deals with the conflicts between investment protection and norms of the different areas of international law. The accommodation of the interests at conflict had to be achieved through the creation of exceptions and defences to the primary aim of investment protection. The old wisdom was that international law was relevant to the process of foreign investment. The theory of internationalization of contracts was based on that premise. But, at the time, the only relevant international law that was considered relevant was the general principle of sanctity of contracts. It was also possible to develop a treaty regime without heeding other principles of international law. Other principles of international law were also in a rudimentary state of development. It is a measure of the extent of the change that international law on foreign investment also developed equally strong principles regarding the protection of the environment, human rights, cultural property and indigenous peoples. Many of these principles have been transformed from aspirational prescriptions over the same period of neoliberal expansion of investment protection into concrete prescriptions of international law.[11] Each of these new interests developed along with strong NGOs, which had a global interest in promoting them so that they came with large pressure groups with countervailing power to meet the power of private interests in promoting investment protection. It became less possible for states to ignore the existence of these interests so that the combination of private and public power that had hitherto characterized international law on investment had to undergo vital changes with public power shifting to espouse the new causes. In that context, defences to liability on the basis of these new interests had to be

---

[11] It was in the 1990s that a strong international environmental law developed with the Stockholm Declaration on the Human Environment (1992). A strong human rights law with the possibility of enforcement through domestic courts had to await later developments. But substantial pressure groups supporting these international law principles began to have an impact on international relations.

6.1 The defences in the treaties and customary law

accommodated. The defences are also significant in that they help to draw a 'bright line' between regulatory takings and compensable takings, as they indicate that in the circumstances in which they are available, the taking should be regarded as regulatory.

The defences that are emerging are a result of a clash of interests or, as some would have it, a clash of hitherto fragmented regimes.[12] Where regimes built on separate values clash, a method of reconciling them will have to be found.[13] Alternatively, in the clash of values on which separate areas of international law have been built during periods of fragmentation of the law, the reuniting of these fragmented areas through their reintegration into common principles will have to be achieved through a process of reconciliation by the construction of a hierarchy of values. In the neoliberal period, a greater value was attached to the protection of foreign investment largely on the basis of the untested assumption that it had the altruistic effect of promoting economic development. That thesis is no longer maintainable. As a result, the law that was built up during the ascendancy of neoliberalism is being dismantled through the recognition of a wide array of defences based largely upon the recognition of the existence of other values of greater significance. Whether the recognition of defences is the way to deal with this problem has to be debated, for defences are based on the existence of the primacy of the rule of liability that they seek to exclude. In the case of investment protection, the argument is that they come lower down in the hierarchy of values that now exist within international law. But it appears to be the way in which the accommodation of the superior normative values is being attempted, as the preservation of the existing system requires that the higher normative values can be accommodated only through their existence as defences. The growing number of defences must be examined. Some of them are coming to be stated in the newer treaties, but since general international law will continue to provide other defences, there cannot be an exhaustible category of such defences.

---

[12] This assumes that human rights, the environment or cultural rights have been built up as separate regimes. They are amenable to such interpretations as they too have institutional mechanisms which support their rules.

[13] Dirk Pulkowski, *Law and Politics of International Regime Conflict* (Oxford University Press, 2014).

308　　BACKLASH THROUGH DEFENCES

6.1.1　National security

Most of the older treaties contained no defences to liability for breaches of the treaty provisions. But some treaties, particularly the US treaties, contained a provision on national security as a circumstance precluding liability. The US view was that a subjective appreciation that circumstances gave rise to a threat to national security was sufficient to give rise to the preclusion of liability. This was the formula the United States had used in the model treaties on the basis of which it negotiated treaties, but the subjective formulation was not used in the US–Argentina treaty. The United States refused to state whether the omission was intentional. Argentina argued in the arbitrations it had to face arising from its economic crisis that the omission was accidental, and that Argentina's subjective appreciation that the economic crisis amounted to a threat to national security was sufficient. But the Argentine arguments have been routinely rejected. It is difficult to understand why a situation that led to widespread hunger in the country, a situation of public emergency resulting in army shootings and the fall of five successive governments within a short span of time could not amount to a national security situation. The Argentinian arbitrations would have terminated expeditiously if the plea had been upheld. It will be long debated as to why such a course was not adopted and what the criteria for national security are. If public emergencies can justify the suspension of human rights, there is no reason to confine the national security situation to wars and similar instances. As a result, the determinations on the issue of national security in the Argentinian awards will always remain suspect. As long as objective situations exist for the invocation of the national security exception, the state should be given a margin of appreciation when it argues that the measures it took were in response to a national security situation.

6.1.2　Necessity

The Argentine cases tested out the defence of necessity available as a general defence to all situations of liability for international wrongs to the fullest extent.[14] The argument that was advanced to the different

---

[14] In the *Case Concerning the Gabikovo-Nagymaros Project* [1997] ICJ Rep. 7, the ICJ stated the situation of necessity as involving 'grave danger to the existence of the state itself, to its political and economic survival, the maintenance of conditions in which its essential services can function, the keeping of its internal peace, the survival of part of its population, the ecological preservation of all or some of its territory'.

6.1 THE DEFENCES IN THE TREATIES AND CUSTOMARY LAW 309

tribunals was that the Argentine economic crisis, in the context of which the alleged wrongful measures causing damage to the claimants were made, constituted both a threat to national security and a situation of necessity. The unfortunate conflation of the two distinct preclusionary situations was to confound the reasoning in the early awards. Necessity, as the Annulment Committee in *CMS* pointed out,[15] is a defence that is relevant only after responsibility has been found, whereas the existence of national security prevented the finding of responsibility. The Argentine effort in pleading necessity was the first in excluding fragmentation as it sought a defence in general international law outside the treaty prescriptions. The early tribunals dealing with the Argentine crisis found it difficult to come to grips with this fact. They were unable to see, or disliked seeing, a difference between the two pleas.

The general view adopted by the tribunals in the early awards[16] was that the exception could not be pleaded in the case because the threat could have been avoided through means other than through devaluation of the peso and the removal of the peg of prices of gas to the American price indices. Evidently, the tribunals were more interested in substituting their own assessment of what should have been done than in assessing the measures in the context of the situation the state found itself in. It is unreasonable to hold that the method chosen to deal with the crisis may not be as good as the alternatives. Neither could it be expected that the same standards be used by every state that faces an economic crisis. The existence of a single standard is the neoliberal solution advocated by the IMF prescription for economic crises. The Asian economic crises had demonstrated that there was no one way out of an economic

---

[15] *CMS v. Argentina* , ICSID, Case No. ARB/01/8, Annulment Award (25 September 2007). The Annulment Committee was strongly constituted with Judge Guilliaume, Judge el Araby and Professor Crawford. It took the unusual step of finding errors as to law, but declaring its inability to do anything about it as it did not have any powers of review as to errors of law, thus undermining the *CMS* Award.

[16] The first three awards, *CMS, Enron* and *Siemens*, were presided over by the same arbitrator, Professor Orrego-Vicuna. Mr Lalonde was arbitrator in two of them. *CMS Gas Transmission Co. v. Argentina*, ICSID, Case No. ARB/1/8 (20 April 2004) (Orrego-Vicuna, Lalonde, Rezek); *Enron Corp. v. Argentina*, ICSID, Case No. ARB/01/3 (22 May 2007) (Orrego-Vicuna, Van den Berg, Tschanz); *Sempra Energy International v. Argentina*, ICSID, Case No. ARB/02/16 (28 September 2007) (Orrego-Vicuna, Lalonde, Morelli Rico). The flawed reasoning in *CMS* permeated the other awards. *LG&E* partially found in favour of Argentina on the defences. *LG&E International Inc. v. Argentina*, ICSID, Case No. ARB/02/1 (3 October 2006). *Continental Casualty v. Argentina* also ruled in favour of Argentina.

crisis.[17] Indonesia adopted the IMF prescriptions subjecting itself to the conditionalities demanded by the IMF. Malaysia, on the other hand, adopted currency controls and came out of the crisis as successfully as Indonesia. Further experience of economic crises arose with the global economic crisis of 2008, which affected both the United States and Europe. The states took different measures, including nationalizations of affected sectors. The ongoing Greek and Spanish crises also demonstrate that the measures that are taken could affect foreign investors adversely along with national investors. In the light of these different episodes, it is unlikely that measures taken relating to economic crises are going to be looked at through the prism of absolute investment protection.[18] Attitudes to the use of the necessity defence will also change as a result. Necessity may prove to be a way of wriggling out of the situation of liability for measures a state takes in such situations. It is evident that later tribunals have not taken the same inflexible attitude towards the defence as the earlier tribunals.[19]

The existence of the draft ILC Code on State Responsibility has muddied the discussion of issue. The draft code's definition of the defence of necessity was narrower than the basis of the defence indicated in customary international law in that it excluded the defence in circumstances where there were alternative methods of avoiding the injury which may prove to be less onerous to the party suffering damage. The fear that states would resort to necessity as an easy way of avoiding responsibility seems to have animated the formation of the ILC's statement of the rules on state responsibility. The authorities relied on do not support the rules stated, particularly the rule that necessity should be excluded where there were less onerous alternatives to the measures taken by the state in response to the situation of necessity.[20] The rule

---

[17] The Asian economic crisis in 1998–9 was a result of the sudden outflow of funds from southeast Asia. The Suharto regime fell as a result of the crisis.

[18] There are pending actions against European states resulting from the economic crisis. *Ping An* v. *Belgium*; There are several against Spain (e.g., *Next Era Energy Global Holdings BV and Next Era Energy Spain Holdings BV* v. *Spain*, ICSID, Case No. ARB/14/11) and Greece (*Cyprus Popular Bank Public Co. Ltd* v. *Hellenic Republic*, ICSID, Case No. ARB/14/16). The *Vattenfall* Case against Germany is well known. Slowly, the boot is getting onto the wrong foot and those who get kicked will be the developed states.

[19] Necessity was successful in later awards in respect of the specific period of the crisis. *El Paso* v. *Argentina; LG&E* v. *Argentina; Continental Casualty* v. *Argentina*.

[20] In the *Torrey Canyon* incident, there were alternative means other than the most onerous one of bombing the container. It could have been dragged away to the high seas. The *Caroline* incident was in the context of the use of force, where the law is usually narrowly stated.

6.1 THE DEFENCES IN THE TREATIES AND CUSTOMARY LAW 311

relating to the absence of alternative means so circumscribes the application of necessity that it cannot be based on sound authority. The situation of necessity requires quick action by the state in difficult circumstances threatening public injury.

The idea that the less onerous course must be followed for the defence of necessity to succeed is unsupported by authority. It is a feature of codification that the view taken of the law, even when erroneous, becomes frozen in the code and comes to be applied. In domestic law, necessity arises largely in situations where a person is faced with alternatives, all of which have disastrous consequences. But the law excuses on the basis of the fact that the defendant had been placed in an unfortunate situation not of his making. It recognizes that the choice has to be made in the context of the situation and that subjective considerations have a role to play. 'Detached reflection cannot be had in the presence of an uplifted knife.'[21] The situation of necessity cannot be treated with preconceived notions. The early Argentine arbitrations set out to refuse the plea and found the ILC Draft Code on State Responsibility a convenient peg on which to hang their preconceived views.

The ILC Draft is not yet a document that has the approval of the different states of the international community through adoption at the UN General Assembly. Its elevation to a status it does not yet have is done only so as to produce desirable results. The desire to give effect to the exclusivity of investment protection found sufficient excuse in the restrictive statement of the defence of necessity in the ILC Draft Code. The Code has been criticized as not containing a reflection of customary law, but is an effort at drafting what the members of the commission considered desirable.[22] There was an uncritical acceptance of whether the ILC Draft Article 25 on necessity in fact stated customary international law. The Draft Article prioritized the 'essential interest of the State towards which the obligation exists' by requiring that the measure taken was the 'only way' of dealing with the situation of necessity. It does not fit in with any logical theory of necessity found in domestic

---

[21] Holmes J. in *Brown v. United States* (1921) 256 US 335. Holmes J. was dealing with self-defence, a situation of necessity as the offender is faced with the alternative of submitting to the act or resisting it. The exculpatory defence is available where he chooses the more damaging alternative over the alternative of retreat, which would have not involved any violence. The law does not require retreat, though the common law once did.

[22] David Caron, 'The ILC Articles on State Responsibility: The Paradoxical Relationship Between Form and Authority', (2002) 96 *American Journal of International Law* 857.

analogues. Neither is the statement supported by the authorities cited as constituting customary international law.[23]

There is little wonder that a schism should open up among the different tribunals that considered disputes arising from the Argentine economic crisis as to the relevance of necessity as an excuse for the measures Argentina took with regard to the crisis. The soundness of stating substantive principles of international law in the form of a code that provides for all circumstances must be doubted in the context of the Argentine cases. Progressively, tribunals have seen the need to move away from the law as stated in the Draft Code on State Responsibility.

The inconsistent awards have shaken the rules in the Draft Code that there should be no alternatives or that the state pleading necessity should not have contributed to it. The basis of the rules in terms of international law in general, and the applicability of the rules to situations of economic crisis in particular, need reassessment. Subjective considerations of the decision-makers faced with choice enter the equation. These are debatable situations of a moral choice. In an economic crisis, the choice is more than moral in that the continued functioning of a state, its security and the well-being of its people are involved. This was so in the Argentinian crisis, where there was a genuine political and economic crisis generated by the outflow of funds that had to be stemmed.

If general principles are a source of international law, the exclusion of necessity when an alternative is present is unsound. The propriety of the choice made, given the urgency of the situation, is a difficult one, which would depend on the precise circumstances. In economic crises, it would depend on many factors, including political acceptability of the choice, the ideological preferences of the government and the international situation. In the moment of tension, bringing the foreign investor into the calculation would have been the least of the worries of the state facing

---

[23] Jurgen Kurz, 'Adjudging the Exceptional at International Investment Law: Security, Public Order and Financial Crisis', (2010) 59 *International & Comparative Law Quarterly* 325, at p. 337, dealing with necessity and its broader meaning in WTO law. Also see Andrew Mitchell and Caroline Henckels, 'Variations on a Theme: Comparing the Concept of Necessity in International Investment Law and WTO Law', (2013) *Chicago Journal of International Law* 93. William Burke-White, 'Investment Protection in Extraordinary Times', (2008) 48 *Virginia Journal of International Law* 307; Andrea Bjorklund, 'Emergency Exceptions: State of Necessity and Force Majeure', in Peter Muchlinski *et al.* (eds.), *Oxford Handbook of International Investment Law* (Oxford University Press, 2008), p. 373; Alvarez, *The Public International Law Regime Governing International Investment*; Diane Desierto, *Necessity and National Emergency Clauses: Sovereignty in Modern Treaty Interpretation* (Leiden: Brill, 2012).

6.1 THE DEFENCES IN THE TREATIES AND CUSTOMARY LAW 313

the public necessity. The tribunals mandate unrealistically that the foreign investment should have been among the foremost considerations. It was not so for the United States or Europe during the global economic crisis; there is little reason why it should be so for Argentina. The cases of Malaysia and Indonesia show the existence of alternatives. The IMF accepted that its prescriptions for Indonesia succeeded only as well as the different method of insulating its economy adopted by Malaysia. The analysis of the existence of alternatives to exclude the defence of necessity by a tribunal, which sits later in comfortable surroundings, is an invidious one.

The rule that the respondent state should not have contributed to the necessity is equally unpalatable. It is difficult to see how the law becomes part of international law. It does not constitute a general principle of law. The respondent state would always be an actor in the situation leading to an economic crisis. In the case of Argentina, it was led into the crisis by following prescriptions of the IMF in adopting liberalization of trade. The United States was led into crisis by imprudent policies based on market fundamentalism. The BIT programme of Argentina itself was in consequence of such a policy change. It had followed the IMF prescriptions throughout the course of the decade, including the period when the crisis broke out. It would be difficult to accuse Argentina of having brought about the crisis. The rule, if it has any validity, cannot be inflexibly applied unless there was some atrocious departure from the accepted norms of dealing with the situation. None could be found in the case of Argentina. The tribunals erred repetitively with a neoliberal conviction that investment protection trumps other considerations.

The law on necessity could be clearly manipulated to suit different levels. The level of the crisis could be underplayed.[24] The strict need for an absence of alternatives could be stipulated. The state could be held to have brought about the situation. The different tribunals adopted variations of this in refusing the plea of necessity. The clear division between the groups of cases indicates another area of disagreement between tribunals. Explanations have to be sought for the division of opinion. Predisposition to results conducive to investment protection did play a role in outcomes.

Situations of necessity involve the making of policies and the taking of measures in pursuance of them. They necessarily involve the exercise of regulatory controls. As the law moves away from strict liability towards

---

[24] See *Case Concerning the Gabikovo-Nagymaros Project* [1997] ICJ Rep. 7, n. 14, above.

recognizing the right of the state to exercise controls over the situation of turmoil, the issue becomes not one of a defence but of whether the substantive law raising responsibility simply does not apply to the measures that are taken not because they are subject to a defence, but because they were in the exercise of the inherent rights of regulatory sovereignty of the state that fall outside the investment treaties. The defence of necessity, as stated in the ILC Draft, does not capture the situation. The inherent rights of the state could resurface in situations of necessity. It does in the case of self-defence, a species of necessity, which is described as an inherent right in the UN Charter. Such rights revive when the life of the state is threatened and a situation of necessity presents itself. Primordial rights, which precede treaty obligations, return to the state when it is in crisis. To say that necessity does not arise when there are less onerous alternatives is as untenable.

The Argentinian arbitrations are an unflattering episode in the life of investment arbitration and, indeed, of international law. The repeated exclusion of the defence by a series of similarly constituted arbitral tribunals resulted in a situation where there was little opportunity for reconsideration of the issue by fresh minds. It was an instance of a wilful force leading the law into a destructive mode. The situation was eagerly seized upon to bring fifty-two arbitrations against Argentina, a state suffering from an economic and political crisis from which it is yet to emerge.[25] The image created of investment treaties was not one of leading to economic development but to economic disaster, with arbitrators and lawyers circling overhead to add to the ruin of a state. Damages running into several billion dollars was not helpful to Argentina in resurfacing from a crisis. The awards brought about an evident tension between neoliberal concern for absolute investment protection dressed in the altruistic garb of global governance, and the rule of law and the sovereign right of the state to protect the public interest in economic survival. Argentina had a heavy price to pay for rejecting the Calvo Doctrine and embracing neoliberalism.

6.2   The expansion of defences

The relevance of the Argentine cases lies in the manner in which the tribunals applied the necessity defence drawn from outside the

---

[25] See the statement of the Government of Argentina indicating an absence of success in restructuring its loans and judgment debts. *The Guardian*, 24 June 2014.

6.2 THE EXPANSION OF DEFENCES 315

investment treaties, indicating different approaches to the creation of defences. Sensitivity to the ground situation that prevailed in Argentina would have found that at least some of the situations that the ICJ identified as constituting situations of necessity were present. The ICJ said these condition existed in situations that involved 'grave danger to the existence of the state itself, to its political and economic survival, the maintenance of conditions in which its essential services can function, the keeping of its internal peace, the survival of part of its population, the ecological preservation of all or some of its territory'.[26] The Argentinian economic crisis involved many of the conditions that the ICJ had identified.

The cases, which upheld necessity, established the fact that the treaties are enmeshed within international law and have to operate within the general system of international law. This ensures that the treaty has to be interpreted in a manner consistent with the principles of international law. The Vienna Convention mandates through Article 31(2)(c) that the context in which any treaty is to be interpreted shall include 'relevant rules of international law applicable in the relations between the parties'. Argentina continuously probed the extent to which it could seek defences outside the investment treaty in other principles of international law.

It is the principle of context of treaty interpretation that provides an opening for the recognition of a wide array of defences that are not stated in the treaties but are present in 'the relevant rules of international law'. These 'relevant rules' have become the basis of the new defences to liability under the investment treaties. In the formulation of its prescriptions, neoliberal concepts have always relied on international law. Thus, the theory of internationalization was that international law applied to the foreign investment contract. Article 42 of the ICSID Convention recognizes the applicability of international law to the foreign investment contract. The investment treaty system works in the context of public international law. The relevance of public international law was accepted at a time when international law had not developed strong competing norms relating to the environment, human rights and other interests. When it did, the inconsistency between the competing interests within public international law had to be resolved. This was done, as explained earlier, through the recognition of new defences.

Increasingly, the newer investment treaties, dealt with in Chapter 7, are including these defences in the treaties. The new defences have enormous

---

[26] *Case Concerning the Gabikovo-Nagymaros Project* [1997] ICJ Rep. 7.

consequences for investment treaties. First, they are applicable to investment treaties, even if they do not include them as defences. Being based on international law, the treaty has to be considered in the context of the whole of international law. Secondly, as they are independently applicable, they may expand and supplement the defences that have already been stated in the investment treaties. The implications of these propositions for investment arbitration are significant. They will move investment arbitration from its existing mooring in inflexible investment protection to consideration of public interest issues that contradict the interest of investment protection in each situation of a dispute. It will complete a transfer of investment arbitration from commercial moorings into the arena of public law. Developing states have consistently argued that the mooring of investment arbitration should be in public law, which tends to emphasize the defeasibility of interests of smaller groups in society to the interests of society as a whole.[27] The usefulness of the treaty system and investment arbitration in the system to foreign investors will be significantly undermined as a result. Yet one could expect neoliberalism to be kept alive despite the changes. One can see that principles of public law favourable to foreign investment are introduced into the subject to counterbalance the developments that favour public interest arguments. There was the rule on legitimate expectations and now there is the proportionality rule. In both instances, the principles were selectively and wrongly used. Yet the game is to keep one step ahead, and arbitrators partial to foreign investment have been attempting to do just that.

Those who argued for the primacy of international law as the basis for inflexible investment protection have been hoist on their own petard as international law has quickly developed competing normative interests, which are perceived as superior to investment protection and as involving not merely bilateral rights and obligations, but multilateral rights and obligations owed to the entire international community. Reconciling these multilateral rights with the bilateral rights created by investment treaties will be a future problem in the area of investment protection. The existence of these multilateral rights will result in defences to liability under investment treaties. Such defences are already stated in the newer investment treaties. But the defences may come to be more extensive than

---

[27] The Western liberal tradition contests this. Studies of European constitutional law are resorted to in bolstering up neoliberal viewpoints in international investment law. But the propositions so created do not have universal validity.

6.2 THE EXPANSION OF DEFENCES 317

those expressly stated in the treaties as the defences operate not only on the basis of the statement in the treaties, but also outside the treaties in general customary international law.

One must have regard to these new defences as they exist in customary international law, which can be drawn on by the respondent state in constructing its own defences to avoid responsibility. These possible customary law defences apply to treaties that do not contain any reference to them. When treaties contain references to them, it must be taken that the reference in the treaty is not exhaustive as to the extent of the defence, which can keep developing in accordance with the evolution of customary international law.

The defences are based on the existence of a hierarchy of obligations, the investment obligations standing lower than multilateral. Where the obligations flow from *ius cogens* norms, clearly, the investment treaty obligations can offer no resistance as they lose force in the face of *ius cogens* obligations. Thus, where the foreign investor had practiced torture,[28] the termination of his investment cannot in any way be questioned under an investment treaty as the treaty obligations lose all force in face of the state's *ius cogens* obligation to prevent torture and the investor's obligation not to use it.[29] Where there are lesser multilateral obligations, they may lend weight to the argument of the state that it was effecting a regulatory taking when a claim is based on expropriation, or that it was acting fairly when a claim is based on the fair and equitable standard. The link between regulatory takings and such defences must be explored as they provide a basis for the identification of takings as regulatory. Likewise, they have an impact on the fairness element in the fair and equitable standard as it would always be fair that the state should give precedence to its multilateral obligations serving global interests. The third possibility is that the international law on the relevant subject, whether it be human rights, the environment or cultural property, has been received into the domestic law through legislation if it is a host state that follows a monist incorporation theory, or has been received through statute into domestic law if it follows a transformation theory of reception of international law. In this case, international law as part

---

[28] These allegations against foreign investors were common in Alien Tort Claims Act cases. The situation in *Doe* v. *Unocal*, where torture and rape, carried out with the complicity of the company, were alleged against a US company, is subject to the jurisdiction of US courts even under the new ruling in *Kiobel* v. *Royal Dutch Shell Petroleum Co.* (2013) 569 US.

[29] The present writer made such an argument in 2001 in Sornarajah, *The Settlement of Foreign Investment Disputes*.

318   BACKLASH THROUGH DEFENCES

of domestic law will always be relevant for the foreign investment trans-action. An investor is bound by domestic laws and can hardly plead wrongful treatment under a treaty if he had violated such laws. The future relevance of public international principles that stand outside the invest-ment treaty principles require examination.

6.2.1 Human rights obligations and investor rights

There is an increasing literature that addresses the conflict between the human rights obligations of a state and its obligations under investment treaties.[30] The major view within international investment law has been that international investment law[31] should be kept insulated from the rest of international law, despite the fact that the two basic foundations of the international investment, the internationalization of the foreign investment contract and the series of investment treaties, are founded in international law and seek to draw legitimacy from it. The technique of fragmentation has aided the instrumentalist vision of the law that empha-sized foreign investment protection. Judge Simma spoke of a prejudice towards commercial solutions 'in the genes' of arbitrators who may regard human rights law as 'intruding in their purely autonomous field, with its ground rules being determined by neo-liberal thought'.[32]

But the onslaught of new forces, such as the NGOs, will ensure that the insulation of the rest of international law is not maintained, and that the interests of a group of stakeholders with vested interests in fragmentation and the separate development of international investment law do not succeed. The developments in the area of international human rights law have been rapid. International investment law, in its present neolib-eral phase, is also of relatively new vintage, with its many doctrines, particularly those relating to the fair and equitable standard, being newly formulated in arbitral awards. The standing of these awards in creating law are weak as opposed to the multilateral instruments in which human rights norms are contained. Even when aspirational, statements

---

[30] Dupuy et al. (eds.), Human Rights in International Arbitration; Bruno Simma, 'Foreign Investment Arbitration: A Place for Human Rights', (2011) 60 International & Comparative Law Quarterly 573.

[31] As opposed to the international law on foreign investment, which seeks to view the subject in the light of international law as a whole. The rival tendency in the literature concentrates on international investment law with a heavy emphasis on investment-based treaty arbitration and the principles that are drawn from it.

[32] Simma, 'Foreign Investment Arbitration: A Place for Human Rights'.

in human rights treaties have a stronger claim to authority than the views of arbitrators.

The relevance of international human rights law stems from the fact that multilateral treaties and other documents on human rights commits both the home state and the host state to the protection and promotion of human rights. They also become globally binding because they constitute customary international law. When states enter into bilateral investment treaties, they carry these commitments along with them. Their capacity to enter into bilateral or regional treaties must be restricted by the existence of these multilateral obligations. States must be taken as not having made obligations contrary to these multilateral obligations. The obligations are binding on foreign investors as well so that if they violate them, there would be liability arising from these violations.[33] The rights under the bilateral investments treaties cannot be exercised in a manner that violates the principles of human rights law.

The home state cannot protect the rights of nationals who have violated human rights either through diplomatic intervention or through means of a treaty. Increasingly, international law will move towards imposing an obligation on home states to prosecute those who have violated human rights extraterritorially. The US Supreme Court recognized the jurisdiction of the courts over American multinational corporations that violate international law while operating in foreign countries under the Alien Tort Claims Act. English courts have recognized the civil liability of parent companies of subsidiaries that cause damage through their operations in foreign states.[34] In these circumstances, it cannot be said that home states create rights in their investors who violate human rights while operating abroad to have their investments protected by treaty principles. They are under a duty to ensure that access to their courts is permitted to those affected by human rights violations in the home states of their foreign investors. Some of human rights law consists of *ius cogens* principles that make inconsistent treaties invalid to the extent of the conflict. Likewise, the nationals themselves could not assert any derived rights under investment treaties if they had acted in violation of human rights principles. Good faith principles

---

[33] Increasingly, international law will move towards the imposition of criminal responsibility on multinational companies and their executives who violate standards of human rights laws.

[34] The High Court has ruled that Shell Petroleum is liable in respect of pollution caused by oil seepage from pipelines affecting the lives of people in surrounding areas (20 June 2014).

require that the foreign investor who claims rights under investment treaties has clean hands. He certainly cannot invoke standards like the fair and equitable standard when fairness is evidently against him as a result of his conduct in violating human rights.

Increasingly, there are home state responsibilities that arise from the operations of multinational corporations whilst abroad, particularly in situations of violations of human rights.[35] At the least, they must ensure that multinational corporations do not take harmful technology out of their states for investment abroad, and they should provide access to justice to those affected by the violations of human rights by multinational corporations.[36] The role of the state in using extraterritorial powers to control abuse of human rights by its nationals is also an increasing phenomenon in international law.[37] Such a role encompasses a corporate national as well. The growing acceptance of these obligations is inconsistent with a home state's rights to protect any corporate national that violates human rights abroad. It may be possible to construct an argument that the home state should withdraw the derivative right of the foreign investor to a remedy under an investment treaty if he had violated an obligation of human rights. In an international law system that increasingly recognizes bystander liability of third states, it would be difficult to argue that the home state of the foreign investor has no duty to prevent its corporate national from complicity in human rights violations through its subsidiaries in other countries. There is an argument for the direct state responsibility of a home state which does not protect the citizens of the host state of its corporate national from human rights violations by its corporate national.

Similar considerations require the host state to act consistently with its human rights obligations. There would be precedent obligations, both in international law and in its own constitutional law, requiring it not to enter into contracts that affect the human rights of its people. The validity of such contracts may have to be subject to human rights audits.[38] Several agencies providing finance for projects require that such an audit is

---

[35] Muthucumaraswamy Sornarajah, 'Linking State Responsibility for Certain Harms Caused by Corporate Nationals Abroad to Civil Recourse in the Legal Systems of Home States', in Craig Scott (ed.), *Torture as Tort* (Oxford: Hart, 2001), p. 491.

[36] The recent decision of the US Supreme Court in *Kiobel* v. *Royal Dutch Shell Petroleum Co.* (2013) 569 US, leaves this proposition unaffected.

[37] This right has been explored in connection with the operation of military personnel whilst on overseas action. But there is no reason why similar principles should not apply to other nationals, including corporate nationals.

[38] Simma, 'Foreign Investment Arbitration: A Place for Human Rights'.

6.2 THE EXPANSION OF DEFENCES 321

made. The onus is greater on the part of the host state as it is subject to human rights obligations created by international law. They are binding both as part of domestic law as well as of international law.

If a human rights violation involving a *ius cogens* principle is involved, clearly there would be no liability in the host state. Rather, the liability of the foreign investor needs to be determined by a tribunal other than an investment tribunal. *Desert Line* v. *Yemen* involves the possibility of genocide as an example of such a dispute. There could be similar examples as where the dispute involves torture or calamities, such as the Bhopal disaster brought about through faulty transfer of technology by the foreign investor that affected the lives of many thousands through massive suffering. Awards have recognised that contracts that include slavery or bribery are inherently invalid.[39] Though the notion of non-arbitrability has not been raised, it is clear that an investment tribunal is inherently incapable of considering such a dispute. Not only is there a requirement that the tribunal should consist of experts in international law in the relevant field, a tribunal that has been set up to consider a narrow issue pertaining to foreign investment should be considered incapable of dealing with broader issues of fundamental concern to the international community.

The second stage at which it becomes relevant is at the jurisdictional stage. Where the predominant features of a dispute disclose that the measures complained of were taken to deal with a human rights issue, there is reason for the tribunal to consider whether there is a case to be made for the violation of the treaty at the jurisdictional phase on the ground that the dispute does not implicate wholly the violation of the investment treaty, but the violation of human rights law over which it has no jurisdiction. Thirdly, as pointed out earlier, at the stage of merits the fact that the measures taken were a response to the violation of human rights within its treaty will always characterize the measure as regulatory. It will counter a claim of expropriation or a violation of the fair and equitable standard simply on the ground that it was necessary to interfere with the rights of the foreign investor either as a sanction for past infringement of human rights of its citizens or to prevent a future violation of such rights in circumstances the foreign investor had set in motion circumstances that would lead to such violation.

---

[39] Judge Lagegren in the *Argentine Bribery* Case, ICC Award 1110, is often cited as authority. For the invalidity of a foreign investment contract based on bribery, see *World Duty Free Ltd* v. *Kenya*, ICSID, Case No. ARB/00/7 (4 October 2006).

Clearly, the relevance of human rights law to foreign investment can no longer be overlooked. There are sufficiently powerful new actors who would ensure that human rights concerns are adequately aired both prior to the making of the investments, during its operation and at the stage of the dispute. The *Cochahamba* water dispute, which led to *Aguas del Tunari* v. *Bolivia*, is instructive of the extent of the role that such NGOs have. As much as the existence of investment treaties may create a regulatory chill, the spotlight that NGOs bring to the malpractices of multinational corporations deters them from bringing arbitrations and from withdrawing from pending arbitrations. NGOs also are active by intervening in arbitrations through *amicus curiae* briefs which are becoming increasingly permitted.

But, so far, the investment tribunals have not considered human rights arguments seriously. The neoliberal predispositions of arbitrators ensure that investment protection is kept distinct from human rights considerations. This has not prevented them from using human rights norms favourable to foreign investment protection such as the rule on proportionality to limit the scope of regulatory expropriation, which is borrowed from European human rights law. As Simma pointed out, arbitrators regard the system as autonomous, 'with its ground rules provided by neoliberal thought'. There is little scope for human rights within this system unless its principles support the neoliberal regime. In the many awards that human rights arguments were raised, they received scant attention. The necessity defence in the Argentinian cases involved humanitarian aspects as the crisis caused widespread hunger. In several cases, there were specific arguments made by Argentina based on human rights.[40] They were rejected on the ground that these arguments related to 'treaties outside the field of investment protection'.[41] Yet arbitrators used the same treaties outside the field of investment protection, principally the European Convention on Human Rights, in support of investment protection.[42] In *Glamis Gold Ltd* v. *United*

---

[40] *Azurix* v. *Argentina*, Annulment Award (2006), at para. 128; *Siemens* v. *Argentina* (2007), at para. 79.

[41] *Azurix*, Annulment Award, at para. 128. The tendency in investment arbitration is to deny a conflict. In *Suez* v. *Argentina*, the tribunal held that: 'Argentina was subject to both international obligations ... Argentina's human rights obligations and its investment treaty obligations were not inconsistent, contradictory and mutually exclusive.'

[42] Apart from the proportionality rule derived from European law, the notion that arbitration awards are property rights used in *Saipem* v. *Bangladesh* ICSID, Case No. ARB/05/07 (30 June 2009) and *White Industries* v. *India*, UNCITRAL, Arbitration (30 November 2011) are derived from European human rights law.

6.2 THE EXPANSION OF DEFENCES 323

States,[43] the tribunal heard and discussed submissions relating to indigenous rights, but did not take them into account in its decisions.

A separate explanation for this phenomena, besides the explanation based on predisposition to neoliberal solutions, is the view that arbitrators have been socialized into a culture that accepts investment protection to the exclusion of other considerations.[44] This argument is similar to the view that commercial arbitrators are prone to taking pro-business views as commercial stability is their primary consideration. It could well be that institutional structures, like the ICSID system, within which investment arbitrators work also induce choices that favour investment protection. The behaviour of the arbitrators is learnt behaviour as they come from a small circle and may be imitating each other's attitudes.

A neoliberal argument seeking to counter recourse to human rights arguments is the argument that the foreign investment protection also involves a human right, the right to property. This argument cannot be taken seriously. As pointed out earlier when considering expropriation,[45] the statements of the right to property do not exist in international documents such as the International Covenant on Civil and Political Rights, and cannot be considered universal rights. When they do appear in regional documents, they are heavily qualified and subjected to the public interest. The best of these documents permit recourse to protection by regional tribunals only after local remedies have been exhausted. The recourse to the argument that the right to property is a human right is a last gasp argument.

Quite apart from the array of human rights that have been articulated in several international documents, there will be a recovery of two broad notions that were eclipsed during the neoliberal period. The retreat of neoliberalism will see the resurfacing of principles associated with the NIEO. Neoliberalism had eclipsed the NIEO, but despite the gleeful reports of its demise, the NIEO remained dormant during the heyday of neoliberalism. It will find resurgence through its principal doctrines,[46] particularly at a time when there is a revival of concerns with global

---

[43] UNCITRAL Arbitration (8 June 2009).

[44] Moshe Hirsch, 'Investment Tribunals and Human Rights Treaties: A Sociological Perspective', in Freya Baetens (ed.), *Investment Law within International Law: Integrationist Perspectives* (Cambridge University Press, 2013), p. 85. Two distinct communities populate human rights and investment protection. There is a cultural distance between them.

[45] See Chapter 4.

[46] Sornarajah, 'The Return of the NIEO and the Retreat of Neo-Liberal International Law'.

324 BACKLASH THROUGH DEFENCES

justice and a cosmopolitan concern with redressing global poverty.[47] Consequently, two ideas of the NIEO will be advanced in the form of human rights arguments.

6.2.1.1 The doctrine of permanent sovereignty over natural resources

Permanent sovereignty over natural resources was once scorned in arbitration as *lex ferenda* and as a rhetorical notion without legal substance.[48] The impact that such a doctrine would have on the sanctity of the foreign investment contract was the reason for giving it short shrift. But the effluxion of time has ensured its acceptance. The ICJ, in the *Armed Activities Case (Congo v. Uganda)*,[49] referred to the UN General Assembly resolutions embodying the principle, recognized its importance and declared it to be a principle of customary international law. Though it did not have occasion to use the principle in the case of the despoliation of conflict diamonds in the Congo by Ugandan troops, it recognized, on the basis of the African Charter on Human Rights,[50] that 'the dispossessed people shall have the right to the lawful recovery of its property as well as adequate compensation'.

Some authors regard the doctrine as constituting *ius cogens*. The view that an investment made in violation of a *ius cogens* right cannot be protected has been stated in at least one investment award. The *Phoenix* Tribunal stated that 'nobody would suggest that ICSID protection should be granted to investments made in violation of the most fundamental rules of protection of human rights like investments made in pursuance of torture or genocide or in support of slavery or trafficking of human organs'.[51] In many of the cases brought under the Alien Tort Claims Act, the international wrong that is often alleged to provide jurisdiction has been violations of *ius cogens* principles. It is quite likely that such violations, if they did occur, will be pleaded, *in limine*, to challenge the jurisdiction of the tribunal.

Where the right of a people to permanent sovereignty over natural resources is violated, as where an elite in power in a state transfers control to a foreign investor in terms that turn out to be disadvantageous to the people, the possibility of recovery of the ownership of the resources

---

[47] On the increasing literature on global justice and poverty, see Amartya Sen, *The Idea of Justice* (London: Penguin, 2005); Pogge, *World Poverty and Human Rights*.
[48] Arbitrator Dupuy in *Texaco v. Libya*.   [49] [2005] ICJ Rep. 168, para. 244.
[50] Article 21(3) of the African Charter on Human Rights.
[51] *Phoenix Action Ltd v. Czech Republic*, ICSID, Case No. ARB/06/5 (15 April 2009).

6.2 THE EXPANSION OF DEFENCES

through cancellation of the contractual rights of the foreign investor would arise. The conflict has to be resolved. In the past, the conflict would have been resolved by emphasizing contractual rights. This was at a time when the status of the doctrine on permanent sovereignty was considered *lex ferenda*. The status of the doctrine as a principle of customary international law is now clearer. The new status of the doctrine introduces considerable uncertainty into the law. In a situation of a contract made in connection with a vital resource with an unrepresentative government, the argument for the defeasibility of the contract at the instance of a later, democratically elected government will be an attractive proposition. There are cases that indicate that resource contracts made in mandated territories could not be considered binding. The reasoning involved is that the mandatory power does not act in consideration of the interests of the people of the mandated territory. That reasoning has application to situations where a state acts to the detriment of its people's interests.

The doctrine makes the state a trustee of the natural resources with a duty to ensure that the resources are used for the benefit of its people. It becomes relevant at two principal stages. First, the state party making the contract in respect of the natural resources must ensure that the contract is not to the detriment of its economy and its environment. Secondly, it must ensure that the operation relating to the extraction of the resources, its subsequent transport and sale are also in accordance with the interests of the people and future generations. The nature of the contracts that are made and the procedures that are to be followed in domestic law now come to reflect these interests. Production-sharing agreements in the oil sector reflect these different concerns and embody within tem the constitutional doctrines that are based on the doctrine of permanent sovereignty as well as the domestic law structures, which have been influenced by the doctrine.[52] Where the foreign investor does not conform to these procedures or fraudulently escapes following these procedures, the validity of its transactions will be affected. The great danger is in situations where the foreign investor is able to make these transactions with elites controlling the government. Since the foreign investor profits from this situation of proximity with the elite, the expectations he forms in the context of that relationship could not be considered legitimate. In such circumstances, succeeding governments seeking to contest these

---

[52] The constitutions of major resource-producing countries contain references to permanent sovereignty over natural resources.

326   BACKLASH THROUGH DEFENCES

arrangements would be acting legitimately. In the resources sector, the right of a people over natural resources will increase in significance. In connection with other rights, such as those relating to the environment, the potency of this right will give the state adequate control over the exploitation of natural resources as well as of ensuring that the foreign investor does not act to the detriment of its economy or its environment. Legal changes that are made consistent with the doctrine will be *prima facie* valid to the extent necessary to give effect to the purposes behind the doctrine. A limit on the doctrine is that the initial contractual obligation should not be excessively affected beyond what is justified by the need to assert the objectives of the doctrine, considering the fact that the making of the foreign investment contract was fully consistent with the doctrine.

The doctrine works in tandem with the principle of self-determination and the rights of tribal and other local communities. Often, it is the lands of these tribal groups and their lifestyles that are affected. Within the larger context of the state, these tribal and local communities have the right to determine their lifestyles and not have them violated by foreign investors or for that matter local investors. There is a duty both on the domestic state as well as the rest of the international community to protect the rights of these groups. In investment law, conflicts between these rights and the rights of such groups have appeared as is evident from the facts of *Glamis Gold Ltd* v. *United States*,[53] in which the area of the mining concession straddled the ancestral sites of the tribal Indians. Where, as in *Glamis*, the host state takes measures to protect the interests of the tribal people, the host state would be acting in reliance of human rights norms and its measures would be clothed with legality.[54]

The contrast is often made with the manner in which the Inter-American Court of Human Rights (IACHR) treated the rights of indigenous people with the way in which investment tribunals discard their relevance. In *Sowhoyamaxa Indigenous Community* v. *Paraguay*,[55] the IACHR recognized the collective rights of the tribal people to their ancestral land, denying the validity of rights transferred by the state to the foreign investor. The Court dismissed the argument that an investment treaty between Paraguay and Germany protected the foreign investor, a German national, on the ground that the Inter-American

---

[53] UNCITRAL Arbitration (8 June 2009).
[54] Judith Levine, 'Interaction of International Investment Arbitration and the Rights of Indigenous People', in Freya Baetens (ed.), *Investment Law within International Law: Integrationist Perspectives* (Cambridge University Press, 2013), p. 106.
[55] IACHR Judgment (29 March 2006).

6.2 THE EXPANSION OF DEFENCES

Convention on Human Rights should take precedence over bilateral investment treaties. The lands could be expropriated and given back to the tribal people, the Court opined, as such expropriation would be in the public interest and would not, on that ground, violate the investment treaty. Here, a 'bright line' for the demarcation of the limits of regulatory expropriation was being drawn. The Court also subscribed to the notion of a hierarchy of rights, holding that the enforcement of a bilateral investment treaty 'should always be compatible with the American Convention, which is a multilateral treaty on human rights that stands in a class of its own and that generates rights for individual human beings and does not depend entirely on reciprocity among States'.

The rights extend potentially to all minority groups which live on their traditional homelands. The issue is also tangled with a potential right to secession as the non-recognition of these rights by the state may strengthen claims to secession. It is therefore in the interests of the host state to ensure the protection of the rights of the traditional communities tied to land when there is a contemplation of alienation of that land to foreign investors. The host state must first examine the legality of such alienation both in terms of its own laws and in terms of international law.

6.2.2   The right to development

This right too received cold treatment from Western international lawyers when first expounded. The view was that human rights consisted of individual rights as, indeed, it did in the Western tradition, and that it could not consist of group rights. As in the case of the doctrine of permanent sovereignty over natural resources, the overwhelming acceptance of it by states, institutions and writers has made this original hostility of little substance. The right to development is now recognized so that the obligation to ensure that economic development eradicating food shortages and hunger is one that rests on the whole of humanity.[56] Coupled with the notion of sustainable development, the notion of a right to development gains even greater traction.

Specific reference is made in documents linking the obligations of foreign investors and the right to economic development. The linkage is evident in the following passage in the conclusion of the Working

---

[56] Stephen Marks, *The Politics of the Possible. The Way Ahead for the Right to Development: Dialogue on Globalization* (Berlin: Friedrich Ebert Stiftung, 2011); Bunn, *The Right to Development and International Economic Law.*

328   BACKLASH THROUGH DEFENCES

Group on the Right to Development which suggest that foreign investment should promote the Millennium Development Goals. It stated that
the right:

> implies that foreign direct investment (FDI) should contribute to local
> and national development in a responsible manner, that is, in ways that
> are conducive to social development, protect the environment, and
> respect the rule of law and fiscal obligations in the host countries. The
> principles underlying the right to development, as mentioned above,
> further imply that all parties involved, i.e., investors and recipient coun-
> tries, have responsibilities to ensure that profit considerations do not
> result in crowding out human rights protection. The impact of FDI
> should, therefore, be taken into account when evaluating progress in
> Goal 8 in the context of the right to development.

More recently, UNCTAD made a study of the relevance of foreign
investment to the notion of sustainable development.[57] It suggested
new policies which will create synergies between foreign investment
policies and economic development, foster responsible investor behaviour by incorporating corporate social responsibility and ensure policy
effectiveness. It advocates a 'balanced approach between the pursuit of
purely economic growth objectives by means of investment liberalization
and promotion, on the one hand, and the need to protect people and
the environment on the other'.[58] The idea of balance is the flavour of the
day, and UNCTAD dutifully follows the beaten path in this but, it
nevertheless recognizes the need 'to protect the people and the environment'. The criticism, of course, is that it seeks to marry the two inconsistent principles of liberalization of foreign investment flows through
investment protection with the state's right to regulate and to impose
standards of corporate responsibility. In the old days, UNCTAD, in
formulating a Code of Conduct on Multinational Corporations, stuck
to one stance without trying to accommodate other possible stances.
UNCTAD itself has gone through periods of evolution in which it has
taken different stances. Nevertheless, UNCTAD's *World Investment
Report* (2012), recognizes the fact that sustainable development is an
objective that now drives the law in the field of foreign investment.
One important component of sustainable development would be the
protection of the rights of people to the natural resources of their state.

---

[57] UNCTAD, *Investment Policy Framework for Sustainable Development* (Geneva:
UNCTAD, 2012).
[58] At p. 8.

6.2 THE EXPANSION OF DEFENCES 329

The international law on development draws its strength from a long assertion of the need for the fundamental restructuring of the international economy, beginning with the UN General Assembly resolutions on the NIEO. Though there were gleeful proclamations of the demise of the NIEO, they were greatly exaggerated. The NIEO never went away. The principles of the NIEO are deeply embedded in the domestic laws of most developing states.[59] Though displaced by the fervour for neoliberalism, the ideas of the NIEO lived on and would be revived in the form of the right to development, the Millennium Goals and, more directly, in recent declarations of the General Assembly requiring the further study of the NIEO.[60] The NIEO's aspirations have always remained latent within international law simply because of the fact that inequalities that exist within the system of international law are a permanent blot on the system.[61] These aspirations have now resurfaced with the failure of neoliberalism and the global economic crisis. They are manifested in diverse ways within international law. In the Doha Development Round, the exceptions claimed for developing countries when dealing with climate change and the dilution of intellectual property rights in the pharmaceutical sector are instances in which developing countries are joining together to assert rights. The resurgence of interest in the international law of development is an indication that the arguments for structural changes needed in the international economic order have been revived.

The legacy of the NIEO is reflected in the new moves to stabilize the right to development, both within human rights law as well as an independent and autonomous right of peoples.[62] Though in eclipse during the neoliberal era prior to the global crisis, the right to development has made a return as an articulated goal of the international community not only because of the failure of neoliberalism, but also because of the

---

[59] Thus, the notion of permanent sovereignty over natural resources is to be found in the constitutions of most resource-producing countries. It also is reflected in contracts used, such as the production-sharing agreements in the oil industry.

[60] Bunn, *The Right to Development and International Economic Law*, at p. 56, refers to the disappointment of the resurfacing of the NIEO expressed by the United States, Canada and EU after the General Assembly Resolution in 2009 reviving the NIEO. The resolution was titled 'Toward a New International Economic Order', A/Res/64/2009 (passed with 124 votes, with 50 abstentions).

[61] Jeffrey Cason, 'Whatever Happened to the New International Economic Order', in Andrew Valls (ed.), *Ethics in International Affairs: Theories and Cases* (Lanham, MD: Rowman & Littlefield, 2000), 200. ons.

[62] Muthucumaraswamy Sornarajah, 'Resurgence of the Right to Development', in Gerald McAlinn and Caslav Pejovic (eds.), *Law and Development in Asia* (London: Routledge, 2012), p. 154.

urgency given it by the NGOs fighting to end poverty and hunger in the world, as well as by writings, including those of a powerful group of political philosophers who question the morality of a world organized on the premise of materialistic progress while the majority of the people of the world live in want and starvation.[63] Economists also decry the fact that neoliberalism had increased the poverty gap. The impact that developments in the area will have on the international law of foreign investment will be significant. The foundation of the law merely on the basis of the protection of multinational corporations on the spurious and untested ground that they generate profits that would seep through to the people can no longer be the foundation for the protection of foreign investment through the law. It is an aged and weary concept that finds little traction in the present world. The right to development is inconsistent with such a basis for the law and cannot co-exist with an unrestricted idea of the absolute protection of foreign investment.

The tussle for the recognition of this conflict is already evidenced in the law. The schism in the awards relating to the definition of investment raised during the preliminary stages of jurisdictional objections indicates the difference of opinion among arbitrators as to whether economic development is a criterion of the definition of a foreign investment protected by the investment treaty.[64] Since the treaties are premised on the ground that they will promote economic development of the parties through investment protection, it is clear that an investment that is detrimental to economic development cannot be a protected investment. That logical premise may be resisted, but both investment treaties as well as the ICSID Convention were accepted by states willing to sacrifice their sovereignty in this regard only on the assumption that economic development would result from the treaties. It would be difficult to accept the view that an investment should be protected even if it cannot have such a result or even if it brought harm to the economy of the state. The right to development bolsters the view that such investment should not be protected and would therefore fall outside the ambit of investments protected by investment treaties. Arbitration tribunals do not have the jurisdiction to assume jurisdiction in respect of such investment. The right to development has the significance that it precludes jurisdiction if

---

[63] Thomas Pogge (ed.), *Freedom from Poverty as a Human Right* (Oxford University Press, 2007); Sen, *The Idea of Justice.*

[64] Diane Desierto, 'Deciding International Investment Agreement Applicability: The Development Argument in Investment', in Freya Baetens (ed.), *Investment Law within International Law: Integrationist Perspectives* (Cambridge University Press, 2013), p. 240.

it can be shown that the investment did not contribute to economic development.

The issue of development assumes significance also at the merits phase. If the evidence led during the arbitration disclosed that the investment was detrimental to the host state's development, it elevates any measure taken to end it to the status of a regulatory measure, which puts it outside the category of measures that require compensation. It enables the identification of the measure as a regulatory measure that would not involve violations of either the expropriation provision or the fair and equitable standard of the investment treaty. It enables the drawing of the bright line between regulatory measures and compensable measures of violation of treaty standards. As such, it becomes relevant at the jurisdictional stage to inquire whether there is any purpose in going to the merits phase. If the merits phase is reached, the regulatory nature of the measure will provide a defence to any cause of action that the claimant established. The right to development may also become relevant as a counterclaim in that it justifies an argument that the threat posed to the development of the state has to be factored into the assessment of any damages a state's measures may cause.

The extent to which human rights considerations will impact on liability for breaches of investment treaty obligations is still to be worked out. One can clearly witness that the process has begun. The distance that has to be travelled to bridge the gap between these two areas is remains great due to entrenched attitudes within the present institutional structures of dispute settlement. The fact is that the assertion of investment protection as the sole aim of international investment law will become progressively eroded as a result of the human rights considerations being taken into account. One must also take account of the fact that these considerations are not the only ones which assail the old position of inflexible investment protection. The fact that there are other areas that similarly cry out for consideration will make the impact of all these considerations appear. Once the breach is made, it is inevitable that all the different considerations will make their impact on foreign investment law. The impact of environmental and other considerations further weakens the traditional position.

6.3 International environmental law considerations

The objective of investment protections will increasingly clash with the aims of environmental protection, which are moving to centre stage as a

332   BACKLASH THROUGH DEFENCES

result of concern with climate change associated with massive consumption and industrialization, and the increasing concern of the law with environmental pollution. Multinational corporations have often been accused of violations of environmental standards. In the few cases relating to investment which have arisen outside the context of investment treaties, tribunals have been accommodative of the fact that a state's intervention in a foreign investment had been motivated by environmental considerations. This would be consistent with the fact that the environmental taking would have been motivated by regulatory considerations and, where there were international law rules mandating the measure, a justification would also arise on the ground that it was consistent with this obligation. This was the widely prevalent view in cases in which the conflict was between an obligation under the foreign investment contract and an obligation under domestic or international laws to protect the environment.

Thus, a World Bank tribunal had previously held that the fact that the interference with the foreign investment was for an environmental purpose justified the interference.[65] Likewise, courts have held that priority must be given to legislation seeking to protect the environmental concerns of a state, particularly when such concerns are mandated by an international convention despite the fact that the action taken would breach a foreign investment contract. On this basis, the Australian High Court justified federal legislation on the ground that it gave effect to obligations to protect the Great Barrier Reef, a protected area under the World Heritage Convention, despite the fact that it stopped sand-mining in the nearby Fraser Island under a concession given by the state government. This incident is interesting in that it posits obligations that are higher than those of investment protection and requires that the higher obligation may justify the displacing of the lower obligation. The possibility of the emergence of a general doctrine to this effect must not be discounted, given the increasing significance that environmental concerns evoke in international law. This is reflected in several multilateral agreements in the field, most of them being capable of affecting the foreign investment transaction. Environmental obligations under the relevant conventions are

---

[65] *International Bank of Washington v. OPIC* (1972) 11 ILM 1216, which involved forestry legislation interfering with a foreign investment contract.

6.3 INTERNATIONAL ENVIRONMENTAL LAW 333

stronger, with definite compliance mechanisms.[66] Diversity of views under different regimes will not help either regime if they remain autonomous and insulated. Investment arbitration's legitimacy is more likely to be undermined if it conflicts with decisions made by environmental institutions, as investment arbitrations are based on weaker mandates. But, given the tendencies within investment arbitration and its institutional structure, the likelihood of a change of mind-set to ensure the emergence of compatible positions is not high. The statement of environmental obligations in broad terms does not help as it enables arbitrators to use existing doctrines such as the proportionality doctrine to ensure investment protection, as the precise investment obligation will always be stronger than a vague environmental obligation. But with newer mechanisms making the environmental obligations stronger,[67] it could well be that a situation will emerge where the need to give effect to the environmental obligations will be more paramount.

There is an increasing literature concerning the interface between international environmental law and the international law on foreign investment.[68] The old cases were premised on the idea that certain interests, such as the protection of the environment, take precedence over the rights of individual foreign investors on the ground that they protect universal and national interests rather than those of individuals. The drawing of such a hierarchy of rights existed in the past at a time when the norms of environmental protection were not strong and may well re-emerge given the greater strength these norms have acquired and the greater global concern with the environment. But, as in the case of human rights, investment treaty arbitration began by taking a view that environmental protection must be kept separate from foreign investment protection.[69]

Investment treaties were taken as giving precedence to the rights of the investors. When the obligation to protect foreign investment arose from an investment treaty, the tribunals began to give priority to the investment treaty obligation rather than to environmental interests. This

---

[66] Elisa Morgera, 'From Corporate Social Responsibility to Accountability Mechanisms', in Rene Dupuy and Jorge Vinuales (eds.), *Harnessing Foreign Investment to Promote Environmental Protection* (Cambridge University Press, 2012), p. 320.

[67] *S. D. Myers* v. *Canada.*

[68] Dupuy and Vinuales (eds.), *Harnessing Foreign Investment to Promote Environmental Protection.*

[69] Early awards dismissed the relevance of environmental considerations. *Santa Elena* v. *Costa Rica; Marion Unglaube* v. *Costa Rica*, ICSID, Case No. ARB/08/1 (16 May 2012); but the more recent awards show sensitivity to environmental concerns.

was despite the fact that a notion of sustainable development had begun to be articulated after the Rio Declaration on the Environment in 1992, which stated that economic development should be achieved having regard to the protection of the environment. The rise of investment treaty arbitration from 1990 was a contemporary phenomenon with the rise of environmental concern. Investment arbitration was, however, promoted in isolation. It was insulated from any competing tendencies. Also, the notion of sustainable development never became specific enough to pose a threat to the obligations a state assumed under an investment treaty. The arbitration tribunal in *Santa Elena* v. *Costa Rica* stated the prevailing thinking when it noted that even takings justified on environmental grounds must be compensated as they are 'similar to any other expropriatory measures that a state may take in order to implement its policies'. Disputes such as like *Santa Elena* may also be regarded as having been decided when the effect of neoliberal thinking was at its highest.[70]

The picture changed as agitations began to be mounted that claimed that was insufficient consideration of environmental interests in investment disputes. The role of the NGOs in leading such agitations had the impact of ensuring that states began to make new treaties incorporating provisions on environmental protection as a consideration. Though originally these provisions were aspirational, their later formulations had specific obligations to take environmental interests into account in making decisions relating to foreign investment. The provisions permitted regulatory interference for environmental reasons, encouraged states not to avoid protecting the environment on the ground that there was an investment protection obligation and encouraged environmental legislation. An OECD study of investment treaties showed that nearly 90 per cent of the treaties made in 2008 contained provisions on environmental protection.[71] That being so, it will become increasingly necessary for tribunals to weigh environmental interests that required the interference of the state and to determine whether they are capable of

---

[70] The three cases, *Santa Elena, Metalclad* and *S. D. Myers*, involved facts which showed that environmental considerations may not have been the real motives behind the decisions taken by the state. Yet the wide dicta in the awards support the view that there was an attempt at insulating investment protection from other values, such as the protection of the environment.

[71] UNCTAD, *World Investment Report* (Geneva, 2014), p. 118; Suzanne Spears, 'The Quest for Policy Space in a New Generation of International Investment Agreements', (2012) 13 *Journal of International Dispute Settlement* 1037.

6.3 INTERNATIONAL ENVIRONMENTAL LAW

displacing the interest in investment protection in the treaty. While the older treaties do not contain provisions on the environment, the newer treaties give an indication as to the new thinking of the states and show a willingness to accommodate environmental factors. Though the prescriptions on environmental protection in the treaties are not strong, arbitration tribunals must pay heed to this change. It would be at the cost of imperilling the system of investment treaty arbitration if arbitrators adhered to the old view that investment protection trumps environmental considerations all the time. This is particularly so not only because investment treaties now contain environmental provisions, but because the movements in environmental protection are so rapid that they are being reflected in multilateral treaties and other instruments. It is difficult to ignore these trends. Such protection becomes relevant even if the investment treaty contains no provision on environmental protection, as the multilateral instruments which contain these standards now constitute customary law and would take precedence over investment protection.

The environmental obligation in a multilateral treaty in conflict with the investment treaty obligation may override the investment treaty obligation, depending whether it has a place higher than the investment obligation in the hierarchy of obligations. It could operate on the obligation of investment protection under the investment treaty by displacing the investment obligation on the ground that the environmental law obligation constitutes a higher norm that is binding on the state. The argument will increasingly be made that the global interests provided for by the obligations of environmental protection under customary international law should have precedence over the investment protection obligation under a bilateral investment treaty. As the argument that foreign investment flows increase as a result of investment treaties is becoming increasingly discredited, it is unlikely the investment treaty obligations will feature high in the hierarchy of treaty obligations or in the values of the international community. The construction of such a hierarchy is increasingly accepted in academic literature.[72]

International investment law has been almost purposefully developed in isolation. Some states, as well as scholars, have ensured that such compartmentalized development aids in the promotion of the sectional interest in investment protection to the detriment of the global interest

---

[72] Vinuales, *Foreign Investment and the Environment in International Law*; Kulick, *Global Public Interest in International Investment Law*.

in environmental protection, as well as the protection of human rights, labour rights, cultural rights and the rights of indigenous peoples. Textbooks on the subject largely deal with the law as developed under the investment treaties, making the subject insulated from the rest of international law. The context in which liability for investment of the aliens arose under the law on state responsibility and the controversies attached to it are quietly forgotten in the process of building up a law on inflexible investment protection. The law is divorced from the context of general international law in which it developed.

The fragmentation that was so effected furthered the neoliberal project of absolute investment protection. But there is now a shift away from such insulation of areas of international law, which had enabled powerful interests to structure the law in compartments and develop it with the esoteric expertise that they could afford to employ. The movement to end such fragmentation of international law has now emerged with vigour. The method of isolating areas of international law and developing them without reference to other obligations and to general principles of international law has been halted. Scholars have called for methods of reconciling conflicts between different legal obligations arising in different areas of international law so that the law can be developed cohesively. These developments coincide with the impact that environmental movements have had in demanding that greater consideration be given to environmental concerns in investment arbitration.

These developments are beginning to show results in investment arbitration. It is possible to see changes taking place in the attitude of tribunals, probably also because the environmental issues are better argued or more starkly presented by the facts. They have arisen in disputes which involve the more powerful states of the world as respondents. These states, such as the United States, Canada and Germany, had hitherto maintained an inflexible standard of foreign investment protection. They have had to argue the disputes on the basis that they had a right to regulate against environmental harm producing a risk to the health of their citizens. In that context, tribunals have clearly articulated the rule that an interference to protect environmental interests should be regarded as an exercise of police powers.

Unlike in *Methanex*, which has limitations regarding existing commitments made by the state, the later statement, without any such reservation, in *Chemtura* v. *Canada*[73] is the more acceptable formulation of

---

[73] UNCITRAL, Award (2 August 2010).

6.3 INTERNATIONAL ENVIRONMENTAL LAW 337

the rule that a state which interferes to protect an environmental interest is making a non-compensable, regulatory expropriation in the exercise of its police powers. The tribunal in *Chemtura* stated:[74]

> The Tribunal considers in any event that the measures challenged by the Claimant constituted a valid exercise of the Respondent's police powers ... [Canada] took measures within its mandate, in a non-discriminatory manner, motivated by the increasing awareness of the dangers presented by lindane for human health and the environment. A measure adopted under such circumstances is a valid exercise of the State's police powers and, as a result, does not constitute and expropriation.

One also finds that multinational companies do not persist with claims when global opposition builds up against a claim that is seen as involving a gross interference with the right of a state to provide basic amenities such as water to its people. Thus, agitation during the pendency of *Aguas del Tunari* v. *Bolivia*, a case involving water privatization, was intense. While it is true that the threat of investment arbitration may have intimidatory effects against a state and deter it from taking regulatory action, equally, bringing an arbitration in a case involving a clear instance of regulation in the public benefit would result in such adverse publicity against a multinational corporation and a perception that it violates standards of good corporate ethics that it may be that adverse publicity would deter the multinational corporation from pursuing such claims. But, as in the case of the tobacco arbitrations,[75] when the very the existence of the multinational corporation is being threatened, the corporation will fight hard on the basis of investment protection norms. It will be interesting to see how the tussle in the tobacco disputes involving a clash of values between protection of investment and the protection of health plays out. On many fronts, there has to be some rethinking done on the issue of investment arbitration.

The nature of the environmental factors taken into account in the more recent awards vary. These have included cases concerning nature

---

[74] Paragraph 266, following *Saluka Investments* v. *Czech Republic*, UNCITRAL PCA, Award (17 March 2006), para. 262, where also the rule is stated without exceptions.

[75] Two arbitrations have been brought by Philip Morris, the tobacco company against Australia and Uruguay regarding their plain paper wrapping and advertisement regulations on the sale of cigarettes. They raise issues relating to the right to health. The conflict between investment protection and human rights and other considerations are starkly brought out in these arbitrations. The tribunal in the Uruguay arbitration has ruled on jurisdiction.

reserves,[76] water rights,[77] indigenous land rights,[78] a ban on carcinogens polluting air,[79] pesticides,[80] wind farms, nuclear power,[81] protection of wild life such as sea turtles[82] and the white puma[83] and waste disposal.[84] But they do show an awareness that it is necessary to take such factors into account. When such attitudes take hold, there will be movement away from inflexible investment protection. But such movement will only enhance the uncertainties that exist in the law as the extent to which environmental factors would be considered relevant would still remain uncertain and will be left to the caprice of each tribunal. No rule can be devised as to the extent of the relevance of environmental factors. That each case will turn on its own facts is to state the obvious. But the effluxion of time will relegate investment protection to a lower position in the hierarchy of values, thereby strengthening defences against liability under treaties. However, it could well be that with entrenched attitudes of giving priority to investment protection, it could be that it will take some time.

In *Suez* v. *Argentina*, Argentina had argued that its measures were justified on human rights grounds. The tribunal dismissed this argument, holding:[85]

> Argentina has suggested that its human rights obligations to assure its population the right to water somehow trumps its obligations under the BITs and the existence of the human right to water also implicitly gives Argentina the authority to take actions in disregard of its BIT obligations. The Tribunal does not find a basis for such a conclusion either in the BITs or international law. Argentina is subject to both international obligations, i.e., human rights *and* treaty obligations, and must respect both of them. Under the circumstances of this case, Argentina's human rights

---

[76] *Santa Elena* v. *Costa Rica*, ICSID, Case No. ARB/96/1 (17 February 2000); *Metalclad Corp.* v. *Mexico*, ICSID, Case No. ARB(AF)/97/1 (30 August 2000).

[77] *Bayview Irrigation District* v. *Mexico*, ICSID, Case No. ARB(AF)/05/1 (19 June 2007); *Vattenfall* v. *Germany*, ICSID, Case No. ARB/09/6 (11 March 2011); *Aguas del Tunari* v. *Bolivia*; *Suez* v. *Argentina*, ICSID Case ARB/03/19 (30 July 2010).

[78] *Burlington Resources* v. *Ecuador*, ICSID, Case No. ARB/08/5 (2012); *Grand River Enterprises Six Nations Ltd* v. *United States*, UNCITRAL, Award (12 January 2011); *Glamis Gold Ltd* v. *United States*.

[79] *Ethyl* v. *Canada*; *Methanex* v. *United States*.

[80] *Chemtura Corp.* v. *Canada*, UNCITRAL, Award (2 August 2010).

[81] *Vattenfall* v. *Germany*.   [82] *Unglaube* v. *Costa Rica*.   [83] *Santa Elena* v. *Costa Rica*.

[84] *Tecmed* v. *Mexico*, ICSID, Case No. ARB(AF)/00/2 (29 May 2003).

[85] ICSID, Case No. ARB/03/19, at para. 240. The *amicus* brief had argued that Argentina's human rights obligation to provide water to its people trumped its obligations under the investment treaty.

6.4 OTHER OBLIGATIONS IN CONFLICT

339

obligations and its investment treaty obligations are not inconsistent, contradictory or mutually exclusive. Thus, as was discussed above, Argentina could have respected both types of obligations. Viewing each treaty as a whole, the Tribunal does not find that any of them excluded the defence of necessity. Therefore Argentina must be deemed to have satisfied the third condition for the defence of necessity.

The passage shows an unwillingness to reconcile the two interests in conflict. The inherent tendency of arbitration tribunals to place investment protection above other considerations is a hindrance to accommodation being reached in such conflicts.

It would, of course, be best if the investment treaty itself was to settle this dispute by ascribing priorities in the event of the conflict.[86] This will accelerate the process of accommodating human rights in a manner that gives it precedence. Unless there is a clear defence based on human rights and environmental rights in the treaty, arbitration tribunals will continue to show reluctance in recognizing the priority of the human rights and environmental standards. The large majority of the treaties still in existence are the old style treaties which give priority to investment protection. The newer ones do not state the position in clear terms. They state an obligation not to reduce environmental standards in order to achieve investment promotion. Such formulae are unhelpful in situation of a conflict between investment protection and environmental standards. A clear treaty formulation stating the priority of environmental goals is what is needed.

6.4 Other obligations in conflict with investment protection

There are other obligations of a state besides human rights and environmental interests, founded in international law, that come into conflict with the state's obligation to protect foreign investment under an investment treaty. Clearly, a state must be conscious of the existence of these other obligations at the time it enters into an investment treaty. But even the most advanced states do not seem to have adequately considered these competing obligations at the time of making investment treaties. Recent cases show a wide variety of instances of obligations from other areas conflicting with investment protection obligations. These must be briefly considered.

---

[86] Vinuales, *Foreign Investment and the Environment in International Law*; Kulick, *Global Public Interest in International Investment Law*, p. 188.

6.4.1   Cultural rights

As in the case of environmental and human rights, clashes are beginning to occur in the areas of obligations relating to cultural rights protected by international conventions[87] and the obligation of investment protection. In *Parkerings* v. *Lithuania*, the fact that a foreign investment project would affect an old city protected by the World Heritage Convention was considered relevant. In *Glamis Gold*,[88] the tribunal did not consider that cultural rights would affect the value of investment protection. The appreciation given to cultural rights in the few awards to consider them vary. A study by Valentina Vadi, surveying the existing awards on the issue of cultural rights, indicated the concerns involved when cultural rights clash with values of investment protection.[89] The neoliberal drive has been to promote cultural homogenization along with common standards of investment protection. The drive for globalization has also been to bring about uniform global patterns of culture as well as governance standards. Cultural diversity is inconsistent with such trends. The issue is not whether the existing investment arbitration awards have taken cultural sensitivities into account, but whether they are the appropriate tribunals to decide the conflict between investment protection and protection of cultural property. The latter concerns the whole of humanity, as the sites and property involved in cases like *SPP* v. *Egypt* and *Parkerings* v. *Lithuania* were of interest to the international community as a whole under the conventions that protected them. Investment protection concerns economists, and their ability to transcend into the realm of culture, a matter for the spirit, must be questioned. A World Bank tribunal like ICSID, whose jurisdiction is invoked only by foreign investors with purely economic concerns, is hardly set up to concern itself with cultural rights. The hope that such tribunals will take adequate account of cultural rights is, given the history of these tribunals and their penchant for exclusive emphasis on investment protection, a vain hope. The reality is the recognition of the fact that interests of significance to the world as a whole must trump the foreign investor's right to protection of his investment under the treaties. In the context of its history, it would be an appeasement to suggest that international investment law can

---

[87] The conventions range from the World Heritage Convention (1972), the Convention on the Protection of Cultural Property in the Event of Armed Conflict (1952), etc.

[88] *Glamis Gold Ltd* v. *United States*, UNCITRAL Arbitration, Award (NAFTA) (8 June 2009).

[89] Vadi, *Cultural Heritage in International Investment Law and Arbitration*.

6.4 OTHER OBLIGATIONS IN CONFLICT 341

accommodate the cultural rights of the different peoples of the world or protect the common cultural heritage of mankind.[90] The drive of the multinational corporation, the principal actor in international investment law, has not been towards such objectives, though lip-service is often paid ostentatiously to demonstrate the contrary.

6.4.2 Indigenous rights

This was already adverted to under human rights. The same considerations as to human rights apply to the protection of the rights of indigenous peoples. The rights of indigenous peoples are also protected by international conventions. These rights often clash with investment protection. Again, tribunals have had to consider such conflicts of norms. They have not given them adequate consideration. While the investor has the right to approach the investment arbitration tribunal, the affected tribal communities do not have such rights. The attitude taken by human rights tribunals to the conflict between tribal rights and investment protection has been different. The issue was addressed in *Sowhoyamaxa Indigenous Community* v. *Paraguay*, where the Inter-American Human Rights Court said that an investment treaty must be compatible with the American Convention on Human Rights. The Court asserted priority for protection of indigenous rights under the Human Rights Convention over investment treaties.[91] The rights of indigenous peoples contain values of significance to humanity and its diversity. The rights of foreign investment cannot displace indigenous rights. It is not necessary to cast such rights in the form of defences when in fact they have priority over rights that arise from foreign investment.

---

[90] Vadi, *Cultural Heritage in International Investment Law and Arbitration*, p. 296, spoke of the possible humanization of international investment law. It is a good idea, as Gandhi said of Western civilization. But the history of investment law is incompatible with humanization. As Vadi herself pointed out (in the first page of her book): 'an international economic culture has emerged that emphasizes productivity and economic development at the expense of the common weal'.

[91] 29 March 2006, IACHR Rep., Ser. C, 146, para. 140: 'Moreover, the Court considers that the enforcement of bilateral commercial treaties negates vindication of non-compliance with state obligations under the American Convention; on the contrary, their enforcement should always be compatible with the American Convention, which is a multilateral treaty on human rights that stands in a class of its own and that generates rights for individual human beings and does not depend entirely on reciprocity among States.'

6.5 Defences: evolution or erosion of investment protection?

It can be argued that progressive systems evolve from strict liability to liability based on fault. One can then say that the evolution of defences is evidence of the process of maturity of the system of investment law and arbitration. Criminal law moved from strict liability towards liability based on fault. It moved from objective fault to subjective fault depending on a precise dissection of the individual offender's actual guilt through defences made available to him. Contract law moved away from strict party autonomy towards actual intention of the bargain through consideration of defences based on capacity and equality of bargaining. The positivist may argue that the evolution of defences in investment law is a sign of similar processes at work, rather than a sign of normlessness and confusion undermining the law and signifying its erosion. It marks, it could be said, the maturing of a system.

The comparison with the evolution of criminal law or contract law is unjustified. The purposes of deterrence of crime or retribution were not destroyed by the evolution of defences in criminal law. Rather, they were enhanced as the punishment of a guiltless man does not serve either purpose. Likewise, ensuring that non-existent or unfair bargains are kept does not enhance the purpose of stability in commerce. In this evolution, there was social acceptance of the changes to such an extent that society now disapproves of a criminal being punished without subjective fault or a contract being enforced without a true bargain. To the extent that analogies have significance, this is not so in the case of investment treaty arbitration based on the inflexible protection of foreign investment. The growing number of defences has tilted the law against the purpose behind the investment treaties, which were asymmetrical in ensuring that the foreign investment was insulated from the control of the host state. The purpose of the defences has been to ensure the recovery of such control to the extent of destroying the fundamental premises on which the regime of treaty-based investment arbitration is built. The object of the defences has been to ensure the recovery of control by states. If the recognition of regulatory expropriation opened up a 'gaping hole' in the system, the recognition of a growing list of defences will possibly lead to the total caving in of the system. The assumed object of the treaties – the facilitation of investment flows due to security of investments – is undermined by the defences which increasingly make such security unsure.

Still, one may argue that arbitration is relevant to the extent that there has to be an external and neutral adjudication of whether the

6.6 CONCLUSION 343

circumstances of the defences have been appropriately invoked by the state. This depends on presuppositions of neutrality. Investment arbitration was created on the basis that the neutrality of the domestic courts cannot be assumed. The situation has now been reached where states cannot assume the neutrality of investment arbitration. This has resulted in the large holes in the system that recognize exceptions such as regulatory expropriation, the tying of fair and equitable treatment to the international minimum standard and, now, the whole array of possible defences. The existence of broad defences will lead to the questioning of the relevance of the system of investment protection under the treaties. The further issue is whether the exceptions that the defences create have eaten up the general scheme of investment protection so as to render the scheme useless. The eventual result would be that foreign investors will lose trust in the system. Theoretically, an issue remains as to whether factors such as human rights and the environment, which stand in a higher rank in the hierarchy of values than investment protection, should receive statement only as defences in investment treaty law.

6.6 Conclusion

The lengthening list of defences to responsibility under investment treaties undermines the system of investment protection under them and adds to the already existing instability created by the lack of unanimity in the application of principles under the treaty or the interpretation of its basic notions. In this sense, the Argentinian cases have unleashed forces that will undermine the bases of such investment protection by ensuring that arguments based on general international law principles that may provide defences are heard. They not only raised the defences made available in the treaties, but also the possibility of defences that are available on the basis of general international law. Proceeding on this basis and aided by the argument that fragmentation of international law should be avoided, the possibility of the existence of further defences arising from obligations created by other treaties conflicting with the obligation of investment protection has been raised. These conflicts arise largely from norms in the human rights and environmental areas. But a wider array of rights exists outside these traditional spheres.

The growing literature on the subject recognizes that the treaties creating these obligations are based on international community interests and recognize the need for global action. The urgency in the areas that are covered gives priority to these obligations over the obligations of investment protection. So far, the investment tribunals which have heard arguments based on global interests have given them short shrift, dismissing them either on the ground that they can co-exist with obligations under investment treaties or construing the facts in such a way as not to give priority to the human rights or environmental concerns.[92] The question has to be fairly raised as to whether investment tribunals are capable of giving adequate heed to issues involving global interests. Merely illustrating the global interests implicated in foreign investment disputes is insufficient.

There is a need to ascribe priorities to the different values which clash. It would almost always be the case that global values must be given priority over the value of investment protection. The shibboleth that investment flows are to the benefit of the poor is as discredited as the notion that colonialism was to uplift the colonized people to a higher standard of civilization. The question that has to be faced is whether the investment tribunal is the proper forum for the resolution of clashes between global values and the value of investment protection of immediate concern to the foreign investor. There are better tribunals which exist to resolve such clashes. The domestic courts should have obvious priority as they are the initial custodians of the human rights and environmental rights of their people, as well as other factors such as cultural rights and indigenous rights. They act as custodians of global interests in cultural rights. When these courts do not adhere to standards, there are other tribunals, such as regional human rights tribunals, which have greater legitimacy to deal with such issues. It would be difficult to think that investment tribunals could have supervisory functions or review powers over the domestic courts exercising such functions. States did not intend them to have such supervisory powers.

The competence of the investment tribunal to deal with global values must be doubted. Their competence under investment treaties were narrowly confined to decide violations of treaty standards. Such tribunals do not have the right personnel to deal with issues involving global interests. The criticism is often made that investment tribunals consist of commercial arbitrators who lack the competence to deal with public law disputes. More important is the criticism that they do not possess the

---

[92] Thus, in *Sempra* v. *Argentina*, the tribunal dismissed the argument that the defence of necessity pleaded by Argentina was justified by human rights considerations. The tribunal said that 'constitutional order was not on the verge of collapse' (para. 79), despite the fact that there were five changes of government within a span of two weeks and the army was shooting hungry people rioting on the streets.

6.6 CONCLUSION 345

mind-set to order the priorities in a conflict between global interests and investment protection. Neither is there any procedure for invoking global rights before investment tribunals. Even if there are public international lawyers on the tribunals, the further question is whether they are vested with the authority to decide questions that implicate the interests of the global community. The competence of the investment tribunal to deal with such problems is sorely lacking. The method of selecting investment tribunal arbitrators is such that tribunals are constituted with arbitrators who have a bias towards business or towards solutions that ensure the continuation of dispute settlement by existing institutions. As a consequence, these arbitrators would not be too conscious of the need to take global interests into account. Their survival in the business of investment arbitration also dictates a decision that is adverse to global interests.

A more vital question is whether a tribunal constituted by two parties to an existing investment disputes should have the power to deal with matters that affect the international community as a whole. This raises the question as to whether there is a doctrine of arbitrability in international law. The matter has been discussed previously. Clearly, as the statement in the *Phoenix* Award indicates, where *ius cogens* principles are involved, an investment tribunal has no jurisdiction simply because the investment, being made in breach of such principles, cannot be protected by the investment treaty as the treaty is inoperative in the event of transactions made in violation of *ius cogens* principles. But where there are lesser obligations, which are still owed to the international community at large, it can be argued that an investment treaty-based tribunal lacks the capacity to pronounce on the issues involving conflicts of these norms. A situation similar to non-arbitrability prevails so that the matter becomes one that can be decided only by a tribunal that is truly competent to decide global issues. It is grossly inappropriate to say that international tribunals assume a life of their own to decide in accordance with global interests. Investment tribunals, historically, structurally and institutionally, lack such competence. Whatever the truth of this proposition may be in other instances where single international tribunals are vested with authority by multilateral conventions, this is not the case in treaty-based investment arbitration where the tribunals are essentially ad hoc tribunals, which derive their jurisdiction from the two states making the investment treaty.

The further question that must be asked is whether global values should be stated as mere defences in a treaty that is designed to protect the narrower value of investment protection. The increase in the number of potential defences to responsibility adds to the instability of the regime created by investment treaties. The suggested changes towards a balanced treaty are based on the incorporation of the potential defences in the investment treaty itself. It does not solve the issues that are raised. The balanced treaties, which are more fully considered in Chapter 7, do not give comfort either to the investor in that they undermine absolute investment protection, which he had under the old treaties, or to the states that have to live with the possibility that arbitrators will be inclined to construe these defences as narrowly as possible so as to defeat their purpose.

7

The search for balance

7.1 Intermediate solutions

There has been a clash of ideologies and interests which has characterized the developments in the past few years of investment treaty arbitration. The interest in investment protection, which has been the sole concern of investment treaties, clashed with the regulatory interests of states in ensuring that public welfare is protected. The ideological preference for building up a law on inflexible investment protection through expansionary interpretation of treaty formulations has clashed with the fundamental rule that tribunals should not go beyond the consent of the parties. Arbitral activism in promoting neoliberal objectives have clashed with the view that such activism will prove to be harmful to the interests of arbitration in the long run. Given these clashes, several solutions have been adopted. Leaving aside the ad hoc solutions to specific problems that have arisen, such as the restriction of fair and equitable treatment by tying it to the IMS standard or the denial of benefits provision to stem the misuse of corporate personality, there have been new fully-fledged attempts at reconciling the issues that have arisen. These have been through the introduction of what are referred to as balanced treaties and the use of the proportionality rule as a means of balancing the interests of foreign investment with the regulatory power of the state. They both search for balance. This chapter analyses the two developments, ending both analyses with assessments of whether they provide adequate solutions to the problems that have arisen.

The two solutions presage change from the earlier moorings of the law in emphasizing foreign investment protection. The first is to ensure that new forms of treaties are made which do not focus on the sole purpose of investment protection, but contain a balance in that there are sufficient exceptions permitting the state to take measures in the public interest. The second is to permit the arbitrator to balance the interests between a norm of protection in the treaty with the regulatory interest of the state in

347

348   THE SEARCH FOR BALANCE

taking measures that interfere with such protection. Such balancing is to be effected by the arbitrators faced with a conflict of interests or a conflict between two different norms. The notions of balancing are drawn from parallels in the domestic constitutional law of Western states. But the theory is wanting for a variety of reasons. The most important among them is that it would be difficult for the decision-maker to apply the balancing theory without his own preconceptions influencing the outcome. Besides, what is loaded into considerations relating to balancing are ideas of a liberal constitutional order which are to be found in Western constitutional systems not acceptable to the plural world in which international investment law has to operate. In that plural world, the values that have to be chosen will be different. Since balancing notions are floated as justifications for the new treaties that have been devised, these new treaties are considered first. The idea of balancing in investment arbitration is considered thereafter.

7.2   Balanced treaties as the solution

This solution is seen by some as systemic reform that is preferable to maintaining the present system, withdrawing from it or the making of band-aid solutions to fix specific problems. It seeks to keep the existing system, but to ensure that a balance is brought about by replacing the old treaties, which emphasized investment protection, with new treaties, which recognize justifications for measures of state intervention in defined circumstances. The purpose of the newer treaties is to create sufficient regulatory space for the state to act in the public interest. Consequently, they are regarded as effecting a balance between foreign investment protection and the regulatory interests of the state. The argument is also made that the new treaties should include the core principles of sustainable development.[1]

The year 2004, which saw the US and Canadian model treaties on investment, could be taken as the year in which these balanced treaties began.[2] They showed a retreat from the model of absolute protection that

---

[1] UNCTAD, which had a history of recommending investment treaties to developing states, now recommends a treaty based on core principles of sustainable development. These principles are explained in the latest *World Investment Report* (Geneva, 2014) issued by UNCTAD.

[2] The ideas were present in earlier treaties, including the draft MAI of the OECD. The effort at an MAI was given up in 1998. The Model Treaty drafted by the International Institute

7.2 BALANCED TREATIES AS THE SOLUTION   349

the earlier US and Canadian model treaties had favoured. The earlier treaties were designed to favour strict protection, though they contained subjective national security exceptions. The 2004 model treaties presaged possibilities of wider exceptions to liability. They contain exceptions to liability when measures affecting foreign investment are taken to protect health and human, animal or plant life, or are taken to protect prudential or economic interests. Environmental protection and labour standards are referred to only to the extent of stating that they must not be reduced in order to pursue foreign investment.

These were early explorations of effecting a balance in the face of the excessive interpretations that had been made of provisions in the traditional investment treaties extending the scope of investment protection. They also contained the ad hoc changes that had been previously made in relation to specific problems. Thus, the fair and equitable treatment standard was tied to the customary law international minimum standard, a change effected by the interpretive note of the NAFTA Commission. Indirect expropriation was subject to the qualification that 'except in rare circumstances' a regulatory taking effected in the public interest would not be compensable.

The significance of the 2004 model treaties was that the United States, the leader in the field of making and sustaining the norms of international investment law favoured by the developed states, along with Canada, was seen as making inroads into a framework of absolute protection on which it had hitherto insisted. The later 2012 US Model Treaty was, according to the statement of the Department of State, similar to the 2004 Model Treaty as 'it maintains language from the 2004 model BIT, in particular its carefully calibrated balance between providing strong investor protections and preserving the government's ability to regulate in the public interest'.[3]

Quite apart from the fact that the United States and Canada were increasingly becoming respondents in NAFTA arbitrations, they were also fast becoming the largest importers of capital, particularly from China, but also from the other newly industrializing countries such as India and Brazil. They had to prepare for a new experience.

---

for Sustainable Development (IISD) was a forerunner of balanced treaties. The IISD Model International Agreement on Investment for Sustainable Development was drafted in 2005. It forms the basis for other model agreements, such as the SADC Model Agreement.

[3] Department of State, Fact Sheet, Bilateral Investment Treaty, Office of the Spokesperson, 20 April 2012.

350   THE SEARCH FOR BALANCE

The Norwegian draft model treaty, released on 19 December 2007,[4] was not accepted in that country due to divisions of opinion. It reflected the thinking that was developing in response both to the unintended interpretations given to investment treaties by arbitral tribunals as well as to concerns that the exclusive emphasis on investment protection did not pay sufficient heed to other interests, such as corporate social responsibility or human rights. The preamble recognizes a wide array of concerns from sustainable investment to prevention of corruption as being the objectives of the treaty. The model treaty subjects expropriation to international law rules, but states also that 'the provision shall not, however, in any way impair the right of a Party to enforce such laws as it deems necessary to control the use of property in accordance with the general interest or to secure the payment of taxes or other contributions or penalties'. The dispute settlement provision is conditioned on a duty to resort to local remedies for a period of thirty-six months. It sets up a joint committee of the parties to review the working of the agreement as well as to review the case law under it. The committee was to have interpretive powers. The draft had a provision on general exceptions enabling the state to take measures to protect health, welfare and morals. It provided separate exceptions for prudential measures, national security, measures covering cultural property and taxation. It did not meet with approval as it did not please Norwegian investors who thought there were too many exceptions, making the treaty useless. It did not satisfy other interested groups, which thought that the treaty did not go far enough in providing for regulatory space. The draft was shelved. Yet it is the forerunner to many of the changes that are being advocated in the field. One could trace the later suggestions that are made for balanced treaties to the ideas that are contained in the Norwegian Model Treaty. The episode indicates that the balanced treaty satisfies none of the stakeholders. Despite this experience in Norway, balanced treaties were seen as the panacea for reconciling conflicts of interest between inflexible investment protection and the need of the state for regulatory space. The two ideas are mutually incompatible, rendering the task of balanced treaties difficult to accomplish.

The United States and Canada released new model treaties in 2012. They did not make dramatic changes to the earlier drafts. There was considerable opposition mounting within the United States to investment treaties, particularly to the investment chapter of NAFTA. The opposition was nationalistic as well as fomented by groups involved

---

[4] For the text, see: www.italaw.com/sites/default/files/archive/ita1031.pdf.

with labour rights and the environment. The global economic crisis also stirred considerable nationalist and protectionist feelings. The draft reflects these concerns by firming up the exceptions in these areas. In the area of taxation, a joint committee of experts is to be created by the two state parties to deal with issues that arise, and it is only if the committee cannot iron out difficulties that a dispute could be submitted to arbitration by the foreign investor. This is a novel technique that has promise. It could cover a wider field than taxation, as was suggested in the Norwegian treaty. The continued involvement with the issue by the executive of both countries with expertise in the problems that arise in the different sectors is a better approach than arbitration by tribunals whose understanding of the issues may not be deep. Besides, it keeps lawyers, with mercenary interests of their own, away from the scene.

Canada used the model in negotiating a treaty with China in 2013. The Canadian treaty with China has caused controversy as investing in resource-rich Canada would be a priority with Chinese state corporations. Canada, presumably, is confident of managing the situation because of the range of exceptions covering regulatory measures. The assumptions of the two parties in making the treaty must have been different. The developed states have begun making balanced treaties. It indicates the fact that the picture is beginning to change in that the developed states are now becoming massive recipients of foreign investment from the newly industrializing states. They see the future possibility of having to defend disputes. They are making preparations for this by ensuring that they have sufficient regulatory space provided in the so-called balanced treaties to ensure that they can avoid responsibility. The United States is yet to lose any arbitration brought against it. It is obviously confident of meeting any claim under the investment treaties brought against it, while maintaining the treaties in the belief that it enables their multinational corporations to defend their investments. This may be possible as the developing host state may lack the expertise to fight claims against it effectively, unless it spends money to hire expensive law firms. In the context of that asymmetry, the balanced treaties favour the interests of the developed states. But one would expect that the balance that developing states make is more heavily tilted towards regulatory interests. What has developed is a battle of model treaties. The developed states' model does contain conservation of regulatory space, but not to the extent of the models of the developing states.

The developing countries have commenced making balanced treaties in the belief that they too can handle the situation if such regulatory space

352   THE SEARCH FOR BALANCE

is conserved in the treaties. The structure of the balanced treaties formulated by the developing countries is different in that they state the
defences to liability in clearer and broader terms. They were also made a
few years after the US and Canadian models in the light of further
developments that had taken place in the intervening years. The main
treaties are the ASEAN Investment Treaty, the SADC Model Treaty on
Investment and the Commonwealth Secretariat draft contained in a
report on the subject of investment treaties. UNCTAD does not have a
model treaty, but advocates inclusion of ten core principles of sustainable
development into investment treaties. The Commonwealth model is
designed with developing countries in mind by an institution that has a
majority of developing countries as its members. It is necessary to consider the impact of these treaties and models.

They are all motivated by the need to achieve investment protection
while preserving regulatory space. The marrying of the two inconsistent
ideas is the balance that is sought to be effected in the different treaties
and they differ significantly. Besides the balance, in the case of regional
treaties, the states may be at different stages of development as well as
possess entirely different political systems.

7.2.1   The ASEAN Investment Agreement

The ASEAN Investment Agreement (2009)[5] is an attempt at a classic
compromise including the traditional statement of the treatment standards and the expropriation clause, with the inclusion of the formula
tying the fair and equitable standard to the international minimum
standard and the exception as to regulatory expropriation. It provides
for several defences to liability. Like the mythical chimera, it contains
inconsistent parts within the same body. It states the traditional treatment standards, but the regulatory scope it permits is extensive. Like all
southeast Asian treaties, it retains the requirement that entry must be
made in accordance with the stringent foreign investment screening laws
that exist in southeast Asian states to be given protection under the treaty.
Arbitration in the region is low because it has been difficult to surmount
this jurisdictional hurdle, as evidenced in the few arbitrations that have
been brought against the states of the region.[6] In fact, knowledge of such

---

[5] ASEAN Comprehensive Investment Agreement (signed on 26 February 2009 in Cha-Am,
Thailand by ASEAN economic ministers).
[6] *Gruslin* v. *Malaysia; Yaung Chi Oo Ltd* v. *Myanmar; Rafat Ali Rizvi* v. *Indonesia; Fraport*
v. *Philippines.*

7.2 BALANCED TREATIES AS THE SOLUTION 353

a requirement is absent among foreign investors. Surveys show that they have seldom sought written authorization at the point of entry, making the investment treaties virtually redundant as a means of investment protection.[7] Many of the laws require that the investment must be specifically approved in writing for the purpose of the protection of investment treaties. The ASEAN treaty keeps this device alive if the domestic laws contain the requirement.[8] This high threshold for jurisdiction is based on the presence of laws regulating entry in the states of the region. There are further provisions that enable the continuous exercise of regulation of the whole process of the foreign investment so that technically any investment that transgresses the law while operating the investment may move it out of the protection of the treaty.

The ASEAN investment treaty recognizes regulatory measures taken to deal with a variety of circumstances. In accordance with developments in some awards, the fair and equitable standard is tied to denial of justice, which means that its invocation is dependent on a prior exhaustion of domestic procedures. A denial of justice occurs only after the domestic courts of the host state have pronounced on the issue. This returns the law to a compromise effected in old customary international law between the United States and Latin American countries, which required the prior exhaustion of local remedies before a claim could arise on the basis of denial of justice. It also anticipates new developments, which go back to the need for exhaustion of local remedies as a precondition for the institution of arbitration proceedings.[9] State responsibility could arise only when the domestic courts had denied remedies. Such denial requires an extraordinary degree of injustice on the part of the domestic courts.

Consistent with what Malaysia did during the Asian financial crisis of 1998, the Agreement permits currency and exchange control measures during circumstances where 'movements of capital cause, or threaten to cause, serious economic or financial disturbance'.[10] Further, Article 14 permits measures to be taken to safeguard balance of payments. There

---

[7] As counsel in *Yang Chi Oo Ltd* v. *Myanmar*, the present writer wrote to all ASEAN states to ask whether they had procedures for giving written consent for purposes of investment treaties. No country, except Singapore, had such formal procedures. It is evident that, as a consequence, the treaties made in the region, which contain this restriction, have little effect. Investors seldom anticipate disputes so that they do not take the precaution of asking for written authorizations triggering the protection of the treaty.

[8] Article 4(a), the covered investment must 'where applicable be specifically approved by the competent authority of a Member State'. The procedures for such approval are stated in Annex 1 of the Agreement.

[9] *Apotex Inc.* v. *United States.*   [10] Article 13(4)(c).

need not be an economic crisis for such safeguards to be taken. The circumstances justifying such measures may be taken in the context of ensuring adequate levels of financial reserves. They must, however, be consistent with IMF Articles. Since the Agreement, the IMF has reported that capital controls may be justified in circumstances where there is a need to keep an adequate financial reserve. The wisdom results from the experience of repeated economic crises. The situation of Argentina, which has still to recover from the fifty-two arbitrations resulting from its exchange controls during its economic crisis, is unlikely to be repeated under the new balanced treaties. Certainly, it will not be repeated under the ASEAN Investment Agreement.

There follow in the ASEAN Investment Agreement four widely phrased defences to liability, apart from a denial of benefits provision that enables the state to determine whether an investor that is controlled by a non-member state's nationals or corporations should be entitled to protection.[11]

The first of the defences relates to measures taken to safeguard balance of payments. This has been dealt with earlier. The circumstances in which such measures can be used are stated broadly, indicating that developing countries have a need to take such measures having regard to their programme of economic development.[12]

Article 17 is a broad provision titled 'General Exceptions'. It states that nothing in the Agreement prevents the taking of any measures that are: (a) necessary to protect public morals or to maintain public order;[13] (b) necessary to protect human, animal or plant life, or health; (c) necessary to secure compliance with laws or regulations not

---

[11] The denial of benefits provision is Article 19.

[12] Article 16(1) states: 'In the event of serious balance-of-payments and external financial difficulties or threat thereof, a Member State may adopt or maintain restrictions on payments or transfers related to investments. It is recognised that particular pressures on the balance-of-payments of a Member State in the process of economic development may necessitate the use of restrictions to ensure, inter alia, the maintenance of a level of financial reserves adequate for the implementation of its programme of economic development.' Restrictions are stated requiring conformity to IMF principles. With the hindsight of economic crises, the IMF principles are to be relaxed.

[13] A footnote states: 'The public order exception may be invoked by a Member State only where a genuine and sufficiently serious threat is posed to one of the fundamental interests of society.' The provision requires objective determination of circumstances justifying the measures, giving competence to the tribunal to determine whether a serious threat did exist. None of the other exceptions are subject to similar constraints. The national security exception is subjective. It is unclear what the distinction between a public interest situation and a national security situation is.

7.2 BALANCED TREATIES AS THE SOLUTION 355

inconsistent with the Agreement;[14] (d) aimed at collecting taxes; (e) imposed for the protection of national treaties of artistic, historic or archaeological value; and (f) relating to the conservation of exhaustible natural resources if such measures are made effective in conjunction with restrictions on domestic production or consumption.

Article 18 is titled 'Security Exceptions', and it states the national security exception in subjective terms. It gives three situations: action relating to fissionable and fusionable materials; traffic in arms; and action in time of war or other emergencies in domestic or international relations. But the article is not limited to the three situations as it states that it includes the situations, 'but is not limited' to them.

One must note that the four Articles capture virtually every measure that could affect the foreign investor. It would be an interesting exercise to see how many of the existing awards under the treaty would have resulted in liability if these provisions had existed in the traditional type of investment treaties. First, it would have been difficult to get over the jurisdictional hurdle simply because there would have to be strict compliance with the entry laws and approval in writing. Indirect control would not suffice due to the denial of benefits provisions. Secondly, the substantive law, the violation of which creates liability, is narrower. Not only is expropriation limited by the exception as to regulatory measures, but there are the other wide limitations. The fair and equitable treatment is based on denial of justice by the local tribunals. There can be no liability for violation of the legitimate expectations of the foreign investor.

Thirdly, there are the broadly stated defences. They are so comprehensively stated that it would not be easy to establish liability in the face of these defences, some of which are subjectively stated. The long list of Argentinian cases would result in an absence of liability had they arisen under the ASEAN Agreement, as the agreement would provide a defence for exchange control measures in times of economic crises. The other cases, which involve measures such as taxation, archaeological sites, environmental measures, health measures and other measures affecting the public interest, would be captured by the exceptions created by the Articles. In this context, the recognition of the substantive rights of the foreign investor are sapped of value by the four provisions of

---

[14] These include: (i) the prevention of deceptive and fraudulent practices to deal with the effects of a default on a contract; (ii) the protection of the privacy of individuals in relation to the processing and dissemination of personal data, and the protection of confidentiality of individual records and accounts; (iii) safety.

356 THE SEARCH FOR BALANCE

the Agreement which recognize wide exceptions to liability. These comments could be made of the later models generated by developing countries. There does not appear to be a balance in the treaty. It is tilted in favour of regulatory control over virtually every facet of foreign investment. It will be interesting to see what arbitrators will make of claims under such a treaty. One may never find out as the chances of such claims succeeding given an honest interpretation of the treaty provisions are extremely slim. As such, prudent advice would be not to bring claims under such a treaty. Unless arbitrators are nakedly intent on circumventing the express provisions of the treaty, it is not very likely that the state will not be able to find justification for the measures it takes against the foreign investor in the broad defences stated in the treaty. The development of the proportionality principle in some awards anticipates a counter in that through it arbitrators arrogate to themselves the reserve power to determine whether the regulatory measure is proportionate to the objective the state seeks to achieve, despite the state's avowal that a defence under the treaty is available. The extent to which such a rule can be adopted under the ASEAN agreement is conjectural.

It is relevant to note that there is considerable displeasure with investment arbitration among the ASEAN states. Indonesia has faced several arbitrations in recent times. It was particularly aggrieved with the acceptance of jurisdiction in *Churchill* v. *Indonesia* on the basis of the Pan-Islamic investment treaty, which does not have strong provisions on jurisdiction. Indonesia has announced that it will not enter into any more investment treaties or renew any existing treaty whose termination period has lapsed. Philippines has not included an investor–state dispute settlement provision in its treaty with Japan. There will be some wariness among some ASEAN states with investment treaties, as there is considerable hostility within the region to investment treaties. The ASEAN treaty itself is a reflection of that hostility in that it seems to be a treaty without much substance from the point of view of the foreign investor.

7.2.2   The SADC Model Investment Treaty

South African Development Community (SADC) is a regional association of southern African states, consisting of Malawi, Mauritius, Namibia, South Africa and Zimbabwe. They are countries rich in mineral resources, and as a result they attract much investment. South Africa, being the leading member of SADC, has a policy of its own on BITs. It had signed many

7.2 BALANCED TREATIES AS THE SOLUTION 357

BITs, but after its experience with some arbitrations based on these BITs,[15] it has suspended its investment treaty programme, announced that it will terminate treaties once the period of the treaty has run,[16] and is against the making of new BITs.[17] Also, the region was subjected to apartheid, a system of rule by white supremacists. In light of this past, the countries of the region take a common position that the historical injustices of the past generated by the severe deprivation of the black population should be redressed by a policy of black empowerment. The argument is that the practice of apartheid is against *ius cogens* norms and that the effects of that practice, which still exist, should be reversed. Towards this objective, legislative programmes were devised to ensure that black people are given privileges in the public sector. The giving of such privileged status would go against the provisions of traditional BITs, which deal with equal treatment with nationals in the national treatment provisions.

This provides the context for the issuance of the SADC Model Bilateral Investment Treaty Template, with a commentary by the Southern African Development Community in July 2012.[18] Made three years after the ASEAN Agreement, the SADC Model contains strict provisions on admission on investments, requiring adherence to existing laws on entry. It is as restrictive as the ASEAN Agreement in stating the investment protection standards. It prefers the non-inclusion of the fair and equitable standard. If it is to be included, it offers two options. The first reads in the essence of the *Neer* standard as a part of the standard.[19] This is justified on the ground that the tying of the fair and equitable standard, as done in the US Model Treaty, has not worked as arbitrators have sought to find ways around such efforts at restriction. The second option is to state a new standard, which it defines as 'fair administrative

---

[15] *Pierro Forresti* v. *South Africa*, ICSID, Case No. ARB(AF)/07/01 (24 August 2010).

[16] South Africa announced the termination of the treaty with Belgium–Luxembourg, and its general policy of letting its investment treaties lapse and not making fresh treaties.

[17] See the Special Note to Article 5: the fair and equitable treatment provision is, again, a highly controversial provision. The Drafting Committee recommended against its inclusion in a treaty due to very broad interpretations in a number of arbitral decisions. It requested the inclusion of an alternative formulation of a provision on 'Fair Administrative Treatment'. Both options are now set out below.

[18] South African Development Community, *SADC Model Bilateral Investment Treaty Template with Commentary,,* SADC Headquarters, Botswana, July 2012.

[19] Article 5(2), as an alternative, the provision would state: 'For greater certainty, paragraph 5.1 requires the demonstration of an act or actions by the government that are an outrage, in bad faith, a wilful neglect of duty or an insufficiency so far short of international standards that every reasonable and impartial person would readily recognize its insufficiency.'

treatment'. In this the SADC Model seems influenced by the current thinking on global administrative law and assumes the existence of external standards of administrative governance, though it takes into account the capabilities of each state in the context of its development. This is an unfortunate inclusion as, if included, it will permit an external tribunal to assess the conduct of a state on the basis of its own subjective standards of administrative governance. It does open the door for the same expansive treatment that is complained of in the case of fair and equitable treatment.[20] It may be based on the view of the proponents of global administrative law who believe in neutral norms in the area when the indications are that they are seeking them exclusively in the public law of European states. One problem that South African official statements advert to is the variance between investment treaty standards and their own public law. The standard for compensation under the South African Constitution, for example, takes into account various factors that reduce compensation from full value, whereas the treaty standards of compensation are higher.

Article 6 on expropriation contains a specific statement that a regulatory taking does not constitute indirect expropriation.[21] The compulsory licensing of patents is also not regarded as expropriation. The compensation criteria reflect the debates that have taken place in the past. Though different forms of the criteria are offered in the model treaty, they take into account the past history of the investment, previous profit made by the investor and other relevant circumstances. The method of valuation suggested is heavily tilted towards the NIEO views on appropriate compensation and moves away from the Hull standard.

Article 8 states the right to repatriation, but is also heavily qualified. It identifies nine circumstances in which such repatriation could be prevented or delayed.[22] There is a time limitation of twelve months for such

---

[20] It is stated to be a South African initiative. This should have been rethought in the context of the South African announcement that it would not be signing any investment treaties in the future.

[21] Article 6.7: 'A [non-discriminatory] measure of a State Party that is designed and applied to protect or enhance legitimate public welfare objectives, such as public health, safety and the environment, does not constitute an indirect expropriation under this Agreement.'

[22] Article 8.3: 'Notwithstanding paragraphs 8.1 and 8.2, a State Party may prevent or delay a transfer through the non-discriminatory application of its law and regulations relating to: (a) bankruptcy, insolvency, or the protection of the rights of creditors; (b) issuing, trading or dealing in securities, futures, options or derivatives; (c) criminal or penal offences and the recovery of the proceeds of crime; (d) financial reporting or record keeping of transactions when necessary to assist law enforcement or financial regulatory authorities;

7.2 BALANCED TREATIES AS THE SOLUTION 359

restrictions. In addition, there are safeguard provisions which enable the state to take measures with regard to capital movements, 'where, in the opinion of the State' there are difficulties of balance of payments, external financial difficulties or difficulties of macroeconomic management. Consultations with the other state party are necessary for suspensions. The provisions on suspension of the right to repatriation are stronger than in other models or agreements. The causes of action created by the SADC Model Treaty for a foreign investor are slim. They are stated in a heavily qualified manner. The technique is illustrated by the right to repatriation, which is stated initially in general terms, but is whittled away with substantial restrictions which are subjectively stated.

The SADC Model Treaty also contains a complete statement of defences. It moves on to create responsibility in the foreign investor under certain circumstances, a definite and progressive change which ends the one-sided nature of the investment treaties. But such responsibility is to be tested out only as counterclaims before arbitral tribunals or as possibly claims brought in civil cases in the home state of the foreign investor. There is no direct effort to create a mechanism whereby a state could sue the foreign investor for the damages it may cause through the same arbitral mechanism created by the treaty.[23] It contemplates obligations in the home state of the foreign investor. An observer who is inclined towards the protection of foreign investment may well be concerned whether the SADC Model Treaty tilts towards the state to such an extent that it makes investment protection otiose. It must also be contrasted with the view of South Africa, the leading state within SADC, that it will suspend the making of investment treaties. The option that South Africa indicates is not to make any investment treaties. Given the major tilt against investment protection, it would be better not to make treaties than have the SADC Model, which cannot achieve any credible investment protection. No investor would risk bringing a claim under a treaty that contains so many subjectively stated defences.

(e) ensuring compliance with orders or judgments in judicial or administrative proceedings; (f) taxation; (g) social security, public retirement or compulsory savings schemes; (h) severance entitlements of employees; and (i) the formalities required to register and satisfy the Central Bank and other relevant authorities of a State Party.'

[23] An exceptional arbitration in which the state sued the foreign investor occurred on the basis of an investment contract in *Indonesia* v. *Newmont* (2004, unreported) (Briner, Schwebel, Sornarajah), where Indonesia sued Newmont for not transferring the shares into local hands as mandated by the contract and the foreign investment laws of the host state.

Part Three of the SADC Model Treaty is innocently titled 'Rights and Obligations of Investors and States'. It begins with the prohibition of corruption (Article 10); includes an obligation to comply with domestic law (Article 11); an obligation on the investor to provide information about the investment for making entry decisions (Article 12); an obligation to make an environmental impact study; an obligation to maintain an environmental management system consistent with international standards (Article 14); an obligation to follow minimum human rights and labour rights (Article 15)' and an obligation to meet corporate governance standards (Article 16). Interestingly, in all these matters the foreign investor has to meet external standards. The justification for the reference to external standards may be found in the notion that the avoidance of fragmentation makes these external standards, found in international law, relevant to the foreign investment process. The SADC Model, in effect, seeks to advance the object of creating a code of conduct for transnational corporations. The effort to do so had failed in the past.[24] It also firms up the statement of defences based on human rights and standards of corporate responsibility.

Article 17 provides for investor liability for civil claims before the home state of the foreign investor. This is a matter argued for by academic scholars and finds fruition in this Article.[25] The notion is that the home state should provide remedies through its courts for harm caused by multinational companies headquartered in its territory acting to the detriment of host state communities. The Article restricts the principle to decisions taken by the parent company within the home state, though this restriction is not made in scholarly writings. This is an unnecessary restriction, as the US Supreme Court, in its decision in *Kiobel* v. *Royal Dutch Shell Petroleum Co.*,[26] states a wider basis of jurisdiction that enables a US court to assume jurisdiction over a multinational corporation acting overseas in violation of international law provided it is an American national or has significant presence within the United States. Yet it is an innovative provision to include in an investment treaty. Reactions to such a proposal in the Western,

---

[24] The United Nations Commission on Transnational Corporations had attempted such a code of conduct. The effort failed due to the opposition of the developed states.

[25] Sornarajah, 'Linking State Responsibility for Certain Harms Caused by Corporate Nationals Abroad to Civil Recourse in the Legal Systems of Home States'.

[26] (2013) 133 Sup. Ct 1659.

7.2 BALANCED TREATIES AS THE SOLUTION 361

capital-exporting states is not likely to be positive.[27] The Article goes further than the proposals of the UN Rapporteur on Transnational Business and Human Rights, John Ruggie, who argued for an obligation of access to the courts of the home state in a more truncated manner.[28] Article 19 seeks to make these obligations imposed on the investor meaningful by requiring any tribunal hearing a dispute to consider whether the violation of the obligations has a mitigation or set-off effect on the merits of the claim or in damages. Such violations could also be the basis of counterclaims. Civil claims could be initiated before domestic courts on the basis of these violations. Standing to do so is given not only to the state or its subdivisions, but also to private persons and organizations.

After stating these obligations, the SADC Model Treaty seeks to establish the rights of states vis-à-vis the foreign investor. Article 20 establishes the right to regulate to ensure development that is consistent with the goals of sustainable development and other legitimate social and economic policy objectives. The right is said to be in accordance with customary international law. A criticism may be that sustainable development is an uncertain concept. The UNCTAD view also is that reform of the investment treaties should be tied to the core principles of sustainable development that are identified in the UNCTAD documents.[29]

Article 21 makes significant inroads into national treatment standards by recognizing a right to pursue development goals. The right enables a state to discriminate in favour of local entrepreneurs, and to enhance local productive capacity and favour local factors in other ways. It justifies the correction of 'historically based economic disparities suffered by identifiable ethnic or cultural groups due to discriminatory measures' in the past. The obvious instances are black empowerment programmes common to the region. Article 22 recognizes the right to establish environmental and labour standards in accordance with internationally accepted standards. This requires the transformation of the international standards into domestic law. The provision, unlike in the case of the 2004 US Model Treaty, creates a legally binding right in the state with regard to environmental and labour standards.

---

[27] The United States has the Alien Tort Claims Act under which it is possible to bring civil actions against multinational corporations present in the United States. There are efforts to curtail the scope of the Act.

[28] Ruggie, *Just Business: Multinational Corporations and Human Rights*, pp. 192–7.

[29] The latest of these UNCTAD documents is the *World Investment Report* (Geneva, 2014), at pp. 128–32.

362 THE SEARCH FOR BALANCE

The Final Part of the SADC Model Treaty is titled 'General Provisions'. The most important section it contains is Article 25 on 'Exceptions'. Subject to non-discrimination,[30] the provision guards against good faith measures taken to protect (a) public morals and safety, (b) human, animal or plant life or health, (c) the conservation of living or non-living exhaustible natural resources and (d) the environment. Prudential measures taken to protect financial markets are excepted, as are taxation measures. There is also an exception of subjectively determined national security interests, which are not circumscribed in any way. The exceptions have been more widely stated than in any existing treaty or model.

The SADC Model Treaty reflects the uniquely exploitative experiences the region has had at the hands of foreign investors, particularly in the mining sectors. It also reflects the association of the model with advice received from NGOs, which have taken to promoting the so-called balanced treaties. The outcome is a document that contains no balance at all. The technique used has been to write in all the traditional rights and standards given by investment treaties, then, wide rights are created in the states to make inroads into the rights and standards as to make the standards nugatory. The issue that arises is why have a treaty of this sort at all? It will not effectively protect investors. The extent of the obligations created in the investor that would lead to counterclaims, the nature of the rights recognized in the state to regulate and the exceptions to liability that are created significantly erode the ability of the foreign investor to maintain a successful claim against the state. The charade serves no interest except of those on the periphery of the relationship, such as arbitrators and law firms. The South African stance of not making investment treaties is a more appropriate one than making a treaty based on the SADC Model. It is unlikely that any developed state would want to make a treaty on the basis of the SADC Model.

7.2.3   The Commonwealth Report and Model Treaty

Though the Commonwealth Report does not contain a definite model of an investment treaty, it does contain alternative formulations that negotiators could use. The report itself prescribes a 'balanced' treaty to the extent that it is replete with a wide variety of defences to liability which

---

[30] A concept truncated by Article 21, which enables discrimination in favour of economic development.

7.2 BALANCED TREATIES AS THE SOLUTION

confirm the fact that in future treaties, if any come about on the basis of the suggestions, there would be wide preclusions relating to measures taken by the state that relate to interests in the areas of environmental protection, human rights, taxation and a variety of public interests. The tendency in the SADC Model Treaty to express them in terms of rights of states rather than in the form of defences is also a noticeable feature of the Commonwealth Model Treaty. The SADC Model is not conclusive on the issue of whether a state acts in pursuance of a right when it takes a regulatory measure or whether it is a defence that can be pleaded after a case against the state has been established, as the Model states both possibilities without distinguishing between a defence and a justification.[31] In either event, the plea would have to be raised after the claim has been established. The trend in the Commonwealth Report is also to build in as many defences into the system as possible, making investment protection virtually take a back seat.

7.2.3.1 Change and balanced treaties

The balanced treaties are seen by some as a 'recalibration' of the system of investment treaty arbitration.[32] This is at least an acknowledgement of the fact that the system needed change. There has been a reaction from states to the excesses that have taken place in the field, particularly the exorbitant interpretations that have been placed on treaty provisions by arbitration tribunals. The recalibration through balanced treaties appears to be a more measured response than a withdrawal from the system. They keep the system alive, but with significant changes that ensure a large number of defences to the state. They move the treaty practice on investment protection away from the lean treaties that contained inflexible standards of investment protection, to treaties that contain broad statements of instances where states' measures interfering with foreign investment on grounds of public interest will not attract liability. But are the balanced treaties the answer to the problems created by investment arbitration?

The view could well be taken that the balanced treaties neither serve the protection of investment nor achieve the aim of conserving the regulatory space of states in a manner acceptable to foreign investors. They move away from the system of absolute investment protection that

---

[31] The distinction is of little significance except from the point of view of blame. In the criminal law, self-defence is a plea in justification, whereas other defences excuse liability. Both have the same effect.

[32] Jurgen Kurtz, 'Book Review', (2012) 106 *American Journal of International Law* 686.

364 THE SEARCH FOR BALANCE

characterized the neoliberal phase of the treaties. They would leave the foreign investor dissatisfied with the extent of the protection he receives as the broad nature of the defences significantly erode the nature of the protection that the balanced treaties provide. If the purpose of the investment treaty is to attract investments – and this is the only raison d'être that can be offered for them – then, the balanced treaties do not achieve that purpose. They remove the only justification (even if flawed) for the investment treaties, as investment protection under them becomes highly tenuous given the broad nature of the defences.[33] The state will have a multitude of ways of justifying the measures it takes against foreign investment. Unless the motives for the measures are flawed, it is unlikely that the foreign investor would be given relief. In some defences such as national security, the subjective decision of the state as to the existence of circumstances supporting them is conclusive. The scope of the defences under the balanced treaties is yet to be tested. The new system may well become a playground for lawyers and arbitrators, but it provides little solace for foreign investors. They signal a reaction of states to the excesses in investment arbitration. The reaction has been to err in the balance to such an extent as to leave the possibility of successful investment claims remote, unless an arbitrator strains meaning in the terms of the treaty to provide relief.

Past experience suggests that restrictions on expansionary interpretations have not worked. In the developing country models, there is still unrestricted access to investor–state arbitration. As with the effort of states to restrict the scope of fair and equitable treatment by tying it with customary international law, arbitrators and lawyers may want to treat such qualifications as not effective in restraining their expansionary tendencies. Thus, arbitrators have found that customary international law has advanced since it was stated in the *Neer* Claim in 1926. They have been creative in seeing such advances in the statements of the ICJ in the *ELSI* Case and in the new arbitral awards, which have stated that the *Neer* standard was not intended to remain static since its statement in 1926. They have discovered other arbitration awards made near the time of *Neer* to show that there were more lax formulations. Likewise, the denial of benefits provisions on corporate nationality have been interpreted

---

[33] A reason given for the termination of treaties by South Africa is that there was nothing to suggest that there were insufficient flows of foreign investment with states like the United States, India or Brazil with which South Africa did not have treaties.

narrowly.[34] Arbitrators may interpret defences restrictively so as to keep open the system of investment treaty arbitration, which has served their own interests well. It may well come to pass that the broad defences that are stated are given a restrictive meaning through new theoretical devices that are introduced into the law. The references that are beginning to appear in the recent awards to a proportionality test may presage this tendency. This may ensure that, despite the balanced treaty, the interests of the foreign investors will be kept alive. The proportionality test, which in itself requires a balancing process, ensures that scope is left for the function of the arbitrator despite wider regulatory space being given to states. Arbitrators could well argue that the defences are available only if the rights of the foreign investor stated in the treaty can be balanced against the rule contained in the defence in the treaty. The issue as to whether the intention of the states to give themselves greater regulatory space will be achieved by the new balanced treaties would largely depend on how arbitration tribunals, which are still given the power of decision by these treaties, will determine the scope of the defences to liability they create.

The change to balanced treaties is the result of states seeking to contain arbitral excess. The reaction of the states indicates that they are still at the bases of the system and have the capacity to destroy it if the need arises. Many Latin American states and others have reacted by withdrawing from investment arbitration and the practice of making investment treaties. The balanced treaties signal the willingness of other states to keep the system alive, though with a large number of defences providing for the taking of measures in defined circumstances. The defences are broad. The arbitrators may react to these developments by seeking to devise supervisory competence over the exercise of the regulatory powers. The emergence of such an attitude is seen in the use of the proportionality doctrine in recent awards. The nature of the competence asserted through the proportionality rule to review the regulatory measures of the states and the defences based on it will determine the future course of the law.

7.3 The proportionality rule in investment arbitration

The proportionality rule is also a construction made in recent arbitrations. It is not stated in the treaties, and is yet another example of the

---

[34] The denial of benefits provision was introduced so as to prevent incorporation of companies as a device for forum shopping. But the provision has been interpreted restrictively. See Chapter 3.

creative interpretation placed on investment treaties by arbitral tribunals. Its discovery is a response to the increasing recourse of states to the rule on regulatory takings as a justification for the measures they adopt. Regulatory measures are also coming to be exempted from liability on the basis of the violation of the fair and equitable standard. It is an avenue by which to closing the 'gaping hole' in investment treaty law created by the recognition of the rule. One could argue that arbitration has kept a step ahead of states so that whenever a rule favouring the state is introduced into treaties, its effect is stunted by an interpretation that gives a role to the arbitration tribunal to determine the extent to which it should apply the innovation in the circumstances of a dispute.

As the possibility of a variety of defences to responsibility under the treaties increase, arbitrators seek to preserve their own power of decision by finding new avenues to exercise control over whether the defences apply to the specific dispute by interpreting the limits of the defence, and also making a proportionality analysis as to the appropriateness of the measure even where it falls within the terms of the defence. The defences in the balanced treaties devolve around the theme that in situations that are defined, as in the case of the general exception for measures taken to protect health or human, animal or plant life, the measures are regulatory. It is such regulatory measures that are tested for validity on the basis of the proportionality rule.

The rule, as in the case of many innovations in this area, has no basis in the formulation of principles in the treaties, but in the assumed power of the arbitral tribunals to create relevant rules. It is an arrogation of a power for which there is no basis in the consent to arbitration. It also does not constitute a general principle of law, as even European systems have not accepted it in totality. But this has been never been a hindrance to arbitral adventurism in the field.

The proportionality rule is a technique used by some European courts when faced with a decision on a governmental measure involving a conflict between an individual's right and the public interest that is contrary the enjoyment of that right.[35] Its current relevance in case law arises in cases where the state seeks to detain an individual on the ground of a charge of terrorism. The texts that discuss the proportionality rule

---

[35] Common law writers readily acknowledge the European origins of the proportionality rule and do not see the need for its use in the common law through displacement of the rule of reasonableness. Sales, 'Rationality, Proportionality and the Development of the Law'. Some common law courts, however, have used the proportionality test in recent times, especially in terrorism cases.

almost exclusively do so in the context of this situation.[36] In such a case, there is a conflict between the right to liberty of the individual and the public interest in his detention in order to remove the threat of terrorism. In such circumstances, some modern courts, faced frequently with the problem in the current troubled times, employ the proportionality test to determine whether the infringement of the individual's right to liberty is justified by an overwhelming public interest. The two interests are balanced in order to determine which the dominant interest should be or whether the end sought to be achieved is proportionate to the suffering caused to the individual. The current concern with the proportionality test in the public law of many legal systems is due to the large number of cases arising out of charges of terrorism against individuals. The use of the test in such circumstances by the European Court of Justice has given an impetus to the test in other systems faced with similar issues. As a result, the proportionality test has become well enunciated in these systems in respect to charges of terrorism. Within the common law systems, there is considerable resistance to the acceptance of the proportionality test.[37] It cannot, as a result, constitute a general principle of law. The prospect of introducing the proportionality rule into investment arbitration is a reaction to the new wisdom that investor–state arbitration has its roots in public law and not in commercial law.

At a time when states have rediscovered customary principles such as regulatory expropriation and the necessity defence and have introduced regulatory rights into the new balanced treaties, the introduction of the proportionality principle to assess the appropriateness of a state exercising its right to protect the public interest against the interests of the foreign investor would give a new lease of life to investment arbitration. It is a development akin to the discovery of the dormant fair and equitable standard as the law on expropriation was becoming emasculated through the assertion of the regulatory expropriation rule. It proves the tenacity of arbitrators and academic supporters to ensure the viability of investment treaty arbitration. As the regulatory space advances and the scope for review of state measures diminishes, the relevance of investment

---

[36] Aron Barak, *Proportionality: Constitutional Rights and Their Limitations* (Cambridge University Press, 2012). There is no reference to the right to property in this text or to the takings jurisprudence.

[37] The US courts have rejected the proportionality rule. There is resistance in other common law jurisdictions. Claudia Gerringer, 'Sources of Resistance to Proportionality Review of Administrative Power under the New Zealand Bill of Rights', (2013) 11 *New Zealand Journal of Public & International Law* 124.

368 THE SEARCH FOR BALANCE

arbitration is maintained through the discovery and application of the proportionality rule.

Looking to public law for answers to issues of foreign investment disputes is not new wisdom. It merely shows the alarming prevarications that occur within the discipline of investment protection that are designed to secure the interests of the foreign investor on the pretext of promoting the economic development of the poorer states. It was not too long ago that developing countries argued that the moorings of foreign investment transactions lay in public law only to be quickly rebuffed. Their argument that the foreign investment transaction was an administrative contract subject to public law was dismissed on the basis that such an idea was a peculiarity of French law.[38] It is interesting that the public law argument assumes a new guise now in order to conserve the power of arbitral tribunals to supervise administrative measures taken by courts.

Its status as a general principle of international law is doubtful. Its only significance is its possible capacity to rescue the relevance of investment arbitration. Its significance to the right to property is limited. There are judgments of the European Court of Human Rights which have used it in the context of a margin of appreciation in considering expropriation. The right to property is stated in relevant instruments on human rights as an attenuated right with the heavy qualification that it is subject to the public interest.[39] The right is not stated in any investment treaty. There is an importation of the right into investment treaties in order to accommodate the proportionality rule.

The formulation of the public interest element in the right to property is such that it is internal to the consideration of the right. It is a theoretical issue as to whether such an attenuated right is fit for the application of any external balancing test. There are also legitimacy issues that arise. One is whether an arbitration tribunal sitting away from the sociopolitical and cultural situation in which the dispute arose should arrogate to itself the right to settle the issues in the dispute using a balancing test that requires an analysis of conflicts of interests within a state with the finality that attaches to awards of investor–state tribunals when it may not be able to sufficiently appreciate the context of the situation. The giving of a margin of appreciation to a state requires a tribunal to be aware of the

---

[38] *Texaco* Arbitration. The view was discussed in Chapter 2.

[39] *Pine Valley Developments Ltd* v. *Ireland*, ECHR, Application No. 12742/87, Judgment (29 December 1991); *Fredin* v. *Sweden*, ECHR, Application No. 12033/86 (18 February 1991).

7.3 THE PROPORTIONALITY RULE

distinct characteristics of the politics of the state, including its ideological and cultural base. The ability of the domestic court to perform such a task is unquestionable. In European law, the margin of appreciation given to a European state and the consequent application of the proportionality test are made in the context of a relatively homogeneous cultural and religious background. Whether this applies to the rest of the world is problematic. Unless the tribunal was enforcing uniform principles of governance for which it has no mandate, it is difficult to understand the basis on which an investment tribunal can have the competence to use the proportionality test. The question is whether a tribunal that is ad hoc and outside the system should be able to examine the correctness of a sovereign state's decision as to what should be done in a given situation of urgency. The power to do this premised on several propositions.

7.3.1 The public law basis of investment arbitration

The view that public law has a relevance to investment transactions is not altogether new. It was, as indicated, an argument advanced in many early arbitrations by developing countries, only for the argument to be dismissed on the ground that it was founded in ideas of French law and could not be universalized as a general principle of law. Thus, the argument was made before arbitration tribunals as well as in literature that a foreign investment agreement was defeasible in the public interest, meaning that where welfare interests of the public require the contract to be extinguished it could be terminated on the theory that public interest dominates the individual interests of the other contracting party. This notion of the defeasibility of state contracts is accepted in the French law theory relating to the 'contrat administratif'. The view was that the state contract was located in public law and that the ordinary principles of contract law could not apply. The state was unlike a commercial contractor. It acts not for its benefit or for profit, but for the benefit of its people so that where circumstances change so as to make the state contract detrimental to the public interest, the state should have the right to terminate the contract. The English court recognized the principle in the *Amphitrite* Case.[40] In this case, which was decided in times of war, Rowlatt J. said:

---

[40] *Rederiaktiebolaget Amphitrite* v. *The King* [1921] KB 500, 503, *per* Rowlatt J.; *Cugden Rutile (No. 2) Pty Ltd & Anor* v. *Gordon William Wesley Chalk* [1975] AC 520, *per* Lord Wilberforce; also *Williams & Humbert* v. *W & H Trade Marks (Jersey)* (1985) 75 ILR 268, at 314–15, *per* Lord Templeman; *Settebello Ltd* v. *Baco Totta & Acores* [1985] 1 WLR

370 THE SEARCH FOR BALANCE

> it is not competent for the Government to fetter its future executive action, which must necessarily be determined by the needs of the community when the question arises. It cannot by contract hamper its freedom of action in matters which concern the welfare of the State.

Amphitrite was not a singular case, an aberration committed in wartime, as is often thought to be. One can find similar dicta in English and Australian cases, indicating that executive discretion should not be curbed when exercised within the limits of the law creating it and when it is designed to serve the public interest. It seems to be a commonplace doctrine, the courts declining to examine the executive discretion vested by statute when used to promote public welfare.

Given this line of authority in English law, it was an uninformed view to state that the potential defeasibility of the foreign investment transaction in terms of public law should be confined to French law. But in *Texaco*, the arbitrator dismissed the view that the foreign investment contract is located in public law on the ground that it is a peculiarity of French law and could not be admitted as a general principle of law. Such a view was stated only so as not to undermine the project of internationalizing the contract which had been embarked upon by the leading scholars in the field. It was an exercise in dissimulation calculated to advance a preferred objective.

The manner of the rejection of the public law argument is instructive. The argument was shunted away by confining its presence to only one legal system, though both fundamental policy as well as a comparative study would have shown that public law features, including defeasibility, were present in the law on state contracts in most legal systems. Common sense dictates the fact that a distinction must be drawn between a contract for the public good, involving what is public property in natural resources or the deployment of assets of the state for public interest projects made by the state, and a private contract made for profit made between traders. Yet such acceptance of this fact was not forthcoming simply because it would defeat the project of constructing investment protection by internationalizing the foreign investment contract. General principles now come to be employed to support the view that the treaties that apply to foreign investment transactions are all about public law, and that a principle of proportionality, created in German law and applied in European law, has become the accepted general principle, which has now

---

1050. Turpin, *State Contracts*; Sornarajah, *The Settlement of Foreign Investment Disputes*, pp. 85–96.

7.3 THE PROPORTIONALITY RULE

become universal international law. Its universality has never been demonstrated. What is convenient for investment protection comes to be passed off, as in the past, as a general principle. The selectivity in the use of this technique is evident.

7.3.2 The proportionality rule

The present move to public law comes from the quarters that are intent on foreign investment protection, quite the reverse from the position in the past when developing country international lawyers sought to reverse internationalization through the use of public law. It is necessary to ask why this reversal in the pattern took place.[41] One possible answer is that there is a need to preserve the system of investment protection that has been set up under investment treaties, as interpreted by a large number of awards made in recent times, from crumbling. Such an erosion of the system is apparent as the old bases of liability have come to be restricted as a result of the reaction of states to the expansionary interpretation given to treaty principles in awards that sought to enhance the protection well beyond what had been intended by states. In doing so, states have revived notions of sovereignty and public law ideas relating to the police powers of states. Such trends limit the scope for arbitral decision as to the propriety of the state measures.

The effort at preserving some possibility of ensuring that the arbitrator could still hold for the foreign investor, despite the fact that the state's measure does not involve responsibility due to its regulatory nature, is to be found in the effort to introduce the proportionality doctrine into the picture. The argument would run that the tribunal still has competence to decide that the public interest objective behind the regulatory expropriation or other measure should be proportionate to the effect on the interests of the foreign investor, thereby enabling a finding in favour of the foreign investor for a lack of proportionality. This will enable every justification or defence that the state pleads to be tested on a proportionality criterion. It would essentially be a utilitarian test.

A second relevance of proportionality concerns the use of the fair and equitable treatment standard. Its use is of recent origin. The standard was

---

[41] Gus Van Harten made the important observation as to the public law features of investment protection under the treaties to make the argument that the state should be given greater leeway to protect public welfare, which was one its most important functions.

raked up in situations where there was no outright taking of property. Usually, the measures taken by the state affect property without involving a transfer of possession. There was difficulty in applying the expropriation provision to such situations. An avenue was found through the dormant fair and equitable standard and the breathing of new meaning into the provision. The usual meaning that was given was that there would be unfairness in situations where the foreign investor was given a legitimate expectation and the measure complained of sundered that expectation. As has been pointed out, this was an administrative law concept. It began to be used without restraint in the early cases to denote a standard of governance that involved a high degree of stability. Some arbitrators began to be concerned with the use of the emergence of this unduly high standard that was expected of the state. In that context, too, proportionality was suggested as a mechanism that could be used in determining whether the standard that was used was appropriate. In this instance, proportionality plays a containing factor.

But the criticism cannot be avoided that both the rule of legitimate expectations and the rule of proportionality, which restrains it, have no basis in the investment treaty. One must have regard to the fact that the proportionality test itself is not used in the language of the treaties. There is no language that enables its inference. It is unlikely that the negotiator of an investment treaty could have anticipated the use of the test, for the test is novel even in the systems of administrative law that recognize it, and its extent and scope are not known in these systems. This seems to be an insuperable objection to its use in investment treaty arbitration. But this simple point has been discarded in the references that can be found in recent arbitral awards that use the proportionality test. For this reason, this fundamental objection to the use of the test that the treaty language nowhere mandates the test or that it could not possibly have been within the contemplation of the states parties to the treaty is not considered at any length. It would appear that the arbitrators who use the test do so without any authority in the treaty text and are clearly exceeding their authority in doing so, but until this is tested out in annulment proceedings on the basis of excess of authority, the fact would be that its use is becoming frequent in investment awards. For this reason, the validity of the use of the test has to be considered. First, the nature of the proportionality test is examined again so that its appropriateness for use in investment arbitration can be determined.

7.3.3   What is the proportionality test?

The purpose of the proportionality test is to ensure that the objective of limiting a fundamental human right is proportionate to the advantage secured to the community. While a state is given a wide margin of appreciation in determining measures that are in the public interest, the courts use a proportionality test to determine whether the state's measure in infringing a fundamental right of the citizen was proportionate to the objective achieved. There would be a balancing of the two opposing interests effected through the use of the test. Technically, to introduce the test into investment arbitration, the investment has to be considered as involving a right to property.

The proportionality test, as indicated, is widely believed to have originated in German constitutional law. It has passed into European human rights jurisprudence, and has been accepted in some courts outside Europe.[42] This favourable account of its origin belies many facts. It is of recent origin, on any account, its limits have not been spelled out and its universality is limited to occasional cases that have adverted to it in some jurisdictions. In others, it has been suggested that the extensive review it vests in the judiciary may be inconsistent with the theory of separation of powers. This is a reason for its rejection in US law. The need for the proportionality rule is said to arise in situations where there are two competing interests, one an individual's right and the other the public interest. The court is required to decide the outcome. The court, in such circumstances, balances the interests involved in the conflict and resolves it in a manner that accords with the interest that has overwhelming factors favouring it. The notion of balancing in situations of conflict of interest is known to the law. The notion of proportionality is used in many instances. Thus, it is used both in domestic criminal law in relation to self-defence, which requires the violence used to repel an attack to be proportionate, and in international law on self-defence where an attack on a state can be resisted only by using measures proportionate to that initial attack. But its use in administrative law is different in that what is opposed is the state's exercise of police powers to regulate in the public interest. It is usually thought of as a power that flows from its sovereignty and is not to be limited through a judicial balancing of competing interests when this would already have been done by the executive which is vested with the task of enforcing policies.

---

[42] Barak, *Proportionality: Constitutional Rights and Limitations.*

374   THE SEARCH FOR BALANCE

In common law systems, the proportionality rule displaces assessment of the rationality of the administrative measure, or what is referred to as the rule of *Wednesbury* reasonableness.[43] The view is that proportionality gives the courts greater power of review than the rule of reasonableness vests in the court, thereby bringing about a shift in the balance of power between the judiciary and the other organs of government. The result is that there is a restriction on the power of the other branches of government. There is displeasure at the idea that separation of powers should be upset through the use of the proportionality rule. A clear division among common law writers has resulted on this basis.[44]

There is a visible use of the theory in recent human rights cases, where the rights of the state in securing national security are pitted against the rights of the individual to his liberty. There is less reference to proportionality in cases involving other types of human rights. The conflict between national security and personal liberty is acute. Its importance lies in the increasing number of cases arising after the 9/11 attacks and the so-called 'war on terror' where suspected terrorists have been detained in the interests of national security.

The transference of the proportionality rule into investment arbitration is made largely on the basis of its use in European Court of Human Rights cases dealing with the right to property. The statement of the right to property in the European Convention on Human Rights contains an internal balance that is required between the interests of the owner and the public interest in the taking of his property. It is implicit in the European Convention that property exists subject to the social will.[45] It is not a situation akin to that of the terrorist cases where what is balanced is a conflict of two rights, the right of the alleged terrorist to individual liberty and the right of society to security from terrorist threats. There is always an internal conflict between the interests of the owner of the property and the state's interest is employing it for public use. It is the

---

[43] Formulated in *Associated Provincial Picture Houses Ltd* v. *Wednesbury Corporation* [1948] 1 KB 223.

[44] Paul Craig, 'Proportionality, Rationality and Review', (2010) *New Zealand Law Review* 265.

[45] Article 1of Protocol 1, of the European Convention on Human Rights provides that: '(1) Every natural or legal person is entitled to the peaceful enjoyment of his possessions. No one shall be deprived of his possessions except in the public interest and subject to the conditions provided for by law and by the general principles of international law. (2) The preceding provisions shall not, however, in any way impair the right of a state to enforce such laws as it deems necessary to control the use of property in accordance with the general interest or to secure the payment of taxes or other contributions or penalties.'

7.3 THE PROPORTIONALITY RULE

state which creates property and determines the manner of use to which it is put. The right to property is different from rights such as the right to life, the right to liberty, the rights against torture and the right against slavery. These are considered non-derogable rights in Article 6 of the International Covenant on Civil and Political Rights. It is in respect of such rights that a true conflict arises between the interests of the individual and those of the public. It does not arise in the case of other, lesser rights. In neoliberal thinking, the right to property may be central. It may be the fundamental basis of the rule of law in the neoliberal vision. But it has no such significance in the law itself. It is very much a lesser right, subject to public interest as a matter of its definition. The right to property is not a core right. It was not contained in the original European Convention on Human Rights. It was introduced by the later protocol. At its inception, it was a right, as the language of Article 1 of Protocol 1 indicates, subject to control by the state in the general interest. The European Court of Human Rights may have changed its status somewhat. The Court turned a statement of the right based on a social democratic vision of property to a right based on a somewhat liberal vision, though it still recognized a police powers doctrine. The Court has used a balancing test to review the legality of administrative measures involving property. It has worked on the idea that there must be compensation, though the extent of the compensation may depend on circumstances. Its views requiring compensation when states undergo economic restructuring during which private property is affected have been criticized as moving away from the law as stated in the Convention.[46] The Court uses the proportionality test only after a wide margin of appreciation is permitted to the state. Whatever the position under the European Court may be, the transference of the law into investment arbitration cannot be accomplished without explanation as to the power of investment treaty tribunals to import a whole system into investment treaty law. The purpose of investment treaties is not to protect the right to property as a human right, but to protect investments, which have to satisfy the definition of investments under the treaty and have to be affected through measures that are prohibited by the treaty. The functions of the European Court and the investment treaty tribunal are different. The European Court has a definite mandate within a system

---

[46] Allen, 'Liberalism, Social Democracy and the Value of Property under the European Convention on Human Rights'; *R. (on the application of SRM Global Master Fund LP)* v. *Treasury Commissioner* [2009] EWCA Civ. 788; Calamita, 'British Bank Nationalizations: An International Law Perspective'.

376 THE SEARCH FOR BALANCE

to interpret the European Convention, even if it goes beyond the original intention of the member states of the European Union. Such a power is lacking in investment treaty tribunals.

7.3.4   References to the proportionality test in arbitral awards

References to the proportionality rule in arbitral awards are recent. They must be taken as a response to the increasing arguments by states that they have inherent rights to take regulatory measures in the public interest. The balanced treaties give credibility to such arguments. But what have been subjected to arbitral decisions in which the test is used are not formulations in the balanced treaties. They are, rather, the treaties that were made in the third phase of the development of the law that contain no effort at balance and are fully intent on securing inflexible investment protection. If the arguments of states that tribunals should not scrutinize regulatory measures are accepted, the role of arbitration in investment disputes will be considerably reduced. The response has been that even in the situation of a reliance on a right to regulate by a state, the arbitral tribunal has a continuing role to ensure that the right is balanced against the equally valid right of the foreign investor to the protection his investment is guaranteed by the treaty. It is likely that this view will prevail when the regulatory justifications contained in the balanced treaties of the fourth phase come to be considered. If the states thought that they had diminished the role of arbitration through the balanced treaties, they were mistaken. Arbitrators have seen fit to dispose of such thoughts through the introduction of the proportionality test, foreshadowing developments leading to the so called balanced treaties with defences stated on the basis of the state's need to regulate.

The proportionality test began to appear in arbitral awards very recently. The pattern that appears is that the arbitral tribunal considers the acceptability of a regulatory right, but reserves the right to examine it to determine whether it satisfies the test of proportionality. The awards may be briefly set out.

In expropriation cases, the notion of proportionality makes its appearance earlier than in other type of cases. Thus, in *Fireman's Fund* v. *Mexico* (2006),[47] citing *Tecmed* v. *Mexico* (2003),[48] the proportionality test is regarded as one of the criteria taken into account when dealing with the

---

[47] ICSID, Case No. ARB(AF)/02/1 (17 July 2006), at para. 176.
[48] ICSID, Case No. ARB(AF)/00/2, Award (29 May 2003), at para. 122.

7.3 THE PROPORTIONALITY RULE

distinction between non-compensable regulatory takings and a compensable expropriation. The inference to be drawn is that proportionality came to be discussed around the time that regulatory expropriation, as a non-compensable form of expropriation, came to be rediscovered. The formulation of the rule on regulatory expropriation brought expansion in expropriation law to a shuddering halt.

With the first textual reference to it in the side letters exchanged at negotiations of the Singapore–US FTA (2004), the regulatory expropriation rule became firmly established. A control device thought up to limit its scope was the proportionality doctrine. This device came to be established first in expropriation cases. The emphasis then shifted to fair and equitable treatment. As seen in Chapter 5, some arbitrators began to state that regulatory measures taken to meet situations involving public interest may be justified even where legitimate expectations are violated. This would also have brought the new doctrine of legitimate expectations that was being developed as the basis of liability for treaty breaches to a shuddering halt if an avenue of preserving it could not be found. The introduction of the proportionality rule proved to be that avenue.

A comprehensive discussion of the proportionality rule takes place in later awards largely in the context of legitimate expectations. The existence of a clear rule on regulatory expropriation may be a reason why liability is transferred to the less exact area concerning the fair and equitable standard. In *Occidental Petroleum Corp.* v. *Ecuador* (2012),[49] proportionality was first discussed as a matter of Ecuadorian law, which was the law that applied to the transaction. The Ecuador Constitution stated that there should be 'due proportionality between offences and penalties'. The principle stated was not one of proportionality in administrative law, but a notion of retribution that punishment must fit the crime. As such, it is a notion of sentencing in most societies and has little to do with proportionality in a general sense affecting interferences with rights. The tribunal conceded that 'at first blush, the provision would appear to be directed toward criminal rather than commercial or administrative matters'.[50] That was no great impediment to a determined tribunal. The tribunal accepted expert evidence that the principle had a wider application in the law of Ecuador. On the face of it, any competent

---

[49] ICSID, Case No. ARB/06/11 (5 October 2012) (Fortier, Williams, Stern). Referred as *Oxy 11* as there was an earlier award with the same name.
[50] Paragraph 398.

378   THE SEARCH FOR BALANCE

lawyer would see that this is an aberration willingly made by the tribunal
to accommodate an innovation that would rescue investment arbitration.

The tribunal then went on to determine the extent of the application of
proportionality in the context of international investment disputes. The
tribunal found it being used in WTO jurisprudence when considering
countermeasures in trade disputes. Then it stated that:[51]

> in the context of administrative action, the most developed body of
> jurisprudence is in Europe. It is very well-established law in a number
> of European countries that there is a principle of proportionality, which
> requires that administrative measures must not be any more drastic than
> is necessary for achieving the desired end. The principle has been adopted
> and applied countless times by the European Court of Justice in
> Luxembourg and by the European Court of Human Rights in Strasbourg.

The tribunal stated that there were four ICSID cases holding that the
principle of proportionality was applicable to fair and equitable treatment.[52] In *MTD Equity*, there is a mere use of the word proportionality.
The dictum counts for little. The other three awards are about expropriation and rely on the jurisprudence of the European Court of Human
Rights. Both *Azurix* and *Tecmed* relied on the European Court's decision
in *James* v. *United Kingdom*.[53] The tribunal then tied the principle in the
European Court's decision to the law in Ecuador. The tribunal returned
to the theme of proportionality in punishment and acknowledged the
difficulty in making decisions on such matters.[54] The case law cited did
not deal with proportionality in the context of the fair and equitable
standard. They were limited to expropriation as the European cases cited
were. The tribunal was conscious of the considerable difficulty in importing European law into consideration of the dispute before it. European
law cannot be converted into a general principle. There is no demonstration that this could be done. In the old days of imperialism, it was easy to
convert European law into international law as the 'civilized' legal systems did not exist beyond Europe. One would have thought such days
were now long gone. In any event, the notion of proportionality does not
even find acceptance in all European systems. There is resistance to it in
English law for the reason that it gives courts too much power of review
over administrative action and upsets the doctrine of separation of
powers. Both in Europe and elsewhere, the proportionality rule is used

---

[51] Paragraph 403.
[52] *MTD* v. *Chile; LG&E* v. *Argentina; Tecmed* v. *Mexico* and *Azurix* v. *Argentina*.
[53] ECtHR, 21 February 1986.   [54] Paragraph 419.

7.3 THE PROPORTIONALITY RULE

only after giving a wide margin of appreciation for the determination of the state that it was acting in the public interest. In some situations, particularly of national security, the investment treaty states that such determination is a matter for subjective decision and is not reviewable. Clearly, the tribunal in *Occidental Petroleum* was hunting fruitlessly for a peg on which to hang the proportionality rule, which it had decided to use. It is another instance of an absence of acceptable reasoning common to investment arbitration.

There are references to proportionality in other awards, but there is no effort to engage in reasoning as to how it comes to be part of the law that is to be applied. In *Arif* v. *Moldova*, there is reference to a balancing exercise in the context of legitimate expectations that takes account of a state's right to regulate, obviously a reference in favour of the state.[55] There was reference to proportionality in *Total* v. *Argentina*.[56] But in these cases, there does not seem to have been any variance to conclusions already reached resulting from the use of the proportionality rule.

In *Rompetrol* v. *Romania* (2013),[57] there is reference to a balancing of competing considerations. But the tribunal was not seeking to apply a proportionality test in any sense. The dispute concerned allegations of harassment of personnel during investigations of alleged crimes. The tribunal characterized the dispute as a novel one that had not arisen frequently in the past.[58] It found that the issue was whether the investor was given fair and equitable treatment. 'There is a paucity of accumulated wisdom as to where to strike the balance in that regard between the legitimate interests of the State and those of the foreign investor.' The tribunal pointed out the interests of the state in pursuing charges of corruption in the course of privatization, but also ruled that this must be done with a standard of fairness. The tribunal stated that the treaty did not immunize individuals from the scope of the criminal law. The balancing exercise was therefore complex. The tribunal ruled that there were no damages that could be proved on the facts. Though the balancing test was referred to, the award does not involve a considered use of the proportionality rule. The dictum, however, suggests that the balancing test is appropriate where the claim is based on the violation of the fair and equitable standard.

---

[55] ICSID, Case No. ARB/11/23 (8 April 2013), para. 537.
[56] ICSID, Case No. ARB/04/01 (27 December 2010), para. 333.
[57] ICSID, Case No. ARB/06/3 (Berman, Donovan, Lalonde).
[58] *Desert Line* v. *Yemen* and *Rafat Ali Rizvi* had features in common.

The references to proportionality are efforts at scurrying to find an alternative basis on which tribunals could review administrative measures of states. It has never been shown how proportionality is relevant to this exercise. The references to the decisions of the European Court fail to mention that the Court uses proportionality only after giving a wide margin of appreciation to the state. In any event, there is nothing in the treaties that gives an arbitration tribunal the power to covert itself into a judicial body that has powers of administrative review over a state's conduct. The treaties never intended to give such power to arbitral tribunals. The attempt to impose a proportionality criterion is yet again an attempt at an expansionary role of arbitration in order to maintain its relevance in the face of the reaction of states to past arbitral indiscretions. This is to compound errors and provoke further action by states. It demonstrates to states that arbitrators have an inveterate bias that prevents visible indication of their intentions in making treaties being given effect. It may slowly lead to the realization that the problem lies with the method of dispute resolution through ad hoc arbitration.

7.3.5   The future of proportionality

There is, as yet, no clear indication that arbitrators will use the proportionality rule each time a regulatory defence is put up by a state. There are indications in a few awards that where a regulatory right is claimed by the state as a justification, the tribunal will balance that right against the interest of the foreign investor to determine whether the measure was justified. There are objections to such an approach which need to be considered:

(i)   There is no justification in the text of treaties to use such a test. The regulatory right is spelled out in balanced treaties. If it is to be subjected to an extraneous test, the treaty would advert to the test being applied. If the proportionality test is applied, arbitrators import the test into the law without any textual basis for such a course.

(ii)   There are no grounds for saying that the test constitutes a general principle of law. The accommodation of a general principle in a treaty is called for if there is room in the treaty for such accommodation. The treaty is clear that the defences justifying regulation are not to be subjected to any extraneous condition. Ordinary

7.3 THE PROPORTIONALITY RULE 381

principles of treaty interpretation would militate against such a course.

(iii) In any event, it will be difficult to demonstrate that the proportionality rule is a general principle of law. In *Occidental Petroleum v. Ecuador*, reliance was placed on the fact that the European Court of Human Rights uses the proportionality rule. The European Court's remedies are engaged after local remedies have been satisfied. The rule is applied only after a wide margin of appreciation is given to the state, and if the measure falls within the margin, the Court will not proceed further. The proportionality test does not arise. Under the European Convention, the balance is internal to the right to property. As indicated, the right to property in the Convention exists subject to the public interest.

(iv) In European law, a wide margin of appreciation is given for the decision taken by a state. It has to be queried whether the situation is the same in investment treaties. The defences recognized in the balanced treaties state the regulatory right in absolute terms. There is no right to property involved in an investment treaty. One has to be constructed. In the overwhelming situations where such an analysis is made, the state's decision that it acted in the public interest is seldom queried.

(v) Outside the European Court, which presumably draws the proportionality rule from German law, the courts of other European states are not uniform in applying the proportionality test. It would be difficult to demonstrate that the test is a general principle of law, even in European states. In English law, the test that is ordinarily applied is one of reasonableness and not one of proportionality. This is a less exacting test, which limits the courts' power of review to egregiously unreasonable measures.

(vi) In many systems, the separation of powers doctrine would prevent the proportionality rule being applied to test whether the legislature or the executive erred. These systems have to be factored in to determine whether the proportionality test is a general principle of law.

(vii) Arbitral tribunals using the test will be performing a creative function which will involve criticisms as to the legitimacy of the exercise.

(viii) The proportionality test calls for the making of highly subjective value judgments. The appropriateness of an arbitral tribunal making such judgment will always be regarded with suspicion.

382   THE SEARCH FOR BALANCE

(xi) The generality and vagueness of the proportionality test means that subjective factors dominate its application. Its use in investment arbitration, an area already criticized for prejudiced views, will have such criticism enhanced if arbitrators were to use the proportionality test as a limit to the exercise of a state's regulatory powers.

So far, the indications are only slight that arbitral tribunals will react to the balanced treaties, which seem to create too many defences in favour of states, by limiting the exercise of the regulatory measures that form the basis of these defences through the use of a proportionality test. There are incipient tendencies in that direction. It could well be that over the course of time a definite tendency could develop that uses the proportionality test. This would defeat the purpose of states that make balanced treaties. But there could be cases in which the wide latitude given to the states in the balanced treaties may do injustice to the foreign investor. A dilemma awaits the development of the law in balanced treaties. The balanced treaties may create more problems than they solve. Given the bias towards investment protection, the urge to develop ways of curbing the right to regulate in the balanced treaties will be great.

The fact is that states may abuse regulatory powers. There is a case for arbitrators reviewing a situation where this occurs. But such reviews will be fraught with charges of bias on the part of the arbitrators. It could well be that overzealous arbitrators may exercise review powers in such a manner as to irk states. If this were to happen, the next step beyond balanced treaties would be to have no treaties at all. One can only hope that arbitral tribunals will proceed with caution when dealing with regulatory measures and do not get enthusiastic about applying tests like the proportionality test.

7.4   Possible changes

The change to balanced treaties has been criticized earlier on the ground that introduces further uncertainties into the law on investment arbitration. It has also been pointed out that the effort to entrench regulatory space in states through balanced treaties may provoke a resort to the application of a proportionality rule by arbitration tribunals. Both trends were seen as not being adequate solutions to the existing problems of investment arbitration resulting from the expansionist adventures that led to the law in the treaties being subverted through interpretation to

7.4 POSSIBLE CHANGES 383

enhance the neoliberal objective of greater investment protection. The balanced treaties will not satisfy foreign investors. The purpose behind them is unclear. If the earlier rationale that the treaties promote flows of foreign investment still holds despite evidence against it, the balanced treaties simply destroy that rationale by making investment protection very uncertain under them. If the rationale is lost, the question remains as to whether it is necessary to make investment treaties at all.

It is said that it is easy to break down existing structures, but that it is difficult to replace them. This is an oblique attack on the inveterate critics of investor–state arbitration. The institution that is attacked is not a venerable one. It rose to prominence in the 1990s, and its decline started in 2004 with the balanced treaties. It is not such a venerable institution in international law that its survival must be assured, particularly when the neoliberal theories which drove it are now defunct. The system has become so toxic that states have found it necessary to withdraw from it. Its termination will not be lamented by many states. The severe critic of it may say that it had become a replacement for colonialism in that it tied the economies of developing states through rules foisted on them via arbitration and through other means of pressure. If that is correct, it is an obnoxious system which must be ended.

It was promoted by the sole hegemonic power whose decline has led to a multipolar world. It created consternation for developing states at difficult times, such as economic crises. The dismantling of the system should not create anxiety, particularly if a more settled one can be found. If the present structure is broken, there are pre-existing structures which still remain valid and will always provide a fall-back position. There is absolutely no evidence to show that the world of investment treaties brought about a better system than the previous systems. There is no evidence to show that it brought economic development to the poorer world. It brought economic development to arbitrators, law firms and to academic aspirants to prosperity. Rather, the anxieties it created through frequent recourse to arbitration, even in times of economic stress to the developing states, stymied policies that could have been taken to avert difficult situations. States like Argentina are saddled with the economic problems created by the heavy damages awarded in the arbitrations on the basis of doubtful interpretations of the law.[59] Vulture funds refuse to

---

[59] See the advertisement of the Argentine government regarding the refusal to settle the debts created by the awards. The vulture funds that bought them for less value from the holders of the awards now claim sums grossly in excess of the price. *The Guardian*, 23 June 2014.

384   THE SEARCH FOR BALANCE

settle debts they bought at less than their value in the hope of tying Argentina down to excessive payments.

The world of investment did function in the past without the present system of treaty-based investment arbitration. Countries like Brazil function quite effectively while staying out of it.[60] There are other avenues of recourse to justice. Contract-based arbitration negotiated by the parties will still remain. The domestic courts, diplomatic protection and international courts do remain and could provide relief. The notion that domestic courts are inadequate may have been true in the past when dictatorships and rudimentary governance existed in many parts of the developing world. That is no longer the case. The rationale for developing the international minimum standard was the absence of secure mechanisms of justice in host states. This may no longer be the case in a majority of the developing states. If it is, there are other methods of recourse to justice available. South Africa has stated its belief that strengthening domestic means of justice to foreign investors is better than having investment treaties. The absence of definite laws on foreign investment and an absence of effective courts was the reason for building up alternative international systems. Neither rationale holds good any longer as most countries have viable legislation on foreign investment and an effective system of courts to provide justice. The local remedies rule is coming to be stressed for this reason as a precondition to treaty-based arbitration.[61] True, it is that failure to provide effective remedies that must enable recourse to international remedies. These exist under the present system.

But now that there is a system that has been built up through investment treaties, the question may be asked whether it can be made more effective. Many suggestions have been made as to how this could be done. The most favoured suggestion is to create a permanent appellate body that will function as an appellate court for all types of investment arbitration. This has been a suggestion put up by a considerable number of scholars. The Appellate Body of the WTO provides the model, but this body works under a single global treaty system. It is unlike investment arbitration, which is based on thousands of diverse investment treaties and free trade agreements.

One can be sceptical as to the validity of the suggestion of a single appellate body. A permanent appellate body will carry with it the defects

---

[60] Brazil is the obvious example. As a South African report pointed out, South Africa did not have investment treaties with its largest investor states: the United States, Brazil and India.

[61] For example, *Apotex Inc.* v. *United States*; UNCTAD, *World Investment Report* (Geneva, 2014).

of the existing system. It will be a superstructure built onto the rotten foundations of the existing system. The personnel who constitute investment arbitration tribunals will transfer to it. The criticism is made that investor–state arbitration is controlled by a very limited group of persons. This oligarchy will be graduated to the permanent appellate body. Whatever biases this group may have will be given legitimacy through this process. True, it is that states that would elect members of the appellate tribunal, but the tribunals where this has been done, including the ICJ, suffer from the fact that there is an inherent domination of these courts by those with greater skills in the law. It is a known fact that nominations made by developing countries to major international tribunals, like the ICJ, are not based on skills but on extraneous factors. An appellate body will not remove the disenchantment with the law that many developing countries have formed of investor–state arbitration. It will, possibly, create procedure to entrench by interpretation notions that are considered unfavourable to the maintenance of a regulatory space for states. A multilateral law on investment protection could well be built up through an international tribunal more efficiently. States do not wish to have such a law as it would impede their regulatory freedom significantly. The location of the appellate mechanism would also be a problem. There is already a considerable body of non-ICSID arbitration,[62] and the appellate mechanism cannot be uniformly applied to the different types of arbitrations that exist at present.

Besides, the law itself is decentralized. It is drawn from single treaties, which are unlike each other. Despite the hype that there are great similarities, the treaties are seldom capable of generating the same law due to textual variations. With the emergence of balanced treaties, the divergences are likely to be greater. The scope of their application differs in accordance with the definition of rights in investment in a diversity of national laws. Appellate mechanisms are premised on the existence of a single legal system of uniform application. This cannot be said of investor–state arbitration. The reasoning used is also diverse. Where analogical reasoning is used to support a point, it could be drawn from a diversity of inconsistent sources.[63]

---

[62] Besides the ICSID, treaty-based investment arbitrations are held under UNCITRAL, ICC, the Stockholm Chamber of Commerce and the London Court of International Arbitration. Other centres also vie for such arbitrations. There are ad hoc arbitrations as well.

[63] Roberts, 'Clash of Paradigms: Actors and Analogies Shaping the Investment Treaty System', at p. 52: 'This decentralization opens the system to a myriad of competing analogies and slows down the process of convergence on a single set of accepted

Within domestic legal systems, the law stated by an appellate court authoritatively can always be changed by the legislature. It is possible to rationalize the structure of the appellate judicial body in a legal system within a democracy on the basis that the legislature, an elected body, can always rectify a decision laying down the law simply by contrary legislation. This will not be the case with an appellate body within investment law. There is no corrective device if there is a perception of error. The process of reconvening the member states that constituted the appellate body would be a cumbersome one. It is unlikely that states would accept the suggestion of an appellate body for investment disputes. If it is correct that philosophical attitudes such as neoliberalism dictate outcomes in investment arbitration, such tendencies will become entrenched within an appellate system that may outlast that philosophical attitude.

An alternative suggested in some treaties is worth considering. It is to have a consultation mechanism consisting of officials of both states prior to the arbitration proceeding. The tribunal could ask for guidance on legal issues from a permanent consultative body. The view was that such a mechanism, modelled on the Article 334 of the EC Treaty, which permits national courts to request advice as to European law from the European Court of Justice, would lead to awards based on consistency as to law. It would be better if the consultation mechanism is established by the states making the treaties. They would then be able to control outcomes in a manner they had intended, rather than have their intentions substituted by third-party mechanisms.

There are other alternatives that could be pursued. The Australian way, now in a state of suspense, is not to have investor–state arbitration. This dispenses with costly arbitration and lifts limitations that freeze regulatory freedom. The extent to which the threat of arbitration freezes such freedom to act in the public interest cannot be calculated. The Australian solution does not leave the foreign investor without recourse to outside arbitration as he can construct this for himself through contract. The Australian courts also provide effective remedies. It would appear that the Philippines government will also follow this approach, as investor–state arbitration is missing from the Japan–Philippines treaty.

One acceptable solution may be to have a screening mechanism prior to arbitration to determine whether there is in fact a need to submit the case to arbitration. This is indicated in many recent treaties in the case of

---

analogies.' The notion that multilateralization brings about uniformity is a contested idea. So, too, the scope of the MFN clause to bring this about remains heavily contested.

disputes relating to taxation, environmental measures,[64] and measures affecting labour standards[65] and prudential services.[66] The technique would be to hold consultations between expert groups of the two states as to whether the measure involves an expropriation, or a determination as to whether the measure is purely regulatory. This ensures the continuing interest of the states in the process of arbitration and flies in the face of the view that there is a complete privatization of arbitration. Arresting privatization is a process that has already been commenced and it should be taken further. The notion that the foreign investor enforces a right of his own when he seeks arbitration is not one that is maintainable in view of these different trends in balanced treaties.

A cue must be taken from these new techniques so that whenever a dispute arises, a permanent tribunal constituted by the two states will initially determine whether there is sufficient justification for the dispute or whether there is a defence disclosed under the treaty. These could be outside the treaty itself, as in the case of necessity, or within the treaty, as in the case of national security. If the parties cannot agree on a defence or on the legal outcome, the dispute could go to arbitration before a panel of arbitrators drawn from a list that both parties maintain. The dispute could be identified by the states prior to the arbitration. The panel could consist of former or serving judges or other qualified persons and experts depending on the nature of the dispute. This will ward against the criticism that investor–state arbitration is limited to a coterie of individuals. It will also neutralize any legitimacy problem as the arbitral tribunal will consist of persons competent to pronounce on the domestic issues of both states as they are drawn from those states. But it may create problems that national judges are not neutral.

The new system should exclude law firms appearing for the parties. There is a problem of inequality in arms in this area, as a developing state, even a large one, needs to hire foreign law firms to defend them in arbitrations. It is a feature of law in developed states that the rich often escape the reach of the law through clever legal defences. The examples of

---

[64] Article XII of the US Model Treaty (2012), refers to requests for consultations on environmental measures.

[65] The US Model Treaty (2012), has a provision for labour standards similar to that for environmental standards.

[66] Article XX of the US Model Treaty (2012), states that the respondent state could ask for a determination by an expert committee formed by both states while the arbitration is in progress as to the status of the measure affecting the financial services sector. The determination that a defence is disclosed will end the arbitration.

388   THE SEARCH FOR BALANCE

it are too numerous to detail, justifying the complaint that bumble bees break through the web of the law while small flies get caught. Investment arbitration is coming to resemble this. Mexico and Argentina has solved this problem to some extent. Dedicated teams of lawyers to defend states could be built up with assistance of NGOs and other institutions. The keeping out of large law firms is necessitated by the fact that this area has been converted into a lucrative legal business. There is also the emergence of third-party funders of litigation. It is time to ease this frenetic activity, which takes the law away from its original purpose of economic development that underpinned the making of the treaties, not the building up of arbitrators, law firms or long queues of young lawyers, both academic and professional, who seek to join in the chase.

Arbitration will remain, despite such reforms, although the frenetic activity in treaty-based arbitration may cease. This activity was not what arbitration was designed for. The specialist institution, the ICSID, was not created with a view to investor–state arbitration, but for arbitration based on contract. Though the possibility of consent through treaties was discussed during the formation of the ICSID, the extent of its later significance could not have been anticipated. The ICSID operated without any experience of treaty-based arbitration for nearly a quarter of a century of its existence. The last few years have exposed the defects in the present system, and it is necessary to make a new beginning in this area in the light of the experience of these years of resistance and change. The balanced treaties or the introduction of a proportionality test to limit regulatory measures are not the answers to the problems that have been created. A more radical change is necessary. This will come about when states begin terminating their treaties and withdrawing from arbitral institutions. Then, contract arbitration will become more significant, and there will be greater use of domestic courts.

8

Resistance and change in international investment law

The last few chapters have dealt with the schisms that have arisen within law on foreign investment protection. These norm conflicts present a crisis of legitimacy for international law on foreign investment. There have been band-aid solutions while the crisis was building up. Ad hoc solutions were adopted, such as the interpretive note of the NAFTA Commission indicating that the fair and equitable treatment standard was to be tied to the international minimum standard of customary international law. Denial of benefits clauses were inserted in order to overcome improper uses of corporate nationality. But such solutions had only limited success as arbitrators, inclined towards inflexible investment protection, found ways of circumventing such quick fixes. Apologists regarded the inconsistent awards as demonstrating the vigour of the system rather than as indicating flaws in reasoning, as conflicts in ideology or as a contest between different approaches to decision-making. The argument was that every sector of the law goes through a phase of development in which tensions are ironed out. It was argued that the design of the system promoted eventual conformity. There was little questioning of inadequacies of the developments or its theoretical fallacies.

The conflicting awards were explained away as based on differences in the formulations of substantive commitments in the provisions of the treaties that were being interpreted, when in fact many of the differences arose as a result of expansionary interpretations of largely similar provisions such as the incorporation of companies to identify corporate nationality or the MFN clause. It was clear that some arbitrators were unwilling to extend the law so as to achieve investment protection, while others willingly did so. These attitudes can be explained on ideological grounds or on grounds of different attitudes to decision-making. The institutional context within which the arbitration took place already favoured inclination towards solutions geared to neoliberal norms that induced the course of decisions towards solutions acceptable to

389

foreign business. Other arbitrators baulked at such expansionism, though they too went along with aspects of the law that had been created. Within arbitration itself, there were no efforts at radical questioning of the system that evolved. Such questioning came from states, NGOs and academic critics.

The malaise in investment arbitration is deep-seated. The legitimacy concerns with it arise from two factors. The first relates to the democracy deficit that is involved in a law made by ad hoc tribunals. Arbitrators have no mandate to make the profound changes they have on the basis of hazy provisions in investment treaties. These tribunals are not accountable. Their decisions, even when wrong, cannot be corrected. One may leave aside the fact that an OECD publication identifies just twelve arbitrators as having contributed to the making of the bulk of the law on the subject, that repeat appointments ensure that the law that arbitrators state continues to be followed and could be buttressed through eager claims to a system of precedent.[1] But the more troublesome fact is that there is ground for questioning the basis on which arbitrators extend the law on the basis of their subjective findings on the policy rationales behind investment. Statistical studies that show that states win arbitrations more often than they lose them are of little significance. The system is seen as affecting the reputation of states, condemns them to pay high damages when they can least afford to do so, exposes them to a multitude of claims arising from the same economic or political situation, and constrains their regulatory efficiency through threats of arbitration.

There is also an absence of ethical values in the type of decisions that have been made. The legitimacy of an international norm must be based on fairness criteria. Neoliberalism has ensured that the aim of liberalization and protection of property rights enhances its philosophy of individualism on the theory that such notions will lead to the trickling down of wealth. The result of the adoption of policies based on this view

---

[1] David Gaukrodger and Kathryn Gordon, 'Investor–State Dispute Settlement: A Scoping Paper for the Investment Policy Community', OECD Working Papers on International Investment, No. 2012/3 OECD Investment Division, Paris, 2012, available at: www.oecd. org/daf/investment/workingpapers. 'For a mechanism that allows parties to choose their arbitrators with only few limitations, it is striking to find that a group of only 12 arbitrators have been involved (typically as one or more of three arbitrators) in 60% of a large sample of ICSID cases (a total of 158 cases out of 263 tribunals). Frequent arbitrators may also serve in other cases as counsel or experts on legal issues' (at p. 45). The charge is repeated in a report by the Transnational Institute, 'Profiting from Injustice: How Law Firms, Arbitrators and Financiers are Fuelling an Investment Arbitration Boom', Amsterdam, 2012.

has been wide and growing disparities in wealth. Globalization has ensured that the picture was repeated in the different countries of the world. In foreign investment, investment flows that are secured through protection given by investment arbitration were justified on the ground of the untested premise that such flows lead to economic development. Investment arbitration is thereby made to rest on a choice of a particular economic philosophy. Arbitrators were not given a mandate to make such a choice for the world or to formulate principles that entrench the choice.

Theories have resulted justifying the making of such a choice. These range from the need to impose a standard of governance, the adoption of the rule of law in economic matters enabling the protection of the right to property, the multilateralization of norms in a globalizing world and the building up of a global administrative law through arbitral award. These justifications are based on the Western liberal tradition pressed into the service of foreign investment protection. The liberal tradition does not demand that the state should not function to the betterment of the society as a whole. Rather, property interests in that tradition are based on the priority of social interests and welfare. In any event, these political and economic theories are inconsistent with the notion of the authoritarian developmental state that is practiced in other parts of the world. Diverse countries such as China, India and Singapore use the model of the developmental state to achieve economic progress. There is nothing to suggest that that economic model is less preferable to other models. The fundamental flaw with neoliberalism is that there is but one model to follow. Investment arbitration subscribes to this single vision of what the model should be. It is not the function of the system of investment arbitration to expand rules so as to accommodate particular visions of economic development and thereby deny the state the role of exercising its regulatory function in the public interest. On any model, this power of the state has to be recognized.

The norms of investment protection created through expansive interpretations lack legitimacy. A norm in society is legitimate not only because it proceeds from identifiable sources of the legal system, but also because the people whom it governs are willing to accept and abide by it. It keeps changing as the different interests of competing groups within the community affected by the norm change, ever reconciling the conflict of interests through the agencies of the law, be it regulatory agencies, courts or the legislature. It also changes as standards of fairness within a community change.

392   RESISTANCE AND CHANGE

In international law, legitimacy is grounded in factors other than power. Private power is often able to manipulate norms in association with the public power of states. For a while, there would be acceptance of such norms due to their low visibility. A case in point is the universalization of intellectual property law through TRIPS until the extent of the change hit the public when it was realized that medicines for widely prevalent diseases were priced highly under patent protection. When the matter becomes visible as a result, the unacceptability of the norm becomes evident in terms of human rights and in terms of public interests. Protests develop against the norm. Consequently, changes have to be instituted. Likewise, investment treaty norms and, more relevantly, the expansion of them by the arbitral fraternity are matters of low visibility, emerging into the public limelight only in recent times as a result of arbitrations involving water rights, the manufacture of carcinogenic substances or tobacco labelling. In South Korea, the *Lone Star* Arbitration involving the claim of a foreign investor in a Korean insurance company in which ordinary people have interests, has caused widespread public concern. The *Cochahamba* water dispute caused global agitations. The low visibility of investment arbitration is no longer possible. The universal interest in such arbitrations is evident and the public aversion to the fact that investment arbitration has become an instrument of protection for foreign investment to the exclusion of other interests such as the environment, health, access to essentials like medicines, electricity and water, positive discrimination to advantage underprivileged groups and human rights is evident. Such visibility is recent. This is so in academic disciplines as well. Previously, investment arbitration attracted little concern among academic international lawyers because of fragmentation and containment within a limited circle. The object was to develop such a law away from the scrutiny of international lawyers from other disciplines. Such a strategy could not succeed for too long. It has now attracted the attention of lawyers from other fields of international law, resulting in a plethora of writing on various areas of international law, which clash with the notion of investment protection.

Change again has had to result in the area. Established interests devise a theory to conserve the existing international law as expanded in investment arbitration through theoretical constructs such as assimilation to principles of comparative public law or the existence of a global administrative law. Those who oppose them have done so on the basis of sectional interests in areas of human rights or the environment. This, again, is a sign of fragmentation as each scholar makes the criticism from the standpoint of his or her own area of international law and not from the point of view of international law as a whole. When the law relating to foreign investment was first structured, the law used was to draw upon rules that facilitated investment protection in the creation of a theory of internationalization. This may have been possible in the past when there were no strong norms on the protection of other global interests. In modern international law, which has developed sufficiently to recognize the protection of a diversity of other interests besides foreign investment, it is necessary to develop an international law that accommodates all these diverse interests rather than tinker with sectors of international law and examine how each sector impacts on the international law on foreign investment. Rather, the effort should be to create an international law on foreign investment that contains the rules of all these different areas and construct a manner of accommodating them in the law. It is inevitable that changes will occur in the law. Such change may include the dismantling of investment treaty arbitration. As far as some states which have pulled out of the system are concerned, the system simply does not exist. Whether others will follow suit, depends on significant remodelling of the existing system. Such changes will only mark yet another change in a cycle of changes.

8.1 Interpreting change

The preceding chapters discussed important developments that have taken place within the international law on foreign investment in the last two and a half decades. It is evident that the law was undergoing tremendous change accelerated by the onset of neoliberal ideology, resistance to such change and further change resulting from such resistance. There was a cycle of changes in which the role of players, the impact of global events, the competing ideological stances and the emergence of a limited consensus in approach was in evidence. It is necessary to see whether these changes could be explained in any meaningful way. This chapter of the work attempts such an explanation. The nature of the cycle of changes in international law on foreign investment in the past has been explored earlier. The explanation in this chapter concentrates on the changes described in this work which occurred with the rise of treaty-based investment arbitration from 1991, the date of *AAPL* v. *Sri Lanka*, to the present. In terms of international law, it is a short period. The dramatic changes took place within a limited period of frenetic activity. The intervening years may be divided into three periods purely for the sake of convenience of discussion of movements during those periods. It then looks at the role that the actors involved in the resulting tussles played in bringing about resistance and change. Section 8.2 explores whether a consensus is emerging or whether richer chaos awaits as the result of these eventful years in international investment law. Finally, the theme is explored as to whether a theory of resistance and change could be formulated to explain the changes taking place within the international law on foreign investment in particular, and international law in general.

8.2   The three periods of change

There were major trends that took place within a short period of time lasting over two decades, resulting in changes to the law being effected. Apologists will analyse the rapidity of the uncertain events as internal to a new and yet unformed law. They would see the law as developed through analogy and reasoning, rather than on the basis of a political and philosophical contest between different ideological forces. The inconsistencies in the large number of conflicting awards would be explained on the basis of the teething troubles of a nascent system that will self-correct in the course of time. Such explanations provide justifications for an internally inconsistent and potentially unjust system created ostensibly to promote economic development of the poorer states, but diverted to perform quite unintended functions of exclusive protection of foreign investment to the detriment of other interests.

These explanations ignore, on the pretext of high science, the external context in which the law was developed. The context of change is always relevant. The different policy goals that characterized different periods, together with the different subjective attitudes of groups of arbitrators to these policy goals, provide better accounts for the changing phases in the law as well as for the conflicts that emerged. For the purpose of analysis, these periods may be identified. The first may be regarded as a euphoric phase begun by the fall of the Soviet Union and the belief that the capitalist system had triumphed. This triggered off the view that there was a need on a global scale to move towards economic liberalization and a trend towards market capitalism. The move towards democracy and market capitalism dominated the phase until the beginning of the next millennium, when there was a massive rise in investment treaties. During this period, the groundwork for launching views favourable to investment protection was laid. The approach to the new millennium witnessed

8.2 THE THREE PERIODS OF CHANGE 395

the Asian economic crisis. Solutions to the crisis, particularly those taken by Malaysia, did not conform to the IMF prescriptions. The new millennium witnessed the Argentine crisis and the bringing of large number of arbitrations. The second period was one in which disenchantment with market-oriented philosophies were beginning to erode the triumph of market capitalism. A decline in the number of investment treaties was becoming visible. Doubts began to be expressed by some arbitrators over the expansionist stances that had been taken in some of the earlier awards. Yet the expansionist adventurism had sufficient vitality to enable new frontiers of the law to be opened up through the fair and equitable standard. The third period is that of the present. In this period, the decline in the number of new investment treaties continues. Many states announced the discontinuance of investment treaty practice and the termination of existing treaties when they came for renewal. Some states withdrew from investment arbitration. Some states discontinued making provisions for investor–state arbitration in their treaties. The new treaties that were made were the so-called balanced treaties, which opened up defences for regulatory measures. One could anticipate greater chaos as a result of such treaties as they do not ensure investment protection to the extent that would satisfy foreign investors and there is uncertainty as to their interpretation. It could also be that there will, as a consequence of balanced treaties, be a move towards other means of investment protection as the newer treaties do not give certainty to outcomes in arbitration. The trends in the current period under the new treaties must await assessment after they become sufficiently visible. The developments are not uniform in the three periods. What is suggested is that there were some strong features in one period, which came to be doubted in others. The three periods may be examined more closely

8.2.1 The period of explosion

Of the three periods, the period of explosion was the longest, beginning clearly in 1990, the date of *AAPL* v. *Sri Lanka*, and ending in 2004, taking in 'the roaring nineties' and the first few years of the new millennium. The three periods are not watertight demarcations. They are made for convenience of discussion to point out that there were distinct features in attitudes at different periods, but that these attitudes shade into other periods as would be the case in any movement within a period of time. The year 2004 is taken as a convenient date as it is prior to the global economic crisis of 2008, and is the year of the model treaties of the United

States and Canada. It also included the early Argentinian cases which showed confidence in declaring expansionary law. It was a period of explosion of the law. From the point of view of making of investment treaties as well as case law, it is easy to chart the explosion of the law in numerical terms. The number of treaties sky-rocketed from around 500 to nearly 3,000 within a decade. After *AAPL* v. *Sri Lanka*, treaty-based investment arbitration took off, with the case-load of the ICSID, which was confined to a few cases arising from contract-based arbitration to over 300 cases arising from treaty-based disputes. The figure, according to the 2014*World Investment Report*, is now over 538.

One important fact was the investment protection chapter in NAFTA (1994). It was nothing but the then existing US Model Investment Treaty cobbled into the free trade agreement. Like other investment treaties, it was aimed at the developing country partner, Mexico. The fact that a large number of cases began to be brought on the basis of the provisions of NAFTA against the United States and Canada presaged an important change. An instrument designed with investment protection in mind was being used against two developed states. The change not only showed the potential for its use in the reverse direction, but took place at a time when the investment picture was itself beginning to change, with the United States being not only the largest exporter of foreign investment, but also becoming its largest importer. The NAFTA disputes and the creative litigation strategies of the lawyers engaged in them changed attitudes to investment law considerably as the United States and, to an extent, Europe were becoming conscious of the fact that their prospects of finding themselves as respondents in such arbitrations was not too far off. The aggressive stance that the United States and Canada had taken in defending the cases brought under NAFTA was to have a profound effect on the law. It led to changes both through the defences they advanced as well as to the new balanced type of treaties the two countries began to make. These developments were restrictive of the law, but did not take place for some time. In the early phases, there was passive acceptance of the developments, as when Canada decided to pay compensation in the *Ethyl* dispute. It was only in the later phase that the United States and Canada began to fight the disputes by advancing defences based on the regulatory rights of a state as in *Methanex, Chemtura* or *Caratube*. It is consistent to say that the early NAFTA situation belongs to the euphoric phase of expansive law, though later the nature of the claims brought against the United States and Canada made them rethink their investment treaties in the light of changed factors.

8.2 THE THREE PERIODS OF CHANGE

More importantly, the nature of the law made under the treaties became expansive, ensuring that the law so made would generate a growth in disputes brought to arbitration. Most of the expansion has been described in this work. It was pointed out in Chapter 3 that there were efforts to expand the scope of jurisdiction under the treaties once the notion of arbitration without privity had become accepted. The scope of corporate nationality as a device for forum shopping had begun as a result of awards enabling the acceptance of such practices. *Fedax* v. *Venezuela* laid the foundations for financial instruments transferred by the original owners being regarded as investments capable of protection under the treaties. The MFN clause was used in order to enhance jurisdiction by removing the limitations that existed in the original treaty that the claimant could rely on. The substantive law regarding claims also underwent expansion. The law on expropriation was broadened so that any act by an agent of a state that leads to depreciation in the value of the property amounts to expropriation. The possibility of the fair and equitable standard of treatment being an alternative ground of claims on the basis that there would be a violation of the standard in the event that the legitimate expectations of the foreign investor were not met came to be discussed. Foundations were laid for the expansion of the substantive law on the basis of the fair and equitable standard as the use of expropriation law became restricted for want of dispossession in the modern types of regulatory measures.

There were continuing efforts to graduate the protection of the foreign investment contract into the sphere of treaty protection. This was done in several ways. One was through the discovery of the umbrella clause, a throwaway provision whose significance had not been fully grasped when it was included in investment treaties. But it was made the focus of efforts to ensure that the contract came to be protected by the investment treaty as the clause endeavoured to protect all commitments made by the host state. Another was to focus on the stabilization clause, the crucial clause in ensuring that legal changes do not affect the contract, and argue that it gave rise to legitimate expectations so that when these expectations were violated, liability for breach of the fair and equitable treatment standard would follow. The vitality of the stabilization clause can be seen in the efforts to keep it viable despite the formulation of a rule on regulatory expropriation.

The extensions were not made in any principled fashion. Rather, they were made by arbitrators jumping on the bandwagon of neoliberalism as if to outdo each other in their zealousness by creating new notions of investment protection. Equally, a firm group of traditionalists, set against expansionism and characterized by a fidelity to the text of the treaty and the extent of the consent of the parties, had emerged. By the end of the period, a crisis of legitimacy had arisen within treaty-based investment arbitration.

By the end of the millennium strong forces had built up against market fundamentalism and investment protection. Repeated economic crises in Russia (1997) and east Asia (1998) led to disenchantment with economic liberalization. Some states adopted measures that were not prescribed by the IMF. In1998 the multilateral investment agreement (MAI), instigated by the OECD, failed due to the persistent efforts of NGOs in the environmental and human rights fields mounting strong campaigns against its use. MAI was a developed country effort to bring about multilateral law among the rich states. The failure of the MAI ensured the rise of new actors on the scene, the NGOs. They emerged during the period of opposition to the MAI when they agitated for greater accommodation of the different interests they espoused in investment law and arbitration. The effort to create a discipline on investment within the WTO similarly floundered as China and India, along with other developing countries, insisted that if an investment discipline was created it should include within it provisions on corporate responsibility and other duties on multinational corporations.

The first period witnessed the rise of investment law, but also the gathering storms. Except in the early years of this period, when the fervour for economic liberalization carried the expansionist notions on its wings, dissent began to set in. It is not possible to identify a precise time when the dissent first arose, but it became visible as the years went by. Perhaps the failure of the MAI in 1998 marked the ending of a period, but it was around that time that the early Argentine cases had begun to experiment with revitalizing the fair and equitable standard. It is better to think in terms of a longer first period. By 2004, it was possible to see clear evidence of dissent and change from earlier premises of absolute investment protection.

But absolute changes never take place, as vestiges of trends set in the earlier period may remain strong as long as the principal actors in the sphere do not lose their power. The principal beneficiaries of the expansionist trends, the multinational corporations, their home states, the arbitrators who are inclined towards a philosophical preference for property protection and law firms that advise multinational corporations are still dominant forces which will resist change so that the tenacity of

8.2 THE THREE PERIODS OF CHANGE

expansionist notions will continue into the next period, as with most changes which are not dramatic enough to displace a paradigm. The stakes are huge in terms of monetary loss for some of the stakeholders, such as multinational companies, arbitrators and law firms, if the advantages of expansionism are abandoned altogether.

8.2.2 The period of conflict

The year 2004 is taken as the beginning of the period of conflict. As indicated, the US and Canada model treaties of 2004 presaged change. Yet just a few years before, the awards in the first few Argentine cases had signalled the opportunity for establishing an expansionist framework. The Argentinian cases are important as the early cases show the expansionist scope of the newly discovered fair and equitable standard, but, as the cases progressed, the exploration of the defences of national security and necessity began to succeed, undermining the inflexibility of investment protection. There were arbitrators who resisted the enhancement of investment protection through the creative interpretation of treaty provisions. The extensions were not supportable in terms of the strict application of the law. Some arbitrators doubted the legitimacy of an investment tribunal taking a role in actively expanding the law and going beyond the consent disclosed in the investment treaty. A classic instance is the dissent of the distinguished French international lawyer, Prosper Weil, who was the president of the tribunal in *Tokios Tokeles* v. *Ukraine* (2004), who expressed the fear that the expansionist trends may come to undermine investment treaty arbitration. The scope and extent of the fair and equitable clause came to be limited in cases like *Saluka*. The use of the MFN clause to enhance jurisdiction initiated in *Maffezini* v. *Spain* was challenged in a series of awards.

The year 2004 may be taken as crucial in this period. It is the year of the US Model Treaty (as well as the Canadian Model Treaty). It was also the year of *Methanex*, where the United States was making the argument that regulations prohibiting a carcinogenic substance used as an additive in petroleum were regulatory measures and therefore could not amount to a compensable expropriation The argument proved successful. That year, when negotiating the Singapore–US FTA, the principal negotiators, in an exchange of letters, signalled that indirect regulatory takings were not to be considered compensable except in exceptional circumstances. The exception contained in the letters passed into a firm statement in the US Model Treaty of 2004. It was actually the rediscovery of a rule that had always existed, but it took the United States to articulate it and to have measures that it had taken vindicated on the basis of the rule on regulatory expropriation.

A new type of balanced treaty took the place of treaties geared solely to investment protection. The period may be taken as lasting until around 2008, the year of the global economic crisis. States were beginning, rather belatedly, to recognize that the policy of minimal market regulation did not provide for market failures. They realized that more assertive action would become necessary in the event of imperfections developing within the market. Such assertive action could be violations of investment treaties, as they would amount to legal changes that depreciate the value of foreign investment. Investment treaties stood in the way of necessary changes. The developed states began to see the need for the creation of regulatory space. They also became conscious of the fact that they were becoming massive recipients of direct investment from industrializing states such as China, India and Brazil. On the political level, the unipolar order under the hegemony of the United States was declining and a multipolar order was coming to replace it. Greater concern with human rights and the environment had to be accommodated. The effect of the growth of NGOs on international politics had to recognized. The moorings of investment treaties, which lay in the North–South divide, was shifting with these developments. New models had to be thought up. New approaches had to be taken to meet new situations.

The result was the spate of balanced treaties recognizing areas in which regulatory measures had to be taken. Defences were provided for measures taken in the public interest. The balanced treaties were favourable towards the recognition of measures taken to protect the environment and labour standards as requiring separate treatment. Taxation and prudential measures in the financial sector were provided for separately. The balanced treaties made by developing country regional associations have been different. They leave no room for any view other than that there is an unreviewable regulatory right in the state to take measures in definite areas of public interest. These treaties move away significantly from the aim of investment protection. They clearly no longer buy into the idea that investment protection given by the treaties is necessary for investment flows that are so beneficial to the host state that it should overlook other considerations.

During this period, the Argentine cases, which arose out of the economic crisis, also began to take a different turn. The early cases showed

8.2 THE THREE PERIODS OF CHANGE 401

that the promises that Argentina had made in order to court foreign investment, such as the tying of gas prices to the American price indices and the parity between the dollar and the peso, had given rise to legitimate expectations that were violated. Compensation became due for the violation of the fair and equitable treatment provision. The plea of necessity that was taken up both under the treaty and as a defence available under public international law was rejected. The outcome in the cases changed. The annulment tribunal in *CMS* was trenchant in its criticism of the award's treatment of the necessity plea. It thought that the plea under the treaty provision should have been considered separately from the customary international law plea of necessity as they function differently. The Annulment Committee ruled that there was an error of law, though it had no power to annul the award on that ground.

The doubt on the scope of the necessity was enhanced when three awards allowed necessity for the period of the economic crisis. The Argentine cases have introduced new uncertainties into the law. The issue of whether arbitral tribunals had assumed jurisdiction without waiting for the exhaustion of the period of eighteen months during which local remedies had to be tried out will also cause problems for existing awards. This is despite a ruling by the US Supreme Court that it will not review such awards. The decision will leave a bitter taste in that there is little means of challenging what was objectively a wrong decision, particularly in view of the fact that a later Argentine case has refused jurisdiction precisely on the point that the waiting period had not been satisfied. As time passes, the appropriateness of the views that a state takes when confronted with economic crises will undergo change. The United States and Europe have undergone similar economic crises, and have taken similar measures, including nationalizations, following the global economic crisis. There are cases arising from the measures that Greece and Belgium took during the crisis. There could be more. One will have to await the awards in these cases to see whether views different from those in the Argentinian cases emerge. As the treaties come to be drafted differently to provide for secure defences for measures such as those taken by Argentina during its economic crisis, it is highly unlikely that disputes like the fifty-two cases against Argentina will be brought to arbitration again.

There were also high-profile disputes that involved Latin American states. None received greater attention than the *Cochahamba* water dispute. It was the result of the privatization of the water supply in the Bolivian city of *Cochahamba*. Bechtel, an American company, had obtained the concession to supply water previously supplied by a public corporation. Its subsidiary raised the price of water by over 50 per cent, leading to riots in the city. Bechtel had to leave, but brought an arbitration under the Bolivia–Netherlands treaty after 'migrating' to the Netherlands. Worldwide protests continued during the arbitration, which lasted for more than four years. The notion of migration and the denial of efforts at *amicus curiae* briefs gave publicity to the case. Bechtel eventually settled the case, but the controversy highlighted the commodification of water by a global company and the denial of the human right to water to the poor of the city. It brought investment arbitration to global attention. Bolivia, obviously, was keen to withdraw from arbitrations after the episode and did so.

Both the Argentine cases as well as the many arbitrations brought against other Latin American states resulted in widespread concern over investor–state arbitration in Latin America. In April 2007, at the meeting of the Bolivarian Alliance for the Americas (ALBA), Nicaragua, Bolivia and Ecuador announced that they would withdraw from the ICSID 'in order to guarantee the sovereign right of states to regulate foreign investment on their territories'. In May 2007, Bolivia denounced the ICSID. Ecuador joined ALBA in May 2007 and also denounced the ICSID. Venezuela followed in January 2012. Withdrawals from the ICSID do not matter unless existing investment treaties are terminated in accordance with their termination provisions. These provisions often permit protection to existing investments for periods of up to ten years. Venezuela now has twenty arbitrations pending at ICSID. It is certain to default on all unfavourable awards, having moved its assets back into its own jurisdiction or into states like China or Russia, which still retain absolute immunity for state assets. Brazil did not sign investment treaties. After its experience with investment arbitration, the only reason why Argentina may want to stay on the bandwagon is the experience it has obtained in defending arbitrations brought by investors. It appears that the interlude of Latin American states with liberalization and privatization is over. Latin America is back to the Calvo Doctrine. At least one part of the world, where the story of international law of foreign investment began, has come a full circle. Having gone from the Calvo Doctrine to liberalization and privatization, Latin America has now come back to the Calvo Doctrine. This analysis will, of course, depend on the political situation remaining the same at least in the near future. The Trans-Pacific Pact (TPP) is an effort to go the other way, but it is not yet complete.

8.2 THE THREE PERIODS OF CHANGE 403

There may be displeasure beginning in other countries as well. In India, the *White Industries* Award, which held that an arbitral award was an asset under the Australia–India BIT and that delay in its enforcement by the local courts would amount to a breach of the fair and equitable standard, has caused consternation. It comes at a time when there are other threats of arbitration against India in several sectors. The bribery scandal involving the allocation of spectrums involve several foreign companies affected by the order of the Indian Supreme Court that all allocations should be cancelled and fresh tenders called. Some foreign companies have threatened to bring arbitrations under BITs. Similarly, in the *Novartis* litigation, the Indian courts have held that the local manufacturing of generic drugs was permissible, resulting again in the threat of arbitration. In the light of these developments, India has shelved future BITs. South Africa has similar reservations after its black empowerment programme was challenged. Indonesia has announced that it will not conclude investment treaties in the future.

Another area in which a storm is gathering is an unrelated area kept away from discussions of the law on investment arbitration involving the increasing concern over the violation of human rights and the environment by global business. Despite Bhopal and similar disasters, the misconduct of global business did not affect the rationale that investment is good for economic development that underpinned investment protection under the treaties and the law made through investment arbitration. With reports by the UN Special Representative on Business and Human Rights that situation was ending. His studies showed the need for concern in the area. It was no longer possible to hold onto the myth that investment flows were always to the benefit of developing host states. There are a growing number of studies on corporate responsibility of multinational corporations. The law that emerges in this field must have an impact on the issue of investment protection. Two separate laws will merge at some future point.

An increasing number of economic studies also began to question the assumption that investment protection through treaties is necessary to promote flows of investment to developing countries. The correlation between the treaties could not be established in clear terms. This resulted in the querying of the making of the treaties, which appeared to involve the surrender of sovereignty for virtually no benefit, the assumption that investment flows take place being unfounded. The period ended with considerable scepticism with the existing network of investment treaties and the system of investment arbitration on which it is based.

404   RESISTANCE AND CHANGE

It is not possible to demarcate the periods precisely, and it is not necessary to do so. The fact is that there was a build-up of factors that had begun to undermine the neoliberal base on which international investment law had been built in the previous period. An essentially asymmetric system was undergoing strains. The holding exercise was in the form of balanced treaties, which were made in the hope that the steam could be released from the pressures that were building up against the system of investment treaties through the accommodation of regulatory space for the state. But the issue that has to be decided is whether such efforts will undermine the principal purpose of investment protection to such an extent that the balanced treaties will prove to be of little use. The balanced treaties serve neither the multinational corporations, as they would fear that the defences that are made will enable them to be put in bad light, nor the states, as their claim to greater regulatory space in the course of arbitral proceedings may frighten future investment away.

8.2.3   The period of uncertainties

This period begins with the global economic crisis, which commenced in 2008 and continues to the present time. In the economic sphere, the neoliberal policies adopted by states came to a halt. The ideas that were prominent in the first period – non-regulation of the market based on the ability of the market to correct itself, economic liberalization of trade, investment and the flows of assets, the emphasis on the right to property, the global protection of intellectual property – became weakened. Policies were no longer fashioned on the basis of these notions. There were riots and demonstrations against what were considered to be the excesses of capitalism in many cities of the Western world. Yet neoliberal tenets have proved to be tenacious, and the efforts to displace them have been superficial despite the need for change. Though changes can be seen, when the smoke clears it could well be that the system survives with a new set of actors in charge.

The global investment picture has undergone significant changes. The rise of Brazil, Russia, India, China and South Africa (BRICS) has meant that these states have rapidly become exporters of capital. They are also becoming states that have sufficient power to influence the course of events in world politics. International law itself has changed from a world that worked under a single hegemonic power to a multipolar order. Small states, such as Singapore, Norway, Dubai and Malaysia,

8.2 THE THREE PERIODS OF CHANGE 405

have accumulated capital that they have put into sovereign wealth funds. These funds are dedicated to making investment overseas. China has a sovereign wealth fund of over US$3 trillion. As state entities became major actors in the field, accommodating them within the existing structures proved to be difficult.

States such as China and India are searching for energy resources, very much like the Western states in the past, and they are making inroads by way of investments into resource-rich regions and countries of the world, in Africa, Canada and Australia. The investment picture has changed rapidly. The United States was wary of Chinese investments, where there were adverse reactions to Chinese efforts to buy UNOCAL shares and other Chinese investments on national security grounds. The use of national security reasons to keep Chinese investments away was resorted to more frequently. At the same time, the United States has been negotiating a free trade agreement with China. Canada has concluded one with China amid much domestic criticism. China seems now to be donning an aggressive mantle in the search for secure investment protection. One cannot read this as a case of China jumping on the bandwagon of Western states. It must be seen as a situation that drives the Western states into defensive positions. Massive investment of the type that China brings involves Chinese control over other economies. Australia, for example, is dependent on Chinese investment in mining for prosperity. Such dependence on a state that is seen as a potential enemy will fuel resentment.

In the context of these changes, inflexible investment protection, which was driven by the United States, can no longer be its goal. The 2012 US Model Treaty reflects this, but one would suspect that there will be further changes in the future to the pattern in that model treaty, conserving a greater amount of regulatory space. A consistent pattern of use of the national security justifications seems to be developing with regard to Chinese investments in the United States, while at the same time there is an ongoing negotiation for an FTA between the two states.

As mentioned in Chapter 7, there will be efforts made to either mend the defects of the existing system, go back to the system which existed prior to the investment treaties or bring about a new system of dealing with disputes arising from investments. The possible changes in this respect were outlined in the final section of Chapter 7. Apart from the balanced treaties and the possibility of the use of the proportionality rule, which was also discussed, there are few other proposals that have been implemented.

The law in the area may have returned to a situation of normlessness that existed when there was an intense conflict between the developed and developing countries, with each group of states contending for different sets of norms. Today, a similar situation prevails despite the fact that there are several investment treaties in the field. The interpretation of their central norms, even where they have some similarity, remains unclear. The confidently made argument that the treaties will lead to multilateralization of the norms, made only a few years ago, is now shaken. It cannot taken seriously. The balanced treaties let back in the ideas of sovereignty that underlay the Calvo Doctrine of the past. They revive so much of national control over foreign investment in times of stress that investment protection is shunted to the back. It is in times of stress that the investor needs protection. This will not be forthcoming as the balanced treaties make the public interest the paramount consideration in these situations of stress.

It may well be that ways of countering these tendencies could be found. The emergence of the proportionality rule may be seen as a way of countering the defences in the balanced treaties as the determination of the state is not taken as final, with the arbitration tribunal asserting that it does have a role in reviewing whether the state's measures were in proportion to what the situation required. But that very process of using such a subjective and indeterminate test will add to the uncertainties in the law. The law is in for another period of tussle with the whip hand being held by the host states. Yet with awards made against them, poorer states are at risk of having them enforced as the US Supreme Court's decision in *Argentina* v.*BG* shows. The inability to pull out of the system for a period of years after termination of the treaty will ensure that the woes of these states will remain for some time.

In the past periods, the private power of multinational corporations acted in tandem with their home states. It would appear that the alliance has now broken up. Developed states find it necessary to protect interests other than those of their corporations. Protectionist sentiment in the guise of national security is seen to be re-emerging. Transfer of jobs out of the state into cheaper locations causes anxiety. States now are moving away from the partnership they had with their private corporations and taking measures solely in the public interest, which means that they cannot subscribe to an international law that inflexibly protects foreign investments.

For entirely different reasons, the interest in preserving sovereign control over foreign investment which developing countries had, is now becoming the same as that which developed states have. Yet multinational corporations, which have accumulated considerable power in the modern world, will not give up their fight to ensure that there are strong laws on investment protection. They can secure them through the use of private power as they, indeed, did in the past by using the theory of internationalization of foreign investment contracts. They will seek to restrict the role of the reserved state power in balanced treaties through finding means of confining such power, either by the restrictive interpretation of the balanced treaties or by formulating new theories, such as the proportionality rule to limit such regulatory power. There will be the usual support for such efforts lent by arbitrators, academics and other players in the field. Whatever methods are chosen, chaos awaits the outcome until the limits of investment treaties as a method of guiding the law are realized. The treaties fulfilled a useful function of attempting clear rules. But now, they seem to be the source of the divisions that have arisen.

8.3   The possible reforms

In the light of the resistance and change that is taking place, there is a need to look at the ways in which there could be reform of the existing system. Several possibilities exist. It is best to itemize them and analyse their effectiveness.

8.3.1   The recognition that the system of investment treaties is a failure so that it should be terminated

Investment treaties brought about an asymmetrical system. They were based on premises relating to economic development that were not provable. The system developed into an uncontrollable mechanism with a multiplicity of stakeholders entering the scene and pulling in different directions. Given this situation, one solution is for the developed state and the developing state that made the treaties to mutually agree on termination or to change of the terms of the treaty so that investment treaty arbitration is ended. It is a fallacy to say that the rights of unilateral recourse to arbitration are not derivative rights. They were created by the states and supplant the right of diplomatic protection of foreign investment by states. To that extent, developed states, conscious of the iniquitous system that has resulted, should step in to ensure that it is not abused. The system that has been created is not to the advantage of any state (except, possibly, small states that would profit by adopting a policy of being a platform state).

The European Community is currently engaged in re-examining its investment treaty programme. It is an opportune time to think in terms of whether the continuation of the system of investment treaty arbitration at the unilateral instance of the foreign investor is an appropriate device in the light of the expansionist abuse that has resulted. Germany may be undergoing such a reappraisal of its treaty programme. Other states must institute similar inquiries and explore mutual termination of the treaties so that a fresh beginning can be made. Wiping the slate clean seems to be the only possible way forward.

8.3.2 Establishing a screening mechanism prior to arbitration

This is a technique that has already been explored in connection with taxation disputes in many of the balanced treaties. The technique requires the tax authorities of the two states to come together to decide on whether there was indeed a power of taxation legitimately exercised. A joint determination that it was so exercised concludes the dispute. The dispute goes to arbitration in the absence of a joint determination. The technique could be extended to all other types of dispute. The existence of the technique demonstrates that the unilateral action of the investor was always considered a derivative action. Its spread to cover all disputes will ensure that there is joint control of the types of dispute that should go to arbitration, thereby eliminating both arbitral activism as well as unscrupulous use of investment arbitration so as to benefit the interests of law firms.

8.3.3 The responsibility of arbitral institutions

Arbitral institutions, particularly the ICSID, were founded on the basis that their existence would promote flows of foreign investment. That has proved not to be the case. Rather, the increase in arbitrations has hindered the progress of developing states as an inhibition has been created against taking necessary action against improper conduct on the part of foreign investors. The ICSID has a responsibility to maintain control of the situation and should actively intervene to ensure that frivolous litigation is not brought against developing states. There is a duty to ensure that recourse to arbitration is not a devise to promote interests other than those of the parties to a genuine dispute. The existing screening role must be enlarged to include instances where the litigation is brought on the basis of expansionary claims as to what the law is. The ICSID bears institutional responsibility to clean the system of its illegitimacy by ensuring that the promised purpose of ICSID arbitration, that it is connected with economic development, is protected. It was on that basis that consent to the ICSID Convention was obtained for the system of investment arbitration.

8.3.4 A return to contractual methods of protection

Given the uncertainties that have arisen within investment treaty arbitration, multinational corporations would be better off going back to the system of arranging their protection through contract, rather than depend on the uncertainties of the investment treaties. The settlement of disputes through investment arbitration will increasingly come to depend on chance rather than certainty in outcome. The composition of the tribunal will matter in how the dispute will be resolved. The existence of a tribunal that consists of activist arbitrators with expansionary visions will decide for the foreign investor. But, the likelihood of being able to constitute such tribunals is becoming increasingly rare as the frequency of challenges to arbitrators ensures that those who will rule on the side of foreign investors are frequently challenged (as indeed are those who have shown a bias towards states). This does not bode well for investment treaty arbitration.

8.3.5 Controlling legal representation in investment arbitration

It must be recognized that overmuch activity of large law firms had much to do with the frenetic developments in the field of investment treaty arbitration. It will cool such activity if representation before arbitral tribunals is confined to selected lawyers on both sides, chosen from a panel approved by the two states that are parties to the investment treaty. Likewise, the arbitrators could also come from former judges and others chosen from a panel selected by the two parties rather than from institutions. This will help to eliminate the cost of arbitration as well.

Innovative ideas should be adopted in this area so that the system that eventuates serves all the different interests adequately and does not benefit only the foreign investors, as the present system does.

410   RESISTANCE AND CHANGE

8.4   Theory of resistance and change

This work has outlined the rapid changes that have taken place in the area of international investment law in a short period of three decades. Three periods of change were identified in this chapter. It was shown that the law shifted as the ideologies and relative power of the actors in the area changed. Except in the first period, where the law was in the firm grip of neoliberalism, the other two periods have witnessed intense conflict and chaos. Few certain legal principles emerged during these two periods. The only positive event to ensue was that the balanced treaties emerged as a compromise, but whether they will accentuate the crisis any further remains to be seen. It is necessary to inquire whether a theory explaining such change can be attempted on the basis of the description of the events that have taken place. This can be tested by the following propositions.

8.4.1   There is relative certainty in the law when it is driven by an uncontested hegemonic power on the basis of an unchallenged ideology it seeks to promote

The law is relatively certain when there is an uncontested hegemonic power interested in formulating the body of laws in a manner that suits the protection of its investors. This is secured through ensuring rights of entry and uniform norms for the protection for foreign investment around the world. Secure rules with effective compliance mechanisms are a necessary part of the system. There will be ready acceptance of such efforts if there is belief that the acceptance of the system is beneficial. The optimum period for securing such protection was the first period described above. Then, the Soviet system, which provided an alternative method of economic organization, folded leaving the United States as the single hegemon. In periods of intense globalization, when strong hegemonic powers with mercantilist projects exist, international law comes to be used to further the goals of private interests. In such past periods, the formation of the British and Dutch East India companies, their expansion and spread across the world was coterminous with the rise in the naval power of their home states. International law formulated several doctrines to aid in such expansion, such as the freedom of commerce, freedom of the high seas, the acquisition of land by conquest and the maintenance of colonial rule over other people. In the first period, the existence of the United States as the single hegemon enabled the shaping of norms favourable to US multinational corporations, which were able to advance their interests as there was an alliance between private and public interests.

The avenues of purveying this system are important. The use of the instrumentality of international law through an existing or newly created international system is necessary. The United States was able to get assistance on this from two international institutions it dominated. The World Bank and the IMF were willing participants in ensuring that such a system of investment protection was brought about. They assisted in spreading the message through persuasion as well as by economic coercion when it came to the granting of loans that a preferred system of laws and measures should be adopted. The conditionalities imposed by IMF when securing loans are well known.

The existence of a well-articulated economic and political philosophy, which drives the legal norms, ensures that the norms are accepted by other states. Neoliberalism was such a philosophy. It held a nearly universal sway in the first decade after the failure of the Soviet Union. The absence of a competing model of norms or their recent failure helps to advance the set of norms espoused by the hegemonic power. This was clear in the first period. The communist system had failed. The capitalist system was the only one left standing. Fervour for the third alternative, the system contained in the NIEO, had diminished in the previous decade, though the alternative models were not entirely demolished. State-based companies were still the basis of the economies of the existing socialist states. The NIEO had seeped into the constitutions as well as the contractual practices of many developing countries. Nevertheless, there was willingness on the part of the developing states to move away from the NIEO. There was a drying up of aid and access to loans from private banks due to the sovereign loan crisis. The context was propitious for the new norms to be accepted.

It is difficult to dismantle systems that have been established completely. This is despite the dominance of the legal order of norms that the hegemonic state seeks to establish. The rules of the system go into abeyance, but are not completely wiped out. They often remain in operation at different levels. The preference to run sectors, such as natural resources, through public corporations survived the wave of privatizations in the developing world. It remains the dominant form in socialist states. Contractual practices that reflect state interests such as the production-sharing agreement in oil continued. Constitutional provisions vesting natural resources in the people could not be wiped out. These were vestiges of the NIEO, which continued to survive despite the onslaught of neoliberal ideas. As pointed out earlier, the gleeful observations regarding the demise of the NIEO were greatly exaggerated.

The success of the norms that were advanced in the first period depended on several factors. First, they were the norms modelled on the US economic and legal system, which were seen as having triumphed over the communist model. Their acceptance was aided by the penchant for imitation of successful models. Secondly, powerful economic and political ideologies were used as the basis of the model. The ground had been prepared for the transformation by powerful US and European leaders, who had accepted the market-led economic models in their own countries. The shift of China to an open-door policy and its evident success, followed by similar shifts in India and Vietnam, aided the widespread adoption of the model. The third factor of an institutional drive behind the model was already indicated. The World Bank and the IMF boosted the model which came to be the focus of what became known as the Washington Consensus.

All changes must have an altruistic justification that cloaks its beneficiaries in a glow of virtuousness. Colonialism was explained as the white man's burden to bring a standard of civilization to the natives of Africa and Asia. The altruistic rationalization in the first period of neoliberalism that displaced competing models was that it was best suited for the economic development of the developing world. Eradication of poverty became the noble purpose that was being served. Economic liberalization benefited the rich states as it enabled markets to be prised open for trade and investment. During the first period, developing states and the newly independent states of the former Soviet Union flocked to join the queue to attract foreign investment by adopting stances that signalled that they were joining the neoliberal club by signing more investment treaties, altering their laws to recognize the right to property and agreeing to international dispute settlement. The East European states, newly released from the Soviet hold, joined in. Latin America abandoned the Calvo Doctrine. There was a global espousal of the neoliberal agenda in the context of which it was able to push through the necessary package of norms that supported investment protection.

The theoretical rationalization was bolstered through other theoretical devices. New justifications were rapidly made. One related to the rule of law redefined so as to emphasize the right to property as the stable theme.

8.4 THEORY OF RESISTANCE AND CHANGE 413

Another was to identify a standard of governance that included property protection as its centrepiece. Investment treaties were interpreted as consistent with the rule of law and the standard of governance that was so necessary for the globalizing world. Multilateralization of these norms became a project.

At the micro-level, these themes found resonance in the arbitral awards that were made in the first period. Arbitrators, as is their wont in their profession, vied with each other to show familiarity with the trends in the field. Once 'arbitration without privity' had been announced, a spate of expansionary awards followed, ensuring that the means of securing jurisdiction' as well as the substantive principles on the basis of which relief could be provided, were expanded.

Change in this period was clearly motivated by a strong ideological commitment to a particular economic philosophy. States followed it through conviction or through imitation in the belief that it assured them of the path to success. Competition was also a factor. States felt that if they did not follow the policies of the other states, they would lose out on the limited foreign investment that was available and miss out on such capital. The fact that the leading international financial institutions supported the economic model made states adopt the model. In the context of this prevailing mood, it was possible not only to promote investment treaty-making, but also gain acceptance for the expansionist rules that investment arbitrators had made through the interpretation of the treaty principles. The fact that a hegemonic power was driving the economic philosophy, using the institutions it commanded and fashioning rules to accord with its preferences ensured the entrenchment of the rules. In the first period, the change could be explained as due to the overwhelming dominance of the hegemonic power and its use of the law as an instrument to drive changes in accordance with its preferred economic model for the world. The total absence of resistance facilitated the entrenchment of the rules so made.

The absence of resistance was due to the fact that the context of change made it difficult for such resistance to emerge. Resistance was later to come from environmental and human rights groups. The rise of the environmental movement or of 'humanity's law' had not yet occurred. It was only towards the end of the century that these movements were to gather strength. Likewise, the movement against fragmentation within academic international law had to await until after neoliberal norms favourable to regime-creating had set in.

8.4.2 In the economic sphere, private power acts in tandem with public to maintain international norms favourable to it

The role of private power in promoting and sustaining international norms that are favourable to it must not be underestimated. Private power is a potent force in international law-making, ignored only because positivism finds it convenient to do so. A convenient curtain is maintained so that the role of private power remains invisible. The lobbying power of business is visible and its role in influencing norms that are preferable to business indirectly is readily acknowledged. But private power can bring about norms and norm changes by itself. This is very visible in the area of international investment law. The use of low-order sources of international law – decisions of tribunals and writings of 'highly qualified' publicists – are manoeuvrable sources of international law. The whole theory of internationalization of foreign investment contracts was constructed through arbitral awards and the writings of publicists. Mercenary publicists have been a phenomenon of international law from the beginning. The internationalization theory in contract-based arbitration was a phenomenon followed by investment treaty, where the same forces were at work. The principal actors in the expansive law-making were arbitrators and academic writers who wrote in support of the norms favourable to business. Many arbitrators were academics who wrote extensively on the subject, often transferring their views into awards. They made each other 'highly qualified' publicists and converted themselves into sources of law. They cited each other. They attempted to build a regime of rules on investment protection.

The leading law firms serviced large multinational corporations. They became innovators of norms and mechanisms of the system of investment protection. Some younger academics, often eager to join the bandwagon that rolled towards huge profits, joined in with academic theses that supported the norms of private power. The academic profession whose role was to stand as a bulwark against power became subverted to its service. The role of private power in making law against the interests of the large majority of the people of the world has been immense. The interplay between public and private power acting in concert towards similar rules of law ensures that the rules are established. Again, this concert brings such overwhelming power to bear that, without strong resistance, the rules favoured become stabilized. But the fact that the system contains rules preferred by overwhelming power serving minority interests carries within it an inherent injustice and, hence, contains the seeds of dissent.

8.4.3 Resistance to the hegemonic order sets in when its inadequacies and injustices become apparent

In the course of this triumphant march of hegemonic neoliberalism, dissent began to simmer. The project of multilateralization that the OECD confidently commenced in 1995 ran into trouble with the NGOs, which mobilized against the MAI, a neoliberal project aimed at developing universal norms of investment protection. Once NGOs entered the fray, a new force had come into the law. The role of the NGOs against the MAI was among the first tests regarding the role of the NGOs in international relations. They lobbied states effectively. They provided a counterbalance to the lobbying power of multinational corporations. Dissent broke out among the developed countries as to the content of the MAI and the project had to be given up. The NGOs continued to resist the expansionary trends and began to counter the new norms on investment protection that were being established. As the norms of inflexible investment protection progressed, resistance again began to build up.

This brings up another facet of change. When a set of norms reaches acceptance, those adversely affected by the change will mount resistance to it, querying the wisdom of such acceptance in the context of the specific interests that they articulate. The NGOs had single agendas. Some were interested in human rights aspects, and saw the investment treaties as absolving multinationals of responsibility in situations where the violation of such rights were involved. Some had interests in the environment. They saw the awards and investment treaties as inhibiting regulatory controls in the sphere. Some had interests in the extent to which the investment treaties gave defence against regulatory protection of cultural rights or the rights of native groups. Some had interests in sustainable development, which brought all the different themes of resistance together. The emergence of such resistance was an important factor in inducing new changes to the law that began to appear. It could well be that the resistance that arose could be ascribed to the next period. But this will not demonstrate the fact that the two tendencies ran together for some time until another change took place and solidified.

Resistance also came from affected states. Latin American states showed their resistance to expansionary bases of the law that was used to impose extensive liability on them by withdrawing from investment arbitration and from treaties. The Argentinian economic crises and the arbitrations that resulted from it demonstrated not only the unfairness of the system, but the manner of expansionist law-making in the early awards. This undermined the treaty system considerably. Other states have now begun to join the bandwagon of dissent or reconsideration. Some of them, such as India, Indonesia and South Africa, are regional leaders.

In the second period, there was a parallel movement in that that rule-making on the basis of power was maintained, but resistance to it built up. Within the system of investment arbitration itself schisms broke out because expansionist law-making is not seen as conforming to the tenets of arbitration based on consent. Yet the vitality of the neoliberal power-based law persists. It goes through mutations in the hope that such new restatements of the rule will be more acceptable. It receives theoretical justification on the basis of revised notions of the rule of law, the need for standards of governance and the emergence of a global administrative law. But the resistance does not accept these rationalisations.

In the context of this contestation, change is again the result. Some states respond by leaving the system. Others seek accommodation by adopting balanced treaties, which change the law from its focus on exclusive investment protection to the recognition of a series of defences based largely on the single interests identified in the resistance by NGOs. The defences are premised on the need to create regulatory space for the states. There are catch-all provisions which are broad, such as measures taken to protect health, morals and welfare of the public. Clearly, there will be concern that the balance tilts too much in favour of regulation.

The change can be seen in a diversity of ways. It can be explained as disenchantment with globalization, presaging a world that makes global law being replaced by an order based on regulatory sovereignty as the failure of free market theories required a return to state supervision of the economy. It reflects the passing of a unipolar, hegemonic order to a multipolar order in which power centres have become diffused as the power of the hegemon recedes due to its overextension. These provide the context that enabled the change to take hold. But they do not change the essential fact that power made law results in resistance.

Where external circumstances favour power, the existing system of rules will continue. Where they favour resistance, the rules must change. Obviously, social phenomena cannot be explained in terms of hard rules. At periods of tension, the law will be kept in a state of flux. That is what is happening in the present third period, where there is a situation of such a heavy clash of normative values that it is difficult to determine

8.4 THEORY OF RESISTANCE AND CHANGE 417

the content of the law. The outcome of arbitrations has become unpredictable as the application of the rules depends on the composition of the arbitral tribunal. The nature of the acrimonious dissents that are becoming common attest to the problems of uncertainty. The outcomes sometimes depend on spurious findings that have no basis in evidence or on arguments of the parties. They depend on the subjective prejudices of arbitrators. The situation results in a chaos that is characterized by normlessness. The competing ideas respond to each other through the formulation of normative rules. The capacity of neoliberalism to change its stances in order to meet resistance is unlimited. The rule changes that take place in arbitrations from the finding of expropriation through the piecing together of acts, to inserting new meanings into the fair and equitable standard, mean that the capacity of neoliberalism to mutate stances is unlimited. Its hydra-headed nature and the power it receives from its supporters ensures its tenacious vitality. This results in a search for new solutions. Until they are found, the normless state will continue.

8.4.4 *The role of justice in resisting power ensures change*

The resistance to norms based on power will seek to promote its aims through articulation of ideas of justice. The great visibility of the search for cosmopolitan global justice is an evident feature in modern international law. This is very evident in the area of international investment law. The address to justice was strong in the articulation of the norms of the NIEO. It has continued into the sphere of international investment arbitration. The norms that were made at the height of neoliberalism clearly favoured business to the detriment of other interests. The charge that they were inimical to the interests of concern to the whole of humanity was easy to make. Specific interests, such as those in human rights and the environment, were able to articulate their proposals effectively by addressing them through arguments based on justice. One could well see that new norms based on a revival of the norms of the NIEO could come to be articulated. Certainly, the revival of interest in the doctrine of permanent sovereignty over natural resources is very much on the cards. The rediscovery of the idea of regulatory expropriation is a resonance of ideas of regulatory sovereignty that underlie the NIEO.

The role of power to transmute into different forms in order to meet resistance should not be underestimated. The recent history of investment protection is replete with examples. When the internationalization of contracts became a defunct theory, powerful interests latched on to the treaty system. A regime was attempted through interpretation of the treaties and through a system for enforcement of awards. When this was challenged, notions of the need for balancing were introduced to meet the resistance. A placatory stance, if successful, may result in the reintroduction of inflexible investment protection with the balance slowly tilting in its favour. The struggle to find a solution will take time.

8.4.5 When resistance mounts, accommodation will be sought that may or may not ease the pressure for change. But the search for accommodation itself is change

The second period was one of dissent to the norms built up during the dominance of the neoliberal model. During this period, the arbitral awards themselves indicated an unwillingness among arbitrators to go along with the expansionary trends. The resistance manifested itself in internal dissension within the system. Reluctance to use the MFN clause to expand jurisdiction is evident in many arbitrations, with a split developing in the awards. Differences also arose in the use of legitimate expectations as a basis for the violation of the fair and equitable standard, which had earlier been the new ford for the law on investment protection. The new balanced treaties came into existence. There was a return to the uncertainties that existed prior to the first period. When resistance bites in, the ensuing period becomes one of uncertainty. The law is then set on a course of normlessness.

The third period ended a phase when the world believed totally in market capitalism and the ability of the market to correct itself without too much state intervention. With it the attendant ideas of economic liberalization and free flows of investment have lost their shine. There is a return to the regulatory state. In the investment sphere, this has been assisted by the perceived need to end fragmentation in international law by recognising that international law on foreign investment must be shaped in the context of other areas, such as the law on human rights and the environment. How this is to be accomplished remains the task. Until an acceptable solution is worked out, the law will remain in a normless state.

There are many ideas that are being discussed. Some of them are unworkable. The notion that states should come together to work out an acceptable solution will never take place simply because the individual interests of the different states do not sufficiently coincide for this to

8.4 THEORY OF RESISTANCE AND CHANGE

happen. The idea that less powerful states could effect a solution is similarly fruitless as the solution has to be accepted by the more powerful states. In the meantime, the present system will continue. Arbitrations will be brought and arbitrators will spew out inconsistent awards based on their perceptions of what the law is, adding to the confusion. States will react by being more recalcitrant in their attitude towards these awards. The fact that enforcement mechanisms will be used to impose arbitral awards will add to the displeasure of states that feel aggrieved by awards based on objectively suspicious law. The balanced treaties will also come to be interpreted. As they contain within them a difficult marriage of inconsistent notions of investment protection and state regulation, the awards based on their interpretation will only add to the chaos, displeasing all the actors whose interests are involved.

There is an idea that a hierarchy of rights could be worked out. This will prove difficult except in the clearest instances. The notion of hierarchies has appeared in other areas of international law. These areas have also been fraught with difficulties when it comes to listing the rights in order of priority.

It is necessary to give up the myth of multilateralization. There is no confluence or coalescence of the law behind any single idea. The larger trends talk of a case-by-case analysis of the situation, decrying the possibility of any certain law or a certain body of applicable principles. It is futile to talk in terms of the creation of customary international law in these situations. It is equally futile to contemplate the possibility of centripetal forces moving the law towards principles when the currently fashionable notion of balanced treaties ties together competing notions of investment protection and regulatory controls.

The fact that the system of treaty-based arbitration is breaking does not mean that there is an absence of a system. There is still the customary law on investment protection, though it was the difficulty concerning the rules of this system that brought about treaties. Most states now have effective domestic courts. The system was designed at a time when these courts were defective and were applying capricious rules of law. Such a situation no longer exists, with the majority of states having efficient and neutral systems of law, so that one main reason for external dispute settlement has disappeared. But, still, there is a need for an external system as there will always be the fear of egregious injustice being done to the foreign investor. The bilateral or regional treaties could still remain to serve as the law as between the parties. The treaties should leave out open-ended phrases such as fair and equitable treatment, which do not have definite content. The problem attends only the method of dispute settlement. It is dispute settlement that has to be fixed. A suggested solution is that the parties construct a permanent body of dispute settlement with designated counsel from within the states to appear before the body. It is only when there is some dispute as to the decision that recourse could be had to a body like the ICSID to settle it. The ICSID will remain relevant for contract-based arbitration. This will exclude to a large extent the involvement of large law firms, which was part of the problem with treaty-based investment arbitration.

8.5   Does the notion of resistance and change apply to other areas of international law?

Resistance and change are frequent in international law, which never remains static. The history of international law is replete with laws made by hegemonic powers undergoing change as a result of resistance emerging from other actors. Slavery is an obvious example where international law changed in response to justice-based ideas. The theory of changes in terms of power and resistance can be applied to other areas of international law. The notion that change results when the rules made by a hegemonic power are resisted, particularly at a time when such power is in decline, is a theory that can be applied to other areas of international law. When hegemonic powers arise, new sets of rules may come to be put in place. The rise of Britain saw this happening, with justifications provided for its navy to traverse the seas, for its commerce to reach other lands and for its military conquests of other people. The hegemonic rise of the United States was similarly accompanied by the conveying of its power through the instrumentality of international law, thereby bringing about important changes. One may identify as instances the global protection of intellectual property, the greater protection of investments and the more liberal rules on the use of force. But, as in past instances, hegemonic power disregards the interests of other people and invites opposition, which is often couched in the form of an appeal to justice. When resistance builds up, change, either through accommodation or replacement of old norms, results. This may be a way to study international law, ensuring that account is taken of the context in which the law is made and functions.

BIBLIOGRAPHY

Books

Adekunle, Adefolake, *Corporate Social Responsibility of Multinational Corporations in Developing Countries*. Cambridge University Press, 2012.

Alexander, Gregory, *Global Debate over Constitutional Property: Lessons from American Takings Jurisprudence*. University of Chicago Press, 2012.

Allen, Tom, *The Right to Property in Commonwealth Constitutions*. Cambridge University Press, 2000.

Alvarez, Jose, *The Public International Law Regime Governing International Investment*. The Hague: Hague Academy of International Law, 2011.

Alvik, Ivar, *Contracting with Sovereignty: State Contracts and International Arbitration*. Oxford: Hart, 2011.

Amerasinghe, Chitharanjan, *State Responsibility for Injuries to Aliens*. Oxford University Press, 1964.

    The Local Remedies in International Law, 2nd edn. Cambridge University Press, 2004.

    Local Remedies Rule, 2nd edn. Cambridge University Press, 2008.

Anderson, Terry and Peter Hill (eds.), *The Privatization Process: A Worldwide Perspective*. Lanham, MD: Rowan & Littlefield, 1996.

Atiyah, Patrick, *The Rise and Fall of the Freedom of Contract*. Oxford University Press, 1986.

Audit, Bernard, *Transnational Arbitration and State Contracts*. The Hague: Martinus Nijhoff, 1988.

Baetens, Freya (ed.), *Investment Law within International Law: Integrationist Perspectives*. Cambridge University Press, 2013.

Banifatemi, Yas, *Precedent in International Investment Law*. New York: Juris Publishing, 2008.

Barak, Aron, *Proportionality: Constitutional Rights and Limitations*. Cambridge University Press, 2012.

Bartholomew, Amy (ed.), *Empire's Law: The American Imperial Project and the War to Remake the World*. London: Pluto Press, 2006.

Benton, Lauren, *Law and Colonial Cultures: Legal Regimes in World History 1400–1900*. Cambridge University Press, 2001.

421

Bhuiyan, Sharif and Philippe Sands (eds.), *International Law and the Developing States: Essays in Honour of Kamal Hossain*. Berlin: Brill, 2014.

Bingham, Lord Thomas, *The Rule of Law*. London: Penguin, 2010.

Bob, Clifford, *The Global Right Wing and the Clash of World Politics*. Cambridge University Press, 2012.

Borchard, Edwin, *The Diplomatic Protection of Citizens Abroad*. New York: Kraus & Co., [1915] 1970.

Bork, Robert, *The Antitrust Paradox*. New York: Basic Books, 1976.

Borschberg, Peter, *Hugo Grotius, the Portuguese and Free Trade in the East Indies*. Singapore: NUS Press, 2011.

Bunn, Isabelle, *The Right to Development and International Economic Law: Legal and Moral Dimensions*. Oxford: Hart, 2012.

Burchill, Richard (ed.), *Democracy and International Law*. London: Ashgate, 2006.

Byers, Michael, *Custom, Power and the Power of Rules: International Relations and Customary International Law*. Cambridge University Press, 1999.

Byers, Michael and George Nolte (eds.), *United States Hegemony and the Foundations of International Law*. Cambridge University Press, 2003.

Cameron, Peter, *Property Rights and Sovereign Rights: The Case of North Sea Oil*. London: Academic Press, 1983.

   International Energy Investment Law: The Pursuit of Stability. Oxford University Press, 2010.

Cassese, Antonio, *Five Masters of International Law*. Oxford: Hart, 2011.

Coll, Steve, *Private Empire: Exxon Mobil and American Power*. London: Penguin, 2013.

Cordonier Segger, Marie *et al.* (eds.), *Sustainable Development in World Investment Law*. The Hague: Wolters Kluwer, 2011.

Corporate Europe Observatory, *How Law Firms, Arbitrators and Financiers are Fuelling an Investment Arbitration Boom*. London: Corporate Europe Observatory, 2012.

Crawford, James, *Brownlie's Principles of Public International Law*, 8th edn. Oxford University Press, 2012.

   State Responsibility. Cambridge University Press, 2013.

Crawford, Neta, *Argument and Change in World Politics: Ethics, Decolonization and Humanitarian Intervention*. Cambridge University Press, 2002.

Crouch, Colin, *The Strange Non-Death of Neoliberalism*. Cambridge: Polity Press, 2011.

Cutler, Claire, *Private Power and Global Authority: Transnational Merchant Law in the Global Political Economy*. Cambridge University Press, 2003.

   The Emergence of Private Authority in Global Governance. Cambridge University Press, 2003.

Davis, Jeffrey, *Justice Across Borders: The Struggle for Human Rights in US Courts*. New York: Cambridge University Press, 2007.

BIBLIOGRAPHY

Desierto, Diane, *Necessity and National Emergency Clauses: Sovereignty in Modern Treaty Interpretation*. Leiden: Brill, 2012.

Dezaley, Yves, *The Internationalization of the Practice of Law*. The Hague: Kluwer, 2001.

Dezaley, Yves and Bruce Garth, *Dealing in Virtue: International Commercial Arbitration and the Construction of a Transnational Legal Order*. University of Chicago Press, 1996.

    Global Prescriptions: The Production, Exportation and Importation of a New Legal Orthodoxy. Ann Arbor, MI: University of Michigan Press, 2005.

Diehl, Alexandra, *The Core Standard of International Investment Protection*. The Hague: Kluwer, 2012.

Dolzer, Rudolf and Margrete Stevens, *Bilateral Investment Treaties*. The Hague: Martinus Nijhoff, 1995.

Douglas, Zachary, *International Law of Investment Claims*. Cambridge University Press, 2009.

Dupuy Pierre-Marie *et al.* (eds.), *Human Rights in International Investment Law and Arbitration*. Oxford University Press, 2009.

Dupuy, Pierre-Marie and Jorge Vinuales (eds.), *Harnessing Foreign Investment to Promote Environmental Protection*. Cambridge University Press, 2013.

Feller, A. H., *The Mexican Claims Commission: 1923–1934*. New York: Macmillan, 1935.

Fox, Gregory and Brad Roth (eds.), *Democratic Governance and International Law*. Cambridge University Press, 2000.

Freeman, Alwyn, *The International Responsibility of States for Denial of Justice*. New York: Longman, Green, 1938.

Friedmann, Wolfgang, *The Rule of Law in a Mixed Economy*. London: Stevens, 1971.

Fukuyama, Francis, *The End of History and The Last Man*. London: Penguin, 1992.

    After the Neocons: America at the Crossroads. New York: Profile Books, 2006.

Gallagher, Norah and Wenhua Shan, *Chinese Investment Treaties: Policies and Practice*. Oxford University Press, 2008.

Garcia, Frank, *Global Justice and International Economic Law: Opportunities and Prospects*. Cambridge University Press, 2012.

Gill, Stephen, *Power and Resistance in the World Order*, 2nd edn. Basingstoke: Palgrave Macmillan, 2008.

Gong, Gerrit, *The Standard of Civilization in International Society*. Oxford University Press,1984.

Gray, Christine, *International Law and the Use of Force*, 2nd edn. Oxford University Press, 2012.

Halper, Stefan, *Beijing Consensus: How China's Economic Model will Dominate the Twenty First Century*. New York: Basic Books, 2010.

Harris, David, *Cases and Materials on International Law*, 7th edn. London: Sweet & Maxwell, 2010.

Harvey, David, *A Short History of Neo-Liberalism*. Oxford University Press, 2005.

Hewart, Lord Gordon, *The New Despotism*. London: Ernest Benn, 1929.

Hirschl, Ran, *Towards Juristocracy: The Origins and Consequences of New Constitutionalism*. Cambridge, MA: Harvard University Press, 2007.

Hofman, Reinisch and Christofer Tams (eds.), *International Investment Law and General International Law: From Clinical Isolation to Systemic Integration*. Baden-Baden: Nomos, 2011.

Humphries, Stephen, *The Theatre of the Rule of Law: Transnational Legal Intervention in Theory and Practice*. Cambridge University Press, 2010.

Kjos, Elisabeth, *Applicable Law in Investor–State Arbitration*. Oxford University Press, 2013.

Jackson, John, *The World Trading System: Law and Policy of International Economic Relations*. Cambridge, MA: MIT Press, 1996.

Jessup, Phillip, *Transnational Law*. New York: Columbia University Press, 1948.

Kinley, David, *Civilising Globalization: Human Rights and the Global Economy*. Cambridge University Press, 2009.

Klager, Roland, *Fair and Equitable Treatment in International Investment Law*. Cambridge University Press, 2011.

Kulick, Andreas, *Global Public Interests in International Investment Law*. Cambridge University Press, 2012.

Leader, Sheldon and David Ong (eds.), *Global Project Finance, Human Rights and Project Finance*. Cambridge University Press, 2011.

Lee, Robert Warden, *Introduction to Roman Dutch Law*. Oxford University Press, 1962.

Lipson, Charles, *Standing Guard: Protecting Foreign Capital in the Nineteenth and Twentieth Centuries*. Berkeley, CA: University of California Press, 1965.

Mandelbaum, Michael, *The Ideas that Conquered the Word: Peace, Democracy and the Free Markets in the Twenty-First Century*. New York: Public Affairs, 2002.

Mann, Francis, *Further Studies in International Law*. Oxford University Press, 1990.

Marks, Stephen, *The Politics of the Possible. The Way Ahead for the Right to Development: Dialogue on Globalization*. Berlin: Friedrich Ebert Stiftung, 2011.

Maurer, Noel, *The Empire Trap: The Rise and Fall of US Intervention to Protect American Property Overseas, 1893–2013*. Princeton University Press, 2013.

McLachlan, Campbell, Laurence Shore and Mathew Weininger, *International Investment Arbitration: Substantive Principles*. Oxford University Press, 2008.

Meyer, Lukas (ed.), *Legitimacy, Justice and Public International Law*. Cambridge University Press, 2010.

BIBLIOGRAPHY

Miles, Kate, *The Origins of International Investment Law: Empire, Environment and the Safeguarding of Capital*. Cambridge University Press, 2013.

Montt, Santiago, *State Liability in Investment Treaty Arbitration*. Oxford: Hart, 2009.

Muchlinski, Peter *et al.* (eds.), *The Oxford Handbook of International Investment Law*. Oxford University Press, 2008.

Nassar, Nagla, *Sanctity of Contracts Revisited: A Study in the Theory and Practice of Long-Term International Contracts*. The Hague: Martinus Nijhoff, 1995.

Nygh, Peter, *Autonomy in International Contracts*. Oxford University Press, 1999.

Orrego-Vicuna, Francisco, *International Dispute Settlement in an Evolving Global Society: Constitutionalization, Accessibility, Privatization*. Cambridge University Press, 2004.

Paparinskis, Martin, *International Minimum Standard and the Fair and Equitable Treatment*. Oxford University Press, 2013.

Parra, Antonio, *The History of ICSID*. Oxford University Press, 2012.

Pauwelyn, Jan, *Conflicts of Norms in Public International Law: How WTO Law Relates to Other Rules of International Law*. Cambridge University Press, 2003.

Peck, Jamie, *Constructions of Neoliberal Reason*. Oxford University Press, 2010.

Peerenbohm, Randall, *China's Long March toward the Rule of Law*. Cambridge University Press, 2007.

Pogge, Thomas (ed.), *Freedom from Poverty as a Human Right*. Oxford University Press, 2007.

   World Poverty and Human Rights: Cosmopolitan Responsibility and Reforms, 2nd edn. Cambridge: Polity, 2008.

Pollan, Thomas, *The Entry of Foreign Investments*: Utrecht, Eleven Publishers, 2006.

Posner, Richard, *Antitrust Law*. University of Chicago Press, 2001.

Pulkowski, Dirk, *Law and Politics of International Regime Conflict*. Oxford University Press, 2014.

Ralston, Jackson, *The Law and Procedure of International Tribunals*. Stanford University Press, 1926.

Rao, Rahul, *Third World Resistance*. Oxford University Press, 2011.

Redfern, Alan and Martin Hunter, *International Commercial Arbitration*, 5th edn. Oxford University Press, 2009.

Reinish, August and Christina Knahr (eds.), *International Investment Law in Context*. Oxford University Press, 2008.

Reisman, Michael *The Quest for World Order and Human Dignity in the Twenty-First Century: Constitutive Process and Individual Commitment*, Hague Academy of International Law, Collected Courses, vol. 351. The Hague: Martinus Nijhoff, 2012.

Rigo-Sureda, Andres, *Investment Treaty Arbitration: Judging under Uncertainty*. Cambridge University Press, 2012.

Rittburger, Volker, *Regime Theory and International Relations*. Oxford University Press, 1993.

Rodrik, Dani, *The Globalization Paradox*. New York: Oxford University Press, 2011.

Rogers, Catherine and Roger Alford (eds.), *The Future of Investment Arbitrations*. New York: Oxford University Press, 2009.

Roth, Andreas, *The Minimum Standard of Treatment as Applied to Aliens*. Leiden: Sijhoff, 1949.

Rothkopf, David, *Power Inc.: The Epic Rivalry between Big Business and Government and the Reckoning that Lies Ahead*. New York: Farrar, Straus & Giroux, 2012.

Ruggie, John, *Just Business: Multinational Corporations and Human Rights*. New York: W. W. Norton, 2013.

Salacuse, Jeswald, *The Law of Investment Treaties*. Oxford University Press, 2010.

  The Three Laws of International Investment: National, Contractual, and International Frameworks for Foreign Capital. New York: Oxford University Press, 2013.

Sasson, Monique, *The Substantive Law of Investment Arbitration: The Unsettled Relationship between Municipal Law and International Law*. The Hague: Kluwer, 2010.

Sauvant, Karl and Frederico Ortino, *Improving the International Law Policy Regime*. Helsinki: Ministry of Foreign Affairs, 2014.

Sauvant, Karl and Lisa Sachs (eds.), *The Effect of Treaties on Foreign Direct Investment*. New York: Oxford University Press, 2009.

Schachter, Oscar, *Sharing the World's Resources*. New York: University of Columbia Press, 1977.

Schefer, Krista Nadakavukaren (ed.), *Poverty and the International Economic Legal System: Duties to the World's Poor*. Cambridge University Press, 2013.

Schill, Stephan, *The Multilateralization of International Investment Law*. Cambridge University Press, 2009.

  (ed.), *International Investment Law and Comparative Public Law*. Oxford University Press, 2010.

Schneiderman, David, *Constitutionalizing Economic Globalization: Investment Rules and Democracy's Promise*. Cambridge University Press, 2008.

  Resisting Economic Globalization. Basingstoke: Palgrave Macmillan, 2013.

Schreuer, Christoph, *The ICSID Convention: A Commentary*, 2nd edn. Cambridge University Press, 2009.

Schreuer, Christoph and Rudolf Dolzer, *International Investment Law*, 2nd edn. Oxford University Press, 2012.

Schrijver, Nico, *Permanent Sovereignty over Natural Resources: Balancing Rights and Duties*. Cambridge University Press, 1997.

BIBLIOGRAPHY

Scott, Shirley, *International Law, US Power: The United States' Quest for Legal Security*. Cambridge University Press, 2013.

Sell, Susan, *Private Power, Public Law: The Globalization of Intellectual Property*. Cambridge University Press, 2003.

Sen, Amartya, *The Idea of Justice*. London: Penguin, 2005.

Serra, Narciss and Joseph Stiglitz (eds.), *The Washington Consensus Reconsidered: Towards a New Global Governance*: New York: Oxford University Press, 2008.

Shea, Donald, *The Calvo Clause: A Problem of Inter-American and International Law and Diplomacy*. Minneapolis, MN: University of Minnesota Press, 1955.

Sikkink, Kathryn, *The Justice Cascade: How Human Rights Prosecutions are Changing World Politics*. New York: W. W. Norton, 2011.

Sloan, Blaine, *The Binding Force of the Recommendations of the General Assembly of the United Nations*. Oxford University Press, 1948.

United Nations General Assembly Resolutions in Our Changing World. New York: Transnational, 1991.

Sornarajah, Muthucumaraswamy, *The Pursuit of Nationalized Property*. The Hague: Martinus Nijhoff, 1986.

International Law on Foreign Investment. Cambridge University Press, 1992 (2nd edn 2004, 3rd edn 2010).

The Settlement of Foreign Investment Disputes. The Hague: Kluwer, 2001.

Stiglitz, Joseph, *The Roaring Nineties: Why We are Paying for the Greediest Decade in History*. London, Penguin, 2003.

Free Fall, America, Free Markets and the Sinking of the Economy. London: Allen Lane, 2010.

Sunstein, Cass, *Free Markets and Social Justice*. New York: Oxford University Press, 1998.

Sutherland, Edwin, *Principles of Criminology*. Philadelphia, PA: Lippincot, 1966.

Tienhaara, Kyla, *The Expropriation of Environmental Governance: Protecting Foreign Investors at the Expense of Public Policy*. Cambridge University Press, 2009.

Tobias, John, *The Right to Health in International Law*. Oxford University Press, 2011.

Toope, Stephen, *Mixed International Arbitration*. Cambridge: Grotius Publications, 1990.

Trebilcock, Michael and Ronald Daniels, *Rule of Law Reform and Development: Charting the Fragile Path of Progress*. Cheltenham: Edward Elgar, 2008.

Trubeck, David and Alvaro Santos (eds.), *The New Law and Economic Development: A Critical Appraisal*. Cambridge University Press, 2006.

Tudor, Ioana, *The Fair and Equitable Treatment Standard in the International Law of Foreign Investment*. Oxford University Press, 2008.

Turpin, Colin, *State Contracts*. London: Penguin, 1971.

428 BIBLIOGRAPHY

UNCTAD, *The Role of International Investment Agreements in Attracting Foreign Direct Investment to Developing Countries.* Geneva: UNCTAD, 2009.

Investment Policy Framework for Sustainable Development. Geneva: UNCTAD, 2012.

Fair and Equitable Treatment: Sequel. Geneva: UNCTAD, 2012.

World Investment Report. Geneva: UNCTAD, 2012.

World Investment Report. Geneva: UNCTAD, 2014.

Vadi, Valentina, *Cultural Heritage in International Investment Law and Arbitration.* Cambridge University Press, 2014.

Vaise, Justin, *Neoconservatism: The Biography of A Movement.* Cambridge, MA: Harvard University Press, 2010.

Van der Walt, Andre, *Constitutional Property Clauses: A Comparative Analysis.* The Hague: Kluwer, 1999.

Van Harten, Gus, *Investment Treaty Arbitration and Public Law.* Oxford University Press, 2007.

Sovereign Choices and Sovereign Constraints: Judicial Restraint in Investment Treaty Arbitration. Oxford University Press, 2013.

Vinuales, Jorges, *Foreign Investment and the Environment in International Law.* Cambridge University Press, 2012.

Voss, Jan Ole, *The Impact of Investment Treaties on Contracts between Host States and Foreign Investors.* Leiden: Martinus Nijhoff, 2011.

Waibel Michael *et al.* (eds.), *Backlash against Investment Arbitration.* The Hague: Kluwer, 2010.

Waldron Jeremy, *The Rule of Law and the Measure of Property.* Cambridge University Press, 2012.

Weeramantry, Romesh, *Treaty Interpretation in Investment Arbitration.* Oxford University Press, 2012.

World Bank, *Towards a Greater Depoliticization of Investment Disputes: ICSID and MIGA.* Washington, DC: World Bank, 1992.

Young, Margaret (ed.), *Regime Interaction in International Law: Facing Fragmentation.* Cambridge University Press, 2012.

Zerk, Jennifer, *Multinational Corporations and Corporate Social Responsibility: Limitations and Opportunities in International Law.* Cambridge University Press, 2006.

Chapters in books

Ackerman, Susan and Jennifer L. Tobin, 'Do BITs Benefit Developing Countries?' in Catherine A. Rogers and Roger P. Alford (eds.), *The Future of Investment Arbitration.* New York: Oxford University Press, 2009, pp. 131–56.

Aisbett, Emma, 'Bilateral Investment Treaties and Foreign Direct Investment: Correlation Versus Causation', in Karl Sauvant and Lisa Sachs (eds.), *The*

BIBLIOGRAPHY

Effect of Treaties on Foreign Direct Investments. Oxford University Press, 2009, p. 395.

Alvarez, Jose, 'The Once and Future Foreign Investment Regime', in Mahnoush Arsanjani *et al.* (eds.), *Looking to the Future: Essays in International Law in Honour of Michael Reisman*. Leiden: Martinus Nijhoff, 2010, p. 607.

'Sovereignty is not Withering Away', in Antonio Cassese (ed.), *Realizing Utopia*. Oxford University Press, 2012, p. 26.

Bjorklund, Andrea, 'Emergency Exceptions: State of Necessity and Force Majeure', in Peter Muchlinski *et al.* (eds.), *Oxford Handbook of International Investment Law*. Oxford University Press, 2008, p. 373.

Braun, Tillman, 'Globalization: The Driving Force in International Investment Law', in Michael Waibel *et al.* (eds.), *The Backlash Against Investment Arbitration*. The Hague: Kluwer, 2010.

Broches, Aron, 'Bilateral Investment Treaties and Arbitration of Investment Disputes', in Jan C. Schultz *et al.* (eds.), *The Art of Arbitration*. Deventer: Kluwer, 1982, p. 132.

Buckley, Ross, 'The Direct Contribution of International Financial System to Global Poverty', in Krista Nadukavukaren Schefer (ed.), *Poverty and the International Economic System: Duties to the World's Poor*. Cambridge University Press, 2013, p. 278.

Cason, Jeffrey, 'Whatever Happened to the New International Economic Order', in Andrew Valls (ed.), *Ethics in International Affairs: Theories and Cases*. Lanham, MA: Rowman & Littlefield, 2000, p. 201.

Dagan, Hannoch, 'Reimagining Takings Law', in Gregory Alexander and Eduardo Penalver (eds.), *Property and Community*. New York: Oxford University Press, 2009, pp. 203–24.

Desierto, Diane, 'Deciding International Investment Agreement Applicability: The Development Argument in Investment', in Freya Baetens (ed.), *Investment Law within International Law: Integrationist Perspectives*. Cambridge University Press, 2013, p. 240.

Hirsch, Morshe, 'The Interaction between International Investment Law and Human Rights Treaties: A Sociological Perspective', in Tomer Broude and Yuval Shany (eds.), *Multi-Sourced Equivalent Norms in International Law*. Oxford: Hart, 2011, p. 211.

'Investment Tribunals and Human Rights Treaties: A Sociological Perspective', in Freya Baetens (ed.), *Investment Law within International Law: Integrationist Perspectives*. Cambridge University Press, 2013, p. 85.

Kingsbury, Benedict and Stephan Schill, 'Investor–State Arbitration as Governance: Fair and Equitable Treatment, Proportionality, and the Emerging Global Administrative Law', in Albert Jan Van Den Berg (ed.), *50 Years of the New York Convention*. Alphen aan den Rijn: Kluwer, 2009, p. 5.

'Public Law Concepts to Balance Investors' Rights with State Regulatory Actions in the Public Interest: The Concept of Proportionality', in Stephan Schill (ed.), *International Investment Law and Comparative Public Law*. Oxford University Press, 2010, p. 75.

Levine, Judith, 'Navigating the Parallel Universe of Investor–State Arbitrations under UNCITRAL Rules', in Chester Brown and Kate Miles (eds.), *Evolution in Investment Treaty Law and Arbitration*. Cambridge University Press, 2011, p. 368.

'Interaction of International Investment Arbitration and the Rights of Indigenous People', in Freya Baetens (ed.), *Investment Law within International Law: Integrationist Perspectives*. Cambridge University Press, 2013, p. 106.

Lillich, Richard, 'The Law Governing Disputes under Economic Development Agreements', in Richard Lillich and Charles Brower (eds.), *International Arbitration for the Twentieth Century*. Irvington, NY: Transnational, 1993.

Morgera, Elisa, 'From Corporate Social Responsibility to Accountability Mechanisms', in Rene Dupuy and Jorge Vinuales (eds.), *Harnessing Foreign Investment to Promote Environmental Protection*. Cambridge University Press, 2012, p. 320.

Santos, Alvaro, 'The World Bank's Uses of the "Rule of Law" Promise in Economic Development', in David M. Trubek and Alvaro Santos (eds.), *The New Law and Economic Development: A Critical Appraisal*. Cambridge University Press, 2006, p. 253.

Schill, Stephan, 'Fair and Equitable Treatment: The Rule of Law and Comparative Public Law', in Stephan Schill (ed.), *International Investment Law and Comparative Public Law*. Oxford University Press, 2010, p. 151.

Schreuer, Christoph and Mathew Weininger, 'Conversations across Cases: Is there a Doctrine of Precedent in Investment Arbitration?' in Peter Muchlinski *et al.* (eds.), *Oxford Handbook of International Investment Law*. Oxford University Press, 2008, p. 1211.

'A Doctrine of Precedent?' in Peter Muchlinski *et al.* (eds.), *Oxford Handbook of International Investment Law*. Oxford University Press, 2008, p. 1188.

Schwebel, Stephan, 'The United States 2004 Model Treaty and Denial of Justice in International Law', in Christina Binder *et al.* (eds.), *International Investment Law for the Twenty-First Century: Essays in Honour of Christoph Schreuer*. Cambridge University Press, 2010, p. 519.

Sornarajah, Muthucumaraswamy, 'Linking State Responsibility for Certain Harms Caused by Corporate Nationals Abroad to Civil Recourse in the Legal Systems of Home States', in Craig Scott (ed.), *Torture as Tort*. Oxford: Hart, 2001, p. 491.

'Fair and Equitable Treatment: Whose Fairness? Whose Equity?' in Frederico Ortino (ed.), *Investment Treaty Law: Current Issues*. London: BIICL, 2007.

BIBLIOGRAPHY

'A Coming Crisis: Expansionary Trends in Investment Treaty Arbitration', in Karl Sauvant (ed.), *Appeals Mechanism in International Investment Disputes.* Oxford University Press, 2008, p. 39.

'Resurgence of the Right to Development', in Gerald McAlinn and Caslav Pejovic (eds.), *Law and Development in Asia.* London: Routledge, 2012, p. 154.

'The Return of the NIEO and the Retreat of Neo-Liberal International Law', in Sharif Bhuiyan and Philippe Sands (eds.), *International Law and Developing Countries: Essays in Honour of Kamal Hossain.* Berlin: Brill, 2014, pp. 32–59.

'The Role of the BRICS in International Law in a Multipolar World', in Vai Io Lo and Mary Hiscock (eds.), *The Rise of the BRICS in the Global Political Economy: Changing Paradigms?* Cheltenham: Edward Elgar, 2014, p. 288.

Soto, Hernando de, 'The Missing Ingredient: What Poor Countries Will Need to Make their Markets Work', in Terry Anderson and Peter Hill (eds.), *The Privatization Process: A Worldwide Perspective.* Lanham, MD: Rowan & Littlefield, 1996, p. 19.

Tudor, Ioana, 'The Fair and Equitable Treatment Standards and Human Rights Norms', in Pierre-Marie Dupuy *et al.* (eds.), *Human Rights in International Investment Law and Arbitration.* Oxford University Press, 2009, p. 310.

Waincymer, Jeff, 'Balancing Property Rights and Human Rights in Expropriation', in Pierre-Marie Dupuy *et al.* (eds.), *Human Rights in International Investment Law and Arbitration.* Oxford University Press, 2009, p. 276.

Wildhaber, Luis, 'The Protection of Legitimate Expectations in European Human Rights Law', in M. Monti *et al.* (eds.), *Economic Law and Justice in Times of Globalisation: Festschrift for Carl Baudenbacher.* Baden-Baden: Nomos, 2007, p. 121.

Wildhaber, Luis and Isabelle Wildhaber, 'Recent Case Law on the Protection of Property in the European Convention on Human Rights', in Christina Binder (ed.), *International Investment for the 21st Century.* Oxford University Press, 2009, p. 657.

Williams, David, and Simon Foote, 'Recent Developments in the Approach to Identifying "Investment" Pursuant to Article 25(1) of the ICSID Convention', in Chester Brown and Kate Miles (eds.), *Evolution in Investment Treaty Law and Arbitration.* Cambridge University Press, 2011, p. 42.

Articles

Allee, Todd and Clint Peinhardt, 'Contingent Credibility: The Impact of Investment Treaty Violations on Foreign Direct Investment', (2011) 62 *International Organization* 401.

BIBLIOGRAPHY

Allen, Tom, 'Liberalism, Social Democracy and the Value of Property under the European Convention on Human Rights', (2010) 59 *International & Comparative Law Quarterly* 1053.

Alvarez, Jose, 'A BIT on Custom', (2009) 42 *International Law & Politics* 17.

Amnesty International, 'Human Rights, Trade and Investment Matters'. London: Amnesty International, 2006.

Bean, Vicki and Joel Beauvais, 'Global Fifth Amendment?' (2003) 78 *New York University Law Review* 30.

Bernadini, Piero, 'Stabilization and Adaptation in Oil and Gas Contracts', (2008) 1 *Journal of World Energy Law & Business* 98–112.

Bogdandy, Armin von and Indo Venzke, 'In Whose Name? An Investigation of International Court's Public Authority and Its Democratic Justification', (2012) 23 *European Journal of International Law* 7.

Bowett, Derek, 'Claims between States and Private Entities: The Twilight Zone of International Law', (1986) 35 *Catholic University Law Review* 929.

Brown, Chester, 'Protection of Legitimate Expectations as a "General Principle of Law": Some Preliminary Thoughts', (2009) 6(1) *Transnational Dispute Management* 3.

Brownlie, Ian, 'The Legal Status of Natural Resources in International Law', (1979) 162 *Hague Recueil des Cours* 245.

Burke-White, William, 'Investment Protection in Extraordinary Times', (2008) 48 *Virginia Journal of International Law* 307.

Cabrol, Emmanuelle, '*Pren Nreka* v. *Czech Republic* and the Notion of Investment under Bilateral Investment Treaties', (2010) 2 *Yearbook of International Investment Law* 217.

Calamita, Jason, 'British Bank Nationalizations: An International Perspective', (2009) 58 *International & Comparative Law Quarterly* 119.

Cantegreil, Julien, 'The Audacity of *Texaco/Calasiatic* Award: Rene-Jean Dupuy and the Internationalization of Foreign Investment Law', (2012) 22 *European Journal of International Law* 441

Caron, David, 'The ILC Articles on State Responsibility: The Paradoxical Relationship Between Form and Authority', (2002) 96 *American Journal of International Law* 857.

Cate, Irene, 'The Costs of Consistency: Precedent in Investment Treaty Arbitration', (2013) 51 *Columbia Journal of Transnational Law* 418.

Chiati, Ahmad el, 'Protection of Foreign Investment in the Context of Petroleum Agreements. (1987) 204 *Hague Recueil des Cours* 1.

Clodfelter, Mark, 'The Future Directions of Investment Agreements within the European Community', (2013) 12 *Santa Clara Journal of International Law* 183.

Cotula, Lorenzo, 'Reconciling Regulatory Stability and Evolution of Environmental Standard in Investment Contracts: Towards a Rethink of Stabilization Clauses', (2008) 1(2) *Journal of World Energy Law and Business* 121.

'The New Enclosures? Polanyi, International Investment Law and the Global Land Rush', (2013) 34 *Third World Quarterly* 1605.

Craig, Paul, 'Proportionality, Rationality and Review', (2010) *New Zealand Law Review* 265.

Curtis, Christopher, 'The Legal Security of Economic Development Agreements', (1988) 29 *Harvard International Law Journal* 317.

Davidson, Nestor, 'Sketches for a Hamiltonian Vernacular as a Social Function of Property', (2011) 80 *Fordham Law Review* 1053.

Delaume, Georges, 'State Contracts and Transnational Arbitration', (1981) 75 *American Journal of International Law* 140.

'The Proper Law of State Contracts Revisited', (1997) 12 *ICSID Review* 1.

Demirkol, Berk, 'Does an Investment Treaty Tribunal need Special Consent for Mass Claims?' (2013) 2 *Cambridge Journal of International & Comparative Law* 612.

Denza, Eileen and Shelagh Brooks, 'Investment Treaties: The United Kingdom Experience', (1987) 36 *International & Comparative Law Quarterly* 908.

Deutsch, Richard, 'An ICSID Tribunal Denies Jurisdiction for Failure to Satisfy BIT's Cooling Off Period: Further Evidence of a Sea Change in Investor–State Arbitration or a Meaningless Ripple?' (2011) *Houston Journal of International Law* 589.

Douglas, Zachary, 'The MFN Clause in Investment Treaty Arbitration: Treaty Interpretation off the Rails', (2011) 2 *Journal of International Dispute Settlement* 97.

el-Kosheri, Ahmed and Tarek Riad, 'The Law Governing a New Generation of Petroleum Agreements: Changes in the Arbitration Process', (1986) 1 *ICSID Review* 257.

Falk, Richard, 'A New Paradigm for International Legal Studies: Prospects and Proposals', (1975) 84 *Yale Law Journal* 969.

Fecak, Tomas, 'Czech Experience with Bilateral Investment Treaties: Somewhat Bitter Taste of Investment Protection', (2011) *Czech Yearbook of International Law* 17.

Finnemore, Martha and Kathryn Sikkink, 'Norm Dynamics and Political Change', (1998) 52 *International Organizations* 524.

Freyer, Dana and David Herlihy, 'Most-Favoured-Nation Treatment and Dispute Settlement in Investment Arbitration: Just How "Favoured" is "Most Favoured"?' (2005) 20 *ICSID Review* 58.

Gallagher, Kevin, 'The New Vulture Culture: Sovereign Debt Restructuring and Investment Treaty Arbitration', Tufts University Ideas Working Paper 02/2011 (2011).

Gaukrodger, David and Kathryn Gordon, 'Investor–State Dispute Settlement: A Scoping Paper for the Investment Policy Community', OECD Working Papers on International Investment, No. 2012/3, OECD Investment

Division, Paris, 2012, available at: www.oecd.org/daf/investment/workingpapers.

Gazzini, Tarcisco, 'The Role of Customary International Law in the Field of Foreign Investment', (2007) 8 *Journal of World Trade Law* 691.

Geiger, Rudolf, 'The Unilateral Change of Economic Development Agreements', (1974) 23 *International & Comparative Law Quarterly* 73.

Gerringer, Claudia, 'Sources of Resistance to Proportionality Review of Administrative Power under the New Zealand Bill of Rights', (2013) 11 *New Zealand Journal of Public & International Law* 124.

Goldhaber, Michael, 'The Rise of Arbitral Power over Domestic Legislation', (2012) 1 *Stanford Journal of Complex Litigation* 374.

Guzman, Andrew, Zachary Elkins and Beth Simmons, 'Competing for Capital: The Diffusion of Bilateral Investment Treaties', (2006) 60 *International Organization* 811.

Hallward-Driemeier, Mary, 'Do Bilateral Investment Treaties Attract Foreign Investment? Only a Bit and They Could Bite', World Bank Policy Research Working Paper No. 3121, World Bank, Geneva, 2003.

International Law Commission, 'Fragmentation of International Law: Difficulties Arising from the Diversification and Expansion of International Law', A/CN.4/L.682, ILC, New York, 2006.

Iyer, Shruti, 'Redefining Investment Regime in India: Post White Industries', (2013) 14 *Journal of World Investment and Trade* 595.

Kingsbury, Benedict, 'The Concept of "Law" in Global Administrative Law', (2009) 20 *European Journal of International Law* 1

Kingsbury, Benedict, Nico Krisch and Richard Stewart, 'The Emergence of Global Administrative Law', (2005) 68 *Law and Contemporary Problems* 15.

Kriebaum, Ursula, 'Regulatory Takings: Balancing the Interests of the Investor and the State', (2007) 8 *Journal of World Investment and Trade* 717.

Kurz, Jurgen, 'Adjudging the Exceptional at International Investment Law: Security, Public Order and Financial Crisis', (2010) 59 *International & Comparative Law Quarterly* 325.

Lalive, Pierre, 'Contracts between a State or a State Agency and a Foreign Company', (1964) 13 *International & Comparative Law Quarterly* 987.

Law Revision Committee, 'The Third Party Rule of Contract for Benefit of the Third Party', Law Comm. 242, Law Commission, London, 1996.

Leader, Sheldon, 'Human Rights, Risks and New Strategies for Global Investment', (2006) 9 *Journal of International Economic Law* 657.

Levinson, J., 'Living Dangerously: Indonesia and the Reality of the Global Economic System', (1998) 7 *Journal of International Law and Practice* 437.

Lowenfeld, Andreas, 'Investment Agreements and International Law', (2003) 42 *Columbia Journal of Transnational Law* 123.

BIBLIOGRAPHY 435

Luca, Anne de, 'Withdrawing Incentives to Attract Foreign Investments', Columbia FDI Perspectives, No. 125, 7 July 2014.

Maniruzzaman, Munir, 'State Contracts in Contemporary International Law: Monist versus Dualist Controversies', (2001) 12 *European Journal of International Law* 309.

'Stabilization in Investment Contracts and Change of Rules by Host Countries', Association of International Petroleum Negotiators, Houston, Texas, 2007.

Mann, Francis, 'The Proper Law of Contracts Concluded by International Persons', (1959) 35 *British Yearbook of International Law* 34

'British Treaties for the Promotion and Protection of Foreign Investments', (1981) 52 *British Yearbook of International Law* 241.

Maupin, Julie, 'MFN-based Jurisdiction in Investor–State Arbitration: Is There any Hope for a Consistent Approach?' (2011) 14 *Journal of International Economic Law* 157.

McNair, Lord Arnold, 'General Principles of Law Recognized by Civilised Nations', (1958) 33 *British Yearbook of International Law* 1.

Mitchell, Andrew and Caroline Henckels, 'Variations on a Theme: Comparing the Concept of Necessity in International Investment Law and WTO Law', (2013) *Chicago Journal of International Law* 93.

Muchlinski, Peter, 'Caveat Investor? The Relevance of the Conduct of the Investor under the Fair and Equitable Standard', (2006) 55 *International & Comparative Law Quarterly* 527.

Newcombe, Andrew, 'Boundaries of Regulatory Expropriation in International Law', (2005) 20 *ICSID Review* 1.

Orrego-Vicuna, Francesco, 'Regulatory Authority and Legitimate Expectations: Balancing the Rights of the State and the Individual under International Law in a Global Society', (2003) 5 *International Law Forum* 180.

'Foreign Investment Law: How Customary is Custom?' (2005) *ASIL Proceedings* 98.

Paulsson, Jan, 'Third World Participation in Investment Arbitration', (1987) 2 *ICSID Review* 1.

'Arbitration without Privity', (1995) 10 *ICSID Review* 232.

Pauwelyn, Joost, 'The Edge of Chaos: Emergence and Change in International Investment Law', (2013), *Social Science Research Network*, SSRN-id 2271869.

Penrose, Edith, 'Nationalization of Foreign Owned Property for Public Purpose', (1992) 55 *Modern Law Review* 1.

Pinchis, Mona, 'The Ancestry of Equitable Treatment in Trade Lessons from the League of Nations during the Inter-War Period', (2014) 15(1) *Journal of World Investment & Trade* 13.

Porterfield, Matthew, 'An International Common Law of Investor Rights?' (2006) 27 *University of Pennsylvania Journal of International Economic Law* 79.

Redfern, Alan, 'The Arbitration between the Government of Kuwait and Aminoil', (1985) *British Yearbook of International Law* 65.

Reisman, Michael and Robert Sloane, 'Indirect Expropriation and its Valuation in the BIT Generation', (2004) 75 *British Yearbook of International Law* 115.

Roberts, Anthea, 'Clash of Paradigms: Actors and Analogies Shaping the Investment Treaty System', (2013) 107 *American Journal of International Law* 45.

Salacuse, Jeswald, 'The Emerging Global Regime for Investment', (2010) 51 *Harvard International Law Journal* 463.

Sales, Sir Philip, 'Rationality, Proportionality and the Development of the Law', (2013) 129 *Law Quarterly Review* 223.

Salomon, Margot, 'From NIEO to Now and the Unfinishable Story of Economic Justice', (2013) 62 *International & Comparative Law Quarterly* 32.

Schill, Stephan, 'Whither Fragmentation? On the Literature and Sociology of International Investment Law', (2011) 22 *European Journal of International Law* 888.

'Deference in Investment Treaty Arbitration', (2012) 3 *Journal of International Dispute Settlement* 577.

Schreuer, Christoph, 'Fair and Equitable Treatment in Arbitral Practice', (2005) 6 *Journal of World Investment and Trade* 357.

Schwebel, Stephen M., 'The Influence of Bilateral Investment Treaties on Customary International Law', (2004) 98 *ASIL Proceedings* 27.

Shemberg, Andrea, 'Stabilization Clauses and Human Rights', Research Paper for the United Nations Representative on Business and Human Rights, United Nations, New York, 2008.

Simma, Bruno, 'Foreign Investment Arbitration: A Place for Human Rights', (2011) 60 *International & Comparative Law Quarterly* 573.

Slaughter, Anne-Marie, 'International Law in a World of Liberal States', (1995) 6 *European Journal of International Law* 1.

Sohn, Louis and Richard Baxter, 'Responsibility of States for Injuries to the Economic Interests of Aliens', (1961) 55 *American Journal of International Law* 515.

Spears, Suzanne, 'The Quest for Policy Space in a New Generation of International Investment Agreements', (2012) 13 *Journal of International Dispute Settlement* 1037.

Stone Sweet, Alec, 'Investor–State Arbitration: Proportionality's New Frontier', (2010) 4 *Law and Ethics of Human Rights* 47.

Trakman, Leon, 'Investor–State Arbitration: Evaluating Australia's Evolving Position', (2014) 15(1) *Journal of World Trade Law* 152.

Transnational Institute, 'Profiting from Injustice: How Law Firms, Arbitrators and Financiers are Fuelling an Investment Arbitration Boom', Transnational Institute, Amsterdam, 2012.

BIBLIOGRAPHY

Van Harten, Gus and Martin Loughlin, 'Investment Treaty Arbitration as a Species of Global Administrative Law', (2006) 17 *European Journal of International Law* 121.

Vasciannie, Stephen, 'The Fair and Equitable Standard in International Investment Law and Practice', (1999) 70 *British Yearbook of International Law* 99.

Veeder, V., 'The Lena Goldfields Arbitration: The Historical Roots of Three Ideas', (1998) 47 *International & Comparative Law Quarterly* 747.

Verdross, Alfred, 'Quasi-international Agreements and International Economic Transactions', (1964) 18 *Yearbook of World Affairs* 230.

Waibel, Michael, 'Opening the Pandora's Box: Sovereign Bonds in International Arbitration', (2007) 101 *American Journal of International Law* 701.

White, Robin, 'Expropriation of the Libyan Oil Concessions: Two Conflicting International Arbitrations', (1981) 30 *International & Comparative Law Quarterly* 1.

Worthstone, Samuel, 'Jurisdiction, Admissibility and Pre-conditions to Arbitration', (2012) 27 *ICSID Review* 255.

Yackee, Jason, 'Do Bilateral Investment Treaties Promote Foreign Direct Investments?' (2010) 51 *Virginia Journal of International Law* 397.

Yen, Trin Hai, 'Interpretations of Investment Treaties', PhD dissertation, Faculty of Law, National University of Singapore, 2013.

INDEX

access to court/justice 319, 320, 360–1
administrative law 49
  administrative
    contracts 114, 368, 369–70
    permissions 200–1
  fair and equitable standard 249,
    261–2, 263, 267, 268–72
  global administrative law 298
  SADC Model Investment Treaty 358
African Charter on Human Rights 324
African states 35, 89, 92, 405
  SADC Model Investment Treaty 352,
    356–62
  See also individual states
Alien Tort Claims Act 64, 241, 319,
  324
aliens 33, 87, 94, 170
amicus curiae briefs 322, 402
analogical reasoning 50–2, 96, 234, 385
annulment of awards 6, 158, 167,
  292, 401
antitrust law 212
apartheid 357
appellate body 384–6
arbitrability, doctrine of 190, 239, 345
arbitration award and underlying
  contract as investments 163–4
arbitration clauses 110–11, 112, 119
Argentina: economic crisis and spate
  of arbitrations 13, 196, 354, 388,
  399, 400–1, 402, 415
  damages 383
  defences 302, 343
    human rights 322–3, 338–9
    national security 308, 309, 399
    necessity 67, 268, 308–15, 322,
      399, 401

enforcement of awards 6
fair and equitable standard 46, 398,
  399, 400–1
  legitimate expectations 265, 266–8,
    273, 274, 277, 279, 282, 292
  US Model Treaty (1987) 56
ASEAN Investment Agreement 189,
  352–6
Asian states 35, 89, 92
  economic crises 47, 309, 395, 398
  See also individual states
audit, human rights 320
Australia 332, 370, 386, 405
autonomy, party 98, 119, 123, 287, 342

balance of payments 353, 354
balanced/newer treaties 5, 28, 46, 400,
  405–6, 407, 418, 419
  ASEAN Investment Agreement 189,
    352–6
  Canada 31, 396
    Model Treaty 47, 219, 251, 348–9,
      350–1
  change and 363–5, 382–3, 385, 387,
    395
  Commonwealth Report and Model
    Treaty 352, 362–3
  customary law 161
  defences 38, 57, 156, 162, 236, 300–2,
    304, 315–16, 346, 400, 416
    environment 236, 334–5, 339,
      400
  proportionality 365, 376, 380, 381,
    382, 406, 407
  SADC Model Investment Treaty 352,
    356–62, 363
  as solution 347–52, 388

INDEX

third phase of BITs 39
United States 31, 396
   Model Treaty (2004). *See under*
   United States
balancing/equilibrium clauses 129,
   132
banks 17, 196–7, 201, 296, 411
Barak, A. 289
Belgium 401
benefits clauses, denial of 183, 189, 354,
   355, 364, 389
bilateral investment treaties
   (BITs) 4, 25, 38–9, 41–2,
   43–4, 48, 94, 294,
   419
   Argentina 267, 308, 313, 338–9
   Bolivia–Netherlands treaty
   402
   Canada–China treaty 172, 351
   converted to multilateral treaties
   181–2
   customary international law 156,
   161, 319
   expropriation 92, 192, 211
   Germany 38, 408
   human rights 319, 338–9, 341
   India 403
   Japan–Philippines treaty 386
   Malaysia–Chile treaty 260
   multilateral obligations 319, 326–7,
   341
   national security 308
   Norway: Draft Model Treaty
   350
   Philippines–Japan treaty 356
   SADC Model Investment Treaty 352,
   356–62
   South Africa 356–7, 359
   UK–Indonesia treaty 174
   See also investment treaties
blood banks 201
Boisson de Chazournes, Laurence
   148–9
Bolivarian Alliance for the Americas
   (ALBA) 402
Bolivia 6, 401–2
Brazil 305, 349, 384, 400, 402
bribery 165–6, 167, 321, 403

BRICS 197, 297, 404
   See also individual countries
British East India Company 20–1, 82,
   83, 100, 410

Calvo Doctrine 33, 35, 66, 191, 314, 402,
   406, 412
Canada 229, 336, 396, 405
   Canada–China treaty 172, 351, 405
   expropriation 195, 229
   Model Treaty 47, 219, 251, 348–9,
   350–1
carcinogens 338, 392, 399
change
   explaining 16–19
   periods of 389–95
     explosion of the law 395–9
     conflict 399–404
     uncertainties 404–7
   phases of law on foreign investment.
     See separate entry
   phases of 19–31
   theory of resistance, and *see separate*
     entry
Chile 260
China 55, 173, 187, 294, 296–7, 305,
   349, 391, 398, 400
   Canada–China treaty 172, 351, 405
   energy resources 405
   extraterritoriality 99
   open-door policy 412
   sovereign wealth fund 405
   state assets 402
   state capitalism 142
   US–China FTA negotiations 405
choice of law clauses 110–11, 119,
   122–8
   Libyan arbitrations 111, 112, 116
   private international law 105
civil law countries 174
civilization, standard of 104, 412
class actions 147, 168–9, 170
climate change 329, 332
codes, foreign investment 17, 36, 121
colonialism 41, 81, 83–4, 85, 100, 114,
   297, 410, 412
common law 51, 229, 229, 261, 367, 374
Commonwealth constitutions 233

440 INDEX

Commonwealth Report and Model
    Treaty 352, 362–3
companies. *See* multinational
    corporations
compensation/damages 7, 67, 358, 375,
    383
    expropriation. *See* compensation
        under expropriation
conflict of laws 94, 105
consent 25, 28, 46, 229, 248, 253, 271,
    275, 276, 294, 296, 366
    jurisdiction beyond. *See separate*
        entry
constitutional theory/law 97–8, 108,
    109, 212, 224, 286
    constitutions 17, 36, 124, 229–33,
        236, 411
    Ecuador 377
    South Africa 358
    Germany 373
    human rights 320
constitutionalization of international
    law 265
consultation mechanism 386
contract law, evolution of 342
contract-based arbitration. *See* interna-
    tionalization of foreign invest-
    ment contracts
contracts, host state and human rights
    320–1
contractual commitments and
    legitimate expectations 282–4
corporate governance 360
corporate nationality 62, 173–7, 364,
    389, 397
    migration of companies 176–7,
        179–83, 402
    'round-tripping' investments 176,
        177–9
corporate (social) responsibility 63–4,
    65, 213, 219, 241, 328, 350, 360,
    398, 403
corporations. *See* multinational
    corporations
corruption 213, 219, 360, 379
    bribery 165–6, 167, 321, 403
costs 67, 69, 80, 190, 409
criminal law 212, 342, 373, 377

cultural heritage/property 7, 130, 135,
    301, 306, 340–1, 415
    expropriation 201, 205, 213, 219, 236,
        238–40
    Norwegian Draft Model Treaty 350
customary international law 244, 247,
    364, 419
    defences 301, 317, 319
    environment 335
    necessity 310, 311, 401
    expropriation 191–2, 193, 194, 203,
        216, 220, 221, 222
    necessity 238
    proportionality 229
    regulatory and non-compensable
        235
    fair and equitable standard and 250,
        251–2, 264, 270
    balancing test 288
    full protection and security 270
    human rights 319
    international minimum standard.
        See separate entry
    investment treaties 39, 40, 43–4, 87,
        156, 161, 167, 353
    natural resources 324, 325
    non-approved investments 167
    state responsibility 90, 91, 92
Czech Republic 18

decolonization 35, 40, 85, 191
defences 64, 300–7, 343–6, 400
    absence of economic development
        162–3, 331
    ASEAN Investment Agreement
        355–6
    Commonwealth Report and Model
        Treaty 362–3
    cultural rights 301, 306, 340–1
    environmental law 301, 302, 306,
        326, 331–9, 343
    evolution or erosion of investment
        protection 342–3
    expansion of 314–18
    development, right to 327–31
    human rights 318–31, 343
    permanent sovereignty over
        natural resources 324–7

INDEX

441

hierarchy in international law 303, 307, 317, 326–7, 332, 333, 335, 338–9, 341, 343

indigenous peoples 301, 306, 323, 326–7, 338, 341

national security 308, 309, 364, 387, 399

necessity 67, 238, 262, 268, 301, 308–15, 322, 374, 387, 401

SADC Model Investment Treaty 359, 360, 363

definition of investment and economic development criterion 150, 151–64, 172, 330–1

denial of benefits clauses 183, 189, 354, 355, 364, 389

'depoliticization' of investment disputes 26–7, 82

development, right to 41, 327–31

diplomatic protection 32, 384

corporate nationality 176, 177

human rights 319

ICSID Convention 82

non-approved investments 167

state responsibility and 86–94

discrimination 357, 361, 362, 392, 403

fair and equitable standard 251, 254–6

Doha Round 214, 329

domestic courts 32, 49–50, 190, 344, 384, 419

home state of foreign investor 99, 319–20

Alien Tort Claims Act 64, 241, 319, 324

SADC Model Investment Treaty 359, 360–1

See also local remedies

domestic law 98, 199, 213, 225, 229

administrative permissions 200–1

ASEAN Investment Agreement 353

defences 311, 317, 321, 325

human rights 321, 325

jurisdiction: investment made in accordance with 164–7, 171

NIEO principles 329

SADC Model Investment Treaty 360, 361

See also constitutional theory; local remedies

Dubai 404

due diligence by investor 278–80

due process 254–6

Dutch East India Company 100, 410

Dutch sandwich 173

economic crises 13, 46, 383–4, 398, 400–1, 415

Argentina: economic crisis and spate of arbitrations. *See separate entry*

ASEAN Investment Agreement 353–4

Asian 47, 309, 395, 398

expropriation 196–7, 219, 221

fair and equitable standard 46

legitimate expectations 265, 274, 282, 292, 400–1

financial instruments 169, 172

global crisis in 2008 15, 54, 142, 310, 313, 351

expropriation 196–7

fair and equitable standard 268, 294, 296

national security 308

necessity 67, 268, 308–15, 322, 399, 401

economic development 81, 84, 85, 104, 107–8, 109, 114, 118, 134, 186, 383

ASEAN Investment Agreement 354

development, right to 327–8

fair and equitable standard 254, 295

ICSID Convention 138

investment treaties and 13–15, 44, 47–8, 403

jurisdiction: definition of investment and criterion of 150, 151–64, 172, 330–1

merits phase 162–3, 331

protection of property 225

screening of foreign investments 166

shell or post-box companies 177, 181

state capitalism 142

Ecuador 402

enforcement of arbitral awards 6, 83, 85, 135, 419
environment 65, 120, 122, 127, 130, 135, 392, 415, 418
  arbitrators 61
  ASEAN Investment Agreement 355
  balanced treaties 236, 334–5, 339, 400
  Commonwealth Report and Model Treaty 363
  conduct of global business 403
  defences 236, 301, 302, 306, 326, 331–9, 343
  environmental impact study 360
  environmental movement 413
  expropriation 205, 213, 214–15, 219, 221, 234, 236–7, 238–40
  global administrative law 298
  global public policy 23
  regulatory controls 201, 415
  SADC Model Investment Treaty 361
  schisms 134
  screening mechanism 387
  stabilization clauses 132
equilibrium/balancing clauses 129, 132
estoppel 265
European Convention on Human Rights (ECHR) 322
  property 223, 225, 227–8, 289, 290, 368, 374–6, 381
European Court of Human Rights 222, 226, 227–8, 229, 289, 290, 295, 368, 373, 374–6, 378, 380, 381
European states 84, 267, 369, 396
  East 18, 280–1, 412
  economic crises 142, 169, 310, 313, 401
  expropriation 197–8
    concept of property 223, 225, 233
  See also individual countries
European Union 51, 300, 408
  European Court of Justice 367, 386
exhaustion of local remedies 33, 190, 323
  ASEAN Investment Agreement 353
  diplomatic protection and state responsibility 90, 91, 92

human rights: individual petition 146, 290
expropriation 34–5, 91–2, 191–3, 244–5, 397
  administrative permissions 200–1
  ASEAN Investment Agreement 355
  basis of expansion of 207–12
    indirect takings 207–10, 243
    tantamount to 45, 63, 192, 203–5, 210–11
  changing concept of property 223–37
  compensation 38, 39–40, 91–2, 191, 192, 193–4, 195, 202, 208, 334
    appropriate 241–2
    formative phase of law on foreign investment 34, 35
    proportionality 198, 206, 211–12, 222, 226–9
    regulatory taking 198, 205, 206, 211–12, 216–20, 222–37, 240, 241–2, 337, 349, 399–400
    SADC Model Investment Treaty 358
    second phase of law on foreign investment 35
  course of law on 193–207
  fair and equitable treatment 206, 207
    bridge to 242–4
  global economic crisis (2008) 196–7
  international minimum standard 192, 223, 244
  Iran. *See separate entry*
  nature of assets held 199–200
  public purpose, lack of 235
  regulatory 118, 121, 128, 132, 195, 200, 205, 206, 208, 210, 417
    compensation 198, 205, 206, 211–12, 216–20, 222–37, 240, 241–2, 337, 349, 399–400
    concept of property 223–37
    defences 317, 321, 326–7, 331, 337
    distinguishing criteria and conserving 237–42
    nationalizations 194
    proportionality 68, 198, 206, 211–12, 222, 226–9, 233–5, 245, 376–7
    reasonableness 220–2, 232, 241

INDEX

revival of 212–20, 302
stabilization clauses 217, 218
stemming regulatory takings tide 220–2
United States 57, 211, 212, 217, 302, 349, 399–400
regulatory controls 201, 237–8
share price fall 196
extraterritoriality 99, 319–20

fair and equitable standard 45, 46, 53, 62, 246–50, 298–9, 318, 397, 398, 399, 417, 419
ASEAN Investment Agreement 353, 355
defences 317, 321, 331
diversity in treaties 250–2
expropriation 206, 207, 242–4
giving content to 252–7
human rights 320
international minimum standard 91, 247, 250, 254
NAFTA Commission 251, 261, 389
treaties 251–2, 349
legitimate expectations. *See separate entry*
SADC Model Investment Treaty 366
financial crises. *See* economic crises
financial instruments 147, 168–73, 201, 397
financial markets 353–4, 362
prudential measures 387, 400
foreign aid 17
formation of contracts 165–6, 167
fraud 165, 177
frivolous claims 80, 408
funding agencies: audits 320

general principles of law
choice of law clause 110, 112
domestic public law 98
expropriation 226, 227, 233
legitimate expectations 133, 253, 293, 295
necessity 312–13
petroleum awards (1950s) 102–7

proportionality 51, 229, 366, 367, 368, 380–1
source of international law 97, 99, 101, 104
genocide 22, 321, 324
Germany 38, 51, 222, 229, 336, 370, 373, 408
globalization 11, 69, 141–2, 266, 391, 410, 416
culture 340
law firms 196
good faith 178, 182, 187, 188, 190, 362
clean hands 319
legitimate expectations 257–61, 263, 265
Greece 310, 401
Grotius, H. 100

health 57, 213, 216, 230, 240, 301, 392
ASEAN Investment Agreement 354, 355
medicines 7, 12, 392
Norwegian Draft Model Treaty 350
right to 12
SADC Model Investment Treaty 362
tobacco disputes 7, 337, 392
hierarchy in international law 238–41, 303, 307, 317, 326–7, 332, 333, 335, 338–9, 341, 343, 419
history 81–6
phases of law on foreign investment. *See separate entry*
Hong Kong 13, 173
Hudson Bay Company 82
human rights 23, 40, 61, 65, 120, 122, 127, 130, 135, 413, 418
absolute sovereignty 22
balanced treaties 400
Commonwealth Report and Model Treaty 363
conduct of global business 403, 415
defences 301, 302, 306, 318–24, 338–9, 343
development, right to 327–31
natural resources 324–7
expropriation 205, 213, 219, 221, 226–9, 233–5, 236–7, 238–41, 321, 326–7, 331

444 INDEX

human rights (cont.)
    individual petition 145–6
    intellectual property 392
    Norwegian Draft Model Treaty 350
    property 68, 164, 289, 290–1, 323,
        368, 412
        ECHR 223, 225, 227–8, 289, 290,
            368, 374–6, 381
        regional tribunals 344
    SADC Model Investment Treaty 360
    schisms 134
    stabilization clauses 132
    torture 317, 321, 324, 375
    water 402

ICSID Convention 60, 152, 168, 172–3,
    271, 330
    annulment 158, 167, 292, 401
    corporate nationality 178, 179, 181,
        182
    diplomatic protection 82
    foreign investment contracts 121,
        122–8, 134, 315
        default law 105
    investment requirement 150,
        151–64, 165, 172
    preamble 138, 157, 190
    seat 161
    teleological interpretation 164–7
    travaux preparatoires 160, 172
    withdrawal of states from 6, 402
ICSID tribunals 2–3, 26, 323, 324, 340,
    388
    contract disputes 2, 122–8, 420
    survival of internationalization
        theory 128–30
    reform: responsibility of 408–9
ignorantia juris non excusat 280
illegality 165, 166, 167, 235
India 55, 173, 305, 349, 391, 398, 400,
    403, 412, 416
    Bhopal 238, 321
    energy resources 405
indigenous peoples 7, 130, 135,
    213, 236, 238–9, 301, 306,
    323, 326–7, 338, 341, 415
Indonesia 310, 313, 356, 403, 416
    UK–Indonesia treaty 174

information
    SADC Model Investment Treaty 360
    intellectual property 12, 101, 214, 329,
        392, 420
    SADC Model Investment Treaty 358
Inter-American Court of Human
    Rights 326–7, 341
International Bank of Reconstruction
    and Development 161
International Court of Justice (ICJ) 136,
    239, 315, 324, 385
International Covenant on Civil and
    Political Rights 234, 323, 375
International Law Commission (ILC)
    state responsibility 90, 92–3, 310–12,
    314
international minimum standard 32–5,
    37, 38, 52–3, 384
    expropriation 192, 223, 244
    fair and equitable standard 91, 247,
        250, 254
        NAFTA Commission 251, 261,
            389
        treaties 251–2, 349
    foreign investment contracts 86–7,
        89, 90–1, 92, 133
International Monetary Fund (IMF) 15,
    43, 310, 313, 395, 398, 411, 412
international trade law 12, 27
internationalization of foreign
    investment contracts 78–9,
    133–5, 315, 407
    diplomatic protection and state
        responsibility 86–94
    exhaustion of local remedies 90,
        91, 92
    international minimum standard
        86–7, 89, 90–1, 92, 133
    national treatment 89
    future relevance 80–1
    history 81–6
    ICSID tribunals and contract
        disputes 122–8
    survival of internationalization
        theory 128–30
    interaction between contract- and
        treaty-based arbitration 130–1
    legitimate expectations 133, 264

INDEX

stabilization clauses 132–3
umbrella clauses 131
internationalization theory 94–102,
    414
Aminoil signals change 116–22
ICSID cases: survival of 128–30
Libyan arbitrations 98, 107,
    111–16, 134
petroleum awards (1950s) 102–7
policy arguments 107–11
interpretation, treaty 60, 149–50, 156,
    159, 162, 186, 187, 189, 381
context: relevant rules of
    international law 315
corporate nationality 174, 178, 183
fair and equitable standard 253–4,
    263–4
purposive or teleological
    interpretation 44, 63, 149–50,
    156, 183, 186, 253–4, 260, 263
investment
economic development criterion and
    definition of 150, 151–64, 172,
    330–1
investment treaties 4, 13–15, 142
appellate body 384–6
balanced/newer treaties. *See*
    separate entry
BITs. *See* bilateral investment treaties
Brazil 384, 402
change, periods of. *See separate entry*
customary law 39, 40, 43–4, 87, 156,
    161, 167, 353
denial of benefits clauses 183, 189,
    354, 355, 364, 389
environment 236, 334–5, 339
fair and equitable standard 269
    diversity 250–2
human rights and right of foreign
    investor to remedy 320
Indonesia 403
interpretation, treaty. *See separate*
    entry
investment flows and 13–15, 44,
    47–8, 403
jurisdiction. *See separate entry*
multilateral agreement on
    investments. *See separate entry*

possible changes 304, 382–8, 407–9
prior consultations and negotiations
    186–8
termination provisions 402, 406
termination of system of 304, 382–4,
    407–8
umbrella clauses. *See separate entry*
Iran 208
Iran–US Claims Tribunal 198–9,
    202–3, 209, 225
Islamic law 96, 103–4
ius cogens 65, 114, 120, 239, 241, 317,
    319, 321, 324, 345
apartheid 357
natural resources 36

Japan 356, 386
joint ventures 199
jurisdiction 3, 5
ASEAN Investment Agreement
    352–3, 355
beyond consent. *See* jurisdiction
    beyond consent
human rights 321, 330–1
ius cogens 324
local remedies. *See separate entry*
Pan-Islamic Investment Treaty 356
jurisdiction beyond consent 57–8,
    136–9, 185–90, 397
corporate nationality. *See separate*
    entry
financial instruments 168–73
most-favoured-nation (MFN)
    clauses 183–5
original sin: 'arbitration without
    privity' 139–43
    extreme adventurism 146–7
    justification 144–6
prior consultations and negotiations
    186–8
restricting arbitral adventurism
    147–50
definition of investment and
    economic development
    criterion 150, 151–64, 172,
    330–1
investment made in accordance
    with host state law 164–7, 171

labour rights/standards 25, 130, 213, 219, 236, 238–9, 240
  balanced treaties 400
  SADC Model Investment Treaty 360, 361
  screening mechanism 387
Latin America 32–5, 92, 188, 365, 401–2, 415
  Calvo Doctrine. *See separate entry*
  United States 86, 89, 92, 353
  See also individual states
lawyers/law firms 29–30, 58, 64–5, 246, 351, 362, 392, 398
  corporate planning 173
  expropriation 205
  investment protection 87–8
  jurisdiction beyond consent 146, 173
  private power and international law 101, 414
  reform 387–8, 409, 420
League of Nations 95
legitimate expectations 98, 243, 248–9, 253, 254–7, 298–9, 316, 397, 418
  administrative law 261–2, 263, 267, 268–72
    global administrative law argument 298
  ASEAN Investment Agreement 355
  contraction of 272–3
  discovery of 50–1, 257–68
  economic crises 265, 274, 282, 292, 400–1
  good faith 257–61, 263, 265
  interaction between contract- and treaty-based arbitration 133
  legitimacy crisis and 291–3
    global administrative law argument 298
    rule of law argument 295–7
    theoretical justifications 293–8
  restrictions on 273–8
    balancing or proportionality test 287–91, 371–2, 377–80
    circumstances of host state 280–2
    contractual commitments 282–4
    due diligence by investor 278–80
    stabilization commitment 284–7

stabilization clauses 121, 132, 264, 270, 274, 282, 283, 284–7, 397
Libyan arbitrations 98, 107, 111–16, 134
licensing systems 200–1
local communities 326–7
  See also indigenous peoples
local remedies 6, 350, 384, 401
  exhaustion of. *See separate entry*

Malawi 356
Malaysia 260, 310, 313, 395, 404
margin of appreciation 146, 227, 234, 235, 241, 289, 368–9, 373, 375, 379, 380, 381
Mauritius 173, 356
Mexican Claims Commission 87, 95, 106
Mexico 34, 35, 388, 396
Middle East 117
  arbitrations and internationalization theory 96–9, 102–7
migration of companies 176–7, 179–83, 402
Millennium Development Goals 328, 329
minority shareholders 199–200, 266
Mixed Claims Commissions
  US and Latin America 87
monism 122, 229, 317
most-favoured-nation (MFN) clauses 62, 183–5, 397, 399, 418–20
multilateral agreement on investments (MAI) 4, 42
  OECD: Multilateral Agreement on Investment 398, 415
multinational corporations 11, 17–18, 21, 28, 59, 81, 330, 398, 406–7, 411
  balanced treaties 404, 407
  corporate nationality. *See separate entry*
  corporate responsibility 63–4, 65, 213, 219, 241, 328, 350, 360, 398, 403
  cultural rights 341
  defences 303
  expropriation 197, 213, 241–2

OECD Guidelines 236
human rights
  extraterritoriality 319–20
  state responsibility 320
international law and 99–102, 120
jurisdiction 146
legitimate expectations 290, 295–6
natural resources 88
non-governmental organizations
  (NGOs) 30, 322, 415
oil sector 88, 96
personality in international law
  20–1, 40, 95, 100, 145
publicity, adverse 337
reform: contractual method of
  protection 409
reorganizations 180, 181
SADC Model Investment Treaty 360
state and private interests 82–3
UNCTAD 328
See also oil industry

NAFTA (North American Free Trade
  Agreement) 16, 53, 56, 195, 204,
  215, 216, 302, 305, 349,
  396
  Commission 251, 261, 349, 389
  legitimate expectations 260–1, 271
  opposition within US 350
Namibia 356
national security 146, 349, 406
  Argentina–US treaty 56
  ASEAN Investment Agreement 355
  Chinese investments 405
  defence 308, 309, 364, 387, 399
  expropriation 195, 234, 236, 238,
    240
  Norwegian Draft Model Treaty
    350
  proportionality 379
  SADC Model Investment Treaty
    362
national treatment 33, 89, 251, 255, 357,
  361
nationality
  aliens, protection of 89
  corporate. See separate entry
  dual 174

nationalization 194, 310, 401
  reprisal 115
natural resources 124, 129, 135, 355,
  362, 411
  sovereignty 36–7, 40, 112, 114, 120,
    122, 192, 324–7, 417
  state corporations 121, 411
nature reserves 337
necessity 67, 238, 262, 268, 301, 308–15,
  322, 387, 399, 401
neoconservatism 19
neoliberalism 39, 47, 62–3, 79, 86, 107,
  131, 304, 336, 390, 391
  Argentina 266, 313, 314
  capacity to change stances/
    conserving 28, 48–54, 316, 416,
    417
  classical view of foreign investment
    81
  cultural homogenization 340
  driving force 10–16
  economic crises 169, 196, 309
  expropriation 195, 199, 204, 206, 214,
    218
    concept of property 223, 225,
      228
  fair and equitable standard 46, 250,
    252, 262, 274, 281, 287, 293,
    295, 316
  hierarchy of values 307
  human rights 322–3
    property, right to 375
  international law, reliance on 315
  jurisdiction 138, 147, 148, 172, 173,
    182
  neoconservatism and 19
  poverty gap 330
  privatization 199
  resisting 54–66
  retreat of 66–8
  umbrella clauses 93
  uncontested hegemonic power and
    410–13
Netherlands, the 84, 402
  corporate nationality 181, 402
    Dutch sandwich 173
    incorporation 174
  East India Company 100, 410

448 INDEX

New International Economic Order (NIEO) 17, 35, 37, 69, 88, 112, 135, 192, 245, 323–4, 411–12, 417
  balanced treaties 39
  development, right to 327–31
  natural resources 37, 324–7, 417
  SADC Model Investment Treaty 358
New York Convention on the Recognition and Enforcement of Foreign Arbitral Awards (1957) 83, 85, 135
Nicaragua 402
Nigeria 230, 236
non-discrimination 357, 361, 362, 392, 403
  fair and equitable standard 251, 254–6
non-governmental organizations (NGOs) 7–8, 23, 55, 65, 205, 213–14, 390, 400, 415, 416
  environment 41, 205, 334, 398, 415
  expansionist norms 45
  external resistance 30
  global interests 31, 306
  human rights 41, 205, 318, 322, 398, 415
    development, right to 330
  lawyers 388
  SADC Model Investment Treaty 362
  single issues 59
norm cascades 22
Norway 404
  Draft Model Treaty 350
nuclear power 338

OECD 334, 390
  Guidelines for Multinational Corporations 236
  multilateral agreement on investment 398, 415
oil industry 88, 411
  internationalization of foreign investment contracts
    concession agreements 99, 111, 116, 117, 119

    petroleum-related contracts 96–9, 102–7, 110, 111–22
  sovereignty over natural resources 36–7, 112, 325
  state corporations 36–7, 121
OPEC (Organization of Oil Exporting Countries) 117
Orrego-Vicuna, F. 266

pacta sunt servanda 97
Pakistan 38
Pan-Islamic Investment Treaty 356
patents 358, 392
Permanent Court of Arbitration (PCA) 271
personality in international law 89, 119
  multinational corporations 20–1, 40, 95, 100, 145
  states 87
pesticides 338
pharmaceutical industry 201, 214, 329, 403
phases of law on foreign investment 31–2
  formative phase 32–5
  universalization of conflicts 35–42
  neoliberal change 43–5
  current phase 45–8, 68–70
    conserving neoliberal regime 48–54
    resisting neoliberalism 54–66
    retreat of neoliberalism 66–8
Philippines 356, 386
police powers 274, 288, 336, 375
  non-compensable takings 193, 212, 218, 230
  to protect public interests 109–10, 217
  See also regulatory *under* expropriation
positivism 20–1, 23, 39, 147, 342, 414
post-box companies. *See* corporate nationality
poverty 29, 324, 330, 412
precedent 4, 45, 50
private international law 94, 105
private power 173, 247, 249, 295, 297, 306, 414

INDEX

fragmentation of international law 305
internationalization of foreign investment contracts 79, 85, 99–102, 105
public and 23–4, 82–3
privatization 11, 12, 199, 266, 337, 379, 401–2, 411
procedural irregularity
challenging arbitral awards 83
production sharing agreements 17–37, 121, 325, 411
property, right to. *See* property *under* human rights
property rights 13, 164–5
changing concept of property 223–37
Iran–US Claims Tribunal 202–3
proportionality 51, 98, 316, 322, 333, 347–8, 365–9, 388, 405
arbitral awards: references to 376–80
ASEAN Investment Agreement 356
future of 380–2
legitimate expectations
balancing test 287–91, 371–2, 377–80
nature of test 373–6
public law basis of investment arbitration 369–71
regulatory expropriation 68, 198, 206, 211–12, 222, 226–9, 233–5, 245, 376–7
relevance of 371–2, 406, 407
United States 51, 373
protection and security 45
fair and equitable standard, and duty to provide full 251, 254–6, 270–1
prudential measures 387, 400
public interest 5, 31, 60, 373, 406
administrative contracts 114
balanced treaties 38, 363, 400, 406
defences 300–1, 314, 316
expropriation 213, 214, 221, 232
without compensation 202, 230
fair and equitable standard 262, 270, 273, 284, 286, 293, 295
human rights
individual petition 146

property, right to 289, 290–1, 323, 368, 374, 381
intellectual property 392
police powers to protect 109–10, 217
proportionality 366–7, 373
regulatory power of state 117–18, 120–1, 122, 127, 128, 130, 132, 206
South Africa 232
purposive or teleological interpretation 44, 63, 149–50, 156, 183, 186, 253–4, 260, 263

racial discrimination 254–6
reasonableness 220–2, 232, 241, 381
Wednesbury 374
reform 382–8
appellate body 384–6
consultation mechanism 386
contractual method of protection 409
legal representation 387–8, 409, 420
permanent body of dispute settlement 420
responsibility of arbitral institutions 408–9
screening mechanism 386–7, 408
termination of system of investment treaties 304, 382–4, 407–8
refugees 164
regional investment treaties 94, 419
ASEAN Investment Agreement 189, 352–6
multilateral obligations 319
renegotiation clauses 127
reorganization, corporate 180, 181
repatriation of assets 358–9
responsibility to protect 241
Rhodes, Cecil 82
Rio Declaration (1992) 334
Roberts, A. 268
Roman law 145
Ruggie, John 361
rule of law 49–50, 64, 295–7, 412
Russia 398, 402

SADC Model Investment Treaty 352, 356–62
Schreuer, C. 247
screening mechanism 386–7, 408
secession, right to 327
self-defence 314, 373
self-determination 22, 40, 122, 326
separation of powers 32, 293, 373–4, 378, 381
shareholders, minority 199–200, 266
shell companies. *See* corporate nationality
Singapore 13, 55, 173, 229, 377, 391, 404
slavery 22, 321, 324, 375, 420
social welfare 301
socialism 225
sources of international law
  arbitral awards 21, 24, 38, 58, 91, 98, 106, 134, 135, 247, 414
  custom 23, 53, 67, 91
    UN General Assembly resolutions 37, 38, 114, 135
  general principles of law 97, 99, 101, 104
  private power 99–102
  writings of 'highly qualified publicists' 21, 24, 38, 58, 98, 99, 134, 135, 247, 414
South Africa 231–2, 356–7, 359, 384, 403, 416
South Korea 13, 55, 392
sovereign immunity 6, 284
sovereign wealth funds 405
sovereignty 90, 97–8, 138, 191, 261, 286, 296, 297, 330, 416
  absolute 22
  concession agreements 99, 111
  natural resources 36–7, 40, 112, 114, 120, 122, 192, 324–7, 417
  police powers to protect public interests 109–10
  right to surrender 119
  stabilization clauses 108, 117–18, 120–1, 286
  subsoil resources 114
Soviet bloc states, former 18, 194
Spain 310
specific performance 113, 114, 116

Sri Lanka 145
stabilization clauses 108–11, 119, 120–1, 127–8, 129–30, 397
  Aminoil 117–18, 135
  ICSID case: *AGIP* v. *Congo* 126
  investment treaty arbitration: role of 132–3
  legitimate expectations 121, 132, 264, 270, 274, 282, 283, 284–7, 397
  Libyan arbitrations 111, 112, 113, 115
  police powers to protect public interest 109–10, 217
  regulatory expropriation 217, 218
standard of civilization 104, 412
state responsibility
  diplomatic protection and 86–94
  financial instruments 169–70
  human rights and multinational corporations 320
  International Law Commission: Draft Code 90, 92–3, 310–12, 314
sustainable development 65, 303, 327, 334, 348, 415
  SADC Model Investment Treaty 361
  UNCTAD 328, 352, 361

Taiwan 13, 55
taxation 212, 213, 219, 221, 237, 387, 400, 408
  ASEAN Investment Agreement 355
  Commonwealth Report and Model Treaty 363
  Norwegian Draft Model Treaty 350
  SADC Model Investment Treaty 362
  US and Canada: model treaties (2012) 351
technology transfer 320, 321
telecommunications 201
teleological or purposive interpretation 44, 63, 149–50, 156, 183, 186, 253–4, 260, 263
terrorism 366–7, 374
theory of resistance and change 410, 420

INDEX

accommodation 418–20
justice 417–18
private and public power 414
resistance setting in 415–17
uncontested hegemonic power
410–13
tobacco disputes 7, 337, 392
torture 317, 321, 324, 375
trafficking of human organs 324
Trans-Pacific Pact (TPP) 402
transition economies 280–1
transnational law 102
formation of contracts 165–6, 167
treaty shopping 181, 182
tribal groups. *See* indigenous peoples

umbrella clauses 62, 93, 131, 243, 284,
397
stabilization clauses 121
UNCITRAL Arbitration Rules 153
UNCITRAL Model Law on
International Commercial
Arbitration 83
UNCITRAL tribunals 153
jurisdiction 159–60
unfair terms 97
United Kingdom 410, 420
colonialism 84
contract law 96, 144, 369–70
East India Company 20–1, 82, 83,
100, 410
extraterritoriality 99, 319
jurisdiction 143
legitimate expectations 50–1, 261, 270
proportionality 378, 381
reasonableness 221, 381
UK–Indonesia treaty 174
United Nations 403
Charter 314
General Assembly 35–6, 37, 114, 135,
329
responsibility to protect 241
UNCTAD 6, 43, 251, 254, 275, 328,
352, 361
United States 11, 15–16, 84, 351, 396,
400, 420
Alien Tort Claims Act 64, 241,
319, 324

Argentina 56, 266, 267, 308
China 405
constitutional law 212, 224
economic crisis (2008) 15, 142, 196,
310, 313, 351, 401
environment 336
expropriation 34–5, 91–2, 195, 196,
197–8
Alien Tort Claims Act 241
concept of property 223–4, 225,
230, 231, 232, 235
Model Treaty (2004) 204, 211, 219,
221, 349, 399
regulatory 57, 211, 212, 217, 302,
349, 399–400
fair and equitable standard
international minimum standard
91, 250, 251
foreign policy 18–19
formative phase of law on foreign
investment 32–5
health 57
intellectual property 101
international trade law 12
Iran–US Claims Tribunal 198–9,
202–3, 209, 225
Latin America 86, 89, 92, 353
Model Treaty (1987) 56
Model Treaty (2004) 39, 47, 56, 156,
348–9, 361
expropriation 204, 211, 219, 221,
349, 399
fair and equitable standard
251, 349
Model Treaty (2012) 56, 349, 350–1,
405
national security 308, 349
proportionality 51, 373
Restatement of Foreign
Relations Law 212, 217, 235
Singapore–US FTA 377
Supreme Court 6, 232, 241, 319, 360,
401, 406
uncontested hegemonic power
410–13

Vasciannie, S. 247
Venezuela 402

452 INDEX

Vienna Convention on the Law of
    Treaties 60, 145, 149, 159, 263,
    315
Vietnam 412
void *ab initio* 167
vulture funds 65, 383

war: civilian property 164
Washington Consensus 11, 43, 412
waste disposal 338
water 7, 337, 338, 392, 401–2

welfare state 212
wildlife 338
wind farms 338
World Bank 15, 43, 124, 163, 332, 411,
    412
   arbitration facility 27, 152, 157, 173
World Trade Organization (WTO) 12,
    64, 214, 384, 398
   Doha Round 214, 329

Zimbabwe 356

For EU product safety concerns, contact us at Calle de José Abascal, 56–1°,
28003 Madrid, Spain or eugpsr@cambridge.org.

www.ingramcontent.com/pod-product-compliance
Ingram Content Group UK Ltd.
Pitfield, Milton Keynes, MK11 3LW, UK
UKHW020349060825
461487UK00008B/588